DISCARDED

THE THEORY OF OIL TANKSHIP RATES
An Economic Analysis of Tankship Operations

M.I.T. MONOGRAPHS IN ECONOMICS

1 *The Natural Resource Content of United States Foreign Trade 1870–1955*
   JAROSLAV VANEK

2 *Iron and Steel in Nineteenth-Century America: An Economic Inquiry*
   PETER TEMIN

3 *Labor Migration and Economic Growth: A Case Study of Puerto Rico*
   STANLEY L. FRIEDLANDER

4 *The Theory of Oil Tankship Rates: An Economic Analysis of Tankship Operations*
   ZENON S. ZANNETOS

5 *Exchange-Rate Devaluation in a Semi-Industrialized Country: The Experience of Argentina 1955–1961*
   CARLOS F. DIAZ ALEJANDRO

6 *Urban Migration and Economic Development in Chile*
   BRUCE H. HERRICK

7 *Unemployment, Money Wage Rates, and Inflation*
   GEORGE L. PERRY

THE THEORY OF OIL TANKSHIP RATES
An Economic Analysis of Tankship Operations

ZENON S. ZANNETOS

THE M.I.T. PRESS
Massachusetts Institute of Technology
Cambridge, Massachusetts, and London, England

Copyright © 1966 by
The Massachusetts Institute of Technology

All rights reserved. This book may not be reproduced in whole or in part, in any form (except by reviewers for the public press), without written permission from the publishers.

Library of Congress Catalog Card Number: 65-27790
Printed in the United States of America

To My Wife

Preface

This study is based on my doctoral dissertation and subsequent related research that I conducted in the area of tankship transportation economics. The essential characteristics of the tankship markets, and the factors that influence the behavior of tanker owners and tanker charterers, have not changed since 1959 when I submitted the dissertation to the Department of Economics at the Massachusetts Institute of Technology. Intervening events provided further evidence that the conclusions reached then are based on fundamental interrelationships of general applicability and which can stand the test of time.

My interest in the area of tankship rate formation started in the spring of 1956, and was stimulated by Professor Morris A. Adelman who became chairman of my thesis committee. To him, and to Professors Charles P. Kindleberger and Robert M. Solow, the other members of the committee, I wish to express my great appreciation for their helpful comments.

To those who assisted me with the original manuscript I once again acknowledge my gratitude. In particular I wish to thank my colleagues Professors Myron J. Gordon, now at the University of Rochester, Thomas M. Hill of M.I.T., Gordon Shillinglaw, now at Columbia University, and Miss Miriam Sherburne of the Sloan School of Management at M.I.T. who offered helpful criticism and suggestions on organization and form.

The Sloan School of Management of the Massachusetts Institute of Technology supported part of the cost of data collection and processing with a grant from the Sloan Research Funds, and the Massachusetts Institute of Technology Computation Center allotted computer time to my research project for many statistical calculations and tests. To those responsible for this aid go my sincere thanks.

The amount and diversity of statistical information supporting this study are quite extensive. The task of collecting this information was extremely complicated because for the major part relevant data are not publicly available. Oil companies collect some data for their internal purposes but often consider what they have as proprietary. Moreover, the information that is available in any one place is usually segmented or specialized, and cannot be readily put together into meaningful time series. It is for all these reasons that I am so appreciative of the assistance I received and continue to receive in my research efforts from industrial sources. A list of those who benefited this study includes executives of oil companies, shipyards, banks, tankship transportation companies, tankship brokerage firms, canal and pipeline companies, tanker owners and operators, government agencies, and numerous firms related to the oil industry and spread all over the world.

Finally, I wish to thank those who toiled most with the finished product: Miss Geraldine Weidman who typed most of the manuscript and who cheerfully and efficiently handled all the details of reproduction showing an immense pride in the final outcome, Mrs. Laurel Townsend, Jr., who expertly assisted with the typing, Mr. John Mara whose drawing skills and craftsmanship are evidenced throughout the book, Mr. Kenan Sahin, a research assistant at M.I.T., who went over the galleys, page proofs, and charts with a keen eye and immense patience, and my wife who contributed in many ways during the various research stages and the final preparation of this book.

ZENON S. ZANNETOS

Cambridge, Massachusetts
September 1, 1964

Contents

1 Introduction   1

2 Expectations and the Behavior of Buyers and Sellers   6
Asymmetry in Expectations   20
Supply and Demand Interactions Under Elastic Expectations   21

   Appendix to Chapter 2   30
Interperiod Maximization of Profit or Utility   30

3 The Shape of the Demand Schedule for Tanker Services — Preliminary Comments   35

4 Rates and Transactions   42

5 Factors Affecting the Supply of Tankships   50
Introduction   50
Spot Rates, Shipbuilding Costs, and Orders Placed — Theoretical Formulations   51
Retirements and Replacements — Theoretical Discussion   57
The Pattern of Ownership — An Institutional Paradox   64
Spot Rates, Shipbuilding Costs, and Orders Placed — Empirical Observations   76
Spot Rates and Orders Placed — Quantitative Evidence   82
Chartering versus Shipbuilding Revisited   94
The Behavior of the Independents versus That of the Oil Companies   97
Spot Rates and Tanker Deliveries   110
Spot Rates and Vessels Scrapped   116
Spot Rates and Slowdowns, Conversions, Repairs, and Tie-ups   126

CONTENTS

6 The Short-Term Supply Schedule   160
    Factors Influencing Transportation Capacity   160
    Definition of Capacity   167
    The Supply Schedule   169

7 Characteristics of the Tankship Markets   174
    Concentration of Ownership in the Relevant Market   176
    Balance Between Production and Refining Capacities   176
    Balance Between Needs and Sources Satisfying such Needs for Each Company by Geographic Regions   178
    The Existence of Tankship Markets   178
    Mobility   179
    Ease of Entry   180
    The Vessel Is the Firm   182
    Absence of Artificial Controls   183
    Summary   184

8 The Formation of Short-Term Rates   186
    Some Further Empirical Observations Regarding Short-Term Rates   199

9 The Long-Term Charter Rate in the Short Run   202

10 Model of Long-Term Rates   215
    Bimodality and Its Impact   227

11 The Long-Term Rates in the Long Run   231

12 A Brief Summary   239

Appendices   246
    Appendix A   Definition of Technical Terms   246
    Appendix B   Method for Conversion of Time-Charter Rates into Spot-Rate Equivalent   249
    Appendix C   Coding Instructions for Data Used   251
    1. Charters
    2. Tie-ups (Monthly)
    3. New Orders (Monthly)
    4. Spot Rates (Monthly)
    5. Gulf Oil Company Charter Data (Format for Multiple-Correlation Card)

Appendix D   Coded Data   262

1. *Charters*
2. *Tie-ups* (*Monthly*)
3. *New Orders* (*Monthly*)
4. *Spot Rates* (*Monthly*)
5. *Gulf Oil Company Charter Data* (*Format for Multiple-Correlation Card*)

Appendix E   Sources of Data Used in Figures   320

Selected Bibliography 321

Index 325

List of Figures

2.1	Demand schedule showing the impact of price-elastic expectations outside R^s.	18
2.2	Theoretical supply schedule affected by price-elastic expectations outside R_1.	18
2.3	Expectations schedules.	20
2.4	Supply and demand schedules.	22
2.5	Supply and demand interactions with asymmetry in behavior.	23
4.1	Scatter diagram of the number of fixtures versus index of spot rates, 1953–1958 (monthly).	43
4.2	Scatter diagram of the number of fixtures in month equivalent versus index of spot rates, 1953–1958 (monthly).	45
4.3	Time series of total number of fixtures, time charters, and consecutive voyages, and index of spot rates, 1949–1958.	46
5.1	Time series of orders placed in T-2 equivalent and index of spot rates, 1949–1958.	78
5.2	Scatter diagram of orders placed versus index of spot rates, 1949–1953 (monthly).	84
5.3	Scatter diagram of orders placed versus index of spot rates, 1954–1958 (monthly).	85
5.4	Rates versus orders placed: quarterly data, 1949–1953.	93
5.5	Rates versus orders placed: quarterly data, 1954–1958.	93
5.6	Cost of vessels per DWT. (Fairplay Index) and spot rates, 1949–1958.	106
5.7	Time series of deliveries and index of spot rates, 1949–1958.	112
5.8	Time series of changes in orders outstanding in T-2 equivalent and index of spot rates, 1949–1958.	114
5.9	Time series of total orders outstanding as percentage of total and working petroleum fleets and index of spot rates, 1949–1958.	116
5.10	Scatter diagram of changes in orders outstanding in T-2 equivalent versus index of spot rates, 1949–1953 (monthly).	118
5.11	Scatter diagram of changes in orders outstanding in T-2 equivalent versus index of spot rates, 1954–1958 (monthly).	119
5.12	Number and average age of vessels scrapped and spot rates, 1947–1958.	121

5.13	Average size of vessels ordered, delivered, and scrapped, 1948–1959.	123
5.14	Plot of vessels, in T-2 equivalent, idle for repairs of below thirty days, between thirty and sixty days, and over sixty days, and tie-ups, 1955–1958.	141
5.15	Time series of idle vessels and index of spot rates, 1949–1958.	142
5.16	Scatter diagram of tie-ups in T-2 equivalent versus index of spot rates, 1949–1958 (monthly).	156
5.17	Scatter diagram of idle capacity as percentage of working petroleum fleet versus index of spot rates, 1949–1958 (monthly).	157
5.18	Scatter diagram of idle capacity as percentage of total fleet versus index of spot rates, 1949–1958 (monthly).	158
6.1	Scatter diagram of operating fleet as percentage of total fleet versus index of spot rates, 1949–1958 (monthly).	170
6.2	Scatter diagram of operating capacity based on working petroleum fleet versus index of spot rates, 1949–1958 (monthly).	172
6.3	Adjusted short-term supply schedule, 1957–1958.	173
8.1	Theoretical time profile of spot rates.	188
8.2	Cobweb adjustment paths.	193
9.1	Charter duration and its impact on charter rates.	210
9.2	Empirical schedules of the structure and level of time-charter rates: the impact of spot rates and charter duration on time-charter rates for 1955, 1956, 1956 by quarters, and 1959.	211
9.3	Long-run convergence of time-charter rates under high and low spot rates: empirical observations for 1957.	212
11.1	Cost per DWT. per annum for vessels of sizes 16,500–100,000 DWT.	237

List of Tables

5.1	World-wide Industry Tanker Tonnage by Age Groups as of January 1, 1959 (Vessels 6,000 DWT. and Over)	62
5.2	World-wide Industry Tanker Tonnage by Size Groups as of January 1, 1959 (Vessels 6,000 DWT. and Over)	66
5.3	World-wide Industry Tanker Construction by Size Groups as of January 1, 1959 (Vessels 6,000 DWT. and Over)	70
5.4	Ownership of Vessels of 6,000 DWT. and Over	72
5.5	New Construction: Vessels of 6,000 DWT. and Over	73
5.6	Total Tonnage including New Construction: Vessels of 6,000 DWT. and Over	73
5.7	Vessel Deliveries by Yards 1956–1958	81
5.8	Contracted Deliveries for Vessels on Order as of January 1, 1959	82
5.9	Zero-Order Correlation Coefficients: Rates vs. Orders	88
5.10	World Tanker Construction Trends 1948–1958 (6,000 DWT. and Over)	91
5.11	Average Price per Deadweight Ton: Japan's Ship Exports 1949–1957	98
5.12	Vessels Scrapped and Spot Rates: Yearly Data	120
5.13	Average Size of Vessels Scrapped, Delivered, and Ordered by Years 1948–1959	122
5.14	Economics of Speed: Port Arthur–New York–Port Arthur	130
5.15	Economics of Speed: Ras Tanura–Antwerp Round Trip Through Canal	131
5.16	Economics of Speed and Suez Tolls: Ras Tanura–Antwerp Round Trip Through Canal at 14.5 Knots and Around Cape at 10 Knots	132
5.17	Repairs and Tie-ups: Capacity Lost in T-2 Equivalent	136
5.18	Capacity Lost due to Repairs	140
5.19	Average Size of Laid-up Vessels	146
5.20	Tie-up Costs	147
5.21	Break-Even Point of the Assumed Marginal Vessel (T-2)	149
6.1	Analysis of Disposition of Foreign-Flag Commercial Petroleum Tanker Fleet: July 1, 1954 to October 1, 1957	164
6.2	Percentage of World Tanker Fleet Trading on a "Spot" Basis	165

7.1	Tankers Owned and under Construction for Five Major Oil Companies and Five Major Independents (January 1, 1959)	175
10.1	Correlation Matrix: Lows: 304 Observations	221
10.2	Multiple Regression Coefficients and Standard Errors: Lows: 304 Observations	222
10.3	Correlation Matrix: Highs: 593 Observations	226
10.4	Multiple Regression Coefficients and Standard Errors: Highs: 593 Observations	227
10.5	F Ratio Tests	228
10.6	Selected Coefficients of Zero-Order Correlation: Subsamples	229
11.1	Five-Year Time-Charter Rates for T-2's	234
11.2	Time-Charter Cost of Operation for Vessels of 16,500 to 100,000 DWT. (1959 data)	235

1

Introduction

Static economic theory states that, given a particular stage of technological development, individual preferences, and resources at a moment of time, all prices in the economic system will be forced to levels at which all markets reach equilibrium. All the adjustments that are necessary for such an equilibrium occur instantaneously and, at the equilibrium price, all the markets are cleared.

In the real world not only do adjustments take time to occur but also the markets are not cleared. A stable equilibrium is achieved in some cases, but only for very short periods of time. Even in these cases, however, the quantities supplied and demanded are a function both of current and of expected prices. As Hicks explains, the current supply of a commodity "depends not so much upon what the current price is as upon what entrepreneurs have expected it to be in the past. It will be those past expectations, whether right or wrong, which mainly govern current output." [1] Similarly, past as well as future expectations determine the position of the current demand curve of a commodity.

The significance of the role of expectations in price determination is very evident in the tankship markets: very few prices of commodities fluctuate as violently as the spot tanker rates. They fluctuate so much mainly because of the present impact of actions that have been initiated in the past by expectations as to future conditions. In particular, short-term supply and demand relationships determine the spot rate in the tankship markets. The spot rate, in turn, greatly influences expectations about the future course of events amplifying expected rate changes. This relative price elasticity of expectations[2] influences the number of

---

[1] Hicks, J. R., *Value and Capital*, Second Edition, Oxford University Press, London, 1953, p. 117. Also see Baumol, J. W., *Economic Dynamics*, The Macmillan Company, New York, 1957, pp. 208–210.

[2] We say that price expectations are elastic if $(\Delta P_f/P_f)(P_0/\Delta P_0) > 1$, where P_0 and P_f stand for present and future (expected) prices, respectively, and ΔP_0 and ΔP_f represent changes in present and future prices.

CHAPTER ONE

orders for new ships on the supply side. It also shifts the demand to the right during periods of high rates, as users of tankers rush to secure tonnage, and to the left during periods of low rates, as users withdraw from the market. The combination of these factors creates essential interrelationships between the supply and demand schedules of one period with those of another, and also generates circular interdependence between supply and demand.

If tankers were a perishable commodity or a ready substitute for other commodities, the impact of misguided expectations would be short lived, although not mild. But such is not the case. Tankers have an economic life of twenty-five years on the average and cannot be used for any important purpose other than the shipment of crude oil and its products, except possibly for transporting grain and ore — which can only be done at a relatively high cost.[3] What is more, the demand schedule for tankers (being a derived demand schedule) exhibits considerable price inelasticity over the greatest part of the relevant price range. A drop in rates, therefore, cannot possibly absorb any excess tonnage,[4] nor can an increase in rates bring about a reduction in the quantities demanded except at a very high rate level.[5] This relative insensitivity in the quantities supplied and demanded occurs because there is virtually perfect complementarity between delivered (imported) oil and tankers.

The purpose of this book is to contribute toward the development of a theory of oil tankship rates. Efforts will be made to identify all the factors that affect the rates in the short run as well as the long run, and wherever possible estimate their impact. Since rates are the

[3] Westinform Service estimates that it costs about $30,000 to $35,000 to clean the tanks of a vessel of 16,500 DWT., and in addition there are costly delays in loading and unloading because the pumping equipment of tankers cannot be used in such trades. W. G. Weston Ltd., London, letter to the author, dated March 3, 1959.

[4] Because of the role that the oil companies are performing in generating the demand expectations and also in supplying a significant portion of the tonnage requirements, the companies aggravate the fluctuations in rates. During periods of high rates they are usually short of tonnage to meet their requirements, and during periods of distress the oil companies enter the market not as buyers but as sellers of their excess capacity. This is similar to the Giffen's paradox, but the symmetry is not real because in the case of tankers we are not dealing with inferior goods.

[5] This high level for an input to a commodity is, as Marshall says, "limited by the excess of the price at which that amount of the commodity can find purchasers, over the sum of the prices at which the corresponding supplies of the other things needed for making it will be forthcoming." Marshall, Alfred, *Principles of Economics,* Eighth Edition, Macmillan & Co., Ltd., London, 1956, p. 317. Within the context of our discussion the "commodity" may be taken as delivered oil and the other supplies as crude oil or products.

rental of tankships, we shall in the process of studying the determinants of tankship rates devote a considerable amount of effort to the economics of tankship building and tankship operation.

The transactions in the tankship markets can be classified into two general categories: the spot,[6] or single voyage; and the period, or long-term, transaction. The rate for single-voyage charters is expressed in terms of a monetary consideration, let us say "dollars" per ton of oil delivered, but the long-term charter rate is usually expressed in terms of "dollars" per deadweight ton (DWT.) per month.

The period, or long-term, charter may refer either to a vessel that is maintained and furnished by the owner with crew and provisions — except for fuel, port charges, and tolls — or to a "bare" boat which the charterer furnishes and maintains. Because the "bareboat" charters constitute less than 1% of all the long-term transactions, the terms "period," "long-term," and "time" will be used interchangeably and will exclude bareboat charters.

In between the single-voyage and the time charters, we find the "consecutive-voyage" charters. As the name implies, consecutive-voyage charters have all the characteristics of the single-voyage charter, but the contract is either for a specified number of such voyages or for as many voyages as can be arranged within a given time period. Although not significant in the past, this form of charter seems to be gaining in importance.

The oil companies now own less than 40% of the total tonnage of vessels of 6,000 DWT. and over. The companies claim that they attempt to supplement their ownership with vessels chartered on a long-term basis, to a total of 90% of their expected requirements. For the remaining 10%, they choose to depend on the spot market.

In an expanding industry such as oil, errors in forecasting transportation needs are to be expected. The trouble is that even a small error in the aggregate demand may necessitate adjustments that generate serious disturbances in a spot market encompassing only about 15% of the total capacity. We must remember that at any moment of time the available supply is in the spot market. As a result, an error of only 5% in the total transportation needs of the industry will be equivalent to 100% of available capacity if only 5% of the total fleet operates in the

---

[6] Note that "spot" is a technical term and in common industrial usage means single voyage. It does not distinguish "futures" from "non-futures" transactions. Both single-voyage and long-term charter agreements may specify either immediate or future delivery. Because contracts for single voyages usually specify "immediate" delivery, the term spot has acquired a one-sided connotation, and unless it is qualified implies *current rate for a single voyage*. It is also for this reason that the "short term" is defined as the time it takes a vessel to complete a round-trip voyage for a specified run.

spot market. Given inelastic demand, heavy opportunity costs, expectations of elasticity different from one, and adjustments that are not instantaneous, the spot rates may fluctuate violently. It appears that this is what has happened historically.

As in any investigation of the factors affecting the price of a commodity, we shall examine the economic data that enter into the determination of the supply and demand schedules of tankship capacity. However, unlike purely theoretical analyses of this sort, which assume a distinct dichotomy between static and dynamic considerations, our empirical study must face the difficult problems of identifying, rather than distinguishing a priori, between these two types of phenomena. As Professor Kaldor said in his critique of Mrs. Robinson's celebrated book,[7] "the apparatus of the 'curves' becomes progressively less useful as one makes the basic assumptions more realistic, since it becomes increasingly difficult to exhibit the conditions of equilibrium by functions of one variable." [8] While in theory we can assume that other things are equal, in practice we do not have the advantage of holding all other variables constant but one so that we can measure the impact of that one. However, static analysis does aid us in understanding the working mechanism of economic forces.[9] The comparison is made here to point out how easy it is to mistake movements along a given demand schedule for temporary equilibria established after the relevant schedules themselves have shifted. Given the existence of shifts, it is in general impossible to determine the slopes of the traditional demand and supply curves.[10]

In the process of investigating the factors which enter into the determination of rates, we shall follow for convenience the tradition of first discussing separately the factors operating through the respective demand and supply schedules. We shall then fuse the two schedules and show how short-term rates are determined.

Once the discussion on the determination of the spot rate is com-

[7] Robinson, Joan, *The Economics of Imperfect Competition,* Macmillan & Co., Ltd., London, 1933.

[8] Kaldor, Nicholas, "Economics of Imperfect Competition," *Economica,* Vol. 1, Nos. 1–4, 1934, pp. 336–337.

[9] As Lionel Robbins said on a slightly different occasion in his "On a Certain Ambiguity in the Conception of Stationary Equilibrium," *Economic Journal,* June 1930, pp. 194–214, "The man who holds that nothing has yet been accomplished (by use of stationary state and static laws) may deserve pity but certainly not respect": p. 194.

[10] When the shifts are "systematic" and the supply and demand schedules are functions of different variables (such as price with a lag on either the supply or the demand side but not both), then of course the parameters can be determined. Allen, R. G. D., *Mathematical Economics,* Macmillan & Co., Ltd., London, 1957, pp. 12–13.

pleted, attention will be focused on the long-term, or period, rates. In this context we shall first suggest and test hypotheses explaining the determination of long-term tanker rates in the short run, and then analyze the factors determining the long-run level of long-term rates.[11]

[11] For the reader who is not acquainted with the terms used in the tankship markets, a glossary is included in Appendix A.

2

Expectations and the Behavior of Buyers and Sellers

Before we proceed with the analysis of the objective factors that affect the supply and demand schedules of tankship capacity, we shall briefly present a hypothesis and the consequent theoretical formulation that we shall test in later chapters. This hypothesis concerns the behavior of buyers and sellers and the influences of this behavior on the shape of the supply and demand schedules. Simply stated, our hypothesis admits elasticities of expectations of a value greater than one, and also a certain degree of asymmetry between the behavior of buyers and sellers. Such an asymmetry of behavior, as we shall show later however, is neither a necessary nor a sufficient condition for stability in the tankship markets. We hope to provide convincing evidence that although the characteristics of these markets create wide price fluctuations, such fluctuations are confined within definable bounds even under the impact of price-elastic expectations.

It has long been assumed that elastic expectations (expectations that the percentage changes in future price levels will be in excess of the percentage changes in present prices) generate explosive price patterns and result in market instabilities. Hicks in his *Value and Capital* [1] states that when elasticities of expectations *all* become equal to one "there is no longer any opportunity for substitutions over time." He further adds: "a system with elasticities of expectations greater than unity, and constant rate of interest, is definitely unstable." [2] Baumol also makes similar observations in his *Economic Dynamics*.[3] The reasoning behind these statements is as follows.

---

[1] Hicks, J. R., *Value and Capital*, Second Edition, Oxford University Press, London, 1953, p. 251.
[2] *Ibid.*, p. 255.
[3] Baumol, J. W., *Economic Dynamics*, The Macmillan Company, New York, 1957, p. 255.

With constant interest rates and elasticities of expectations all equal to one, people will not alter their pattern of preference between present and future transactions, because prices increase or decrease in the same proportion and in real terms remain unchanged. In other words, the tangents to the relevant points on the indifference curves will keep the slope that they had before the price change. With elasticities of expectation greater than unity, where future normal prices are expected to rise or fall permanently and proportionately more than the present price changes, an increase in prices will induce the buyers to *accelerate expenditures* and the sellers to *accelerate input but postpone output*. This will further increase prices, increase demand, and so on, ad infinitum. The opposite will occur in the case of a price decrease if elasticities of expectations are greater than one.

The assumption of a constant interest rate may be somewhat unrealistic under the influence of elastic expectations, and the only case where it does not affect interperiod substitutions is that of unitary elasticity. In effect the latter happens also to be the case where even a variable interest rate *may* not affect any product markets, with the possible exception of the money (or securities) market itself for reasons independent from the rest. That is to say, although people may choose to borrow or lend money to take advantage of the expected change in the interest rate,[4] yet they may in no way change their stock of goods if their expectations in the nonmonetary markets are unit elastic.[5] Under all other conditions (whenever expectations are not unit elastic) the cost of carrying inventory will be an important factor that will undoubtedly influence purchasing plans.

If we now consider the money market as a part of the total system under symmetry in expectations, we shall find it necessary to make certain changes before the theory is applicable. First, we shall have to redefine unitary elasticity so as to take into account the impact of the

---

[4] In this case the people who borrow will have to evaluate, over the relevant investment horizons, the expected cost of keeping money idle versus the expected gain due to a later increase in interest rates. Those who lend must consider the expected gain that they will realize if they lend now against the expected loss of utility that they will suffer by being deprived of the use of their money earlier.

[5] If money is borrowed ahead of the point of need to take advantage of lower interest rates, then the stocks of other goods may be affected even under unitelastic expectations if the expected future normal price of these goods *before the change in present prices occurs* is higher than the present price. It all depends upon these price differences versus the value attached to liquidity; that is, it depends upon the conditions that determine whether the opportunity cost of idle funds over the relevant period is zero or positive. Let us notice again, however, that this situation will occur only in cases where people are indifferent as between present versus future transactions in all markets but that of money.

cost of capital,[6] and then derive a coefficient of expectations for interest rates to cover the case of people who are either short or long in liquid funds.[7] The amount of funds held by people can be assumed to have been determined either by choice or by initial endowments.

In addition to the assumption of symmetry of expectations among buyers and sellers, Hicks' formulations relating to elastic expectations further assume monotonicity in the functions relating present to future price changes, constant marginal utility of money, and absence of aversion to risk. Without these assumptions interperiod substitutions may cease and thus curb explosive price patterns.

After staying dormant for quite a few years, interest in elasticities of expectations and dynamic stability has been aroused by a series of publications.

Enthoven and Arrow in an article that appeared in *Econometrica*[8] have shown that expectations need not necessarily create instabilities in an otherwise stable system. Their conclusions, which are an extension of Metzler's theorem[9] to the case of nonstatic expectations, relate stability to "extrapolative expectations" and to the reaction of the system to a change in expected future prices. In their words ". . . a necessary and sufficient condition for the stability of the system with any expectation is that $1/K_i > b_i \eta_i$ for all markets . . . (i.e.) the coefficient of insensitivity of prices to excess demand be greater than the destabilizing force of the extrapolative expectations." [10] An extension of the Enthoven-Arrow theorem to other classes of matrices appeared in Arrow and McManus, "A Note on Dynamic Stability." [11] Finally Arrow and Nerlove[12] by assuming "adaptive" rather than "extrapolative" expectations have shown that the degree of inertia of the system to a change in

---

[6] It must be pointed out here that "small changes" in interest rates may not affect the relevant cost of capital of firms and individuals. Consequently the investment behavior of individuals under these conditions will be the same as in the case of constant interest rates.

[7] The importance of a relevant coefficient of expectations for interest rates may be seen in the following simple illustration. If the prices for all goods go up by 10% in a year, then the holdings in these goods of each person will increase in monetary terms by 10%. This will not be so, however, in the case of the current monetary value of liquid funds if the interest rates increase by 10%.

[8] Enthoven, Alain C., and Kenneth J. Arrow, "A Theorem on Expectations and Stability of Equilibrium," *Econometrica*, Vol. 24, No. 3, July 1956.

[9] Metzler, Lloyd A., "Stability of Multiple Markets: The Hicks Condition," *Econometrica*, Vol. 13, No. 4, October 1945, pp. 277–292.

[10] Enthoven and Arrow, *op. cit.*, p. 290.

[11] Arrow, Kenneth J., and Maurice McManus, "A Note of Dynamic Stability," *Econometrica*, Vol. 26, No. 3, July 1958, pp. 443–454.

[12] Arrow, Kenneth J., and Marc Nerlove, "A Note on Expectations and Stability," *Econometrica*, Vol. 26, No. 2, April 1958, pp. 297–305.

expected future prices does not affect the stability of a dynamic system which is stable under static expectations.

The conclusions reached in the articles just mentioned are not insignificant but appear to have been somewhat prejudiced, nonetheless, by the assumptions of the extrapolative and adaptive nature of expectations. As Mills[13] points out in the case of adaptive expectations, since prices are assumed to follow a smoothed-out path based on actual prices, which in the long run are assumed to converge, expectations will also converge.

With this brief discussion on the impact of elastic price expectations on the stability of general market equilibria, we shall now examine the theoretical consequences of an assumption that dynamic forces operate in tankship building and tankship transportation markets.[14] Since we shall be interested in partial equilibria, our task will be easier in some ways than that of investigators dealing with conditions relating to general equilibrium analysis. Budgetary constraints and shifts in wealth that may not operate in the general case will definitely curb interperiod substitutions in partial analysis. Yet in other ways the task of the empirical investigator is more complicated because any theoretical model that he develops must be sufficiently realistic and devoid of excessively simplifying assumptions so that it can withstand the empirical test for validity.

The nature and dynamics of the fluctuations in the tankship building and tankship transportation markets are much more complicated than those described by the classical cobweb theorem or the cattle and hog cycles. Ships are not as perishable as cattle, hogs, or wheat, so the production cycle does not fully determine the duration of the price cycle.[15] In fact, as we shall show later, the interrelationship between tankship services and tankship building is such that the price upswing in the tankship services market may be (and usually is) reversed before the output that was initiated by dynamic anticipations reaches the final market. Furthermore, it appears that in the tankship markets we are presented with a strange situation where the short-run *expectations* of

---

[13] Mills, Edwin S., "The Use of Adaptive Expectations in Stability Analysis: Comment," *The Quarterly Journal of Economics*, Vol. LXXV, No. 2, May 1961, pp. 330–335.

[14] This topic was also explored in 1939 by Jan Tinbergen: see *Selected Papers*, L. H. Klaasen *et al.*, Editors, North-Holland Publishing Company, Amsterdam, 1959, pp. 1–14; and also by Tjalling C. Koopmans, *Tanker Freight Rates and Tankship Building*, Haarlem, 1939.

[15] Within the life span of tankships, which is about twenty-five years, we can observe several price cycles even for reasons purely endogenous to the supply side of the market. It all depends upon the time distribution and magnitude of the various supply quantities as these enter and are withdrawn from the market. This topic will be expounded later.

the operatives will often appear ex post facto to be *rational* [16] while the *behavior* of these operatives is *irrational*.[17] In other words, through their behavior, which appears to be irrational, those who operate in the tankship markets influence the actual price to the extent that it confirms their expectations. Another peculiarity of the tankship markets that is worth mentioning relates to the organizational structure of the petroleum industry. Tankship transportation, the rates of which are determined under conditions that approximate perfect competition,[18] is an input to a good whose final price seems to bear little if any relationship to its marginal cost, especially in the short run. Consequently wide rate fluctuations are to be expected, especially if one also considers the loss of good will or penalty through default of contractual commitments.

If we ignore for the time being the nature of expectations, to the extent that in the final analysis we are interested in determining the impact of price changes on the quantity demanded, at any moment of time, the Slutsky-Hicks formulation for the consumer equilibrium presents a very convenient avenue of exploration.[19] Although this formulation was originally developed to analyze the static income effect and the income-compensated substitution effect of a price change on the quantity demanded at a moment of time — for the purpose of maximizing utility for a single period — yet, as we show in the Appendix to this chapter, it is also applicable in the case of interperiod substitutions.[20]

In effect this implies that the various amounts of commodities, which an individual plans to purchase, are substitutes or complements not only at that moment of time but also over time. In the absence of price-elastic expectations, therefore, an increase in the price of a commodity

---

[16] Price expectations are defined as rational if expected prices are an unbiased estimator of actual prices.

[17] For example, in late 1956 during the Suez Canal crisis there were instances of charterers who signed agreements for delivery of vessels in 1962 to commence a rental engagement of ten years' duration. And this at a time when shipyards were accepting orders for a three-year delivery. The rental rates were high enough to allow banks to lend up to 90% of the cost of the vessels that were to be built for these commitments and be sure of repayment of such loans out of the net rental in five years. So one wonders how much information is wasted in practice.

[18] See Chapter 7, "Characteristics of the Tankship Markets."

[19] This formulation is otherwise known as the "fundamental equation of value" or the Allen-Hicks formulation. See Hicks *op. cit.,* Mathematical Appendix to Chapters 2 and 3, pp. 307–314; also Allen, R. G. D., *Mathematical Economics,* Macmillan and Co., Ltd., London, 1957, pp. 658–664.

[20] See "Interperiod Maximization of Profit or Utility" at the end of this chapter. This result was also alluded to by Jacob L. Mosac in *General Equilibrium Theory in International Trade,* The Principia Press, Inc., Bloomington, Indiana, 1944, p. 122.

will decrease the consumption of the commodity and increase that of its substitutes both currently and in the future. If, however, expectations are that a price increase will occur in the future, then this will lead to an increase in current consumption of the commodity if it is a substitute for future consumption of that very same commodity. On the other hand it will lead to a decrease in current consumption if there is complementarity among the amounts of the commodity consumed over time.

There is another comment that we must make concerning the Slutsky-Hicks formulation. The theory underlying the latter was aimed at describing consumer or household behavior. Does this therefore imply that it is inapplicable in the case of intermediate goods or goods whose demand is derived? In our opinion the answer is no, because even consumer goods may be considered as intermediate to final utility or satisfaction and consequently face derived demand. There are no impairing differences between marginal rates of substitution which are based on industrial marginal physical productivities and consumer marginal utilities, nor are there any weakening compromises of theory if we assume that industrial budget constraints operate in the same way as do those of the individual consumer. Consequently, although the Slutsky-Hicks formulation was originally developed to apply in the static case of consumer equilibrium, we find that it also applies in the case of interperiod maximization of utility, as well as in the case of non-households.

Our investigation of the impact of price-elastic expectations on partial market stability over time will still be in terms of short-run analysis. In doing this, no restrictive assumptions will be made as to any specific pattern of expectations, either extrapolative or adaptive. It will be shown that such price movements are bounded and that at least one-way stable equilibria can occur in markets affected by price-elastic expectations. Such expectations, we shall later point out, will in the long run cause cyclical price patterns in the tankship markets without the necessity of cyclical demand.

Whenever a market is at a short-run equilibrium we shall assume that there exists a price level P_f which the operatives in the particular market expect to prevail in the future. Changes in this expected future price level are assumed to be a function of the changes in the present price. In this respect this formulation borrows from Arrow-Nerlove[21] rather than Enthoven-Arrow[22] in that we are using an "expected normal price," but in our case this expected normal price is taken before any changes in the present price P occur. As long as the market is at an equilibrium

---

[21] Arrow, Kenneth J., and Marc Nerlove, *op. cit.*, pp. 297–298.
[22] Enthoven, Alain C., and Kenneth J. Arrow, *op. cit.*, p. 289.

point, only static expectations are assumed to prevail, and the latter determine the expected future price level. There is no reason, however, why it must be concluded that static expectations necessarily imply a future price level equal to current prices. For example, technological economies of scale both internal as well as external may still operate on the long-run supply schedules in a way that allows a determination of the future price level under static conditions. We assume, therefore, that the level is affected by factors endogenous as well as exogenous to the particular market but that the future price level *under static conditions* can be derived from *objective* data before any changes in present prices occur.

It seems logical to assume that a price range exists around each stable short-run equilibrium within which prices may move without setting into motion dynamic expectations. A price movement beyond this range, however, which we call the "price range of strict static relevance," will cause dynamic interperiod substitutions.[23] The magnitude of this range is determined, we believe, by the characteristics of the particular market; these cannot be included satisfactorily in a general formulation but nonetheless do not affect the general conclusions that can be drawn from this discussion.[24] Although this assumption is rather unnecessary and may appear to be somewhat gratuitous at this stage, it is introduced nonetheless in the hope that it will help the reader to follow our subsequent discussion.

In considering the impact of price-elastic expectations on the equilibrium of a single market, we shall assume that cross price effects are negligible and that the only substitutions that can occur are of an interperiod nature. The latter assumption may seem to be restrictive but in actuality it is not, for if we can prove that short-run stability at various points of time under such conditions is possible, then this will certainly be true if we assume that other prices and quantities can move freely in order to stabilize the markets, unless, of course, complemen-

---

[23] If prices move in discontinuous jumps the assumption of a price range of static relevance will be workable as well as realistic. Only in cases of a continuous monotonic price "drift" may it fail, but here again the drift may be due to shifts in the short-run equilibrium point rather than be the result of disequilibrating price movements.

[24] The characteristics that we have in mind include: the type of end use of the product (how urgent are the needs that it satisfies); if an input factor is concerned, the imputed profit to this input; the range over which the supply schedule is elastic (that is to say, the range beyond which even the most inefficient suppliers not only cover their full cost but also realize satisfactory profits). In general we can say in a vague way that this range is bounded by limits beyond which prices cannot be explained by "normal" and objective data.

tarities exist.[25] In our case, however, the goods offered over the various time periods are substitutes and not complements. Furthermore, and this as a justification for the choice of dealing with short-run rather than long-run equilibria, if we can show that no short-run price is unbounded at any point of time then we can conclude that long-run prices are not explosive, even though not necessarily stable. In order to see the realism of arguments on the production plan we may take the markets to be intermediate to a final product, the latter being either physical product or utility.

For the convenience of the reader the special notation that will be used in the subsequent discussion is summarized here:

E = the price of elasticity of expectations defined as $(\partial P_f/\partial P)(P/P_f)$

where P_f stands for the future price level and P for the present price. The lower-case subscripts b and s will be used to denote the price elasticity of expectations of buyers and sellers, respectively. The range of E is assumed to be finite.

E_D = the price elasticity of demand defined as $(\partial Q/\partial P)(P/Q)$
$E_{D,M}$ = the income elasticity of demand
E_{D,P_f} = the elasticity of demand with respect to future price
R^s = the price region of strict static relevance, namely the set of all prices around the static equilibrium such that dynamic price-elastic expectations are absent

Let us assume that the demand for a noninferior product X at any moment of time may be represented by

$$Q = K + f(P_f)$$

where K is a constant representing the demand under static expectations,[26] at which time $f(P_{f_0}) = 0$. Under dynamic expectations, $f(P_f) \neq 0$ and $P_f = g(P)$.[27]

We shall now proceed to determine the impact of interperiod substitutions on the quantity of a commodity demanded at any moment of time.

From Equation 2.23 in the appendix and for $s = 0$, we have

$$\partial Q/\partial P = -Q(\partial Q/\partial M) + (\partial Q/\partial P)_{\pi = \text{const}} \qquad (2.1)$$

[25] In the case of tankers, which is our main concern, while it is true that the chartering of tankship services and tankship building are alternatives over the long run (time horizon of at least two years), these are not substitutes in the short run. Consequently, the assumptions of negligible cross price effects and no substitutions, other than of an interperiod nature, are quite realistic.
[26] Alternatively, K may be set $K = f(P)$ within R^s.
[27] Actually, $\Delta P_f = f(\Delta P)$.

where the first term on the right-hand side represents the income effect of a price change and the second term the income-compensated substitution effect.

If $E_b < 1$, then $(\partial Q/\partial P)_{\pi=\text{const}} < 0$; but $\partial Q/\partial M > 0$ if X is not an inferior good; therefore, $\partial Q/\partial P < 0$. The latter implies that whenever the price of X goes up to the extent that future prices are expected to increase proportionately less, the quantity demanded goes down, thus creating excess supply which restores equilibrium. If the price goes down because future prices again are expected to decrease proportionately less, the quantity demanded increases, creating excess demand which restores the market to its previous equilibrium position. In the case where $E_b = 1$ (expectations of unitary elasticity) and there exists no interference from the purely monetary markets, there will be no interperiod substitutions, that is to say $(\partial Q/\partial P)_{\pi=\text{const}} = 0$, but the total effect may be negative because of budgetary considerations. That is to say, the income effect $-Q(\partial Q/\partial M)$ is negative and will thus tend to restore equilibrium.

If now, $E_b > 1$ then the income-compensated substitution term $(\partial Q/\partial P)_{\pi=\text{const}}$ is positive because $Q = f(P_f)$ and $P_f = f(P)$; and consequently,

$$(\partial Q/\partial P)_{\pi=\text{const}} = (\partial Q/\partial P_f)(\partial P_f/\partial P) \quad (2.2)$$

$$(\partial Q/\partial P)_{\pi=\text{const}} = E_b E_{D,P_f} Q/P \quad (2.3)$$

where E_b stands for the elasticity of expectations of buyers and E_{D,P_f} for the elasticity of demand (income-compensated) with respect to future prices. The value of E_{D,P_f} is positive whenever $E_b > 1$; consequently, $(\partial Q/\partial P)_{\pi=\text{const}} > 0$, indicating that the income-compensated substitution effect will cause an increase in the quantity demanded of a good, if present prices increase, and cause a decrease if prices decrease because of price-elastic expectations.

The income effect $-Q(\partial Q/\partial M)$, however, is negative because $\partial Q/\partial M > 0$ since we are dealing with noninferior goods.

Equation 2.1 therefore becomes

$$\partial Q/\partial P = (E_b E_{D,P_f} Q/P) - Q(\partial Q/\partial M) \quad (2.4)$$

If we multiply both sides of Equation 2.4 by P/Q and simplify we obtain

$$E_D = (E_b E_{D,P_f}) - (PE_{D,M})Q/M \quad (2.5)$$

where E_D is the price elasticity of demand, and $E_{D,M} = (\partial Q/\partial M)(M/Q)$ or the income elasticity of demand.

It can be seen from the appendix that M, the total money available, can be safely taken to be bounded, since we are dealing with partial equilibria and do not assume identity in the expectations of each and every person with respect to each and every market at any moment of time. Furthermore, the interest rate and budgetary constraints that definitely operate in any particular market at any moment of time set an upper bound to the available monetary resources.[28] A much stronger statement can be made in the case of nonhouseholds (industrial operations), where each decision-making subentity of the firm operates under budgetary constraints. As a result, when both E_{D,P_f} and $E_{D,M}$ are mathematically well behaved, are positive and finite, and the elasticity of expectations of buyers E_b is also positive and finite, then by the "Archimedean property"[29] there exists a P^* for which in Equation 2.5

$$P^* E_{D,M} Q/M > E_b E_{D,P_f} \qquad (2.6)$$

Inequality 2.6 implies that for all $P > P^*$, $E_D < 0$ even though $E_b > 1$; therefore, before prices reach infinity the demand schedule will assume a negative slope and Q will approach zero uniformly. This sets an upper bound for prices. Later we shall examine the probable consequences of a price reversal.

Below the initial equilibrium point, a disturbance accompanied by elastic expectations will send prices to zero unless the magnitude of $E_{D,M}$ is such that it will eventually reverse the trend and make E_D negative before the origin is reached.

Intuitively it is obvious that even with price-elastic expectations any price movements must be bounded, so the theoretical conclusions that

[28] Under identity in expectations with respect to every market at any moment of time and symmetry of expectations between buyers and sellers, we may be presented with a rather academic case where

$$M = \int_{t=1}^{N} P_t Q_t e^{-rt} \, dt$$

may not be bounded. For example let us assume that the buyers of inputs Q'_i, for $i = 1$ to m, derive their monetary resources from the ownership of products Q_j, ($j = 1$ to n). If elastic expectations operate in both the Q_i and Q_j markets for some i and j, then M may not be bounded if the net result is for Q_j prices to increase by a factor $e^{r't}$ where r' is greater than r, and for all practical purposes close to infinity. We said that this case is rather academic because the wealth of such individuals will be on paper until they enter the market to realize them. Otherwise they will have no cash budget at all, and consequently carry very limited if any transactions. If on the other hand they do enter the market then they will sell at a finite price and so establish a finite budget. We must further add, however, that the probability of such an occurrence under partial analysis and absence of identity in expectations is infinitesimal.

[29] The "Archimedean property" states that for any two real numbers $a > 0$ and $b > 0$, there exists an integer for which $na > b$. For proof see Birkhoff, Garrett, and Saunders MacLane, *A Survey of Modern Algebra*, The Macmillan Company, New York, 1949, p. 69.

16   CHAPTER TWO

we reached should not come as a complete surprise. Undoubtedly, there must be a prohibitive price beyond which there will be no transactions. Similarly, since we are dealing with noninferior goods, it is not logical to expect ad infinitum negative purchases (sales by users) at negative prices, even if we allow for inventory carrying charges. As we shall show later, in the tankship markets we often observe negative purchases at negative prices, but the latter are still bounded by the expected out-of-pocket cost involved in keeping vessels idle.

On the basis of the foregoing relationships we can conclude that only if the resources are unlimited (actually infinite with zero interest) or, alternatively, if (*a*) the income elasticity of demand is infinitesimal (the reciprocal of infinity) and (*b*) the purchase of a given commodity utilizes "a very small portion" (reciprocal of infinity) of a given budget will price-elastic expectations cause indeterminate or explosive price patterns in any one market. Assumptions such as these, however, are quite unrealistic, especially if the commodity is an intermediate good. In the latter case the budget is a function of the demand of the final product, and the highest purchase price will be that which will absorb all expected profit and result in a loss equal to the penalty of default of contractual obligations (or loss of "good will").

In Inequality 2.6, the quantities M, $E_{D,M}$, and E_{D,P_f}, that is to say the income, income elasticity of demand, and elasticity of demand with respect to future prices are all properly discounted whenever necessary by the relevant cost of capital and for the appropriate time periods because we are dealing with interperiod substitutions.

Turning now to the shape of the demand schedule, we find that elastic expectations create four definite price regions and, depending on the magnitude of $E_{D,M}$, very probably a fifth below the initial static equilibrium. These regions are

$$R_1 = \{P_i : P_i \epsilon R^s\} \qquad \text{for } 0 \leq E_b \leq 1 \tag{1}$$

and where by definition the total effect of a price change $\partial Q/\partial P$ is negative.[30] As the reader may remember, this is the region we previously called the price range of strict static relevance, because we feel that it is only logical to assume that dynamic (price-elastic) expectations are not excited unless the market receives a jolt. Small price movements around an equilibrium point are to be expected.

If we do not make this assumption, the region R^s will shrink to a point and result in an unstable equilibrium. In such a case, even the slightest

---

[30] The special notation used here, for example $R_1 = \{P_i : P_i \epsilon R^s\}$, should be interpreted as follows: The region R_1 is the *set of all* prices P_i *such that* P_i *is included* in region R^s.

movement away from the equilibrium point on either side will cause wild fluctuations.

$R_2 = P_{ii} : P^* > P_{ii} > P_i$ for $E_b > 1$ and total effect $\partial Q/\partial P > 0$ (ii)

$R_3 = P_{iii} : P_{iii} \geq P^*$ for $E_b > 1$ and total effect $\partial Q/\partial P < 0$ (iii)

$R_4 = P_{iv} : P_i > P_{iv} > P_L$ for $E_b > 1$ and total effect $\partial Q/\partial P \geq 0$ (iv)

(where P_L, the *low* price, equals zero if the fifth region R_5 does not exist), and finally, depending on the value of $E_{D,M}$,[31]

$R_5 = P_v : P_v \leq P_L$ for $E_b > 1$ and total effect $\partial Q/\partial P < 0$ (v)

The shape of such a schedule appears in Figure 2.1.[32] The range and slope of the various demand segments have not been chosen to be representative of anything specific; therefore, no quantitative importance should be attached to this particular choice. The reader may also notice that in Figure 2.1, the quantity Q is a function of present price P, although previously in the process of developing our theoretical formulations we assumed $Q = K + f(P_f)$; that is to say, we assumed that Q is a function of P_f. The reasons for the change are mainly three:

1. In dealing with interperiod substitutions caused by expectations, we are concerned with the impact of these expectations on the present quantity demanded. But these expectations are initiated by changes in present prices. Consequently, it is not the particular expected level of future prices that is important, but the relative changes in that level. And to repeat again, the changes ΔP_f are in our analysis a function of ΔP, and they are the only important consequence of a present price change.

2. Given any expected future price before any change in present prices, with the aid of a coefficient of expectations directly relating present to future changes, we shall be able to arrive at the level of future prices. This complication is, however, unnecessary for our exposition. Since there is no way of obtaining objective observations of future prices, we must be content in dealing with the manifestation of their existence and measuring with the aid of substitutes.

3. If we wish to derive relationships which can be used for decision making, it is not enough for the related entities to be observable. They must be observable soon enough to allow for forecasts and analysis, and thus enable changes in behavior if necessary. As a result, the value of the prognostic qualities of approximate relationships are often great enough to more than offset the damages caused by functional impurities.

[31] Actually if the region R_5 is to be empirically observable, the effect of $E_{D,M}$ is necessary but not sufficient. We must also have a relevant supply schedule in that region, which implies that the costs of exit from and re-entry into the market are such that they will generate offers from suppliers at prices in region R_5.

[32] This demand schedule may be considered by some as a cutout from a multi-dimensional surface; that is to say, the regions outside R^s may be thought of as the loci of temporary intertemporal equilibria. We do not believe so, but even if it were so, still, as we should shortly argue, it would make no difference.

To summarize then, in Figure 2.1 our choice of $Q = f(P)$ rather than $Q = f(P_f)$ was dictated by empirical realities. Such a compromise, as we have argued, is not really damaging and will aid us in our subsequent analysis of the tankship markets. We shall show later that there exists a

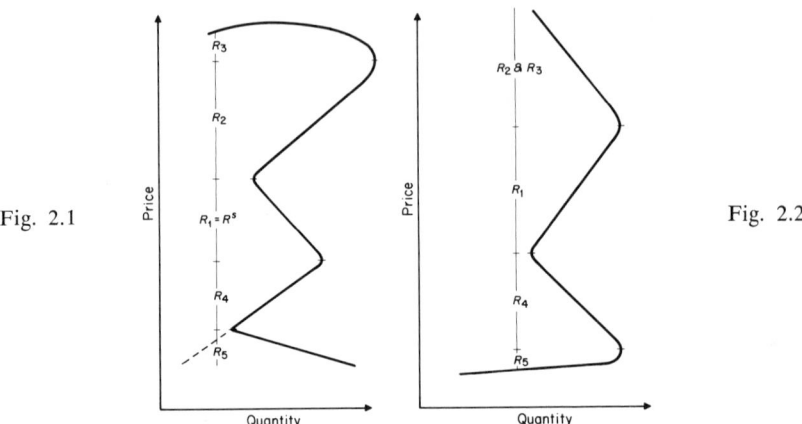

Fig. 2.1

Fig. 2.2

Figure 2.1. Demand schedule showing the impact of price-elastic expectations outside R^s.

Figure 2.2. Theoretical supply schedule affected by price-elastic expectations outside R_1.

very close similarity between the theoretical schedule of Figure 2.1 and the empirical demand schedules of tankships and tankship transportation.

As we have already mentioned, implicit in Hicks' formulation is the notion of complete symmetry in the expectations of buyers and sellers in all markets. With the knowledge of the shape of our hypothetical demand schedule (which is shown in Figure 2.1), we can easily prove that partial equilibria outside R^s are possible, even under symmetry which implies that $E_s > 1$ whenever $E_b > 1$. It is obvious that the necessary and sufficient conditions for an equilibrium above R^s rest with the relationship between the slopes (magnitude) of the demand and supply schedules in regions R_2 and R_3. By assumption (symmetry in expectations) the supply schedule in these regions is of negative slope.[33] Such an equilibrium point, whenever it exists, must be in region R_3 and will only be stable from below unless we assume reversibility in the demand and supply schedules. Region R_2 is a price range of instability, because for the whole range the supply schedule will be of negative slope while the slope of the demand schedule will be positive.

[33] In the case of consumer goods, because the income effect for *suppliers* is positive rather than negative (as it is in the case of buyers), we may get supply schedules of more pronounced negative slopes in regions R_2 and R_3.

Equilibria below R^s can exist depending not only on the relative magnitude of the slopes of the supply and demand schedules but also on the magnitude of $E_{D,M}$. All the prices in region R_4 constitute potential unstable equilibria for the same reasons that make R_2 a region of instability.[34] The slope of the supply schedule in region R_4 is expected to be negative in the case of consumer goods, not only because of the assumed symmetry in price-elastic expectations between buyers and sellers, but also because of the impact of the budget (income) effect on the suppliers. As their income goes down because of the drop in prices of the goods they possess, they will tend to supply more and consume less of the affected commodities. There will be a price, however, at which it will be catastrophic for them to produce, and as a result they will withdraw from the market. This occurrence will undoubtedly precipitate a change in expectations from elastic to inelastic and further accentuate the positive slope of the supply schedule. It is for this reason that in region R_5, if it exists, we may find stable equilibria, but these points are only stable from above unless, again, reversibility in the schedules is assumed.

Figure 2.2 depicts the shape of a supply schedule under the impact of price-elastic expectations. Its general outlines are similar to those of the demand schedule shown in Figure 2.1. Because of the assumption of symmetry in expectations between buyers and sellers, however, the two schedules are "out of phase." We must stress that only in the case where suppliers can adjust instantaneously do we expect to observe such a schedule.

Finally, another comment on the demand schedule as shown in Figure 2.1. Whether the regions outside R^s are caused by purely interperiod substitutions generated by elastic price expectations, as we have assumed, or else generated by shifts in an otherwise nonexistent static demand schedule, and which shifts have their origin in price expectations, it is actually immaterial. In other words, it makes no difference if the regions outside R^s are the loci of shifts in an assumed static demand schedule of the traditional shape, as long as such a traditional schedule never exists in these regions. We believe, however, on the basis of empirical observation, that this is not the case. Under the circumstances described, the schedule as shown in Figure 2.1 is the only relevant schedule in our estimation, and if shifts do occur, because of the elastic price expectations, the whole schedule with all of its regions shifts. These same arguments can be made for the supply schedule.

---

[34] This of course assumes that a relevant supply schedule exists in this whole region because only if the sellers' refusal price is less than P_1 will the supply and demand schedules intersect in region R_4 for an unstable equilibrium. If the refusal and re-entry prices of the suppliers happen to be included in R_4, then R_5 does not exist and at least one-way stable equilibria may be observed in region R_4.

Asymmetry in Expectations

If we now assume asymmetry in the behavior of buyers and sellers — or at least manifested asymmetry — we shall find that buyer-elastic expectations may not be allowed to bloom fully. The time period over which such elastic expectations will operate will not extend beyond the production cycle or the time it takes to produce a sufficient shift in the supply schedule and cause a price precipitation.

Figure 2.3 presents one type of asymmetrical pattern of expectations

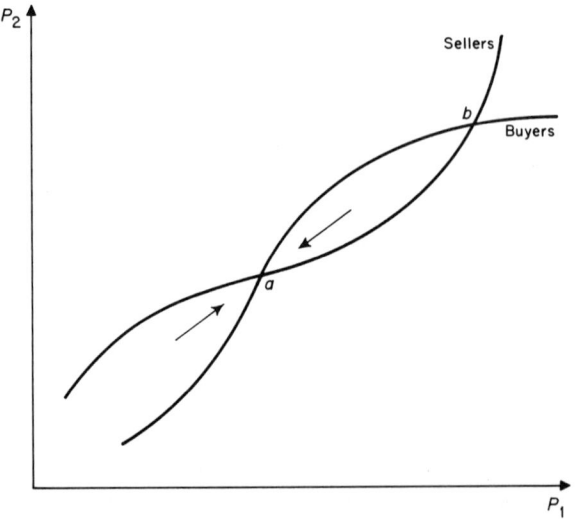

Figure 2.3. Expectations schedules.

and nonuniformity of functions. It shows that as the demand increases eventually the expectations of the sellers become elastic and those of the buyers inelastic, thus bringing forth the excess supply which will eventually satisfy the increased demand and, in the absence of any lag between cause and effect, guarantee a return to stability. The pattern of expectations assumed in Figure 2.3 implies the existence of demand schedules with positive slope, at least for certain price ranges.[35] The slope of the supply schedule, however, will not in general change the sign of its traditional slope but will become more elastic.

In a case where expectations are compounded and alternate between

---

[35] No particular significance should be attached to the numerical value of the slopes of these two schedules of expectations.

elastic and inelastic we may get a pattern of interweaving supply and demand schedules. It all depends upon the magnitude of the difference between the coefficients of expectations of buyers and sellers whether or not such a "braid" effect is obtained. If it does materialize, then stable equilibria will alternate with unstable equilibria. In case interweaving is not achieved, then the presence of dynamic expectations will not be destabilizing, because the asymmetry in the behavior of sellers will generate the necessary excess supply (unless of course the supply and demand schedules happen to coincide). If instability is averted, then the pattern of expectations may not leave any observable empirical trace.

It is not unreasonable to assume that expectations alternate between elasticity and inelasticity, if the market stays long enough at an equilibrium point, before it goes into a spin again. And this is because the "memory" of those operating in the market may not last long enough to recall how the market came to rest at that particular equilibrium point. Consequently, any equilibrium point may be taken to be the normal static equilibrium, and a move away from it will excite price-elastic expectations.

Finally we must note that on the basis of empirical observations it may be very difficult, if not impossible, to distinguish between the case of asymmetric expectations with interwoven pattern and symmetric expectations, unless more than one cycle in expectations materializes.

Supply and Demand Interactions Under Elastic Expectations

As a means of studying the impact of expectations on market equilibria, especially whenever shifts in the schedules are also present, nine schedules of supply and demand are shown in Figure 2.4. Schedule I shows the traditional normal long-run demand schedule, which assumes "all other things equal" with the exception of the price change of the particular commodity. In cases where dynamic expectations are assumed to be operating and to be a function of present price changes, a static demand schedule as shown in Schedule I with zero elasticity of expectations is very improbable.[36] Any real price movement will generate dynamic expectations which, in turn, will increase the quantity demanded in the short run rather than decrease it, because of shifts in the short-run investment possibility schedules at the various points of time.

Schedules II through IX present demand schedules exhibiting the im-

---

[36] If it is assumed that the elasticities of expectation are zero, then we revert to the case of static stability. See Hicks, *op. cit.*, pp. 245–282.

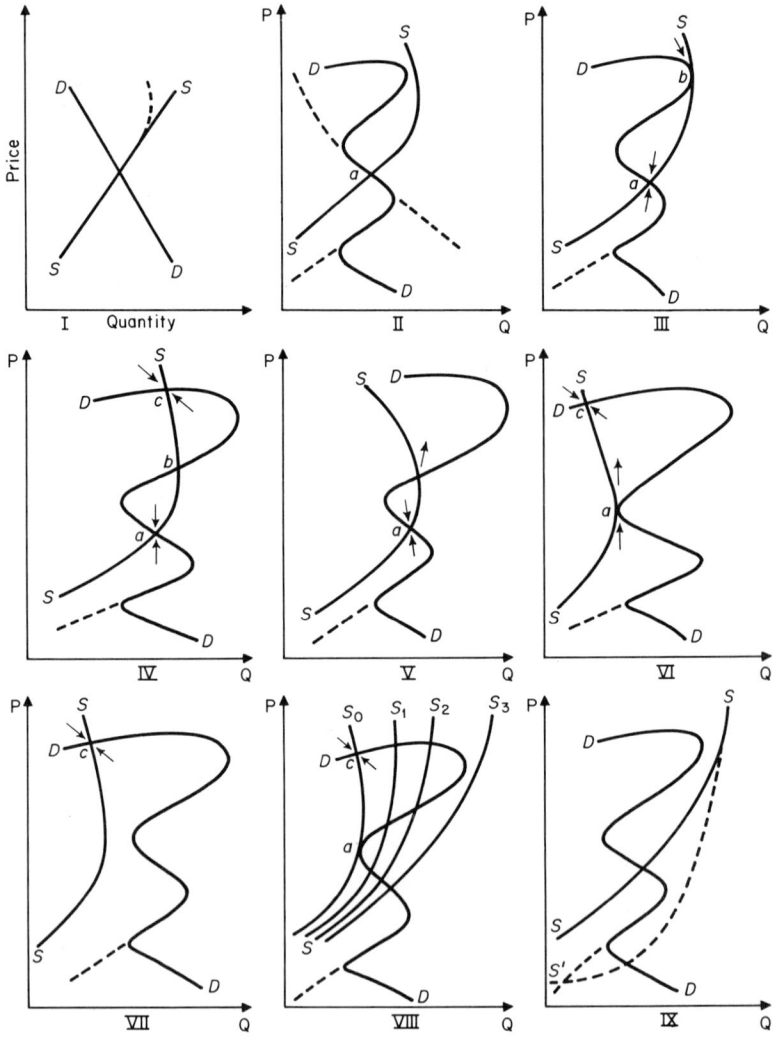

Figure 2.4. Supply and demand schedules.

pact of price-elastic expectations of the type that we have assumed,[37] and symmetric behavior between buyers and sellers. The end points of these schedules take the shape shown because of the income effects of price changes and the shape of the expectations schedule. As for the

[37] To be exact, these schedules are not based on the elasticity of expectations as defined by Hicks, *op. cit.*, p. 205, but on *coefficients of expectations* as used in smoothing functions. The reason is that the notion of the elasticity of expectations "does not tell us what the expected price *is* but merely *how it changes* when present price changes." Baumol, *op. cit.*, p. 210. However, such a distinction does not in any way affect our exposition.

supply schedules, to the extent that the impact of the dynamic expectations cannot be felt instantaneously because of the length of the reaction and/or the production cycle, they should be of the traditional shape. Consequently, we have chosen to show the supply and demand interactions under both sets of assumptions. Figure 2.4 depicts supply schedules of the traditional shape, because of slowness in the reaction of the suppliers, and Figure 2.5 shows the consequences of the assumption that the suppliers react without excessive time delays. It must be noted again at this time that what we have said concerning the demand schedules has nothing to do with dynamic shifts in demand or shifts over time in the quantity demanded due to reasons other than expectations. Our analysis up to this point is still in terms of comparative statics but with an elasticity of expectations not necessarily zero. That is to say, our arguments imply that some dynamic factors work in a certain manner to cause even the *applicable* short-run demand schedule to assume, as of a given moment of time, a shape different from the traditional.

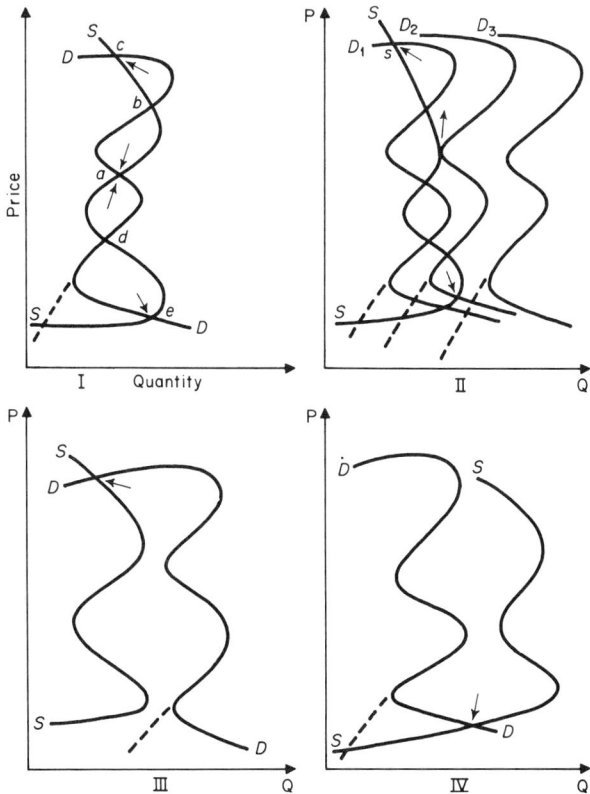

Figure 2.5. Supply and demand interactions with asymmetry in behavior.

DELAYED REACTION OF SUPPLIERS

Schedule II of Figure 2.4 shows a market at equilibrium, even though the supply and demand schedules are under the impact of price-elastic expectations. Because of the assumption underlying Figure 2.4 — that the reaction of the suppliers is not instantaneous — the impact of expectations on the supply side is limited to a counterclockwise rotation of the supply schedule.

We notice in Schedule III that once something happens and causes a shift to the right in the demand schedules[38] (such as the Korean War and the Suez crisis in the case of tankships), a movement away from the temporary equilibrium *a* will occur. Prices will rise, which may condition expectations about further shifts. Depending on the intensity of the shock, the initial rise in price may be confined between *a* and *b,* in which case it will tend to gravitate toward *a* before a secondary shift in demand occurs; or it may go beyond *b*. In the latter case, because *b* is a stable equilibrium from above but not from below,[39] the price may drop all the way toward *a* or stay *temporarily* at *b*, depending on how wide and swift are the adjusting oscillations. The amplitude of these oscillations will depend upon the severity of the original shock and the net effect of possible secondary shocks that may oppose each other. More shifts may occur, however, because the initial rise in price may set such shifts in motion. From the second shift on, the relative intensity of the opposing movements will determine the direction of the rate fluctuation. In addition to shifting the demand schedule to the right, the original shock and the rate of change in prices may cause a clockwise rotation of the demand schedules.

A possible sequence of shifts may take the markets through Schedules IV to IX. Schedule IV of Figure 2.4 shows that prices could rest (if sufficient time were allowed to end the oscillations) at either *a* or *c*, but not at *b* because *b* is unstable. Schedule V shows that above *b* the price moves "skyward," possibly not only because of the shifts in demand but also because of shifts toward the left in the supply schedules. The latter

[38] This implies expectations about shifts in all envisioned schedules in the future and not shifts caused by substitutions between years. The same results are obtained if the supply schedules shift to the left (because of retirements of facilities). As we shall show later, shifts in the supply schedules are very critical for the operations in the tankship markets and can create cyclical patterns in tankship rates.

[39] Below *b* but above *a* the quantity supplied at each intermediate price is greater than the quantity demanded; hence the price will tend toward *a*. But we notice that the same situation exists above *b*, which will make *b* a stable equilibrium from above, but not from below.

shifts, shown better in Schedules VI and VII, may occur if the owners have had time to react to the elasticity of their expectations or reach the elastic point on their expectations schedule. The next possible shift in demand, therefore, may establish c of Schedules VI and VII as the only stable equilibrium.

The market now enters its most critical and precarious stage, and it is ready for a reversal. It cannot stay long at point c for one of several reasons.

1. The demand schedule may not be reversible.[40] This will make point c a stable equilibrium only from below and not from above. Consequently any price fluctuation, in such a case, will be destabilizing and will create chaos and panic.

2. The withdrawal of the buyers, because of the budget effect, may be taken by the sellers as an indication of reversal in expectations. Such an assumption may generate excess supply, which will cause precipitation in prices.

3. The expectations of buyers may actually change, when they withdraw from the market, and cause shifts to the left in the demand schedules. As a result the market may go back through the stages depicted by Schedules III and II.

4. Under the impact of price-elastic expectations, the sellers accelerate input and postpone output whenever prices rise. The acquisition of additional capacity will undoubtedly shift the supply schedules to the right as shown in Schedule VIII. Consequently, and even if the demand schedules are reversible, the emergence of new capacity will ultimately throw the market into a swift decline. After the oscillations exhaust themselves, the schedules of supply and demand may appear as in Schedule IX, generating overcapacity and short-run equilibrium prices below "normal" full cost.

On the basis of the schedules presented in Figure 2.4, one can readily see that markets which exhibit the characteristics that we postulated are prone to excess capacity and depression. The movements about the normal short-run equilibrium point occur very swiftly, in both directions. The falls are always of greater magnitude than the rises because the region of static relevance is bypassed on the downfall. It appears that markets affected by price-elastic expectations laboriously work their way out of overcapacity and depression to reach the region of static relevance for a short respite, in order to plunge again into another adventure. Thus the fate of those operating in these markets is to alternate between a few months of exhilaration and many years of misery.

[40] It is very probable that the demand schedules are not reversible, outside the region of strict static relevance. As soon as prices start sliding downward, elastic expectations will dictate withdrawal from the market, which will further accentuate the downfall. Thus the downward movement in prices occurs very swiftly. Similarly, whenever prices go up sufficiently, elastic expectations take over immediately.

INSTANTANEOUS REACTION OF SUPPLIERS

If the suppliers react instantaneously to the various manifestations of price changes and the elastic expectations of buyers, then the supply schedule will assume the shape shown in Figure 2.2. Above the region of strict static relevance the supply schedule will bend backward more sharply as the suppliers adjust to their elastic expectations. Below the static region we now find a price range over which the supply schedule will assume a negative slope, before it reverses itself and proceeds to the origin as prices fall.

The results of supply and demand interactions under these circumstances will not be significantly different from those that we have just considered. The only major difference, as can be seen in Figure 2.5, will be found below the static region. We notice that because the supply schedule becomes negatively sloped and then reverses itself two more equilibria are established. The one at point d is unstable, but the equilibrium at e is stable at least from above.

The fluctuations in a market affected by elastic expectations, symmetric buyer-seller behavior, and instantaneous supplier reaction are undoubtedly more violent and wider. Otherwise, we can readily see by comparing Figures 2.4 and 2.5 that the over-all market behavior in both cases is similar.

SUPPLY AND DEMAND INTERACTIONS WITH ASYMMETRY IN BEHAVIOR

Finally, let us examine the consequences of an assumed asymmetry in the behavior of buyers and sellers. If the sellers do not or cannot react instantaneously, then this case is similar to the one we examined under "Delayed Reaction of Suppliers." The analysis made and conclusions reached then are still valid. The only difference is that the inelastic expectations of the suppliers will cause a clockwise rather than counterclockwise rotation of the supply schedule, and may not cause much surplus capacity. Consequently, although the fluctuations will not be eliminated, yet the duration of the price cycles may be shortened.

If the suppliers react without excessive delays their stabilizing influence is even more pronounced. Whether or not such a market can avoid completely the erratic fluctuations inherent in the schedules of Figure 2.4 no one can tell on an a priori basis. It all depends upon the magnitude of the coefficients of expectations of buyers and sellers, and the impact of such on the quantities supplied and demanded at the various prices.

Of the two assumptions governing the speed of supplier reactions (instantaneous versus lagged), the most realistic is the one that assumes delayed reaction. There is usually a "lead time" between input and output, and if fixed capacity (capital equipment) must be acquired, then the delays are further increased. As a result we observe that whether behavior is symmetric or asymmetric the results in general are the same, that is to say, elastic buyer expectations generate wide price fluctuations. These prices are bounded from both above and below and some of the equilibria are stable at least "one way." However, as we have already noted, even the stable equilibria are prone to be temporary under the impact of price-elastic expectations.

These statements raise a number of questions concerning the quantitative attributes of the turning points and the ranges of the supply and demand schedules. Taking first the demand schedule, we believe that the range of its region of strict static relevance R^s is determined by the normal long-run supply schedule at any moment of time. The cost functions of the suppliers are more or less known, consequently, costs and "reasonable prices based on such costs" are expected to play a major role in defining the range within which such strict static influences will reign.[41]

Once prices move beyond this range, however, and each buyer cannot *by himself* account for this move on the basis of objective data available to him, he automatically assumes that dynamic factors are operating either on the investment possibility schedules or on the production functions. Being in a completely unstructured situation, he assumes that others know what he does not, his expectations become elastic, and subjective elements rather than "reasonable prices based on costs" influence his behavior. This will continue up to the point where new objective evidence enters to force him to reconsider his behavior and awake to face reality. The new evidence under falling prices is in the form of complete withdrawal of the sellers from the market — when they cannot cover their short-run variable costs, less any costs necessary for deactivation and subsequent reactivation of their facilities — and under rising prices complete elimination of all the profit imputed to the product.

For intermediate products, under rising prices, the turning point occurs at the price that eliminates any profit or utility out of the final product. In fact the input price may go beyond the point of such profit elimination from the final product because of the imputation of any loss of good will due to stockouts. Consequently the greater the profit margins and/or loss of good will associated with a final product, the

---

[41] In the tankship service markets, in particular, costs are known to the buyers (the oil companies) because the latter also operate vessels. Furthermore the "firm," as we shall later observe, is under normal operating conditions quite simple (the vessel), and consequently its technology can be easily duplicated.

greater the range of the demand schedule over which elastic expectations will prevail to create a positive slope.

Turning our attention now to the supply schedule, we believe that although it is established under expectations symmetrical with those operating on the demand schedule, it seems logical to assume that such symmetry is only adopted by the sellers as the latter observe the behavior of the buyers. In other words, the suppliers being closer to objective data take their cue from the manifested behavior of the buyers. Consequently the *real* expectations schedules that influence the behavior of the buyers and sellers may not be exactly symmetrical or qualitatively identical. First of all the reactions of the sellers may be lagging a little behind those of the buyers, but more important than that, the final turning points of the demand schedule may be taken by the sellers as implying a change in expectations. As we have already seen, the income (budget) effects of price changes will cause the turning points, and as a result the demand schedule will assume negative slope although expectations are still elastic. So, even though there may be a *manifested* symmetry, it may hide a certain degree of asymmetry in the *real* expectations schedules. In either case, however, as we have repeatedly stressed and shown during our analysis, the results are the same.

What are the intuitive justifications behind such assumed *manifested* symmetry in the expectations schedules of buyers and sellers?

1. All the reasons that justify symmetry in expectations — and asymmetry in transaction behavior — over R^s, the price range of strict static relevance.

2. Transaction asymmetry in behavior appears to be a fact of life. Although with the culmination of an exchange transaction the utility of both parties is enhanced, yet every concession by one during the bargaining stage is a net benefit to the other.

3. It is inherent perhaps in human nature, and also implied in game-theoretic behaviors, to assume that the willingness of an opponent automatically implies the need for a reconsideration on the part of the other. So, in effect, and even if the sellers are willing to sell all they have at a certain price, once they see a lot of buyers wanting to purchase their product they withdraw from the market to reconsider.

To summarize, we have thus far shown that when dealing with partial market stability, equilibria can occur with elasticities of expectation of buyers greater than unity, although such equilibria may be very temporary. Prices are not explosive, although they may follow a fluctuating pattern within bounds. Whether the expectations of the sellers are elastic or inelastic does not actually affect the qualitative attributes or general nature of the interactions. Inelastic expectations for the suppliers will reduce the destabilizing influence of the elastic expectations of the buyers, but in all probability will not eliminate it, especially in cases where production is not instantaneous.

Leaving this theoretical but also general discussion of the shape of the demand and supply schedules, we shall now turn our attention to the tankship service market and comment on the factors that affect its demand schedule.

Appendix to Chapter 2

Interperiod Maximization of Profit or Utility

We shall prove here that the Slutsky-Hicks formulation[42] for the consumer equilibrium in the static case (maximization of utility in any one period), applies also to the case of interperiod substitutions.[43] Namely, we shall show that the solution of the n good case at any one moment of time applies in principle to the case where the choice is between purchases of the same good at n different points of time, for maximization of utility over a plan covering at least two time periods. This process of budget allocation among periods within a plan is termed here an interperiod substitution.

Let us assume that a consumer attempting to maximize his utility, or a producer of some good, uses as input a commodity X. The quantity Q_t of X that he needs at any moment of time t (for $t = 0, 1, \cdots, n$), is derived from his final utility function or the demand of his final product, respectively. The price P_0 of this input at time $t = 0$ is determined by market considerations, and so are its prices $P_1, P_2, \cdots, P_n$ at times $t = 1, \cdots, n$ in the future. On the basis of the relationship between these prices, optimal purchasing plans may be developed given activity budgets and forecasts.

It is assumed here that the final good or utility cannot be produced instantaneously with the mere acquisition of the input, and that the input can be stored without any significant loss in utility. The latter assumption is necessary for the existence of interperiod substitutions, while the former, although not vital for our arguments, introduces some realism in the designation of input and output as two different products. Probabilistic uncertainty may be introduced in manufacturing plans, manufacturing time cycles, demand, delivery times, etc., and still not disturb

---

[42] See Hicks, *op. cit.*, pp. 307–314; and Allen, *op. cit.*, pp. 658–664.
[43] See also Mosak, *op. cit.*, p. 122.

our assumptions of static conditions as long as the type of probabilistic distributions and their parameters are known with certainty. Inventory stocks may thus be established even under static conditions, but purchasing plans will nonetheless be influenced in such cases by the needs of mainly one time period. Under static conditions, the producer will have no reason to deviate consciously from the original plan. Nor would he during any one period purchase more than what he needs for his "current" production plans, unless the P_i of any two periods differ by more than the carrying charges associated with the financing and storing of such excess inventory over the necessary period of time. Once dynamic expectations about future price levels enter into the picture, however, a producer will generally buy more than his current needs if prices are expected to rise, and less if prices are expected to fall. So his demand for X may be represented by $Q = K + f(P_f)$, where K is a constant[44] and P_f stands for the future price level. Under strictly static price expectations and stationary demand of the final product that uses X as an input, $f(P_f) = 0$ and $Q = K$.

For any input purchase plan we assume that the rational producer or consumer will allocate his purchases to the various periods in such a way as to maximize the present value of his profit or utility function.

$$\pi(Q_0, Q_1, Q_2, \cdots, Q_n) \tag{2.7}$$

under the constraint that

$$M \geq \sum_{t=1}^{n} P_t Q_t e^{-rt} \tag{2.8}$$

where r is the applicable interest rate or cost of capital, and M is the present value of his monetary resources (owned or borrowed). Under budgetary restrictions where a series of yearly budgets B_t is available,

$$M = \sum_{t=1}^{n} B_t e^{-rt} \tag{2.9}$$

The quantities Q_t that the producer or consumer will buy at the various prices P_t will thus be determined by maximizing

$$\pi + \mu(M - \sum_{t} P_t Q_t e^{-rt}) \tag{2.10}$$

where μ is a Lagrange multiplier, and a function of both M and prices.

At the equilibrium we have

---

[44] Actually K is a function of present prices under static conditions. We chose this expositional oversimplification because we wished to show the impact of dynamic considerations on the static demand schedule (quantity demanded at any moment of time).

APPENDIX TO CHAPTER TWO

$$\partial\pi/\partial Q_t - \mu P_t e^{-rt} = 0 \qquad (t = 0, 1, \cdots, n) \tag{2.11}$$

and

$$\sum_t P_t Q_t e^{-rt} = M \tag{2.12}$$

which imply that the present values of the net marginal profits imputed to the last units of quantities Q_t purchased during the various periods $t = 0, 1, \cdots, n$ must all be equal to their prices discounted for t periods and multiplied by μ the marginal utility of money. This is true for all t.

If we designate $\partial\pi/\partial Q_t$ with π_t, we then get from Equation 2.11

$$\pi_0/P_0 = (\pi_1/P_1)e^r = (\pi_2/P_2)e^{2r} = \cdots = (\pi_n/P_n)e^{nr} = \mu \tag{2.13}$$

From Equation 2.13 we notice that interperiod equilibrium occurs when the marginal rates of substitution π_i/π_j are equal to the price ratios properly discounted.

Equations 2.11 and 2.12 will determine the various quantities Q_0, Q_1, $\cdots$, Q_n purchased at the various points of time.

Now observe the effect of changes in M and prices. By substituting $\partial\pi/\partial Q_t = \pi_t$ and taking the partial derivative of Equations 2.11 and 2.12 with respect to M, we get

$$\left. \begin{array}{l} \sum_t \pi_{st}(\partial Q_t/\partial M) - P_s e^{-sr}(\partial \mu/M) = 0 \qquad (s, t = 0, 1, \cdots, n) \\ \sum_t P_t e^{-rt}(\partial Q_t/\partial M) = 1 \end{array} \right\} \tag{2.14}$$

Substituting for P_t in Equation 2.14, $P_t = \pi_t e^{rt}/\mu$, as derived from Equation 2.11, we have the equivalent

$$\left. \begin{array}{l} \sum_t \pi_{st}(\partial Q_t/\partial M) - \pi_s(1/\mu)(\partial \mu/\partial M) = 0 \qquad (t = 0, 1, \cdots, n) \\ \sum_t \pi_t(\partial Q_t/\partial M) = \mu \end{array} \right\} \tag{2.15}$$

By Cramer's rule the solution of the above equation is

$$(\partial Q_t/\partial M) = \mu(D_t/D) \qquad (t = 1, 2, \cdots, n) \tag{2.16}$$

where D is the determinant value of the matrix of coefficients in Equations 2.15 with cofactors D_t and D_{st}.

From the equilibrium conditions we obtain no information concerning the sign of D_t, a result which implies that with an increase in income the demand for a product may increase or decrease. The latter situation occurs with inferior goods.

Second, we take the case where a price, say P_s, is increased or is expected to increase all other prices with M remaining for the moment the

MAXIMIZATION OF PROFIT OR UTILITY   33

same. Again, we substitute $(\partial \pi/\partial Q_t) = \pi_t$ and differentiate Equations 2.11 and 2.12 with respect to any P_s to get

$$\begin{aligned}
\sum_t \pi_{it}(\partial Q_t/\partial P_s) - P_i e^{-ir}(\partial \mu/\partial P_s) &= 0 \quad (t = 0, 1, \cdots, n), \quad (i \neq s) \\
\sum_t \pi_{st}(\partial Q_t/\partial P_s) - P_s e^{-sr}(\partial \mu/\partial P_s) - \mu e^{-sr} &= 0 \\
\sum_t P_t(\partial Q_t/\partial P_s) e^{-tr} + Q_s e^{-sr} &= 0
\end{aligned} \quad (2.17)$$

Substituting $P_t = \pi_t e^{tr}/\mu$ in Equation 2.17 we obtain

$$\begin{aligned}
\sum_t \pi_{it}(\partial Q_t/\partial P_s) - \pi_i(1/\mu)(\partial \mu/\partial P_s) &= 0 \quad (i \neq s) \\
\sum_t \pi_{st}(\partial Q_t/\partial P_s) - \pi_s(1/\mu)(\partial \mu/\partial P_s) &= \mu e^{-sr} \\
\sum_t \pi_t(\partial Q_t/\partial P_s) &= -\mu e^{-sr} Q_s
\end{aligned} \quad (2.18)$$

We again use Cramer's rule to obtain the solution in terms of $\partial Q_t/\partial P_s$, which is

$$(\partial Q_t/\partial P_s) = -\mu e^{-sr} Q_s(D_t/D) + \mu e^{-sr}(D_{st}/D) \quad (2.19)$$

Substituting Relation 2.16 in Equation 2.19 and letting $X_{st} = \mu D_{st}/D$, we get

$$(\partial Q_t/\partial P_s) = -Q_s(\partial Q_t/\partial M)e^{-sr} + X_{st}e^{-sr} \quad (2.20)$$

The result in Equation 2.20 is nothing more than the Slutsky-Hicks formulation discounted by the appropriate time value of money and for the relevant time periods.[45] The term e^{-rs} is invariant with respect to both income and prices, consequently Equation 2.20 constitutes a proof that the fundamental equation of value theory applies to the case of interperiod substitutions.

In Equation 2.20 the first term on the right-hand side gives the income effect of a price change on the demand, and the second, the income-compensated substitution effect. We shall use Equation 2.20 in the following form:[46]

$$(\partial Q_t/\partial P_s) = [-Q_s(\partial Q_t/\partial M) + (\partial Q_t/\partial P_s)_{\pi=\text{const}}] \quad (2.21)$$

where

$$(\partial Q_t/\partial P_s)_{\pi=\text{const}} = X_{st}$$

[45] The number of periods depends on the numerical values of t and s. If we are concerned with the present, of course $t = 0$.

[46] We must always remember that whenever we use this relationship to assess the impact of interperiod substitutions the terms are appropriately discounted.

In Equation 2.21 we can let $t = s$ to obtain Equation 2.22 which gives us the effect of a price change of a good on the quantity demanded in the period that the price change occurred.

$$(\partial Q_s/\partial P_s) = [-Q_s(\partial Q_s/\partial M) + (\partial Q_s/\partial P_s)_{\pi=\text{const}}] \quad (2.22)$$

3

The Shape of the Demand Schedule for Tanker Services — Preliminary Comments

In order to obtain an appreciation of the shape of the static demand schedule of tankship services, we must go through several steps of sequential analysis and derivation. Tankship services add spatial utility to crude oil, which, in turn, is an input to refined oil: some of the refined products are intended for ultimate consumer use (for example, gasoline is used as an input to consumer transportation and pleasure, and heating oil for comfort) and others are still further inputs to products of various sectors of industrial activity and defense effort. Tankship services, incidentally, enter again at this stage by adding spatial utility to the refined products.

The region of strict static relevance R^s of the demand schedule for tankship services is, from all indications, very inelastic because of the inelasticity of the demand for petroleum products.

We believe that the demand (short-run and intermediate) for petroleum is inelastic for the following four reasons:

1. Substitution of sources of energy is highly limited because of the heavy capital investment required in converting from one source of energy into another.[1] The cost of oil, therefore, is only a very small fraction of the total cost of the output. As a result, any change in the price of oil will have no appreciable effect on the cost of the final product or service, and will not force substitution of inputs.

2. Technical substitutability, except in the very long run, is usually very low or nonexistent. For certain major uses petroleum and its products have no substitute. Gas turbines and commercial atomic reactors may become competitive with oil-generated power plants only in the very distant future.

3. The structure of the oil industry (institutional-geographical type of

---

[1] My former colleague Gordon Shillinglaw of Columbia University informs me that the new generating plants of electric power companies have built-in flexibility that allows substitution of sources of energy. This will make the demand schedule of fuel oil more elastic.

CHAPTER THREE

constraints) allows the oil companies to pursue in the short run production policies that are independent of the cost of any single input factor. The marginal cost of the greatest part of all oil produced is so small, as compared to its final price, that normal increases in the price of inputs, such as tanker transportation, cannot possibly equalize prices with marginal costs. This would be particularly true in the aggregate if oil were free to flow to any market.

The notion of average replacement cost of the capacity used does not enter into managerial decision making, in this particular case, mainly because

(*a*) We are concerned with the short run, and an extensive one at that, since the productive life of some of the existing oil fields is quite long, and

(*b*) the range of potential replacement costs is so great as to render any average meaningless because of the extensive variance surrounding it. Only if we assume that each individual firm faces, because of *its own* experience, a replica of the statistical universe of the industry will the notion of an average replacement cost be meaningful in managerial decision making.[2]

4. Finally, the existence of regulating agencies and "shut-in" capacities shows that the total demand for oil is inelastic. The price changes that we observe are neither the result of demand elasticity nor of efforts to shift the demand schedule for the industry. These changes are caused by attempts on the part of small operators to enlarge their own share of the market (or to get rid of excess inventories) by regional and seasonal adjustments of oil flows, or by pure miscalculations[3] on the part of some producers. Inciden-

---

[2] Even in this case, however, there is no way of knowing whether the "current" replacement cost can serve as a datum for the cost of the particular "future" capacity which will replace the one presently used. In other words, one is not only concerned with the probabilistic distribution, the mean and variance, of replacement costs *at any moment of time* but also with the distribution over the means, their average and variance *over time*.

[3] There is no doubt that miscalculations do occur often, even with the experts. Data furnished by a few oil companies show that the errors in forecasted year-to-year *changes* are between 30% and 41% of the actual changes. Even on aggregates, errors of 5% (cumulative) are not uncommon. See McIntosh, A. F., "Petroleum Demand Past and Future," paper delivered to the 1957 annual meeting of the A.P.I. and summarized in the January 1958 issue of the *Petroleum Press Service,* London, pp. 5–7. Also, one may take the yearly reviews and forecasts of the Transportation Coordinator of the Standard Oil Company of New Jersey, which have appeared regularly for several years now in the December issue of *The Oil Gas Journal,* and compare the forecasts made in one year with the actual results reported in the following year. Because storage is costly and because the marginal cost of oil is low, temptations toward occasional dumping should be expected. This observation particularly applies to small operators whose market share is so small that they hope they can unload before retaliation occurs. On the impact of stocks on prices see "Massive Improvision," *Petroleum Press Service,* January 1957; "The Economic Role of Stocks," *Petroleum Press Service,* October 1957; "Stockpiling Oil for Europe?" *Petroleum Press Service,* December 1957, pp. 449–451; and also the "Market Reports" that appear at the end of each monthly issue of the *Petroleum Press Service.*

tally, the fluctuations that occur in the product prices do not necessarily imply cost push caused by the raw materials.

On the subject of posted versus delivered prices, it is only fair to mention that things are not as simple as they appear to be.[4] The "net back" to the producer does indeed fluctuate, depending on market transportation costs as we have implied in the third reason given above, but this statement is true mostly in the case of "marginal" sales.[5] Since most sales are covered by long-term agreements, we would only notice the impact of freight rates on these sales if the accounting system of the producer were geared to register opportunity costs.

Where then does all this lead us? It shows that changes in transportation rates may induce changes in other factors but will not decrease or increase the quantity of transportation services demanded in the short run.

In summary, then, we conclude that the region of strict static relevance of tankship services is inelastic because[6]

1. Transportation is an input to a factor the demand for which is inelastic.
2. Ocean transportation is very specialized; hence, technically the substitution of other input factors for it is almost impossible, especially in static terms.
3. The cost of transportation is only a small fraction of the total cost of the final product that uses it as an input.
4. The institutional and geographical constraints operating in the oil

---

[4] For general but spotty information on prices, see *Produits Petroliers En Europe Occidentale,* United Nations, Geneva, March 1955; O.E.E.C., *Oil, the Outlook for Europe,* Paris, 1955, Chapter 11; Higgins, E. A., *Oil prices in 1957* (11 pages), paper presented before the Institute of Petroleum in London, December 1957; *Oil Bunker Prices,* Westinform Shipping Report No. 31, January 1955; *Developments in Oil Bunker Prices,* Westinform Shipping Report No. 91, August 1957; "The Drop in Prices," *Petroleum Press Service,* March 1958, pp. 82–84; "Prices under Pressure," *Petroleum Press Service,* March 1959, pp. 85–87; O.E.E.C., *Europe's Need for Oil,* Paris, 1958, Chapter 6.

[5] Most of the crude oil is sold on a delivered basis yet there is no organized market at delivery points. Consequently, in order to determine the impact of transportation rates on the "net back" a producer receives on the "marginal" sales, we have to study the level versus the structure of discounts given. The posted prices at the producing centers are not usually real prices but only indices on which discounts are given.

[6] The reader will undoubtedly recognize in these conditions Marshall's "laws" of derived demand (see Marshall, Alfred, *Principles of Economics,* Eighth Edition, Macmillan & Co., Ltd., London, 1956, Chapter 6). To the latter, Samuelson, in his *Economics,* Fourth Edition, McGraw-Hill Book Company, Inc., New York, 1958, pp. 523–525, has postulated a fifth principle to take care of cases of oligopoly. For general discussion see also Frankel, P. H., *Essentials of Petroleum,* Chapman and Hall, Ltd., London, 1946.

markets allow the operatives to pursue production plans relatively independently of the cost of inputs, especially in the short run.

5. Changes in transportation costs force other factors to adjust in such a way as to lessen the impact of *own* price changes on the quantity of transportation demanded.[7]

So much for the region of strict static relevance of the demand schedule.[8] But is there anything that we can say about the imprint of the dynamic expectations on demand? In particular, can we determine the shape assumed by the demand schedule because of interperiod substitutions? These questions are very vital because we should like to know whether a hypothesis, as expounded in Chapter 2, represents empirical reality.

If we simply record the number of transactions completed at the various prices (rates), we shall fail somewhat to obtain a demand schedule for one or a combination of the following reasons:

1. The number of transactions by itself, even though important, is not sufficient, since each transaction has more than one dimension. An agreement may cover one voyage for a specified run, consecutive voyages, or an extended time duration. Size and speed also have bearing upon capacity, and this will not be reflected in the number of transactions.

2. Transactions completed do not necessarily imply quantity demanded at the respective rates. In contrast to the theoretical determination of competitive equilibria, recontracting does not take place in practice, and markets are therefore not cleared. Thus the completed transactions, however defined, may represent only intermediate equilibria achieved by operatives having only partial knowledge of the alternatives. As a result, the completed transactions may not reveal the total impact of the market forces.

3. Lags may be present, so that the price prevailing in one period may not be the result of factors operating in the same period, but may be influenced by factors of previous or even future periods.

4. Finally, all the other things that are assumed equal under static conditions may not remain equal in practice.

Most of the objections presented in the first category can be removed by translating transactions into time equivalents. This entails the arduous task of converting *trips* into time duration by taking into consideration the speed of the chartered vessels and round-trip distances. This approximation ignores *size and speed* differences among vessels *on time charter,* yet sample checks showed that the "time-cost" of the prohibitive number of calculations necessary for perfection would far outweigh its benefits, and would not change at all the nature of our con-

---

[7] By impacts of *own* price changes we mean $\partial x_i / \partial P_i$ (total effect). The latter is contrasted to $\partial x_i / \partial P_j$ (total effect) which shows the total impact on the demand for x_i caused by a change in the price p_j of *another* commodity x_j.

[8] The reader may also wish to glance over Koopmans, T. C., *Tanker Freight Rates and Tankship Building,* Haarlem, 1939, pp. 23–49.

clusions. In fact if the refinements were made, they would have accentuated the impact of interperiod substitutions on the demand schedule. As we shall show later, during periods of rising prices not only the number of transactions increases but also the average time duration of each contract and the percentage of transportation capacity operating on time charter increase.[9] That is why any refinements will further strengthen the proof of our hypothesis. For these reasons, it was decided for the purposes of this book to stop at the first level of refinement.[10]

Overcoming the shortcomings of the data caused for the reasons given in the second category above is not an easy task, because it is in general virtually impossible to determine the amount of demand that remained unsatisfied at the various prices, especially if such an attempt is made long after the events took place. On the other hand, it may not be necessary for us to make an estimate of such quantities. If the scatter diagram of transactions — either in number or time equivalents — versus rates gives us the expected results, then the most refined cases must do likewise. If we fail in our first approximation, however, then we must find ways to estimate the unsatisfied demand.[11]

Luckily, we do have a readily available means for obtaining a more representative demand schedule than that given by the number of completed transactions. Expectations, as we shall soon show, affect the tankship building and tankship service markets in the same manner. The difference between the demand schedules of these two markets may be one of degree but definitely not one of substance. The number of orders placed for new vessels is more or less representative of the quantity demanded at the various prices because of the particular short-term notions that apply in these markets. For example, orders are placed for delivery over a period of two to six years. Thus, the supply schedule of shipbuilding is flexible and does not permit price fluctuations as wide as those observed in the tankship service markets. More important, however, is the fact that this flexibility of the supply schedule allows, in the short run, for more orders (almost all) to be accommodated. As a result, the effective supply schedule follows approximately the outline of the demand schedule, and the orders placed represent more closely the quantities that the owners of tankships demand at various prices. In effect, we are allowed to observe for each

---

[9] See Chapters 4 and 6.

[10] The size and speed range of tankers over the time period covered by this analysis were not as yet great enough to cause serious problems because of such simplification. Furthermore, the large vessels were not many and most of them were chartered on "private terms."

[11] The relationships are not reversible; that is, if the first approximation succeeds, it implies a success for the refined case. If the latter succeeds, however, we cannot conclude that the same thing applies to the first approximation.

price change an approximation of the complete impact of expectations on the quantity demanded before another price change again occurs which in turn will create new expectations, and so on ad infinitum.

For measurements of elasticities of demand with respect to future prices[12] (the result of elasticities of expectations), the tankship building markets thus afford a laboratory of great value. This applies of course to observations concerning the net result of both strictly static and dynamic considerations because, as we have already explained, it is very difficult (as well as of no great practical significance) to separate the purely static from the dynamic effects, as reflected in the effective demand schedule at any moment of time.[13]

Finally, if we are given evidence of an elasticity of expectations greater than unity, by time series analysis we may be able to determine whether or not lags are present. To overcome any undesirable consequences of the assumptions that everything else remains fixed, we could adjust if it were essential for the major factors that cause shifts in the static demand schedules. One must be careful, however, not to color the impact of price changes and thus conceal rather than reveal. Often, the factors that operate on the demand schedule may have had their origin in the price movements, consequently adjustments under such circumstances are not only unnecessary but also harmful.

A very important consideration mitigating the impact of other factors in our case is the excessive speed with which events occur. In a short period of two months tankship rates may change by a factor of 7, so it is rather improbable that external primary effects may be operating on the demand continuously and with such an intensity during this

---

[12] As previously explained, the region of a demand schedule exhibiting the effects of dynamic impacts may be taken by some as reflecting nothing more than the locus of intermediate equilibria established after expectations have caused the demand and supply schedules to shift. But such a distinction is immaterial as long as the demand schedule is never double valued in such a price region. If such a definition is adopted, however, we must be careful to distinguish between shifts that shape the effective demand schedule outside the region of strict static relevance, and shifts in the total demand schedule (all price ranges, static and dynamic alike). The analysis followed here is still one of comparative statics even though the system is, to use Professor Samuelson's terminology, "dynamic and causal" or "stochastical and non-historical." See Samuelson, Paul, "Dynamics, Statics, and the Stationary State," *Review of Economic Statistics,* Vol. XXV, No. 1, February 1943, pp. 58–68. Also Samuelson, *Foundations of Economic Analysis,* Harvard, 1947, Chapter 9.

[13] If we are dealing with derived demand schedules we can assume on the basis of our previous arguments that the *own* strictly static substitution as well as income effects are negligible. Consequently, the strictly static short-term demand schedule is very inelastic. Hence, the shape of the dynamic shifts in expectations will determine the deviations from the inelastic pattern of the demand schedule.

period of time as to cause such drastic results — especially when the pattern is repeated over time.

With the preceding qualifications in mind we shall now analyze the relationship between short-term rates and transactions (fixtures), but shall return to this topic of measurement later, when we discuss the shipbuilding markets, so that we can compare the empirical schedules of tankship service and tankship building demand.

4

Rates and Transactions

In this chapter we shall present empirical approximations to the demand schedule for tankship services. To obtain a schedule valid for all possible prices we must choose a time period covering at least one rate cycle.

During the ten years between 1949 and 1958 that we have used for the purpose of this study, the tankship markets went through two complete rate cycles. If we define a cycle as the period from trough to trough, we find that the first cycle lasted from July 1949 to July 1954, and the second one from July 1954 to July 1958.[1]

Because of the time element involved, transactions were tabulated only from July 1953 to the end of 1958, thus covering only one complete cycle in short-term rates. Since we shall later compare this schedule with that of tankship building over both cycles, no information is lost because of such omission. Furthermore, in the course of our analysis in this chapter we shall present sufficient information to convince the reader that our conclusions also apply in the case of the cycle from July 1949 to July 1954. The sources of the data used are explained in Appendix E.

Figure 4.1 presents a scatter diagram of spot rates versus the number of fixtures transacted. The rates for homogeneity were converted into cents per 1,000 ton-miles carried. Even though no consistent pattern amenable to quantification is observed, it is obvious that expectations based on spot rates exercise a considerable impact on the number of fixtures. It will be noticed that the observations plotted in Figure 4.1 take the rough form of a large numeral 3. Expectations appear

[1] After a short period of false signs of recovery in the fall of 1958, the rates slid again and in the summer of 1959 reached approximately the levels of the summer of 1958. See Davies & Newman, Ltd., *Tanker Market Report,* London, July 31, 1959.

to turn elastic somewhere between $1.10 and $1.35 per 1,000 ton-miles. Beyond $1.30 per 1,000 ton-miles, the rates and the number of fixtures are positively correlated, with a turning point in expectations (from elastic to inelastic) occurring around $1.80 per 1,000 ton-miles.

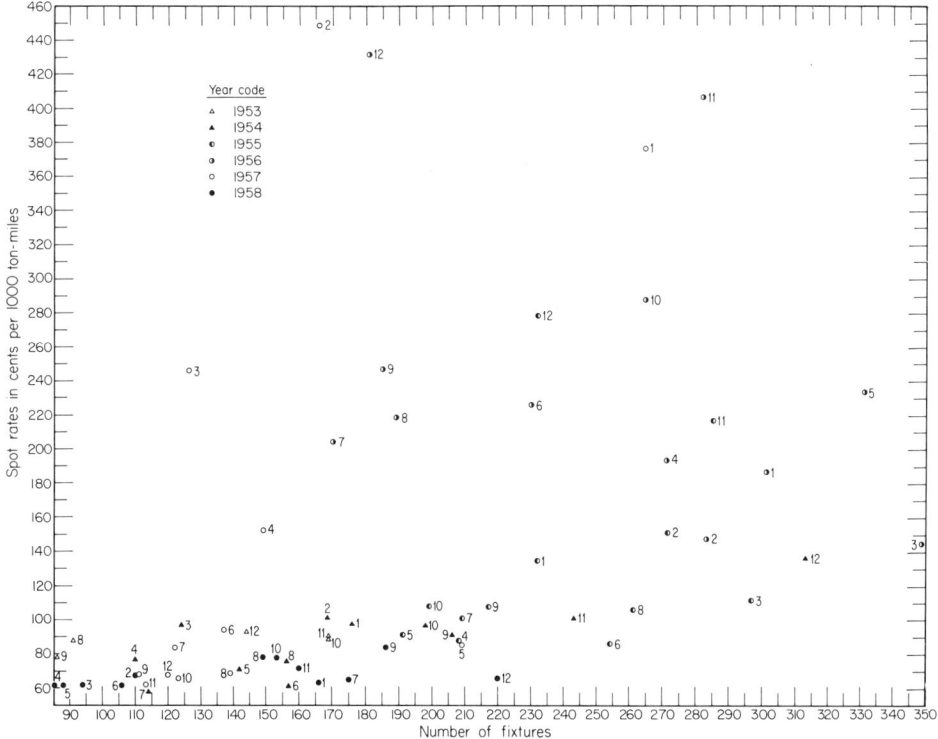

Figure 4.1. Scatter diagram of the number of fixtures versus index of spot rates, 1953–1958 (monthly).

A withdrawal from the market occurs between $2.00 and $2.30, with the number of transactions falling from a high of 348 in March 1956 (333 in May), to 170 in July 1956. Then comes a zone of uncertainty between $2.30 and $2.70, where expectations fluctuate between elasticity and inelasticity, followed by another turning point and elastic expectations around $2.80 and $3.00. Finally, there is a negative correlation beyond $4.10.

In order to appreciate the relationship between rates and transactions we can trace the time profile of the interactions presented in Figure 4.1. The loop followed by rates and transactions in 1957 indicates that the demand schedule may not be reversible.

If this pattern is to be admitted as evidence it is necessary to make sure that cause and effect are not confused. That is, we must ascertain that the observed pattern is not the result of temporary shifts in demand irrespective of rates; if it were it would make the fixtures *consistently and at all levels* rate determining but not rate determined.

To resolve the issues raised in the previous paragraph, we shall go through the following simple exercise in logic. First, if the rates mainly reflect the results of temporary shifts in demand (given fixed short-run supply) and are not accompanied by any dynamic considerations, then the charters contracted during periods of high rates should be mostly of short-term duration: if the expectations of the operatives concerning the future are unaltered, the number of long-term charters transacted should be negatively correlated with rates, and the rate of shipbuilding activity should not be affected. Indeed, in the case of shipbuilding, the fact that it normally takes between fifteen and twenty-five months to complete a vessel indicates also that there is no reason why an accepted temporary scarcity should lead to future surpluses.

Second, if forecasts of long-term considerations are mainly involved in the patterns of market behavior, then the consequences of a shift in current demand and an increase in rates will depend on whether rate expectations are inelastic, unit elastic, or elastic.[2]

Given inelastic rate expectations, an increase in rates due to shifts in demand will postpone rather than increase fixtures, especially charters of long-term duration. At most it may cause an influx of voyage charters, whereupon the operatives will wait until the normal shifts in the supply schedule restore equilibrium. Orders for new ships may be increased, but only up to the point of full shipyard capacity.

Unit elastic expectations will not change interperiod behavior because they leave the relative positions of periodic purchases within a plan unaltered.

If expectations are elastic, the necessary mechanism for cyclical freight rates is established when the initial disturbance occurs. The increase in rates will generate interperiod substitutions which will make the demand schedule assume a positive slope. In addition, the elastic expectations may generate shifts in demand, shifts which in turn will cause further increases in rates, elastic expectations, interperiod substitutions, and so on. Orders for new vessels will also be generated, and a similar cycle will be established in the shipbuilding markets. This process will continue until either expectations change from elastic to inelastic, as operatives recognize their previous error, or new deliveries

---

[2] If both short-term and long-term considerations are involved, then the consequences of a shift in demand can be decomposed into the two categories just analyzed. In such cases the short-term considerations will dominate.

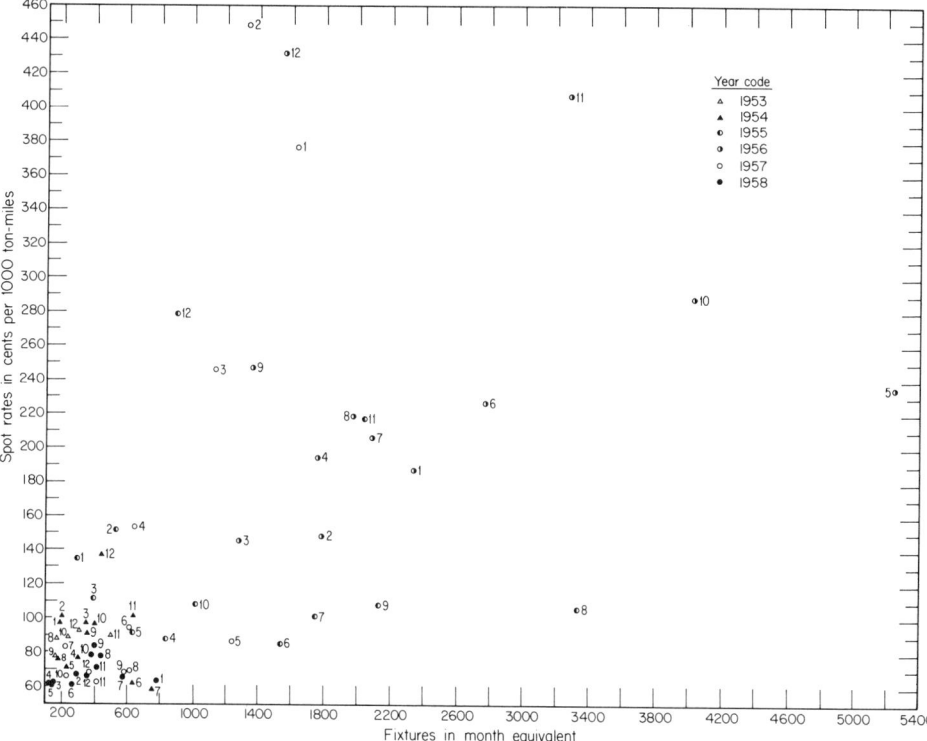

Figure 4.2. Scatter diagram of the number of fixtures in month equivalent versus index of spot rates, 1953–1958 (monthly).

in vessels cause such shifts in the supply schedule as to decrease rates and, consequently, change expectations.[3]

Once rates start falling elastic expectations take over again. Buyers will interpret a fall in prices as a signal of future price declines of greater consequence. As a result, the operatives will at this point postpone orders of all kinds, thus prolonging the depression in the tanker service markets and also creating a future tonnage shortage which will give rise to another disturbance; therefore, a cyclical demand pattern is not necessary to the mechanism of cyclical rates. Changes in demand may bring about a change in the duration as well as in the intensity of the cycle but will not eliminate it.[4] In addition, the suddenness and

[3] Also, the process may stop if the inelasticity of the expectations of the sellers and their risk functions are such that they can bring forth enough "short selling" to satisfy the buyers.

[4] Similar observations were also made by Koopmans for the period before the Second World War. See *Tanker Freight Rates and Tankship Building*, Haarlem, 1939, pp. 148–167.

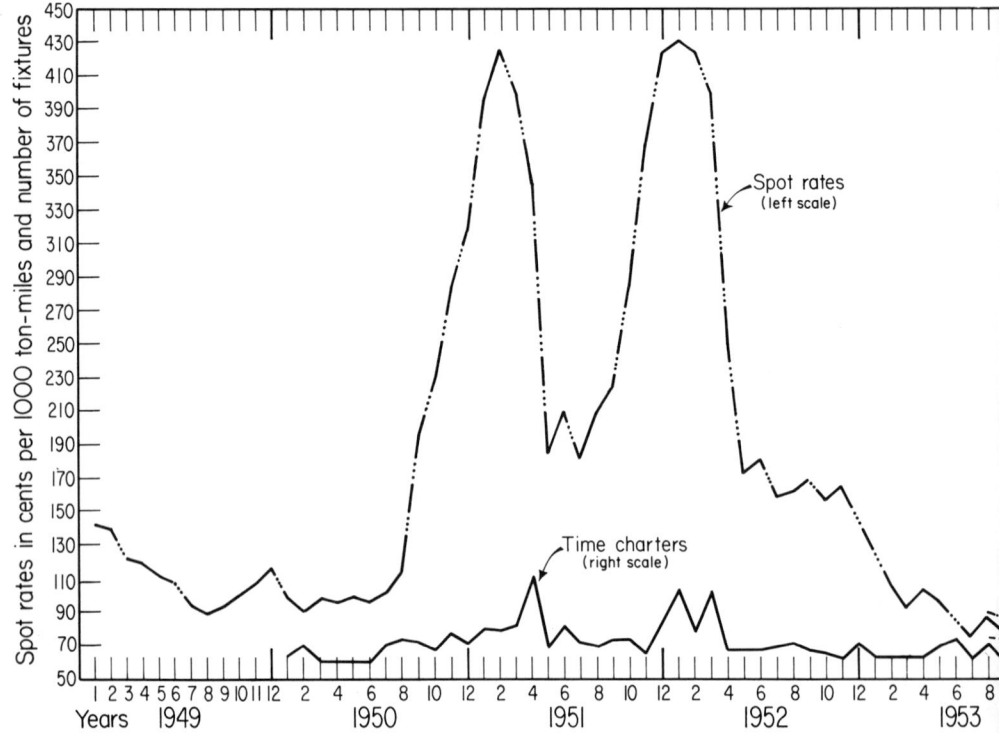

Figure 4.3. Time series of total number of fixtures, time charters,

magnitude of the rate changes may influence the intensity of expectations, which, in turn, may influence the amplitude of the cycles.

Turning to more quantitative evidence, we present in Figure 4.2 the scatter diagram of rates versus fixtures translated into month equivalents, thus giving a weight to each transaction that approximates its importance. Figure 4.2 shows a pattern that is not in substance different from that of Figure 4.1. The over-all shape of the two schedules is the same but the fluctuations in transactions, when measured in terms of months of commitments, tend to be greater. For example, the range of monthly fixtures in terms of numbers of transactions is between 85 and 348, while the months of duration vary between 50 and 5,250. The full impact of rates on fixtures *in terms of carrying capacity* is much greater than that shown in Figure 4.2 because the latter exhibit assumes that vessels on voyage and time charter are uniformly distributed with respect to size and speed, whereas in fact vessels on time charter are generally larger and faster. Consequently, the validity of any conclusions drawn on the basis of Figure 4.2 would be greater if the carry-

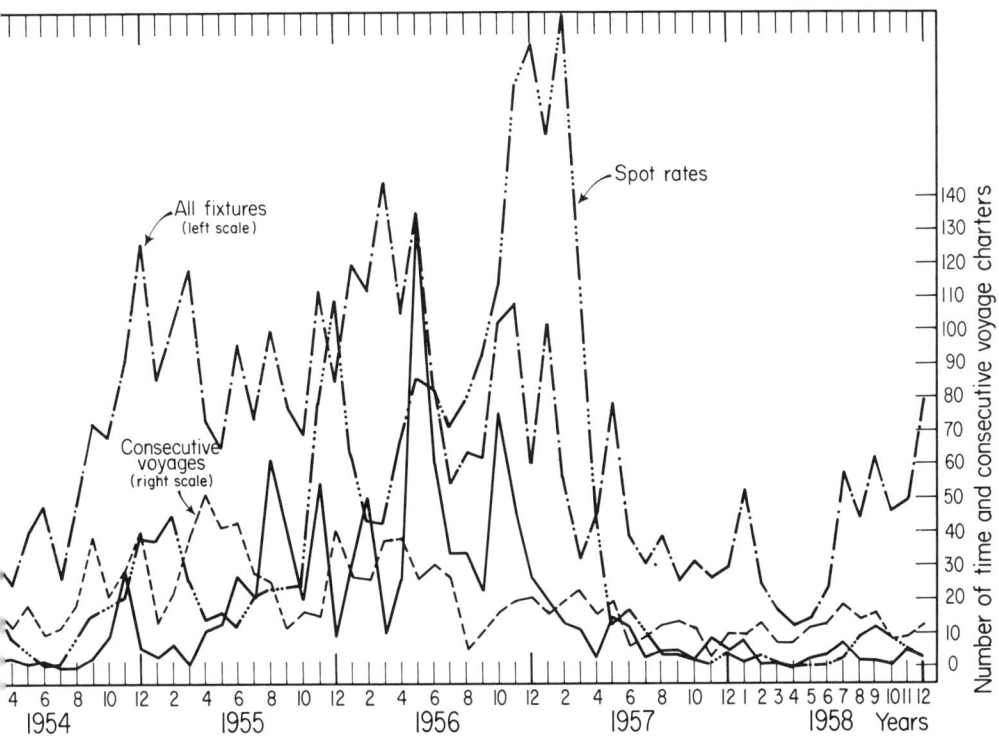
and consecutive voyages, and index of spot rates, 1949–1958.

ing capacity adjustment had been made. Figure 4.2, therefore, is a "conservative" representation of the effect of rates on fixtures.[5]

There is no doubt that the observations in these two exhibits bear the impact of elastic expectations, at least within certain ranges. Not only does the number of all fixtures increase with increasing rates, but also the number of months over which contracts are made. Of 897 time charters of definite time durations contracted between 1950 and 1957, approximately 66% were contracted at a rate of $1.30 per 1,000 ton-miles and over.[6] Furthermore, the duration and lead time (time period between the signing of the contract and the delivery of the vessel) show significant differences which strengthen our conclusions. The average time duration over which the contracting parties

---

[5] We must also remember that during periods of high rates and complete reservation of facilities, a certain amount of unsatisfied demand must be expected. This is another conservative aspect of our empirical schedules.

[6] Of the 134 transactions that were rejected, only 23 were contracted at rates below $1.30 per 1,000 ton-miles.

were bound during periods of high rates was eighty-five months,[7] while it was only fifty-six months during periods of low rates. The average

Rate Per 1,000 Ton-Miles	Duration of Charter in Months	Lead Time in Months	Sum of Duration and Lead Time	No. of Fixtures	Average No. of Fixtures Per Month
$1.30 and over	61.1	24.1	85.2	593	16.0
Below $1.30	45.5	10.5	56.0	304	6.5

number of fixtures contracted per month was 16 at rates of over $1.30, and only 6.5 at rates below $1.30 per 1,000 ton-miles. Variance analysis indicates that in every case the sample means are different at the 99% confidence level. Were it not for elastic expectations, such behavior would not have been observed.

With wildly fluctuating time series one cannot very easily distinguish leads from lags. Figure 4.3 presents the time series of spot rates (1949–1958), the number of time charters transacted between 1950 and 1958, the consecutive-voyage charters from August 1953 to December 1958, and the total number of all transactions (spot, consecutive voyage, and time charter) completed between August 1953 and December 1958. Prior to 1956, data indicate that the charter time series were in approximate phase and moving in the same direction as rates. For the year 1956, however, the data show a tendency on the part of short-term rates to lag behind transactions. Whether this apparent change was due to existing as against anticipated needs or to the stage of the expectations schedules is not clear. There is evidence, however, that the oil companies were cognizant of the possibility of a Middle East crisis and a Suez blockade long before these actually occurred.[8] Their consideration of the eventuality of unrest in the area must have influenced chartering as well as shipbuilding activity. Also, many of the time charters contracted during the Korean War years may have expired early in 1956, thus causing the disturbance needed to set the whole system in motion. We must stress again, however, that, with elastic expectations,

---

[7] This meant that on the average the contracts consummated during the Suez crisis would have expired during the latter part of 1963. Conceivably the availability of all this tonnage, coupled with the present tie-ups and orders outstanding, might have prolonged the depression in the tankship markets beyond 1963.

[8] See Petroleum, *The Antitrust Laws and Government Policies*, S. Res. 57, U.S. Government Printing Office, Washington 25, D. C., August 27, 1957, pp. 83–84, where it is stated that the State Department was studying in March 1956 the possible effects of a Suez Canal closure. Undoubtedly the oil companies were the source of such information to the State Department.

the end result (cyclical movement) will be the same no matter whether the initial impetus to a rate change comes from the supply or the demand side.

Finally, let us reiterate that in markets where recontracting does not exist the transactions completed do not represent the actual quantities demanded at the various rates. When shortages develop the transactions actually completed conceivably become fewer and fewer as rates increase, while the excess demand becomes greater and greater as a result of elastic rate expectations. A possibility such as this cannot be tested with the data presented here, but will affect the time series in a fashion approximating that shown in Figure 4.3.

5

Factors Affecting the Supply of Tankships

Introduction

There is little that can be done to increase tanker capacity in the short run. Conceivably, operatives could increase the operating speed of tankers and also utilize voyage and port times more efficiently to cut down delays. In either case, however, the costs increase sharply and the short-term supply schedule becomes almost vertical beyond the point of full capacity.

If the short run is made somewhat longer, but still not as long as the shipbuilding cycle, capacity may be somewhat expanded by the inflow of dry cargo ships, whalers, and grain or ore carriers. These vessels, however, as well as tankers, are specialized means of transportation; consequently, conversion or change of trade is costly. Thus one would expect such conversions to happen only when tankship rates are high in relation to rates in the markets from which capacity might be diverted.

These arguments imply that the only significant changes in capacity occur through shipbuilding activity. In what follows, we shall analyze the factors affecting shipbuilding as a preparatory step to our discussion of tankship rate formation.

In general the number of orders placed for new vessels will be affected by four main considerations or a combination of such. Although listed separately for purposes of exposition, these influencing factors are not necessarily independent of each other. In fact, as we shall soon point out, some of them are vitally interdependent. These factors are the following:

1. The spot rates (rentals) in the tankship markets and the expectations generated by such rates.
2. The cost of shipbuilding.
3. The rate of technological obsolescence and the age distribution of the

existing vessels. Technology and age determine remaining economic life, consequently they affect retirements and replacements of vessels.

4. The pattern of ownership within the industry as colored by the existing institutional considerations. Often, the existing capacity for the industry may be more than sufficient at any moment of time but new orders may be generated by the desire of the operatives either to change or to sustain their share of ownership.

Tanker rates are the motivating force behind each of these factors. However, the impact of rates on new orders differs, depending on the medium through which such impact operates. For this reason the discussion of the factors influencing new capacity will be separated into three broad classifications, one to consider the impact of spot rates and shipbuilding costs, another to analyze the influence of economic life expiration on replacements, and finally a section to consider the influence of institutional factors. The reader is requested to keep this separation in mind especially where interactions among the three classifications are present.

Spot Rates, Shipbuilding Costs, and Orders Placed — Theoretical Formulations

Orders placed in general appear to be closely related to the spot rates,[1] suggesting that movements in spot rates shape expectations about the future. Spot-rate-induced expectations also indirectly affect the elasticity of expectations with respect to the level of shipbuilding costs through their effect on orders placed. We may thus define

$$O_t = f(R_s, C_s) \tag{5.1}$$

where O_t stands for orders budgeted for period t, and R_s, C_s stand for the spot rates and cost of shipbuilding respectively, both in the short run.

If we assume that the function can be differentiated, we can approximate the change in orders placed because of changes in spot rates and the cost of shipbuilding by taking the differential of our function.[2]

---

[1] We shall show later that during periods of low rates "budget" effects and technology may encourage orders and give a negative slope to the demand schedule.

[2] The differential is really the principal part of the infinitesimal change in $f(x,y)$ due to changes of Δx, and Δy in the independent variables x and y. The total change is given by

$$\Delta f(x, y) = [\partial f(x, y)/\partial x] \Delta x + [\partial f(x, y)/\partial y] \Delta y + \varepsilon_1 \Delta x + \varepsilon_2 \Delta y$$

where ε_1 and ε_2 are infinitesimals approaching zero with Δx and Δy.

The differential is defined as the first two terms of the right-hand side. As for the error involved in neglecting $\varepsilon_1 \Delta x$ and $\varepsilon_2 \Delta y$, we can estimate it by applying Taylor's theorem.

CHAPTER FIVE

Then

$$df(R_s, C_s) = [\partial f(R_s, C_s)/\partial R_s] \Delta R_s + [\partial f(R_s, C_s)/\partial C_s] \Delta C_s \quad (5.2)$$

For small changes, increments dR_s and dC_s may be defined as[3]

$$dR_s = \Delta R_s \quad \text{and} \quad dC_s = \Delta C_s \quad (5.3)$$

Each price change is accompanied by two effects on the demand of a particular commodity, the income-compensated substitution effect and the income effect.

The income-compensated substitution effect of the first term on the right-hand side of Equation 5.2 can be expressed alternatively, *ceteris paribus*, as

$$([\partial f(R_s, C_s)/\partial R_s] \, dR_s)_{\pi=\text{const}} = [(\partial O_t/\partial R_s)(R_s/O_t)]O_t/R_s \, dR_s \quad (5.4)$$

$$([\partial f(R_s, C_s)/\partial R_s] \, dR_s)_{\pi=\text{const}} = E_{O_t,R_s}O_t/R_s \, dR_s \quad (5.5)$$

$$([\partial f(R_s, C_s)/\partial R_s] \, dR_s)_{\pi=\text{const}} = O_t E_{O_t,R_s}\overline{R}_s \quad (5.6)$$

where E_{O_t,R_s} stands for the spot rate elasticity of demand for tankship orders, other things equal, and $\overline{R}_s = dR_s/R_s$.

Notice that Equation 5.6 is not the static substitution effect of the Fundamental Equation of Value Theory (Slutsky-Hicks formulation). If our relationship were X_{rs}, namely the static income-compensated substitution effect on the demand for new shipbuilding due to a change in spot rates, then, because of symmetry, X_{rs} would be equal to X_{sr}, or $\partial X_s/\partial p_r = \partial X_r/\partial p_s$.[4] This relationship does not exist, however, in the shipbuilding and ship service markets. First of all, ordering new ships and renting on spot for a single voyage are neither substitutes for each other, nor, from the static point of view, complements. Many such single-voyage cycles will be completed before the new ships that are ordered appear in the market. Hence, for the case considered here, X_r (orders for new vessels) and X_s (spot charters) *are complements only indirectly through dynamic expectations.* Furthermore, and even if we were considering long-term rates,[5] only by making the additional assumption that the lead time from rental contract to ship delivery is the same as the lead time from ship construction contract to new ship

---

[3] Notice that Δx and dx are arbitrary increments of x, with no assumptions made as to their exact magnitude.

[4] Hicks, J. R., *Value and Capital*, Second Edition, Oxford University Press, London, 1953, Mathematical Appendix, pp. 307–313. Also Allen, R. G. D. *Mathematical Economics*, Macmillan & Co., Ltd., London, 1957, Chapter 19. For our purposes X_r stands for new orders, p_r for the cost per deadweight ton for building a vessel, X_s for spot charters, and p_s for spot rates.

[5] To be exact, *the rate* applicable to a charter of duration equal to the life of a new ship.

delivery could the orders for new vessels and the long-term charters be considered as substitutes *in static terms*. And this consideration could only be applicable to the oil companies. Let us not forget, however, in conjunction with the last qualification that over 60% of all tonnage is owned by the so-called independents. Furthermore, our assumptions about equality of lead times and charter durations are extremely unrealistic.

In terms of total market demand, therefore, *shipbuilding and ship services, both in the short and in the long run, will be found at any moment of time to be complementary because of dynamic anticipations*. After all, the demand for shipbuilding is derived, ships being the only inputs of importance to ship services. This complementarity, however, does not necessarily imply that there is a *static* income-compensated substitution effect $X_{rs} < 0$, unless we assume an applicable demand schedule of the traditional negative slope. The latter assumption, however, we found to be meaningless and repudiated by empirical reality. Furthermore, we have seen that our X_r and X_s (new ships and ready ship services) are meaningfully related only in the dynamic sense. Intertemporally, however, any entities are substitutes. To show the latter interrelationship, we can restate Equation 5.6 as follows, using the formulations developed in Chapter 2.

$$[(\partial f(R_s, C_s)/\partial R_s)] dR_s)_{\pi = \text{const}} = O_t E_b E_{O_t, R_f} \bar{R}_s \quad (5.7)$$

where E_b is the rate elasticity of expectations of buyers.

The preceding relationship (Equation 5.7) is positive or negative depending on E_b and E_{O_t, R_f}, and gives us the impact of dynamic expectations on orders because of shifts in the investment opportunity schedules. In our case E_b is greater than one, E_{O_t, R_f} is positive, and the whole income-compensated substitution effect is positive.

In addition to the dynamic effects of changes in spot rates on orders placed, given by Equation 5.7, there is also a static income effect comparable to that of any other price change. This is expressed as

$$I_{R_s} = (\partial I/\partial R_s)(\partial O_t/\partial I) dR_s \quad (5.8)$$

Under fixed budget assumptions $\partial I/\partial R_s = F_t$, the present available fleet,[6] and consequently Equation 5.8 becomes

$$I_{R_s} = F_t(O_t/I) E_{O_t, I_R} dR_s \quad (5.9)$$

where $E_{O_t, I_R} = \partial O_t/\partial I)(I/O_t)$ represents the income elasticity of orders due to changes in rates.

Turning now to the second term on the right-hand side of Equation

---

[6] The relationship is positive because a rate change will increase rental incomes of available vessels.

CHAPTER FIVE

5.2, we can derive a relation similar to Equation 5.7 for the effect of shipbuilding costs on new orders placed.

$$([\partial f(R_s, C_s)/\partial C_s] \, dC_s)_{\pi=\text{const}} = (O_t/C_s)E_{O_t,C_s} \, dC_s \quad (5.10)$$

$$([\partial f(R_s, C_s)/\partial C_s] \, dC_s)_{\pi=\text{const}} = O_t E_{O_t,C_s} \overline{C}_s \quad (5.11)$$

$$([\partial f(R_s, C_s)/\partial C_s] \, dC_s)_{\pi=\text{const}} = O_t E_b E_{O_t,C_f} \overline{C}_s \quad (5.12)$$

where $E_{O_t,C_s} = (\partial O_t/C_s)(C_s/O_t)$ represents the present price (cost) elasticity of demand, *ceteris paribus*, $\overline{C}_s = (dC_s/C_s)$, E_b the price elasticity of expectations,[7] and E_{O_t,C_f} the elasticity of demand with respect to future shipbuilding costs.

Equation 5.11 gives us the substitution effect (income-compensated) caused by changes in the cost of shipbuilding (*own* price effect). In the case of tankers this static substitution effect — as it refers to substitution of another commodity for tankers in period t — is virtually nil. However, there is an interperiod substitution caused by the elasticity of expectations which will affect the orders of one period versus another. If expectations are elastic, the substitution effect is positive;[8] if they are inelastic, it is negative. This result is shown more clearly in Equation 5.12.

The income effect of a shipbuilding cost change on the demand for new vessels is

$$I_{C_s} = (\partial I/\partial C_s)(\partial O_t/\partial I) \, dC_s \quad (5.13)$$

Given again a fixed budget

$$(\partial I/\partial C_s) = -O_t$$

and

$$I_{C_s} = -O_t(O_t/I)E_{O_t,I_C} \, dC_s \quad (5.14)$$

where $E_{O_t,I_C} = (\partial O_t/\partial I)(I/O_t)$, or the income elasticity of orders due to changes in the cost of shipbuilding.

The foregoing income effect I_{C_s} is only static[9] and always negative because new tankers are not an inferior commodity.[10]

---

[7] Because the two markets that we are analyzing are related, we assume that the coefficients of expectations are the same in both. If not, a proper identification will be necessary.

[8] This does not necessarily imply that the shape of the static indifference curves is different from what we naturally expect it to be, namely, concave up. Here $\partial O/\partial C_s$ evidenced in static terms is really equal to $(\partial O/\partial C_f)(\partial C_f/\partial C_s)$ where C_f = expected future costs. If we limit ourselves to periods t and $t+1$ only, C_f is the cost for O_{t+1}. Therefore O_t and O_{t+1} are substitutes.

[9] Notice that the relevant income effect rules over the budget plan.

[10] Our previous observation on the behavior of the oil companies when charter rates are low (which behavior gives rise to Giffen's paradox similarities) refers to tanker service availability, not shipbuilding. What is more, the relationship is

If we now consider the total effect on new orders which are brought about by changes in shipbuilding costs, we notice that the substitution effect (Equation 5.12), which is expected to be positive, may be offset by the negative income effect (Equation 5.14). The direction of the net effect will thus depend upon the size of the shipbuilding budget, the coefficient of expectations, and the change in orders placed with respect to the change in real income, all other things being equal.

In summary, the direct expected impact of changes in spot rates and construction costs on orders placed during a period is expressed by

$$df(R_s, C_s) = O_t E_b E_{O_t, R_f} \bar{R}_s + F_t(O_t/I) E_{O_t, I_R} dR_s \\ + O_t E_b E_{O_t, C_f} \bar{C}_s - O_t(O_t/I) E_{O_t, I_c} dC_s \quad (5.15)$$

$$df(R_s, C_s) = O_t E_b (E_{O_t, R_f} \bar{R}_s + E_{O_t, C_f} \bar{C}_s) \\ + (O_t/I) E_{O_t, I} (F_t dR_s - O_t dC_s) \quad (5.16)$$

where $E_{O_t, I_R} = E_{O_t, I_c} = E_{O_t, I}$.[11]

Equation 5.16, as defined, shows that the value of $df(R_s, C_s)$ depends on two interperiod substitution effects and two static income effects. These substitution effects are due to the expectations as shaped by the movements in the spot rates and the cost of shipbuilding, respectively, and are positive or negative depending on the sign of the elasticity of expectations. If expectations are elastic, and there are many indications that this is the case, then the two terms are positive.

In terms of absolute magnitude we expect $E_{O_t, R_f} \bar{R}_s$ to be greater than $E_{O_t, C_f} \bar{C}_s$ because of the higher volatility in spot rates as compared to shipbuilding costs, although E_{O_t, R_f} itself, being relatively indirect, may be smaller than E_{O_t, C_f}.

The two static income-effect terms oppose each other, and this is clearly evident in $(F_t dR_s - O_t dC_s)$. As we have seen, changes in spot rates not only affect dynamic expectations in such a way as to shift the investment opportunity schedules, but they also affect the current incomes of those who control tankship capacity. When rates are rising, this income effect, which is proportionate to the tankship capacity con-

---

asymmetric. The positive sign of the income effect in the tankship service markets arises, in the case of the oil companies, not because both $(\partial I/\partial R_s)$ and $(\partial Q/\partial I)$ are negative, but because both are positive. This shows that the input may be price determining rather than being itself determined by the price of the final product.

[11] Notice that in real life the various E_{I_t} may not be equal. If, for example, shipbuilding is granted a fixed budget on the basis of a total over-all budget, given price relationships, production possibility schedules, and expectations as of that moment of time, any real income effects due to changes in C_s may affect only the shipbuilding budget. On the other hand, since the cost of transportation is part of the delivered product cost, the income effects of a change in R_s will affect the over-all budget and thus may result in E_{O_t, I_R} being less than E_{O_t, I_c}.

56 CHAPTER FIVE

trolled but not necessarily owned, generates more orders.[12] The other income effect is definitely negative and is due to changes in the cost of shipbuilding. Its magnitude depends on the shipbuilding budget and the income elasticity of orders placed. The net result on new orders will depend upon whether the people operating in these markets feel richer because of the increase in rentals or poorer because of the increase in the cost of their capital equipment.

Because the demand for shipbuilding is derived, we do not expect the income elasticity to be very significant. Rather, we expect orders placed to be relatively inelastic with respect to income. In either case, as long as short-term rates increase ($dR_s > 0$), the net result of the two income effects is expected to be positive, since F_t is normally greater than O_t,[13] and dR_s is normally greater than dC_s.[14] Both dR_s and dC_s move in the same direction, so our statements relating to their respective magnitudes are valid in absolute terms.

As Equation 5.15 shows, then, the most important factors influencing orders placed are the elasticities of expectation generated by the movement in short-term rates. Unless the *own* income effect counterbalances the tanker-rate income effect, only a reversal in rates can arrest the flood of orders. The conditions under which such a reversal can occur were analyzed in Chapter 2. The cause and effect manifestation, of course, is not instantaneous. It takes time, and orders may lag behind spot rates by a few months; but we shall come back to this point later.

Before closing this discussion, we must mention that changes in C_s may be expressed as an implicit function of R_s. There is strong evidence that such a relationship exists, especially when shipbuilding is beyond

---

[12] Notice that the independents will not benefit by an amount proportionate to the capacity that they own but only to the extent of the capacity they have available for charters. In contrast the oil companies will benefit by an amount proportionate to the capacity they own or have under charter (if such capacity is not engaged in transporting oil on a delivered basis under old contracts), minus the differential they will now have to pay to cover existing tonnage deficiencies.

Even though during periods of high rates one would expect to find most of the orders being placed because of the income effect to come from the oil companies, in actuality this is not the case. As a result of the financial agreements that the oil companies and independents are willing to negotiate, the benefit to the independents is in proportion to both the capacity they currently have available for charters and some of the capacity they will have in the future. Physical delivery of the ship may run anywhere from months to years (in one case, over ten years), and agreements are sometimes made for ships that do not exist, even on the drafting board.

[13] Figure 5.7 shows that at its peak O_t was 96% of F_t, in September 1957 (aftermath of the Suez crisis). However, not all of the existing fleet was available for rechartering or recontracting.

[14] It is safe to claim that on the average dR_s is at least twice as great as dC_s.

the full capacity point.[15] Because of the latter qualification, we feel that it is better to consider C_s as an independent variable. Our formulation, however, can easily be adapted to account for a change of C_s from an independent to a dependent variable.

Retirements and Replacements — Theoretical Discussion

The number of orders placed will also be affected by the retirement program (scrapping) for old and obsolete vessels. This rate of scrapping is really a function of three main considerations:

1. The age distribution of vessels as of a moment of time.
2. The rate of technological change and the rate of introduction of such change.
3. The level of expected charter rates.

At the outset we must stress that the analysis in this section is an approximation of a much more complicated formulation that involves present values. The simplified analysis is preferred, however, for purely expositional purposes because it is easy to follow. A more sophisticated method is included in the last footnote to this section.

An uneven age distribution in the existing fleet will create uneven replacement programs, other things being equal. In the absence of technological change, given expectations of long-term remunerative rates, a ship will be replaced if and only if $TC_i - AVC_0 < 0$, where TC_i represents the total cost per unit of capacity of a new ship similar to the one to be retired and AVC_0 represents the average variable cost of the old ship.[16] This argument assumes that the average variable cost of a ship increases with age.

Technological obsolescence will affect replacement programs if it results in a total cost for a new ship (not necessarily similar to the one for which replacement is contemplated) lower than the average variable cost of the existing ship: $TC_j - AVC_0 < 0$. If TC_j is less than TC_i a ship will be replaced even though $TC_i - AVC_0 > 0$.

Low spot rates will accelerate retirements during depressed periods if the current rate R_0 is lower than AVC_0 and the expected revenue per unit of remaining capacity is lower than AVC_m, where AVC_m represents the average variable cost over the longest possible physical life as con-

---

[15] During periods of excess capacity, a more sophisticated dynamic system is needed to express the relationship between C_s and R_s in terms of the number of years of orders carried on the books of the shipyards.

[16] The TC_i includes the cost of capital and takes into consideration any trade-in or scrap value of the old ship; AVC_0 considers also the cost of lay-up in case the ship is now, or is expected to be, idle.

trasted to economic life. To the extent that AVC increases with age, AVC_m will be greater than AVC_0. Consequently, if the expected revenue per remaining unit of capacity is lower than AVC_0, such revenue will certainly be lower than any AVC_i.

Therefore, even if $TC_i > TC_j > AVC_0$, the vessel will be scrapped if the expected revenue will not cover the out-of-pocket costs per unit of remaining capacity (that is, $R_m < AVC_0$). However, given $R_m < AVC_0$, a replacement will not be ordered unless either $TC_j < R_m$ or the expected rate R_m is an intermediate rate that will govern only over a period of time not greater than the life of the existing vessel. As long as the long-term rate R_L is greater than TC_i or TC_j, then an order for replacement will be initiated sometime in the future. Nevertheless, the relationship between R_m and R_L will determine the timing of the replacement order. For example, if $R_m = R_L > TC_j$, then the replacement order will be initiated at once; if, on the other hand, $R_m < TC_j < R_L$, the new order will be placed if and only if the period over which R_m is expected to rule is less than or equal to the shipbuilding lead time t_s, and provided that the average variable cost of the old ship over t_s, AVC_{t_s}, is greater than the total cost per unit of capacity of the new ship TC_j.

Formalizing the above argument, we observe that, of the eight different interrelationships between TC_j, AVC_{t_s}, AVC_0, R_m, and R_L, the following three cases are important. If (a), $TC_j > AVC_{t_s}$, and $R_m < AVC_0$, and $R_L > TC_j$, then the old ship will be scrapped. An order will be placed, however, only if the low rate R_m is not expected to rule over a period exceeding the shipbuilding lead time t_s. (This of course implies $t_s = m$ because if t_s is greater than m, then, depending on the tie-up costs, it may be advisable to keep the old vessel, since $TC_j > AVC_{t_s}$.)

On the other hand, if (b), $TC_j < AVC_{t_s}$, and $R_m > AVC_0$, and $R_L > TC_j$, the old ship will not be scrapped, but an order will be placed. Scrapping of the old ship will await the point at which AVC exceeds the expected rate R_m.

Finally, if (c), $TC_j < AVC_{t_s}$, and $R_m < AVC_0$, and $R_L > TC_j$, then the old ship will be scrapped and an order will be placed only under the same conditions that we stated under a.

All the other possible relationships are either inadmissible (four of them imply $R_L < TC_j$) or else are of no interest to us (for example, $TC_j > AVC_{t_s}$, $R_m > AVC_0$ and $R_L > TC_j$).

If $R_L > TC_j$, then in every case orders are placed when either (i) $TC_j < AVC_{t_s}$, or (ii) $R_m < AVC_0$, and $AVC_{t_s+1} > R_{m+1} \geq TC_j$ for $m \geq t_s$.

If the rates in the short run are lower than AVC_0 and the ship is laid up, its average variable cost increases by the average variable cost of the lay-up. This condition, in effect, causes $TC_j < AVC_{t_s}$ (even in cases where the average variable cost of the old ship, *excluding tie-up cost,* is lower than TC_j), and thus hastens retirements and new orders.

This discussion shows that initially a certain number of orders Q_A will be placed purely because of the age of the existing vessels. We have noticed, however, that charter rates may either prolong or hasten this replacement point because, if a ship is to stay in operation, $R_m - AVC_0$ must be positive.[17] The lower (or higher) R_m, other things being equal, the sooner (or later) a vessel will be retired (kept idle or in service) given the fact that AVC_t increases with t.

In addition to Q_A, a quantity Q_T will be ordered because of technological considerations. Obsolescence cuts the economic life of vessels, and retirements take place earlier than originally expected. The criterion that determines replacement in this case is the difference between the total cost per unit of capacity of the new ship and the average variable cost of the old vessel. As in the case of Q_A, the expected charter rates will also affect Q_T. For those vessels that are already tied up or are expected to be tied up because of low rates, the average variable cost per unit of remaining capacity is increased by the average idle and recommissioning cost AIC, thus accelerating retirement.

The question of course is how this impact of replacements affects our previous formulation as expressed in Equation 5.16. When rates are high and the fleet is employed, expectations will in all probability overshadow any other consideration, and Equation 5.16 will govern. Under such circumstances, the relevant Q_A will be included in the quantities ordered because of the dynamic substitution effects. Such a contribution will be over and above any purely speculative quantity. In addition, a part of Q_T will be involved, which is determined by $TC_j - AVC_{t_s} < 0$, where AVC_{t_s} *does not* include any tie-up costs, since remunerative employment exists.

When rates are low, however, both Q_A and Q_T will be greater than they would be at high rates because of the expected cost of idleness. What determines the size of replacement orders in this case is the difference between the total cost of the new ship and the average variable cost of the old one, where the average variable cost of the old ship includes also the expected average idle cost. Namely, a vessel will be replaced if $TC_j - (AVC_{t_s} + AIC_{t_s}) < 0$, where AIC_{t_s} represents the expected average idle and recommissioning cost over the period t_s (shipbuilding lead time), provided, of course, that $R_{t_s+1} \geq TC_j$. It is to be

---

[17] For the shortest short run, a vessel may be kept in operation if $R_s - (AVC_0 - MIC) > 0$, namely, as long as the short-term rate plus the expected marginal idle costs are greater than the AVC_0. Keeping the vessel in operation under such circumstances is a distress measure and applies only in cases where R_t for $t > s$ is expected not only to cover AVC_t but also to compensate for previous out-of-pocket losses.

expected that the "profit squeeze" imposed by low rates will force the operators to introduce cost-saving technological innovations, thus eliminating all the inefficient units under their control.

To complete Equation 5.16 we must add the following term which covers the increase in orders caused by retirements or scrappings S:

$$\Delta O_{t,S} = \sum_{i=1}^{n} V_i c(AIC_{t_s})_i [(AVC_{t_s} + AIC_{t_s})_i - TC_j] \qquad (5.17)$$

provided that

$$AVC_{t_{s+1}} > R_{t_{s+1}} \geqslant TC_j$$

In Equation 5.17, $\sum_{i=1}^{n} V_i$ represents all the vessels which cannot find remunerative employment and whose average variable cost plus average idle cost during t_s is greater than the total cost of their expected replacement. The first factor (AIC_{t_s}) guarantees that the whole term will be zero if the short-term rates cover out-of-pocket costs and the ship expects to stay employed. Finally, c is a scalar which determines whether the unit of measurement for replacement is ton for ton or not. The provision that $AVC_{t_{s+1}} > R_{t_{s+1}} \geqslant TC_j$ is to guarantee that upon completion of the new vessel its expected charter rate will at least cover its full cost, a requirement that must be satisfied before undertaking to build a new vessel. Furthermore, to replace the old vessel it is necessary for the expected total cost per unit of capacity of the replacement to be lower than the expected average variable cost per unit of capacity of the vessel to be replaced. The latter comparison is only valid over the period during which the old vessel was expected to be employed.[18]

---

[18] In practice, the problem is not as simple but, in general, one can adapt economic tools (see Fisher, Irving, *The Theory of Interest*, Macmillan Company, New York, 1930, especially Chapters 6, 7, 8, for his "second approximation") for purposes of alternative decision making in everyday reality. For example, given R_t and R_t' as the rate per unit of capacity expected in period t for the old and the new vessel respectively; C and C' as the respective capacities AVC_t and AVC_t' as the average variable (out-of-pocket) costs per unit of capacity in period t for the old and the new vessels; $n - m$ the expired life of the old vessel; S_o the present scrap value of the old vessel; S_m and k_m the values of the old and new vessel, respectively, m years from now, if any; r the subjective rate of return; K and K' the initial investments in the two vessels respectively; then initially for each alternative to be considered we must have

$$\sum_{t=1}^{m} C(R_t - AVC_t)(1 + r)^{-t} + S_m(1 + r)^{-m} - S_o > 0 \qquad (1)$$

and

$$\sum_{t=1}^{m} C'(R'_t - AVC'_t)(1 + r)^{-t} + k_m(1 + r)^{-m} - K' > 0 \qquad (2)$$

In order to choose the new over the old, the following must hold:

While on the subject of technology, we must mention that its effect in the tankship service markets is surplus producing. Namely, the value of scalar c in Equation 5.17 is greater than one. *In industries such as this in which the technological economies of scale are so pronounced, surplus is the natural consequence of the general increase in the size of the most efficient units.* For example, during 1956–1958, the average size of the ships on order was twice that of the ships in operation. Obviously then, one-for-one replacement introduces a much greater capacity than is needed, especially when it occurs in periods of depressed markets and excess tonnage. Owners who contemplate replacements of more than one unit will undoubtedly attempt to reconcile capacities, but there are many owners of one or a few vessels, and replacements by these owners will expand capacity. Furthermore, the replacement may have to be one for one if the vessels must operate in dispersed geographical locations at the same time.

We can now summarize the results of Equations 5.16 and 5.17:

1. If expectations are uniformly *inelastic*, a negative correlation should be observed between short-term rates and orders placed. The lower part of the demand schedule will be more elastic because of Equation 5.17. At very high rates (still under the assumption that expectations are inelastic) the positive income effect of one of the two income terms may give the schedule a positive slope if it counterbalances all the other effects, *but such an occurrence is very improbable,* as can be attested by examining Equation 5.16.

$$\sum_{t=1}^{m} [C'(R'_t - AVC'_t) - C(R_t - AVC_t)](1+r)^{-t} + (k_m - S_m)(1+r)^{-m} - (K' - S_0) > 0 \quad (3)$$

If $R'_t = R_t$, the previous equation simplifies to

$$\sum_{t=1}^{m} (C \times AVC_t - C' \times AVC'_t)(1+r)^{-t} + (k_m - S_m)(1+r)^{-m} - (K' - S_0) > 0 \quad (4)$$

The previous relationship represents the first approximation of the present worth of economic value (under certainty); but in order to apply to present-day reality we must further adapt it to reflect the impact of taxes, because the government for tax purposes recognizes the accrual principles of income determination, principles which distinguish between cost and amortized expense, and also between realized and deferred income. Thus Equation 4 under straight-line depreciation becomes

$$\sum_{t=1}^{m} (C \times AVC_t - C' \times AVC'_t)(1+r)^{-t}(1 - \text{Tax Rate}) + [(K \times m/n) - S_0](\text{Tax Rate})$$
$$+ (k_m - S_m)(1+r)^{-m} + \sum_{t=1}^{m} (k'/n' - K/n)(1+r)^{-t}(\text{Tax Rate}) - (K' - S_0) > 0 \quad (5)$$

Equation 5 may be modified further to reflect probabilistic uncertainty, but such modification of necessity will be based on individual value judgments and will in no way alter basic premises of decision making. In these relationships we assumed discrete accumulation of income and expense streams.

TABLE 5.1

WORLD-WIDE INDUSTRY TANKER TONNAGE BY AGE GROUPS AS OF JANUARY 1, 1959
(Vessels 6,000 DWT. and Over)

Ownership	Total		0 to 5 Years 1954–1958			6 to 10 Years 1949–1953			11 to 15 Years 1944–1948			16 to 20 Years 1939–1943			21 Years & Older 1938 & Prior		
	No.	T-2	No.	T-2	%	No.	T-2	%	No.	T-2	%	No.	T-2	%	No.	T-2	%
OIL COMPANIES																	
Allied/Ashland	1	.3	—	—	—	—	—	—	—	—	—	—	—	—	1	.3	100
Atlantic Refining	19	25.2	5	7.5	30	3	6.4	25	6	6.1	24	4	4.2	17	1	1.0	4
British Petroleum	167	151.1	40	61.6	41	56	44.7	30	44	29.4	19	22	12.7	8	5	2.7	2
Caltex	60	64.7	7	13.1	20	12	11.1	17	40	39.9	62	—	—	—	1	.6	1
Cities Service	15	25.9	7	17.9	69	—	—	—	7	7.0	27	1	1.0	4	—	—	—
Continental Oil	1	1.0	—	—	—	—	—	—	—	—	—	1	1.0	100	—	—	—
Gulf	54	78.1	15	30.5	39	13	21.4	28	16	17.3	22	8	7.9	10	2	1.0	1
Hess	7	7.2	1	1.0	14	—	—	—	2	2.1	29	4	4.1	57	—	—	—
Paragon	6	9.2	2	5.2	56	—	—	—	2	2.0	22	2	2.0	22	—	—	—
Petrofina	9	12.2	5	8.4	69	3	2.8	23	1	1.0	8	—	—	—	—	—	—
Pure Oil	2	2.1	—	—	—	—	—	—	1	1.0	48	1	1.1	52	—	—	—
Richfield	3	2.9	—	—	—	—	—	—	1	1.2	41	2	1.7	59	—	—	—
Sinclair Refining	13	16.0	2	4.7	29	2	3.5	22	—	—	—	8	7.5	47	1	.3	2
Shell	223	206.9	81	108.1	52	25	23.3	11	56	41.0	20	34	19.9	10	27	14.6	7
Socony-Mobil	30	38.9	8	14.0	36	3	5.8	15	4	4.1	11	14	14.5	37	1	.5	1
Standard Oil (California)	23	27.1	1	1.2	4	7	12.2	45	11	10.5	39	3	2.6	10	1	.6	2
Standard Oil (Indiana)	12	9.7	—	—	—	—	—	—	3	1.2	12	4	5.3	55	5	3.2	33
Standard Oil (New Jersey)	123	178.5	41	84.5	48	18	32.3	18	32	31.0	17	26	26.8	15	6	3.9	2
Standard-Vacuum	19	22.3	4	6.6	30	2	3.5	16	10	9.7	43	3	2.5	11	—	—	—
Sun Oil	15	19.2	2	4.1	22	2	4.1	22	3	3.1	16	6	6.5	33	2	1.4	7

FACTORS AFFECTING SUPPLY OF TANKSHIPS

Texas Co.	48	58.0	14	22.4	39	10	14.2	24	11	10.2	18	12	11.0	19	1	.2	—
Tidewater	15	33.6	8	27.0	80	—	—	—	6	6.0	18	—	—	—	1	.6	2
Union Oil	7	9.5	2	5.3	56	1	1.1	12	1	1.0	10	3	2.1	22	—	—	—
Other Oil Companies	34	38.1	12	21.1	55	10	8.8	23	6	4.8	13	2	1.6	4	4	1.8	5
Total Oil Companies	906	1,037.7	257	444.2	43	167	195.2	19	263	229.6	22	160	136.0	13	59	32.7	3
INDEPENDENT COMPANIES																	
Andreadis	9	17.3	6	14.1	82	2	2.2	13	—	—	—	1	1.0	5	—	—	—
Barber Oil	10	12.7	—	—	—	3	5.6	44	6	6.1	48	1	1.0	8	—	—	—
Carras	8	12.7	5	9.8	77	—	—	—	2	1.9	15	1	1.0	8	—	—	—
Goulandris	37	75.1	20	51.0	68	8	15.1	20	5	5.3	7	4	3.7	5	—	—	—
Hendy, Joshua	2	2.1	—	—	—	—	—	—	1	1.4	67	1	.7	33	—	—	—
Kulukundis	15	19.5	12	16.8	86	1	.9	5	1	1.1	6	1	.7	3	—	—	—
Kurz	30	33.8	4	7.0	21	2	2.2	7	4	4.2	12	20	20.4	60	—	—	—
Lemos	11	26.8	9	24.7	92	1	1.1	4	—	—	—	1	1.0	4	—	—	—
Livanos	28	44.2	17	32.0	72	9	10.0	23	2	2.2	5	—	—	—	—	—	—
National Bulk	36	88.2	12	48.0	54	8	18.2	21	11	15.9	18	4	5.3	6	1	.8	1
Niarchos	64	117.5	27	68.9	59	20	31.6	27	5	5.0	4	12	12.0	10	—	—	—
Nicolaou	4	3.9	—	—	—	3	3.3	85	—	—	—	—	—	—	1	.6	15
Nomikos	4	6.0	3	4.7	78	1	1.3	22	—	—	—	—	—	—	—	—	—
Onassis	44	65.1	19	33.3	51	9	16.7	26	9	9.0	14	5	4.8	7	2	1.3	2
Vergottis	6	10.3	2	4.9	48	4	5.4	—	—	—	—	—	—	16	—	—	—
Wang	7	6.2	—	—	—	—	—	—	4	4.0	65	1	1.0	4	2	1.2	19
Other Independent Companies	1,398	1,524.4	518	747.0	49	412	418.4	27	187	168.3	11	108	89.4	6	173	101.3	7
Total Independent Companies	1,713	2,065.8	654	1,062.2	51	483	532.0	26	237	224.4	11	160	142.0	7	179	105.2	5
GOVERNMENT COMMERCIAL	84	63.7	11	11.5	18	31	29.6	46	5	4.2	7	10	6.7	11	27	11.7	18
TOTAL WORLD COMMERCIAL	2,703	3,167.2	922	1,517.9	48	681	756.8	24	505	458.2	14	330	284.7	9	265	149.6	5

2. If, on the other hand, rate and shipbuilding expectations are uniformly *elastic,* outside the region of strict static relevance R^s, then the demand schedule for orders above R^s will definitely be of positive slope (until the spot rates drop or $O_t dC_s$ counterbalances all the other terms at very large O_t). Below R^s the demand schedule may show "schizophrenic" tendencies because of the partially opposing effects of Equations 5.16 and 5.17, and the income effect of changes in shipbuilding costs. Orders placed at very low rates may thus oscillate for a while intermittently, tracing two relevant segments of demand, one of negative and the other of positive slope. Once the effects of the replacement programs of inefficient vessels exhaust themselves and also the order-producing effects of the term $O_t dC_s$ are satisfied, then the demand schedule definitely assumes a positive slope and veers toward the origin.

3. Finally, if the expectations of those operating in the tankship markets are not uniformly elastic, the "demand" schedule of orders placed will change from one of positive to one of negative slope around the points where the expectations schedules change from elastic to inelastic.[19]

The Pattern of Ownership — An Institutional Paradox

Our previous statements about replacements must now be qualified to allow for variations in the pattern of tanker ownership. If the tankship markets were purely competitive[20] under a stationary state and with ships of equal age and size evenly distributed among the many owners, we would need to look only at the aggregate quantities to determine market behavior. That is, it would be possible to determine the number of new orders needed to meet the stationary-state requirements by examining the total existing fleet. The same is true in the case where the markets are highly organized. Then a central agency can coordinate the number of orders placed in order to meet the total requirement for transportation and at the same time avoid unwanted surpluses.

If we look at replacements from the point of view of the empirical investigator, however, the problem is unfortunately more complicated. While it is true that no single owner owns more than approximately 7% of the total capacity (see Table 5.1), yet approximately 34% of the present total capacity (for vessels of 6,000 DWT.) is owned by oil companies. This, in effect, introduces an imperfection, because employ-

---

[19] As we have previously shown in Chapter 2, the assumption of expectations schedules of nonuniform elasticity is not necessary for the final turning points (top and bottom) of the demand schedule. The income effect will eventually take over and give a negative slope to the demand schedule even under uniformly price-elastic expectations.

[20] Later on we shall introduce an extensive discussion on the organizational behavior of tanker markets. See Chapter 7, "Characteristics of the Tankship Markets."

ment for this tonnage is not secured competitively.[21] Conceivably some or all of the oil companies, for reasons purely known to themselves, could at any time decide to increase their share of the total tonnage (own more and charter fewer ships from the independents) while the total market abounds with surpluses. Namely, decisions by oil companies to purchase additional tonnage may be made independently of current *aggregate* market conditions.[22] When their long-term needs are greater than the capacity controlled, the oil companies have the choice of ordering vessels or securing tonnage on long-term charter, regardless of any surpluses that some other owner may or will have.[23]

The impact of changing technology and the age distribution of vessels owned by the independents and the oil companies may again, in the absence of any "regulating agency," generate orders while surpluses exist in the aggregate. Table 5.2 shows that an age disproportionality of vessels exists with the various owners, as well as in the aggregate. Other things being equal, lumpiness in orders placed should then be expected, which in turn will affect future replacements. Given normal conditions and a mature industry, new orders greatly depend on deliveries made twenty or so years before.

For the reasons discussed here, orders were being placed during the post-Suez period while cancellations were mounting. For example, during the first half of 1958, orders were placed, *mostly by oil companies*,[24]

---

[21] As previously mentioned, only in times of surpluses does this tonnage compete directly in the market.

[22] In the general case, this claim may not be technically correct. In some cases the decisions to increase ownership shares is aimed at mitigating the conditions that have caused the undesirable market situation and uncertainty. But in so doing the oil companies aggravate rather than improve the situation, because they enter into the market exactly when they should have stayed out. Furthermore, the oil companies cannot succeed in eliminating these undesirable conditions, given the many uncertainties surrounding their forecasts of oil demand as well as the geographic sources of oil supply. See Koopmans, Tjalling C., *Tanker Freight Rates and Tankship Building,* Haarlem, 1939, Part III (Section 8).

[23] The magnitude of this choice on the part of oil companies is really limited. Certainly they cannot afford to have enough vessels for their maximum expected needs because of the costly surpluses of tonnage thereby created. Such surpluses benefit only the small oil producers who do not own transportation facilities. Furthermore, to the extent that we expect the relative needs of each individual company to fluctuate on the average more than those of the industry, the "independent" tankship market is necessary for pooling the risks inherent in such uncertainties, and its elimination will be very costly for the oil companies and the industry. See also the summary at the end of Chapter 7.

[24] It seems that the oil companies follow the independents advantageously on the downswing but disadvantageously on the upswing. The independents, because of their flexible organizational structure, react faster.

TABLE 5.2
WORLD-WIDE INDUSTRY TANKER TONNAGE BY SIZE GROUPS AS OF JANUARY 1, 1959
(*Vessels 6,000 DWT. and Over*)

Ownership	Total		Average DWT.	Deadweight Class										
				6,000–16,000		16,001–20,000		20,001–30,000		30,001–40,000		40,001–50,000		50,001–60,000	60,001 Plus
	No.	T-2		No.	T-2	No.	T-2	No.	T-2	No.	T-2	No.	T-2	No.	T-2	No.	T-2
OIL COMPANIES																		
Allied/Ashland	1	.3	6,150	1	.3	—	—	—	—	—	—	—	—	—	—	—	—
Atlantic Refining	19	25.2	21,310	—	—	14	14.8	—	—	5	10.4	—	—	—	—	—	—
British Petroleum	167	151.1	16,340	110	66.3	29	27.4	6	10.6	21	44.0	1	2.8	—	—	—	—
Caltex	60	64.7	17,660	5	3.4	50	50.4	—	—	5	10.9	—	—	—	—	—	—
Cities Service	15	25.9	25,720	—	—	8	8.0	—	—	7	17.9	—	—	—	—	—	—
Continental Oil	1	1.0	16,740	—	—	1	1.0	—	—	—	—	—	—	—	—	—	—
Gulf	54	78.1	22,860	7	4.8	19	20.1	16	26.4	12	26.8	—	—	—	—	—	—
Hess	7	7.2	16,990	—	—	7	7.2	—	—	—	—	—	—	—	—	—	—
Paragon	6	9.2	24,040	—	—	4	4.0	—	—	1	2.2	1	3.0	—	—	—	—
Petrofina	9	12.2	21,620	1	.8	5	5.0	1	2.0	2	4.4	—	—	—	—	—	—
Pure Oil	2	2.1	16,380	—	—	2	2.1	—	—	—	—	—	—	—	—	—	—
Richfield	3	2.9	16,360	—	—	1	.7	2	2.2	—	—	—	—	—	—	—	—
Sinclair Refining	13	16.0	19,350	4	2.7	5	5.1	3	5.3	—	—	1	2.9	—	—	—	—
Shell	223	206.9	15,970	112	61.6	86	91.1	6	11.2	18	40.1	1	2.9	—	—	—	—
Socony-Mobil	30	38.9	20,170	3	2.7	18	18.5	6	11.4	3	6.3	—	—	—	—	—	—
Standard Oil (California)	23	27.1	18,910	4	2.5	13	13.4	6	11.2	—	—	—	—	—	—	—	—
Standard Oil (Indiana)	12	9.7	13,790	7	3.9	2	2.0	3	3.8	—	—	—	—	—	—	—	—
Standard Oil (New Jersey)	123	178.5	22,500	12	6.6	56	57.0	33	58.6	22	56.3	—	—	—	—	—	—
Standard-Vacuum	19	22.3	19,420	1	.6	13	12.2	4	7.0	1	2.5	—	—	—	—	—	—
Sun Oil	15	19.2	20,090	2	1.3	9	9.7	—	—	4	8.2	—	—	—	—	—	—

Texas Co.	48	58.0	19,200	14	10.2	23	25.8	9	16.0	—	—	2	6.0	—	—	—	—
Tidewater	15	33.6	33,910	1	.6	6	6.0	—	—	—	—	4	12.5	4	14.5	—	—
Union Oil	7	9.5	21,480	3	2.1	3	3.2	—	—	—	—	—	—	1	4.2	—	—
Other Oil Companies	34	38.1	19,130	13	6.9	8	8.3	9	14.1	4	8.8	—	—	—	—	—	—
Total Oil Companies	906	1,037.7	18,830	300	177.3	382	393.0	104	179.8	105	238.8	10	30.1	5	18.7	—	—
INDEPENDENT COMPANIES																	
Andreadis	9	17.3	29,200	—	—	4	4.3	—	—	5	13.0	—	—	—	—	—	—
Barber Oil	10	12.7	20,250	—	—	7	7.1	3	5.6	—	—	—	—	—	—	—	—
Carras	8	12.7	24,290	—	—	5	5.3	1	1.9	—	—	2	5.5	—	—	—	—
Goulandris	37	75.1	30,420	1	.7	9	9.6	12	23.9	7	16.9	8	24.0	—	—	—	—
Hendy, Joshua	2	2.1	16,780	1	.7	1	1.4	—	—	—	—	—	—	—	—	—	—
Kulukundis	15	19.5	21,140	1	.7	8	8.3	4	6.0	2	4.5	—	—	—	—	—	—
Kurz	30	33.8	18,280	—	—	24	24.3	6	9.5	—	—	—	—	—	—	—	—
Lemos	11	26.8	35,660	—	—	2	2.1	—	—	7	18.5	2	6.2	—	—	—	—
Livanos	28	44.2	24,130	2	1.5	12	13.2	8	13.7	4	9.9	2	5.9	—	—	—	—
National Bulk	36	88.2	39,150	1	.3	9	10.6	5	7.5	10	22.0	3	8.4	1	3.7	7	35.7
Niarchos	64	117.5	27,700	—	—	18	18.0	18	27.2	17	39.6	11	32.7	—	—	—	—
Nicolaou	4	3.9	16,180	1	.6	3	3.3	—	—	—	—	—	—	—	—	—	—
Nomikos	4	6.0	24,020	—	—	1	1.1	2	2.7	1	2.2	—	—	—	—	—	—
Onassis	44	65.1	22,970	3	2.0	13	13.1	21	32.2	4	8.4	3	9.4	—	—	—	—
Vergottis	6	10.3	25,690	—	—	—	—	4	5.4	2	4.9	—	—	—	—	—	—
Wang	7	6.2	16,070	2	1.2	5	5.0	—	—	—	—	—	—	—	—	—	—
Other Independent Companies	1,398	1,524.4	18,470	449	301.3	627	663.2	208	300.5	104	229.8	10	29.6	—	—	—	—
Total Independent Companies	1,713	2,065.8	19,960	461	309.0	748	789.9	292	436.1	163	369.7	41	121.7	1	3.7	7	35.7
GOVERNMENT COMMERCIAL	84	63.7	13,790	51	26.3	27	27.6	4	5.2	2	4.6	—	—	—	—	—	—
TOTAL WORLD COMMERCIAL	2,703	3,167.2	19,390	812	512.6	1,157	1,210.5	400	621.1	270	613.1	51	151.8	6	22.4	7	35.7

68 CHAPTER FIVE

for a total of 1,750,000 DWT., while cancellations must have been close to 5,000,000 tons, giving a net *decrease* in new orders placed of approximately 200 T-2's. Also, for the second half of 1958, 1,400,000 DWT. of new orders were placed, but cancellations brought down the net new orders placed to only 1.3 T-2's.[25]

The impact of the institutional considerations discussed here is expected to manifest itself only on the downswing. When rates are high and expectations elastic, the whole industry behaves in only one fashion. Each owner places orders because others have begun ordering, and no one thinks of costs and prices. With rates low, however, the soul searching and re-examination begins. It is exactly at this stage that the institutional factors enter.

It is reasonable to assume that the oil companies dislike[26] low tanker rates mainly because rate depressions disturb their long-term contractual bargaining. Furthermore, under depressed market conditions the oil companies do not "realize" any return on their tankship investment, and this may disturb the transportation divisions who are looked upon as second-class citizens. If most of the oil produced by a particular company is sold on a delivered basis and the company successfully resists pressures for renegotiations of old contracts and discounts, then the low rates *on any new charters transacted* will affect favorably the total profits of an integrated firm. This profit, however, applies *only* to the marginal capacity obtained at low rates, and will all be imputed to the production activity. Such an occurrence will be of little consolation to the managers of transportation departments who operate under budgetary constraints and notions of accounting profit centers. In case the company has to yield and renegotiate or grant discounts, then the total profit will be reduced, other things being equal, but again the brunt of the squeeze will be felt by the transportation activity, which will have to justify its existence. In either case, however, whether the delivered prices reflect the low transportation rates or not, the small oil companies that do not own their own vessels and usually depend on the spot market tend to benefit much more from low rates than do the

---

[25] The figures for orders placed were derived from Jacobs, John I., *World Tanker Fleet Review,* June 30, 1958, p. 2, and December 31, 1958, p. 4, and Table 10. The figures refer to vessels of 10,000 tons dead weight and over.

It must be stressed that our figures refer to tanker cancellations only. In addition to cancellations, orders may either be converted to dry cargo orders or postponed. Usually postponements are another dimension of cancellations, because those who place the orders may request such postponements in periods of uncertainty until the market trends become more definite.

[26] Industrial sources claim that this is not so. Our discussion, therefore, may be directed to "what should be" rather than to "what is."

rest, and this, of course, does not please the large integrated firms.[27]

In general, it appears advantageous to the large oil companies (in terms of profits and competition) to shield the delivered and posted prices from the fluctuations of the spot tankship market. In the absence of any restraining force, such fluctuations, due to spot rate movements, will occur because of differences in the transportation intensity of the various crudes and products intended for a given market. If price adjustments are not made, there will be more than one price for the same homogeneous product in the same market, a factor which will influence the buyers to move en masse from one supplier to another. The relative rigidity of the posted prices[28] implies that the emphasis is placed on delivered prices, although no such prices are officially quoted. The emphasis on delivered prices is very logical, nevertheless, because it guarantees price equalization at the consumer markets.

Unless the producer has some control over transportation, he cannot very well exercise control over delivered prices nor, consequently, over rates of production. Such uncertainty is very costly and, to eliminate it, the oil companies may attempt to increase their tonnage in the hope of reducing their dependence on chartered vessels. The irony is that the oil companies do not realize that their own behavior is instrumental in determining the market outcome, and they react in a manner that prolongs the depression in the tankship markets and aggravates future cycles.[29]

The consequence of the Suez Canal frenzy may be seen from a comparison of the tonnage owned with the tonnage under construction, shown in Tables 5.1 and 5.3 respectively. These comparisons show that on January 1, 1959 the nine largest owners of tankers among the oil companies had vessels on order and under construction equal to 80% of their total ownership at that date, while the comparable figure for the independents — listed by name in Tables 5.1 and 5.3 — was only 35%. Of course, what *part* of this discrepancy is the consequence of faster reaction by the independents, who may have ordered and received most of their vessels before the oil companies placed their orders, we do not exactly know, but we can safely infer that it is not very sig-

[27] The source of displeasure lies in potential competition. Looking at delivered prices, low transportation cost tends to equalize competitive positions because it reduces the advantage that the large firms normally enjoy in production. Consequently, the small producers may be encouraged to penetrate into new markets during periods of low rates.

[28] There is another reason for the rigidity of posted prices. The U.S. depletion allowance of 27.5% is based on actual revenues from production.

[29] This paragraph refers to *individual* action and not to any cooperative action among the oil companies.

TABLE 5.3

WORLD-WIDE INDUSTRY TANKER CONSTRUCTION BY SIZE GROUPS AS OF JANUARY 1, 1959
(*Vessels 6,000 DWT. and Over*)

	Total			Deadweight Class											
				6,000–16,000		16,001–20,000		20,001–30,000		30,001–40,000		40,001–50,000		50,001–60,000		60,001 Plus	
Ownership	No.	T-2	Average DWT.	No.	T-2	No.	T-2	No.	T-2	No.	T-2	No.	T-2	No.	T-2	No.	T-2
OIL COMPANIES																	
Allied/Ashland	—	—	—	—	—	—	—	—	—	—	—	—	—	—	—	—	—
Atlantic Refining	—	—	—	—	—	—	—	—	—	—	—	—	—	—	—	—	—
British Petroleum	57	141.1	36,840	14	14.5	5	6.4	—	—	12	27.6	18	57.7	—	—	8	34.9
Caltex	13	37.3	43,090	—	—	1	1.2	—	—	4	9.0	6	18.5	—	—	2	8.6
Cities Service	3	13.0	65,000	—	—	—	—	—	—	—	—	—	—	—	—	3	13.0
Continental Oil	—	—	—	—	—	—	—	—	—	—	—	—	—	—	—	—	—
Gulf	23	61.1	38,880	—	—	1	1.2	6	12.2	10	26.0	3	8.7	—	—	3	13.0
Hess	—	—	—	—	—	—	—	—	—	—	—	—	—	—	—	—	—
Paragon	3	6.5	32,270	—	—	1	1.3	—	—	1	2.2	1	3.0	—	—	—	—
Petrofina	—	—	—	—	—	—	—	—	—	—	—	—	—	—	—	—	—
Pure Oil	—	—	—	—	—	—	—	—	—	—	—	—	—	—	—	—	—
Richfield	—	—	—	—	—	—	—	—	—	—	—	—	—	—	—	—	—
Sinclair Refining	2	3.3	24,500	—	—	—	—	2	3.3	—	—	—	—	—	—	—	—
Shell	45	101.4	33,760	—	—	15	18.0	—	—	21	48.7	4	12.2	—	—	5	22.5
Socony-Mobil	15	42.1	41,860	—	—	2	2.5	2	4.2	—	—	11	35.4	—	—	—	—
Standard Oil (California)	10	34.7	51,900	—	—	—	—	—	—	—	—	7	21.7	—	—	3	13.0
Standard Oil (Indiana)	—	—	—	—	—	—	—	—	—	—	—	—	—	—	—	—	—
Standard Oil (New Jersey)	53	158.0	43,790	—	—	—	—	—	—	23	56.3	27	86.7	—	—	3	15.0
Standard-Vacuum	4	7.6	28,390	2	1.9	—	—	—	—	1	2.6	1	3.1	—	—	—	—
Sun Oil	3	10.0	47,750	—	—	—	—	—	—	—	—	3	10.0	—	—	—	—

Texas Co.	11	29.4	39,660	—	—	2	2.6	—	—	2	5.2	7	21.6	—	—	—	—
Tidewater	15	59.3	59,190	—	—	—	—	—	—	—	—	6	18.4	—	—	9	40.9
Union Oil	2	8.5	60,000	—	—	—	—	—	—	—	—	—	—	2	8.5	—	—
Other Oil Companies	12	28.6	35,600	1	1.0	1	1.1	1	1.4	3	6.4	6	18.7	—	—	—	—
Total Oil Companies	271	741.9	40,600	17	17.4	28	34.3	11	21.1	77	184.0	100	315.7	2	8.5	36	160.9
INDEPENDENT COMPANIES																	
Andreadis	—	—	—	—	—	—	—	—	—	—	—	—	—	—	—	—	—
Barber Oil	6	18.8	46,000	—	—	—	—	—	—	—	—	6	18.8	—	—	—	—
Carras	3	9.9	47,530	—	—	—	—	—	—	—	—	3	9.9	—	—	—	—
Goulandris	10	27.5	40,990	—	—	—	—	—	—	5	12.7	5	14.8	—	—	—	—
Hendy, Joshua	—	—	—	—	—	—	—	—	—	—	—	—	—	—	—	—	—
Kulukundis	3	4.8	23,970	—	—	2	2.6	—	—	1	2.2	—	—	—	—	—	—
Kurz	4	13.1	45,370	—	—	—	—	—	—	—	—	4	13.1	—	—	—	—
Lemos	—	—	—	—	—	—	—	—	—	—	—	—	—	—	—	—	—
Livanos	5	10.9	31,780	—	—	—	—	2	3.6	3	7.3	—	—	—	—	—	—
National Bulk	3	21.0	104,520	—	—	—	—	—	—	—	—	—	—	—	—	3	21.0
Niarchos	7	26.5	55,790	—	—	—	—	2	3.3	1	2.7	—	—	—	—	4	20.5
Nicolaou	—	—	—	—	—	—	—	—	—	—	—	—	—	—	—	—	—
Nomikos	—	—	—	—	—	—	—	—	—	—	—	—	—	—	—	—	—
Onassis	14	53.7	56,640	—	—	—	—	1	1.7	3	8.0	2	6.4	—	—	8	37.6
Vergottis	2	4.9	36,650	—	—	—	—	—	—	1	2.2	1	2.7	—	—	—	—
Wang	—	—	—	—	—	—	—	—	—	—	—	—	—	—	—	—	—
Other Independent Companies	459	971.3	31,770	4	3.4	133	169.5	70	117.8	151	353.3	85	258.7	4	14.2	12	54.4
Total Independent Companies	516	1,162.4	33,700	4	3.4	135	172.1	75	126.4	165	388.4	106	324.4	4	14.2	27	133.5
GOVERNMENT COMMERCIAL	23	30.8	20,000	11	6.4	2	2.6	1	1.7	9	20.1	—	—	—	—	—	—
TOTAL WORLD COMMERCIAL	810	1,935.1	35,600	32	27.2	165	209.0	87	149.2	251	592.5	206	640.1	6	22.7	63	294.4

nificant. During the Suez Canal crisis and the two years immediately following, the lead time from order to delivery was *over* twenty-two months. Consequently, not many orders initiated by the crisis could have been delivered by December 31, 1958, even under the hypothesis that the independents react faster.

Tables 5.4, 5.5, and 5.6 provide ample evidence that on January 1,

TABLE 5.4

OWNERSHIP OF VESSELS OF 6,000 DWT. AND OVER

	Oil Companies		Independents		Governments	
	1	2	1	2	1	2
January 1, 1957						
% of Total Vessels	36.0		60.7		· 3.3	
% of Total Capacity		35.1		62.5		2.3
July 1, 1957						
% of Total Vessels	35.6		61.2		3.2	
% of Total Capacity		34.5		63.3		2.2
January 1, 1958						
% of Total Vessels	35.0		61.9		3.1	
% of Total Capacity		34.1		63.9		2.1
July 1, 1958						
% of Total Vessels	34.0		62.9		3.1	
% of Total Capacity		33.1		65.0		2.0
January 1, 1959						
% of Total Vessels	33.5		63.4		3.1	
% of Total Capacity		32.8		65.1		3.1

Source of Data: Transportation Coordination Department, Standard Oil Company, New Jersey.

1957, the oil companies owned 36% of the total number of vessels but only 35.1% of the total carrying capacity. The corresponding figures for the independent fleet were 60.7% and 62.5%, showing that the race toward larger vessels was started by the independents. By January 1, 1959, the difference in percentages of ownership became greater, showing that the independents were the first to place orders. The latter observation is substantiated by Table 5.5, which shows that the share of the oil companies in the backlog of orders had increased steadily and significantly, while that of the independents had followed the opposite trend. This trend, which occurred after the drop in rates, is consistent with our hypothesis that the oil companies follow the independents, but that by the time the consequences of their reactions are manifested they will be attempting in vain to assert their independence from the tanker market during periods of low rates. We further notice in Table

FACTORS AFFECTING SUPPLY OF TANKSHIPS 73

TABLE 5.5

NEW CONSTRUCTION: VESSELS OF 6,000 DWT. AND OVER

	Oil Companies		Independents		Governments	
	1	2	1	2	1	2
January 1, 1957						
% of Total Vessels	27.7		72.3		0.0	
% of Total Capacity		31.7		68.3		0.0
July 1, 1957						
% of Total Vessels	29.8		70.2		0.0	
% of Total Capacity		35.2		64.8		0.0
January 1, 1958						
% of Total Vessels	29.1		68.1		2.8	
% of Total Capacity		34.2		62.9		3.0
July 1, 1958						
% of Total Vessels	32.4		64.3		3.3	
% of Total Capacity		37.6		59.7		2.7
January 1, 1959						
% of Total Vessels	33.5		63.7		2.8	
% of Total Capacity		38.4		60.0		1.6

Source of Data: Transportation Coordination Department, Standard Oil Company, New Jersey.

TABLE 5.6

TOTAL TONNAGE INCLUDING NEW CONSTRUCTION:
VESSELS OF 6,000 DWT. AND OVER

	Oil Companies		Independents		Governments	
	1	2	1	2	1	2
January 1, 1957						
% of Total Vessels	33.6		64.1		2.3	
% of Total Capacity		33.6		65.1		1.3
July 1, 1957						
% of Total Vessels	33.7		64.1		2.2	
% of Total Capacity		34.8		64.1		1.1
January 1, 1958						
% of Total Vessels	33.2		63.8		3.1	
% of Total Capacity		34.1		63.4		2.5
July 1, 1958						
% of Total Vessels	33.6		63.2		3.2	
% of Total Capacity		35.0		62.8		2.3
January 1, 1959						
% of Total Vessels	33.4		63.2		3.4	
% of Total Capacity		34.9		63.2		1.9

Source of Data: Transportation Coordination Department, Standard Oil Company, New Jersey.

5.5 that the vessels ordered by the oil companies were larger. Of the total number of vessels under construction on January 1, 1957, 27.7% belonged to oil companies and 72.3% to independents. In terms of carrying capacity, however, the share of the oil companies was 31.7% and that of the independents 68.3%. By December 31, 1958, 33.5% of all vessels under construction, representing 38.4% of total carrying capacity, were for the oil companies and 63.7%, for 60% of carrying capacity, were for the independents. As shown previously in Table 5.2, on December 31, 1958 the average size of the company vessels under construction was 40,600 DWT., against 33,700 DWT. for the independents.

The combined figures of existing tonnage and new construction are presented in Table 5.6; they reveal that the oil companies have increased their share of ownership slightly in the post-Suez period, which again may serve to substantiate our assertion about the behavior of oil companies during periods of low rates and tonnage surpluses. Although the oil companies may follow behind the independents in terms of reaction time they are not outdone.

We feel that the institutional constraints will not affect appreciably the otherwise great number of orders generated by price-elastic expectations during periods of high rates, but will probably combine with retirements to cause the lower part of the demand schedule to assume a greater elasticity than otherwise.[30] The reasons for such an effect are the disproportionality of age and size distribution within the industry — namely, an intra-industry mismatch of existing surpluses and needs for new tankers for replacement purposes — and the role that the oil companies play. The oil companies, as we have argued, will probably assert their independence from market fluctuations exactly at the time that surpluses manifest themselves for the industry as a whole.[31] We have also pointed out that, given the existence of economies of scale in tankship building and tankship operation, orders placed are by nature surplus producing. Ancillary technologies (harbor facilities, refineries, storage, etc.) continuously advance, and markets keep on growing, thus allowing the utilization of larger and larger vessels. Consequently, because of size indivisibilities, replacements introduce more capacity than is lost to retirements. Finally, to the extent that the somewhat asymmetric behavior of the oil companies during low rates combines to produce a uniform impact (more orders), it is expected to be dis-

---

[30] This may be shown as an oscillation because the impact may be discontinuous.

[31] Because the surpluses are manifested in the tankship service and not in the tankship building markets, the oil companies do not necessarily benefit from lower shipbuilding prices.

equilibrating. In magnitude, however, the orders initiated by institutional considerations are minor relative to those placed when rates are high. We may say that they are only of an adjusting nature, bringing the ratio of owned versus chartered capacity to the "desired" equilibrium. Because the independents in general react faster to changes in rates,[32] their orders disturb the desirable ratio of ownership of the major oil companies. Consequently, the big companies may place orders later — when spot rates are low[33] and after the independents withdraw from the shipbuilding market — in order to restore this presumptive equilibrium. Although these orders placed under conditions of excess transportation capacity may be disequilibrating in the short run and the intermediate run, they may be long-run equilibrating *under conditions of cyclical demand*.

The number of tankers under construction may also be influenced by the domestic policies of various countries. Some governments take national pride in having vessels flying their flag, while others may attempt through legislation to encourage shipbuilding activities in their countries. Presumably such efforts by governments are intensified during periods of depressed market conditions and excess shipbuilding capacity. The actual contribution of these pressures to the number of orders placed is not known but it can be safely assumed that it is relatively insignificant. In the United States, where several attempts have been made in the past to aid the shipbuilding industry,[34] such programs did not

---

[32] Often the oil companies do not react in time, not because they do not want to do so but because of their inflexible organization structures. As an illustration of what may happen, consider the following actual case. During the Suez crisis, the tanker department of a major oil company requested funds for new vessels in its budget. The request went through the proper channels and was returned for "more details." The details were furnished and after study the finance committee approved the appropriation initially. This meant that negotiations with shipyards were approved but actual authorization for fund expenditure would await another application at the time the contract was to be signed. Orders were placed but by this time spot rates had fallen. Consequently, in the authorization funds were cut and some orders had to be cancelled. The whole process took approximately twelve months. Such a delay between decision and action is not evident with the independents.

[33] Notice that this statement refers to tanker rates and not shipbuilding costs. The latter may still be high, or even at their peak, since shipbuilding costs seem to lag a few months behind spot rates.

[34] For details see: Shields and Company, *Financing the United States Merchant Marine,* Shields and Company, New York, May 1958; Subcommittee of the Committee on Interstate and Foreign Commerce hearings before the United States Senate, e.g. *Merchant Marine Study and Investigation,* Pursuant to S. Res. 50, Part I, June 21–22, 1949, U.S. Government Printing Office, 1949; *New Ship Construction Program,* Pursuant to S. Res. 13, April 21–22, 1955, U.S. Government Printing Office, 1955; *Tanker and Cargo Tankship Charter and Construction,* On S. 3877, June 13, 1956, U.S. Government Printing Office, 1956.

materially affect the orders for tankers. It is still more attractive to own and operate a vessel under a foreign flag, even though the owner must forgo the benefits that accrue to the U.S.-flag vessels operated under the various maritime acts.

A study of the shipbuilding statistics shows that the backlog of orders outstanding in the United States lags behind the cycle of spot rates by approximately one year, indicating that orders are determined by rates.[35] Quantitatively, during 1955–1959, the tankship orders placed with United States yards have fluctuated between 1.6% and 8.1% of the world total, which shows that any legislative effect on orders, however important it may be for the domestic industry, is not expected to affect the world total in any significant manner.

Spot Rates, Shipbuilding Costs, and Orders Placed — Empirical Observations

A strict empirical test of the validity of our theoretical formulation is impossible because of the lack of adequate data. Information on spot rates and orders placed has been accumulated, and all the details of changes in their magnitudes are known, but the available information on shipbuilding cost is sketchy and rather unreliable. Because the contract price is considered confidential information, it has been impossible to put together a *reliable and continuous* time-series index of the cost of shipbuilding in order to quantify monthly changes.[36] Furthermore, each contract contains its own particularities. As a result, and even if the agreed price of contracts were known on the basis of the contractual provisions, extensive and complicated calculations would be necessary before all contracts could be brought down to a homogeneous basis. Therefore, an indirect approach must be used in deriving an index for shipbuilding costs and the demand schedule for new vessels.

Figure 5.1 demonstrates the existence of a close relationship between orders placed and spot rates, the correlation being much greater during the 1954–1958 cycle. With proper adjustment to eliminate known impurities the similarities between the two time series become even more

---

[35] This lag is due to several factors: (*a*) protracted negotiations take place before the signing of a contract. So the initiation of an order and the award do not occur at the same point of time; (*b*) construction statistics usually appear when construction orders are signed. Between the award of the contract and the construction authorization there may be a time lag due to administrative red tape and details; (*c*) the fact that foreign yards are approached first since they are less expensive.

[36] Although secrecy seems to be breaking down, the absence of continuity in data is still with us.

striking. Let us take, for example, the "unexplained" influx in orders during August and September of 1957. An analysis of some contracts which were placed by oil companies in August–September of 1957 showed beyond doubt that the majority of the orders analyzed were initiated (and often concluded but not announced) in January–March of 1957. As the spot rates started falling, the oil companies started protracting the negotiations and putting demands for concessions. In one case an order for *four* tankers of 40–45,000 DWT. each was placed in February 1957 with Italian yards, at $275 per DWT., *but was not announced*. In September of 1957 an announcement was made that this company placed an order for *five* "supertankers" of 40–45,000 DWT. each. What actually happened was that the Italian shipyard, not wishing to lose a good customer, finally offered to build *five* vessels instead of four for the total price originally agreed upon. So the net result was that the oil company got a free vessel (effectively the cost per DWT. came down to $225), the February transaction became a statistic in September, the backlog of the Italian yard increased, but the shipbuilder did not get any additional revenue.

The relationships shown in Figure 5.1 and the qualitative detail behind the empirical observations provide strong support for the assumption that the spot-rate expectations of the users of tankship services are elastic,[37] and the belief that the magnitude of the initial shock determines the swiftness of the response and the magnitude of the fluctuations. The fact that the Suez Canal crisis affected a greater percentage of the tankship capacity than the Korean War may explain the quantitative difference between the two cycles. Of course, the value of the elasticity index is not always the same, depending upon the point of measurement on the expectations schedule.

Let us recapitulate briefly our arguments about the demand and supply schedules for tankships, and relate these arguments to available qualitative empirical evidence as a preparatory step to the discussion of the quantitative relationship between spot rates and orders.

At the beginning of a rate movement the expectations of the users of tankers seem to be inelastic because the users are reluctant to believe in the permanency of such movement, especially if the disturbance is small and rates have been at a constant level for a relatively long time. Users seem to feel that such movement is a temporary deviation from an equi-

---

[37] The notion of elasticity of expectations applies to changes from "what prices would have been" and has nothing to do with the level of magnitudes. Namely, if we say that expectations are elastic at a point and $(\partial P_t/\partial P_0)(P_0/P_t) > 1$, we have no reason to deduce that $P_t > P_0$. Also, when we make a statement concerning price elasticity of expectations, it applies to all prices in the future for all $t > 0$.

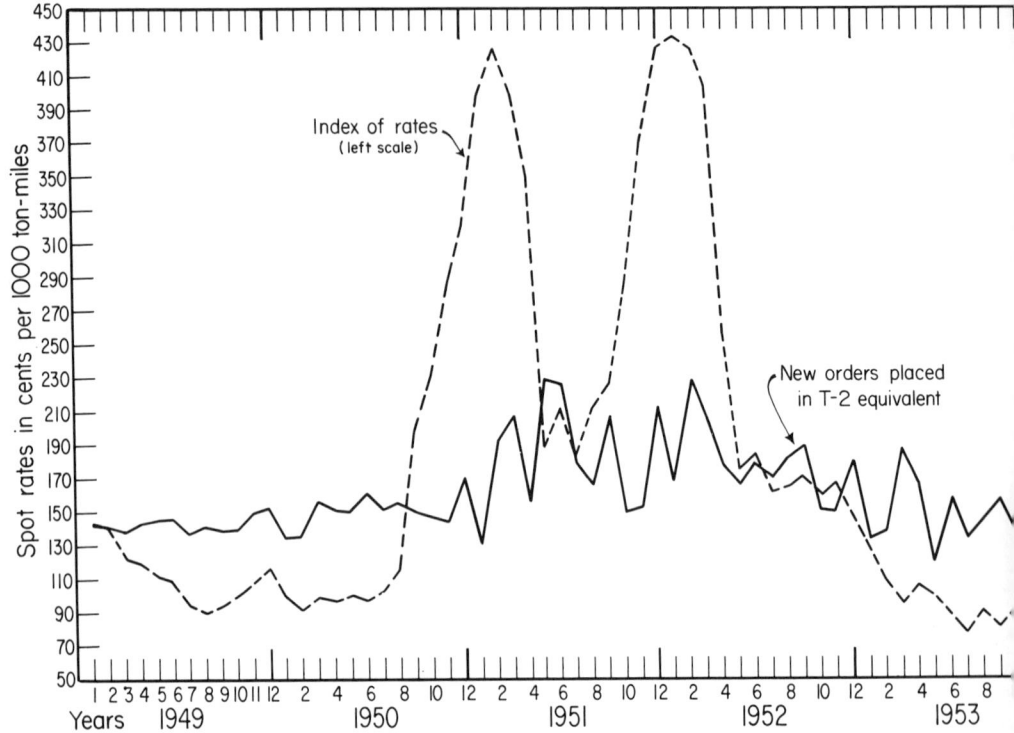

Figure 5.1. Time series of orders placed in T-2

librium level which necessitates vigilance rather than action. As the rate movement gains momentum, however, their expectations become more and more elastic, until finally a level is reached beyond which logic tells them that rates cannot be expected to rise in the long run. In between this final turning point and the original equilibrium there may be some pause for reflection, and withdrawal from the market, but it does not usually last long. Although such pause, incidentally, will change the slope of the effective demand schedule from positive to negative and then back again to positive, it does *not necessarily* imply that expectations also changed temporarily from elastic to inelastic and then back to elastic again.

Implicit in such a spot-rate elasticity of expectations is the belief not only that the present cause of the shift in demand for tankship services is real but that manifestations in the future will be even greater. Therefore, the logical reaction of the owners of tankship services is to place more orders with shipbuilders, thus causing shifts in the shipbuilding schedules.

As a result of such shifts in the shipbuilding schedules we expect to

FACTORS AFFECTING SUPPLY OF TANKSHIPS

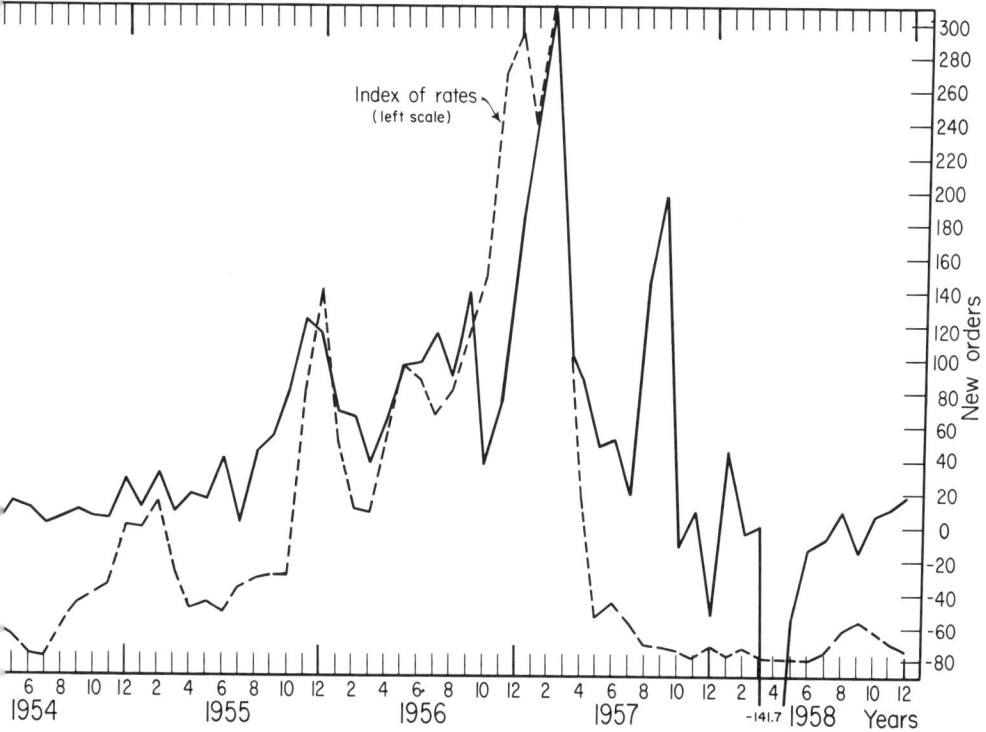

equivalent and index of spot rates, 1949–1958.

observe a secondary reaction pattern molded by changes in shipbuilding costs. Even though the pattern of behavior in the tankship building markets is not believed to be as elastic as the spot-rate expectations schedule,[38] it is expected to enhance the shifts in the demand for vessels and to possess all the qualitative attributes of the spot-rate schedule of expectations. As soon as prices per DWT. start their upward trend, the shipbuilders rush to accept orders and, in general, become very accommodating. They promise early delivery, omit escalation clauses (that is, quote fixed prices), grant liberal credit terms, and so on. This situation, however, does not last long; soon the shipbuilders play "hard to get" and assume the upper hand with demands for the total payment even before delivery, escalation clauses, and five-to-six-year delivery schedules.[39] At the same time, instead of devoting all their capacity to

[38] What we wish to say here is that expectations in the tankship building market *are elastic* but the coefficient of expectations may not be as great as the one operating in the tankship transportation market.

[39] See Jacobs, John I., *World Tanker Fleet Review,* December 31, 1957, p. 6; and also issues of June 30, 1956, p. 4; and December 31, 1958, p. 6.

shipbuilding, they start employing part of their organization efforts to expansion, thus cutting their current capacity somewhat for the purpose of building future capacity.[40]

It is unlikely that the observed behavior of the shipbuilders is due to real reasons rather than expectations. It seems that they start with inelastic expectations, which become more and more elastic as the price per DWT. is bid upward. Evidence shows that at first they postpone expansion and devote all their capacity to the construction of ships, but after they fill their order books for four or five years to come (something which does not take long to achieve given the reactions of those operating in these markets), their expectations become elastic and they switch some of their efforts to expansion.[41] In addition, the shipbuilders raise demands for better and better terms. Some of them even set the promised delivery date far enough in the future to allow themselves leeway for the expected "prize contracts."

For example, Table 5.7 shows that the Japanese yards in 1957 had a yearly capacity of at least 140 T-2 equivalents; yet in late 1956 and very early in 1957 these yards were quoting deliveries beyond 1962.[42] A glance at Table 5.8 shows that for Japan the years beyond 1960 were very lean indeed, which explains why the Japanese yards were the first to show signs of weakness.[43] Yet, to repeat again, they were refusing in late 1956 and early 1957 orders for delivery prior to 1962. This type of behavior cannot be explained satisfactorily, unless we assume elastic expectations. The total backlog of orders with Japanese yards on December 1958 was less than two and a half years of activity.

Although the expectations schedules of buyers and sellers may be somewhat out of phase we believe that there is a parallelism in the observable behavior between the two sides of the market. Prices, however, are neither explosive nor are they perpetually establishing new lows, for reasons that we expounded when we analyzed the patterns of behavior

---

[40] The notion of cutting output for the sake of expansion is the essence of Professor W. W. Rostow's early business-cycle explanations in economic history. Traces of this thinking are found in his *British Economy in the Nineteenth Century,* Oxford, 1948, and Gayer, Arthur D., W. W. Rostow, and Anna J. Schwartz, *The Growth and Fluctuation of the British Economy 1790–1850,* Two volumes, Oxford University Press, Oxford, 1953.

[41] For more discussion on the theoretical issues of expectations, see Baumol, J. W., *Economic Dynamics,* The Macmillan Company, New York, 1957, pp. 83–115; Hicks, *op. cit.,* pp. 250–251.

[42] Really they were even reluctant to accept orders according to reliable sources. To contrast this situation with what happened later see *Westinform Shipping Report No. 129,* 1959, pp. 2–6.

[43] According to *The New York Times* of Sunday, March 22, 1959, page 16S, "Shipyards all over the world were reported as quoting fixed prices again. In recent years shipyards have insisted on escalation clauses in contracts."

TABLE 5.7
VESSEL DELIVERIES BY YARDS 1956–1958

	Deliveries in the 12-Month Period Ending:				
Country of Building	Dec. 1956	June 1957	Dec. 1957	June 1958	Dec. 1958
United States	9.8	21.0	26.8	26.4	53.0
United Kingdom	52.4	51.9	52.9	46.5	50.1
Canada	—	—	.3	.3	—
Sweden	21.0	24.5	38.4	44.5	48.6
Norway	7.1	6.6	10.8	15.2	17.2
Denmark	1.7	4.7	6.1	9.3	12.4
France	9.3	18.5	26.3	23.1	22.9
Spain	3.3	2.2	1.1	4.5	5.3
Netherlands	19.9	12.9	18.6	22.2	23.4
Italy	9.0	7.8	12.3	28.0	35.3
Belgium	4.8	2.4	1.5	7.3	11.0
Japan	75.5	104.6	128.4	140.6	129.4
Germany	10.0	6.3	16.0	25.1	29.1
Portugal	—	—	—	1.0	1.0
Yugoslavia	—	—	—	—	—
Greece	—	—	—	—	—
Formosa	—	—	—	—	—
Australia	—	—	—	—	—
Total	223.8	263.6	339.5	394.0	438.7

Source: Transportation Coordination Department, Standard Oil Company, New Jersey.
Figures expressed in T-2 equivalents.

operating in the tankship transportation markets. As the current cost of shipbuilding rises, the users of vessels move on an elastic expectations schedule, causing compounding shifts in the demand schedules facing the owners. The process gains momentum up to a point as we move in a northeasterly direction. These shifts do not bring about a balance in supply and demand, but are, instead, disequilibrating, forcing prices to very precarious levels. Finally, the budget effects force the buyers to withdraw from the market and may also influence the expectations of the users of vessels to become inelastic. This latter change, however, is not necessary, since withdrawal is otherwise guaranteed.

The price in the meantime may have reached a lofty yet shaky temporary equilibrium (on that part of the supply schedule that bends backwards) when suddenly not only the quantity demanded diminishes but the demand schedules may also show signs of shifting to the left (because the users withdraw from the market as a consequence of the

TABLE 5.8

CONTRACTED DELIVERIES FOR VESSELS ON ORDER AS OF JANUARY 1, 1959

Country of Building	Under Const. as of 1/1/59	Vessels Contracted for Delivery in:					Total Backlog of New Construction
		1959	1960	1961	1962	1963 and Beyond	
United States	76.5	81.8	39.4	16.8	—	—	138.0
United Kingdom	33.2	91.1	62.8	67.7	36.1	66.5	324.2
Canada	2.7	2.6	2.6	—	—	—	5.2
Sweden	25.5	72.2	71.9	55.0	40.7	31.6	271.4
Norway	7.5	14.1	13.2	21.8	19.6	45.6	114.3
Denmark	8.8	16.6	13.8	4.5	14.1	12.3	61.3
France	20.6	26.9	34.5	23.5	21.9	—	106.8
Spain	4.5	10.1	10.8	1.8	1.2	23.7	47.6
Netherlands	11.9	33.0	36.7	36.5	14.9	4.9	126.0
Italy	36.3	44.5	22.3	16.6	13.4	—	96.8
Belgium	13.2	8.7	7.7	4.7	6.1	1.3	28.5
Japan	56.8	139.8	118.1	48.0	17.7	12.3	335.9
Germany	26.1	58.4	45.8	70.5	23.7	33.2	231.6
Portugal	—	—	—	1.8	—	—	1.8
Yugoslavia	1.3	4.3	6.4	2.1	—	—	12.8
Greece	—	—	1.6	1.6	—	—	3.2
Formosa	2.4	2.4	2.4	—	—	—	4.8
Australia	—	—	2.2	—	—	—	2.2
Total	327.3	606.5	492.2	372.9	209.4	231.4	1,912.4

Source: Transportation Coordination Department, Standard Oil Company, New Jersey.
All figures are in T-2 equivalents.

budget effect and possibly a change in their expectations), and the supply schedules start shifting to the right as the new capacity added in response to the elastic expectations of the owners becomes operational. It does not take long for the price to reach its peak, but it takes even less time for it to reach the bottom.

Violent fluctuations of this sort are typical of the tankship markets. We shall return to them later (to show their adjustment paths) when we discuss the formation of short-term (spot) charter rates.

Spot Rates and Orders Placed — Quantitative Evidence

To give operational content to the theoretical relationships governing orders for new vessels, we need to have, among other data, monthly time series of shipbuilding costs. The latter type of information is not available both because it is often considered proprietary and because transactions for tankship building do not occur continuously. Furthermore, as we have already stressed, there is often a time lag of a few months between the initiation of a contract and the announcement of the award (if it is announced and its terms made public).

In looking for a substitute for shipbuilding costs, we naturally focused our attention on tanker rates. Intuitively we can justify the choice because tanker rates induce expectations which affect orders and shipbuilding costs. We have, however, a more objective reason for such choice. On the basis of statistical relationships that we derived between changes in spot rates and changes in the Fairplay[44] index for the cost of a new vessel if it were in stock, the movements in short-term rates can explain 86.5% of all changes in shipbuilding cost. Consequently, we decided to approximate the value of our function by deriving a relationship between tanker rates and orders placed.

Figures 5.2 and 5.3 present scatter diagrams of monthly spot rates per 1,000 ton-miles versus monthly orders placed for the periods 1949–1953 and 1954–1958, respectively. Examining first Figure 5.2, we notice that for the total range of rates the correlation between orders placed and spot rates appears to be positive. Such a relationship, however, is not uniform. If we connect the monthly movements in rates[45] and orders placed, especially for 1951 and 1952, we find that these movements describe "loops" as if moving on the periphery of a crude figure eight. This is consistent with our hypothesis that spot-rate expectations are elastic and that the whole demand schedule exhibiting the impact of interperiod substitutions shifts to create the multiple loops. Any reversal in the direction of the demand schedule between the region of static relevance and the upper bound may be caused, as we have already explained, by temporary withdrawals for reappraisals, temporary changes in expectations, purely stochastic reasons, or failure of our measurement system to record unsatisfied demand.

Of the above-mentioned factors the first two are interrelated, and "purely stochastic reasons" as the motivating force behind the changes must be discounted, because of the regularity of the turning point of the schedules shown in Figures 5.2 and 5.3. There is no doubt that our observations may have failed to record the full impact of price-elastic ex-

---

[44] *Fairplay* is a London nautical publication which twice a year provides an index for vessel costs, (*a*) for a new vessel if ready, and (*b*) for a vessel if ordered.

[45] The readers may remember that these years include the Korean War. The movements in rates were caused by temporary tonnage shortages and the expectations created by the conflict. Our notation gives the month and the year for each observation.

84 CHAPTER FIVE

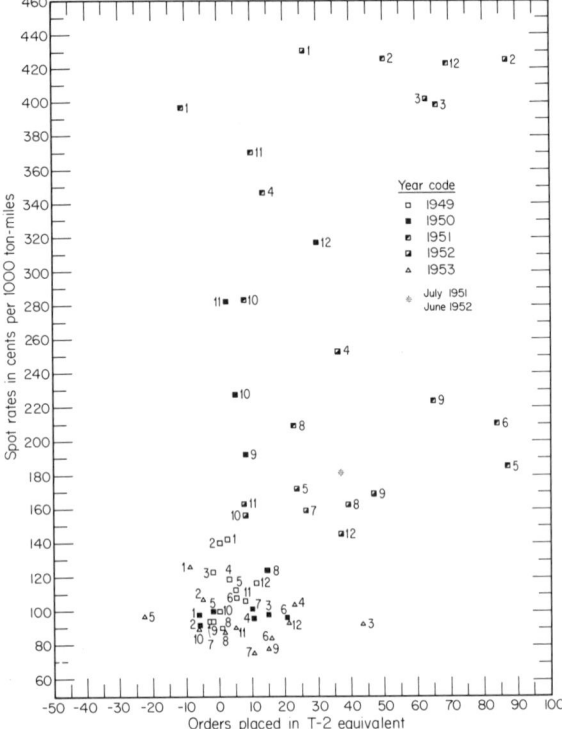

Figure 5.2. Scatter diagram of orders placed versus index of spot rates, 1949–1953 (monthly).

pectations, especially within the price regions over which symmetry exists in the expectations of buyers and sellers. Although the operations in the tankship building markets are flexible enough (with supply stretching to meet demand) to mitigate the impact of such occurrences, they may not eliminate it completely. We have already noticed how the Japanese shipbuilders discouraged orders by quoting protracted deliveries (over six years). If a backward-bending supply (before it shifts far enough to the right) is influencing our observations, then what appear to be "temporary withdrawals for reappraisals" and "temporary changes in expectations" are nothing more than consequences of the deficiencies in our measurement methods. It seems to us after extensive analysis that this last observation offers the most plausible explanation. Note, however, that the hypothesis that price-elastic expectations are present is in no way impaired.

The lower part of the exhibit shows that there may be turning points in expectation at about $1.30–$1.40 per 1,000 ton-miles, at $2.80, and finally at $4.20. As we shall see later, a rate of $1.30–$1.40 per 1,000 ton-miles is remunerative for most ocean tankers, especially for vessels of T-2 size and over, and thus may lie at the boundary of the region of strict static relevance.

When we were discussing the theoretical relationships developed earlier in this chapter, we mentioned that at very low rates we should not be surprised to find what we then called some "schizophrenic" tendencies in our schedules because of the opposing effects of expectations on orders (substitution versus income effects) and the scrapping-replacement programs. This is clearly shown in Figure 5.2, which offers further evidence of the validity of our formulations.

What appears to be a turning point in expectations at $2.80 may only be the result of what we previously called deficiencies in measurement methods. Otherwise we cannot explain such an abrupt (as well as regular, as Figure 5.2 shows) change in expectations, from elastic to inelastic and then back to elastic, unless we assume that the operatives have no memory at all and every time prices move away from an equilibrium (stable or unstable) a new set of elastic expectations is created.

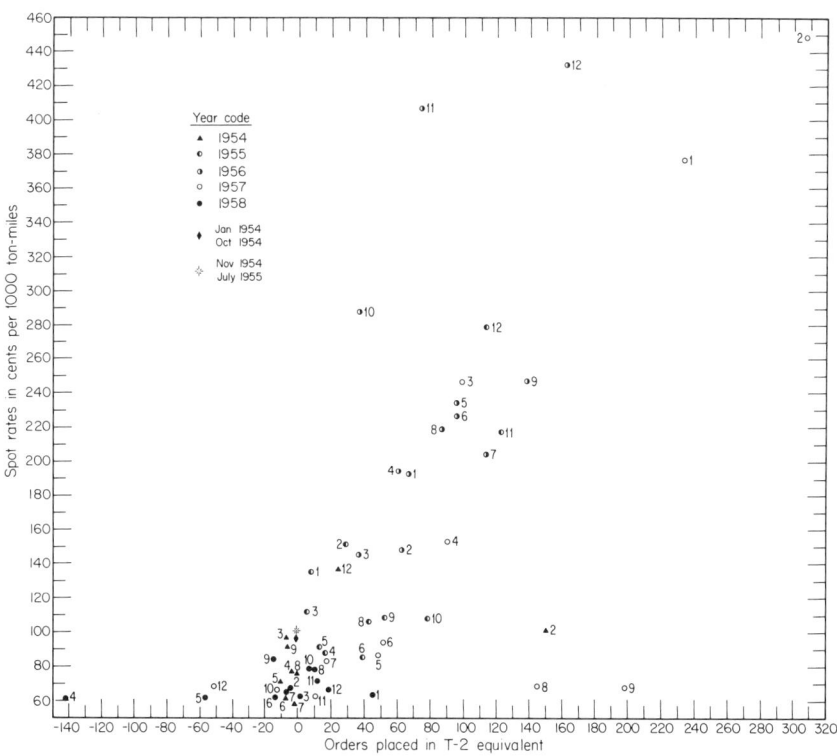

Figure 5.3. Scatter diagram of orders placed versus index of spot rates, 1954–1958 (monthly).

Finally, the uppermost turn at $4.20 is no doubt due to the budget effect that we have previously explained in detail.

Turning now to Figure 5.3, we notice that what we have just observed concerning the years 1949–1953 also applies to the period 1954–1958. It is interesting in this conjunction to trace the rate movements in 1956 and 1957 and compare them with those of 1951 and 1952. The qualitative similarities are indeed amazing, both in terms of the general shape and also swiftness of movements. Without the presence of price-elastic expectations such similarities would be very improbable. Furthermore, under static conditions no one would expect to observe a sevenfold change in prices and orders placed in the short period of a few months.

The impact of expectations and the result of replacement programs were much more pronounced during the 1954–1958 period, as shown by the fourfold increase in the range of orders placed. As seen in Table 5.2, the age distribution of tankers is skewed because of the war-built vessels; hence, the replacement programs will be extensively influenced by such skewness.

Rate expectations during the Suez crisis appear to have taken the market through a complete cycle in a short period of six months, thus causing orders to trace a big loop. At low rates, the opposing effects of expectations (cancellations versus budget effects) and the replacement programs define the end points of a range of approximately 340 T-2's, from plus 200 to minus 142. Within this amazingly large range, smaller fluctuations (oscillations) are observed, all, incidentally, with rates between 60 and 70 cents per 1,000 ton-miles.

Even though the pattern of orders placed, with respect to changes in the level of spot rates, is qualitatively the same for both five-year periods, we notice some quantitative dissimilarities. In addition to the already observed greater range of movement of orders placed, as influenced by the spot-rate elasticities of expectations and the replacement programs, we also notice the following:

1. The lowest point reached by the spot rates during the 1949–1953 period was about 75 cents per 1,000 ton-miles, against 58 cents for the 1954–1958 period.

2. The critical turning point of expectations at low levels seems to be $1.30–$1.40 against about $1.10–$1.20 for the two time periods respectively.

3. The highest level reached by spot rates during the 1949–1953 period was $4.30 per 1,000 ton-miles, as compared to $4.49 for the 1954–1958 period.

These quantitative dissimilarities can all be explained in terms of the changes in the size composition of the tankship fleet. As we shall see later, because of economies of scale in tankship building and tankship operation, the newer larger vessels can operate at a lower cost. Consequently, any replacement of marginal vessels will bring about a drop in the cost curves of the industry. During the 1948–1953 cycle the marginal vessel was 12,000 DWT. The influx of orders generated in 1951 and 1952, and the subsequent retirement of obsolete vessels, made the T-2, a vessel of 16,500 DWT., the marginal vessel during 1954–1958.

The out-of-pocket cost of the marginal vessel during 1948–1953 was approximately 77 cents per 1,000 ton-miles of oil carried (or U.S.M.C. minus 50%), and that of a T-2 was 61 cents (or U.S.M.C. minus 60%). Rates, however, can go below out-of-pocket cost, because of the alternative costs of keeping the vessel idle. Consequently, a difference around 16 cents per 1,000 ton-miles in the refusal rate should be expected.

The same thing can be said about the upper bound of the region of strict static relevance, which appears to be $1.30–$1.40 versus $1.10–$1.20 in the two respective cases. Since the idea of a "fair rate" (including a fair return on investment) for the vessels operating at any moment of time is a static notion, behavior should be influenced by current cost considerations in static terms[46] unless dynamic expectations enter into play. In our case, the turning points are $1.30–$1.40 versus $1.10–$1.20 for the respective time periods, the discrepancy being due we feel to the average full-cost differentials of the vessels operating during the two time periods under consideration.

At first glance it may appear that the highest levels reached by spot rates during the two cycles are inconsistent with our previous findings and arguments. Actually this is not the case, and the results are very consistent if we examine the role of uncertainty in planning. The larger the vessel, other things being equal, the greater the risk of underutilization. Consequently, during periods of great uncertainty (low rates), all the benefits of economies of scale are conceded to the charterer as an inducement. When rates are high, however, and especially with price-elastic expectations, there is no uncertainty in anyone's mind concerning full utilization. If anything, the charterers feel uncertain as to whether they will find enough vessels to satisfy their magnified needs. As a result the large tankers will command a premium equivalent to the operating-cost efficiency realized by other complementary operations, if risks of underutilization are absent and all other conditions are assumed to be identical.

If what we have just observed is valid, namely, that at low rates the influences on orders placed are the result of static cost effects and the budget-replacement activities, we would expect to find a negative overall correlation between rates and orders outstanding at low rates, but a

---

[46] This should be particularly true in our case because the oil companies, who are the "buyers" of tankship services, operate their own fleets and thus know the cost functions of their suppliers.

positive correlation at high rates. Table 5.9 gives us an indication that this is so. We notice that the zero-order correlation coefficients[47] are all negative and that some of them are very significant for periods of low rates, particularly for the coefficients of correlation of rates with changes

TABLE 5.9

ZERO-ORDER CORRELATION COEFFICIENTS: RATES VS. ORDERS

	Lows	Highs	Both Together
Nonlogarithmic			
Spot Rate vs. Orders Outstanding	−.238	.0784	.2060
Spot Rate vs. Changes in Orders Placed*	−.855	.0772	−.2742
Index of Expectations† vs. Orders Outstanding	−.291	.6363	.0345
Index of Expectations vs.			
Changes in Orders Placed	−.826	−.4010	−.5864
Logarithmic Relation			
Spot Rate vs. Orders Outstanding	−.6487	.1154	
Spot Rate vs. Changes in Orders Placed	−.8836	.0342	
Index of Expectations vs. Orders Outstanding	−.7029	.1038	
Index of Expectations vs.			
Changes in Orders Placed	−.8120	.4882	

* The "Changes in Orders Placed" are the percentage ratio of orders placed in period t (defined as a percentage of orders outstanding at the beginning of the period) over the respective magnitude of period $t-1$.

† The "Index of Expectations" is based on short-term rates and is derived in Chapter 10. Briefly stated, this is a "weighted" index of rates prevailing over the previous four months.

in orders placed. The logarithmic derivation is even more significant, which indicates that behavior in the tankship markets may be conditioned much more by rates of change in the relevant parameters than by absolute levels. Of course this much we expected from our theoretical discussion.

When rates are high the respective correlation coefficients are not as significant as when rates are low, with the exception of the correlation between the index of expectations and orders outstanding (nonlogarithmic relation). The direction of the relationships, however, is positive, with the exception of the correlation between the index of expectations and the changes in orders placed. Knowing that the correlation between the index and orders outstanding is positive and fairly significant, the negative correlation between the index and the changes in orders placed may indicate the existence of measurement impurities. The index is developed under the assumption that expectations are influenced by dis-

[47] These are partial correlation coefficients of the first order and were obtained as part of the multiple regression and correlation 704 program that will be discussed later.

tributed lags. So it is a "smoothed-out" short-term rate. In contrast, the changes in orders placed are very volatile. Furthermore, the date of record, as we have already explained, may not coincide with the date of initiation of the contract, and during periods of high rates the amount of orders placed does not necessarily equal the quantity demanded (we suspect that it is smaller). The last qualification can explain the low correlation coefficients under high rates, which correlation coefficients are nonetheless positive with the exception of the one relating the index of expectations and changes in orders placed.[48]

We cannot exclude the possibility that what we observed may be due to or colored by real lags between impetus and manifestation of the impact. Such lags will affect particularly any relationships based on rates of change or differences, as contrasted with levels. Because events occur so fast, however, and the operatives do not allow examination of their minutes, it is very difficult to distinguish real from impure lags.

Evidences of lags real or otherwise may be detected in Figure 5.1, which presents a plot of the time series of spot rates and orders placed. Also, lags are the cause of the difference between the correlation coefficients of "Spot Rate vs. Orders Outstanding" (.0784) and "Index of Expectations vs. Orders Outstanding" (.6363).

To ascertain the existence of delayed reaction, we introduced lags into the monthly series for the total period 1949–1958, but the results proved somewhat disappointing. The only significant relationship — a correlation of .7069 between orders placed and spot rates — was obtained when a three-month lag was introduced in the data.[49] For this reason, instead of attempting to obtain improvements by experimenting further with shifts in the time series,[50] it was decided to correlate quarterly rather than monthly data.

[48] To eliminate volatility, we defined "changes" in orders placed in terms of ratios. This, however, introduced impurities in that in absolute terms the changes may be increasing but as percentages they may be decreasing.

[49] If we look at Figure 5.1, we notice that the lags are not uniform, a possible indication that the elasticity of expectations depends on the previous point of temporary equilibrium. Namely, an alternating sequence of elastic and, again, inelastic expectations may be repeated each time a deviation from a temporary equilibrium occurs.

[50] Just to satisfy curiosity, five-month moving averages centered on the third month were attempted, but they gave no better results than those obtained with three-month lag. In multiple regression and correlation analyses, moving averages centered on the present time period impair the predictive value of the relationships. It is like inquiring what certain magnitudes will be X months from now to determine one value for the current period. If it is simple regression, however, and the smoothing is done only for the dependent variable, a relationship based on a moving average (if not centered at the terminal point) will aid prediction. It will, in effect, tell the behavior of the dependent variable that will satisfy the equation.

90 CHAPTER FIVE

If our hypothesis about the average elasticity of orders with respect to rates is correct, the coefficients of regression and correlation between average quarterly rates and quarterly orders placed should be positive. The negative correlation that is believed to exist at low rates will be buried (if the data are not stratified) because it is valid for such a short range, only approximately 40 cents out of 400.

Table 5.10 shows the quarterly data that were used to correlate the net orders placed with the corresponding rates for the years 1954–1958. During these years, incidentally, we have witnessed a complete cycle in rates and orders placed, and our observations, therefore, will not be disturbed by accidental stratifications.

The results of the correlation are quite encouraging. The regression equation explaining orders placed in T-2 equivalents is

$$Y = -55.75 + 1.36X$$

where X represents the short-term rate in cents per 1,000 ton-miles. The correlation coefficient between X and Y is $r = .88$, and the coefficient of determination is .78, which is very satisfactory. The standard error of estimate is 98.33 T-2's, and the standard deviation, 208.

We notice that the regression coefficient is positive *and greater than one*, and that the regression equation shows that only at low rates should we expect cancellations of orders. The point of zero orders of about 41 cents, as given by the equation, is not correct, because of the abrupt change at low levels and also because of the impact of the replacement programs that we have already explained.

In addition to the nonlogarithmic regression we attempted one of the form

$$\log Y = a + bX$$

This was done in the hope of getting a better picture of the point of zero orders. The results are given in the following regression equation:

$$\log Y = 4.885 + 0.00527X$$

with a correlation coefficient of .7, a coefficient of determination of .5, and a standard error of estimate of .522. In order to avoid negative numbers, the dependent variable Y in the foregoing equation is defined as 200 plus actual orders placed in T-2's.

Obviously the semilogarithmic correlation between orders placed and rates is not as good as the previous correlation. The coefficient of determination has dropped from .78 to only .5. The point of zero orders,[51] however, occurs under the logarithmic formulation at 84 cents per 1,000

---

[51] When we refer to the point of zero orders, we imply zero *net* orders placed. Namely, where orders placed minus cancellations equal zero.

TABLE 5.10

WORLD TANKER CONSTRUCTION TRENDS 1948–1958
(6,000 DWT. and Over)

Year	On Order As of 1st of Each Quarter		Deliveries During Each Quarter		New Orders Placed During Each Quarter		Av. Rate Per 1,000 Ton-Miles ($)
	No.	T-2's	No.	T-2's	No.	T-2's	
1948							
1st	249	212.5	2	1.5	71	80.7	
2nd	318	291.7	12	8.6	59	82.9	
3rd	365	366.0	8	5.3	49	51.4	
4th	406	412.1	29	25.2	48	40.4	
Total			51	40.6	227	255.4	
1949							
1st	425	427.3	12	10.7	(15)	(8.5)	1.35
2nd	398	408.1	24	26.5	13	13.4	1.13
3rd	387	395.0	23	25.0	(4)	(4.2)	.93
4th	360	365.8	37	41.3	15	16.4	1.08
Total			96	103.5	9	17.1	
1950							
1st	338	340.9	28	28.9	6	4.7	.96
2nd	316	316.7	27	29.0	26	28.3	.97
3rd	315	316.0	30	28.2	26	32.7	1.40
4th	311	320.5	41	40.7	36	32.3	2.75
Total			126	126.8	94	98.0	
1951							
1st	306	312.1	20	21.4	94	112.9	4.06
2nd	380	403.6	38	36.0	151	182.6	2.47
3rd	493	550.2	26	25.2	89	126.2	2.04
4th	556	651.2	46	46.7	67	94.3	3.59
Total			130	129.3	401	516.0	
1952							
1st	577	698.8	25	27.5	117	179.1	4.18
2nd	669	850.4	37	42.4	75	96.5	2.02
3rd	707	904.5	31	36.6	69	111.9	1.63
4th	745	979.8	54	57.1	56	73.0	1.55
Total			147	163.6	317	460.5	
1953							
1st	747	995.7	32	44.3	15	23.7	1.08
2nd	730	975.1	46	55.5	17	15.6	.95
3rd	701	935.2	50	57.7	—	13.6	.80
4th	651	891.1	59	74.3	6	13.0	.91
Total			187	231.8	38	65.9	

TABLE 5.10 (cont.)

Year	On Order As of 1st of Each Quarter		Deliveries During Each Quarter		New Orders Placed During Each Quarter		Av. Rate Per 1,000 Ton-Miles ($)
	No.	T-2's	No.	T-2's	No.	T-2's	
1954							
1st	598	829.8	50	65.6	(7)	(10.9)	.98
2nd	541	753.3	49	63.0	11	16.0	.70
3rd	503	706.3	55	75.7	3	10.2	.75
4th	451	640.8	64	90.7	17	34.5	1.12
Total			218	295.0	24	49.8	
1955							
1st	404	584.6	51	66.0	30	53.0	1.32
2nd	383	571.6	32	41.7	13	52.1	.88
3rd	364	582.0	33	46.3	41	101.8	1.05
4th	372	637.5	47	71.8	219	368.2	2.01
Total			163	225.8	303	575.1	
1956							
1st	544	933.9	36	58.4	88	163.6	1.60
2nd	596	1039.1	26	43.6	119	246.4	2.18
3rd	689	1241.9	33	55.1	164	361.1	2.23
4th	820	1547.9	36	66.7	182	416.7	3.76
Total			131	223.8	553	1187.8	
1957							
1st	966	1897.9	31	57.3	203	551.8	3.57
2nd	1138	2392.4	45	95.5	73	214.6	1.11
3rd	1166	2511.5	48	89.9	93	271.3	.73
4th	1211	2692.9	55	98.0	(13)	(38.7)	.65
Total			179	340.7	356	999.0	
1958							
1st	1143	2556.2	44	86.7	(70)	(172.4)	.64
2nd	1029	2297.1	71	124.6	(27)	(51.1)	.61
3rd	931	2121.4		104.3		(20.6)	.76
4th	863	1996.5		115		46.3	.72
Total			430	430.6			
1959							
1st	810	1935.1	62	125.5			
2nd	735	1764.5					

Source of Data: Orders and Deliveries: Transportation Coordination Department Standard Oil Company, New Jersey.
Rates: U.S. Maritime Administration, Washington, D. C., and Addison Outwater and Associates (Tankship Brokers), New York.

ton-miles, which is quite an improvement (as far as the empirical observations indicate) over the 41 cents per 1,000 ton-miles indicated by the linear formulation. As will be noticed in Figure 5.3, the upper limit of the rate range for negative net orders placed was at approximately $1.00 for the 1954–1958 period, and the lower limit at $.58. The value of $.84 given by the semilogarithmic correlation is, therefore, in agreement with the observed range.

The scatter diagrams of the quarterly data of rates and orders placed for the two time periods 1949–1953 and 1954–1958 are presented in Figures 5.4 and 5.5. The observations that we made when examining the monthly data of Figures 5.2 and 5.3 appear to apply also in the case of the quarterly data.

Summarizing briefly the results of our qualitative and quantitative analysis, we can definitely say that the expectations of the buyers in both the tankship building and tankship chartering markets are generally price elastic. It may be difficult to understand such behavior, especially since statistics on orders outstanding are available to operatives and

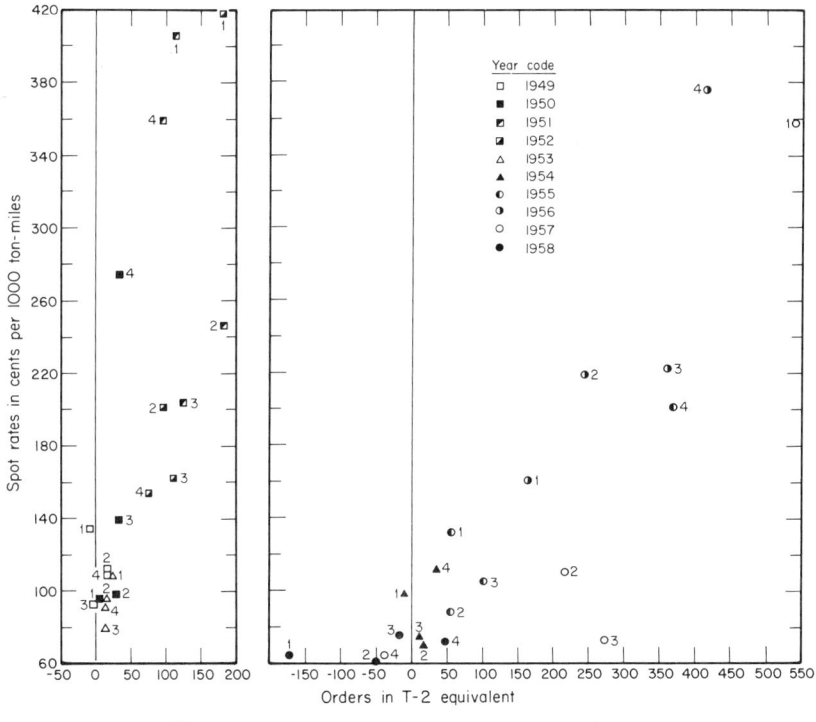

Fig. 5.4. Fig. 5.5.

Figure 5.4. Rates versus orders placed: quarterly data, 1949–1953.
Figure 5.5. Rates versus orders placed: quarterly data, 1954–1958.

are "conservatively" dependable.[52] One would think that the backlog of orders outstanding at any moment of time would be taken into consideration by the operative in shaping plans. Only under conditions of pure competition are the operatives ignorant of the interdependence of their action, and only complete naïveté can explain absolute disregard of published data.

Chartering versus Shipbuilding Revisited

Now that we have completed our discussion on both the chartering and the shipbuilding demand schedules,[53] and have commented on their similarities, let us focus attention on a few of the differences that we have observed.

Both schedules, as shown in Figures 4.1, 4.2, 5.2, and 5.3, have the general characteristics of the schedule presented in Figure 2.1. The demand for chartering, however, is proved to be more positively elastic. Its turning points are more pronounced, indicating that the rate elasticity of expectations is stronger in the tankship service market. There are very good reasons for the latter observation:

1. The breadth of the spot market is limited, and, consequently, conducive to wide rate fluctuations. What is more, the market gets narrower as the rates rise. These relationships imply that any upward revision of aggregate transportation needs equal to, let us say, C_a per cent of the total, will be manifested as $\Delta C_s = (T/S) \times C_a$ where ΔC_s stands for the percentage increase in demand for vessels in the spot market, T for total capacity, and S for the transportation capacity available in the spot market. Let us again point out that whether or not the demand is for long-term charters, as long as these are prompt[54] the charterers have to satisfy their needs out of the small capacity available in the spot market.

2. Unlike shipbuilding, the notion of capacity in the *prompt spot market* is very well defined. Of the long-term charter requirements, of course, only part is prompt, and the rest extended. For the extended part, admittedly, "short-chartering" suffices. That is to say, vessels that are being built or are operating under charter can enter the submarket of future employment at any time, and be chartered in the same way that new vessels, which are not even on the drafting board, are contracted for extended deliveries. But

---

[52] What we wish to state here is that these statistics may be understated because of lags. But even with lags the backlog of orders outstanding is impressive.

[53] Even though for convenience we shall be using the term "demand," we really refer to the locus of intermediate intertemporal equilibria of schedules that exhibit the impact of price-elastic expectations.

[54] For the reader who is not familiar with the industry, an explanation is due. Transactions are for either prompt or future delivery. Single-voyage or spot charters are usually for prompt delivery; but time (or period) charters are *usually* for future delivery when rates are high, and prompt when rates are low.

there is nothing in the shipbuilding market that corresponds to the prompt chartering submarket, since the shipbuilders do not keep inventory of completed or even semicompleted vessels. Furthermore, "buyers" know that it takes time to build a vessel. Consequently, the fact that their impatience is tempered by this realization allows for more flexibility in the shipbuilding capacity available at any moment of time.[55]

3. With charters, because most of them are negotiated through brokers, the market is somewhat similar to other commodity exchanges and, as a result, the reaction to supply and demand considerations is very prompt. In shipbuilding, however, agreements are reached through private negotiations and often the terms of contracts are not readily available, thus causing market imperfections. That is why there is plenty of information on charters — for anyone who wants to uncover it — but very little on actual shipbuilding costs. Given that cost information is very vital for the generation of price-elastic expectations, the insufficiency of information on the provisions of shipbuilding contracts tends to mitigate the impact of expectations.[56]

4. The administrative processes involved in chartering and shipbuilding are different. Chartering decisions are usually made at relatively low levels in the organizational hierarchy, while shipbuilding decisions have to go through the gamut of the capital-budgeting process. As a result the reaction time in chartering is much shorter. The time delay which is introduced in shipbuilding serves, comparatively, as a stabilizing factor unless it happens to be equal to the time difference between two consecutive rate cycles. (The probability for such an occurrence is very small since elastic expectations generate enough surplus to create prolonged depressions.)

Another cause of time delays between impulse and response in shipbuilding is the amount of detail which has to be negotiated. In chartering, contractual provisions are so standardized that a telephone call (such as a person places with his stockbroker) usually suffices. In shipbuilding, however, the contracts are very lengthy, legalistic, and elaborate in detail.

Because of the factors just mentioned, the shifts in the demand schedules and the consequent fluctuations in rates are expected to be much more violent in chartering than in shipbuilding. Furthermore, we would expect the shipbuilding time series to lag behind the chartering and spot-rate series because of different lead times between contracts and vessel deliveries.

The following may illustrate the differences in the fluctuations that are characteristic of the two markets. During the Suez Canal crisis in Feb-

[55] Conceivably the impatience function relating acquisition for future delivery decreases exponentially with time, and as a result the marginal impatience for any period beyond the normal shipbuilding duration is very small.

[56] Conceivably secrecy may generate exaggerated rumors which may spread like "wild fire." That rumors exist in the tankship building markets there is no doubt. In fact these are often intentional. To the extent, however, that a lot of administrative red tape precedes the placement of contracts, enough time elapses to "cool off" somewhat the excited spirits.

As time goes by, information on shipbuilding costs is expected to become available more freely, especially as more and more yards enter the international competition.

96   CHAPTER FIVE

ruary 1957, spot rates reached a peak of over $4.50 per 1,000 ton-miles only to tumble down to 85 cents per 1,000 ton-miles in May 1957, and reach the bottom in November of the same year at about 62 cents. That is, in less than three months the rates dropped to less than 20% of their peak value, and six months later to about 14% of the peak value. In contrast, shipbuilding prices reached their peak at the same time, but only by the end of 1957 did these show serious signs of weakness, and then mostly in Japan[57] because of its excess capacity. The initial drop was about 25% of the peak value, and it was not until the latter part of 1958, namely, at least eighteen months from the peak period, before the cost of shipbuilding reached approximately 50% of its peak value.[58]

Possible differences in the elasticities of the lower part of the two demand schedules may betray further dissimilarities between tankship chartering and tankship building markets. As we have previously argued, in this price region the net income effect of *own* price changes is probably positive in the tankship service markets — because of the ownership and control of tankship capacity by the oil companies — but in the tankship building markets, there are two income effects and these oppose each other. In the latter case it is expected that the positive income effect will be stronger than the negative for the greatest part of the range of rates, except for the two extremities, where the negative income effect will probably be greater. This may explain the flatness of the top and especially the bottom part of the demand for new vessels, and also warn that — other things being equal — slight differences may be observed in the levels of rates at which the two demand schedules change slopes.

The impact of the income effects may not be the sole reason, however, behind such differences in the levels of the turning points. Since the orders for new vessels are determined for the greatest part by tanker rates, the shipbuilding markets, as we have already pointed out, may lag a little behind.[59]

---

[57] See Jacobs, John I., *World Tanker Fleet Review*, December 31, 1957, p. 6; also "Japanese Shipping and Shipbuilding," *The Shipping World*, March 26, 1958, pp. 329–330.

[58] According to the *Petroleum Press Service*, September 1958, pp. 326–329, and Jacobs, John I., *World Tanker Fleet Review*, December 31, 1958, p. 6, the bottom price for 45,000–65,000 tonners was around $145 per DWT. during the last quarter of 1958, but *The Shipping World* of June 3, 1959, p. 543, reports that a "tough bargain" was obtained for a 47,000 DWT. vessel in Japan at $140 per DWT. in the second quarter of 1959. For smaller vessels the prices are higher, but the drop from the peak is of comparable magnitude.

[59] Because rates move so fast and so much when above the static, long-run-equilibrium level, this lag may not be significant with respect to time, but it could cause a *rate-level* lag of turning points.

Finally, since the oil companies not only withdraw from the market at low rates but also enter into the spot market in order to *relet*[60] their surpluses, the lower part of the demand schedule for charters will be more positively sloped than will that for shipbuilding. At "rock-bottom" prices, both demand schedules may acquire negative slopes, but for different reasons. The slight increase in chartering activity at distress rates may be due to the entry of tankers into other trades — grain, molasses, etc. — while, in the case of shipbuilding, the negative slope may be due to the income effect of *own* price changes, and the replacement — and readjustment — programs that we have explained previously.

The Behavior of the Independents versus That of the Oil Companies

It has been argued previously that certain asymmetry of expectations between buyers and sellers is more typical than symmetry, although empirically expectations may be manifested as symmetric. Furthermore, evidence was presented suggesting that in *shipbuilding* the expectations of the sellers (shipbuilders), except at the very end of a price upswing, are rather price inelastic. If parallelism (symmetry of expectations) were applicable, we should expect those who use tankers as inputs (the independents and the oil companies) to postpone ordering ships to as late a future date as possible. This we found not to be the case, however, and the manner in which orders were placed in the past proved the expectations of the ship owners to be elastic.

The behavior of the ship owners is indeed amazing, not only because they choose to ignore published data on the backlog of orders but also because, historically, the cost of shipbuilding has tended not to remain at abnormally high levels longer than the average duration of ship construction.[61] It appears, therefore, that the ship owners who place contracts with deliveries stretching beyond, let us say, two years are doubly naïve. But of course this is what creates the shipbuilding cycle.

Unfortunately, because of scanty information on shipbuilding con-

---

[60] A "relet" is a sublet.

[61] It seems that there is a tendency toward shorter average construction periods. In 1959 some yards could deliver a ship in about one year. The "Universe Apollo" of 104,500 DWT. was delivered to the Universe Tankship Company for chartering to Gulf Oil Company in about seven months by the Kure Shipbuilding Company of Japan. In this case, however, the shipbuilding and tankship companies both belonged to Ludwig's interests. This is a record time; the normal range in 1959 was between fifteen and twenty months.

98 CHAPTER FIVE

tracts, there are no reliable, consistent, and continuous statistics of costs that make it possible to trace the changes from month to month and from year to year.[62] We can form an idea of the relative fluctuations, however, by studying the export statistics of the Japanese Ministry of Commerce.[63] The data presented in Table 5.11 indicate that the shipbuilding cost fluctuations may lag behind the rate fluctuations but, nevertheless, are following the same course. However amazing these cost fluctuations may appear, they do not tell the whole story. What we present in Table 5.11 are not actual cost data of *orders placed* during

TABLE 5.11

AVERAGE PRICE PER DEADWEIGHT TON:
JAPAN'S SHIP EXPORTS 1949–1957

Year of Delivery	Av. Size (DWT.) per Vessel Delivered	Av. $/DWT. For Tankers Delivered*	Av. Rate per 1,000 Ton-Miles
1949	17,400	129	1.12
1950	4,200	159	1.52
1951	18,430	186	3.04
1952	20,560	202	2.35
1953	33,000	141	.94
1954	31,510	114	.89
1955	33,496	135	1.32
1956	35,432	174	2.44
1957	50,131	210	1.52
1958		185†	.68
1959		160†	
1960		145†	

Source: Shipbuilding Data: AALL and Co., Ltd., Tokyo, Japan.
Rates: Same as in Table 5.10.
* Notice that these are not the average prices for ships contracted in that year. These are averages for the cost of ships delivered.
† Our estimates assume no disruptions like the Suez crisis or wars. The 1959 contract prices for Japanese yards were approximately $145 per DWT. for supertankers of 45,000 tons (J. I. Jacobs & Co., Ltd., *World Tanker Fleet Review*, December 31, 1959, p. 4).

the respective years but rather averages of historic contract prices for *vessels delivered*.[64] The year-to-year fluctuations in the cost of orders

[62] The continuity of information is also affected by the way orders are placed. During periods of low rates, the "buyers" withdraw from the market in concert. Published data show that there was no single contract negotiated during the first half of 1959.

[63] Data included in a nineteen-page report on shipbuilding, issued by AALL & Co., Ltd., in January 1958.

[64] Because the data of Table 5.11 represents cost of delivered vessels, there is a lag of at least a year between the cost series and spot-rate time series.

placed, therefore, must be much greater than what is shown here. Furthermore, averages do not reveal the range of fluctuations unless the data are uniformly stable. During the 1949–1959 period the cost of shipbuilding fluctuated between $120 and $300–$325 per DWT. These costs do not include contracts awarded to United States shipyards, which are always higher.

Policy makers of various companies have been asked on several occasions why they rush at inopportune moments, and the answer always seems to be about the same. "When someone starts running, you start running after him. You run not because you want to, but because someone else started it. Things happen extremely fast; when you get into a stampede, you do not pause to ask questions. Our consolation is that our competitors are making the same mistakes as we do." Both oil companies and independents are susceptible to this hysteria as far as shipbuilding is concerned. The only difference is that the independents on the average lead the oil companies by about six months;[65] otherwise they seem to be moving on a similar schedule of expectations. When we move to the area of chartering, however, where the two perform opposing functions, we notice that the symmetry no longer holds and the independents behave like sellers and the oil companies like buyers.

The independents, of course, may have more excuse for rushing into the shipbuilding market with orders than the oil companies, because ships are used as inputs to their only final product, namely, transportation services. In this respect there is no substitute. The oil companies, however, are in a more flexible position both in the short run and the long run, and this should dictate more cool calculations. Flexibility is afforded them because transportation is an input to further inputs, and conceivably they could reschedule runs, deplete inventories temporarily at the refinery, or even postpone delivery to their customers. What is more, the fact that at any moment of time they own vessels for a substantial portion of their transportation needs and have an equally substantial portion on long-term and consecutive-voyage charters, usually running over the immediate future, allows them a flexibility not afforded the independents.[66] Finally, the independents are fighting for a share of the transportation market and cannot increase their share without taking

---

[65] Notice that this delayed response of the oil companies may be good or bad depending on the point of the price cycle at which they enter the market. Conceivably, what we observe may not be the result of a lag in expectations, but rather a manifestation of administrative "red tape."

[66] For the period of 1954 to 1957, the oil companies controlled either through ownership, time charters, or consecutive-voyage charters between 80% and 91% of the total world fleet.

100   CHAPTER FIVE

the risk of excess capacity.[67] But what is the excuse of the oil companies, who consider shipping as an ancillary evil?

The hysteria of the oil companies does have some basis however. The opportunity costs involved, in case of disruption of transportation, are so high that the producers are willing to pay the ransom. The cost of the Middle East oil, which is the most transportation intensive, was once estimated at 25 cents per barrel,[68] only a small fraction of the cost of competing oils. Furthermore, refinery shutdowns are costly, and shut-in crude in the Middle East could benefit no one, be it the consumer, the producer, or the countries' political rulers.

As in the case of the shipbuilders, there are also indications of initial inelasticity in the expectations of the independents with respect to charter rates. Of course, not all of them move at the same time from the inelastic to the elastic part of their schedule. For example, during the Suez crisis the expectations of the Greek shipowners[69] turned elastic too soon; they have been proved wrong, together with the oil companies, whose over-all behavior indicated almost infinite elasticity of charter-rate expectations.

The over-all (shipbuilding and chartering) behavior of the majority of the independent tanker owners seems to be rational, though asymmetric, if we assume that the strategy of the oil companies is known and that *specific vessels or shipbuilding contracts are necessary for charter agreements*. When the charter-rate elasticity of expectations for the oil companies is greater than one (expectations elastic), and the behavior of the companies is consistent, the best strategy for the independents is to behave as if they have elastic shipbuilding-cost expectations,[70] even

[67] The irony is that most of the risk during the Suez crisis was taken over by the oil companies, which provided long-term charters for ships not even contracted for. The independents with the oil company's signature on the charter could mortgage the hire and thus obtain money for building the vessel. According to information provided by one of the banks that specializes in such loans, in some cases the charter was so high that the bank could afford to give up to 90% of the cost and still get its money back from the net hire in five to seven years—and this with an economic life for the vessel of approximately twenty-five years.

[68] This figure was quoted in *Le Prix des Produits Pétroliers en Europe Occidentale,* study prepared by the Secretariat of the Economic Commission for Europe, United Nations, Geneva, March 1955, p. 17. The figure was derived from data contained in the 1952 Oil Agreement between Iraq and the Iraq Petroleum Company. In addition to the cost of production, there was at that time a royalty of 23 cents per barrel. See also Ozanne, Henry, "Super-Tankers Threaten United States with $2 Middle East Oil," *World Oil,* April 1949, p. 51.

[69] See Jacobs, John I., *World Tanker Fleet Review,* December 31, 1957, p. 5.

[70] In many cases the independents have not ordered the ship until they secured a charter for it. They have, therefore, quite a lot to gain and relatively little to lose by accepting such an arrangement. The extent of the risk in such cases is determined by the level of the rate and the length of the charter.

though they may not. Such strategy will be rational if the total premium that they expect to pay in order to build at time t_0 is less than the net value of the discounted stream of the *premiums* that they expect to receive from its initial charter. They will thus have the tonnage to satisfy the increase in demand for future deliveries (of charters) that was triggered by a short-term excess demand, but at the same time they are contributing to the long-run instability of the market.

The fact that the time period over which rates will be low is extended with each additional vessel built does not seem to enter into the independents' planning for at least two important reasons:

1. The tankship transportation markets are not well organized, consequently "prudence" (in view of the consequences of overbuilding) does not prevail. And this is because the independent shipowners do not realize the interdependence of their behavior at the time of the decisions.

2. As long as the original time-charter agreement gives a good probability that the major part, if not all, of the initial investment will be recovered in the first few years of the life of the vessel, then the independents will be foolish not to invest. Most charters granted by oil companies during the Suez Canal crisis were at such high rates and of long enough duration to guarantee recovery of the investment (even at high shipbuilding prices) in approximately seven years. Consequently, and even if the independents realize the interdependence of their plans, they should invest under such circumstances.

In order to analyze the consequences of a decision to build "now, versus later," we must divide the planning horizon into five parts.

(i) The time period m of the initial charter agreement of duration k, over which the vessel will be operating if delivered at time t_0 at a cost C_0, versus being delivered at time t_m at a cost C_m.

(ii) A time period starting at t_m, the time that the vessel will be delivered at a cost C_m if not built at t_0, and extending up to t_k (that is to say, the period of overlap of the original time charters of the alternative vessels).

(iii) The time span between t_k (the point of expiration of the original charter of the early vessel) and $t_{k'}$ (the point of expiration of the charter of the late vessel).

(iv) The time period between $t_{k'}$ and t_n (the point of expiration of the life of the late vessel).

(v) The time span between t_n and t_{m+n}, that is to say, the number of years by which the new vessel will outlast the old.

Before we proceed with the analysis let us denote (and also summarize previous relevant notations):

R_0 = the yearly time-charter revenue of the early vessel.
R_m = the yearly time-charter revenue of the late vessel.
OC = the out-of-pocket operating costs of the early vessel per year.
OC' = the out-of-pocket operating costs of the late vessel per year.
R_L = the long-run time-charter or spot-rate revenue that is expected to prevail beyond the initial time-charter agreements.

k = the duration of the initial charter of the early vessel.
k' = the duration of the initial charter of the late vessel.
n = the life of the vessels in years.
C_0 = the cost of the early vessel.
C_m = the cost of the late vessel, ordered m years later.
S = the scrap value of the early vessel at time t_n.
S' = the scrap value of the late vessel at time t_{n+m}.
i = the cost of capital or subjective rate of return.

The relevant considerations during the various time periods (i) through (v) that we must use later are

$$\sum_{t=1}^{m}(R_0 - OC)_t(1+i)^{-t}(1-\text{tax rate}) + \sum_{t=1}^{m}(C_0/n)(1+i)^{-t}(\text{tax rate})$$
$$- C_0 + C_m(1+i)^{-m} \quad (\text{i})$$

$$\sum_{t=m+1}^{k}[(R_0 - OC) - (R_m - OC')]_t(1+i)^{-t}(1-\text{tax rate})$$
$$+ \sum_{t=m+1}^{k}(C_0 - C_m)/n(1+i)^{-t}(\text{tax rate}) \quad (\text{ii})$$

$$\sum_{t=k+1}^{k'}[(R_L - OC) - (R_m - OC')]_t(1+i)^{-t}(1-\text{tax rate})$$
$$+ \sum_{t=k+1}^{k'}(C_0 - C_m)/n(1+i)^{-t}(\text{tax rate}) \quad (\text{iii})$$

$$\sum_{t=k'+1}^{n}(OC' - OC)_t(1+i)^{-t}(1-\text{tax rate})$$
$$+ \sum_{t=k'+1}^{n}(C_0 - C_m)/n(1+i)^{-t}(\text{tax rate}) + S(1+i)^{-n}(1-\text{tax rate}) \quad (\text{iv})$$

$$\sum_{t=n}^{n+m}(R_L - OC')_t(1+i)^{-t}(1-\text{tax rate}) + \sum_{t=n}^{n+m}(C_m/n)(1+i)^{-t}(\text{tax rate})$$
$$+ S'(1+i)^{-(n+m)}(1-\text{tax rate}) \quad (\text{v})$$

If

$$(\text{i}) + (\text{ii}) + (\text{iii}) + (\text{iv}) - (\text{v}) \geq 0 \quad (5.18)$$

and

$$\sum_{t=1}^{k}(R_0 - OC)_t(1+i)^{-t}(1-\text{tax rate})$$
$$+ \sum_{t=k+1}^{n}(R_L - OC)_t(1+i)^{-t}(1-\text{tax rate})$$
$$+ (C_0/n)\sum_{t=1}^{n}(1+i)^{-t}(\text{tax rate}) + S(1+i)^{-n}(1-\text{tax rate}) - C_0 \geq 0$$
$$(5.19)$$

then the independents should invest even though their shipbuilding-cost expectation may be inelastic.

In the foregoing formulations we made the assumption that R_L is the same for both vessels. Our analysis is not dependent on such an assumption, but it was made because it agrees with empirical realities. First of all the time difference between t_k and $t_{k'}$ (the difference between the expiration dates of the two alternative original charters) is not great. Empirical evidence (already presented) shows that the average duration of time charters transacted during periods of high rates is approximately fifteen and a half months longer than the duration of the time charters signed during low rates. If we add to the duration of the charters the lead time between agreement and vessel delivery then the difference increases to thirty months.

Past history shows that spot rates and shipbuilding costs do not remain at high levels longer than twenty months. Consequently, the value of m is expected to be between two and three years, and under the conditions postulated for our analysis R_L will be approximately the same for both vessels. Furthermore, we must not forget that the lead time can be manipulated within limits.

To the extent that the rate elasticity of expectations of the charterers is greater than unity, the satisfaction of both Equations 5.18 and 5.19 is guaranteed and is only a matter of time on a rising market. During the downturn, orders will be postponed unless $(C_m(1 + i)^{-m} - C_o) > 0$ is large enough to counterbalance the negative rate effect, a condition that is unlikely to occur since tanker rates fluctuate much more than shipbuilding costs. We would thus expect postponement of orders and even cancellations on the downturn. Furthermore, during depressed periods the charterers practically withdraw from the market; hence the whole question of the existence of a time-charter rate is almost entirely academic. Even if we do find an R_o and R_L, it is very improbable that this fact will satisfy the conditions of Inequality 5.19.[71]

Before leaving the discussion of Inequality 5.19 we should like to use it and resolve a seemingly paradoxical occurrence. We can show that the *average spot rate* over the life of many vessels currently operating will be below the vessels' long-run average cost. Many people observing this cannot understand why "people are so stupid to invest in tankers." Relationship 5.19 will help us realize that the investors are not stupid after all. What the cursory observer does not realize is that many of the vessels operating in the spot market have secured over their life span at least one long-range time charter at rates high enough to help recover most, if not all, of the fixed investment. Once the investment is recovered, then the vessel can "afford" to operate below long-run average cost as long as the rate is above out-of-pocket cost.

---

[71] See *The Financial Times* of Thursday, April 17, 1958, "Outlook for Shipping — Mr. Niarchos' Views."

104   CHAPTER FIVE

On the basis of the intrinsic characteristics of the tankship markets we can make the very strong statement, that the probability is very great that the average spot rate applicable to *any* vessel over its life span will be lower than its long-run average cost. What is strange is that only very few of the most astute independent operators see in this the opportunity for an arbitrage and sign time-charter agreements at high rates which they fulfill by entering the spot market.

Our conclusion that the independents should order vessels even when their shipbuilding-cost expectations are inelastic was based, among other things, on the very fundamental assumption that specific vessels or contracts for such vessels are necessary for the consummation of charter agreements. However, we find that this assumption is not universally true, indicating that *on the average* the expectations of the independents in the shipbuilding market are elastic rather than inelastic. That is to say *they behave like buyers*. Otherwise, the independents would be found selling short on the upswing, namely, signing time-charter agreements but postponing orders until later.

During the period covered by this study, and especially during periods of high rates, many time charters were given specifying the vessels desired in the most general terms — specifying, for example, just size and nothing more — rather than naming *specific* ships, but the independents have lost potential fortunes by choosing to run to the bank first and then to the shipbuilder.

Consequently, whether the shipbuilding-cost expectations of the independents are elastic or inelastic, they *are manifested as elastic*,[72] which leads us to the following observations and rules that relate final market demand to derived demand.

1. To determine the behavior of buyers and sellers in a derived market, one must look into the final market.

2. If the users' price elasticity of expectations in the final market (with respect to a change in *own* price) is greater than unity, then the elasticity of expectations of the users with respect to the cost of the derived factor will also be greater than unity. If it is less than unity, it will be true in the derived market also.

3. If the price expectations of the suppliers of the final product are less than unity, then expectations with respect to the derived factor cost will in all probability be *revealed* as being symmetric with those of the users of the final product. If expectations are elastic in the final market, they will also be elastic in the derived market.

Our previous conclusions on the "asymmetric symmetry" of expectations of buyers and sellers seem to hold with the independents and the

---

[72] This manifestation of elasticity indicates that the oil companies should not always consider the reaction of the independents as an *external* guide for action. Such a practice often leads to a vicious circle of reasoning.

oil companies. Table 5.5 shows how the independents led the oil companies into the shipbuilding market and then again led them in withdrawing from it.[73] That the net result of the expectations of both oil companies and independents in the shipbuilding market is "final-market-rate" elastic is also shown by the Fairplay semiannual index of shipbuilding costs.[74] Figure 5.6 shows that both Fairplay cost indices move in the same direction as do spot rates, and that the cost of building the Fairplay standard ship is a smoothed function of the price of a "stock boat." [75]

If we forget the impact of factors that affect the over-all trend (in our case inflation), we notice that when charter rates are high the price of the stock boat is higher than the cost of building one, and vice versa. Unfortunately, we cannot exactly determine whether this difference is due to objective economic reasons or to expectations. In other words, the premium during periods of high rates may be due to

1. The time cost of income that a ready vessel can earn while another vessel is being built;
2. The loan value of the charter of an operating vessel which is bigger than that of a vessel under construction, because the latter does not earn income during the construction period; or
3. The premium that oil companies are willing to pay to satisfy their assumed urgent needs.

Under low rates, the major objective reason that may explain such deviation is the cost of idleness of a ready vessel during the construction period of a new one. On the other hand, we must not exclude the possibility that at least part of such deviation between the two cost indices of Figure 5.6 may be caused by the *inelastic charter-rate* expectations of the independents.

The fluctuations in the cost indices of Figure 5.6 could be the result of and be consistent with the behavior of either the independents or the oil companies, because

1. If the observed fluctuations are the result of the behavior of the independents, they show that the expectations with respect to shipbuilding cost are or are manifested as elastic, and the independents thus prefer to buy now.[76] This behavior, incidentally, is consistent with both elastic *charter-rate* expectations (if they buy the ship to "store" it)[77] or inelastic (if they buy

[73] See also *Petroleum Press Service*, September 1958, pp. 326–329.

[74] *Fairplay*, semiannual issues (January and July), 1949–1958.

[75] A "stock boat" is a finished vessel on inventory. This idea is used for comparative purposes only, because inventories of new vessels are a very rare phenomenon.

[76] Escalation clauses are included in the contracts only on the upswing. In some cases, 100% of the cost is covered by such clauses, which means that the quoted price represents only the *basic cost* of the shipbuilding contracts.

[77] This is only a theoretical possibility; storage in conjunction with our discussion should imply chartering on spot and postponing time chartering for the proper

CHAPTER FIVE

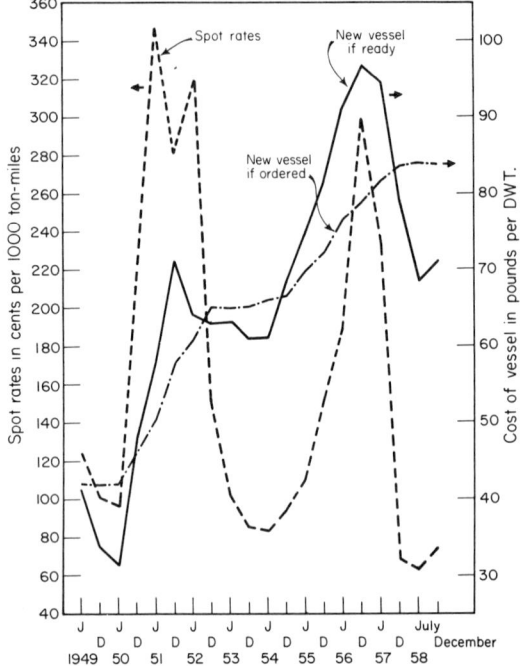

Figure 5.6. Cost of vessels per DWT. (Fairplay Index) and spot rates, 1949–1958.

the ship to take advantage of present rates that they do not expect in the future). The eagerness of the independents to charter their vessels on a long-term basis shows that they buy vessels to use them and not to store them. We can conclude, therefore, that they have *inelastic charter-rate* expectations at least for the main part of their expectations schedule.[78] The existence of inelastic expectations in the charter market, however, is a sufficient condition as we have shown previously for a revealed elastic schedule in the tankship building market.[79]

2. If, on the other hand, the fluctuations are due mainly to the behavior of the oil companies, they are again the result of elastic expectations — but now in both markets, the main one being, of course, the tankship service market.

---

future period. However, there is at least one case where the shipbuilders have built a stock boat (a vessel that has not been ordered) to utilize excess capacity caused by the depressed markets in 1958. See J. I. Jacobs' *World Tanker Fleet Review,* December 31, 1958, p. 4.

[78] We are informed that the independents did not particularly like time charters of less than five years' duration.

[79] We can even make a stronger case (but it is not necessary) because, as we have already argued, evidence points out that the independents *behave* like buyers and betray real — not only manifest — elastic expectations in the tankship building markets.

Thus, whether the movements in the prices of ready vessels and the cost of building are due to the behavior of the independents, or the oil companies, or both, they are manifested as the net result of elastic expectations in the tankship building markets.

As for the chartering market (where the behavior is opposing), empirical evidence shows that the independents moving on the inelastic part of their schedule were at first adding to their orders chiefly as they were chartering. Later, in exuberance — "after all, no one expected this collapse in rates," [80] — they began placing orders with no charter security and with promises for escalations and cash on delivery. At the end of the first quarter of 1958, only 41.8% of all the ships under construction were "fixed" (had charter agreements waiting). Listed by flag of registry, the percentages of chartered new buildings were as follows: [81]

British	21%
Liberian, Panamanian	31
Norwegian	58
Swedish	69
French	50
Italian	60
Danish	25

The number and the characteristics of time charters that are contracted on high, against those on low, rates provide further interesting evidence of the expectations of the oil companies versus those of the independents. For the period of 1950 to 1957, the consistent time-charter data that we shall analyze later are comprised of 897 observations, of which 304 were contracted when the spot rates were low and 593 when they were high. In terms of monthly averages the respective figures are 6.5 and 16 transactions. The lead times (from agreement to ship delivery) were 10.5 months and 24.1 months, respectively, and the duration of the time charters was 45.5 months for the period of low rates versus 61.1 months for the period of high rates. Variance analysis shows that the contrasted means are not the same at the 1% significance level. Actually we can make even stronger statements in all cases. This fact, in our estimation, indicates elastic rate expectations on the part of the oil companies and probably inelastic (at least for parts of the rate range) for the independents.

With this discussion as background, we can appreciate the impact of the behavior of the oil companies and the independents on tanker rates.

---

[80] Niarchos' interview with *The Financial Times, op. cit.*

[81] The data were provided by Captain Conway of the Cosmopolitan Transit Lines. The British flag percentage seems to be low. Probably orders for the then newly formed tankship companies of British Petroleum and Shell were considered as unfixed.

CHAPTER FIVE

Expectations can swiftly bring about sequential shifts in demand, but because the supply schedules, especially in the short run, cannot change without the passing of time, rates move from the bottom to the peak, and vice versa, in a matter of months.

As we shall see later, the normal static supply schedule is very elastic up to the point of full capacity[82] (this is part of the normal long-run schedule), and then becomes very inelastic (i.e., it follows the short-run schedule). This shape exists because the most efficient unit in operation (even if one assumes no ancillary technological constraints) is not large enough to be a significant percentage of total capacity. It can be duplicated; hence, entry is not restricted. Beyond normal capacity, however, the only way one can increase capacity in the short run is by increasing the speed at which the vessels are operated, which is a very costly proposition.[83]

The result, under the circumstances that we have sketched here, is that a shift in demand to the right of the point of full capacity can send the short-term rates skyward. This rise, in turn, triggers new orders for ships and also shapes expectations about future rates. But rates also move downward, and we can visualize what will happen if expectations about the future are not realized.

Before ending this section, let us mention what policy planners of the oil companies said on several occasions during interviews. They claim that they do not attempt to maximize profits but to minimize the cost or penalty of a wrong decision. One of them went so far as to admit that they operate under the assumption that they are always making the wrong decisions and plans. They behave, therefore, in their implementation of plans, in a manner that they hope will minimize the penalties. On the basis of this type of thinking, and with constant marginal utility of money, one will undoubtedly arrive at an optimum solution by including among the penalties of the alternatives the opportunity costs of decisions.[84] There is one important qualification, however. This solution will be arrived at only if there is a symmetry of expectation in assigning values in the process of arriving at a certainty equivalent.[85] If this prefer-

---

[82] The definition of full capacity is vague because of the various dimensions of capacity. We shall return to this discussion later.

[83] Normal speed, in practice, is defined as the point beyond which the speed can increase only by a proportionate increase in shaft horsepower to the third power and above. Fuel consumption varies directly with SHP; hence, above normal speed S, a speed of $S(1 + x)$ can be achieved only at a cost of $F(1 + x)^n$ where $n > 3$.

[84] In this way, for every pair of alternatives the revenue side advantages of one alternative will appear as penalties of another.

[85] For a description of the process, see any of the many articles on expectations and uncertainty. Professor Shackle in his *Time in Economics,* North-Holland Publishing Company, Amsterdam, 1958, provides a whole chapter on "Decision

ence toward risk minimization tends to ascribe relatively more value to the avoidance of anguish because of losses (by "imaginative anticipation," to use Professor Shackle's terminology)[86] than to the joy due to the anticipation of gains, then asymmetry will arise in the translation of the expected gains of one alternative into the opportunity costs of another. Under such circumstances, risk minimization and profit maximization will not give identical solutions.[87]

The so-called principle of conservatism that is applied in managerial decision making may be due largely, if not completely, to an asymmetry in assigning weights to the avoidance of anguish versus the experiencing of joy in the process of translating expectations. This principle will not only result effectively in higher costs relative to revenues at the different points of time over which the decisions will rule, but will also dictate higher discounting rates for the revenue streams as compared to those applied to the cost streams.

The conservative entrepreneur tends to believe that the forecasted value of costs of a particular year will prove to be below the actual costs, and the forecasted revenue above the actual costs, not because of price movements but because of the greater weights assigned to the avoidance of anguish caused by losses. This process of weighing costs and revenues leads him to a conservative *forecast*. Then, to cope with the uncertainty inherent in the stationary assumption on the basis of which he has developed his forecast, he will apply a discounting factor to the streams of costs and revenues. Usually the uncertainty due to dynamic phenomena is incorporated into the expected rate of return; but because of the asymmetry of anguish versus joy, the effective discount rate applied to the cost stream is lower than that applied to the revenue stream.[88] This process is not, of course, applied either consciously or consistently. In fact, the inconsistency in the application of such a process may be one of the main factors that lessens the impact of bad decisions.[89]

---

and Uncertainty," pp. 35–66, and also a reading list on pp. 62–65. Also see Baumol, *op. cit.,* pp. 86–91, and his bibliography.

[86] *Op. cit.,* p. 41.

[87] If we consider more dimensions to the uncertainty problem, namely, uncertainty with respect to risks inherent in plans, and uncertainty with respect to plan intensity, then the deviation from profit maximization because of these asymmetries will be greater.

[88] Those whose imaginative anticipation equates on a "one-to-one" basis a present loss with a future one apply a zero discount rate to the cost stream.

[89] On the basis of what we have said concerning asymmetry, consistency under conservatism implies noncancellation of the revenues and costs of a particular year. It also implies that the expected revenues of one alternative cannot be considered as opportunity costs of the other alternative but should be netted against other revenues.

110 CHAPTER FIVE

It is not unnatural to expect policy planners to use risk minimization (in terms of certainty equivalent) because losses are concrete and are more painful than the thought of profits that would have been realized had the decision been different. If a decision has not resulted in eventual losses, probably no one will question its wisdom or compare it with former alternatives now perhaps forgotten.[90] The accounting system of the firm certainly will not pick up and trace the consequences of alternatives that have not been implemented, nor will it point at the fact that although a decision led to adverse consequences it was dictated by the most efficient decision-making processes. As a result, executives have a greater probability of survival if they avoid risk and aim for the *status quo*.[91]

Finally, the behavior of the operatives in the tankship markets (elasticities of expectations, ordering, chartering, etc.) may prove to be a little more rational than our analysis has indicated, if examined in the context of an expanding industry. With a positive long-term trend, mistakes will be washed out. The question, however, arises: Why make such costly mistakes and look to the long-term trend for salvation?

Spot Rates and Tanker Deliveries

If we assume a normal period of between fifteen and twenty-four months for the completion of a vessel,[92] it follows from our previous findings that the peaks in tankship deliveries will lag behind the peaks of orders placed by at least the average shipbuilding lead time. If we now allow for the "frictional" postponement of deliveries at times of saturated construction berths and also consider some lag between spot rates and orders placed, we shall find that vessels will be delivered in increasing numbers reaching their peak some two to two and a half years after the spot rates *have passed* their peak.

Figure 5.7 presents a plot of monthly spot rates (per 1,000 ton-miles)

---

[90] Another and more simple explanation of the risk minimization behavior may be found in the shape of the entrepreneur's utility surface. He may be at a point where the slope is zero.

[91] There is of course a mild counterbalancing effect. The averaging process of accrual-accounting allocations tends to smooth out extremes in performance, but from observation we can confidently say that this does not encourage risk taking.

[92] This average lead time changes. During the early postwar years, it took on the *average* three years to build a vessel; by 1956 the lead time was reduced to about two years, and in 1958 it was between fifteen and eighteen months. The latter figure may have been inflated because of the desire of shipowners to postpone completion as much as possible during depressed market conditions.

against deliveries in terms of T-2 equivalents.[93] It is obvious that the upward trend in deliveries had not exhausted itself as of the end of 1958. If we assume an average lead time of eighteen months in shipbuilding, on the basis of the pattern of orders placed, we could expect that the rate of deliveries would not decrease until sometime in 1959. On the basis of the arguments given and the evidence presented in Tables 5.7 and 5.8, we would have expected the 1959 deliveries to exceed 7,000,000 DWT. or 50 T-2 equivalents, and this in fact occurred.

The data used in Tables 5.7 and 5.8 came originally from *Lloyd's Register of Shipbuilding Returns* and are based on scheduled deliveries for vessels of 6,000 DWT. and over. Usually, however, there is an overflow, and John I. Jacobs & Company, Ltd. in their *World Tanker Fleet Review*[94] report the following for tankers of 10,000 DWT. and over as of December 31, 1958.

Year	No.	Scheduled Deliveries DWT.	T-2 Equiv.	Expected Deliveries DWT.	T-2 Equiv.
1959	256	7,992,850	542	7,000,000	475
1960	190	6,753,650	443	6,250,000	406
1961	148	5,532,450	372	5,000,000	336
1962	69	2,882,300	198	4,250,000	292
1963	40	1,842,850	128	2,500,000	173
1964/5	13	628,100	44		

The significance of these figures is that most of these orders were placed in response to changes in spot rates, but because of the shipbuilding lead time these tankers will be entering the market at times when economic or market conditions may not be very favorable. Only if the high short-term rates at the time the majority of orders are initiated accurately reflect the long-term expectations will disaster be averted. In case the short-term rates are the result of only short-term market interactions, then the *peak in orders placed will occur at and most probably after the peak in short-term rates* (because of the elasticity of expectations), *and consequently deliveries will reach their peak long after the impetus that generated them has disappeared.* Unless another *unexpected* need appears to utilize this new capacity as it enters the market its impact will be destabilizing and very painful.

The lessons of the past are very easily forgotten, as is shown by the works of Koopmans, Tinbergen, and recently of Westinform Service.

[93] The data on deliveries were provided by the Transportation Coordination Department of the Standard Oil Company of New Jersey, which compiled these from Lloyd's Register.

[94] December 31, 1958, pp. 4–5.

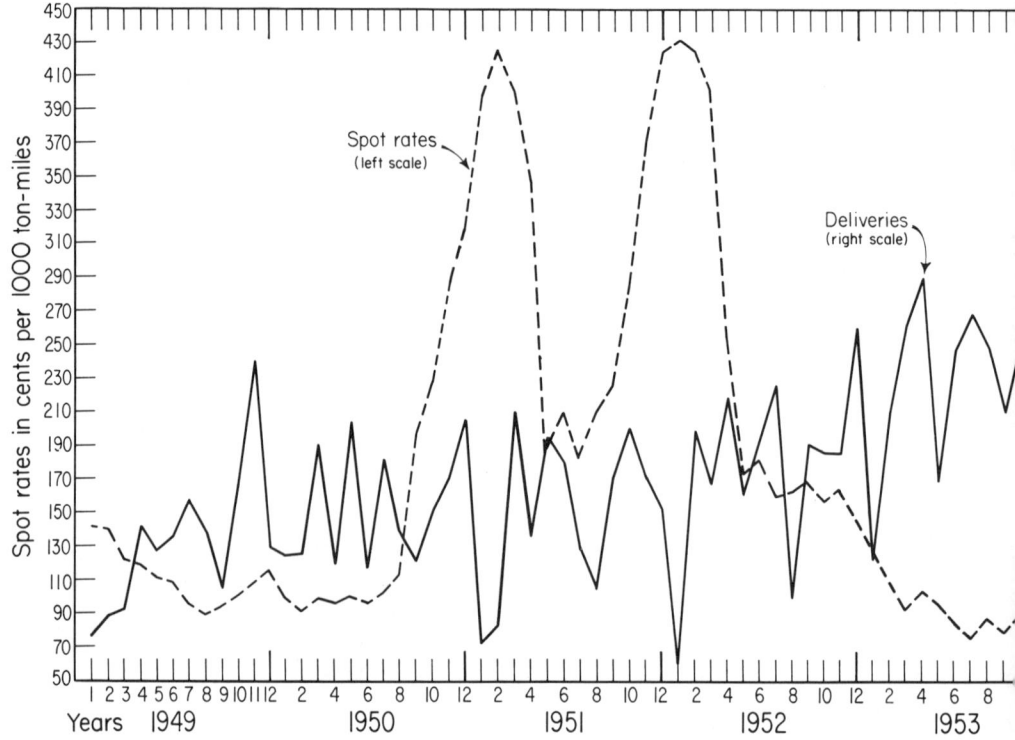

Figure 5.7. Time series of deliveries

Westinform Shipping Report No. 118[95] attempted an analysis to show a parallel between the shipping crises of the 1930's and of the "post-Suez" period. The value of this report is at best questionable because of its analytical weaknesses.[96] It contains some statistical information,

[95] *Lessons of the 1930's,* September 1958, 7 pages. This report was the sequel to an article written by the President of W. G. Weston, Ltd., Mr. W. G. Weston, for *Fairplay,* July 3, 1958.

[96] It defines peaks and troughs by "highest and lowest points," which depend on the time period chosen, neglecting any intermediate fluctuations which may qualify as cycles; it neglects shipbuilding construction, but attempts to relate tonnage launched with "World Seaborne Trade." It indulges in a lot of implicit theorizing and arrives at conclusions by definition. For example, it defines "Effective World Fleet" as *total fleet less ships idle* and then concludes that changes in the "effective size of the world fleet almost exactly correspond with changes in seaborne trade, although the operating factor, freight rates, is related in a much less exact manner," *op. cit.,* p. 5. The conclusions reached by Westinform are all expressed in terms of leads and lags from the peaks and troughs of "world seaborne trade," but very little explanation is given of such leads and lags. Then, assuming that the same relationships apply to the present period, Westinform makes projections to predict recovery in the tankship markets.

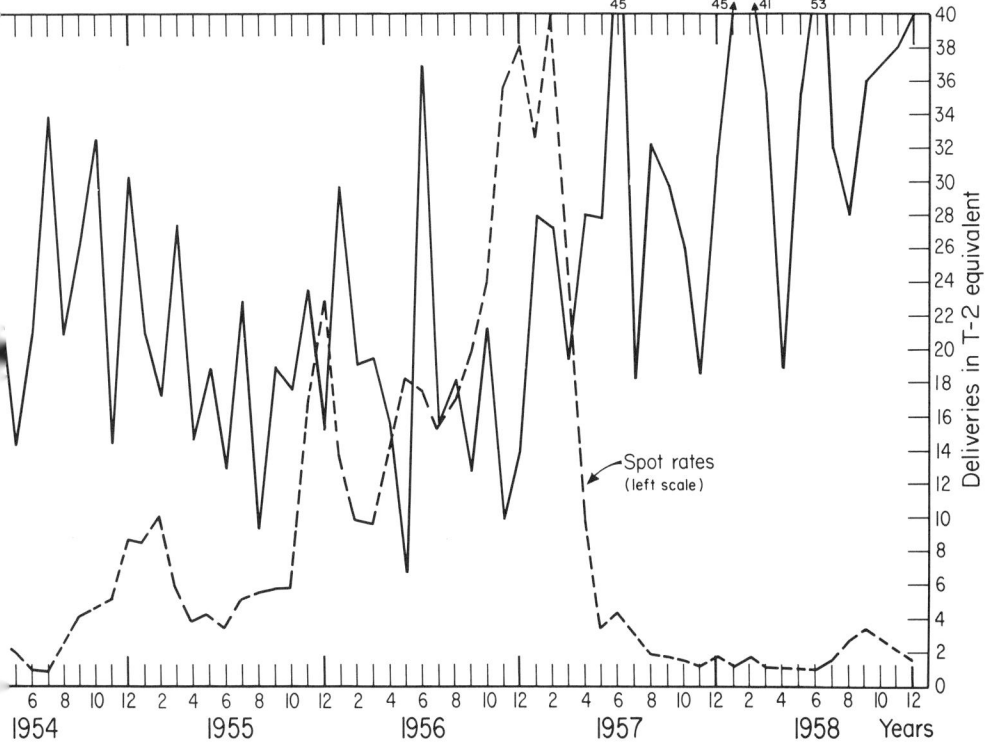

and index of spot rates, 1949–1958.

however, which, although it may not qualify on the basis of scientific standards of accuracy,[97] is indicative of a parallel between the two periods.

The relationship between oil movements and transportation needs is indisputable. We can argue, nevertheless, that many of the links in the chain of cause and effect are more revealing than the end points. Our contention is that seaborne trade affects the short-term demand for transportation, and the effect is naturally reflected in the level of short-term rates. The rates condition expectations that generate orders for vessels when rates are rising, and cause both rates and orders to spiral. The ordered vessels, however, because of the shipbuilding lead time, increase future rather than present capacity. Also, we have provided evidence that the relationship between rates and orders placed is relatively strong and that *orders begin to decline only when, or after, the rates do*. Consequently, the *increments* to future capacity will continue

[97] When compared with data included in Koopmans, *op. cit.*, pp. 186–204, the Westinform data (excluding faulty definitions of peaks) appear out of phase by about three months to a year.

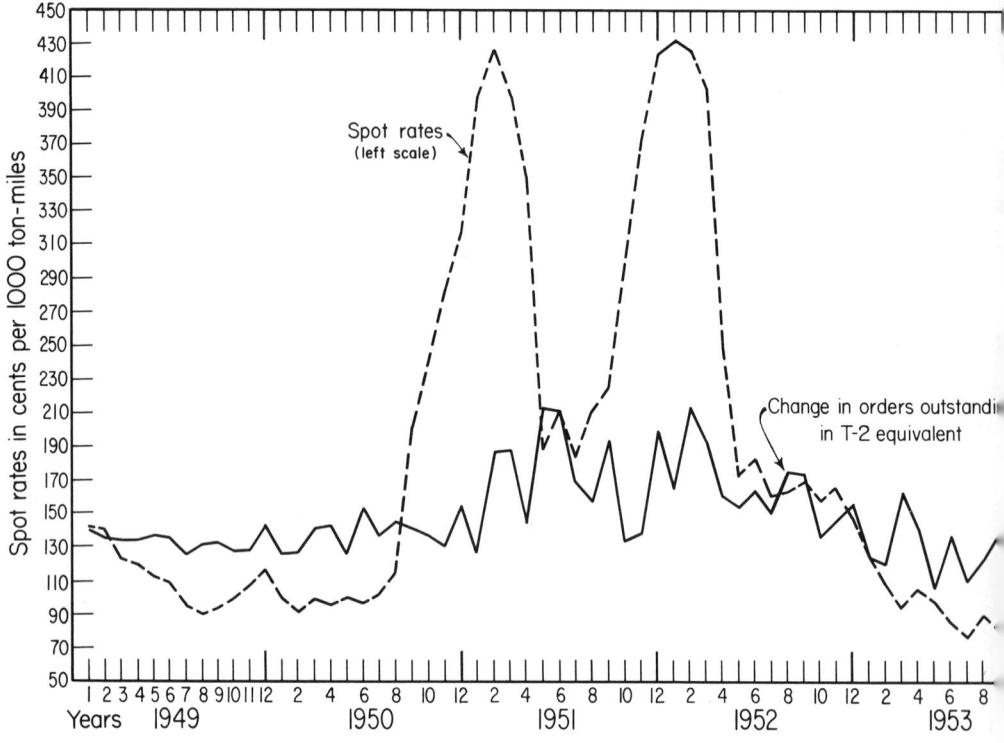

Figure 5.8. Time series of changes in orders outstanding

beyond the point where the need that generated them has been satisfied or has even created surpluses. It is abundantly clear that the impact of deliveries which appear a few years later, after, let us repeat, *the satisfaction of the need that initiated them*, will create chaotic conditions.

The net result of the impact of rates on orders can be seen in Figure 5.7, and in Figures 5.8 and 5.9. Figure 5.8 shows the time-series comparison between changes in orders outstanding and spot rates. We notice that the peak in the changes to the backlog of orders was reached seven months after the peak in rates.[98] To illustrate the relationship between the magnitudes of orders outstanding and the tonnage in existence during those periods, we show in Figure 5.9 the time series of orders as a percentage of total fleet and working petroleum fleet.[99] During the Suez

[98] As we have previously pointed out this time difference may be exaggerated by time lags between the initiation and announcement of orders.

[99] The working petroleum fleet is defined as vessels operating. It is composed of total tonnage minus government-owned and special-purpose vessels, and ships idle over thirty days (for repairs or lay-up). The working petroleum fleet figure is somewhat inflated by the inclusion of all repairs and maintenance of under thirty days.

FACTORS AFFECTING SUPPLY OF TANKSHIPS   115

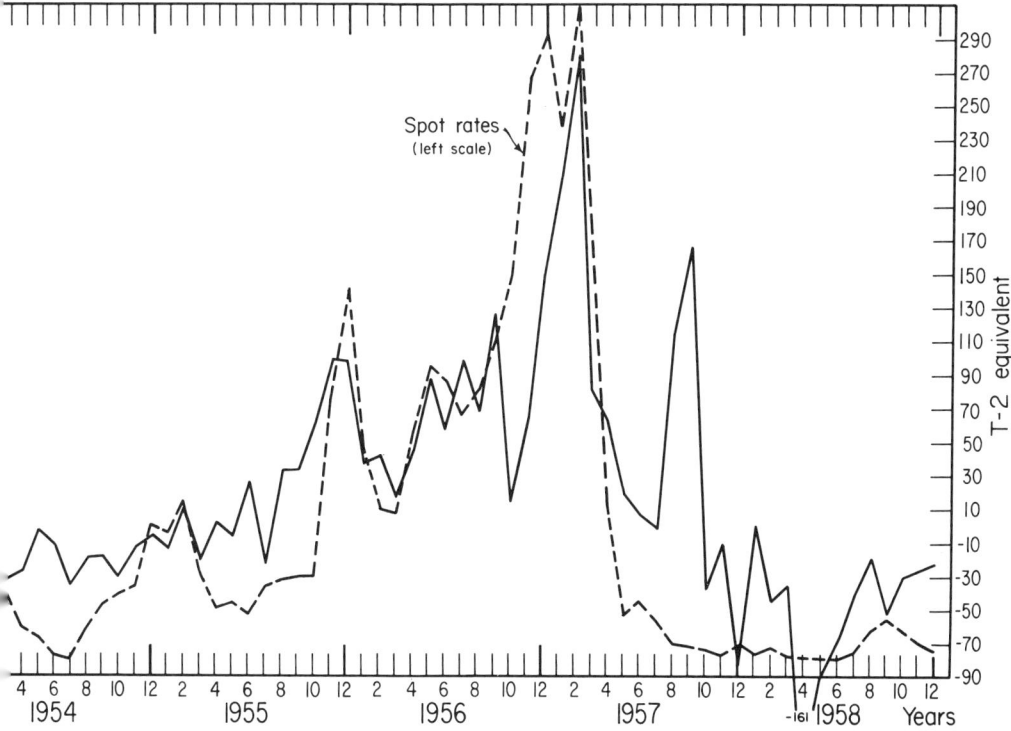

in T-2 equivalent and index of spot rates, 1949–1958.

Canal frenzy, orders flooded the shipyards to such an extent that at the peak, in September 1957, orders outstanding were about 94% and 112% of the total fleet and working petroleum fleet, respectively. Such a backlog is indeed staggering if we realize that the fleet at this time was approximately equal to 2600 T-2 equivalents. The relationships depicted in Figure 5.9 occurred in spite of the new records in deliveries that were being established during this period. In Figures 5.10 and 5.11 we present a scatter diagram of the net changes in orders outstanding (in terms of T-2 equivalents) versus spot rates, for the periods 1948–1953 and 1954–1958, respectively. The results indicate that even the *net changes* are positively correlated with rates.

The arguments just presented are in general agreement with those presented by Koopmans and Tinbergen in their classic works.[100] The difference between our analysis and theirs on this score rests mainly on the degree of quantitative evidence, the shape of our demand schedule

---

[100] See Koopmans, *op. cit.*, pp. 160–172, where Tinbergen's work is also discussed.

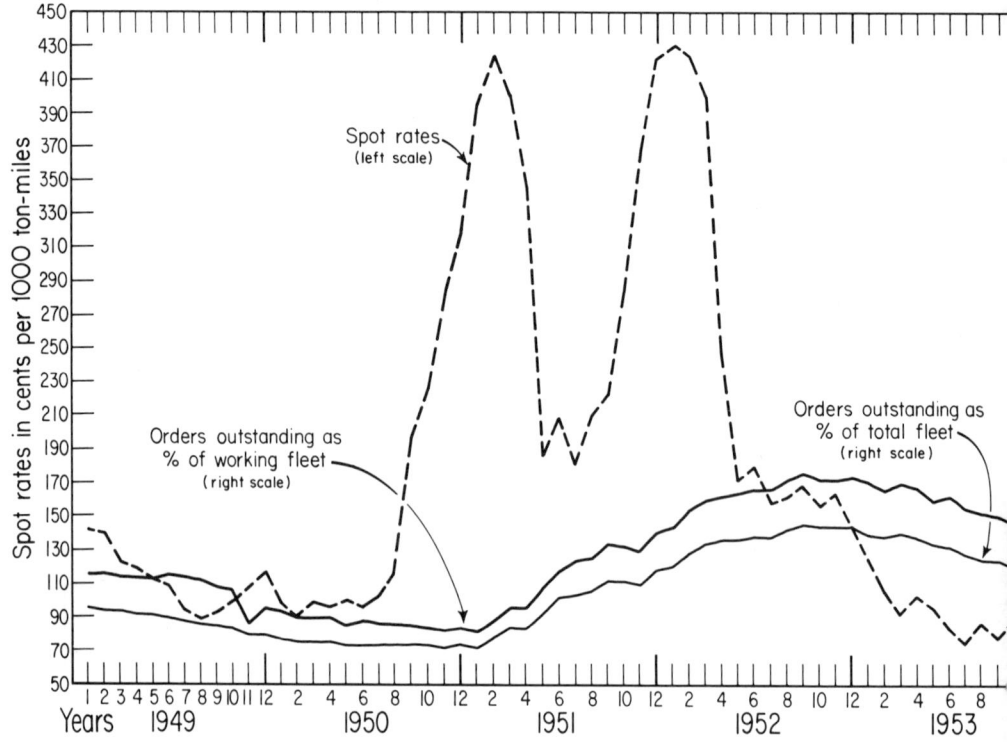

Figure 5.9. Time series of total orders outstanding as percentage of

(due to dynamic expectations), and the particular reaction patterns of the operatives.

Spot Rates and Vessels Scrapped

Prior to this point, we have discussed the factors that cause shifts to the right in the supply schedule of tonnage. We shall now turn to the causes of shifts to the left, or contraction of capacity.

Contraction of supply may occur either permanently or temporarily; that is, it may affect either the long-run or the intermediate supply schedules. In the former category we may classify scrappings or permanent retirement of vessels, while in the latter we may include slowdowns, extended repairs, conversions to dry cargo, grain carriers, etc., and finally tie-ups. Some of the aforementioned factors, such as conversions, are of relatively little importance; and extended repairs and slowdowns, although quantitatively important in the aggregate, are variable within narrow and more or less definable limits.

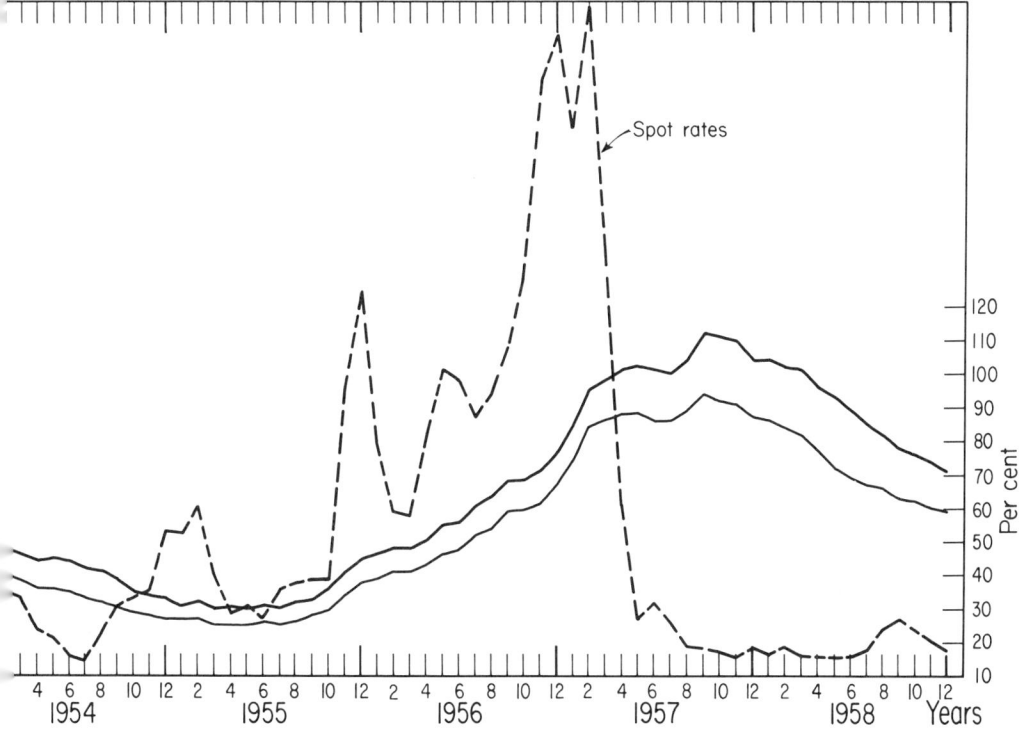

total and working petroleum fleets and index of spot rates, 1949–1958.

We shall analyze in this section the factors that govern permanent retirements, leaving the contractions of the short-run and intermediary nature to subsequent discussion. Some aspects of permanent retirements (scrappings) of vessels have been presented in conjunction with our discussion of their impact on orders placed. We have pointed out there that the relationship between the short-term and the expected rates over the remaining life of the vessels, on the one hand, and out-of-pocket cost of operation and tie-up, on the other, determines whether a vessel will be scrapped, tied up, or operated.

As there is so much fluctuation and uncertainty in rates in the long run, it is quite probable that the owners of vessels base their expectation on the only concrete evidence that they have, that is to say, the existing spot rates. Therefore, we would expect the number of vessels scrapped to be inversely related to spot rates. Furthermore, if our previous theoretical conclusions are valid, the age of vessels retired and the short-term rates should be positively correlated.

Table 5.12 presents the yearly data for the number of vessels sold for scrap, the capacity which indicates the average size of the vessels

118 CHAPTER FIVE

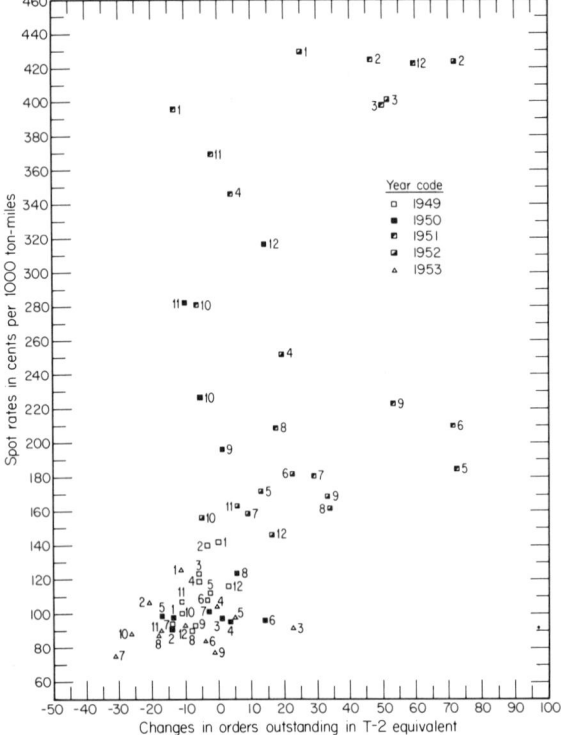

Figure 5.10. Scatter diagram of changes in orders outstanding in T-2 equivalent versus index of spot rates, 1949–1953 (monthly).

involved, the average life of such vessels, and the average spot rate for each year between 1947 and 1958. The same data are plotted in Figure 5.12, and show very convincingly that the number of vessels scrapped and the spot rates are moving in the opposite direction, while the age of the vessels retired increases with the spot rates. The downward trend in the average age of vessels retired is caused by the advance in technology, which continuously changes the size composition of the tanker fleet.

As we have stressed in discussing retirements and orders placed, retirements and replacements are two distinct actions from the economic point of view and should be so treated. Failure to do so will result in erroneous theoretical conclusions, such as those reached by Koopmans and Einarsen on this subject.[101] By defining as "replacement" any order that preceded or followed by twenty-four months the sale or retirement

---

[101] See Koopmans, *op. cit.*, pp. 156–158.

FACTORS AFFECTING SUPPLY OF TANKSHIPS   119

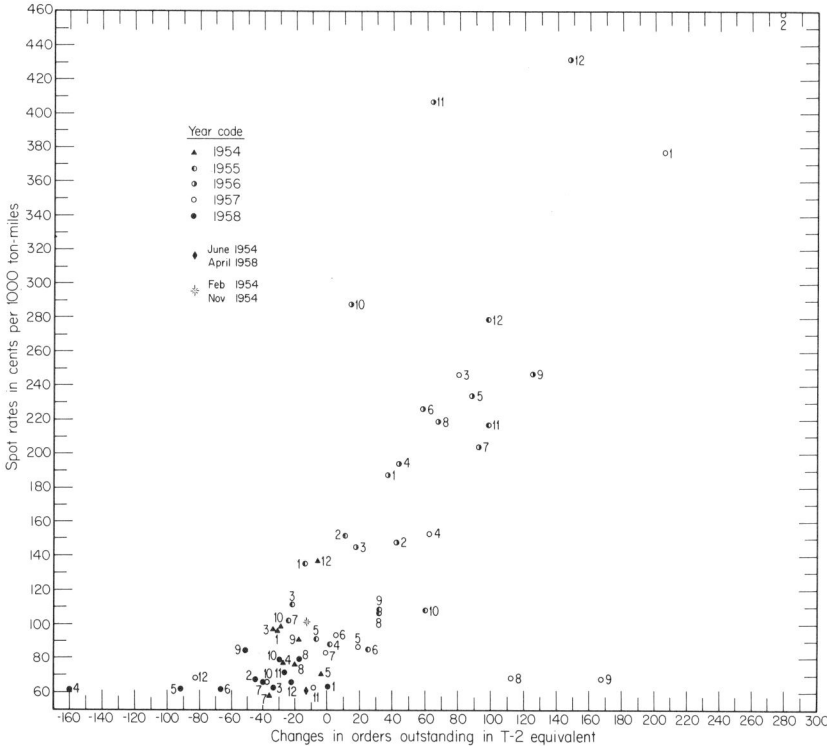

Figure 5.11. Scatter diagram of changes in orders outstanding in T-2 equivalent versus index of spot rates, 1954–1958 (monthly).

of a vessel, Einarsen's data, Koopmans concluded, show "that the conditions which stimulate new investment also favor replacement." [102]

There is no theoretical reason requiring sale or retirement of a vessel only after an order for its replacement has been placed or the replacement itself has been received. Or, to invert the argument, there is no reason why the placing of an order or the receipt of a presumed replacement should cause the economic value of an existing vessel to vanish. As the day follows the night so do low rates follow years of inflated rates. Because these rate fluctuations occur often and are violent, and rates rise and fall in less than twenty-four months, Einarsen found enough sales and retirements to associate with orders placed, and vice versa. If it were not for these violent changes, we are confident that the data would have refuted such a hypothesis, *especially during periods of high rates.*

[102] *Ibid.,* p. 158.

TABLE 5.12

VESSELS SCRAPPED AND SPOT RATES: YEARLY DATA

Year	1 No. of Vessels	2 T-2 Equivalent	3 Average Age in Years	4 Av. Yearly Spot Rate per 1,000 Ton-Miles
1947	8	3.1	29.5	2.20
1948	4	1.8	29.5	2.66
1949	42	19.0	30.1	1.12
1950	16	6.1	32.0	1.52
1951	6	2.3	38.2	3.04
1952	5	2.0	36.6	2.35
1953	56	25.0	29.6	.94
1954	70	37.9	29.0	.89
1955	55	25.7	30.2	1.32
1956	10	4.2	31.4	2.44
1957	16	8.0	26.4	1.52
1958	37	20.5	25.1	.68

Source of Data: 1 and 2, Transportation Coordination Department, Standard Oil Company, New Jersey.
    3, *Register of Tank Vessels of the World*, Standard Oil Company, New Jersey.
    4, For 1947 and 1948, Conrad Boe, Ltd., Oslo, Norway.
       For 1949–1956, United States Maritime Administration.
       For 1957 and 1958, Addison Outwater and Associates, New York.
Note: For the 1958 data the average life of vessels scrapped by the oil companies was 21.9 years versus 28.9 for the independents.

A *small* number of retirements will occur regardless of rates; however, the greatest number of such retirements will take place, we believe, on *low* spot rates, in spite of any orders outstanding for the owners of the vessels retired. Why should an owner who is able to secure remunerative employment for his old vessel refuse it? On the other hand, if an operator sees that he has no prospects for remunerative employment over what now seems to be the remaining economic life of his vessel, and therefore decides to retire the vessel instead of keeping it idle, why should he order a replacement if the prospects for employment of the new vessel when it appears in the market are not promising? Would he not naturally wait until he is somehow assured about the immediate future?

We have pointed this out on purely theoretical grounds before, and Figure 5.12 gives us empirical evidence that the correlation is negative between rates and vessels retired. Further, the average age of the vessels retired is positively correlated with rates and not negatively as the Einarsen-Koopmans argument would imply. If the variability in the average age of vessels scrapped is so great between years, is not this an indication that a uniform time period (twenty-four months for example) between replacements and scrappings, or scrappings and replacements, is lacking? Why should there be a difference of over six years between the average lives of vessels scrapped in 1955 and 1958, respectively? If we accept such differences as part of calculated replacement-scrapping plans, we shall in effect be asserting that the owners knowingly cut the economic life of their vessels, which is illogical. It is one thing to accept naïveté, but this degree of irrationality is inadmissible.

To summarize briefly, we have already provided empirical evidence that spot rates and orders placed are positively correlated. The same relationship also exists between spot rates and fixtures (vessels hired). So the higher the spot rate, the greater the flood of orders both for new vessel construction and for rental of existing vessels. At levels such as those reached by spot rates on the upswing even the most inefficient vessels can secure remunerative employment, consequently, no one in his right mind will retire a vessel at high rates unless he has to do so. At low rates, when most of the retirements will take place because of

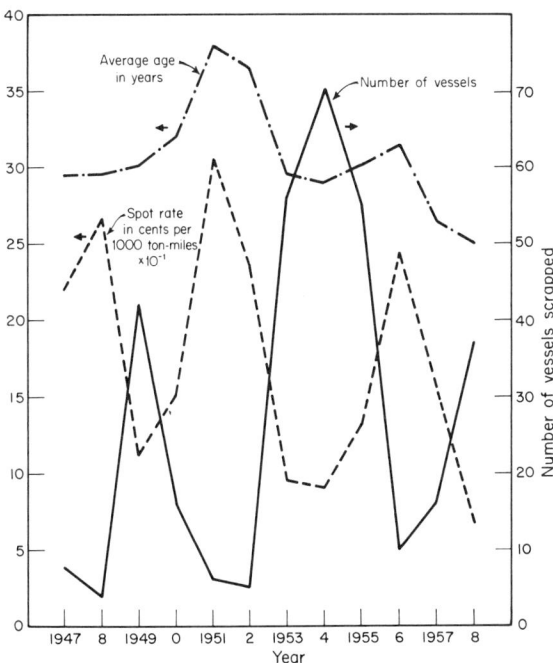

Figure 5.12. Number and average age of vessels scrapped and spot rates, 1947–1958.

CHAPTER FIVE

the expiration of the economic value of vessels, retirements may not necessarily generate replacements but only reduce the existing surpluses. Technological innovations of a substantial nature will be introduced more likely when rates are high and most of the new vessels are ordered. During periods of low rates, the pressure for technological changes will be aimed most probably at reducing the cost of operation of existing vessels in order to increase their profitability and postpone the expiration of economic life of surplus vessels.

It appears, then, that replacement orders are the *result* of the expiration of the economic value of old vessels, which is more likely to occur at low rates. But when replacements do occur, only under conditions of stationary stability would we expect a one-to-one correspondence between retirements and orders placed. In industries such as this, where the firms enjoy internal economies of "unit" scale, replacements on a vessel-for-vessel basis are surplus conducive.

Table 5.13 presents the average sizes of the vessels scrapped, de-

TABLE 5.13

AVERAGE SIZE OF VESSELS SCRAPPED, DELIVERED, AND ORDERED BY YEARS 1948–1959

Year	Average Size per Vessel in T-2 Equivalent			Av. Rate per 1,000 Ton-Miles
	Scrapped	Delivered	Ordered	
1948	.45	.80	1.12	2.66
1949	.44	1.07	1.06	1.12
1950	.38	1.01	1.04	1.52
1951	.38	.99	1.26	3.04
1952	.40	1.11	1.45	2.35
1953	.45	1.24	1.74	.94
1954	.54	1.36	1.96	.89
1955	.47	1.39	1.90	1.32
1956	.42	1.70	2.15	2.44
1957	.50	1.90	2.80	1.52
1958	.55	1.94	*	.68
1959 (Jan.–Apr.)	N.A.	2.04	*	

Source of Data: Transportation Coordination Department, Standard Oil Company, New Jersey.
For rates see Table 5.12.
N.A. = Not available.
* Periods of extensive cancellations.

livered, and ordered yearly, for the years 1948 to the end of April 1959. The same data are graphed in Figure 5.13. These exhibits are convincing evidence that replacements cause surpluses in the tankship markets. The average size of the vessels delivered during the various years was

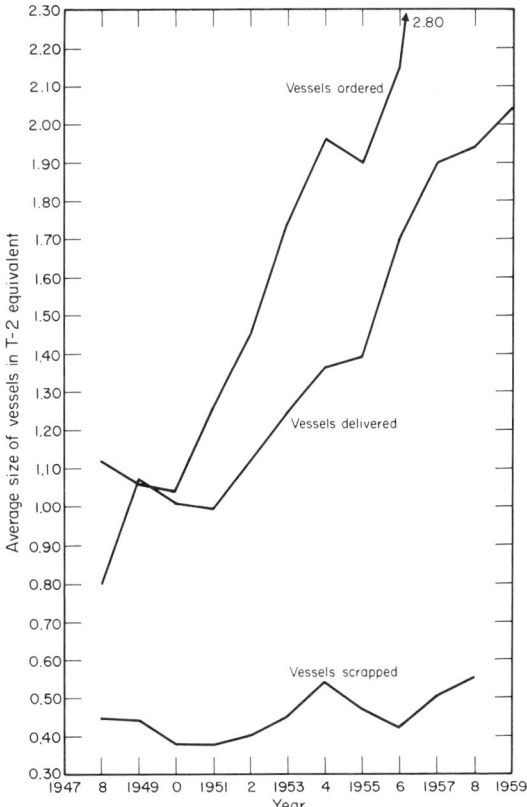

Figure 5.13. Average size of vessels ordered, delivered, and scrapped, 1948–1959.

anywhere from two to four times as large as the average size of vessels scrapped. Even more impressive is the comparison between the sizes of vessels scrapped and orders placed: the average size of the latter, in 1957, was 5.6 times greater than that of the vessels retired. One must not, however, forget that replacements are still a very small fraction of the orders placed, given elastic price expectations. One glance at Column 2 of Table 5.12 will convince us that even if we assume that all vessels retired were replaced, such orders cannot account for more than 1% of all orders placed during periods of high rates when the avalanche of orders occurred.[103]

[103] On May 1, 1959, despite cancellations, postponements, and conversions of over 3,000,000 tons during the last quarter of 1958 and a record delivery of 2,500,000 DWT. (163.3 T-2's) between January and April 1959, orders were outstanding for 718 vessels, a total of over 26,000,000 DWT., equivalent to 1729.7 T-2's or approximately 55% of the total fleet (idle and operating) of January 1, 1959.

124   CHAPTER FIVE

Now that we have raised the issue of technology versus size, let us digress for a minute and observe that although economies of scale are necessary for the trend toward mammoth tankers, yet the speed of introduction of larger sizes does not always depend upon purely economic considerations. The pride and rivalry of the various tanker operators, especially independents, have contributed extensively to the rapid change from the era of the T-2 to that of the 100,000 tonner. It was not long ago that the war-built T-2 (16,500 DWT. and with a speed of 14.5 knots) was the queen of the seas. In 1948–1949, the shipbuilders were already delivering 27,000 tonners that could achieve average speeds of 16 knots. Three years later the industry was thinking in terms of 37,000 DWT. vessels, but one independent operator (Onassis) set his sights even higher. The "Tina Onassis," delivered in 1953, was 45,222 DWT. and achieved speeds of 16.5 knots. Then came the challenge from another operator (Niarchos), in the launching of the "World Glory" (45,509), to which the former responded by building the ill-fated "Al Malik Saud Al Awal" (46,548 DWT.).

While this rivalry was stealing the headlines, Ludwig (National Bulk Carriers, Inc. and Universe Tankships, Inc.) quietly walked away with the prize. Since 1955, when the "Sinclair Petrolore" (56,080 DWT.) was delivered, Universe Tankships has held the record. "Sinclair Petrolore" was followed in 1956 by the "Universe Leader" of 85,515 DWT., and in January 1959 by the "Universe Apollo" of 104,500 DWT.[104] To "challenge" Ludwig, Onassis early in 1957 ordered two vessels of 105,000, and Niarchos one of the same size. These were later changed to 106,500 DWT., but the post-Suez depression forced Onassis to cancel his orders[105] and Niarchos to postpone action for a year. Niarchos' vessel, which is now being built, is the largest under construction.[106] We expect, however, that the race for size will not end here.

No matter how great the economies of scale achieved with vessels of 100,000 DWT., the industry cannot afford such inflexibility *if it is applied universally*. Only regularly scheduled distant runs can be entrusted to such vessels, provided the harbor facilities, storage capacity, refinery throughput capacity, and market size permit their use. For this

---

[104] There were three more vessels of 104,500 DWT. each under construction for Universe Tankships as of July 1959, and rumors were circulated about plans for tankers between 160,000 and 200,000 DWT.

[105] Because these vessels were part of a "transfer out and build in U.S." agreement with the U.S. Government, Onassis got into trouble. To our knowledge, final decision on one of the two vessels had not been taken as of July 1959.

[106] During the Suez crisis it was rumored that Niarchos requested from shipyards details for a vessel of 160,000 DWT., but, together with the rates, rumors subsided.

reason it is not expected that the *number* of such vessels will increase drastically in the near future, especially because of actions by the independents (unless of course they first obtain a charter agreement). It is more natural for the oil companies to own big vessels, because the uncertainty of their utilization in such rigid circumstances is less.[107] Because no independent would take the risk of having such a tanker remain idle or operate in the spot market, most of the supertankers operate under long-term charters of ten or more years' duration.[108]

Figure 5.12 also shows, on the basis of the 1958 data, that the average life of the vessels scrapped by the oil companies was 21.9 years versus 28.9 for the independents. This fact indicates that the oldest vessels used by the oil companies are not older or less efficient than those of the independents. From data furnished by the Transportation Coordination Department of the Standard Oil Company of New Jersey, we find that on January 1, 1959, 3.1% of the vessels owned by the oil companies were 21 years old or older. The corresponding percentage for the independent fleet was 5.1%. On January 1, 1958, the relevant data were 3.8% for the oil companies and 5.8% for the independents. Because the oil companies have secure employment for a certain amount of tonnage, the 1958 data, if they are applicable to all other years, may reveal the competitive character of the tankship markets. As the labor cost of the oil companies is high relative to that of the independents, competition will force the former to scrap their vessels earlier.[109]

Another point that comes out of Figure 5.12 is worth mentioning. The average life of the vessels scrapped in 1958 has no parallel in the period under observation. This may be the result of a combination of the technologies of scale enjoyed by the industry and the consequent

---

[107] Table 5.3 shows that the average size of the vessels under construction on account of the oil companies was 40,600 DWT., and that of the independent vessels 33,700 DWT. on January 1, 1959.

[108] The history of the vessels of 65,000 DWT. and over shows the following: in 1957, five vessels of 65,000 and one of 85,000 were chartered for ten years by the Texas Company for Middle East-U.S. trade; two other vessels of 65,000 and 68,000 DWT., respectively, were chartered by Standard-Vacuum (Stanvac) for fifteen years for Far Eastern trade. In 1958, two 87,400 DWT. vessels were chartered for fifteen years for Far Eastern trade by Stanvac. The "Universe Apollo," according to the *Shipping World,* was to be delivered to the Gulf Oil Company for a fifteen-year charter to operate between the Persian Gulf and Japan. Source of information: Conrad Boe reports of Oslo, Norway; Addison Outwater & Associates (Brokers) of New York, and the *Shipping World and World Shipping,* Vol. CXXXIX, No. 3415, Wednesday, December 10, 1958, London, p. 501.

[109] The oil companies have an advantage over the independents in that they use bunkers which they themselves produce. This argument, however, will apply only in the case of spot, and even here only in cases where bunkers are in excess supply.

obsolescence, and the extreme severity of the present depression in the tankship markets.

Finally, Table 5.13 shows that the average size of vessels scrapped is inversely related to tanker rates. This further strengthens our arguments that spot rates determine the greatest part of the retirements in a given year.[110]

In summary, we can say that retirements of vessels are negatively correlated with rates and for this reason are equilibrating. To the extent that they are quantitatively insignificant,[111] however, the retirements have not caused in the past, and are not expected to cause in the future, sufficient contraction in the supply schedules to restore equilibrium in a depressed market.

Spot Rates and Slowdowns, Conversions, Repairs, and Tie-ups

We shall now turn to the factors that affect the short-term and intermediary supply schedules. These factors are slowdowns, conversions to day cargo vessels, extended repairs, and, most important of all, tie-ups.

SLOWDOWNS

It is a little odd and rather unfortunate that the economics of slowdowns (and of course speed-ups when rates are high) have not been determined empirically. In the naval architecture and marine engineering literature, we read that the shaft horsepower (SHP) and fuel consumption vary proportionately with speed to the nth power. This n at "cruising speeds" is equal to 3, and at maximum speed equal to 4, according to Manning.[112]

Not being qualified on matters of marine engineering, we shall not delve into the engineering aspects of speed but shall point out their economic significance by making use of the relationships between speed

---

[110] The smaller vessels are usually less efficient, and hence are the first to be retired. As rates go down, relatively larger and larger vessels become uneconomical.

[111] In the next chapter we shall show that because of the extensive inelasticity of the normal supply schedule *beyond full capacity* small changes can prove very important. This is not in conflict with our present arguments because retirements occurring during periods of low rates are usually caused by existing surpluses, abundance of deliveries, and expectations which are rate elastic.

[112] Manning, George C., *The Theory and Technique of Ship Design*, The Technology Press of the Massachusetts Institute of Technology, Cambridge, 1956, p. 45.

FACTORS AFFECTING SUPPLY OF TANKSHIPS 127

and fuel consumption derived by marine engineers.[113] The main purpose in slowing down a vessel is to save fuel, but capacity is lost in the process. It is necessary, therefore, to balance the cost of such loss of capacity against the savings from fuel. Immediately it is evident that fuel costs will be an important factor in problems of this nature. The question now is, how do we get an index of the cost of lost capacity?

In periods of low rates we can find tonnage very easily. Conceivably, then, we can define the cost of lost capacity in terms of the amount of money that has to be paid to transport an equivalent amount of oil by hiring more vessels in the spot market. Clearly, we are discussing the case of the oil company, since for the independent who operates in the spot markets[114] the problem is simply one of maximizing revenue over the life of the vessel.

Let us now formalize the above arguments. Let S represent the cruising speed of a vessesl per hour, M the round-trip distance, K the number of days in port per round trip, N the number of trips per year, F the fuel consumption in barrels or tons per day at sea, and f the fuel consumption per day in port. Then, on the basis of 330 operating days per year,[115] the capacity of a vessel is $330 \times S \times 24$ miles; and the number of trips

$$N = \frac{330 \times S \times 24}{M + (24 \times S \times K)} \qquad (5.20)$$

The number of steaming days D is

$$D = 330 - N \times K \qquad (5.21)$$

and the yearly fuel consumption C for steaming and in port

$$C = (330 - N \times K) \times F + N \times K \times f \qquad (5.22)$$

or

$$C = 330F - N \times K(F - f) \qquad (5.23)$$

If we now assume that for speeds $S(1 - r)$, where r stands for the

---

[113] On this aspect we feel that the engineers flounder as much if not more than economists do on engineering aspects. See Manning, *op. cit.*, p. 41, where he sets as the criterion of economic efficiency for operating vessels "the ratio of the relative gross revenue to that of operating cost." Also see Benford, Harry, *Engineering Economy in Tanker Design,* Society of Naval Architects and Marine Engineers, paper presented at the December 1956 meeting, 98 pp., whose economic evaluation (pp. 38–48 especially) is full of such misconceptions.

[114] Spot-market operations are necessary for this discussion because on long-term charters the charterer pays for the fuel.

[115] About thirty–thirty-five days of repairs were considered normal in 1958–1959 on foreign-flag vessels. Later we shall question the validity of this figure.

percentage reduction in speed, there is a corresponding fuel reduction represented by $F(1-r)^n$,[116] we can find

$$C' = 330F(1-r)^n - N' \times K[F(1-r)^n - f] \quad (5.24)$$

where

$$N' = \frac{330 \times S(1-r) \times 24}{M + [24 \times S(1-r) \times K]} \quad (5.25)$$

The savings then are equal to the difference of $(C - C')$ multiplied by the cost of fuel p.

$$(C - C')p = p[330F[1-(1-r)^n] - K \times F[N - N'(1-r)^n] \\ + K \times f(N - N')] \quad (5.26)$$

In the above expression, the first two terms on the right-hand side represent the savings due to the lower fuel consumption while steaming, and the third term, the savings due to lower fuel consumption in port. Notice that the latter is *not* due to lower fuel consumption per day in port but to fewer days in port because of fewer trips during the year. Finally, if we add to Equation 5.26 the savings due to port charges (again because of fewer trips and, hence, fewer port visits) we get

$$\text{Yearly Savings} = p[330F[1-(1-r)^n] - K \times F[N - N'(1-r)^n] \\ + K \times f(N - N')] + (N - N') \times P \quad (5.27)$$

where P is the port charge per visit.

The loss in capacity at first approximation is equal to

$$L = (\text{DWT.} - M - B) \times (N - N') \quad (5.28)$$

where M stands for crew and vessel supplies, and B for bunkers (vessel fuel).

Because a reduction in bunkers will allow a further increase in carrying capacity, however, Equation 5.28 is inflated by a fraction or all of the following quantity: $N' \times [(C/N) - (C'/N')]$. The exact nature of this quantity will depend on the refueling schedule followed by the vessel. In cases of low rates, the vessels prefer to load at the source (low-cost point) all the bunkers they need for the round trip, as the loss in marginal revenue is more than offset by the decrease in fuel costs.

This discussion leads us to a second approximation for L:[117]

---

[116] We may assume that for a few knots *below* normal cruising speed the fuel consumption varies with the square of the speed; at around $S(1 \pm r)$, F becomes $F(1 \pm r)^3$, if r is small; and for positive r beyond, F becomes $F(1+r)^4, \cdots$, $F(1+r)^\infty$.

[117] Conceivably, with longer trips M will increase, which may counterbalance part of the additional capacity gained by the reduction in bunkers. However, supplies are not as important quantitatively as bunkers. As for B, it is equal to $[(330F/N) - K(F-f)] \times (1.10)$, showing that the greater the distance the lower

$$L = (\text{DWT.} - M - B) \times (N - N') \times q[(C/N) - (C'/N')] \quad (5.29)$$

where q is a factor less than or equal to unity.

Knowing the savings and the loss in capacity, we can now find the upper limit that our savings will allow us to pay in order to recover such capacity. Hence, if the spot rate R is

$$R < \text{Equation 5.27} \div \text{Equation 5.29} \quad (5.30)$$

then it pays to slow down the owned vessels and acquire additional tonnage to recover the loss in capacity.[118]

After the Suez crisis and the ensuing drop in tanker rates, many oil companies, among which were British Petroleum, Shell, and Standard Oil Company of New Jersey, slowed down their vessels to save on fuel cost. In addition, it was rumored that around the middle of 1957, British Petroleum instructed all of its vessels of 20,000 DWT. and over to use the Cape route at low speed, and thus save a further amount due to the Suez Canal tolls. For such routes, we must add on the right-hand side of Equation 5.27 the term $N \times D$ to account for the canal dues, where D stands for the total dues per trip.

The above-mentioned formulations were used to determine the critical spot rate for the Port Arthur to New York run and the Ras Tanura to Antwerp round trip. For the latter we have also computed a variation in order to demonstrate the impact of the Suez Canal tolls.

On the basis of the data[119] shown in Table 5.14, it seems advantageous to slow down a T-2 from 14.5 knots to 10 if the spot rate is lower than U.S.M.C. minus 58% (or $1.20 per ton delivered) and the cost of bunkers is not less than $2.65 per barrel ($17.23 per ton).[120] For the Ras Tanura to Antwerp trip of 12,880 miles by way of the Suez Canal, according to Table 5.15, the savings in fuel costs are sufficient to permit the chartering of vessels in the spot market at rates no higher than U.S.M.C. minus 49.0%, or $5.58 per delivered ton of oil. These figures are based on the assumption that half of the bunkers are bought at Ras Tanura, at $18.40 per ton, and the other half at Antwerp, at $26.25 per ton.

---

the capacity (paying cargo) of a vessel. The factor 1.10 is an approximation of the safety allowance required by law.

[118] In cases of excess owned tonnage, the alternatives are to slow down or tie up. Here, however, expectations about intermediate prospects must enter; these will be discussed later. Notice that in the case of slowdowns and spot chartering the companies preserve utmost flexibility. As rates go up, they can increase the speed of their own vessels and stop chartering.

[119] The operating data were provided by Mr. M. D. Cooper, President, The Marine Brokerage Company of New York.

[120] We can use the relationships that we derived to determine the impact of changes in the cost of bunkers on the most efficient speed for operating tankers.

TABLE 5.14

ECONOMICS OF SPEED: PORT ARTHUR–NEW YORK–PORT ARTHUR

1. Port Arthur–New York–Port Arthur	\= 3,680 miles	
	At 14.5 Knots	*At 10.0 Knots*
2. Days steaming per trip	10.6	15.3
3. Days in port per trip	3.0	3.0
4. Total	13.6	18.3
5. Number of trips per year (330 days)	24.3	18.0
6. Total number of steaming days per year	258.0	276.0
7. Total number of days in port per year	72.0	54.0
8. Bunkers per day steaming (bbls)	300	150
9. Bunkers per day in port (bbls)	100	100
10. Total bunkers per year	84,700	46,700
11. Capacity in barrels occupied by bunkers per trip	3,500	2,600
12. Savings by reducing speed		
Bunkers 38,000 barrels at $2.65/bbl		\= $100,700
Port charges (24.3 − 18.0) × 2,200 per trip		13,860
Total		$114,560
13. Loss in capacity		
15,620 tons per trip × (24.3 − 18.0)		\= 98,406 tons
Less gain because of Item 11		
$= \dfrac{900 \times 18}{6.5}$		(2,500)
		95,906 tons
14. Equating rate 114,560/95,906 or	$1.20 per ton delivered which is approximately U.S.M.C. *minus* 58%	

Source of Data: Marine Brokerage Company, Inc.

If all the bunkers are loaded at Ras Tanura where the cost is lower,[121] then the savings due to the differential fuel-oil consumption decrease; however, capacity also decreases because of the displacement of paying cargo by the additional bunkers. These substitutions change the critical spot rate to $5.33 per ton of crude oil delivered, or U.S.M.C. minus 51.5%, thus further illustrating the impact of bunker prices on slowdowns, especially on long routes.

Finally, Table 5.16 presents the impact of the Suez Canal tolls on transportation under depressed tanker market conditions.[122] It shows that

---

[121] Obviously it is better for a vessel to load all bunkers at the point of minimum cost as long as the tanker rates are lower than the cost differential. In our case, the cost difference is $7.85 per ton. Consequently, it pays to load all bunkers at Ras Tanura as long as the spot rate is less than $7.85 per ton of oil delivered, or U.S.M.C. minus 28%.

[122] The comparisons shown in Tables 5.15 and 5.16 refer to vessels that can go through the Suez Canal loaded, i.e., 42,000 DWT. and below. For the mammoth tankers the comparison will be similar to that carried in Table 5.14.

TABLE 5.15

ECONOMICS OF SPEED:
RAS TANURA–ANTWERP ROUND TRIP THROUGH CANAL

1. Ras Tanura–Antwerp–Ras Tanura	= 12,880 miles through Suez	
	At 14.5 Knots	*At 10 Knots*
2. Days steaming per trip	37	54
3. Days in port per trip plus 2 for Canal	5	5
4. Total	42	59
5. Number of trips per year (329 days)	7.86	5.60
6. Total number of steaming days per year	290	301
7. Total number of days in port and Canal per year	39	28
8. Bunkers per day steaming (bbls)	300	150
9. Bunkers per day in port and Canal (bbls)	100	100
10. Total bunkers per year	90,900	47,950
11. Capacity in barrels occupied by bunkers per trip	11,600	8,600

12. Savings by reducing speed (assume bunkers loaded at half points)
    Bunkers   42,950 barrels or 6,600 tons
    Ras Tanura   3,300 at $18.40   = $ 61,000
    Antwerp   3,300 at $26.25   87,000
      Total for bunkers $148,000

    Port charges   (7.86 − 5.60) × $3,500   7,830
    Canal tolls   (7.86 − 5.60) × $13,200   29,832
                                                       $185,662

13. Loss in capacity
    15,300 tons/trip × 2.26   = 34,578
    Less gain because of Item 11

$$= \frac{3{,}000 \times 5.6}{6.5 \times 2} \qquad\qquad \begin{array}{r}(1{,}292)\\ \hline 33{,}286\end{array}$$

14. Equating rate $185,662/33,286   or $5.58/ton delivered which is approximately U.S.M.C. minus 49.0%.

12′. Savings by reducing speed if all bunkers are loaded at point of minimum bunker cost
    Bunkers 6,600 tons × 18.40   = $122,000
    Port charges and Canal tolls   37,662
    Total $159,662

13′. Capacity lost
    14,400 tons per trip × 2.26   = 32,544
    Less gain because of Item 11

$$= \frac{3{,}000 \times 5.6}{6.5} \qquad\qquad \begin{array}{r}(2{,}585)\\ \hline 29{,}959\end{array}$$

14′. Equating rate $159,622/29,959   or $5.33 per ton delivered (U.S.M.C. minus 51.5%)

TABLE 5.16

ECONOMICS OF SPEED AND SUEZ TOLLS: RAS TANURA–ANTWERP ROUND TRIP THROUGH CANAL AT 14.5 KNOTS AND AROUND CAPE AT 10 KNOTS

1. Ras Tanura–Antwerp–Ras Tanura around Cape both ways = 22,540 miles
2. Ras Tanura–Antwerp–Ras Tanura through Suez both ways = 12,880 miles

	At 14.5 Knots	At 10 Knots
3. Days steaming per trip	37.0	93.9
4. Days in port plus 2 days for the Canal transit	5.0	3.0
5. Total	42.0	96.9
6. Number of trips per year (329 days)	7.86	3.4
7. Total number of steaming days per year	290.0	318.8
8. Total number of days in port and Canal per year	39.0	10.2
9. Bunkers per day, steaming (bbls)	300	150
10. Bunkers per day, in port and Canal	100	100
11. Total bunkers per year (in barrels)	90,900	48,840
12. Capacity in barrels occupied by bunkers per trip	11,600	14,365

13. Savings by reducing speed (bunkers loaded at half points)
    Bunkers   42,060 barrels or 6,500 tons approximately
    Ras Tanura   3,250 at $18.40   = $ 59,800
    Antwerp   3,250 at $26.25   85,310
      Total for bunkers $145,110
    Port charges (7.86 − 3.4) × $3,500   15,610
    Canal tolls   7.86 × $13,200   103,752
      Total savings $264,472

14. Loss in capacity in tons
    15,300 tons per trip × 4.46   = 68,238
    Plus loss because of Item 12   732
                                                68,970 tons

15. Equating rate $264,472/68,970   or $3.83/ton delivered
    (U.S.M.C. minus 64.86%)

13'. Savings by reducing speed if all bunkers are loaded at the point of minimum bunker cost
    Bunkers 6,500 × 18.40   = $119,600
    Port charges and Canal tolls   119,362
      Total savings $238,962

14'. Capacity lost
    14,400 tons per trip × 4.26   = 61,344 tons
    Plus loss because of Item 12   1,464
      Total loss in tons   62,808

15'. Equating rate = $238,962/62,808   or $3.80/ton delivered
    (U.S.M.C. minus 65.14%)

Source of Data: Marine Brokerage Company, Inc.

the Cape route would be justified only if the rate is lower than U.S.M.C. minus 64.86% ($3.83 per ton delivered), assuming bunker prices of $18.40 and $26.25 at Ras Tanura and Antwerp, respectively. If all the bunkers are loaded at Ras Tanura, the critical spot rate further drops to U.S.M.C. minus 65.14%, or $3.80 per ton of oil delivered. The evidence demonstrates that the Suez waterway is the most economical route for the vessel that can traverse it, even under excessively depressed market conditions.

Slowdowns have not actually affected tankship capacity by between 25% and 27%, as we might calculate from the data presented in the exhibits. The probable reason is that the low spot rates were caused by excess tonnage in the possession of the charterers in the first place, and under such circumstances the alternatives confronting the oil companies are to slow down their vessels or to tie them up. If the outlook for excessively depressed rates covers an extended time period, then it will be more economical for the operators to lay up their vessels and thus save wages and subsistence costs, which in the case of the oil companies are higher than for the rest of the industry.[123] What is more, it is doubtful whether many operators have considered the economics of speed, although, at the rates prevailing since April 1957, they would have been wise to do so. The operators may appear irrational in neglecting the economics of speed while at the same time worrying about size, but there are possible reasons for this asymmetry. Size comparison and related decisions are *ad hoc* decisions made only once over the life of a vessel. In contrast, speed calculations must be made continuously because, as we have seen, they are a function of distance, spot rates, and bunker prices among other factors. For this reason, the operators may be reluctant to reconsider the matter of speed often, especially if one considers the cost of rescheduling.[124] Another possible reason may lie in the cost, to the oil companies, of surplus bunkers which they themselves produce.

It is believed that slowdowns affect only an insignificant part of the total fleet and that for all practical purposes their impact on total capacity may not be greater than that of frictional unemployment. The Transportation Coordination Department of the Standard Oil Company of New Jersey has estimated that the impact of these slowdowns has

---

[123] Even under these circumstances, however, the oil companies will benefit if they slow down the vessels on time charter, tie up all vessels whose out-of-pocket cost minus relevant lay-up costs is higher than the market rate, and satisfy any further needs through spot charters.

[124] The majority of large operators (especially the oil companies) have electronic data-processing installations. Consequently, a simple program can take care of such calculations whenever necessary.

CHAPTER FIVE

resulted in what they call a "hidden surplus" of about 5% of the operating fleet.[125] Although the supply schedule has, on the surface, remained unchanged as a result of these slowdowns, the demand schedule has been shifted effectively to the right.[126] The result has been an apparent but inflated growth in the operating petroleum fleet of the world of 9.9% in 1957, and of approximately 6% in 1958. As the rates increase, this "hidden surplus" is eliminated, thus causing leftward shifts in demand and arresting the recovery of rates. In the meantime, some owners, encouraged by the temporary recovery of rates, may put tie-ups into operation, further depressing the rates, causing slowdowns again, and so on until the whole fleet returns to operation at full capacity. These short-term dynamic (circular) considerations will cause rate fluctuations under depressed conditions, but such fluctuations are expected to be confined within very narrow limits because of the quick response from the operatives.

CONVERSIONS

The conversions are quantitatively insignificant. Because the tankers are extremely specialized vessels, the cost of conversion is relatively high. Only under very remunerative conditions in other markets such as grain, ore, and molasses will transfers occur, and even in these cases, because of the characteristics of these markets, only the smallest and most uneconomic vessels will normally be lost to other types of trade. This is clearly shown in the data now presented. Moreover, a loss of an average of fifteen T-2's per year from a market of over 3,000 T-2's is quite unimportant.

Year	No.	Conversions T-2 Equivalent	Average Size in T-2 Equivalent
1954	22	10.4	.46
1955	47	29.8	.63
1956	26	18.0	.69
1957	6	3.3	.55

[125] We believe that slowdowns should have caused a much greater impact on the operating fleet. Since this phenomenon occurs at a time when the relevant supply schedule is almost horizontal, because of the excessive surplus, its impact on rates will be transitory.

[126] Given the shapes of the supply and demand schedules, whether the manifestation of an impact appears as a shift in demand instead of supply, or vice versa, makes little difference. Because of the operations of the oil companies, some people may even consider that the acquisition of company vessels causes leftward shifts in demand rather than rightward shifts in supply.

REPAIRS

Finally, we come to the extended repairs and the tie-ups. According to the experts, the average duration of the yearly repairs is twenty-five to thirty days for vessels using United States repair yards, and thirty-five to forty days for vessels using foreign yards. It appears that the difference between the average repair periods is primarily due to variations in productivity rather than to the type of repairs performed. These figures, if accurate, will place the over-all average around thirty-five days because the majority of vessels use European and other foreign yards.

The aforementioned figures were provided by people connected with the oil companies and may be somewhat inflated if based only on their own experience. The oil companies are known to be usually more meticulous, but in our opinion many of the independents save on idle repair time (off hire) not through carelessness but mainly as a result of considerable preparatory as well as ancillary work performed by the crew while the vessel is on hire at ports. Characteristic are two statements: one was made by the president of the tankship subsidiary of a large oil company who expressed satisfaction at having his vessels operate 329 days a year on the average; while his counterpart in an independent company stated that if the average idleness of his vessels because of repairs exceeded fifteen days per year, he felt that they were not doing so well.

If we accept a mean value of, let us say, 35 days around which the duration of repairs is normally distributed,[127] we shall find the probability very small indeed that repairs will stretch over 60 days. Table 5.17, however, shows that the capacity of vessels under repairs more than sixty days sometimes even exceeds that of the vessels under repairs between thirty and sixty days. This fact may indicate that repairs are extended during periods of uncertainty and thus serve as an intermediary step to lay-up.

In general, we can say that the *level* of repairs, expressed as a percentage of the operating fleet including vessels under repairs, depends upon

1. The efficiency or technology of repair yards, and
2. The spot rate existing at the time.

Developments in the technology of ship repairing will reduce the

---

[127] The distribution is expected to be skewed if not multimodal because the age and size of the existing fleet are not normally distributed, but we have no data to test any hypothesis.

CHAPTER FIVE

TABLE 5.17

REPAIRS AND TIE-UPS: CAPACITY LOST IN T-2 EQUIVALENT

	Under 30 Days	30–60 Days	Over 60 Days	Tie-ups
January 1, 1955		30.0	25.5	72.2
February		30.0	30.2	59.3
March		26.9	35.4	54.0
April		50.8	26.8	55.8
May		78.5	30.5	55.4
June		81.7	34.9	59.9
July		69.8	55.8	57.0
August		65.1	65.3	49.5
September		56.8	71.8	43.8
October		46.4	66.6	36.0
November		45.4	53.8	31.1
December		45.6	43.6	21.5
Yearly Average: T-2's		52.25	45.0	
Per Cent of Total Operating Capacity		2.4%	2.1%	
January 1, 1956		44.6	33.2	17.0
February		44.7	31.2	14.4
March		55.2	30.1	11.4
April		62.5	34.4	8.9
May		88.3	32.3	9.9
June		65.0	46.3	8.7
July		71.7	43.3	6.9
August		77.2	41.5	6.9
September		84.0	45.9	6.4
October		70.5	44.4	5.3
November		65.2	33.1	5.0
December		33.6	40.8	4.6
Yearly Average: T-2's		63.5	38.1	
Per Cent of Total Operating Capacity		2.85%	1.7%	
January 1, 1957		35.1	27.8	2.3
February		48.2	17.7	.8
March		39.8	24.9	.1
April		71.3	29.2	1.4
May		106.4	26.1	4.1
June		100.4	46.0	8.7
July		96.1	43.4	21.6
August		88.6	50.0	35.7
September		115.0	41.3	64.6
October		102.9	45.0	88.8
November		86.8	37.3	109.1
December		63.9	33.1	124.8
Yearly Average: T-2's		79.5	35.2	
Per Cent of Total Operating Capacity		3.25%	1.43%	

TABLE 5.17 (Continued)

	Under 30 Days	30–60 Days	Over 60 Days	Tie-ups
January 1, 1958	70.1	48.9	24.8	166.7
February	77.6	49.0	19.4	203.2
March	68.3	52.4	17.0	229.3
April	67.0	68.1	12.6	283.7
May	77.6	87.3	10.1	334.6
June	102.2	74.6	12.7	350.2
July	94.2	73.9	15.8	335.3
August	92.4	81.8	16.7	286.8
September	107.4	69.7	18.8	272.4
October	100.6	69.6	21.3	256.0
November				263.0
December				233.0
Yearly Average: T-2's	85.7	67.5	16.9	
Per Cent of Total Operating Capacity	3.35%	2.64%	0.66%	

Source of Data: Transportation Coordination Department, Standard Oil Company, New Jersey.

average time required for yearly repairs, thus causing a downward trend in capacity lost. As for the spot rate, it will, we believe, affect the level of repairs by inducing ship owners to postpone, hasten, or prolong repairs. If the rates are high, the owners, especially the oil companies, will even be willing to pay overtime in order to have the repairs finished early. The opposite will occur in the case of the independents if their expectations are elastic. Under declining rates, the owners who have excess capacity will at first attempt to perform any necessary repairs while waiting for the rates to improve. If the rates improve and employment is secured, repairs are finished and the vessels go into operation; but if the rates continue to be low, the repairs are extended as long as hope for a reversal exists. Once such hope is lost, the vessels are tied up.[128]

These arguments do not apply in the case of vessels under long-term contractual agreements. Such contracts provide that the "owners under-

[128] Tying up vessels is rather costly, and many of the costs, such as preparatory repairs and "bottom" painting, launches, and rental of river or other basins, do not vary proportionately with the number of days the vessels are tied up. Statistics on costs of lay-up are very spotty, and even those who are in a position to know profess ignorance. Figures were given — for a year's tie-up and reactivation — ranging from $20,000 per vessel to $350,000. The U.S. Maritime Administration spent $380,000 per vessel to activate eight T-2's during the fall of 1956, but these vessels were in permanent lay-up for at least three years before activation. According to the same source, reactivation costs without repairs are estimated at $60,000 per T-2. We shall return to the cost of tie-up later.

take that nine months after the vessel was last dry-docked and at the expiry thereafter of each nine months of continuous use under the charter they will put the vessel in dry dock and clean and paint her bottom at their expense as soon . . . thereafter as Charterers place the vessel at Owners' disposal. . . ." [129] It is natural for the charterers to prolong the nine-month period if employment exists, but to take advantage of this provision exactly at the end of the nine months if the ships are idle, because the time taken for repairs is "off hire," and added on to the end of the period covered by the contract. At most, then, the rates will normally affect the incidence but not the duration of repairs of vessels chartered on long term.[130]

The incidence of repairs is also affected by seasonal fluctuations in the trade. Since the late fall and the winter months are the busiest for fuel-oil and spring gasoline stock-up, and the summer months the least busy, repairs are scheduled for the summer and early fall. Hence, the number of repairs is expected to increase in periods of low rates and in the summer, and, conversely, to reach the bottom during periods of high rates and during the winter months of each year.

In summary, we would expect to find that technology and spot rates affect the level of repairs. The impact of technology will cover the total fleet, but the spot rates will affect the duration of repairs of the oil company vessels and those of the independents trading in the spot market. The spot rate will also affect the incidence of repairs, but not the duration, for vessels on long-term charter, as also will the seasonality of demand. We do, however, expect the seasonality of demand to affect the spot rate, with the result that we may not be able to distinguish very clearly between these two impacts. It may also be very difficult to distinguish the impact of spot rates on the level (duration) from that on the incidence of repairs.

To prove our contentions, we must have information on the distribution of vessels by repair intervals. Unfortunately, however, there are no data indicating the percentages of the total fleet (in T-2 equivalents) that usually complete the yearly repairs in less than 30 days, between 30 and 60 days, and over 60 days. The only consistent information available for the total period 1949–1958 is in terms of capacity idling over 30 days for either repairs or tie-ups. By subtracting the known tie-ups we can determine the total capacity idle for repairs extending

[129] Bes, J., *Tanker Chartering and Management,* C. De Boer, Jr., Amsterdam, 1956, p. 113.

[130] There is the case of an oil company which in late 1956 asked the owner of some of the vessels it operated under charter to forgo "off-hire" repairs and continue the vessels on charter pay. Necessary repairs were performed during port calls and dry-docking was postponed.

over 30 days. But this is not sufficient because, as we have previously mentioned, the idle capacity because of repairs requiring less than 30 days is thus included in the "working petroleum fleet." Since we have information only for 1958 concerning repairs of 30 days and under, we shall use the 1958 data in our attempts to resolve the issues confronting us.

U.S. Maritime Administration data show that approximately 50% *of all capacity lost* in 1958 was for repairs of less than 30 days, 40% for repairs of between 30 and 60 days, and 10% for repairs extending beyond 60 days. If we now assume that vessel sizes are uniformly distributed between the repair intervals,[131] the relationships between total capacity (number of vessels of uniform size) repairing under 30 days, between 30 and 60 days, and over 60 days must be proportional to 50:18:2.7, or 70.7% of total versus 25.5% versus 3.8%. Multiplying these percentages by mid-values of 20,[132] 45, and 75 days, we arrive at an estimated average repair period of 28.5 days, which seems to be more realistic than that assumed by the oil companies. If we assume a mid-value of 15 for the first interval, the average repair period becomes 25.2 days per year.

For the year 1958 itself, we have all the information available and can check directly. The data in Table 5.17 show

Repair Interval	% of Yearly Capacity Lost	Average Days per Year for Fleet
Under 30 days	3.35	12.2
30–60 days	2.64	9.6
Over 60 days	0.66	2.4
Total	6.65	24.2

An average, then, of 24.2 days of each vessel's yearly capacity was lost to repairs in 1958, which is very close to the time duration we found earlier by assuming uniform repair intervals. (In our subsequent discussion we shall use, whenever the calculations necessitate, 25 days as representative of the average duration for repairs for the years 1954–1958.)

---

[131] We may be assuming too much here, because the newer vessels require fewer repairs and the largest vessels are the newest. However, the duration of repairs and size are positively correlated even if not directly proportional. Inasmuch as these two factors offset each other, our assumption will not falsify reality.

[132] The mid-value here is intentionally increased because for all practical purposes no vessel is expected to spend less than 10 days for repairs. One case of 8 days is known by the industry, and this occurred at the height of the Suez crisis. The fact, however, that the range is confined between 10 and 30 days does not necessarily preclude skewness in the distribution within the interval.

Of course, 1958 was a year of extensive tie-ups, or a period of "certainty" as far as the future was concerned, which may mean that some owners chose not to repair their vessels before tie-up. To the extent, however, that our percentages are in terms of non-tied-up capacity, this discrepancy is for the most part corrected. Furthermore, not many operators will neglect the *necessary* repairs of their vessels, because such negligence will more than catch up with them when the vessel is once more readied for operation. It is expected, nevertheless, that the decision to tie up will affect repairs of over 30 days duration by eliminating all repairs in lieu of tie-up and possibly cutting down some repairs of over 30 days that are necessary only for vessels expected to be in operation.

Table 5.18 shows that the percentage of the non-tied-up fleet capacity

TABLE 5.18

CAPACITY LOST DUE TO REPAIRS

Year	Capacity Lost Due to Repairs of Over 30 Days in T-2 Equiv.	Percentage of Non-Tied-up Fleet Capacity	Av. No. of Days Capacity Lost for Repairs of Over 30 Days	Tie-ups Yearly Average as % of Total Fleet	Av. Rate per 1,000 Ton-Miles
1949	116.9	10.6	38.6	3	1.12
1950	76.6	6.2	22.6	1	1.52
1951	69.5	5.1	18.6	0	3.04
1952	85.5	6.0	22.0	0	2.35
1953	65.8	4.3	15.7	3	.94
1954	72.0	4.1	15.0	6	.89
1955	97.3	4.5	16.4	2	1.32
1956	101.6	4.6	16.8	0	2.44
1957	114.7	4.7	17.2	1	1.52
1958	84.4	3.3	12.0	9	.68

Source: Transportation Coordination Department, Standard Oil Company, New Jersey.
For rates, see Table 5.12.

lost because of repairs extending over 30 days is definitely, but not uniformly, declining. We chose here to show yearly data so that we might overcome the impact of seasonal periodicity, which undoubtedly must affect repairs, in the oil trade. There is some evidence that repairs are "inflated" during some years, especially the years immediately preceding those of extensive tie-ups, but the evidence that this is due to procrastination of the tie-ups is inconclusive. It may be that the post-Korean War trend toward lower figures indicates more efficient utilization of repair time, and the year-to-year variability may be indicative only of "ability to pay" for repairs. Whatever the reason, the difference between the capacity lost in 1949 and that lost in 1958 is quite significant, especially for long-run supply schedules as inelastic as those of tankers.

Because we are dealing with movements that are affected by time lags, expectations, costs, and many qualitative factors, we cannot rely on yearly figures alone for our analysis of repair data, but must also look into monthly movements. Figure 5.14 shows the plot of repairs of 30 to 60 days, 60 days and over, tie-ups, and (for 1958) repairs of under 30 days. We observe in this figure a consistent trend toward lower capacity losses because of repairs extending over 60 days, which may be the result of efficiency; but except for this and a possible upward trend in repairs of 30 to 60 days, the data do not help us in any conclusive way. The upward trend in repairs of 30 to 60 days is possibly due to "repairs in lieu of tie-up," because it occurs in the middle part of 1957 just before extensive tie-ups take place. Note how later on in 1957 the repairs of 30 to 60 days and especially those of over sixty days decrease extensively as tie-ups increase. The peak reached in June 1955 may be due to a combination of (*a*) vessels deactivated (note that the tie-ups decrease substantially) and (*b*) seasonal repairs.

To study the movements in total idle capacity and to observe the

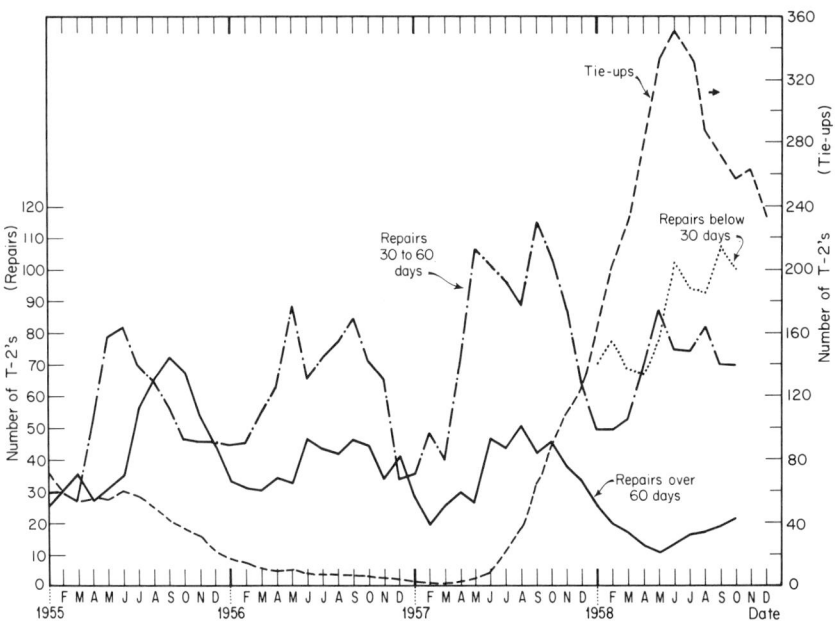

Figure 5.14. Plot of vessels, in T-2 equivalent, idle for repairs of below thirty days, between thirty and sixty days, and over sixty days, and tie-ups, 1955–1958.

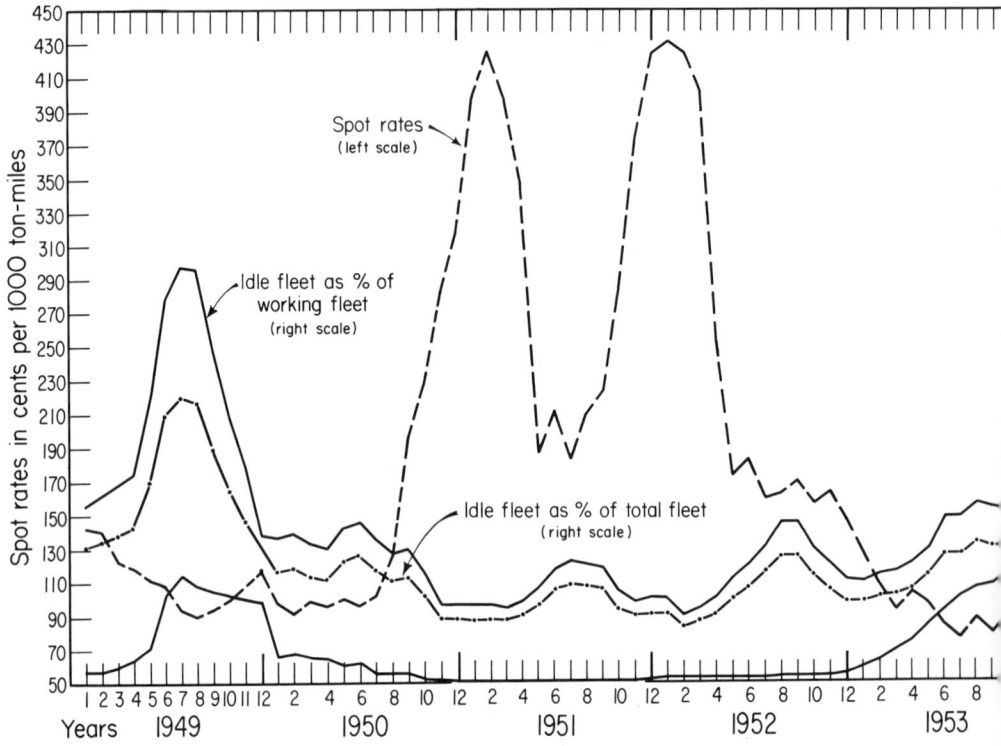

Figure 5.15. Time series of idle vessels

impact of seasonal trade on repairs, we now turn to Figure 5.15. The term "idle" appearing here indicates all capacity idle for thirty or more days for repair and tie-up. It is evident from the exhibit that the level of repairs is not constant and that it is affected by rates. The presence of technological impacts, even though not very vivid, can be inferred from the levels reached by the idle fleet during the two periods of record rates, namely the Korean conflict and the Suez crisis. Although the lowest point reached during the former period was 3.2% of the total fleet, the corresponding figure during the Suez crisis was 2.4%. As we have seen in Table 5.18, there is a definite downward trend in the percentage of capacity idle due to repairs of over 30 days. Even if we assume that changes in technology — or imitation by some countries of the technology of others — chiefly affect the longer repairs, the observed trend will also be present in the total sum of all repairs.

Figure 5.15 further shows that *within any one year* there is a periodicity in idle capacity, and gives evidence that this periodicity can be attributed to repairs regardless of movements in tie-ups. It is evident that the short-term rate affects such periodicity. Also, to the extent that

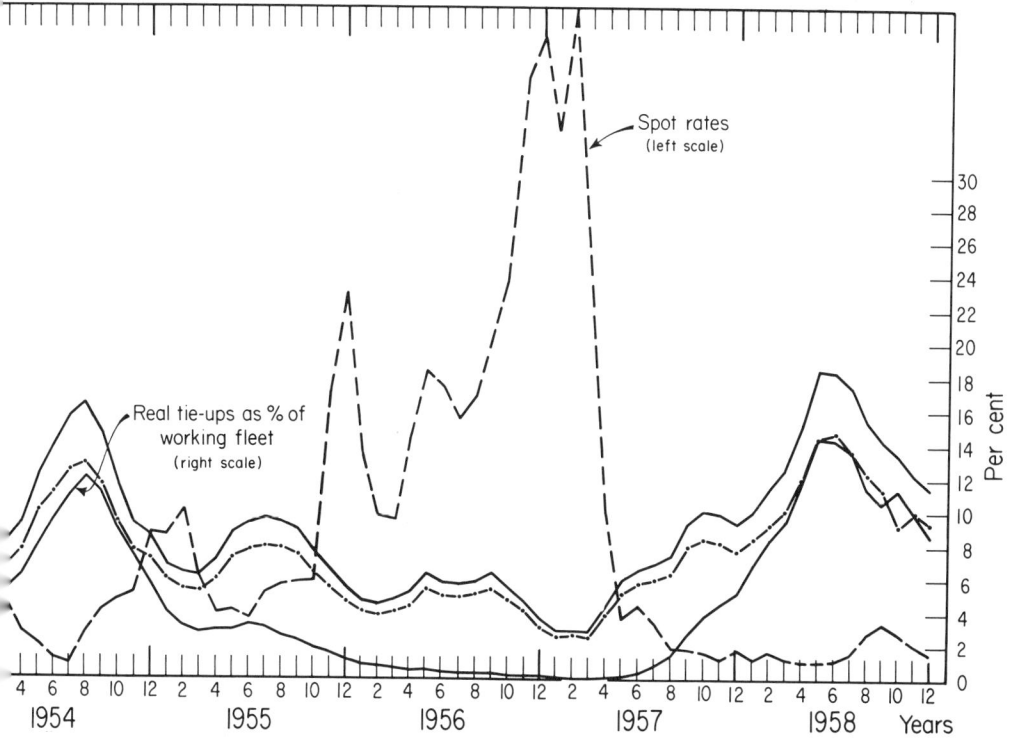

and index of spot rates, 1949–1958.

the rate movements lead those of idle capacity, we may conclude that the pattern observed in idle capacity is due to shifts in demand rather than to anticipations operating on the supply side. Such seasonal shifts in demand are expected and discounted by those operating in the tankship markets, and thus future expectations are not altered unless a deviation from the usual pattern occurs. Hence, the seasonal fluctuations in idle capacity because of repairs are equilibrating.

In summary, the incidence as well as the level of repairs is expected to vary with the spot rates. During periods of low rates, repairs are extended as long as uncertainty prevails. Once the near-future course of rates becomes clear, however, vessels are taken away from "extended repairs" and led to tie-up. That is why repairs tend to decrease once tie-ups start rising. The extent to which *necessary* repairs are inflated by *extended* repairs does not in our estimation exceed 1.5% of the non-tied-up capacity. A regular periodicity in repairs due to the seasonality of trade is observed, but both this variation and the impact of extended repairs seem to be equilibrating. Finally, the level of repairs seems to be affected also by the state of technology in ship repairing, as evidenced by the downward postwar trend in the average duration of repairs extending over 30 days.

TIE-UPS

We have pointed out earlier that during periods of low rates and uncertainty the vessel owners will attempt to keep their vessels afloat in the hope of finding remunerative employment for them. As long as this surplus tonnage is competing in the market, however, hopes for improvement in rates cannot materialize. Naturally, each owner hopes that all the others will tie up their vessels first; but as soon as some major owner loses hope and starts extensive tie-ups, all the rest take this as an indication of extended depression and, paradoxically, do likewise, even though they originally started with a "let someone else do it" attitude.

Before the stage of tie-ups, and while their expectations are inelastic, the owners as a first measure attempt some slowdowns and extended repairs until there is no doubt in their minds about the immediate future. During this period of uncertainty, the spot rates settle not at the normal average variable cost of operation, but even lower. Any owner who foresees a period of unemployment — if he insists on a rate that covers normal average variable costs — will undoubtedly adjust his refusal rate to reflect the average out-of-pocket idle costs over such a period of would-be idleness.

There are two types of potential idle costs: costs due to idleness in a state of operational readiness, and lay-up cost. The owners will stay in operational readiness only if employment is foreseen in the immediate future or if the tie-up costs are greater than the costs of idleness in operational readiness.

Clearly, an assumption that the cost of tie-up is greater than the cost of idleness in operational readiness, if correct, would imply negative rates and zero tie-ups. We can therefore dismiss it outright. We do expect, however, to find operators accepting any short-term rate that is greater than the variable operating cost minus the average out-of-pocket idle cost per unit of capacity involved.

In our attempts to collect data on tie-up costs, we were confronted with a very confusing array of irreconcilable figures. Many sources did not explain — presumably did not really know — the components of the figures they quoted. Such figures, therefore, could not be used at all. Only the tanker brokers[133] seemed to possess detailed data, and it

---

[133] Mainly, Marine Brokerage Co., Inc., and to a lesser degree, Cosmopolitan Transit Lines, both of New York.

is on their figures (after separating those relevant for economic decision making) that we shall base the following discussion.

The key role in our exposition inevitably will go to the marginal vessel. The out-of-pocket operating costs of such a vessel will be vital, because these costs enter into the determination of the point at which withdrawal from the market occurs. Besides, it is the operating cost of the marginal vessel that determines the upper limit, and hence the going rate in the market under conditions of firm (full-capacity) demand.

Now what are the characteristics of this marginal vessel? Does it have to be the smallest vessel in operation? In theory it may be, but not in practice, because there is no recontracting and no single market. For this reason the marginal unit for empirical research purposes must be important in terms of capacity. If not, its impact will be at most of a fleeting nature, not lasting long enough to be observed.

Luckily we do have such a unit in the tankship markets, the war-built T-2. Inasmuch as approximately 13% of total fleet capacity in 1959 is accounted for by such vessels, there is no doubt as to their importance in rate determination. In markets where the short-term supply schedules are as inelastic as those of tankships, the marginal unit is expected to define the range of the turning points; and because of its significant contribution to capacity, it will undoubtedly be found to play a very important part also in defining the lower limit of the rates.

It is evident that the smallest unemployed unit will be the first to withdraw from the market. Although with the existence of long-term contracts not all of the smallest vessels will be the first out of employment, certainly the smallest of the unemployed vessels will be laid up first. This much is indicated by Table 5.19 which traces the monthly developments in 1958. The average size of the vessels tied up increased steadily up to June; then, with the withdrawal from tie-up of the larger vessels, the average size dropped gradually from .95 T-2's to .82.

The marginal size of the vessels tied up presents an even better picture of how the sizes respond to rates and expectations. Up to June 1958, the vessels in tie-up were increasing, and the average size of tankers tied up increased from .93 to 2.20 T-2 equivalents in just four months. Then, with the seasonal repair absorbing some capacity, the short-term rates responded, causing a change in the expectations of some owners, who thought that this was a sign of revival and consequently reactivated their vessels. Unfortunately, the owners seemed to react faster to increases in rates, and to adopt a "wait and see" attitude on decreases. The reactivation, of course, created surplus tonnage in operating readiness, which pushed the rates from their best level for the year of 84 cents down to 66 cents per 1,000 ton-miles.

TABLE 5.19

AVERAGE SIZE OF LAID-UP VESSELS

Date	Av. Size of All Tied-up Vessels in T-2 Equiv.	Rate per 1,000 Ton-Miles	Av. Size of Vessels Tied up or Withdrawn from Tie-up	Adjusted for Vessels Withdrawn and Scrapped	Av. Size of Ships Scrapped
1-58	.70	63			
2-58	N.A.	67			
3-58	.86	62	.93	.93	None
4-58	.88	61	.96	.96	None
5-58	.91	61	1.52	1.52	.40
6-58	.95	61	2.20	2.20	.68
7-58	.90	65	(1.48)	(1.67)	.53
8-58	.89	78	(1.16)	(1.20)	.40
9-58	.85	84	(2.27)	(2.27)	None
10-58	.84	78	(1.06)	(1.06)	None
11-58	.85	71	(1.53)	(1.87)	.50
12-58	.82	66	(1.26)	(1.68)	.57

Source of Data: Transportation Coordination Department, Standard Oil Company, New Jersey.

The size of the vessels reactivated did not present any consistent pattern, with the exception that all these vessels were larger than a T-2. This may indicate that expectations were mixed among the owners of laid-up capacity, who reacted in different ways.

We have previously noticed in exhibits such as Figure 5.15 that tie-ups lag behind the rate movement during the downturn by several months. This reluctance is admittedly due in part to the uncertainty that sudden changes produce, but it also involves some practical economic considerations. We refer specifically to the cost of tie-ups.

As Table 5.20 shows, the greatest part of the tie-up cost is a fixed outlay of approximately $20,000. Depending on the distance between loading and unloading points, this is equivalent to 39–43 cents per 1,000 ton-miles, or between 23.2 and 27.3 U.S.M.C. points, if the tie-up period extends for only one month. Many owners may be tempted, as a result, to undercut the going rate, hoping that by the time their trip ends the market conditions will be better. This, however, is a vicious circle. Once rates are cut because of surplus tonnage, there is a tendency for the same process to be repeated, because at each new round of negotiations the initial tie-up costs make the refusal rate 23 to 27 U.S.M.C. points lower than it would have been otherwise. In fact, once an owner permits himself to enter such an agreement, the probability that he will repeat it is strong. It is like waiting for a bus rather than walking to a short-distance destination. The longer one waits, the greater the temptation to continue

TABLE 5.20

TIE-UP COSTS

Duration of Tie-up in Months	Incremental Cost	Cumulative* Total Cost in $	Approx. Cost in Cents per 1,000 Ton-Miles of Capacity Lost		Approximate U.S.M.C. Points	
			P.G./U.K.	US.G./N.Y.	P.G. to Europe	US.G./N.Y.
1	25,298	25,298	39.2	43.0	23.2	27.3
2	5,298	30,596	23.8	26.0	14.0	16.8
3	5,298	35,894	18.7	20.3	11.0	13.0
4	5,298	41,192	16.0	17.6	9.2	11.3
5	5,298	46,490	14.4	15.8	8.6	10.2
6	5,298	51,788	13.3	14.6	8.0	9.3
.	.	.	.	.	.	.
.	.	.	.	.	.	.
.	.	.	.	.	.	.
n	5,298	20,000 + (n × 5,298)	≈8.2†	≈9.1†	≈4.9†	≈5.9†

Source of Data: Marine Brokerage Company, New York; Cosmopolitan Transit Lines, New York; *U.S.M.C. Rate Schedule* (Robert T. Jones, Inc., New York).

* At the end of the tie-up period, if not shorter than six months or at the end of a year from the last bottom painting, whichever comes first, approximately $10,000–$12,000 are needed for painting. However, most of this cost ($10,000) would have been necessary had the vessel been in operation. In addition, a certain amount of preventive maintenance purely due to tie-up is necessary which may be done continuously or at the reactivation point. This cost is approximately $1,000 per month minimum, and is included here.

† For n large enough the values approach these figures asymptotically.

P.G. stands for Persian Gulf; U.K. for United Kingdom; US.G. for U.S. Gulf; N.Y. for New York.

waiting, only because one has waited that long already. Inherent in such behavior is the belief that, like the expected change in the gambler's luck, the revival of rates (the bus) will eventually arrive, and the longer the period of waiting the closer the point of reward.

The expectations of the owners who behave in the manner described in the previous paragraph are rate inelastic like those of all the other owners who may tie up their vessels during this period of uncertainty.[134] The difference in behavior is due to the fact that the duration of the uncertainty and expected unemployment is shorter in the eyes of those who stay in the market. The charters transacted at distress rates are of one voyage duration at a time and are accepted by the owners in lieu

[134] Because rental services are perishable (cannot be stored to be sold later), and a significant amount of out-of-pocket cost is involved in staying in readiness, there is a strong pressure on the owners either to accept low rates or to tie up their vessels. Such behavior, therefore, may not necessarily be due to elastic expectations.

of tie-ups in the hope that market conditions will soon improve. Incidentally, once undercutting starts, there need not be many cuts before the rates reach the floor, nor does the system need many participants to operate. As long as there are just a few owners who are willing to remain in the market idle but in readiness, the existence of the larger vessels guarantees that market prices will eventually reach a level lower than the out-of-pocket minus the expected tie-up cost for most T-2 vessels.

It is indeed surprising, in view of the figures of Table 5.20 (if correct), that the owners do not withdraw their tonnage as soon as the rate falls below the out-of-pocket cost point. Why they wait months before they decide to tie up their vessels it is difficult to understand. Many of the voyages undertaken during depressed periods barely yield, as we shall see shortly, over out-of-pocket minus *initial* tie-up cost. The reason is that the expectations of most owners about employment at remunerative rates are inadvertently spoiled by those vessels whose contractual agreements begin a month or so later, by crew costs that some owners consider fixed or unavoidable, and by ships that are to be relocated. These latter vessels can afford to take virtually any rate as long as it is positive.

The behavior of the tanker owners and operators clearly indicates either that the data shown in Table 5.20 are wrong or that the owners overestimate the cost of tie-ups. If the data are correct, and if we may assume uncertainty over, let us say, a six-month period, no operator should accept any contracts at a rate below out-of-pocket cost less 10 U.S.M.C. points, because the average tie-up costs over a six-month period are between 8 and 9.3 U.S.M.C. points. However, many contracts for T-2's are negotiated at much lower rates.

Another possible explanation of the reluctance to tie up vessels may lie in prestige factors, hesitance to admit mistakes, and even some administrative costs of decision making (changing plans). This last, incidentally, was found, in visits with various people in the industry, to be a real consideration. Apparently, nonroutine decision making is painful, or at least bothersome, and many people would rather forgo profits than overcome their own reluctance, as well as that of their superiors, in order to act in time. This is especially true in the case of the oil companies, because of their cumbersome organizational structure.

To find the critical rates for the marginal vessel, we have calculated and presented in Table 5.21 the "break-even" point of a T-2 under foreign flag. The present cost, excluding minimum return on investment, appears to be $1.15 per 1,000 ton-miles for the Persian Gulf–Antwerp trip and $1.12 for the Maracaibo or Port Arthur–New York run.[135] Al-

---

[135] U.S. coastal trade is restricted to U.S.-flag vessels. Use of the foreign cost figures here is made only for comparative purposes.

TABLE 5.21

BREAK-EVEN POINT OF THE ASSUMED MARGINAL VESSEL (T-2)
(Italian Crew, Foreign Flag)

	Annual Cost	
Wages (40 men)	$ 76,336	
Seniority, Vacation Leave, Social Insurance	18,316	
Overtime	25,225	
Provisions at $1.75 per Man-Day	25,550	
Repatriation and Manning	15,000	
Insurance and Other Premiums	22,242	
Stores and Expendable Equipment	31,025	$213,694
Repairs and Maintenance		100,000
(1) Subtotal		$313,694
Miscellaneous and Off-Hire Costs	$ 10,000	
Hull and Machinery Marine Insurance	43,316	
War Risk Insurance	2,009	
Excess Liabilities Insurance	365	55,690
(2) Total before Fuel, Port Charges, Tolls, Depreciation, and Overhead		$369,384
Allocated Costs		
Management Overhead	$ 21,900	
Depreciation (20 Years Straight Line)	158,400	
Interest (5% on Average Investment)	79,200	259,500
(3) Total Excluding Fuel, Port Charges, Tolls		$628,884

Fuel, Port Charges, Canal Tolls	Persian Gulf–Antwerp	Maracaibo or Port Arthur–N.Y.
Fuel	$249,400	$224,455
Port Charges	27,510	52,000
Canal Tolls	103,752	0
(4) Total	$380,662	$276,455

(5) Out-of-Pocket Costs

	Persian Gulf–Antwerp	Maracaibo or Port Arthur–N.Y.
Subtotal (1)	$313,694	$313,694
Fuel, Port Charges, Tolls (3)	380,662	276,455
Total, Annual	$694,356	$590,149
(6) Total Tons Delivered, Annually	120,258	383,940
(7) (5)/(6)	$5.80	$1.54
or U.S.M.C. *minus*	47.0%[a]	46.0%[b]
or A.T.R.S. *minus*	48.4%	46.0%
per 1,000 Ton-Miles	$ .90	$ .89

CHAPTER FIVE

TABLE 5.21 (Continued)

		Persian Gulf–Antwerp	Maracaibo or Port Arthur–N.Y.
(8)	(3 + 4)/(6)	$8.43	$2.42
	or U.S.M.C. *minus*	22.6%[c]	17.3%[d]
	or per 1,000 Ton-Miles of Delivered Oil	$1.31	$1.28
(9)	Adjustment to Bring Repairs Down to 25 Days: U.S.M.C. Points	1.0[e]	1.0
(10)	Wages Adjustment U.S.M.C. Points	2.0[f]	2.3
(11)	Representative Full Cost Including Interest (Items 7, 8, 9) U.S.M.C. *minus*	25.6%	22.5%
	per 1,000 Ton-Miles of Oil Delivered	$1.26	$1.23
(12)	Representative Full Cost Excluding Interest U.S.M.C. *minus*	31.7%	29.8%
(13)	per 1,000 Ton-Miles	$1.15	$1.12

Source of Data: Marine Brokerage Company, Inc., Association of Ship Brokers and Agents, Inc.

[a] U.S.M.C. flat (100%) is $10.90 per ton delivered.
[b] U.S.M.C. flat (100%) is $2.85 per ton delivered.
[c] Overhead, 1.7 U.S.M.C. points; depreciation, 12.3 points; interest, 6.2 points; insurance, 4.3 points.
[d] Overhead, 2.0 U.S.M.C. points; depreciation, 14.4 points; interest, 7.2 points; insurance, 5.1 points.
[e] To bring the repairs down to what we found is the representative level.
[f] Italian wages are the second highest foreign wages. The adjustment of $25,000 per year brings wages closer to the foreign average.

though this cost may be the relevant one under conditions of full capacity,[136] it is the out-of-pocket cost that determines the withdrawal of the fleet under depressed market conditions.

The costs usually avoided when the vessel is in tie-up include wages, all the relevant costs associated with the crew, and repairs and maintenance due to operations. To cover these costs, a T-2 under foreign flag and with an Italian crew must receive $5.80 per ton for the Persian Gulf–Antwerp run and $1.54 per ton delivered for the Maracaibo or Port Arthur–New York trip, that is, approximately U.S.M.C. minus 47% and U.S.M.C. minus 46%, respectively, or $.90 per 1,000 ton-miles for the Persian Gulf employment and $.89 per 1,000 ton-miles for the Western Hemisphere trade.

Because 35–36 days idleness for repairs seems excessive[137] and because, furthermore, the wages received by Italian crews are the second

---

[136] The reader may remember that for the 1954–1958 period we have observed a turning point of expectations at around $1.10–1.30 per 1,000 ton-miles. See the discussion on "Spot Rates, Shipbuilding Costs, and Orders Placed — Empirical Observations."

[137] See the discussion on "Repairs."

highest foreign wages in the free world,[138] adjustments have been made to approach the median cost of a T-2. With these changes, the minimum rate required to cover the out-of-pocket costs of a T-2 is around U.S.M.C. minus 50%. This, however, is not the refusal rate, because the owners must consider the cost of tie-up. With the latter included, the theoretical lower limit of the refusal rate drops to around U.S.M.C. minus 73% for the Persian Gulf–Antwerp trip and approximately U.S.M.C. minus 77% for the Maracaibo or Port Arthur–New York trade.

One would not expect to observe *average* levels of this sort for an extended time period, for several reasons:

1. It does not seem logical that the owners will consider only one month's tie-up costs while negotiating for employment extending over several months. The round-trip distance, for example, between the Persian Gulf and most North European countries takes about one and a half months. Furthermore, as time goes by the owners may naturally consider a time duration greater than that of a trip.

2. The brokerage fees which are paid by the owner are approximately equivalent to 2% of the total "hire" involved.[139]

3. The owner must be offered some inducement, however small, to keep in operation.

The first consideration would increase the refusal rate by at least 10 to 12 U.S.M.C. points to reflect out-of-pocket cost of operation less two months' average tie-up cost, the second consideration by 2 points, and the third consideration by probably 3 to 5 points. As a result, the *average* lower limit of the refusal rate for a T-2 would be found around U.S.M.C. minus 60%, or around $.62 and $.68 per 1,000 ton-miles depending on the route.[140] This we shall call the "T-2 lay-up rate."

So much for the average. Let us again point out, however, that single transactions at lower rates (deviations from the averages) will occur because

1. Vessels which can fit a voyage in between re-employments may be willing to accept lower rates than those just specified, because their only out-of-

---

[138] French crews are the highest paid, see Metcalfe, James V., *Principles of Ocean Transportation,* Simmons-Boardman, New York, 1959, p. 281.

[139] During depressed periods these fees may go as high as 4.5 percentage points because of efforts by more than one broker to secure employment for a vessel.

[140] Notice that the U.S.M.C. scales are not equalized. Thus, the use of the U.S.M.C. scales without specification of the route or conversion to 1,000 ton-miles equivalent rate is very misleading. We have seen this from the results of Table 5.21 where the various approximations to the full cost of a T-2 varied by as much as 5.3 U.S.M.C. percentage points. We now notice also that U.S.M.C. minus 60% will give $.62 per 1,000 ton-miles for the Maracaibo or Port Arthur–New York route but $.68 for the Persian Gulf–Antwerp run.

CHAPTER FIVE

pocket costs under such circumstances are the cost of the fuel and the port charges. (The labor cost, which is unavoidable in cases such as this, is approximately equivalent to 16.6 U.S.M.C. points for the Persian Gulf run and 19.5 points for the U.S. trade.)[141]

2. Tankers on their way to a loading port or place of tie-up may accept a cargo at lower rates because in such a case their marginal cost is practically zero.

3. Many oil companies have crew employment policies such that the wages become in effect unavoidable. Whenever their surplus vessels appear in the market as "relet," therefore, they can afford to accept a lower rate than usual for the same reasons as given under the first consideration above.[142]

As for the average rates in the markets, we have said that the refusal cost of the T-2's will govern, because these vessels comprise such a significant percentage of the total capacity. In general, the rates would drop below the T-2 refusal rate only if the shifts in demand to the left and/or supply to the right create surpluses greater than the total capacity of vessels of T-2 size and smaller. Sometimes, however, due to the imperfections in the spot markets created by the long-term contractual agreements,[143] many supertankers may be seeking employment at the same time and may thus force the rates temporarily to a point below the T-2 critical rate. We do expect, however, to find that in general the prevailing rate is based on the T-2 refusal cost, in which case

---

[141] Even though fixtures indicating absolute wage fixities are not very common, some transactions for T-2's were concluded in 1958 around U.S.M.C. minus 70%–75% and even some at U.S.M.C. minus 80%. See, for example, the fixtures of *World Trade* reported the week ending January 31, 1958, and *Arabia Maru* reported the week ending May 1, 1958, both fixed at U.S.M.C. minus 80%. (Reported by Davies & Newman, Ltd., of London.) Both these vessels were "relets," and the rate agreed indicated a complete fixity of crew costs.

[142] The fact that the employment policies of the oil companies lower the refusal rate explains why, when beset by excess capacity, the oil companies prefer to tie up vessels that they have on long-term charter and operate their own, even though the latter may be less efficient than the former. The reason, let us repeat, is that the marginal cost of the chartered vessels is higher because of the crew costs. If a chartered vessel is tied up, any savings accruing to the owner because of such tie-up are returned to the charterer. Among these savings is the cost associated with the crew. The above may be behind the difference in the average age of the tie-up fleets of the independents and the oil companies. The average age of the ships tied up in December 1958 and belonging to the major independents was 11.0 years, while that for the oil company vessels was 14.7 years. Most of the tied-up vessels belonging to the independents were on long-term charter agreements with oil companies.

[143] Such imperfections allow T-2's to operate, when on long-term charter, while existing supertankers and new buildings of the supertanker size may be seeking employment at their effective marginal cost of around U.S.M.C. minus 70%–75%, or even be led to tie up.

it will not only cover the out-of-pocket cost of the supertankers but will also contribute toward their fixed costs.

We shall now turn to some empirical quantitative evidence on the relationship between rates and tie-ups. Even though the oil companies and the independents are motivated by somewhat different considerations in their decision to tie up vessels, this makes little difference from the practical point of view, in our estimation.

It is true that the oil companies in periods of surpluses will at first stop chartering[144] and will tie up their own vessels, or vessels chartered by them, only if their transportation needs are lower than the capacity at their disposal. Thus, the factors governing company tie-ups emanate from the transportation needs of the oil companies, and not from the level of short-term rates. However, to the extent to which oil companies can place their vessels in the spot market in cases of excess capacity if they find the rates remunerative, they will tie up vessels only under depressed rates.

Theoretically, because of the dual role of the oil companies, we may argue that the oil company tie-ups, unlike those of the independents, constitute an external factor independent of rates and are thus rate determining and not rate determined.[145] But really what difference does it make? Is it not, in the first instance, the existence of unemployed vessels that causes spot rates to drop? As previously pointed out, we are not only observing continuous movements along the supply and demand schedules in static terms; we are also witnessing shifts in such schedules. Does it matter whether such a situation was created by curtailment of the demand resulting from the withdrawal of the oil companies from the spot market, or by the failure of the demand to keep up with the new supply, or from a combination of both? Given the shape of the demand schedule (as affected by interperiod substitutions and with its "schizophrenic" tendencies at low rates), and the infinite elasticity of the short-term schedule below full capacity, it really makes no difference at all. The same results can be obtained under any hypothesis.

[144] This is only true at the beginning of the downturn. Once the depression has set in and caused company-owned vessels to be laid up, it may be found more advantageous to enter the spot market for short-term needs than to make outlays for reactivation. That is, as long as the spot rate is lower than the out-of-pocket cost of operation to the companies plus the net reactivation cost (including the cost of all "fixities" such as extended crew commitments that are marginal with the decision less the alternative tie-up costs) averaged over such short term, the companies will cover their short-term needs through the spot market. There is ample evidence that this is being done.

[145] Koopmans, op. cit., Section 7. He states, however, that "the conclusions drawn . . . would prove to be largely independent of the hypothesis adopted. . . ." p. 138.

154 CHAPTER FIVE

We have already observed, in conjunction with rates and orders placed, that in nonstatic terms there is a certain degree of circular interdependence between rates and the position of the demand schedule, indicating that rates do affect and are affected by shortages and surpluses.[146] Furthermore, the spot market continues to exist and in fact may be the only active market under depressed conditions, and the oil companies are free to enter the market with their excess tonnage. Thus, even though low rates are not a sufficient condition for company tie-ups, they are a necessary one.

The arguments presented above also apply in the case of the independents, because approximately 77% of the independent tonnage (approximately 51% of the world total) is at any moment of time operating outside the spot market on long-term charters to the oil companies. The impact of these charters is no different from that of the oil company needs for tonnage. That is, some vessels may still be employed, even though the rate is below the relative *normal* lay-up point, merely because they are either owned or controlled through charters by oil companies. However, the emphasis on the word *normal* implies that these vessels will be affected also by the spot rate and that their effective lay-up point may for particular reasons be lower than that of comparable vessels in the spot market.

How then are these theoretical imperfections expected to affect the tie-up schedules? Admittedly they will introduce imperfections by causing efficient vessels to be tied up while less efficient ones operate. Such imperfections, however, will not in any essential way impair the key role of the short-term rates in determining tie-ups, for the following reasons:

1. The larger vessels that have lower normal tie-up points will be typically found on long-term charters,[147] thus leaving the inefficient vessels in the spot market.

2. Approximately 15% of the world total capacity is operating in the spot market, and this quantity is more than enough to give us empirical evidence of the relationship between rates and tie-ups, especially since the range of the tonnage operating in the spot market varies from 20% under depressed market conditions to 8% during periods of strong demand.

---

[146] Under such circumstances — unless measured during periods of very swift rate movements — empirical indices of static elasticity are dangerously misleading. This is especially true in the case of demand schedules which are measured on the basis of quantities bought and sold, not demanded, at the various rates.

[147] There are several reasons for this: (*a*) the construction may have been initiated by a charter; (*b*) these are "specialized" vessels because of their size, and cannot be used without advance planning. As a result, in order to achieve the economies of such specialization, these vessels must be assigned to *continuous specialized* runs; (*c*) the opportunity cost of idleness in the case of large vessels is extensive and the owners do not wish to risk unemployment.

3. The company-owned capacity is affected by the spot rate because the spot market serves as an outlet for oil company surplus tonnage.

4. The provisions included in time charters give options to the charterers to lay up the chartered vessels, "in which case the hire provided for under this charter shall be reduced by the amount by which the Owners can reasonably reduce the expenditure otherwise falling upon them. . . ."[148] The expenditures that can be "reasonably reduced" are the wages and other costs associated with the crew, such as subsistence, bonuses, insurance, and some vessel costs such as stores (but not fuel for the engines).[149] In effect, the chartered vessels may be affected by the short-term rates as much as any other vessel, even though for different reasons. Their effective lay-up point may not be as high as that of vessels of comparable size operating in the spot market, but *it may be higher* than that of the company-owned vessels because of the costs associated with the crew.[150]

5. Because of the existence of a minimum quantity below which the demand does not fall (i.e., part of the demand schedule is determined independently of rates, and hence is infinitely inelastic in static terms), it is the "marginal" quantity that is of interest to us. Hence the capacity operating in the spot market will set the price.

For the reasons just expressed, no attempt will be made to separate the tie-ups into those coming from spot-market operations versus those under the control of the oil companies. Nor would the latter be further subdivided into company-owned vessels and those chartered on long term.

Figure 5.16 presents a scatter diagram of the vessels tied up (expressed in T-2 equivalents) versus the spot rates by months for the years 1949–1958. We do notice that there is an extensive range of rates over which tie-ups vary only slightly; then, at a rate of approximately $1.10–$1.20 per 1,000 ton-miles, withdrawals become heavier until finally the schedule becomes completely horizontal at around $.90 per 1,000 ton-miles. These observations are in complete agreement with our expectations that we based on purely theoretical considerations.

The quantitative relationship between tie-ups and rates is best expressed by

$$y \text{ (tie-ups)} = .1 + 41.1/x^2$$

The correlation coefficient was found to be .78 with a coefficient of determination of .6, which is a respectable relationship. The rate x is

---

[148] Bes, *op. cit.*, p. 112.

[149] For complete list see Bes, J., *Chartering Shipping Terms,* C. De Boer Jr., Amsterdam, Fourth Edition, 1956, p. 55.

[150] Koopmans' analysis was based on the premise that "The reduction in these items through the laying-up of the vessel does not, therefore, enter into the charterer's calculations," which is incorrect, unless the stipulations of time charters have changed since Koopmans' study, for which we have no evidence. See his *Tanker Freight Rates and Tankship Building, op. cit.,* p. 111.

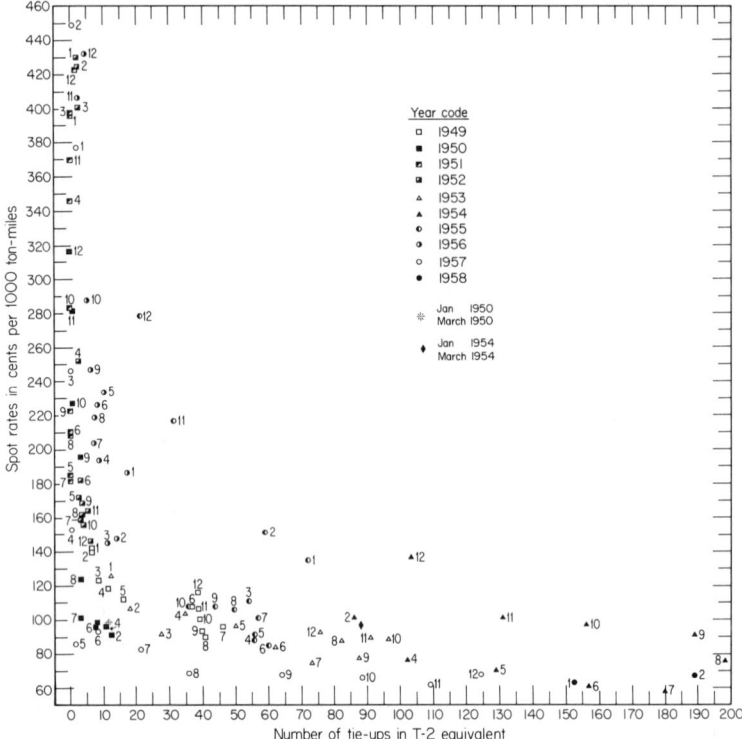

Figure 5.16. Scatter diagram of tie-ups in T-2 equivalent versus index of spot rates, 1949–1958 (monthly).

expressed in dollars per 1,000 ton-miles and is a weighted index of the average rates for the various runs. The method of computation of this rate is explained in Chapter 10, "Model of Long-Term Rates."

Equations of the same form were also fitted to the specific data of the various trades (Western versus Eastern Hemisphere) to check for differences between the various runs, and also between United States coastal and all other trades to observe the impact of rates on U.S.-flag versus foreign-flag vessels.[151] No significant differences were found, with most of the correlation coefficients being around .78, plus or minus five percentage points. The lowest correlation coefficient was .71 and applied to the following equation

$$y = 2.3 + 17.9/x^2$$

where y stands for the foreign tie-ups in T-2 equivalents and x for the Persian Gulf–United Kingdom rate per 1,000 ton-miles.

[151] With the exception of a protectionistic premium that affects the *level* of rates in U.S. tankship markets, there are no basic differences between the United States and global market operations and rate determination.

FACTORS AFFECTING SUPPLY OF TANKSHIPS   157

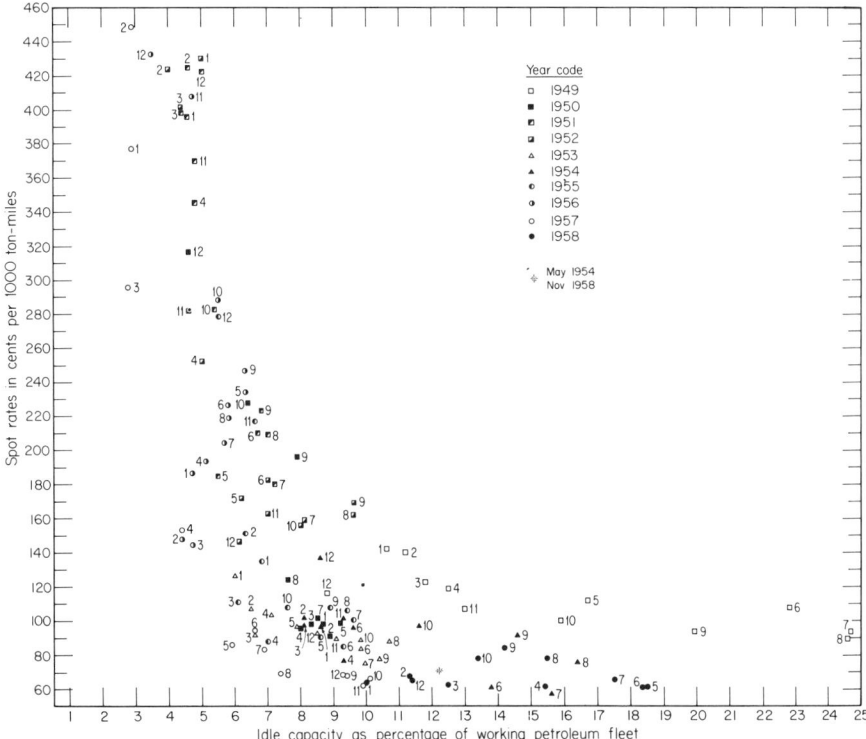

Figure 5.17. Scatter diagram of idle capacity as percentage of working petroleum fleet versus index of spot rates, 1949–1958 (monthly).

Empirical relationships based on tie-ups, expressed in absolute terms of T-2 equivalents over a period of ten years, may be somewhat misleading, because the industrial capacity has increased by over 250% during this period. Furthermore, as we have argued previously, part of the idleness for repairs is, for all practical purposes, in lieu of tie-ups. For these reasons, we have calculated the tonnage idling either for repairs of over thirty days[152] or for tie-ups, expressed it as a percentage of the working petroleum fleet and total tanker fleet capacity, and presented the results in Figures 5.17 and 5.18, respectively. As expected, the data show more cohesiveness, and the correlations between idle tonnage and rates are significantly strengthened. The strongest relationship between rates and idle tonnage occurs when the latter

---

[152] Admittedly there are some "repairs" of over thirty days which are legitimate. To the extent, however, that these approximately represent a constant percentage of capacity over time, their inclusion in the idle fleet will not falsify the results of our formulations, although it will push the lower part of the schedule to the right.

158   CHAPTER FIVE

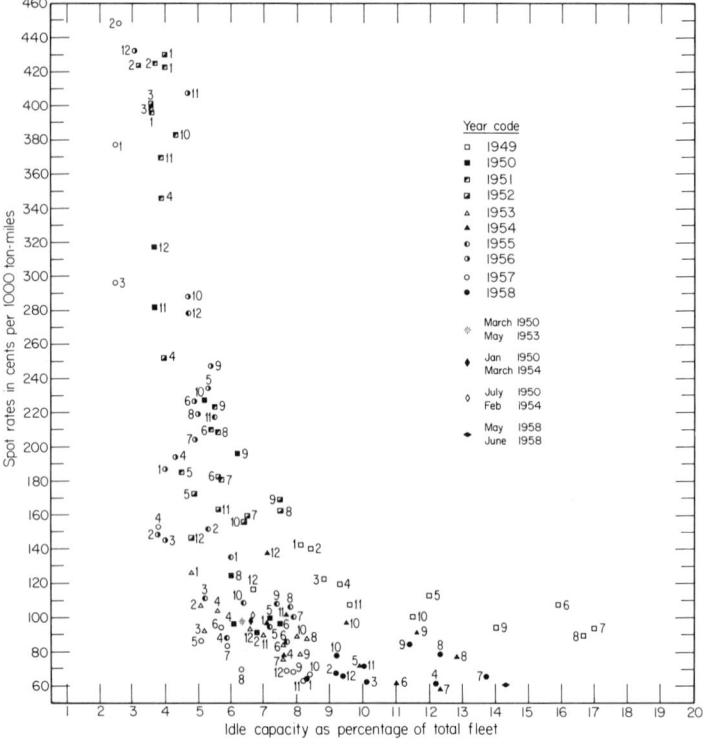

Figure 5.18. Scatter diagram of idle capacity as percentage of total fleet versus index of spot rates, 1949–1958 (monthly).

is taken as a percentage of total tankship capacity and is given by the equation

$$y = 3.25 + 2.515/x^2$$

with a coefficient of correlation of .912, showing that approximately 83% of the average variation in the percentage tie-ups is explained by the short-term rate.

The response of owners to the movement in rates is not "lightning-prompt." We have seen in Figure 5.15 that the tie-ups reached their peak about nine months after the rates had reached and remained relatively close to the bottom, even though the vessels in tie-up started responding in less than two months after the rate had reached the full cost of a T-2. Our arguments do not necessarily imply that tie-ups lag behind the rate movements by nine months. What we observe may be due chiefly to the infinite elasticity of the normal and short-term supply schedules below full capacity and to the infinite inelasticity of the short-term supply schedule above the critical full capacity point. This we believe is true, but one should expect some lag behind the rates because

1. After a swift somersault by the short-term rates, the owners would naturally undergo a period of uncertainty.

2. It takes some time, however short the duration may be, for the vessels to discharge their existing contractual obligations. For the single-voyage contracts this may be approximately a month to a month and a half (if we allow also for the lead time between contract and date of delivery). The remaining life of the long-term charters will not contribute to this time lag because, as we have previously explained, the considerations leading to the tying up of the chartered vessels, if these are surplus, are not different from those applying to vessels operating in the spot market.

3. Tie-ups are not always reported when they occur, and that is why many revisions are made later in the data. Such shifts between incidence and reporting, however, do not usually cause discrepancies of longer duration than a month.

To ascertain the existence of such short-term lags of the tie-ups behind the spot rates, we have taken a three-month running average of the idle tonnage (as a percentage of the total tanker capacity) and plotted it against rates. The results did not prove to be materially different from those presented in Figure 5.18.

Finally, a comment on the difference between the 1949 and 1958 data is in order. The 1949 observations appear to follow a course that indicates about 30 cents per 1,000 miles difference in the critical lay-up points, or approximately 20 U.S.M.C. points for the Maracaibo–New York run. This deviation is no doubt due to the change in the average size of the tanker fleet and the economies of scale that accrue from it.

6

The Short-Term Supply Schedule

Having completed our general discussion of the factors that affect the supply of tankships, we are now ready to concentrate on the short-term supply schedule. This discussion will be based for the most part on material explored in previous chapters, especially in the chapter dealing with rates and idle capacity.

The short-term supply schedule, by definition, depicts the various quantities of a commodity the producers are willing to supply at different prices, under conditions of limited freedom, for adjustments in capacity. All these possibilities refer in theory to the same point of time, that is, they are considered to exist simultaneously. Is it possible then to determine empirically the shape of such a schedule, especially since empirical observations refer to different points of time? The answer to the question just posed is, yes, though what one determines is an approximation to theoretical perfection.

We have explained that we expect the short-term supply schedule to be very inelastic beyond the full-capacity level and very elastic below. Because the notion of capacity and the permissible adjustments to such capacity are vital to the definition of the particular short-term schedule (out of the many possible schedules covering short-runs of different durations) we shall now refer once again to the role of the various factors affecting capacity. After that, we shall determine the elasticity of the supply schedule.

Factors Influencing Transportation Capacity

The transportation capacity available at any moment of time can be changed by any one or a combination of the following:

1. Deliveries and/or retirements.
2. The amount of ballasted traffic (and crosshauling).
3. The speed of existing vessels.
4. The inflow of whalers, ore carriers, and other special-purpose vessels into the oil trade.
5. The magnitude of idleness for repairs, loading, and unloading.
6. Tie-ups.

Because each of these factors will affect supply schedules of different time duration, we must at this point decide on our definition of "short-term." At the outset it is obvious that we can ill afford to define our short run as one extending over a period of time long enough to allow for new entry or permanent exit of capacity, in response to shifts in demand that have occurred during the *same* time period. On the other hand, we do not wish to revert to the notion of the shortest of all possible short runs, namely, the *market supply curve*. The latter schedule will be mostly vertical, with deviations from the vertical occurring because of pure speculation and not because of marginal costs. In between, we can find short runs during which the capacity is fixed both in quality and quantity, with the exception of new capacity that has been initiated by conditions independent of the present demand and prices.[1]

DELIVERIES AND/OR RETIREMENTS

To assume independence of *deliveries* from *current* demand and prices may sound somewhat illogical, in view of our previous proof of circular dependence, yet, if necessary, such a concession must be made if we are to approach everyday reality. What is more, we have found that rates and orders placed are positively related, but that deliveries — as a consequence of the circularity — follow exactly the opposite path. This implies that significant shifts in the supply schedules will occur during low rates but, because the elasticity of the schedules in this price region is infinite, the impact of deliveries will be harmlessly buried.[2]

---

[1] This is a deviation from the usual meaning of short term. See, for example, Marshall, Alfred, *Principles of Economics*, Eighth Edition, the Macmillan Co., Ltd., London, 1956, pp. 306–311; Bishop, R. L., *Unpublished Manuscript*, Book II, Chapter 1, pp. 21–22; and Viner's celebrated "Cost Curves and Supply Curves," reprinted in Viner, Jacob, *The Long View and the Short*, The Free Press, Glencoe, Illinois, 1958, p. 54.

[2] If deliveries change the size composition of the fleet extensively, then the supply schedule may shift downward and assume a more horizontal shape. For this to happen, however, the new vessels must go into the spot market. As we have seen, most vessels are built after long-term charter agreements have been obtained, so they may be identified. As a result we do not expect this to be a very critical consideration.

During periods of high rates, on the other hand, when shifts will impart elasticity to an otherwise infinitely inelastic schedule, deliveries will be relatively small and rather impotent. Furthermore, there are two more avenues that we can and will follow, to eliminate the impact of deliveries.

1. We shall assume that for each given rate there is a supply quantity equal to a fixed percentage of total capacity, regardless of any changes in the composition of the fleet. This is tantamount to assuming that the rightward shifts in total capacity are proportional to the changes in operating capacity.[3] We expect to find later that the assumptions on which the above is based are not exactly correct and that changes in the composition of the fleet will affect the short-term supply schedule mostly through the increase in average size and the consequent economies of scale. The manifestation of these impacts will be in the form of a wide range of values below the point of infinite inelasticity. That is, the turning points from elasticity to inelasticity will tend to gravitate downward, as will the lower limit of lay-up values.

2. To bring our definition of short term closer to the theoretical one, we plan to eliminate deliveries from our supply schedules. This will have to be a crude approximation, because during periods of surpluses there is no way of knowing whether the new ships replace existing ones, which will consequently have to be scrapped or laid-up, or whether the new vessels themselves become idle.

For the purpose of this approximation, we shall assume that during periods of surpluses the monthly tie-ups are inflated by an amount equivalent to the new deliveries during the month, and we shall reconstruct the supply schedules. No adjustment, however, will be made during periods of rising rates and tonnage shortages.

The arguments presented here concerning the new deliveries apply also in the case of retirements, but with the impact on the supply schedules reversed. As we have seen previously, however, the retirements are quantitatively insignificant and do not merit any special consideration.

So much for the deliveries and retirements. We shall now take the rest of the supply factors one by one, and see what adjustments we shall have to make to arrive at the short-term supply schedule.

BALLASTED TRAFFIC

The ballasted traffic does affect capacity significantly; however, geographical constraints and institutional factors limit the efficiency that

[3] Because the changes are proportional, any measure of elasticity that is based on total capacity will remain unchanged. This is, in effect, what Tjalling C. Koopmans assumed in his *Tanker Freight Rates and Tankship Building*, Haarlem, Netherlands, 1939, Section 6, pp. 59–105. This measure of elasticity is not correct; it should be based on operating and not total capacity. The discrepancy at high rates, however, is small because most of the fleet is operating.

can be achieved in this area. The independents are always attempting to cut down the distance of their ballasted trips, and sometimes succeed in doing so through contracts of affreightment.[4] According to the last report of the old Suez Canal Company,[5] southbound oil was only 2.8% of the northbound, indicating that roughly 97.2% of the tanker capacity operating in the Persian Gulf–Europe trade goes back to the loading point in ballast.

Unfortunately, we cannot determine the amount of total ballasted capacity utilization. The Suez Canal data are not representative of world-wide oil movements because the trip through the Canal is one of the voyages for which we least expect oil to substitute for ballast. We suspect that the greatest efficiency in this respect is achieved by vessels operating between the Persian Gulf and the United States East Coast. Instead of returning to the Persian Gulf in ballast, these vessels may proceed to Maracaibo to accept a load for Europe, thus utilizing part of their return capacity.

We do not believe that the total carrying capacity is affected to any great extent by reductions in ballasted traffic, for the following reasons:

1. Only the vessels operating in the spot market can contribute to such efficiency because presumably the tonnage under the control of the oil companies is always utilized in the most optimal way. Thus, only approximately 15% of the total world capacity is potentially involved.

2. The Persian Gulf–United States run at its peak was employing only 6.2% of the total tonnage. Consequently, if we assume uniformity in the charter-mix under which the fleet operates in the various runs, only 1% of the world fleet will be operating in the Persian Gulf–United States trade under spot-charter agreements. As a result the potential impact of the ballasted capacity utilization for this run is less than .5% of the total fleet.

Because the amount of capacity operating in the spot market varies inversely with the spot rates, we would expect more efficiency in ballasted traffic utilization during periods of low rates. Furthermore, it is during periods of depressed market conditions that the operators are hard pressed to make ends meet. During periods of high rates, it is more profitable for vessels to hurry back to the main loading ports than to waste valuable time at the unloading area attempting to find new cargo which may be unremunerative.[6]

[4] Under these agreements, the shipowner undertakes to carry a specified number of tons of oil between two ports over a certain time period, but he is usually free to use any vessel he wishes and also to time the deliveries within the specified period to his best advantage.

[5] *The Suez Canal,* S.O.P. Press, Cairo, 1956, p. 21. Also see their *Survey of the Future of the Suez Canal Company,* Ebasco Services, New York, 1957, p. II-2.

[6] The buyers, knowing that the vessels will have to go in ballast to the loading ports, naturally try to strike a bargain based on out-of-pocket costs.

OPERATING SPEED

The economics of speed have been explained under our discussion of slowdowns, and we pointed out that the cost of fuel enters into the determination of the level of speed in a vital way. The importance of fuel costs becomes even greater for higher-than-normal speeds, because the shaft horsepower — and hence fuel — required to propel a vessel varies proportionately with the increase in speed to the fourth power and over.[7] If the price of bunkers (fuel oil) increases with the increased activity, or through sympathetic pressure, then the use of speed-ups for the purpose of increasing capacity will undoubtedly soon be checked. Furthermore, if we exclude the tonnage that operates in the spot

TABLE 6.1

ANALYSIS OF DISPOSITION OF FOREIGN-FLAG COMMERCIAL PETROLEUM TANKER FLEET: JULY 1, 1954 TO OCTOBER 1, 1957

Date	Owned by Oil Companies	Time Charters	Consecutive-Voyage Charters	Single-Voyage Charters
7/1/54	46.362%	27.590%	11.002%	15.046%
10/1/54	44.762	28.469	11.150	15.619
1/1/55	44.053	27.427	9.124	19.396
4/1/55	44.155	26.645	9.163	20.037
7/1/55	44.254	27.364	8.968	19.414
10/1/55	44.542	29.126	9.548	16.784
1/1/56	43.809	28.578	10.632	16.981
4/1/56	44.005	30.118	10.913	14.964
7/1/56	43.337	29.630	11.586	15.447
10/1/56	43.086	29.626	14.061	13.227
1/1/57	42.732	31.286	14.154	11.828
4/1/57	42.268	31.213	15.512	11.007
7/1/57	41.595	33.184	16.461	8.760
10/1/57	41.234	33.320	16.944	8.502

Source of Data: Marine Transportation Department, Socony Mobil Oil Company, Inc.

markets, there is no empirical evidence that the oil companies increase the speed of their fleet when the rates are high. Given the ex post facto proof that when the rates are high the oil companies continue to draw upon the few vessels remaining in the spot market — while harboring

[7] Starting from 10 knots and a fuel consumption of 150 barrels per day, the speed of a T-2 can be increased by 45% to its normal 14.5 knots while the fuel consumption rises by 100% to 300 barrels per day. For a further increase of 1.5 knots, however, the fuel consumption increases to approximately 435 barrels per day.

surpluses — thus further stimulating the spot rates, we can confidently conclude that the speed of the fleet under the control of the oil companies does not change. After all, why should they speed up since in the short run they have surplus capacity?

In a study of the 25,000 or so transactions completed over the last twelve years, we have been unable to discover even a single relet on high rates, although surpluses exist. This indicates beyond any doubt that the chartering activity during periods of high rates is initiated by future expectations and not by short-term needs. How else can we explain the increase in long-term contracts during such periods (see Tables 6.1 and 6.2), the increase in lead times (between contract and delivery date), and the increase in contract durations?

TABLE 6.2

PERCENTAGE OF WORLD TANKER FLEET TRADING ON A "SPOT" BASIS

Date	Percentage	Date	Percentage
7/1/54	15.0	4/1/56	15.0
10/1/54	15.6	7/1/56	15.4
1/1/55	19.4	10/1/56	13.2
4/1/55	20.0	1/1/57	11.8
7/1/55	19.4	4/1/57	11.0
10/1/55	16.8	7/1/57	8.8
1/1/56	17.0		

Source of Data: Marine Transportation Department, Socony Mobil Oil Company, Inc.

Our conclusion, then, is that only the dwindling tonnage remaining in the spot market may be affected by speed-ups, but as it is such a small fraction of the total capacity, its influence, if any, will be very small — in the neighborhood of 1% at most.[8]

SHORT-RUN SUBSTITUTES

The total capacity of the specialized vessels (those used for whaling, carrying ore, molasses, vegetable oil, etc.) is not greater than 2% of the oil tankship capacity. Therefore, even if all these could enter freely into the oil trade, their impact would be limited. In addition to the long-term contractual commitments that will undoubtedly inhibit the movement of the specialized fleet, there is the problem of the cost of conversion.

[8] As a result of the Suez Canal crisis, the percentage of the world fleet operating in the spot market was only 8.8% on October 1, 1957. On April 1, 1955, it was 20%. See Tables 6.1 and 6.2.

It is doubtful that a capacity equal to even 1% of the total oil fleet capacity can be contributed by outside sources.

IDLENESS DUE TO REPAIRS, LOADING, AND UNLOADING

Repairs may be cut, and there is evidence that this has happened when rates have been high. Here again, however, the capacity involved, if we include improvements in technology, is not greater than 1%–1.5%. As for idle port time, it is quite expensive under any circumstances, and conscious efforts are made to eliminate it, regardless of rates. Beyond a certain point, however, the costs associated with *preparedness of the shore installations* become so prohibitive that it is unwise for anyone to attempt it.

So far, we have considered all the factors that contribute to the increase in capacity, and found that if we exclude deliveries, which from the theoretical point of view are an intermediate or long-run impact, the rest do not constitute any important source of short-term expansion. Utilization of ballasted traffic is more likely to appear under depressed or normal market conditions, and even in such cases its impact is not significant. Speed-ups are very expensive and, because of the consequences of elastic expectations, are not practiced. Conversions of other vessels into oil tankers cause shifts in the short-term schedules for which we must make adjustments. Luckily, however, the capacity flowing into the tankship market from this source is not expected to be even .5% of the total tanker capacity. Finally, we have said that repairs may be cut, and we expect that this cut will increase total capacity by approximately 1%–1.5% of total capacity. Such an impact will shift the vertical portion of the supply schedule to the right.

Our general conclusion, on the basis of the evidence uncovered, is that the short-term schedule for tankship services is extremely inelastic beyond the point of theoretical full capacity. (We shall postpone defining this "theoretical full capacity" until after we have finished our discussion on the factors that operate on the short-term supply schedule below full capacity.)

TIE-UPS

When rates are low and surpluses begin to appear, the unemployed vessels are forced out of the market. We have explained earlier how the various stages of idleness succeed each other, and shall not repeat the discussion here. Because of such withdrawals from the active market, the supply schedule assumes a slope; but on the basis of purely theoretical considerations the value of such a slope, below the turning point, is expected to be close to zero.

The elasticity of the lower part of the supply schedule is due mainly to the existence of a rather homogeneous marginal capacity of considerable magnitude. As of January 1, 1959, approximately 13% of the total carrying capacity was contributed by T-2's constructed during World War II. In addition, another 5.8% of the total capacity consisted of prewar vessels of 10,000 DWT. and over, but these vessels were used mainly for special trades such as cargo and products for markets that were not amenable to mass distribution. Consequently, the prewar tonnage, with the exception of periods of abnormally high rates, will be able to compete only in specialized segments of the total market. It is expected, however, that these vessels will enter into other areas of the market in periods of excess demand. Thus, at best, this tonnage will help define the region of unit elasticity of the supply schedule.

Once this special tonnage withdraws from the market, the rates are expected to reach very quickly the lower limit of the T-2 lay-up point, which we have previously defined and calculated as being between 62 and 68 cents per 1,000 ton-miles (depending on the route). When the rates go below, let us say, 70 cents per 1,000 ton-miles, massive withdrawal of these T-2's occurs, which renders the short-term supply schedule very elastic. If, on the other hand, the rates go slightly above 70 cents per 1,000 ton-miles, many of these vessels will be reactivated and thus arrest the recovery of rates. This process will be continued until demand, or expectations about future demand, absorb all the tonnage in tie-up.

We may ask what guarantees that a homogeneous marginal capacity of sufficient magnitude will always be available. Perpetual availability of such blocks of tonnage is clearly necessary to impart generality to our previous conclusions. Luckily there is such a guarantee in the cyclical movements of tankship building and the advance in technology, which together generate new favorite sizes with each new shipbuilding boom.

There are certainly other factors that contribute to the elasticity of the lower part of the short-term supply schedule, the most prominent being the marginal operating costs of vessels and the average tie-up costs. Because of the "time fixity" of most of the operating costs and the "size fixity" of most of the tie-up costs, the lay-up rate of vessels narrows and the marginal capacity is increased by the tonnage of neighboring sizes.

Definition of Capacity

If we define theoretical full capacity in terms of ton-miles of cargo carried and use an approximate 3% of the world total one-way carrying capacity for ballasted capacity utilization, we find that the feasible (economic) carrying capacity of the fleet on the basis of the 1958 data does not exceed 40.2% of the total. In other words, if we define as total capacity the aggregate ton-miles that a vessel can carry when steaming 365 days per year, we find that only 40.2% of this absolute is used. Repairs are expected to take away approximately 7% of the total, and port calls 15%,[9] thus leaving only 78%. Ballasted traffic will further reduce this by 37.8%, leaving 40.2% as the maximum usable capacity.

Because the average distance over which oil is carried does not remain constant, the usefulness of ton-miles of oil carried is somewhat limited as a measure of capacity. Taking, for example, the capacity of a T-2 operating between Maracaibo and New York versus the same vessel operating between the Persian Gulf and Antwerp, we find that the capacity differential is approximately 11%,[10] and in favor of the longer run. For a short-term schedule as sensitive as that of tankships, at or near full capacity, such a difference is statistically very significant. Furthermore, the entry and exit of vessels will cause shifts to a short-term schedule based on such a measure.

Instead of ton-miles we have decided to use the notion of "operating fleet as a percentage of the total fleet," and for the measurement of the elasticity of supply we shall use an index based on the "working petroleum fleet" rather than the total fleet, because such an index depicts changes in the level of employment more accurately.

The "operating fleet" is defined as the total fleet less the tie-ups and vessels idle for over thirty days. The reason we exclude vessels idle longer than thirty days is that we believe some idleness is in lieu of tie-ups. Ideally we should also have excluded some repairs of less than thirty days, because if repairs of over thirty days are inflated, surely those of less than thirty days must also be. However, with the exception of 1958, we do not have any data for such repairs, consequently we shall assume that all repairs of less than thirty days are essential.

Inherent in our definitions of capacity and the exclusion of extended repairs is the premise that normal idleness due to essential repairs lasting over thirty days is a constant percentage of capacity. This may not be exactly true in the long run because of changes in the size and age composition of the fleet, but we feel, nonetheless, that even in the long

---

[9] This percentage is based on the 1958 employment figures of the fleet and is likely to change with the geographical distribution of oil sources and markets. The longer the oil has to travel, the lower this lost capacity will be.

[10] The T-2 capacity for the Maracaibo–New York run is roughly 700,000,000 ton-miles, and for the Persian Gulf–Antwerp trade 775,000,000 ton-miles. The difference is due to the number of days spent in port.

run such an assumption is much less harmful than the acceptance of all *stated* repairs as *necessary* repairs. In the short run, which is the focus of our attention, the impact of such changes in the age and size composition of the fleet on the *extended* repairs will not cause perceptible changes. Any short-run impact on repairs of less than thirty days is reflected in the available capacity, by our inclusion of such repairs as part of the "operating fleet."

Exclusion of repairs of less than thirty days from the available capacity would imply either that these repairs are not a necessary part of readiness, an assumption which is not correct, or that they are a constant percentage of available capacity — in which case it will be of little consequence whether these repairs are included or excluded. So our decision was to include them in available capacity as an essential part of the operating fleet, realizing that such inclusion may introduce some error (which we cannot separate) caused by repairs of less than thirty days in lieu of tie-up. In trying to assess the quantitative significance of such an error we must realize that the probability for such occurrence is very small, especially in periods of high rates. Furthermore, the amount of repairs of less than thirty days at any moment of time may not exceed 4% of the total capacity, as can be seen in the 1958 data of Table 5.17. To summarize then, although our calculations include some elements of error their quantitative impact is insignificant even for a schedule as sensitive at high rates as the short-run supply schedule.

The "working petroleum fleet" differs from the "operating fleet" in that it excludes, in addition to tie-ups and repairs of over thirty days, government-owned vessels operating in the oil trade and special purpose vessels.[11]

The main disadvantage of our definitions of capacity is that these do not record the impact of speed-ups or the efficiency of utilization of the ballasted traffic. However, the contribution of these two factors to capacity is negligible, especially within the regions of sensitivity of the supply schedule.

The Supply Schedule

Figure 6.1 presents the scatter diagram of the monthly "operating fleet as a percentage of the total fleet" versus spot rate per 1,000 ton-miles. The striking feature of the exhibit is the inelasticity of the schedule for operating-fleet values of 95% and beyond. The critical rate seems to be around 90 cents per 1,000 ton-miles, which, as we have seen (cf.

---

[11] Those carrying molasses, vegetable oils, ores, and chemicals; and depot ships, lake tankers, etc.

170   CHAPTER SIX

Table 5.21), represents the out-of-pocket costs for a T-2. It is also very interesting that, below 70 cents per 1,000 ton-miles, the short-term schedule becomes infinitely elastic and the rate seems to be settling around 61 cents, which is very close to what we found as the refusal rate for a T-2.

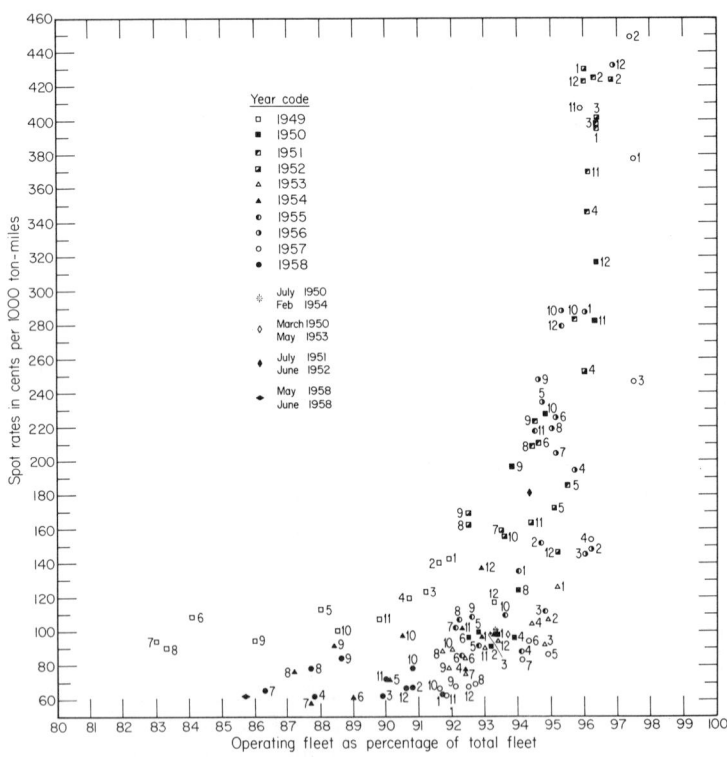

Figure 6.1. Scatter diagram of operating fleet as percentage of total fleet versus index of spot rates, 1949–1958 (monthly).

The upper part of the schedule possibly shows evidence of bending backward, but not in any pronounced fashion. If the schedule does actually bend backward, it may be exhibiting the impact of elastic expectations and speculation based on them.

By definition, the difference between 100% and each observation at the various rates represents the capacity idle because of tie-ups or for repairs of over thirty days.[12] Any change, therefore, in the average duration of repairs of over thirty days will cause shifts in the schedule. Evidently such a shift took place during 1957, and the schedule shows that

SHORT-TERM SUPPLY SCHEDULE 171

the average duration of repairs must have decreased by approximately five and a half days during the year.

Another point that merits mention is the width of the elastic part of the schedule. It indicates that the average lay-up rate of the marginal vessels has decreased over the ten-year period by no less than 30 cents per 1,000 ton-miles. Of course, not all the range (width) in values can be attributed to lower marginal costs. Some variation undoubtedly is due to expectations, as the 1949 data clearly show. Possibly this is an instance in which elastic *short-term* expectations caused early withdrawals, during both the downswing and the recovery of rates.

To obtain statistical measures of the elasticity of supply, we need data on the percentage changes in the employed capacity. The definition of working petroleum fleet is such that it gives us the best approximation of what we want. It excludes commercial vessels belonging to governments, which are not amenable to the calculus of marginal costs, as well as vessels operating in special trades that for all practical purposes constitute separate markets. Therefore, changes in the idle capacity expressed as a percentage of the working petroleum fleet will give us the best approximation to the numerator of the elasticity formula.

The short-term supply schedule, based on the working petroleum fleet, is shown in Figure 6.2. The general characteristics of this schedule are not different from those observed in Figure 6.1. Up to 92% of "capacity" the elasticity is infinite, but the schedule suddenly becomes unit elastic around 93%. Between 93.0% and 94.1% the index of elasticity is approximately .656; it changes quickly to 0.02 between 94.1% and 95.6%, and remains at approximately 0.02 up to 97.2%. From then on — beyond $2.50 per 1,000 ton-miles — the elasticity is zero.[13]

To avoid shifts in the supply schedules, which plague statistical analysis, we should collect data during periods of rather rapid price changes, preferably during downward movements. The latter will guarantee that there will be little interference from shifts in the observations caused by movements from the short-term to the intermediate schedules. We have such a period of ideally fast price changes starting with January 1957.

The 1957 and 1958 data, adjusted for deliveries and plotted against rates, are presented in Figure 6.3. In adjusting for deliveries, we assume

---

[12] In effect, the equation for the supply schedule is based on that of Figure 5.18: Operating Fleet $= 96.75 - 2.515/x^2$

[13] These results show that the "frictional unemployment" and any necessary repairs extending over thirty days do not exceed 3% of the total working petroleum fleet.

172   CHAPTER SIX

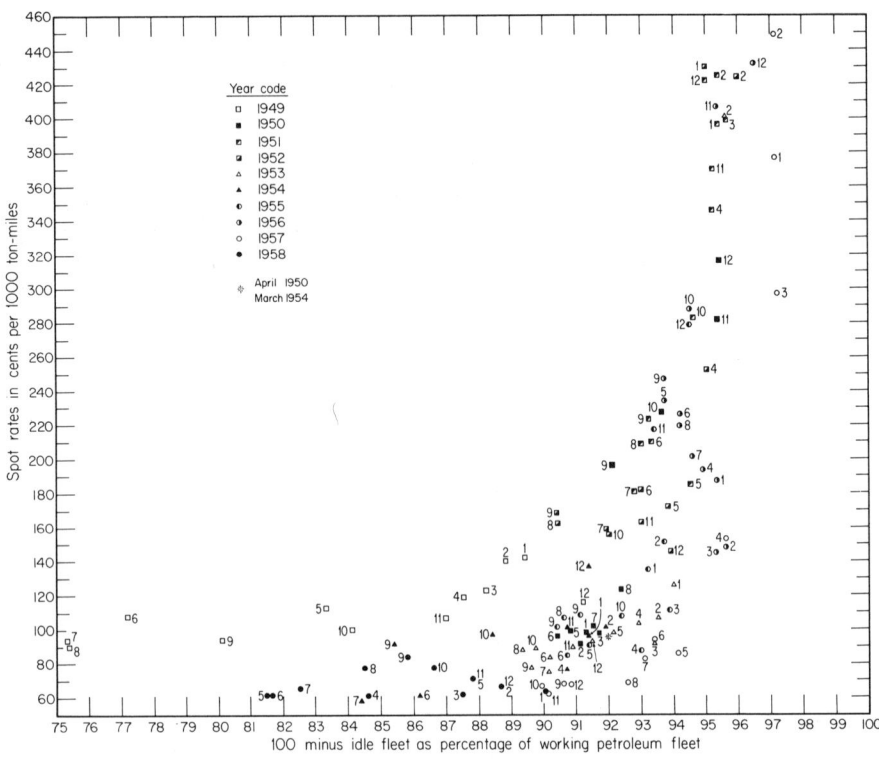

Figure 6.2. Scatter diagram of operating capacity based on working petroleum fleet versus index of spot rates, 1949–1958 (monthly).

that the new deliveries take employment away from the existing fleet, and therefore we subtract from the idle fleet an amount of tonnage equivalent to the capacity delivered. The results of this exhibit have really exceeded our best expectations; there is a perfect correspondence between the empirical schedule and what we expected to find on the basis of purely theoretical deductions. The encircled observations represent the result of temporary rate changes, during the months of August, September, and October of 1958 (see Figure 5.15) with consequent reactivation of tonnage. Because the expectations about demand were not sustained, the rates returned to their prior level but left more fleet actively seeking employment than before.[14] This occurred during the fall months, when as a result of winter inventory build-up seasonal shortages are usually observed, and so it set the stage for another performance similar to the one that took place about twelve months before. These surplus vessels remain in the market for a while seeking

[14] This is one of the causes of the flatness of the short-run supply schedule below the point of full capacity.

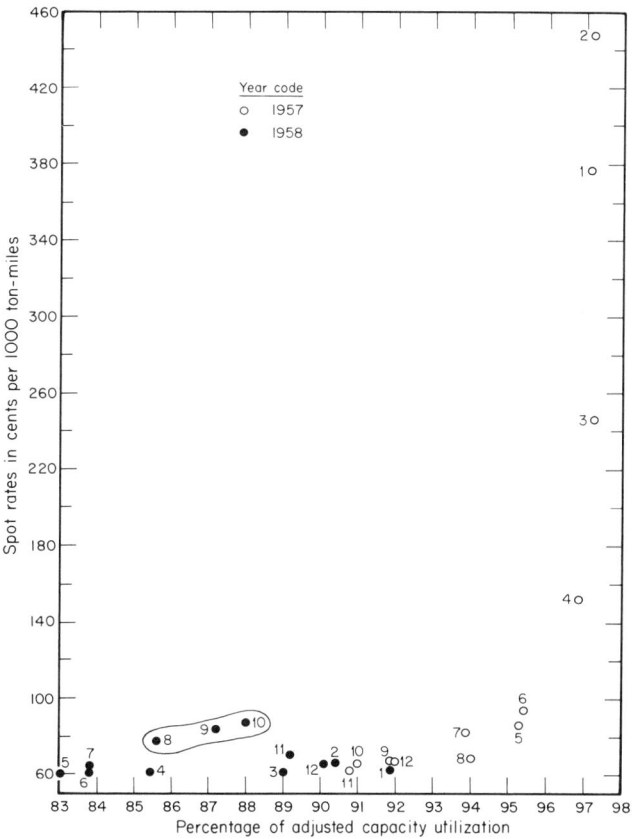

Figure 6.3. Adjusted short-term supply schedule, 1957–1958.

employment until disillusionment leads them back to tie-up a few months later. We read in the July 1, 1959, *Tanker Market Report* of Davies & Newman, Ltd., London:

Events in the tanker market during the past month followed very closely the pattern set during the preceding two or three months. The laid-up fleet has continued to increase, and now stands at around 440 vessels totalling 7,395,000 tons deadweight, a further increase during the month of 20 vessels of about 395,000 tons deadweight.

7

Characteristics of the Tankship Markets

In view of what we have previously said about the organization structure of the oil industry, we would expect the tankship markets to be oligopolistic in terms of both ownership and effective behavior. If the producers and distributors of crude oil are vitally affected by fluctuations in tankship rates, because these fluctuations are reflected in the posted *as well as* delivered prices for oil, then the only solution is to stabilize the cost of transportation. Otherwise any change in the cost of transportation will upset the very delicate balance that exists between the prices of the oil originating from the various geographical regions and destined for the major consuming markets. So, on first glance we would expect the ownership of tankers to be heavily if not totally concentrated in the hands of the major oil producers. This, however, is not the case, which implies that any price stability that may exist in the oil markets is not achieved through *ownership* or *control* of transportation facilities.[1] As of January 1, 1959, there were over 600 tanker owners with none owning more than 7% of the total capacity available, so complete control by a few is out of the question.

If we glance at Table 7.1, we notice that there is much more concentration of ownership among the oil companies than there is among the independents. The five major oil producers (or associated companies) own approximately 68% of all capacity owned and constructed by oil companies. This should of course be expected given the influence these companies exercise on oil trade. We must add, however, that the ownership of all the oil companies combined is not greater than 34% of the world total, consequently the ownership of the five largest oil companies is only 23%–24% of the world total. The five major in-

[1] This does not imply that the cost of transportation is left to become an exogenous factor. The impact of transportation may still be eliminated by arrangements that favor a delivered price with all the profit imputed to production.

CHARACTERISTICS OF TANKSHIP MARKETS

TABLE 7.1

TANKERS OWNED AND UNDER CONSTRUCTION FOR FIVE MAJOR OIL COMPANIES AND FIVE MAJOR INDEPENDENTS
(*January 1, 1959*)

Companies	Ownership	Construction	Total
Oil Companies			
Standard Oil Co. (N.S.)*	201	166	367
Shell	207	101	308
British Petroleum	151	141	292
Gulf	78	61	139
Caltex	65	37	102
Total above	702 (67.5%)	506 (68%)	1208 (68%)
Total all Oil Companies	1038 (100.0%)	742 (100%)	1780 (100%)
Independents			
Niarchos	118	27	145
Onassis	65	54	119
National Bulk Carriers	88	21	109
Goulandris	75	26	101
Livanos	44	11	55
Total above	390 (19%)	139 (12%)	529 (16.4%)
Total all Independents	2066 (100%)	1162 (100%)	3228 (100%)
Total of above 10 majors	1092 (35%)	645 (34%)	1737 (34.7%)
World Total	3104 (100%)	1904 (100%)	5008 (100%)

Source of Data: Tables 5.1 and 5.3.
* Includes Standard-Vacuum: 22 T-2's owned and 8 T-2's under construction.

dependents, on the other hand, do not control more than 19% of the independent capacity, or 13% of the world total. Their share of the construction in progress is even less, being 12% of the total construction initiated by independents and about 7% of the total world-wide tanker construction.

Looking at the combined ownership of the five major oil companies and the five major independents, we find that 1.5% of owners control 35% of the total world tonnage. On the basis of purely quantitative information, as a result, we would say that although no one owns more than 7% of the total the remaining 65% of capacity is so thinly dispersed among 98.5% of the owners that a few of the majors could control the market if they behaved accordingly. Such control will be much easier, as well as vital, to establish in a market such as that of tankships which is influenced by price-elastic expectations, and which is so sensitive to small variations in capacity when it reaches 95% of total utilization. Do the tankship markets then operate under the impact of oligopolistic influence? The answer is no! Although logic as well as ownership composition could imply the contrary, the tankship markets operate more like perfectly competitive markets. Let us now analyze the reasons behind this paradox.

Concentration of Ownership in the Relevant Market

Although both oil companies and independents own vessels, for purposes of rate determination the relevant market is the spot market and the latter is usually composed of the independent fleet only. The vessels of oil companies rarely enter into the spot market, and when they do enter it is only during periods of depressed rates.

The concentration among the independents is not very great. In spite of this, because of the inelasticity of the supply schedule at 94% of capacity utilization and beyond, and the infinite elasticity below 92%, any one who has at his disposal 3%–4% of capacity can very effectively exercise price leadership and organize the market. This, however, does not happen because no one has all his vessels in the market at any moment of time. To reduce the risk of unemployment, multiunit owners space the availability of their vessels by accepting time charters for 75% to 90% of the capacity they own. As a result, the concentration of ownership of vessels operating in the spot market at any moment of time is very small indeed, with no one owning more than 1% of the available capacity.

So the spot market is the relevant market, and it is in this that we look for clues of tankship-market behavior.

Balance Between Production and Refining Capacities

Our discussion on the impact of concentration on the structure of the tankship markets drew upon empirical observations to show "what is," that is to say, that there is no significant or effective concentration of ownership in the tankship markets, especially in terms of what is available in the spot market at any moment of time. One may ask, however, why should it be so? Is there not enough motivation for the oil companies either to organize the markets or to eliminate them completely?

There are several reasons for the relatively low degree of concentration which also explain why the oil companies are not, and cannot feasibly be, self-sufficient in transportation. One of these reasons is the imbalance between the production and refining capacities of each of *several* oil companies. Once such imbalance is admitted then the oil companies cannot preserve their autarchy in planning or their independence of action even if an initial understanding about posted prices is reached. Oil companies must as a result decide on sale prices, and transportation costs then become critical. Self-sufficiency in transportation by all will obviously create surpluses and costly waste. It is also obvious that complete dependence of some oil companies on others for transportation capacity (reflected in terms of delivered oil) will not be satisfactory. No one will accept the arbitrary decision of someone else as to what constitutes a fair transportation charge.

The facts which motivate behavior in this case are clear, as far as the oil companies are concerned: (*a*) fluctuations in transportation costs are considered undesirable and must somehow be eliminated as a consideration in pricing decisions, and (*b*) it is realized that no one can impose his will upon the rest because no one can afford to be completely self-sufficient. As a result, those who are endowed with excess production capacity have to choose between two feasible alternatives. They can either (i) sell on both F.O.B. and C.I.F. basis but establish the C.I.F. price in a way that will make the buyer indifferent between F.O.B. and delivered basis, or (ii) sell on F.O.B. basis only and have the buyers provide means of transportation, either owned or chartered.

It is obvious that the oil companies cannot strictly adhere to an F.O.B. price. Fluctuations in transportation costs will be reflected in the cost to the buyer and will affect his purchasing plans. Whenever rates are low, given a certain pattern of F.O.B. prices, the oil which travels the longest will be relatively favored, and when rates are high the one closest to the buyer will be in the most advantageous position. Such possible changes in sources of supply will undoubtedly introduce a lot of uncertainty in the sales budgets and production plans of oil companies, and also possibly leave the oil companies to the mercy of those who may happen to control transportation. So an F.O.B. price is not practical.

Selling on a delivered basis, therefore, is the only solution to the dilemma facing the oil companies. The difference between the F.O.B. and delivered price, however, must not be higher under normal conditions than the market cost of transportation (or what it would have cost the buyer if he had his own vessels). In fact, in order to eliminate some instability from their sales and investment plans, the producers may offer an incentive in terms of lower transportation costs, and so encourage them to choose a delivered price.

We must notice that under both alternatives i and ii, the market price for transportation services will be established under competitive conditions. In the first case, an integrated oil firm will not allow anyone to interpose a transportation price, between production and refining and between refining and the consumer, which includes monopolistic rent. To guard against such an eventuality the oil companies will be forced to obtain their own transportation capacity, at least for part of their total needs. In the C.I.F. case the transportation cost that is included in the delivered price must be based on *long-run* costs of tankship services and must include the minimum return that is necessary to keep the required investment in the industry. It cannot be higher than long-run cost because otherwise the buyers will prefer to buy on an F.O.B. basis and own their own vessels (or charter from independents.) Once such a long-run cost is established and included in delivered prices, the owners of vessels operating in the market cannot price their services on a different basis. So, under either alternative the tankship markets will operate in a manner approaching perfect competition.

Balance Between Needs and Sources Satisfying Such Needs for Each Company by Geographic Regions

Given that geological accidents determine the location as well as the quantity of oil produced, the probability is quite large that there will be imbalances between the needs of the oil companies in the various geographic locations and the resources available to them in those regions. Such an occurrence will encourage the producers to exchange (barter) their oil to eliminate excessively wasteful crosshauling. As a result the barterers will find it necessary to establish transportation rates that are objective and acceptable to all the parties involved. To be sure, no rate will be universally acceptable unless it is established in a "competitive" market, or else is based on long-run cost. For the latter to be broadly acceptable it must be the result of known technology of operation and of production functions that can be reproduced. Here again these conditions are characteristic of perfectly competitive markets.

The Existence of Tankship Markets

The arguments that we have thus far presented point out the necessity for company-owned vessels and an independent tanker market. The oil companies cannot afford to operate under an unstable oligopolistic situation, nor would they be willing to become completely dependent on someone else by relinquishing control of transportation facilities to a monopolist. Consequently, they must own vessels for at least part of their transportation needs if they are to preserve their independence of action. On the other hand, they cannot afford to be completely self-sufficient because they will then be creating surpluses and wasteful crosshauling. For these reasons there must be a tankship market.

The tankship markets are the consequence and not the reason for the perfectly competitive conditions under which tanker rates are established. These markets operate in a manner similar to the stock market. The owners of vessels normally report the availability of their tankers to brokers, who, through their offices in the various parts of the world, attempt to place these vessels with customers who have transportation needs. On the demand side of the market, the oil companies and other people who need vessels register their needs with brokers, who try to match supply and demand in total and also bring about an equilibrium in the markets by geographic areas.

There are cases of transactions that occur outside the organized markets, for which the parties get together on a private basis without intermediaries. More often than not, these transactions are for time charters of extensive duration. This practice of by-passing the brokers, however, does not diminish the importance of the organized market nor does it affect its perfectly competitive nature. The spot rate as established in the tankship markets serves as a basis for the private agreements, but the brokerage fee is avoided as in the case of private real estate sales.

Mobility

The existence of a tankship market and tanker brokers does not by itself guarantee that the markets will behave in a perfectly competitive manner. For example, no one can claim that the real estate markets are *ipso facto* perfect. In the case of tankers, however, we have a unique feature in the form of mobility, which encourages competition even further.

Mobility is very vital not only because it reduces the cost of exit from a particular *market,* but also because it serves toward global equalization of supply and demand. The *total* amount of capital invested in tankships, as well as in any other type of a vessel, is mobile, and as a result the productive capacity is not fixed in any geographic area. Although this mobility does not result in a costless entry and exit from the *industry,* no doubt it does allow some flexibility even on that score. For if the total investment is mobile as a *going concern,* naturally the resale price will be higher than it would have been had the concern been dismantled and sold in pieces.

Normally in other forms of investments in capital equipment once the capital has been committed it is for the greatest part completely sunk in the geographic area. An individual can get out of the venture either through sale on a going-concern basis, and of course at a price reflecting the estimate of the buyer as to the risk and profitability involved in that particular industry and geographic area, or by means of physical transfer of all movable assets which, again, cannot be achieved without a considerable loss. The respective economic forces in the tankship markets are different however. Capital is mobile in that the owner of a tankship can move his whole firm from port to port, and hence enter into different geographic markets with very little cost. This characteristic makes for a more competitive international market because it tends to equalize rates by balancing supply and demand.

A question now arises as to whether this observation is pointing out one of the difficulties the oil companies face or will face in any attempt to control tankship tonnage capacity for oil price regulation. In the early history of the oil industry in the United States, before the industry became international and the tanker an important mode of transportation, control of railroads meant control of the markets. Why then do we not find a comparable situation today? Is it by accident or by design that the oil companies own only a small share of the total transportation capacity? The answer of course is that it is by no means an accident. Economic and institutional considerations make it impossible for anyone to control the market. Some of these factors we have already pointed out, and more we shall discuss shortly, but mobility is one of the most important determinants of the character of the tankship markets. In the case of railroads the greatest part of the capital investment is fixed, not only in terms of time extending over several tanker life cycles but also in a physical sense. For these reasons the cost of entry and exit from the industry and specific geographic markets is much heavier in the case of the railroads than in the case of tankers. That is why it is difficult for absolute control and monopolistic conditions to flourish in the tankship markets.

Ease of Entry

We have argued under "mobility" that it is easy to move tankers from market to market and so at the same time facilitate *exit* from the industry itself. Now we shall examine the question of *entry* to the industry.

One thing that strikes the empirical analyst of tankship operations is the relative absence of *obvious over-all* administrative and financial economies of scale. As a result, a tanker owner needs no administrative superstructure in order to operate efficiently. When the vessels are away from their home base the owners can very efficiently relinquish day-to-day operational control to the captain of the vessel, use the offices of tanker brokers at the various ports for employment if necessary, and use local suppliers for essential stores.

The presence of brokers may not necessarily imply the absence of economies of scale of an over-all administrative or financial nature, especially if we include in these managerial activities a risk optimum. It may indicate rather that the scale necessary for achieving some or all of these optima for the firm is so large that it will be uneconomical for anyone to achieve it given the present market needs. Either hypothesis, however, points out that the *feasibly* optimum scale for the firm is so small as to make it very easy for anyone to enter the market.

Since the over-all optima for the firm are not instrumental in inhibiting entry into the industry, we shall now examine whether the size of the operational units presents any problems. Taking the largest vessel afloat in 1959, we find that it is not greater than .002% of total capacity. Consequently, and even if the largest vessel available represents the most efficient size for *all purposes,* there will be a need for over 500 such vessels to satisfy the total transportation requirements of the industry. As everyone knows, however, there are all sorts of limitations restricting the use of these large vessels, such as loading and unloading facilities, refinery capacities, and market needs; so the *average* optimum size, given these limitations, may not be greater than .0004% of total capacity, thus pointing out that approximately 2,500 vessels may be required to satisfy industrial needs. Under such conditions entry into the industry is quite easy.

The financial risks that the owners undertake when they invest in tankers need not be great either. We have already noticed that at the time when most ships are ordered the owners do not have to finance the building of the vessels themselves. Usually the banks, insurance companies, and trust funds provide up to 80% and sometimes even 90% of the needed capital on the basis of a bona fide charter agreement. We have also shown that during periods of strong demand and a shipbuilding boom the length of the time charter tends to increase; consequently, it is not unreasonable for a bank to expect to collect the total amount of the loan in five years out of the net charter rental. Such an arrangement removes most of the financial risk from the plans of the owner and leaves enough capacity beyond the expiration of the original charter so that the owner can realize a healthy profit over the remainder of the life of the vessel. It is also for this reason that such a vessel, following the original charter agreement, may continue operating in the spot market at rates below long-run average cost and still prove to be a wise investment decision. The financial institutions do not necessarily take undue risks in this case because first of all, as we have said, they arrange that the proceeds from the charter should be applied directly toward the payment of the loan installments and they also require an insurance policy to cover their investment in case of a natural disaster. All in all then, the only prerequisites for obtaining the money to build a vessel are the building plans and a charter signed by an oil company.

In summary then, entry into the industry is relatively easy, because: (*a*) over-all administrative and financial optima are not operationally present; (*b*) the optimum size of the average operational unit is very small, so, given the transportation needs of the industry, there is room for over 2,000 such units; and (*c*) capital for investment in tankers is rather plentiful and relatively riskless.

The Vessel Is the Firm

One important conclusion that emerges very clearly from our discussion under "mobility" and "ease of entry" is that for all practical purposes, the *vessel is the firm*. Administratively, it is under the jurisdiction of its captain for most of the time. Only loose supervision can be exercised by the home office because, given the distance that separates the point of action from the point at which over-all administrative control rests, effective central control cannot be exercised. The farther the distance, other things being equal, the looser the control. Furthermore, the nature of the decisions that are characteristic of tankship operation necessitates flexibility for quick action. The expected loss due to idleness and indecision at a far-away port until the feedback control mechanism operates to transmit new directives is far greater than the expected loss because of suboptimal decisions on location by the captain. In addition to what was just stated, we must not forget the traditional role of the captain of a ship. He is the master of his vessel with the power to perform many more functions than those falling under any notion of liberal administrative theory. He crosses international boundaries, operates under international laws, and whenever necessary, he is the law. All these arguments show why administratively the vessel is the firm.

Now what are the economic reasons for and the consequences of such an administrative entity? We have already mentioned the fact that the optimum size of the vessel is very small relative to the total capacity for the industry. This economic rationale, however, carries with it certain implications that are embodied in the existence of a neat and *separable* unit of capacity, the vessel. The first implication is that economic planning may be carried out on a vessel-to-vessel basis independent of anything else. Each vessel can pursue its own independent employment. Because of the absence of any administrative superstructure, and with no knowledge or preoccupation about fixed costs, decisions are likely to be made on an out-of-pocket and opportunity-cost basis. As a result the price mechanism operates as in the case of perfect competition where the price is equal to the marginal cost of the marginal vessel in operation.

A second consequence of the notion that every vessel is a firm is the relative absence of complementarities of resources. Because complementarities of resources are rather absent the vessel can fit into the organizational structure of any firm and perform as effectively as if it were still in the parent organization. Consequently, whenever excess capacity exists, and because the cost of such excess capacity in terms of out-of-pocket expenditures is very high, there is a tendency for the oil companies to throw their surpluses into the market and relet to other oil companies or to the independents. Arrangements such as these are unique and are not found in many other types of productive facilities, for example, in manufacturing.

Finally, there is a further consequence of the absence of complementarities in the fact that technology of operation is common to all. Complete knowledge of technology is characteristic of perfectly competitive operations. Of course some may say that it is not clear which is the cause and which is the effect. Frankly, it makes no difference because the end result is the same. We feel that the technology of tankship operations is very simple and generally well known to potential entrants, yet even if it is not otherwise known, since it is the practice of the oil companies to relet their excess capacity, technology can become common knowledge very rapidly.

There is ample empirical evidence that the vessel is treated as the firm: (*a*) charters very rarely fail to mention specific vessels; (*b*) the independents in their discussions treat the vessels as continuous projects; (*c*) vessels are being built irrespective of over-all market considerations; and (*d*) contracts for new buildings are initiated and financed by charter agreements.

All of the above arguments point to one thing, the perfectly competitive nature of tanker markets.

Absence of Artificial Controls

Related to our arguments on mobility is the issue of artificial controls. The operation of tankships is one of the least controlled because it is international. With the exception of the United States coastal trade that is by law limited to tankships flying the flag of the United States and a few partial protectionistic attempts by France, Italy, and Japan, the routes are not pre-empted to the ships of any particular country. In this way economic rather than any other type of considerations are paramount. We must also notice that there are no franchises on routes, as one finds in other modes of transportation, thus contributing further to the competitive nature of the markets.

Summary

We have shown thus far that the tankship markets, which on the basis of common sense and on a priori characteristics should be imperfect, operate like perfectly competitive markets. Having resolved this paradox we shall now summarize several other characteristics of tankship operations.

Because the spot market is always very thin, consisting of 10% to 15% of total capacity, it is very excitable. Given this and elastic expectations, we may find in many cases that the oil companies follow a leader in the wrong direction, and further accentuate the fluctuations in the market. Such leadership, however, does not bring about stability as the "price leadership" of oligopolistic markets, but rather accentuates the chaotic conditions of a perfectly competitive market in which the operatives make decisions on erroneous information. For example, when tonnage demand is low, many oil companies withdraw from the tanker market because they own enough tonnage and have enough charter commitments to last them in the forseeable future. In addition, their stocks of oil may be such that they can afford to postpone transportation for quite a few months to come. Their withdrawal from the market, however, may be interpreted as a loss of confidence in the tanker market and an expectation for further weakening which in turn may induce the smaller charterers to withdraw. This indeed results in further weakening which justifies the otherwise unjustifiable expectations that induced it. In other words, while the expectations of the major oil companies are biased and unjustifiable, they can by their behavior influence the behavior of other operators who in turn may react by withdrawing from the market. Their withdrawal can cause a precipitation in the rates and thus ex post facto bring about a justification of the original biased expectations. The opposite, of course, can occur in periods of excess demand. So, leadership in the tankship markets widens the fluctuations and causes further instability.

Another characteristic of the tankship market is that the fortunes of all are tied together. Because of the oligopolistic nature of the end-product markets and the overlapping territories in which the oil products sell, an increase or decrease in total demand will affect all the producers in more or less the same qualitative way. In other industries, one geographic region may be depressed while others prosper and thus changes may affect the various firms differently depending on the geographic area that they serve. In the oil industry, however, one is dealing with a universal market for a more or less homogeneous and highly substitutable product, so that any change will affect all of them in the same direction. Hence the demand for tonnage either skyrockets or goes to the bottom for all at the same time.

What we have just said refers to the direction of the impact and not to the quantitative magnitude of changes in the individual transportation needs. To the extent that all oil companies share the same total demand, given any particular demand level, we expect most of the covariances between the transportation needs of oil companies to be negative. This implies that the variance for the total industrial needs is less than the sum of the variances faced by the individual users of tankships. It is for this reason that the operations of the tankship markets serve toward more efficient utilization of tonnage by mitigating the risk and reconciling surpluses and deficits.

8

The Formation of Short-Term Rates

All the necessary analysis leading to the formation of short-term tanker rates has been presented in the previous chapters; here we shall recapitulate our findings and bring a few points into clearer focus.

At the outset we showed that the elasticity of demand for oil is very small. The elasticity becomes smaller the shorter the duration of time covered, but even for a schedule of a year's duration the elasticity index of the demand for oil is not far from zero.

Then we turned our attention to the supply schedule and proved that, short of a shipbuilding cycle, the supply schedule is very inelastic beyond full capacity. The lower part of the supply schedule, by contrast, is very elastic because of the refusal rate of the marginal vessels. The latter constitute a substantial part of total capacity; hence, within the relevant range of fluctuations in capacity, the lower part of the supply schedule is completely horizontal. The change from elasticity to inelasticity occurs within less than two percentage points of total capacity, and indicates that a shift in the demand by as little as 1% around the critical area will be enough to create fortunes or disaster. With an elasticity of supply of .02 immediately beyond full capacity, a shift in oil demand of 1%, and a consequent shift in transportation demand of 1.66%,[1] will increase rates by no less than 83%.

---

[1] From the data presented by Kahle and Kelley at the Fifth World Petroleum Congress on May 30, 1959, on "The Role of Sea Transportation in the Petroleum Industry," one can see that for the period 1950–1958 requirements have increased by an average factor of 1.66 for every percentage increase in oil-demand transportation. The factor of 1.66 refers to a relative and not absolute change. In absolute terms we find that the transportation requirements increase by an average of .536 T-2's for each million U.S. barrels of increase in petroleum production. The marginal rate has been increasing steadily and over the time span covered by this study appears to be .64 T-2's, indicating that petroleum is transported over longer and longer distances.

The behavior of the buyers and sellers attracted a considerable amount of our attention. We have shown that the expectations of the buyers over the whole range of prices are definitely price elastic. Given this price elasticity of expectations, we then proved that once a disturbance occurs it is sufficient to create perpetual circularity in the tankship markets. The oil companies will rush into the market to secure an increasing share of the existing tonnage, adding further impetus to rate increases. The manifestation of an increase in tonnage demand will be further magnified in the spot market, because only an average of 15% — less during periods of high rates — of the total tonnage operates in the spot market. Thus a 1.66% increase in demand for tonnage comprises at least 11% of the spot capacity.

Orders for new vessels will be initiated by expectations during periods of rising rates and will only stop when rates start declining. This relationship implies evidence of surpluses — leftward shifts in demand — even before the deliveries start appearing in the markets; but even excluding such a possibility, the deliveries will eventually shift the supply schedule to the right and depress the rates.[2] That is, the downturn will occur even if the demand schedule does not shift to the left.

The elasticity of the lower part of the supply schedule is nearly infinite. Consequently, rates will reach the lay-up point of the marginal vessel very fast, and the continuous inflow of new tonnage will cause extensive lay-ups. The latter will guarantee that rates will remain depressed until either the demand catches up with the available capacity or the excess supply disappears through attrition.

Because orders are placed mostly during periods of high rates, they will create irregular but continuous discontinuities in the attrition rate and will probably also create continuously discontinuous shortages. With elastic expectations, shifts in demand will further accentuate the amplitude as well as the duration of the rate cycle unless these shifts occur at a time of shortages.

The shape of the short-term supply schedule provides evidence that rate stability and equilibria *in the short run* may be possible only at the lower (elastic) part of the schedule. It is true that extremely short-

---

[2] Surpluses may occur before new vessel deliveries start, for four main reasons. The first three of these reasons operate through the demand, and the fourth through the supply. (1) The expectations may turn inelastic and thus effectively shift the demand schedule to the left. (2) Usually many of the transactions are completed for future delivery (the lead time increases with the rates.) If such transactions are purely anticipatory or speculative, then surpluses will become evident as soon as the ships are turned over to the charterers. (3) The chartering activity may serve as a "catharsis" of impulses. After the buyers exhaust a lot of energy by ordering they may see the transparency of their expectations and so withdraw from the market. (4) The impact of short selling may be enough to shift the supply schedule to the right and precipitate a downfall in rates.

lived equilibria may occur at any rate but are so unstable, because of the expectations that operate in these regions, that we wonder whether they merit the name. Only at the bottom of rates does some certainty finally prevail, as evidenced by the number of tie-ups. Everywhere else we expect to observe extensive fluctuations. Equilibria at low rates are possible only because both the normal short-term and the market supply schedules are infinitely elastic.

The position of the tankship supply and demand schedules is also affected by other circularities of shorter duration, such as seasonal trade, repairs, and the individual needs of big users. These fluctuations will, in effect, give an irregularly wavy appearance to the surface of the bigger rate cycle, as shown in Figure 8.1. This raises the question of

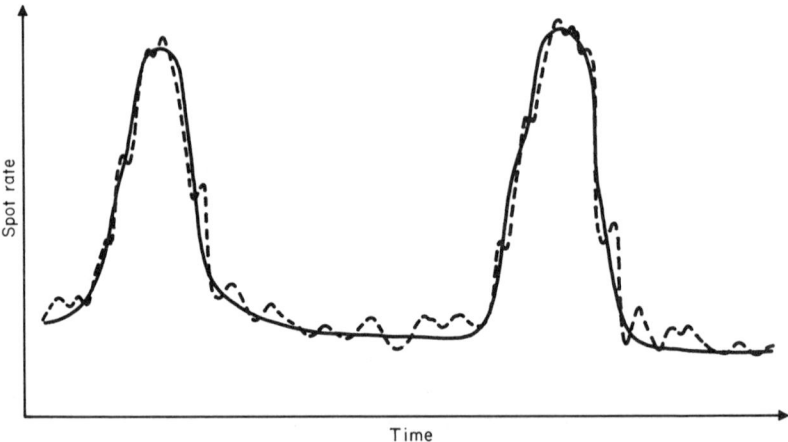

Figure 8.1. Theoretical time profile of spot rates.

whether any equilibria exist with so many overlapping fluctuations. This is a matter of taste, but it seems to be more in line with traditional theory if the answer is no. In our opinion, since the fluctuations at low rates are persistent and occur within narrow ranges of definable levels (the lay-up rates of the marginal capacity), these levels qualify as short-term equilibria. Thus, there is no one equilibrium but a definable range within which these may be found at low rates. No similar range can be observed during periods of excess demand.

Is there anything that we can say about the intermediate or long run? Do we expect to observe any equilibria? To answer these questions we must analyze the short-run "adjustment paths" over two consecutive production periods. If we find that there is a tendency for repetition, then what applies to the short run must also apply to the long run. That is, if the adjustments show no tendency in the short run — any short run — to approach the relevant long-run (static) equilibrium, then there is long-run instability.

The reader may already have observed similarities between the tankship markets and the classical cobweb theorem.[3] For example, we have, as in the classical theorem, perpetual naïveté and adaptive expectations in accordance with existing prices.

As Akerman has shown geometrically[4] and Nerlove analytically,[5] with adaptive expectations, the following constitutes a necessary and sufficient condition for a return to equilibrium after a disturbance.

$$(1 - 2/a) < s/d < 1$$

where a stands for either the coefficient of expectations or adjustment (and $0 < a \leqslant 1$), s for the slope of the supply schedule, and d for the slope of the demand. For $a = 1$, this formulation reduces to the traditional cobweb conditions of convergence.

Let us stress that whether we are attempting to observe short-run or long-run cobweb reactions, we must concentrate on studying the normal short-term and market supply schedules. It is true that for long-run purposes the relevant short-term supply schedules will be farther to the right because of "permanent" capacity increases. Nevertheless, any oscillations around an alleged equilibrium point must meet the short-term schedules first, regardless of total capacity. The previous argument may not be relevant in the theoretical cases of instantaneous adjustments of the supply schedules, but it is definitely of vital importance to empirical reality with irreversibilities of supply.

If we apply the cobweb condition to our case, a will have to be greater than unity and will show that the values of s/d for which the oscillations converge are confined between -1 and 1. Such conditions could only be satisfied if the slope of our short-term supply schedule were uniformly inelastic. The infinite elasticity of the lower part, below full capacity, would render our system unstable unless the market supply schedule is likewise infinitely elastic. In addition, we have the complications generated by changes in the slope of our effective demand

---

[3] See Ezekiel, Mordecai, "The Cobweb Theorem," *The Quarterly Journal of Economics,* Vol. LII, 1938, pp. 255–280; Buchanan, Norman S., "A Reconsideration of the Cobweb Theorem," originally in *Journal of Political Economy,* February 1939, pp. 67–81, and reprinted in *Readings in Economic Analysis,* Vol. 1 (General Theory), Clemence, Richard V., Editor, Addison-Wesley Press, Inc., Cambridge, Massachusetts, 1950, pp. 46–61; Akerman, Gustav, "The Cobweb Theorem: A Reconsideration," *The Quarterly Journal of Economics,* Vol. LXXI, No. 1, February 1957, pp. 151–160; Nerlove, Marc, "Adaptive Expectations and Cobweb Phenomena," *The Quarterly Journal of Economics,* Vol. LXXIII, No. 2, May 1958, pp. 227–240.

[4] Akerman, *op. cit.,* p. 152.

[5] Nerlove, *op. cit.,* pp. 233 and 236.

schedule. On the basis of the cobweb criteria of convergence, therefore, no definite conclusion can be drawn about the stability of the tankship-market equilibria.

If the traditional cobweb assumption is to apply to the tankship markets, we must further make the following qualifications:

1. *Pure Competition*

Underlying the cobweb oscillations is the assumption that the "producers" behave as pure competitors. Their output is determined by "present" prices and the belief that such prices will continue. Furthermore, each "producer" decides independently, not realizing his interdependence on the decision of others or the effect his output will have on the market. In the tankship transportation market we do not have the ideal competitive conditions, as evidenced by the efforts of the oil companies to reduce their dependence on the independents. We have pointed out earlier that the tankship transportation markets behave in a nearly perfectly competitive manner not because of the existence of *all* the preconditions of perfect competition, but in spite of several aspects of the institutional environment. *What we observe in the tankship markets is a paradox.* Also, the price expectations operating in the tankship markets are not exactly identical to those inherent in the cobweb assumption of uniformity because, in our case, we have observed a certain degree of asymmetry in the behavior of buyers and sellers. Furthermore, we have argued that even a manifested complete symmetry in expectations may not necessarily imply that the sellers have in reality price-elastic expectations, but that they may react rationally to the elastic expectations of the buyers. Empirical evidence shows that the independents are motivated by a mixture of the above hypotheses, and that the expectations of sellers are price elastic over certain price ranges.

To the extent that a great many orders for new vessels are placed only after a contractual agreement between oil companies and independents is entered (that is to say a signed charter), pure independence of supply and demand is not preserved. There is a certain amount of "coupling" of partial behavior. In spite of this partial interdependence of supply and demand, however, the pattern of orders placed during rising rates leaves little doubt that the greatest part of each "new" supply is initiated without regard to *over-all* interdependencies. Especially little heed is paid by any one buyer or seller to the interdependencies between his actions and those of the remaining buyers and sellers in the industry. In fact, a number of new sellers enter into the market during periods of high rates. Had they realized their mutual interdependence the new sellers would not have entered into the market at that time, and the existing sellers would not have placed orders for vessels. Having obtained the charter they should have waited for the downturn to buy existing vessels that are going begging for business. The same arguments can be made even more strongly concerning the behavior of buyers.

2. *Reversibility of Supply*

The cobweb theorem assumes that the supply schedule remains unchanged, implying complete reversibility and perfect adaptability during contractions, without any complications arising from any "reserve" capacity caused by previous expansions.[6] Unlike such assumptions of complete

---

[6] See Buchanan, *op. cit.*, pp. 46–48.

perishability of capacity (i.e., that the investment in one period will not benefit or influence the capacity or output of another period), the supply schedule of tankship transportation is irreversible and, as a result, prior mistakes carry into the future.[7]

3. *Infinite Inelasticity of the Market Supply Schedule*

Although this assumption is not explicitly stated, it is implied in the assumption of output perishability. In modifications of the original cobweb theorem that mention "stocks,"[8] the market supply schedule is still depicted as very inelastic at all levels, with the exception of some deviations to the left from the vertical because of replenishment and perhaps some speculative enlargement of stocks.[9] Such assumptions imply zero storage cost, but because the present price is expected to govern in the future, everyone prefers to sell at once instead of store for future sale. Only at a price equal to zero does the market supply schedule become infinitely elastic. Contrary to the above assumptions, in the tankship markets expectations over a period of intermediate and long-run duration are rate inelastic under depressed conditions even though they are elastic over the short run. The cost of tie-up also sets a positive lower limit below which rates do not go under normal circumstances; hence the market supply schedule becomes infinitely elastic much before reaching zero and thus confines the fluctuations.

4. *Point versus Continuous Input and Output*

The markets that have been traditionally associated with cobweb phenomena are related to agriculture, and for good reasons:

(*a*) The productive processes in agriculture are usually initiated at the same time and do not require continuous input. This is important because cancellations would otherwise occur.

(*b*) The initiated agricultural production all matures at approximately the same time, thus preventing any "successive quantitative adaptations."

In the tankship markets, orders are placed as a result of rates, but both the capital inputs and the output are continuous. The penalties of cancellation are usually heavy — if construction is far along — so cancellations may be discouraged. As a result, the total output initiated by a period of high prices may not be affected very substantially by subsequent events. However, all vessels ordered are not expected to be completed at the same time, because of the different processes applied by the different shipyards and also because of the intentional prolongation of many contracts after a decline in rates.

The differences between agriculture and other industrial production, which we have just expounded, led Akerman to state that the cobweb reasoning applies outside of agriculture only to a very limited degree.

---

[7] Akerman has made a distinction between the long-term normal supply, short-term normal supply, and market supply curve. He did not assume complete intraperiod reversibility, but his emphasis on the normal long-run schedule betrays an assumption of complete interperiod adaptability. See Akerman, *op. cit.*, pp. 151–152.

[8] Akerman, *op. cit.*, and Nerlove, *op. cit.*

[9] Akerman, *op. cit.*, p. 152.

In his words, other processes "are started and consequently come to an end at different successive points of time and are in that way open to successive quantitative modifications." [10]

Because of the irreversibilities just mentioned and the absence of a definite "production period," [11] the static long-run equilibrium of tanker rates, if any, around which oscillations occur will be continuously changing as new capacity becomes available. This new capacity, as we have previously shown, will flow in continuously, but will reach its peak between two to three years after the decline in rates. Thus, new long-run static equilibria will be created continuously, and oscillations will have an altogether different point of reference all the time.

Another and very important conclusion that we can derive from this is the simultaneous existence of cobwebs of different duration. While the main center of gravity is the relevant static long-run equilibrium, the oscillations around such a point are spun by smaller cobwebs — and even if it remains constant. These movements are similar to those of the solar system. The sun, like the static long-run equilibrium, is the center of "the universe," with planets spinning around it and satellites orbiting around the planets. The latter, like the strings of the cobweb, are sometimes closer to the sun but never reach it.

In summary, these qualifications modify but do not completely destroy the applicability of the cobweb theorem to the tankship transportation market. We shall now show geometrically the impact of the cobweb interactions on the supply of tankship capacity and the formation of tanker rates.

Figure 8.2 shows a demand schedule[12] exhibiting the impact of interperiod substitutions caused by price-elastic expectations, and with tanker rates resting at an imaginary equilibrium point a. Suddenly the demand shifts to the right and there is an excess demand.[13] Let us for the moment assume that the short-term supply schedule shifts to the right, to meet the excess demand, and that it now runs through the long-run capacity point I. The spot rate then climbs upward to point b or b' depending on the severity of the shock created by the original shift; for this reason some fluctuations may occur between points b and b'.

This increase in rates affects the expectations of the oil companies

---

[10] *Ibid.,* p. 160.

[11] The duration of the so-called "production period" is positively related to the intensity of the original impact, implying that no uniformity exists between the duration of the various rate cycles.

[12] The lower part of the demand schedule is exaggerated for illustrative purposes.

[13] A real shift in demand is not required to bring about an increase in rates and cobweb interactions. A temporary market shortage may jolt the equilibrium and, depending on its intensity, may initiate cobweb oscillations.

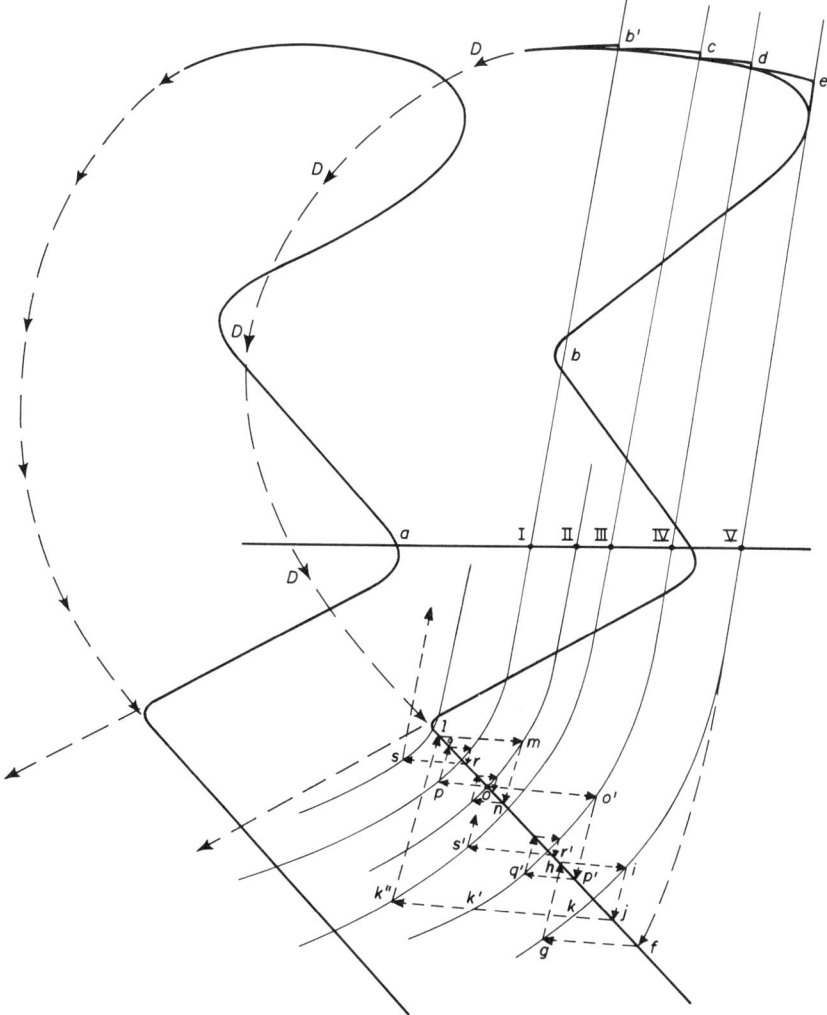

Figure 8.2. Cobweb adjustment paths.

and the independents, who respond by initiating orders for new vessels. At the same time, the chartering activity is accelerated because of elastic rate expectations, thus possibly causing further shifts in the demand schedule.

The upper limit of rates will be defined by that rate which will absorb all the profit imputed to production.[14] At this point the income effect,

---

[14] Given that the distance of the main market from the alternative sources of supply is not equal, then the rate corresponding to this turning point should be equal theoretically to the value of the nearest oil in the market of price

because of the new charters, will become negative and counterbalance the positive interperiod substitution effect that was initiated by price-elastic expectations. Whether the expectations of the oil companies change from elastic to inelastic when the income effect becomes negative is immaterial, but it is a little unreasonable to exclude this possibility completely. To repeat, however, such an assumption is not necessary for our conclusions.

Once up there the spot rate will remain temporarily at high levels until one of the following possibilities occurs: (*a*) the supply schedule may shift to the right through points such as II, III, IV, and V; (*b*) the demand may shift to the left because of a change in expectations; or (*c*) the demand schedule may be irreversible, in which case the withdrawal of the buyers because of the income effect will automatically and promptly cause a serious precipitation in prices. This last possibility will cause the demand schedule to follow path *D*.

All three of these possibilities have their merits and may in fact be operating at the same time. The last two will undoubtedly bring about a faster reaction. Of these two, empirical evidence gives credence to the irreversibility of the demand schedule, with price-elastic expectations still operating. That is why the decline occurs so swiftly; because once it starts, with price-elastic expectations, it cannot stop until the bottom is reached.

Let us now suppose that the demand does not shift, that the demand schedule is reversible, and that all depends on the supply schedule.

---

equalization, plus the opportunity cost of refinery shutdowns (or loss of good will) and minus the marginal cost of crude production. It is amazing that there is so much similarity between the turning points of the two rate cycles studied. We get the feeling that there must be some objective reason behind this, but the author has not succeeded in uncovering it. The only positive statement that we can make is the following. During the Suez Canal crisis the critical market was Europe, and that is where the point of equalization must have shifted to attract the oil from the Western Hemisphere. The Caribbean oil with AFRA transportation was approximately $4.17 per barrel in the London market (i.e., $1.17 for transportation plus $3.00). Whether by coincidence or functional relationship, the *average* spot cost of transportation for the Persian Gulf crude was $4.18, but some transactions went as high as $4.64. We may question the use of AFRA for purposes of marginal economic analysis, since it is a weighted average rate of all existing contracts both spot and long term (the company-owned vessels are multiplied by the average rate of the long-term contracts). Nevertheless, it is used in industry for long-term agreements as an indicator of the cost of transportation so it must influence decision making.

If a functional relation does exist between the cost of transportation from the Persian Gulf and the "delivered" price of the Caribbean oil, then it appears that the marginal imputation of value to the Persian Gulf oil was close to zero. Actually under our assumption it was equal to the opportunity cost of refinery shutdowns and loss of good will.

We assume this because we wish to show the independence of our arguments from demand considerations.

The supply schedule may shift for one of the following reasons:

1. The vessels ordered because of the high spot rates will eventually be delivered and thus increase the capacity available.
2. Capacity may be increased "effectively" by short-chartering for future delivery.

The response of deliveries to high rates will be immediate, but at first not significant because of the time it takes to build a vessel; it may be six months to a year before the impact of the new deliveries is felt. Chartering for future delivery, however, does satisfy needs immediately because the greatest part of such needs is only psychological and not real, extended and not immediate.

The shifts in supply, for the foregoing reasons, will create slight downward pressure on rates and fluctuations at points such as c, d, and e; and finally, the slightest addition to actual or effective capacity will send the rates sliding downward to point f. These downward movements in rates usually follow the market supply schedule. Consequently, the rates may reach a lower point than that indicated by the normal short-term schedule at the same quantity. The slight slope is given to these market supply schedules to indicate some withdrawal from the market either for real or purely speculative reasons. The slope of the price path (upward) is also given a slight positive slant to indicate some enlargement of capacity due to speculative recommissioning of vessels.

For industries such as ship operation in which economies of scale are still realized, the normal long-term as well as the normal short-term supply schedules will shift, but because these shifts will only affect the level and not the quality of the cobweb adjustments, we leave them out.

Let us now observe how rates fluctuate during periods of surpluses. These fluctuations will occur between the static long-run equilibrium and the refusal rate of the marginal vessel. Because of the low rates at point f, the quantity offered in the market drops to g, following the short-term schedule through long-run point V. This decrease is due to the shift from the market supply to the normal short-term schedule. At this point we shall assume for purely illustrative purposes that all the vessels are still in the market and that the short-run supply schedule remains unaltered for a while. With quantity offered at such low rates, the latter may be bid up to level h, which brings forth quantity i, depressing the rates again to level j.

Seeing that rates are very low and the prospects for improvement dull, some owners may get discouraged and decide to tie up their vessels. This means that quantities k' and k'' instead of k are offered at that rate level, and active capacity is shifted to the short-term schedule running through the static long-run capacity point III. The cobweb will now gravitate upward, fluctuating successively through points *l, m, n, o, p, q, r,* and *s*. Some of the capacity that has previously been tied up, if it has not been permanently retired, may be encouraged by relatively higher rates and come out of tie-up, causing a shift to another short-term supply schedule corresponding to a new long-run static capacity point such as IV. So the cobweb is spun through points such as *o', p', q', r'* and *s'*.

These movements up and down the lower part of the demand schedule will continue, but will be confined entirely below the long-run supply schedule, as long as there is excess capacity that can be enticed when rates are high and discouraged (tied up) when rates are low. Finally, and even without rightward shifts in demand, attrition through permanent retirements will exhaust all the "reserve" capacity, and the cobweb will follow points similar to *p, q, r, s* spinning to the left. One of these leftward movements will go past the relevant demand schedule and then a new "production cycle" begins.

Notice that the static long-run equilibrium, even with assumptions of demand stability, has been approached but never reached, except incidentally. In actuality, because it takes so long for the rate to rise above the doldrums of the lay-up point, we do expect changes in the relevant long-term equilibrium point. Hence the "long-run" equilibrium is unstable.[15]

In conclusion, we have found that oscillations are characteristic of the tankship markets. These oscillations are confined, having as a lower boundary the refusal rate of the marginal vessel and as an upper boundary the price at which the income effect becomes negative and sufficiently large to counterbalance the interperiod substitution effect. (At this point the market may also get a gratuitous jolt from a concomitant but unnecessary change in expectations.) Stability of equilibria at a rate higher than the full cost of the most marginal vessel is inconceivable because of the impact of rates on orders placed. Even without any other influence, the shifts in supply initiated by the high rates will cause a rate downfall.

Under depressed market conditions the rates will be bound by the "lay-up rate" of the marginal vessels, and the short-run, cobweb-like oscillations will be converging toward some short-run equilibrium point. The slopes of the short-term and market supply schedules guarantee such convergences.

Because of the tie-up and recommissioning of vessels, the relevant short-run equilibria and their corresponding static long-run equilibria

---

[15] See Baumol, J. W., *Economic Dynamics,* The Macmillan Company, New York, 1957, p. 114, for a comment on this point.

will be shifting from left to right, and vice versa, confining the oscillations in rates within a relatively narrow range. The latter is due mainly to the quick response of the owners to the rate movements, and to their ability to respond quickly. Eventually, however, the readily available excess capacity will either be in use or retired. As a result, rates will approach the static long-run equilibrium, swiftly go beyond (to the left), and start another rate cycle.

The rates, therefore, will finally approach the relevant static long-run equilibrium point but will not stay there. This conclusion and the fact that the position of such equilibria changes indicate that the tankship markets are in the long run unstable.

Let us explore an apparent inconsistency between the following two statements that we have made:

1. That there is a convergence toward short-run equilibria, under depressed rates.
2. That the static long-run equilibrium is approached but the system is unstable in the long run.

First of all, we must remember that there are cobweb cycles of different durations and what we called "suns," "planets," and "satellites." Because of the shifts in these short-term equilibria, the short-term cobwebs continue ad infinitum. Nevertheless, the oscillations around any one *fixed* short-term equilibrium are converging. Because the fixity of the relevant short-term schedules is transitory, as vessels are activated and deactivated, the convergence will continually have a different point of reference. The area within which these potential short-term equilibria exist is on the lower part of the demand schedule, it is well defined and predetermined by the capacity available and the reaction patterns of the suppliers. We cannot, however, say the same thing about the long-run equilibria. As a consequence of the convergence of the short-term cobweb movements under depressed market conditions, we can only concede that a static long-run equilibrium must be approached from below. Why? Because these points of convergence, including some long-run equilibria, are all located on the same demand schedule if we assume no shifts and a well-defined demand.

We cannot therefore, even purely as a matter of preference, refer to these short-term points of convergence as *stable* short-term equilibria, nor can we concede that the static long-run equilibria are stable *from below*. Even though the long-run equilibria are approached from below they are bypassed very swiftly. As soon as we step above, the wide fluctuations in rates and the production cycle start all over again. What guarantees that the rate will not be confined below the static long-run equilibrium? The natural attrition of capacity and any of the seasonal

198   CHAPTER EIGHT

or other short-term occasions of excess demand [16] assures us that it will not.

Thus we have shown that the static long-run equilibria are at most *stable from below but not from above,* and because of this the system is unstable, implying that the turning point in expectations and demand occurs very close to the static long-run equilibrium near the full cost of the marginal unit, and is in complete agreement with the empirical evidence we have presented earlier.

It is inherent in the system that rates linger at low levels most of the time over the life of a vessel.[17] What, then, encourages investment in the industry? The outlook is really not so glum for several reasons:

1. The deviations of the rate from the full cost of the marginal vessel are greater on the upswing than the downswing. During the 1954–1958 cycle, the peak was approximately 350% of the estimated full cost of a T-2, while the trough was only 50%. This indicates that each month of operation at rates corresponding to the peak can offset five months of operation at "rock-bottom" rates.

2. We have shown that the lowest rate will be set by the lay-up point of the marginal vessel. Thus with the prevailing rates, all the other vessels – to the extent that their cost of operation is lower – will not only cover their out-of-pocket costs, but also part of all their fixed costs. We shall later provide evidence that the economies of scale made possible by progress in the technology of shipbuilding and other ancillary industries are quite substantial and are still accruing, creating obsolescence continually. Thus the marginal vessel of today was not the marginal vessel of yesterday; it was able therefore to secure full-cost-remunerative employment over most of its life.

These arguments suggest, however, that once all the technological economies of scale — external as well as internal to the industry — are reaped and the industry reaches maturity, the period of depressed rates will become quite critical for all the vessels operating in the spot market.[18] Conceivably, however, the behavior of the operatives in an industry is conditioned by the dynamic prospects of the industry itself. If this hypothesis is true, and there are reasons to believe that it is, then once an industry exhausts all of its economies of scale and reaches its ultimate stage of maturity (stationary state), the expectations prevailing in the industry may no longer be rate elastic.

3. The average capacity trading in the spot market is approximately 15% of the total and is composed of either the inefficient vessels or the speculative ownership of big tanker operators whose vessels are for the most part on long-term charters. So the impact of short-term rates is felt

---

[16] We may possibly get an egg to stand on end, but with the slightest disturbance it will topple over.

[17] Because of the infinite inelasticity of the short-term supply schedule beyond full capacity and the fact that yearly shipbuilding capacity is at least 7,000,000 DWT. (approximately 15% of existing capacity), the boom is not expected to last more than six to twelve months under normal conditions.

[18] Under assumptions of complete certainty and stability, there will be no need for a spot market.

directly by only a small share of the total market. Those vessels that operate in the spot market at any moment of time must have operated or will operate under at least one long-term charter agreement over their life span. As a result their owners may have had or will have opportunities to recover their investment in these ships. The vessels that seek long-term employment will only be affected if the long-term rates are sensitive to the short-term levels. To this topic, however, we shall return a little later.

It is mainly for these reasons that we believe the lot of the tanker owners is not so bad in general, even though the spot rate may, on the average, be below the long-run average cost of a vessel over its life span.

Some Further Empirical Observations Regarding Short-Term Rates

We have seen in the various figures depicting short-term rates the time profile of the rate movements. The empirical observations corroborate fully the inferences drawn from our theoretical formulations, which are shown graphically in Figures 8.1 and 8.2.

The spot rates, over the ten-year period that we examined, range from a low of 58 cents to a high of $4.49 per 1,000 ton-miles of oil carried. These rates are expressed in monthly averages, and reached their highest point in February 1957 and their lowest in July of 1954.[19] The rise as well as the decline in rates occur very swiftly, as both theoretical and empirical evidence shows. Of the two parts of the rate cycle, the upward climb will be slower because of the tortuous approach toward the normal static long-run equilibrium point. Once the excess capacity is eliminated and the static long-run equilibrium point is bypassed, then the climb picks up speed. The distance to be covered, however, is shorter on the upswing because of the existence of temporary intermediate equilibria. In contrast, during a rate decline the spot rate slides on the market supply schedule and drops all the way to the refusal rate of the marginal vessels. Taking the 1954–1958 cycle, which had a single peak,[20] and adjusting for normal seasonal rate variations, we find that it took fourteen months for the spot rates to reach their peak. We also observe that once the full cost of the marginal vessel is reached (around $1.30 per 1,000 ton-miles) then the changes in the level of spot rates become wider, often causing rates to double in a

---

[19] Since the lowest rate reached after the Suez crisis was 61 cents during April, May, and June 1958, the bottom of the depression had not been reached in 1959. Given economies of scale and changes in the size composition of the fleet, we would expect the rate to reach a lower level than the 58 cents of July 1954.

[20] The various phases of the Korean war compounded the cycles and did not allow the first one to be completed in the middle of 1951.

matter of two months. During the decline, rates dropped to 19% of their peak level in only three months, and reached the marginal cost (about 90 cents per 1,000 ton-miles) of a T-2.

If we analyze the 119 monthly variations in the average spot rates for the years 1949 through 1958, we find that 49.2% of all differences were positive and 50.8% were negative. This uniform distribution of first differences at first glance may be attributed to the presence of a random walk, which would negate our theory concerning a systematic influence of price-elastic expectations. A deeper analysis shows that a random walk is not present.

By developing a transition probability matrix, we find that the probability is .61 that a positive change will be followed by another positive change, and only .39 that a positive change will be followed by a negative change. Given a negative change, then the probability is .605 that the following change will also be negative and only .395 that it will be positive. The symmetry between the two sets of probabilities should be expected because the number of positive and negative changes is uniformly distributed. What is important is the significant difference in the conditional probabilities, implying the existence of price-elastic expectations.

Of all positive differences that followed another positive difference, 38% were of the same[21] magnitude, 29.5% were greater, and 32.5% were smaller than the preceding change. Of the negative changes, 34.3% were of the same magnitude, 31.5% were greater, and 34.3% smaller than the preceding negative change.

To ascertain whether there is a difference between the changes that occur around the temporary short-run equilibria and those that occur in the regions in which price-elastic expectations operate, we analyzed the changes by size. Taking all variations in spot rates, the probability is .49 that a change will be confined within plus or minus 10 cents of the previous rate level. Of these changes 86.3% occurred around the short-run equilibria at low rate levels (around the out-of-pocket cost of the marginal vessel). If we enlarge the price interval a little, we find that the probability is .655 that a change will be confined within plus or minus 20 cents of the previous rate.[22] Of these changes approximately 86% occurred around the possible short-run equilibria, and were all preceded by a change not greater than plus or minus 20 cents.

Once a change occurs, either up or down, of a magnitude greater than 20 cents per 1,000 ton-miles (there are 62 such cases out of 119), then

[21] We define "same" as being within 10 cents, because our probability states were defined by intervals of 10 cents each.

[22] Of all changes, 56.3% were confined within plus or minus 20 cents and had already been preceded by a similar change.

we find that the probability is zero that the following change will be of the same magnitude. What is more, the probability is only .032 that the new rate will be within plus or minus 10 cents of the previous price, given that the previous change was over plus or minus 20 cents per 1,000 ton-miles. Taking the complement of the above probability we see that if an absolute change greater than 20 cents occurs, then 96.8% of the new changes will be greater than plus or minus 10 cents. The comparable figure for a change greater than plus or minus 20 cents, given a previous change greater than plus or minus 20 cents, is 90.3%. Coupled with our previous findings that a positive change is followed by another positive change with a probability of .61, and a negative change by another negative change with a probability of .605, these results show how explosive the rate movements are until they hit the two reflecting barriers. The latter are represented by the rate at which the negative income-budget effect forces the charterers to withdraw from the market when rates are high, and the withdrawal rate of the marginal vessels when the rates are low.

In addition to the presence of price-elastic expectations, the results presented in this section indicate that the tankship transportation market is very unstable in the long run. The only fluctuations that are confined within a narrow range are those occurring around the short-run equilibria. Even these short-run equilibria, however, are not stable.

9

The Long-Term Charter Rate in the Short Run

In trying to find the "quantitative essence" of the "long-term charter rate," we shall be besieged inevitably by all sorts of difficulties, intrinsic, expositional, and of detail.[1] The "thing" exchanged for such a rate is not homogeneous, and even if it were, its value would depend on many short-term as well as long-term considerations.

For these reasons, it may be advisable to separate our discussion of the determination of long-term charter rates into two parts, depending on the duration of the influences that operate on long-term rates. We shall find, of course, that many of the factors that affect the long-term charter rate in the short run do likewise in the long run. However, there are distinct qualitative differences in the results of some of these impacts which necessitate such a dichotomy.

In the present chapter, we shall deal with the various factors that affect the long-term charter rates in the short run. Initially, we shall provide theoretical arguments on the qualitative contribution of each one of the relevant parameters, and then we shall proceed to analyze empirical evidence.

We believe that of all the nonrandom factors, the following are the most important determinants of the long-term rates in the short run:

1. The short-term rate as of a moment of time.
2. The expectations about the future that short-term rates create.
3. The status of tie-ups at the particular point of time.
4. The level of orders outstanding.
5. The size of the particular vessel.
6. The type of the propulsion system of the vessel (whether steam turbine or diesel).
7. The duration of the charter agreement.

[1] "Long-term charter rate," as used here, refers to the rate of other than single-voyage charters. Later, we shall make a distinction between the applicable rates for charters of different "long-term" durations.

8. The lead time between the agreement and the delivery of the vessel.
9. The type of cargo carried by the vessel whether "clean" (gasoline and other refined products) or "dirty" (crude oil).
10. The type of currency in which payment is made.

Because some of these factors, such as the first four, are transient, their impact is expected to be manifested only in the short run. Others are more lasting, however, because their origin lies in objective data, and they are therefore also expected to appear in our discussion of the long-run level of the long-term charter rates.

We shall be treating many variables as independent for practical reasons and not because of the existence of functional independence. For example, we have shown in the previous chapters that the short-term rates affect expectations, new orders, and also tie-ups. Accordingly, we may argue that the latter do not qualify as independent variables. This much is conceded. Nevertheless, the impact of short-term rates on orders and tie-ups, for example, is much more lasting than the level of short-term rates itself; therefore, orders and tie-ups merit individual consideration. For similar reasons, rates of change in certain variables may explain more than the levels, and later we shall test this possibility also.

Let us now take the short-run determinants of long-term rates one by one and analyze their theoretical impact.

1. The short-term rate is expected to influence the long-term rate both on the upswing and during periods of low spot rates, for reasons similar to those operating in the money markets.[2] Unlike the money market rates, however, as we shall see shortly, the long-term tankship rate is expected to be lower than the short-term, under normal conditions.

If we assume certainty and exclude "economies of scale" in long-term contracts, the long-term rate would be approximately equal to the arithmetic average of the current spot rate and the expected spot rates over the interval covered by the long-term contract.[3] For this reason alone, it is obvious that the long-term rate will not fluctuate as much as the short-term rate, and that at any moment of time short-term and long-term rates will be equal only if the expected average value of the future short-term rates, properly discounted, is equal to the current spot rate.

If we now remove the aforementioned restrictive assumptions, we notice that differences may arise between long-term and short-term rates for any one or a combination of the following reasons:

(a) There may be demand uncertainties and expectations over the

---

[2] See Hicks, J. R., *Value and Capital,* Second Edition, Oxford University Press, London, 1953, pp. 141–152 and 163–170; also Keynes, J. M., *The General Theory of Employment, Interest and Money,* Macmillan & Co., Ltd., London, 1936, Chapter 13; and Kalecki, M., *Studies in Economic Dynamics,* Allen and Unwin, Ltd., London, 1943, pp. 32–47.

[3] See Hicks, *op. cit.,* p. 145. The relation will be only approximate because of the time shape of the spot rates over a given interval.

period covered by the long-term contract. Thus, if the current spot rates are considered excessively high, the long-term rates will be lower than the short-term rates, and vice versa.

(b) Because of the risks inherent in the operations of the spot market, the short-term rate will normally be higher than the long-term rate. These risks, unlike those in the money markets, are not due to fears of default, but mainly to fears of unemployment. As we have previously explained, the oil companies resort to the spot market for their marginal needs in order to minimize the amount of idle tonnage. To lure tankships to the spot market, however, the charterers must offer higher rates to compensate the speculators for the risks transferred to them. And, incidentally, the premium of the short-term over the long-term rate must be sufficient to attract the marginal speculator and must make it worthwhile for the most inefficient vessels in the spot market to stay in operation.

(c) Even if we exclude the risk of unemployment, it is logical to assume that there is some subjective value to the certainty of plans. If this is true, then the short-term rate must be higher than the long-term rate by an amount that will compensate the marginal entrant into the spot market for the trouble of entering into frequent negotiations. Conceivably this "trouble premium" could be smaller for the big tankship owners, because they can enter the market and make coincidental agreements of long-term and short-term duration.

(d) In addition to the "trouble premium," the long-term contracts save on time spent for decision making and are administratively more simple and less costly for both the charterer and the owner. The brokerage fee, which is usually paid by the owners, contributes to the savings that accrue with long-term contracts, even though it is a flat percentage on the total contractual consideration. To the extent that under a single-voyage charter the owner pays for the fuel, canal tolls, port and pilot charges, etc., which the charterers pay under a time charter, the brokerage fee will be relatively higher for vessels trading in the spot market. Furthermore, the brokerage fee sometimes rises from a normal rate of 1.25% to 2.5% of the contract price because of multiple listings that are necessary under depressed market conditions.

(e) Finally, and an important consideration, there is a real money value to a long-term charter, in that it can be mortgaged. Many independents follow this practice of financing because they save on interest. In cognizance of the security behind a long-term charter agreement, the banks not only are more willing to lend money on two signatures (one of which is that of a secure oil company) rather than one, but also make concessions in the interest rate commensurate with the reduction in risk.

In summary, the long-term rates are expected to move in the same direction as the short-term rates but will not exhibit the erratic fluctuations of the spot rates. For subjective and objective reasons, mainly the latter, the short-term rate is expected to be sufficiently higher than the long-term rate to induce the marginal speculators and marginal vessels to stay in the spot market. Somehow the speculators must be compensated for the risk they undertake — which risk of unemployment is shifted to the spot market by the oil companies. Only during periods of depressed market conditions may the long-term rate be higher than the short-term, but because the spot-rate fluctuations are so narrow under such circumstances, the difference between spot and long-term rates will not be great.

2. As we have argued earlier, the expectations of the "buyers" in the tankship markets are over-all price elastic. This implies that the short-term rates will affect the long-term rates indirectly, through expectations. It is only logical to assume that if a buyer expects the short-term rates to increase proportionately more in the future than the present rate increase, he will also expect future long-term rates to follow in sympathy. In fact the impact of expectations, based on spot rates, may be so great as to distort any correlation between short-term and long-term rates. That is, once the short-term rates generate expectations they may become captives of their own creation.

3. Tie-ups will affect long-term rates, as of a moment of time, because these vessels form a ready reserve on which the charterers may draw. We have shown that as long as this reserve exists, the level of rates cannot improve. Thus, the greater the capacity tied up the lower the long-term rates will be.

4. Orders are mostly determined by spot rates but are not as transient as rates because of the shipbuilding lead time. For this reason, high levels of orders outstanding (backlog) are compatible with periods of both high and low rates. When rates are rising, orders rise with them, and the level of orders outstanding as of that moment has no direct adverse impact on the current long-term rates because of the expectations prevailing. During rate depressions, however, with all the surpluses that are brought about, orders outstanding condition expectations and thus affect "future" rates, especially if many of these vessels do not have charters waiting for them upon completion. In general, however, we would expect to find a positive correlation between total orders outstanding and long-term rates even under depressed market conditions, because with the drop in rates new orders are no longer placed and the deliveries and the cancellations bring about a reduction in the level of orders outstanding.

5. The size of vessels plays a vital role in the determination of rates because the industry still enjoys internal technological economies of scale. The savings that accrue with size are very substantial, and theoretically should be reflected in both the short-term and the long-term rates. Because of the risks involved in operating large vessels in the spot market, however, not many vessels of the supertanker size are found there under normal conditions. These vessels are likely to accept single-voyage charters only during depressed periods because under such circumstances their only alternative is tie-up.[4] We have shown, however, that the refusal rate of the marginal block of vessels usually sets the price in a depressed market. Furthermore, inasmuch as many of these large vessels accept employment with "part-cargo" because many spot charterers cannot utilize them at full capacity, the refusal rate of the marginal vessel may not cover much more than the out-of-pocket cost of these supertankers. Consequently, the rates are equalized and the economies of scale are buried in underutilization of capacity during depressed market conditions.

[4] The largest vessel that we observed in the spot market was one of 44,000 DWT., but this was only for one voyage. There may have been other cases, however, both of larger vessels and of voyages of longer duration which did not come to our attention.

CHAPTER NINE

The impact of the economies of scale, then, is felt mostly in the long-term market. We shall now examine the qualitative features of this impact on the rates.

Because it is necessary under conditions of excess demand to raise the level of rates to attract vessels of smaller and smaller sizes, the impact of size on long-term rates (as measured by partial correlation coefficients) will be more visible in a high spot market. When rates are low and most of the smaller vessels are tied up, only the larger vessels are potential entrants into the long-term market; and for this reason alone the *visible* influence of size on long-term rates is likely to be small.

6. The economics of tanker propulsion are very complicated, not because of conceptual difficulties but because of the absence of reliable empirical information. With reliable data, the analysis itself would not be different from the one presented in the footnote under "Retirements and Replacements" and in the main text under "Slowdowns." The available data are not only "colored" and incomplete, but are not even finalized. Because the technology is still rapidly developing, the comparisons between the diesel engines and turbines are particular and not universally applicable. Up to 1957 the diesel engines could not develop more than 15,000–16,000 shaft horsepower (SHP), while turbines could go up to 25,000. This limited the use of diesel to vessels of about 35,000 DWT. With "supercharge" a diesel could be fitted to propel a tanker of 40,000–45,000 DWT. Now, however, plans are made for diesels of 25,000 SHP, which, if successful, will again bring the diesel engine into competition.

Assuming then that both steam turbines and diesels can be used for any vessel size, let us consider briefly the pros and cons of this confused subject.[5]

The main advantage of diesel propulsion is that it achieves greater thermal efficiencies, converting a greater percentage of fuel energy into mechanical power at the shaft. It is estimated that the diesel achieves 40% thermal efficiency (it consumes .35 lb. of fuel per SHP hour), while the steam turbine converts only 25% into mechanical power (.575 lb. per SHP hour).[6]

These data imply that the diesel consumes about 40% *less* fuel than a steam turbine of equal output, thus increasing the vessel's carrying capacity by saving on bunker space. However, the total fuel cost may be higher for the diesel vessel because it uses a distillate (diesel oil) and the steam turbine uses a residual oil.[7] The cost of the diesel oil ranges, depending on the source, from 150% to 180% of the "Bunker C" fuel oil used by turbines. Furthermore, the diesel engine does not use more than 80% to 85% of the

---

[5] The reader who is interested in getting more details is advised to read with a critical attitude: "Speed and Power Economics of Big Tankers," *The Oil Forum*, Vol. IV, No. 3, March 1950, pp. 113–116; Møller-Guldberg, *Comparison Between Steam-Turbine and Diesel-Driven Tankers of 24,000 D.W.T.*, Burmeister & Wain, Copenhagen, 1956, 11 pp.; Jung, Ingvar, and Gunnar Ohlsson, "Technical and Economic Data for Turbine-Powered Tankers," *International Shipbuilding Progress*, Vol. 4, No. 38, October 1957, pp. 531–541; "The Advancing Diesel," *Petroleum Press Service*, October 1957, pp. 335–369; "Diverse Trends in Ships' Propulsion," *Petroleum Press Service*, pp. 375–378.

[6] See *Fairplay*, October 30, 1958, p. 1048, and "The Advancing Diesel," *op. cit.*, p. 366.

[7] A little later we shall discuss the case of diesels using heavy fuel oil.

shaft horsepower developed[8] (versus 100% for the turbine), which implies that a diesel vessel probably cannot achieve the speed of a comparable steam-driven tanker, thus losing some of its capacity advantage.

In addition to differences in the quantity of bunkers and speed, the difference in carrying capacity between the diesel and the steam-driven vessel is affected by the following factors, all of which seem to favor the steam turbine:[9]

(a) Both the weight and the area occupied by diesel installations are greater than those of steam turbines.

(b) The diesel engines are more delicate than the steam turbines and require longer repair times.

(c) Because the diesel vessel uses small auxiliary steam installations for loading and unloading, it is not as efficient at port (turn-around time) as the steam-driven vessel.

The cost of operating a motor ship is greater than that of the steam vessel, because of the following factors:

(a) Higher initial investment, because of the bulkier construction of diesels.

(b) Higher maintenance costs, because of the intricacy of the diesel engine.

(c) Greater crew requirements for the engine room.

(d) Requirements for auxiliary units for heating, loading, and unloading, because steam is not available.

On the basis of these factors, it appears that the steam turbine is superior to the diesel from the economic point of view. However, many operators prefer diesels because of the controllability of diesel power. The latter, it is claimed, allows better maneuverability and easier steering.

During the last three years, many diesel vessels have been fitted with special equipment that enables them to use heavy residual oils (fuel oil). These special facilities, which supposedly have a ten-year life and are not very costly,[10] are used to preheat and purify the fuel. The savings in fuel cost are of course substantial, but evidently corrosion necessitates frequent

---

[8] Jung and Ohlsson, *op. cit.*, pp. 536–537.

[9] See Bes, J., *Tanker Chartering and Management*, C. De Boer, Jr., Amsterdam, 1956; also Jung and Ohlsson, *op. cit.*, p. 531. Møller-Guldberg dismiss (b) and (c) of the claimed capacity disadvantages of diesel (there may be a conflict of interest here since their firm produces diesels) and conclude that "the advantage of the diesel-engined ship is so enormous that hardly any responsible shipowner can decide in favor of turbine ships without having very pressing reasons for doing so," p. 11. The aforementioned analysis appears to be somewhat biased. In contrast, Jung and Ohlsson say that "the turbine vessel only needs to save a few days a year for loading or discharging or owing to shorter repair times, and it will be economically superior," p. 538. The empirical data that they present show that a steam-driven vessel usually spends 295 days at sea, versus 275 for the diesel (p. 539), which is more than enough to counterbalance the capacity advantage and any fuel economy of the latter. Both articles mentioned assume that the diesels operate on heavy fuel.

[10] The *Petroleum Press Service*, October 1958, p. 377, claims that the cost is £20,000–£25,000 while Bes, in his *Tanker Chartering and Management*, p. 42, says that it is £10,000.

replacements of the cylinder liners and piston rings. According to Bes[11] this cost is approximately £2,000 per year.

If the data correspond to the actual costs of conversion, there is no doubt that the converted diesel engine is more economical than the regular diesel. In fact, the whole investment is recovered in one year out of the savings in fuel cost, which are approximately $300 per day on a T-2 size vessel. As for the relationship between the costs of operation for a converted diesel and a geared turbine, it seems that these costs are now equalized for vessels of small sizes, with the diesel a slight favorite.

The above excursion into the economics of diesel versus turbine engines provides us with all the information that we need to assess the effect of propulsion on long-term rates. Under a long-term charter agreement the charterer pays for the fuel, port charges, and canal dues, but all the other operating expenses such as crew costs, repairs, and maintenance are the responsibility of the owner. Consequently, if we assume full capacity, the vessels that are most economical in fuel consumption are expected to command a premium, since the savings from fuel consumption will accrue to the charterer.

Because capacity is also affected the criterion of vessel choice then reduces to fuel cost minimization per unit of capacity, provided that the opportunity cost of the capacity lost is not greater than the over-all savings achieved. *This applies only to the region of elastic supply.*

According to the *Petroleum Press Service*[12] and Bes,[13] the converted diesel vessel has been commanding higher charter rates for the reasons just explained. However, we feel that the *regular* diesel will not command higher rates than the turbine vessel but, on the contrary, possibly lower rates.

Data on the categories of the propulsion systems of the particular vessels are available, but unfortunately no information exists on conversions. For this reason this variable will not be used in our formulation explaining the long-term rate.

7. The duration of the charter agreement, as we have explained during our discussion of the relationship between the short-term and the long-term rate, will affect the long-term rate because of

(*a*) The uncertainties and expectations concerning the movement in spot rates over the period that the long-term contract covers.

(*b*) The risks of unemployment that are eliminated by the long-term agreement.

(*c*) The nuisance of frequent contracts.

(*d*) The savings in the administrative costs and the brokerage fees.

(*e*) The mortgageability of the long-term contracts.

Because of the uncertainties in the movement of short-term rates over an extended period of time, it is natural to expect decisions to be made on the basis of deviations from the static long-run costs. This is the only objective criterion available to the owners and will logically serve as a point of departure, especially for those whose imaginative anticipation of future short-term conditions is not very strong. The deviations from this cost-based, long-term rate will be determined by the short-term conditions that are expected

---

[11] *Op. cit.,* p. 42.
[12] October 1958, p. 378.
[13] *Op. cit.,* p. 43.

to prevail, but will grow fainter and fainter as the duration of the charter is extended.

For long-term contracts which do not extend beyond the foreseeable future, the difference between the long-term and the short-term rates will be mainly caused by (*a*), the expectations concerning the movement in spot rates over the period covered by the contract. This impact is expected to cause long-term rates higher than the "current" short-term rates (but still below the relevant static long-run cost) in periods of excess supply, and lower than the existing short-term rates (but now above static long-run costs) in periods of excess demand. These differences are due to the imaginative anticipation of the turning points and the future levels of rates on the part of the people who operate in the tankship markets. Furthermore, there are certain aspects of security that force the charterers to yield during periods of low rates and the owners during periods of high rates.

With a long-term contract extending *beyond* the time period that imagination can penetrate, the influence of factors (*b*) through (*d*) will be reflected in the level of long-term rates but will be very small, merely because the imaginative anticipation beyond a period of, let us say, five years will at best be very weak. The mortgageability of the long-term charter, however, may have *definite and discernible* influences, which become stronger the longer the duration of the charter because its value can be translated into a "present worth equivalent," especially in cases where other sources of capital are closed to the vessel owner. Even in this case, however, an extension of the duration of the charter beyond, say, seven years will not benefit the shipowner, because banks do not, as a matter of policy, grant loans on charters extending beyond five to seven years. The loanable value of a charter, of course, may still change because of the charter rate, but not because of the duration of the contract, if the bank expects a repayment out of the net "hire" in a maximum of seven years.

Even though some of the "unilateral" benefits accruing out of long-term contracts apply also to the charterers (for example, the risk of being caught short of capacity, the trouble of entering the market, and the administrative-cost saving), the owners still benefit much more than the charterers, and therefore we would expect, *under normal conditions,* most of the savings to be conceded to the oil companies. The bargaining position of the big charterers is strengthened by the fact that they own and control a considerable amount of transportation capacity whenever they enter the market, and as a result, their needs are not as immediate as those of the owners. Whenever the oil companies enter the market for long-term charters of five to ten years, the exact timing of the agreements is rather immaterial because the companies have some flexibility as a result of the capacity they control. For the independent, however, every day of idleness is costly as the idle costs are not postponable, and he is therefore under more pressure.

The concession of most of the savings of the long-term contracts to the charterers will then cause slight downward shifts to the "current" long-term cost that is used as a guidepost for determining the long-term rate of contracts of different durations. These movements must not be confused with shifts caused in the long run by changes in the composition of the fleet, which we shall discuss later. Here we refer to the same static long-run costs but looked at successively in relation to charters of different duration.

If we now put together the impact of factor (*a*) with that of factors (*b*) through (e), the relationship between the short-term and the long-term rates of different durations may appear as shown in Figure 9.1.

What we here call "normal rate" is nothing more than the hypothetical normal long-term rates based on static long-run costs. The slightly negative

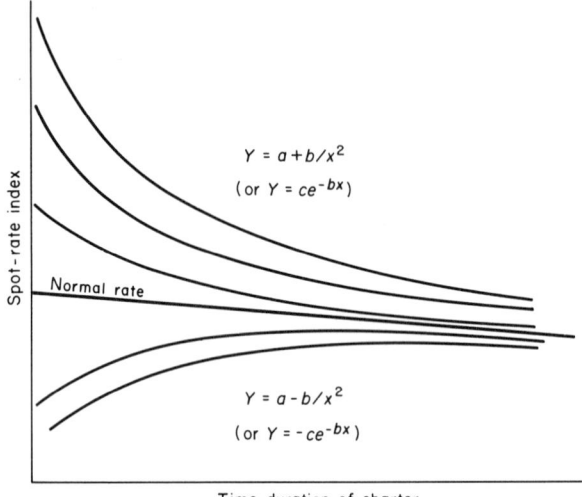

Figure 9.1. Charter duration and its impact on charter rates.

slope is due to factors (b) through (e) as previously explained.[14] Factor (a) will cause these transcendental curves to approach the "normal rate" from above and below as the duration of the charter is lengthened.

Theoretically, there is an infinity of such curves corresponding to the infinite number of possible short-term rates. When the spot rate is below the *normal* long-term rate, the market long-term rate will tend to be greater the longer the duration of the contract.[15] On the other hand, when the short-term rates are very high, the market long-term rates will be lower the longer the charter's duration.

Because of the disproportionate fluctuations of the spot rates above versus below the normal (static) long-term rate, the lower part of the previous graph is flatter. Thus we would expect stronger empirical relationships between the market long-term rates and the duration of the charters under high rates. Furthermore, if our theoretical arguments are valid, the range within which rates for charters of very long duration move must be very narrow, indicating the great degree of independence of the long-term rates from current market conditions.

[14] A slightly negative slope may also be caused by anticipations of economies of scale over the life span of the charter agreement. If the charterers expect that even the most efficient of the existing vessels will become rather semiobsolete in a few years, they will undoubtedly discount heavily the benefits to be accrued during the last few years of the charter.

[15] The negative slope of the "asymptote," namely the normal rate, may upset this relationship. The market long-term rate may increase with the duration of the charter *up to a certain point* and then turn downward reversing the relationship.

Although we have been talking in terms of the static long-term rate, we must not forget that there is considerable heterogeneity in the tankship markets because vessels are not identical. Their speed may be different, their propulsion system, their pumping capacity, and also their construction. All these heterogeneous characteristics, however, can be reduced into homogeneous objective data and can be accounted for in the relationship between size and long-term rates. Once such "quality differentials" are accounted for, then all long-term charter rates for charters of equal time duration are equalized in the market to a very great extent.

The process of translating time-charter rates into a homogeneous basis, although manageable, is rather complicated. It requires a conversion of the stated capacity of a vessel into tons of oil that the vessel can potentially deliver and then calculation of the cost per ton of delivered oil. Obviously the run will affect the calculations, not only because the longer the run the smaller the potential deliveries but because for any one vessel the carrying capacity is not a linear function of the distance. The days in port for loading and unloading and the time spent traversing canals are mostly fixed per trip, irrespective of the size of the vessel and the distance covered. As a result, one must first choose a run, take the particularities of the vessel and the terms of the transaction, and then calculate the spot-rate equivalent of a time charter. An illustration of the method used for converting time-charter rates into spot-rate equivalent can be found in Appendix B at the end of this book.

In order to study the relationship between the duration of charter agreements and charter rates, we have converted into spot-rate equivalent the rates for all time charters transacted between 1950 and 1961, over one thousand all together. For the conversion we used the Curaçao–London–Curaçao run. The empirical evidence fully confirms the inferences that we made on the basis of purely theoretical considerations. Figures 9.2 and 9.3 present some of the results, the rest being of a similar nature. The trend lines were drawn "freehand" to go through the mid-values of the transactions. With the exception of 1959, during the years depicted in the figures there

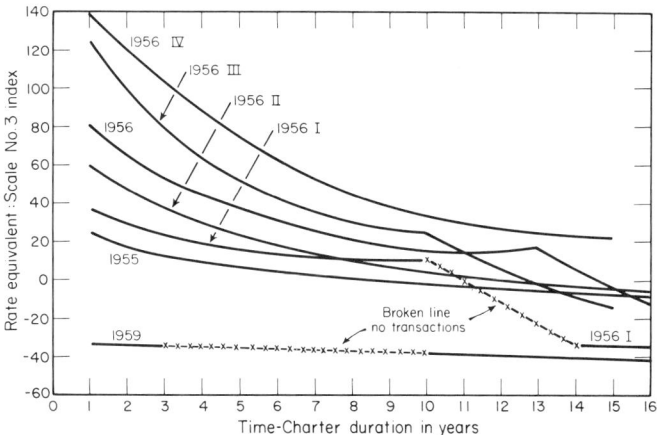

Figure 9.2. Empirical schedules of the structure and level of time-charter rates: the impact of spot rates and charter duration on time-charter rates for 1955, 1956, 1956 by quarters, and 1959.

was a sufficient number of observations to allow generalizations. In 1955 there were 219 time-charter agreements, 383 in 1956, 64 in 1957, and 30 in 1959.

During periods of normal or high spot rates, as can be seen in Figure 9.2, the longer the duration of the contract the lower the rate. Although the rates for a time charter of one year's duration in 1955 and 1956 ranged from Scale plus 25% to Scale plus 140%, we see that the ten-year time charters were separated by only 30 points. These results were expected. As we have previously explained, the longer the duration of the contract the greater the influence of objective considerations. The difference between the 1959 trend line and the asymptotes approached by the 1955 and 1956 charter rates is due to the change in the composition of the total fleet, which shifted downward the static long-run supply schedule for the industry. The orders generated by the Suez crisis were mostly for vessels of 40,000 DWT. and over, and some of these vessels were in operation in 1959.

In order to observe the impact of spot rates on time-charter rates for contracts of different time duration, we separated the 1956 data by quarters. During 1956, rates increased progressively from an average of $1.60 in the first quarter, to $3.76 per 1,000 ton-miles in the last quarter. This can be inferred also from Figure 9.2, because the rate for a time charter of one year's duration is not very different from the spot rate. The results shown in Figure 9.2 confirm very definitely the theoretical schedules of Figure 9.1, during periods of spot rates higher than normal.[16]

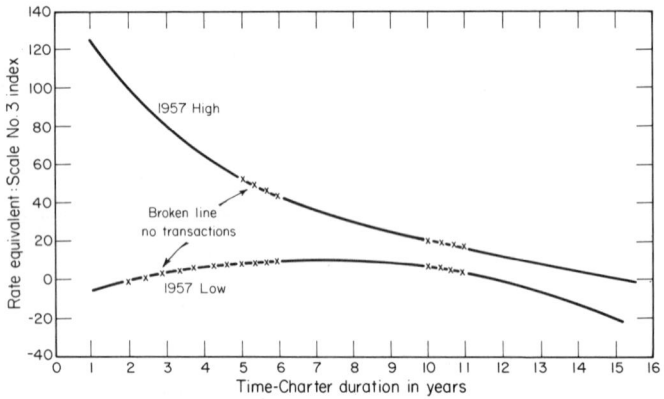

Figure 9.3. Long-run convergence of time-charter rates under high and low spot rates: empirical observations for 1957.

The spot rates during 1957 plummeted from a high of $4.49 per 1,000 ton-miles reached in February to a low of 62 cents approached in November. With the exception of the first quarter of the year, the remainder of 1957 was a year of tanker market depression. For this reason, we chose 1957 to illustrate what happens to the time-charter rate as the duration of the charter increases under high and low spot rates. The results are shown in Figure 9.3.

---

[16] In terms of the Scale index, the full cost (including financial charges) of a T-2 is approximately Scale plus 10%.

We notice how the two schedules converge toward Scale plus 10%, which happens to be approximately the full cost of a T-2, as the duration of the charter increases to nine years. From then on the schedule under high rates resumes its downward trend more decisively, while the lower schedule reverses itself. The reasons for this behavior of the schedules, for time charters of eleven years and over, are not only of a short-term nature (elimination of risks of unemployment, nuisance of frequent contracts, savings of administrative and brokerage costs, and mortgageability of the charter) but also reflect the impact of expectations of technological changes. If there is sufficient probability that the chartered vessels will become obsolete during the tenure of the agreement, this expectation will no doubt influence the charter rate. Finally, we notice that the slope of the 1957 schedule under low rates is not very steep because of the narrow range separating the static long-run rate from the short-run equilibria under low rates.

8. Related to the duration of the charter is the lead time, or the period between the signing of the charter agreement and the actual delivery of the vessel. The lead time is expected to affect the long-term rates because of the uncertainty and expectations concerning the short-term rate over the lead-time period. This, as we have already observed, is one of the factors that affect the relationship between the long-term rates and the duration of the charters.[17]

The correlation between the long-term rates and the lead time is expected to be positive under low spot rates and negative when spot rates are high. This implies that the longer the lead time, the higher the long-term rate will be under depressed market conditions; and the opposite, during periods of strong demand. Again, as in the case of the duration of the charters, the relationship between the lead time and the market long-term rate will be stronger during periods of excess demand because of the greater fluctuation in spot rates on the upswing.

9. The rate should be affected by the type of cargo carried because of the cost of corrosion. That is why tankers intended for clean trade command a premium.

A detailed analysis of the cost of corrosion is not needed for our purposes.[18] Long-term fixtures, unlike single voyages, do not normally specify the type of cargo, with the exception of a provision that the vessel may not be used for more than three years in clean trade.[19] On the assumption that only about 30% of the tankship capacity is, at any moment of time, carrying gasoline and other products, the necessity for separating the long-term mar-

---

[17] Even though the net manifestation of the impacts of lead time and charter duration on long-term rates is similar, some of the reasons behind such impacts are different. For example, the urgency of the charterers' needs attaches penalties to lead times at high rates and to premiums during depressed market conditions. No such impact operates through the duration of charters. Furthermore, the longer the lead time, the lower the loan value of the charter, while the opposite is usually true with charter duration.

[18] The reader who is interested in the problems of corrosion may wish to leaf through the papers presented at the midyear and annual meetings of the American Petroleum Institute. The latter's Division of Transportation is very active on matters of corrosion protection.

[19] Bes, *op. cit.*, p. 123. Evidently the three-year limit is independent of the time-charter duration.

ket into clean and dirty trade is obviated because the clean trade can be fitted into the three-year limit, excluding exceptional cases. The case is different, however, in the spot market, but for single-voyage charters details exist. The brokers' reports listing the spot transactions separate the "clean" from the "dirty" trade, and indicate that there is a differential of approximately 20 Scale points in favor of the tankers operating in the "clean" trade.

10. Finally, the type of currency in which payment is made should also affect the long-term rate. However, this information is not often available. The transactions are mostly in dollars or sterling, but even though the majority of the payments are made in these two currencies the designation is presumably more indicative of the central markets where the transactions occurred than of the currency of the actual payments.

Therefore, currency, the type of cargo, and the type of propulsion will be left out of the model that we shall test empirically to quantify the impact of the factors that operate on long-term rates and which we have analyzed theoretically.

10

Model of Long-Term Rates

We shall now explain quantitatively the variation in long-term rates by means of a statistical model. In this respect we shall assume that the relationship between rates and the independent variables is linear, if not in the natural at least in the logarithmic form. This assumption, though an oversimplification of what we believe to be a complicated transcendental function, is suggested by the graph depicting the theoretical relationship between short-term, market long-term, and "normal" long-term rates. The model and several variations to it will be tested by means of multiple-regression and correlation analyses.[1]

Our first analysis covers the period between 1950 and 1957 and depicts long-term rates as a function of nine independent variables as follows:

x_1 = index of short-term rates (monthly)
x_2 = duration of the charter (in months)
x_3 = lead time between charter agreement and vessel delivery (in months)
x_4 = size of the vessel (in DWT.)
x_5 = index of short-term "adjustment" (monthly)
x_6 = vessels idle as percentage of the working petroleum fleet (monthly)
x_7 = index of change in x_6 (monthly)
x_8 = orders outstanding as a percentage of the working petroleum fleet (monthly)
x_9 = index of change in new orders placed (monthly)

The index of short-term rates is a weighted index of the average monthly rates per 1,000 ton-miles for the various runs. The weights

[1] One other analysis of this sort came to our attention and benefited our work. Alvin Karchere of Caltex studied the time charters for tankers for the period of August 1956 to August 1957, and kindly furnished the writer with a copy of his "interim report," 11 pp.

assigned approximate the average significance of the oil flows in terms of tankship capacity utilization during the period 1950–1957. If we let

a = the average monthly rate per 1,000 ton-miles for the Caribbean–United States run

b = the average monthly rate per 1,000 ton-miles for the Persian Gulf–United States run

c = the average monthly rate per 1,000 ton-miles for the U.S. Gulf–north of Cape Hatteras run[2]

d = the average monthly rate per 1,000 ton-miles for the Persian Gulf–United Kingdom run

e = the average monthly rate per 1,000 ton-miles for the Caribbean–United Kingdom run

The index $x_1 = (3a + 3b + 6c + 8d + 4e)/24$

Rates b and d have been adjusted for the canal tolls by subtracting 10 cents per 1,000 ton-miles for the Persian Gulf to the United States trade, and 13 cents per 1,000 ton-miles for the Persian Gulf to the United Kingdom trade. The total round-trip toll is approximately 87.5 cents per ton of oil carried.

Variables x_2, x_3, and x_4 do not need any explanation, but x_5 does. What we call here the index of short-term "adjustment" is a "smoothed-out" function of the short-term rates. Our purpose in introducing this variable is to test whether immediate expectations are shaped by the "current" spot rates alone, or whether some form of distributed lag operates on expectations. Furthermore, this index may provide us with at least a qualitative indication of the elasticity of expectations.

The method followed in arriving at the index of adjustment is similar to that used in demand analysis when distributed lags are introduced.[3] We shall assume that the charterers condition their behavior by relative changes in the levels of rates, implying an exponential adjustment path.

Let us denote A_t as the index of actual changes in spot rates between period t and $t - 1$, and E_t as the expected index of the relationship between the spot rates of the same periods. We define

---

[2] We have given some weight to the U.S. rates, although the market is restricted to U.S.-flag vessels, to account for the "sympathetic pressure" which tends to equalize the market rates and eliminate differentials over and above the protectionist premium.

[3] See, among others, Koyck, L. M., *Distributed Lags and Investment Analysis,* North-Holland Publishing Company, Amsterdam, 1954; Chow, Gregory C., *Demand for Automobiles in the United States,* North-Holland Publishing Company, Amsterdam, 1957; Nerlove, Marc, *Distributed Lags and Demand Analysis for Agricultural and Other Commodities,* U.S. Government Printing Office, Washington 25, D. C., June 1958. The latter reference also contains summaries of other works in this area.

$$A_t = R_t/R_{t-1} \tag{10.1}$$

where R_t and R_{t-1} stand for the level of spot rates in periods t and $t-1$, respectively, and

$$E_{t+1} = A_t + a(E_t - A_t) \tag{10.2}$$

These definitions imply that if $A_t < 100$ there has been a decrease in rates, and if $A_t > 100$ there has been an increase. This type of "index" will exclude negative values which may cause us difficulty in a logarithmic formulation.

Equation 10.2 implies that the *expected* index of change in rates between periods t and $t+1$ is equal to the *actual* index of change between periods t and $t-1$ plus a factor a times the difference between the expected and actual changes between periods t and $t-1$. In this respect, as long as the actual and expected indices are the same, we assume in effect that the operatives will expect a percentage change in the rates for the next period equal to the one that occurred in the previous period.[4]

Equation 10.2 is a difference equation, the general solution of which is

$$E_{t+1} = \sum_{k=0}^{n} a^k(1-a)A_{t-k}$$

Alternatively we can arrive at the solution algebraically. From Equation 10.2, by rearranging we get

$$E_{t+1} = (1-a)A_t + aE_t \tag{10.3}$$

but

$$E_t = A_{t-1} + a(E_{t-1} - A_{t-1}) \tag{10.4}$$

or

$$E_t = (1-a)A_{t-1} + aE_{t-1}$$

and

$$aE_t = a(1-a)A_{t-1} + a^2 E_{t-1} \tag{10.5}$$

Hence Equation 10.3 becomes

$$E_{t+1} = (1-a)A_t + a(1-a)A_{t-1} + a^2 E_{t-1} \tag{10.6}$$

where again

---

[4] Alternatively, we may assume that the "percentage rate of change" is measured in terms of a uniform absolute base, be this U.S.M.C., Scale, or any other base. In this case, if we assume continuity of our functions, our index becomes

$$A_t = R_t/R_{t-1} = R_0 e^{nr_t}/R_0 e^{nr_{t-1}} \quad \text{or} \quad \ln A_t = n(r_t - r_{t-1})$$

The latter may be taken to denote the actual difference in the percentage rates of change in spot rates between periods t and $t-1$; because our subdivisions of each period $t-(t-1)$ may be taken as equal, we have

$$\ln A_t = r_t - r_{t-1}$$

$$a^2 E_{t-1} = a^2(1-a)A_{t-2} + a^3(1-a)A_{t-3} + \cdots + a^n(1-a)A_{t-n} \quad (10.7)$$

and substituting in Equation 10.6 we get finally

$$E_{t+1} = (1-a)A_t + a(1-a)A_{t-1} + a^2(1-a)A_{t-2}$$
$$+ a^3(1-a)A_{t-3} + \cdots + a^n(1-a)A_{t-n} \quad (10.8)$$

If we now substitute for A_t the value as given by Equation 10.1 we get

$$E_{t+1} = (1-a)R_t/R_{t-1} + a(1-a)R_{t-1}/R_{t-2} + \cdots$$
$$+ a^n(1-a)R_{t-n}/R_{t-n-1} \quad (10.9)$$

Some of the officials of the oil companies we visited spoke about the alleged use of the so-called "50% rule." Those who use it claim that they always cut differences in half, whenever and wherever these arise, and behave as if the adjusted figures are the actual figures.[5] We shall assume, as a result, that $a = .5$, in which case we get

$$1 - a = .5$$
$$a(1-a) = .25$$
$$a^2(1-a) = .125$$
$$a^3(1-a) = .0625$$
$$a^4(1-a) = .03125$$

Let us assume for practical purposes that any period whose impact is less than 5% of the combined impact of the periods following it will be insignificant in the shaping of expectations. Hence our index becomes

$$E_{t+1} = .50(R_t/R_{t-1}) + .25(R_{t-1}/R_{t-2}) + .13(R_{t-2}/R_{t-3})$$
$$+ .06(R_{t-3}/R_{t-4}) \quad (10.10)$$

In addition to the index of short-term adjustment, we shall use variables based on idle vessels, orders outstanding, and orders placed, in order to attest the significance of intermediate and somewhat long-term influences on long-term rates.

We have previously defined the "working petroleum fleet" as the total fleet minus government-owned vessels, special purpose ships, and vessels idle either because of tie-up or for repairs extending beyond thirty

---

[5] The "50% rule," according to at least one high official of an oil company, is applied also to plans made on the basis of forecasts. One can easily prove that, if such a practice is used by a substantial segment of the industry, the only salvation may be erroneous forecasts in the right direction of a magnitude equal to twice the would-be actual. Otherwise, if estimates are always correct, by cutting the implementation in half the rate cycle will be aggravated and the cobweb effects will be even more pronounced. The probability of correct forecasts, however, is not very great, and even in the remote possibility that the "50% rule" is consciously and consistently applied, we do not expect such practices to aggravate the rate cycle further.

days. Variables x_6 and x_8 are both based on the working petroleum fleet.

Variables x_7 and x_9 are approximations of rates of change and are based on idle capacity and new orders placed, respectively. The rate of change in idle capacity is measured as the ratio of the idle capacity of period t, as a percentage of the working petroleum fleet of period t, to the respective magnitudes of period $t - 1$. As for x_9, it represents the ratio of new orders placed in period t, as a percentage of the orders outstanding at the beginning of the period, to the new orders of period $t - 1$, as a percentage of the orders outstanding at the beginning of $t - 1$.[6]

The "universe" that we are about to analyze consists of 1,048 long-term charters — time charters only, not consecutive voyages — which, according to the brokers, comprise over 95% of all the transactions of the period under observation. Of these 1,048 observations, 129 had to be rejected because they were followed by options for an extension of the contracts, and 6 more because they were bareboat charters.[7] For certain computer runs an additional sixteen observations were eliminated because they involved vessels under 9,000 DWT.

The statistical models that we shall discuss were tested at the M.I.T. Computation Center.[8] The preparatory work,[9] excluding the time spent on collecting data, consumed over 2,500 man-hours; and the processing of the data required about 5 hours of computer time. The subsequent analysis of the results of course consumed many hours, and some of the implications of our original findings indicated further avenues of research exploration that we are pursuing now.

In the belief that there are qualitative differences in the impacts of some of the variables on long-term rates during periods of high and low rates, respectively, we decided to test and see how significant such differences are. We therefore separated all long-term transactions into two samples, depending on whether the short-term rate at the time was over or under $1.30 per 1,000 ton-miles,[10] and subjected the long-term rate means to variance analysis. The test shows that we cannot say anything at a critical value of 1%, but for a 95% confidence level the means of the two samples are definitely different. Because of these results, it was decided to run the data in two samples as highs and lows.

Without exception, every test indicated that the logarithmic formula-

---

[6] New orders placed are defined as 1,000 + new orders (all in T-2's) to avoid negative numbers due to cancellations.

[7] Under a bareboat charter agreement, the owner delivers a "bare" vessel and the charterer has to man it, provide for the crew, etc., as if the vessel were his.

[8] We wish to express our appreciation for the use of the computation facilities.

[9] Developing the coding instructions, coding, punching, and sample testing the data.

[10] This rate was chosen as representing the upper limit of the full cost of a T-2.

tions were better. This much we did expect from the theoretical discussion presented in the chapter on the long-term rates in the short run. (See especially the discussion on the relationship between the short-term and the market long-term rates and also on the impact of the duration of the charter on long-term rates.) For this reason, we shall present here only the results of the logarithmic regression and correlations; but first we wish to issue this warning. Many of the assumptions on which the mathematical theory of correlation is based are at best only approximated by empirical reality. The significance of the results that we shall present lies principally in the qualitative relationships that they reveal. We shall now proceed with the quantitative evidence.

Table 10.1 presents the correlation matrix under low rates. The regression equation giving the best fit is

$$\ln Y = 5.23 + .752 \ln X_1 + .004 \ln X_2 + .029 \ln X_3 - .213 \ln X_4 \\ - .550 \ln X_5 + .0004 \ln X_6 - .195 \ln X_7 + .197 \ln X_8 + .140 \ln X_9$$

The correlation coefficient for this regression equation is $r = .644$, giving a coefficient of determination $r^2 = .415$ and a standard error of estimate of .157. Theoretically, the coefficients of this regression equation show the respective elasticities, or the percentage impact on the long-term rates of percentage changes in the variables.

The standard errors of the slope coefficients of the regression equation are

Intercept:	1.116	X_5:	.181
X_1:	.131	X_6:	.109
X_2:	.011	X_7:	.049
X_3:	.009	X_8:	.028
X_4:	.030	X_9:	.056

At a critical level of 5% (two tails), the coefficients for X_2 (duration of the charter) and X_6 (idle capacity as percentage of the working petroleum fleet) are not significant (are unstable) whereas all the others are highly significant. It is not surprising to find some instability in view of the high intercorrelation that exists between our independent variables. Such a correlation between variables, however, should not be taken necessarily to imply a direct relationship, because any two variables may be influenced by one or more other variables in such a manner as to give a strong mathematical relationship.[11] In our case we know that the short-term rates affect several of our variables, and there is a resulting tendency toward some distortion. There is another reason, however, for the instability of the coefficient of time-charter duration. As we have shown in Figure 9.3, there is a tendency for a reversal in

[11] Hoel, Paul G., *Introduction to Mathematical Statistics,* Second Edition, John Wiley & Sons, Inc., New York, 1954, pp. 121–122.

TABLE 10.1

CORRELATION MATRIX: LOWS: 304 OBSERVATIONS

	X_1	X_2	X_3	X_4	X_5	X_6	X_7	X_8	X_9	Y	Significance of r_{iY} 95% Confidence Level
X_1 (Short-Term Rate)	1.000	.125	.106	−.102	.844	−.571	−.594	−.649	−.884	.062	No
X_2 (Duration of Charter)		1.000	.639	.509	−.014	−.108	.051	−.033	−.091	−.010	No
X_3 (Lead Time)			1.000	.439	−.022	−.030	.076	−.002	−.065	.078	No
X_4 (Size)				1.000	−.253	−.091	.080	.188	.076	−.164	Yes
X_5 (Index of Adjustment)					1.000	−.245	−.626	−.703	−.812	−.112	No
X_6 (Idle Capacity)						1.000	.639	.151	.611	−.289	Yes
X_7 (Change in X_6)							1.000	.325	.620	−.195	Yes
X_8 (Orders Outstanding)								1.000	.571	.299	Yes
X_9 (Change in Orders Placed)									1.000	.026	No

the schedule depicting the relation between rate and time-charter duration during periods of low spot rates. At first, the time-charter rate tends to increase as the duration of the charter is extended, but then it turns downward. We notice that the regression coefficient is close to zero, and can easily assume a negative sign. As for idle capacity, again when rates are low, in one sense the greater the number of vessels that are tied up the fewer will be available in the spot market and the greater the probability for employment for the rest at somewhat remunerative levels. Again in this case the regression coefficient is almost zero, showing the presence of conflicting forces.

To assess the relative importance of the coefficients of regression in determining the dependent variable, we have derived, and present in Table 10.2, the standardized or "beta coefficients." The latter indicate

TABLE 10.2

MULTIPLE REGRESSION COEFFICIENTS AND STANDARD ERRORS: LOWS: 304 OBSERVATIONS

Variable	Regression Coefficient	Std. Error in Reg. Coef.	Beta Coef.	Std. Error in Beta Coef.
Intercept	5.226	1.116	5.954	1.663
X_1	.752	.131	.824	.144
X_2	.004	.011	.025	.063
X_3	.029	.009	.188	.060
X_4	−.213	.030	−.398	.056
X_5	−.550	.181	−.571	.188
X_6	.0004	.109	.004	.123
X_7	−.195	.049	−.391	.097
X_8	.197	.028	.453	.066
X_9	.140	.056	.319	.126

$\ln Y = 5.226 + .752 \ln X_1 + .004 \ln X_2 + .029 \ln X_3 - .213 \ln X_4 - .550 \ln X_5 + .0004 \ln X_6 - .195 \ln X_7 + .197 \ln X_8 + .140 \ln X_9$.
$r = .644$.
$r^2 = .415$.
Standard Error of Estimate $= .157$.

the increase in the dependent variable resulting from an increase of one standard deviation in the independent variable.[12] Comparing the non-standardized with the beta coefficients, we notice that the only change in rank occurred between X_8 and X_4. Otherwise the results do not present any surprises. The reason for the change in rank between X_8 and X_4 is that orders outstanding as a percentage of the working petroleum fleet X_8 change considerably during periods of low rates. Reductions

---

[12] Arkin, Herbert, and Raymond Colton, *Statistical Methods,* Barnes & Noble, Inc., New York, 1957, pp. 96–97.

in the numerator due to deliveries and cancellations are not fully offset by withdrawals from the working fleet, consequently the coefficient fluctuates within a wide range. This can be seen in Figure 5.9. As a result the standard deviation of X_8 is relatively large.

Because of the compensating quantitative adjustments that are re-reflected in the regression coefficients of a multiple regression equation, it was decided that the zero-order correlation coefficients r_{iY} should be tested for significance. The zero-order correlation coefficients[13] indicate the mathematical relationship between two variables, and can be found in Table 10.1. If we take the data of the column under Y and test their reliability, we find that we can say with 95% confidence that the first three independent variables are insignificant, the fourth significant, the fifth insignificant, the next three significant, and the last one insignificant.[14] *The only reliable* relationships that we find under low rates are

Size versus time-charter rate	(negative correlation)
Idle capacity versus time-charter rate	(negative correlation)
Changes in idle capacity versus time-charter rate	(negative correlation)
The level of orders outstanding versus time-charter rate	(positive correlation)

These results are in complete agreement with what we expected on purely theoretical considerations.[15] Size reflects the economies of scale and, as we have argued before, will be negatively correlated with long-term rates under any circumstances. Idle capacity will of course be small when rates are high and great when rates are low, and the level of orders outstanding will move in the same direction as the rates.

The other coefficients of zero-order correlation, even though insignificant, indicate results in agreement with our predictions. The short-term rates are positively related with the long-term rates, as is the lead time, the latter because under low rates the normal long-term rate is approached from below. The duration of the charter is negatively correlated with long-term rates indicating that the negative slope of the normal long-term rate schedule may be quite pronounced.[16] The regression coefficient for X_2, however, which theoretically indicates in a logarithmic formulation the charter-duration elasticity of long-term rates, is positive, showing the great instability of the relationship.

---

[13] These are sometimes called partial correlation coefficients of the *first order* (nonstandardized).

[14] For a standard test see Hoel, *op. cit.*, p. 124.

[15] See Chapter 9, "The Long-Term Charter Rate in the Short Run."

[16] We have explained before that under low spot rates we expect the market long-term rate to increase with the duration of the charter up to a point, and then turn downward. The reversal is caused partly by objective savings and partly by anticipations of the impact of technological changes (which are expected to occur during the tenure of the charter) on the cost curves of the industry.

Another important conclusion may be deduced from the sign of r_{Y5} (long-term rates versus adjustment index) if this is also valid during high rates. To the extent that the relationship between the spot rates and the long-term rates is positive and the correlation between the index of adjustment and the long-term rates is negative, we may conclude that the behavior of the oil companies does not follow a "smoothed-out" reaction path based on short-term rates. This may also be seen from the regression coefficients of X_1 and X_5, which are $+.752$ and $-.550$, respectively.

Finally, the sign of the zero-order correlation coefficient between the change in orders placed and the long-term rates is positive, indicating the impact of elastic expectations both on orders placed and on long-term rates.

The relationship between the independent variables and the long-term rates under periods of high rates is given by the following regression equation.

$$\ln Y = 2.405 + .154 \ln X_1 - .046 \ln X_2 - .063 \ln X_3 - .198 \ln X_4 \\ - .353 \ln X_5 + .030 \ln X_6 - .440 \ln X_7 + .449 \ln X_8 + .657 \ln X_9$$

The coefficient of correlation r is .698, the coefficient of determination r^2 is .487, and the standard error of estimate is .233. The latter is higher than .157, the standard error of estimate under low rates; yet the correlation is greater under conditions of excess demand (highs), indicating that the standard deviation of the long-term rates is so much greater under high rates that it more than offsets the difference in standard errors.[17] The respective standard deviations (logarithmic-geometric) are .203 under low and .323 under high rates; but again the greater variability of the long-term rates under conditions of excess demand (high) was to be expected on purely theoretical grounds.

The standard errors of the intercept and the slope coefficient are

Intercept:	.503	X_5:	.062
X_1:	.030	X_6:	.020
X_2:	.017	X_7:	.066
X_3:	.010	X_8:	.040
X_4:	.027	X_9:	.071

[17] As we know in general, $r = \sqrt{1 - S_{y \cdot x}^2 / S_y^2}$ where $S_{y \cdot x}$ is the standard error of estimate or the standard deviation *around the line of regression*, and S_y is the standard deviation around the mean value of y. That is, r measures the improvement in the estimate of a variable due to its relationship with another variable. Therefore, other things being equal, the greater S_y is the larger the coefficient of correlation. This does not necessarily imply, of course, that a change in S_y will not affect $S_{y \cdot x}$, but there is no reason to expect a proportional change. Failure to realize this relation often leads to misuse and misinterpretation of the importance of the coefficients of correlation.

The only one of the regression coefficients that is insignificant at a critical level of 5% (two tails) is X_6, or the variable indicating idle capacity; and again, as in the case of "lows," the coefficient has the wrong sign. By studying the changes in the coefficients caused by the introduction of new variables, we find that under "highs" X_6 is stable and has the proper sign until X_9 is introduced. Under "lows" its sign is changed by X_7, and its significance completely ruined by X_9. A possible explanation for all this may lie in a curious interrelationship that was accidentally established by our measurement rules between X_6 and X_9. As can be seen in Tables 10.1 and 10.3, the variables X_6 and X_9 are positively correlated. Logic tells us that the relationship should be negative. The positive correlation exists because during low rates deliveries and cancellations reduce X_9; but deliveries also increase the working petroleum fleet. As a result, X_6 is reduced because it is expressed as a percentage of the working petroleum fleet. Evidently the percentage increase in tie-ups is less than the percentage increase in capacity. During periods of high rates, although new orders may be increasing in an absolute sense they may decrease as a ratio of existing orders because of the high level of orders outstanding. So again a spurious correlation is established here between X_6 and X_9. Another possible explanation may lie in the existence of lags.

Turning now to the contribution of the independent variables, as shown in Table 10.3, we find that it is significant at the 95% confidence level for every one but X_7. This is not surprising because under periods of excess demand the level of idle capacity reaches a lower limit and cannot drop much below that.

The relative importance of the various X_i in determining Y is shown by the beta coefficients presented in Table 10.4. The change in orders placed still seems to bear the most significant quantitative impact[18] on the long-term rates, followed by the changes in idle capacity and orders outstanding. The most significant rise in relative importance is in the lead-time coefficient, and the greatest setback occurs in the index of adjustment, both of which changes are not surprising.

If we now compare the respective r_{iY} of Tables 10.1 and 10.3, we notice how much stronger the relationship is between most X_i and the long-term rates under "highs." The short-term rate, with its greater variability above what we previously called the short-term normal equilibrium, also pulls the long-term rate with it and creates greater dispersion above the normal long-term rate than below it. With this greater disper-

---

[18] Let us stress again that this does not necessarily imply a direct relationship. Orders and idle capacity serve mostly as objective indicators of "intermediate" expectations. Furthermore, these relationships are valid only within the confines of the multiple-regression model.

TABLE 10.3
CORRELATION MATRIX: HIGHS: 593 OBSERVATIONS

	X_1	X_2	X_3	X_4	X_5	X_6	X_7	X_8	X_9	Y	Significance of r_{iY} 95% Confidence Level
X_1 (Short-Term Rate)	1.000	.052	.161	−.055	.201	−.052	−.081	.115	.034	.211	Yes
X_2 (Duration of Charter)		1.000	.509	.475	−.114	.066	.233	−.034	.201	−.312	Yes
X_3 (Lead Time)			1.000	.456	−.115	.062	.129	.087	.106	−.317	Yes
X_4 (Size)				1.000	.022	−.063	.132	.208	.063	−.383	Yes
X_5 (Index of Adjustment)					1.000	−.205	−.551	.104	−.488	−.174	Yes
X_6 (Idle Capacity)						1.000	.299	−.457	.146	−.167	Yes
X_7 (Change in X_6)							1.000	−.401	.884	−.043	No
X_8 (Orders Outstanding)								1.000	−.429	.254	Yes
X_9 (Change in Orders Placed)									1.000	.105	Yes

TABLE 10.4

MULTIPLE REGRESSION COEFFICIENTS AND STANDARD ERRORS: HIGHS: 593 OBSERVATIONS

Variable	Regression Coefficient	Std. Error in Reg. Coef.	Beta Coef.	Std. Error in Beta Coef.
Intercept	2.405	.503	3.340	.465
X_1	.154	.030	.172	.033
X_2	−.046	.017	−.099	.037
X_3	−.063	.010	−.244	.037
X_4	−.198	.027	−.279	.038
X_5	−.353	.062	−.218	.039
X_6	.030	.020	.056	.037
X_7	−.440	.066	−.492	.074
X_8	.449	.040	.451	.040
X_9	.657	.071	.676	.073

$\ln Y = 2.405 + .154 \ln X_1 - .046 \ln X_2 - .063 \ln X_3 - .198 \ln X_4 - .353 \ln X_5 + .030 \ln X_6 - .440 \ln X_7 + .449 \ln X_8 + .657 \ln X_9.$
$r = .698.$
$r^2 = .487.$
Standard Error of Estimate = .233.

sion, the theoretical path of the market long-term rates will have to make more pronounced adjustments in order to approach the normal long-term rate from above than from below. This much is indicated not only by X_{1Y} but also by X_{2Y}, X_{3Y}, and X_{4Y}.[19] Only the idle capacity and the change in it are stronger under "lows" because idleness, after all, is a characteristic of low rates.

Finally, we notice that the correlation between the index of adjustment and the long-term rates is negative, while that between the short-term and long-term rates is positive. This supports our previous contention that expectations and reactions are not smoothed out; and that the so-called 50% rule, as applied to the whole industry, may be more myth than reality. Expectations are no doubt price elastic.

Bimodality and Its Impact

Frequency distributions of some of the variables indicate the existence of bimodalities. This much is also indicated by an analysis of the means and the standard deviations of the variables.

In order to ascertain the significance of these bimodalities, we have divided the "highs" and "lows" into samples on the basis of vessel size,

---

[19] Those who wish to see the theoretical justification for these statements should refer to Chapter 9.

TABLE 10.5
F RATIO TESTS

1. *Lows by Size:* Mean = 1.125 (in natural logarithm)

Class	No. of Observations	r	r^2	$\bar{Y}$
9,000–29,999 DWT.	270	.622	.388	1.126
30,000 and over	26	.902	.814	1.108
F = .003				

Hence we can say that the means are the *same* with 99% confidence.

2. *Highs by Size:* Mean = 1.378

Class	No. of Observations	r	r^2	$\bar{Y}$
9,000–29,999 DWT.	450	.677	.458	1.403
30,000 and over	119	.825	.681	1.280
F = 11.8				

The means are *different* at 99% confidence level.

3. *Lows by Charter Duration:* Mean = 1.121

Class	No. of Observations	r	r^2	$\bar{Y}$
1–59 months	124	.554	.301	1.051
60 and over	163	.691	.477	1.174
F = 50				

The means are *different* at 99% confidence level.

4. *Highs by Charter Duration:* Mean = 1.384

Class	No. of Observations	r	r^2	$\bar{Y}$
1–59 months	123	.794	.631	1.551
60 and over	438	.519	.269	1.337
F = 102				

The means are *different* at 99% confidence level.

5. *Lows by Years:* Mean = 1.121

Class	No. of Observations	r	r^2	$\bar{Y}$
1950–1953	37	.815	.664	1.055
1954–1957	250	.684	.464	1.130
F = 59				

The means are *different* at 99% confidence level.

6. *Highs by Years:* Mean = 1.387

Class	No. of Observations	r	r^2	$\bar{Y}$
1950–1953	173	.751	.564	1.290
1954–1957	391	.666	.444	1.430
F = 85				

The means are *different* at 99% confidence level.

duration of charter, and historical time period. These six samples, of two subsamples in each, were then subjected to the same multiple regression and correlation analysis as used for the total statistical universe, and also to analysis of covariance. All the tests, with the exception of the subdivision of the "lows" by size, indicated that the means of the samples were different at 99% confidence level. The multiple correlation coefficients ranged from a low of .519 to a high of .900, but beyond these quantitative differences the *over-all* results did not change qualitatively. (The details for the samples are given in Table 10.5.) Some *particular* results, however, were brought to light by the analysis just given which are quite interesting and give additional weight to some of our previous claims:

1. We have previously argued *and also substantiated* that under both low and high short-term rates, the long-term rates will be negatively correlated with size. Now we find that for vessels under 30,000 DWT., *under depressed market conditions only*, the relationship between size and long-term rates is positive.[20] (See Table 10.6.) This we cannot understand unless it is due to

TABLE 10.6

SELECTED COEFFICIENTS OF ZERO-ORDER CORRELATION: SUBSAMPLES

	Lows	*Highs*
Size below 29,999 DWT.	$r_{1Y} = .339$	$r_{1Y} = .225$
	$r_{4Y} = .183$	$r_{4Y} = -.206$
Size 30,000 DWT. and over	$r_{1Y} = -.065$	$r_{1Y} = .355$
	$r_{4Y} = -.325$	$r_{4Y} = .640$
Charter Duration below 59 Months	$r_{1Y} = .235$	$r_{1Y} = .425$
	$r_{2Y} = .082$	$r_{2Y} = -.055$
Charter Duration over 60 Months	$r_{1Y} = .119$	$r_{1Y} = .100$
	$r_{2Y} = -.110$	$r_{2Y} = -.090$

the reluctance of the owners to reactivate the larger vessels until the rates are remunerative. As we pointed out when discussing tie-ups, the part of lay-up costs that varies with time is relatively fixed with respect to size. Consequently, the out-of-pocket lay-up cost per unit of capacity is lower the larger the vessel and, as a result, the greater the reactivation rate.[21] It is very difficult to believe, however, if we consider the economies of scale in tankship operation, that the minimum reactivation rate will increase with size. Another possible explanation of the observed relationship may be the fear of idleness beyond the offered contract. Even though the average cost

[20] We have tested with other subclassifications and found that the turning point occurs between 25,000 and 26,000 DWT.

[21] The minimum reactivation rate is equal to the out-of-pocket cost of operation per unit of capacity less the out-of-pocket cost of tie-up.

per unit of capacity is smaller the larger the vessel, on an absolute basis the cost of idleness in *operational readiness* is greater. Hence, unless the probability is great that the reactivation will be permanent, the owners may leave their vessel in tie-up. In this case, again, we do not believe the owners attempt to penetrate that much ahead into the future.

These operations do not apply to vessels of over 30,000 DWT. because vessels of the latter sizes are rarely found in tie-up, for reasons previously explained. Thus, for these vessels the economies of scale are reflected in the negative correlation.

2. The relationship between short-term and long-term rates was found to be positive under both "lows" and "highs." Table 10.6 shows, however, a very slight negative relationship under low rates for vessels of 30,000 DWT. and over.[22] The reasons given under the first category above may also operate here, but the results may also indicate that when rates are low and the smaller vessels are led to tie-up the remaining vessels may benefit from the consequent improvement in rates. When conditions improve, however, and the vessels in tie-up are reactivated, the resulting competition forces concession of all the economies of scale to the charterers.

3. The coefficient of zero-order correlation between charter duration and long-term rates under "lows" for charters of less than five years duration is positive, while the respective coefficient for charters of over five years is negative. In our theoretical discussion we concluded that the relationship would be positive but that the slope of the normal long-term rate might reverse this relationship. Evidently, (*a*) the negative slope of the schedule is pronounced, and (*b*) the asymptote (normal long-term rate) is approached rather quickly (in a period of less than five years).

4. Further evidence of (*b*) is provided by the relationships between the short-term and the long-term rates. The zero-order correlation coefficients and the regression-equation coefficients point out that under both "highs" and "lows" the adjustment is exponential and that it is wider and more pronounced during periods of high rates. Under both cases, however, the evidence substantiates our belief that beyond a time period that the imaginative anticipation can penetrate, it is the cost-based, normal long-term rate that serves as a guidepost.

[22] This correlation coefficient is not significant, but the difference between .339 and —.065 is significant.

11

The Long-Term Rates in the Long Run

In the previous chapters, we analyzed in detail all the factors that affect the long-term rates, but we considered them only from the short-run point of view. Now we turn to discussion of the changes that will occur with the removal of the static assumptions.

Our previous conclusions on the relationship between the long-term rates and all the factors affecting it may be summarized as follows:

$$R_L = R'_s - a - b + (d/n)(R_s - C)$$

where

R_L = the long-term rate

R'_s = the normal short-term rate, which under certainty would also guarantee the necessary return on investment to keep (perpetuate) fixed capital in the industry

a = the risk premium that the spot market commands because of the fears of unemployment

b = the "trouble premium" and all the "objective savings," due to administrative costs, brokerage, and mortgageability of the charter, that accrue with long-term contracts

d = a factor of proportionality

n = the duration of charter

R_s = the maximum average short-term rate expected to govern over period n

C = the full cost to the industry, including the minimum necessary return on fixed capital

Factors a and b are functions $f(n)$ and $g(n)$, respectively, and they will approach a limit as n approaches its maximum value. As for $(d/n)(R_s - C)$, it represents the impact of expectations, which, as we found, is greater the higher the spot rates R_s and the shorter the duration of the charter n. As n approaches its maximum value, the whole factor becomes insignificant, showing that the longer the duration of the contract the greater the dependence on objective data.

If we now go from the long-term rate in the short run to the long-term rate in the long run, we find that both R'_s and C will change, whereas all the rest will remain more or less unaffected. This is so because the changes in R'_s and C are caused by changes in the long-run costs of the industry.

In the tankship service markets, as previously explained, technological economies of scale still exist, and in this chapter we shall estimate their significance, since these are so influential on long-term rates.

From our beta coefficients for highs and lows, and the respective standard deviations, we find that under "lows" for every 1,000 DWT. change in size, the long-term rate changes by $-.054$ dollar, and under "highs" by $-.0144$ dollar. The difference in the respective figures may be due, in the absence of errors, to

1. The bargaining power of the two parties, which results in a *smaller* concession of the economies of scale on the upswing than on the downswing, and
2. More pronounced economies of scale at the early stages of size.

We must not, however, depend only on our regression coefficients for this estimate because

1. We feel that the *quantitative* exactness of regression models is not always reliable.
2. Our regression equations represent linear approximations of non-linear relationships.
3. Even if we do get a reliable quantitative indicator from a linear regression model, it will still not reflect the total impact of the economies of scale because, as we have just mentioned, the portion of the "savings" of size conceded will sometimes be greater than others, depending on the bargaining position of the contracting parties.[1]

Before we proceed with an analysis of the cost of operation, we must mention that the traditional operations of the time-charter markets cause one of the factors contributing to the economies of scale to assume a different role. Because the costs of fuel, together with port charges and canal tolls, are paid by the charterer under a time-charter agreement, we expect to find that the more efficient vessels (because of fuel

[1] Even in the absence of stringent institutional constraints, the rates for vessels of different sizes would be equalized in the market in such a way as to allow part of the economies of scale to the buyers. The latter must be compensated for the inflexibility — storage capacity, refining capacity, limitations of market size, etc. — that the large vessel imparts.

consumption) will reduce the visible impact of scale on the cost of the transportation under conditions of both surpluses and shortages.[2]

Unlike the spot market in which the rate is given in homogeneous units (a certain monetary consideration *per ton of oil delivered*), in the time-charter market there is no one rate, but there are several *rates* for vessels of different sizes, for different lead times, and for different charter durations. Under such circumstances it is impossible to establish a representative time-charter rate for the total market, unless a representative size and charter duration are picked. Most of the indices and graphs that purport to represent a market rate for time charters are often misleading.[3] If, of course, we can find many transactions of the same duration and involving vessels of the same size, then an index can be developed to show the rate movement in that *particular* submarket. As we have indicated in previous chapters, however, the number of time-charter transactions seems to be a function of rates, thus implying that there are periods during which very few or no transactions occur. Consequently, it is impossible for anyone to establish empirically an average rate which is at the same time meaningful.

Knowing that (*a*) the T-2 has been the most common vessel during the last decade, and (*b*) about 50% of all the time charters were for five years duration, we have developed an index for a five-year time charter for T-2's. The results are shown in Table 11.1 and substantiate our reservations concerning the use of such indices. We notice that in 1954 there were no five-year time charters given to T-2's, in 1958 there was only one, in 1953 there were three, and in 1950 four, while in 1955 there were thirty-eight. The average long-term rate seems to be moving in the same direction as the short-term rate and, as expected, exhibits far narrower fluctuations than the short-term rate index. Aside from these observations, however, we cannot conclude anything on the basis of single transactions.

Just as we cannot substantiate either on theoretical or empirical grounds the use of a single long-term rate in the short run, neither can we do so in the long run. Consequently, the most logical approach toward establishing a time-charter rate in the long run is that of a *particular* cost analysis with projections based on it.

Table 11.2 presents what we call the "time-charter cost of operation"

---

[2] The cost of fuel per DWT. per year falls from about $15.20 for a T-2 to $11.23 for a 100,000 DWT. vessel, both considered in the Persian Gulf–United Kingdom trade (Cape route both ways for the 100,000 DWT. vessel).

[3] These graphs and indices are usually developed by tanker brokers. The London Award which depicted the cost of a two-year time charter has given way to AFRA, but the latter is not really a time-charter index for going rates.

TABLE 11.1

FIVE-YEAR TIME-CHARTER RATES FOR T-2's

Date	No. of Transactions	Average Rate	Spot-Rate Index
1950			
February	1	$2.70	.91
November	3	3.05	2.82
1951			
January	1	3.25	3.96
February	2	3.55	4.25
March	1	3.20	3.98
May	1	3.90	1.85
June	1	3.70	2.10
September	1	3.00	2.23
November	1	3.50	3.70
1952			
January	3	4.35	4.30
February	2	3.85	4.24
March	2	4.00	4.01
May	1	4.00	1.72
September	1	4.10	1.69
October	1	4.55	1.56
1953			
January	1	3.40	1.26
November	2	3.00	.90
1954			
None			
1955			
June	4	3.10	.85
July	7	3.25	1.01
August	9	3.40	1.06
September	8	3.35	1.08
October	6	3.40	1.08
November	4	3.50	2.17
1956			
January	2	3.70	1.87
April	6	4.00	1.94
July	5	4.05	2.04
August	1	4.25	2.19
September	2	4.20	2.47
October	2	4.20	2.88
November	2	4.75	4.07
1957			
January	1	4.40	3.77
June	1	4.45	.94
July	1	4.31	.83
November	1	3.43	.62
December	3	3.45	.68
1958			
June	1	3.10	.61

Source of Data: Columns 1 and 2, Conrad Boe, Ltd. (Brokers), Oslo, Norway. Column 3, the same as Table 5.12.

TABLE 11.2

TIME-CHARTER COST OF OPERATION FOR VESSELS OF 16,500 TO 100,000 DWT.
(1959 Data)

	Deadweight Size									
	16,500	20,000	30,000	40,000	50,000	60,000	70,000	80,000	90,000	100,000
Cost Per Annum										
Wages, Provision, Insur. etc.	213,694	223,450	234,350	250,700	261,600	277,950	288,850	299,750	316,100	327,000
Repairs and Maintenance	110,000	120,960	147,850	173,600	201,600	228,480	255,360	282,240	308,000	336,000
Vessel Insurance	45,690	56,060	77,710	98,160	116,690	135,460	153,790	172,130	192,270	212,120
Overhead	21,900	22,000	22,000	22,000	22,000	22,000	22,000	22,000	22,000	22,000
	$391,284	422,470	481,900	544,460	601,890	663,890	720,000	776,120	838,370	897,120
Per DWT./Annum	24.24	21.12	16.06	13.61	12.04	11.06	10.29	9.70	9.32	8.97
Depreciation and Interest on Fixed Investment (8%)	253,440	296,000	410,400	518,400	616,000	715,200	812,000	908,800	1,015,200	1,120,000
Per DWT./Annum	15.36	14.80	13.68	12.96	12.32	11.92	11.60	11.36	11.28	11.20
Total Cost Per DWT./Annum (Excluding Fuel, Port Charges, Canal Tolls)	39.60	35.92	29.74	26.57	24.36	22.98	21.89	21.06	20.60	20.17
Voyage Charter Equivalent A.T.R.S.	−20%	−27½%	−40%	−46½%	−51%	−53½%	−56%	−57½%	−58½%	−59½%
General Information										
Crew	40	41	44	46	48	50	53	55	58	60
Construction Cost/DWT.	$192	185	171	162	154	149	145	142	141	140
Total Cost in $M	3,168	3,700	5,130	6,480	7,700	8,940	10,150	11,360	12,690	14,000
Repair Cost in $M	100	108	132	156	180	205	230	254	277	300

Source of Data: Marine Brokerage Company, Inc., New York.

for vessels from 16,500 to 100,000 DWT. The total cost per DWT. per year varies from a high of $39.60 ($3.30 per DWT. per month) for a T-2 to $20.17 ($1.68 per month) for a 100,000-ton vessel. In terms of voyage-charter equivalents, the rate drops from A.T.R.S. minus 20% to A.T.R.S. minus 59.5%.[4]

The economies of scale realized by operators of large vessels are actually more pronounced than is indicated by Table 11.2. This is so for two reasons:

1. A DWT. of capacity of a large vessel is greater in terms of actual carrying capacity than a DWT. of a small vessel because the speed of larger vessels is normally greater. For example, while the speed of a T-2 (16,500 DWT.) is 14.5 knots, some larger vessels travel at 16.5 knots.

2. The fuel consumption per DWT. of capacity decreases as the size increases. For example, a 19,500 DWT. motor-driven vessel normally consumes 28 tons of heavy fuel oil and 1.5 tons of diesel oil per day of steaming, while an 86,000 DWT. motor vessel consumes only 58 tons of heavy fuel oil and 2 tons of diesel oil per day.

If we look at the two general components of the cost of Table 11.2, we find that the greatest reduction in costs occurs because of the crew requirements. As shown in Figure 11.1, the economies of scale due to the shipbuilding costs taper off much faster than the crew costs.

With such a great range of costs, no doubt remains that the long-term market consists of many components that could easily qualify as separate markets. This subdivision, of course, introduces imperfections in the long-term markets, and we can no longer talk about rate equalization as in the spot market. In the case of the long-term rates the question arises: equalization to what? All this provides further evidence that only cost can serve as a guidepost in the long-term markets, as we have been claiming all along for several other reasons. Let us mention again, however, that this adherence to a cost-based rate does not imply that the owner retains no part of the economies of scale. Part of the latter must stay with the owner to compensate him for the greater risks (costlier unemployment and more limited use); another part must go to the charterer to compensate him for the inflexibility introduced into his operations; and the incidence of the remaining part will be determined by the prevailing market forces. It is only in this way that rate equalization can be understood in the long-term markets.

Our regression model has shown that for every 1,000 DWT. change in size, the long-term rate changes by $−.054 during periods of low

[4] To find the voyage rate equivalent, one has to find the time duration of the trip (round-trip distance), multiply by the time-charter rate per day, add fuel, port charges, and canal tolls, and divide by the amount of cargo carried, thus arriving at a rate per ton of oil delivered, instead of rate per DWT. per month or day. See Appendix B.

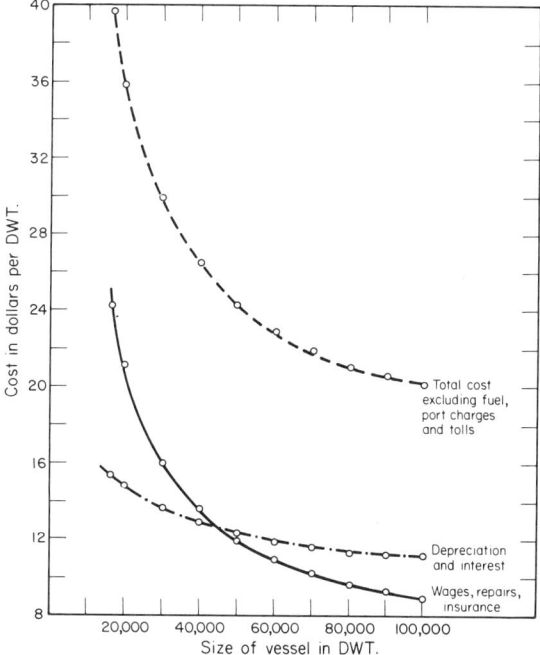

Figure 11.1. Cost per DWT. per annum for vessels of sizes 16,500–100,000 DWT.

rates and $-.0144 during periods of excess demand. We shall now test and see how this compares with objective economic data.

Because the mean size of vessels chartered under low rates is 17,912 and the standard deviation 7,413, we shall assume a critical (two tails) value of 5% and see how the cost behaves when size increases from, let us say, 16,500 to 30,000 (actually it should be 17,912 ± 14,826 but there are no vessels at the lower end). From Table 11.2 we notice that the total cost falls from \$3.30 per DWT. per month to \$2.48, a drop of \$.82 per DWT. per month. According to the regression model, the rate changes by $-.054$ times 13.5, or \$.73, which is a very good approximation of \$.82. Furthermore, since we observed a tendency for a positive relation during low rates for small sizes, we must actually test at the upper end of the spectrum. Thus we find that the difference in cost between 20,000 DWT. and 30,000 DWT. is 51 cents according to Table 11.2, while our model predicts 54 cents. Under high rates, on the other hand, the mean is 22,255 and the standard deviation 19,439; thus, we shall test between 20,000 and 60,000 DWT. vessels. The cost per DWT. per month at 20,000 is approximately \$3.00, and at 60,000 DWT. is \$1.92, showing a difference of \$1.08 per DWT. per month. The regression model gives us $-.0144$ times 40, or only 58 cents. The difference between 30,000 and 60,000 DWT. vessels is given as 56 cents per DWT. per month by Table 11.2, and 43 cents by the model.

The difference between cost and predicted rate under high rates may be due to any one or a mixture of the following reasons:

1. The assumptions of linearity in our model.
2. The impact of wide spot-rate fluctuations which will tend to shift the time-charter rate upward.
3. The bargaining power of the negotiating parties, which will determine the deviations from long-run costs (after the risks on both sides are considered). Under periods of excess demand, the wide fluctuations of the spot rate and the charterers' expectations develop a market climate favorable to the owners. With elastic expectations, then, it is only natural for the charterers to concede to the owners a greater part of the economies accruing to size under high rates than under low rates. It is the charterer who is under pressure during periods of excess demand and the owner during periods of excess supply.

The question of what will happen to the long-term rates in the long run is still with us. On the basis of the results shown in Table 11.2, there is no doubt that the trend will be downward as the composition of the fleet slowly changes. The level in an AFRA rate in the future will definitely be decreasing. However, such changes in the average level of long-term rates are not expected to be more than gradual.

Fluctuations around this downward average normal long-term rate are to be anticipated in the average market long-term rate because of expectations and the relationship that exists between the short-term and the long-term rates; but again these are short-run considerations and have no more than a transient impact on the long-run level of the long-term rates.

12

A Brief Summary

We shall now briefly summarize our findings, chapter by chapter, and then conclude with a statement on the implications of this study for managerial purposes.

In Chapter 1 we suggested that traditional static economic analysis does not explain how rates are formed in the tankship markets. We have indicated that a substantial price movement away from normal rates (the theoretical equilibrium point) will create expectations that future rates will increase proportionately more than present prices. These expectations will then cause those in the market to change their purchasing plans, and shift their purchases from future to present periods. Such shifts (interperiod substitutions) will affect the demand schedules of both ship chartering and shipbuilding.

The impact of expectations on the amounts of tanker services demanded at the various rates is immediate, but in the case of tankship building the increase in orders for new vessels will not be reflected in the available tankship capacity until sometime later because of the construction lead time. Given this difference in the timing of the impacts of rate expectations on the available supply and demand, we concluded that short-term (spot) rates are formed by the interaction of the demand schedule as affected by price expectations and the usual static supply schedule. The empirical shape of these two schedules was consequently given extensive treatment.

Chapter 2 was devoted to a theoretical discussion of the influence of price expectations on the stability of rates. The traditional as well as current theories on this subject were discussed, and they proved to be based on the assumptions that both buyers and sellers are influenced by price changes in the same manner (symmetric expectations) and that their expectations have no turning points (uniform schedules). According to existing theory, therefore, elasticities of expectations greater than unity, that is to say, expectations that prices in the future will increase proportionately more than at present, cause market instability because prices will be either increasing or falling continuously.

Having extended the use of the fundamental theory of value to the case of producer goods and interperiod profit maximization, we applied the Slutsky-Hicks formulation and analyzed the impact of a present price change on interperiod substitutions in terms of income-budget effects and income-compensated substitution effects. We found that even under the traditional assumptions of symmetry in the behavior of buyers and sellers price-elastic expectations do not necessarily create perpetually explosive price patterns. The price movements are bounded because of the budget effects, and one-way stable equilibria can occur outside the region of normal rates. Alternatives to the traditional hypothesis were then suggested, some of which assume (*a*) asymmetry of behavior between buyers and sellers, (*b*) regular but nonuniform schedules of expectations, (*c*) alternating patterns in expectations, (*d*) "zero" memory for buyers and/or sellers, and (*e*) immediate or delayed reaction on the part of the sellers. In each case a relative stability is guaranteed in the sense that prices are bounded and rather tractable, although capable of wide fluctuations, in markets which are affected by expectations of elasticity greater than one and where the applicable demand schedules have slopes that alternate between positive and negative values.

Chapter 3 dealt with the shape of the demand schedule for tankship capacity. Considerable discussion was devoted to the relationship between the demand for oil and that of tankship tonnage in order to establish the theoretical shape of the demand schedule. The tonnage demanded *in the absence of price expectations* was found to be virtually unaffected by price movements (infinitely inelastic), and we therefore attributed the difference between such infinite inelasticity and the elasticity of the empirical demand schedule to interperiod substitutions as caused by expectations.

The shape of the empirical demand schedules was the subject matter of Chapter 4. The empirical approximations to what we have called demand schedules revealed the impact of price expectations. This implies that once an initial disturbance of significant magnitude occurs, which Chapter 5 guarantees, the necessary mechanism for cyclical tanker rates is established. The initial change in rates will generate expectations about future price changes and will thus cause shifts in purchases and chartering activities from future to current periods (interperiod substitutions). These shifts, if we assume fixed supply, will cause further price increases, which in turn will affect expectations, and so on. In addition to movements along a demand schedule with positive slope (outside the region of strict static relevance), consecutive shifts in the demand schedule may also occur, further aggravating price movements and chartering as well as shipbuilding activities. This spiral will continue until either expectations change from elastic to inelastic (for reasons originating outside the rate movement), the buyers withdraw from the market because of the negative budget effect, or the supply schedules shift and reverse the movement in rates. Once such a reversal occurs, prices will plummet. The drop in prices will automatically turn the "speculative" purchases into surpluses. The latter will be especially pronounced if elastic expectations still operate, because such expectations will dictate reverse interperiod substitutions (postponement of orders). Prices will then remain at very low levels, fluctuating below "normal" until the next disturbance occurs, caused either by normal attrition or pure accident, to repeat the cycle. It is for these reasons that cyclical demand is not necessary for the mechanism of cyclical prices in the tankship markets.

Chapter 5 presented a detailed analysis of the factors affecting the supply schedule of tankship services. New orders placed and tie-ups were proved to be the most important factors affecting the supply schedule. Our theoretical formulations showed that the changes in orders placed are governed mainly by two interperiod substitution effects and two static income effects, caused by changes in spot rates and tankship building costs. The two substitution effects are the result of expectations generated by spot rates and shipbuilding costs, respectively, and they are positive or negative depending on the price elasticities of expectations in the tankship service and tankship building markets. The two income effects oppose each other, but the net result is expected to be positive, *as long as spot rates increase,* because of the greater price fluctuations in the tankship service market. When spot rates rest at a very low level, the income-budget effect due to tankship building costs most likely takes over and results in some orders for replacement of old vessels, and paradoxically also for expansion. Consequently, the analysis shows that given price-elastic expectations, the majority of orders are placed during periods of very high spot-rate and shipbuilding cost levels, some at very low tankship building costs and excessively depressed tanker rates, and *very few* orders are placed during periods which one may consider as normal. Technological changes in tankship building normally appear during periods of depression, but even if this were not so, only when tanker rates are very low will technological obsolescence be manifested to threaten the economic life of existing vessels. The impact of technology, therefore, is mostly incorporated in the orders for replacement, and this impact is normally surplus producing because of the increasing average size and efficiency of newer vessels.

Another factor affecting orders is the pattern of ownership of existing capacity. It appears on the basis of available evidence that most big oil companies order some vessels during periods of surplus capacity, for the industry, in the hope of reducing their dependence on chartered vessels and to bring their ownership back to some "desirable" level. This does not imply that they follow countercyclical purchasing policies. The greatest part of their orders is placed when rates and shipbuilding costs are high. The painful awareness, however, that they have gone through a stampede makes them anxious to rid themselves as much as possible of the condition that generated it by becoming more self-sufficient. We have shown, nonetheless, that the existence of an independent market is necessary for the over-all efficiency of tankship transportation; therefore such behavior on the part of the oil companies serves only further to protract the rate depression.

Considerable discussion was devoted to the differences between the expectations and behavior of the oil companies and the independents. We have shown analytically that the *manifested* behavior of the independents is consistent with either price-elastic or inelastic expectations, as long as the oil companies have elastic expectations. The conditions under which the independents will order vessels, if their expectations are inelastic, were then fully analyzed.

The empirical evidence supports our contention that expectations in the tankship building market are elastic. This observation applies to both the oil companies and the independents, although the coefficient of expectations is greater in the case of the oil companies and their reaction pattern lags behind that of the independents. Vessels are ordered by both the oil companies and the independents mainly when rates are high, and do not appear in the market until after tanker rates have dropped.[1] As a result, depressions are prolonged and the preconditions for cyclical replacements (and shortages) are established.

Vessels scrapped were found to be independent of the conditions that generate orders for new vessels. In fact, spot rates and vessels scrapped are negatively correlated, implying that normal replacements do not affect orders in any significant way when rates are high.

The economics of slowdowns, repairs, and tie-ups were extensively discussed. Although important savings can be realized if the speed of vessels is varied depending on spot rates, there is little evidence that many tanker operators take advantage of such practices. Repairs and tie-ups were found to be related because operators find it advantageous to wait out periods of uncertainty by stretching out necessary repairs. When hope is lost, the vessels are led to tie-up.

---

[1] The shipbuilding costs lag behind tanker rates. Consequently, even after the latter drop shipbuilding costs may be at their peak for a while.

The empirical schedule of tie-ups is almost L-shaped, betraying that capacity cannot be increased in the short run and that massive withdrawals occur at low rates. That is to say, on the basis of tie-ups we should expect to observe an infinite inelasticity in the short-term supply schedule above *practical* full capacity, and infinite elasticity below.

The factors that affect the short-term supply schedule were discussed in Chapter 6. It was shown that the short-term supply schedule is infinitely inelastic beyond full capacity and extremely elastic below. The capacity that separates the elastic from the inelastic part of the short-term supply schedule is not greater than 2% of the total, and the range of rates within which such transformation occurs is approximately 40 cents per 1,000 ton-miles, out of a total range of approximately $4.00.

The tanker markets paradoxically operate in a fashion resembling perfect competition. The various reasons behind this paradox were analyzed in Chapter 7. It was pointed out that institutional considerations in the final markets for oil, and imbalances between the production and refining capacities as well as between geographical regions for the various oil companies, necessitate an independent tanker market. Self-sufficiency for all oil companies would therefore imply perpetual instability and chronic surpluses. In addition to the factors just mentioned, the mobility of capital, which reduces the cost of exit from any particular market and serves toward global equalization of supply and demand, the ease of entry caused by exceptional methods of financing and risk elimination, the absence of large administrative and financial optima which permit the vessel to operate as a firm, and the absence of excessive artificial national and international controls, all contribute toward the perfectly competitive climate of the tankship markets.

Chapter 8 dealt with the formation of short-term rates. It showed that the shape of the demand schedule in the region affected by inter-period substitutions will cause violent fluctuations in the spot rates above normal rates (the static long-run equilibrium point). Because of the extreme inelasticity of the supply schedule in this region, the fluctuations will be swift and extensive. Rates will remain at high levels until expectations, short-selling, or new capacity precipitate a downturn, and then they will slide continuously until they reach the tie-up cost of the marginal capacity. There, rates will remain fluctuating below normal rates (the static long-run equilibrium) until either shifts in demand or attrition eliminate the excess capacity and create shortages. When this takes place, spot rates will be forced above the full cost of the marginal vessel, will influence expectations, shifts in demand, etc., and will start another cycle.

The adjustment paths followed by spot rates are similar to those of the classical cobweb theorem. We have found, however, that there are many cobwebs within cobwebs (i.e., cobwebs of different durations occurring simultaneously) in the tankship markets. These fluctuations have the static long-run equilibrium as a central focus, but they are not expected to reach and remain at such an equilibrium because it is unstable. Consequently, spot rates are fluctuating either temperately below the static long-run equilibrium point or violently above it.

Chapter 9 analyzed the factors that influence long-term charter rates in the short run. The analysis suggested that the long-term and the short-term rates will move in the same direction and that the long-term rates will not exhibit the volatility of the spot rates. There will be real differences (not for fuel, etc.) between the levels of the two rates, however, because of (*a*) the uncertainties and expectations over the period covered by the long-term contract, (*b*) the unemployment risks inherent in the operations of the spot market, (*c*) the subjective value of certainty, (*d*) the administrative savings made possible by the long-term contracts, (*e*) the loan value of the long-term charters and (*f*) the expected savings due to improvements in technology over the tenure of the time charter.

As the duration of the charter lengthens, the long-term rates are expected to approach the normal long-term rate from above during periods of high rates and from below during depressed market conditions. Because of the negative slope of the normal long-term rate, the long-term charter rates during periods of excess demand may show signs of bending backward as the duration of the contract lengthens.

The theoretical formulations explaining the formation of the long-term rates in the short run were subjected to multiple-regression and correlation analysis, and the results proved very satisfactory. The model and the analyses to which it was subjected are found in Chapter 10. It is shown that under periods of low rates the most significant factors affecting the level of long-term rates under depressed market conditions are the size of the vessel (negative impact), the changes in idle capacity (negative), and the level of outstanding orders for new vessels (positive). Under periods of high rates, the most important factors shown by the regression model to affect the long-term rates are the outstanding orders for new vessels (positive relation), the size of the chartered vessel (negative), the level of spot rates (positive), the duration of the charter (negative), and the lead time from contract to delivery (negative). The quantitative significance of these factors as well as the ranges and extent of their applicability were extensively analyzed.

Finally, Chapter 11 suggested that because of the heterogeneity among vessels and the absence of a representative number of transactions it is impossible to draw any definite conclusions about *the* long-term rate in the long run. On the basis of our analysis included in

Chapters 9 and 10, however, which suggested that the normal long-term rate is based on cost, we drew the conclusion that the level of long-term rates (in general) will be moving downward, reflecting the economies of scale that tankship transportation is still realizing.

Tankship operations have for years been based on intuition. This study provides an analytical framework for an understanding of the market forces that determine tanker rates and quantitative relationships that can be used to shape management policy in the areas of tankship building, tankship operation, and tankship chartering. Once the fundamental relationships that are expounded and integrated in this book are fully understood, then managers will not only be in a better position to make decisions whenever the opportunity arises but, more important, they will be able to design an information system that will give warning signals of impending events. The analysis of the factors behind the supply and demand schedules provides the foundation for such an information system. The latter need not be very complicated. For example, the relationship between capacity utilization and spot rates, which is depicted in the short-run supply schedule, can serve as the basis of a simple but effective system, especially if the latter is geared to carry out the consequences of expectations generated by price changes. The actual design of a comprehensive managerial information system has not been among the purposes of this volume, but it is an area that occupies part of our present research efforts.

Appendix A

Definition of Technical Terms

AFRA
: The Average Freight Rate Assessment (AFRA) is supposed to show the average cost of a ton of oil delivered. Thus it is not a current index but a mixture of current and historic costs intended to show at any moment of time the cost of oil in transit.

A.T.R.S.
: This term stands for the American Tanker Rate Schedule. It is an index aimed at substituting U.S.M.C. The latter is found unsatisfactory because it covers large areas under the same rate and also because it includes the canal tolls as a part of the basic rate.

Bareboat Charter
: This type of agreement provides for the delivery of a "bare" vessel to the charterer. The latter assumes responsibility for providing crew, provisions, supplies, fuel, and whatever else is needed.

Charter
: As used in the tankship markets a charter is a contract.

Clean
: Clean refers to cargoes of gasoline and other refined products.

Consecutive-Voyage Charter
: Similar to single-voyage but for either an extended number of "consecutive" trips or extended time period.

Contract of Affreightment
: An agreement providing for the transportation of a given amount of oil between two ports over an extended period of time but on such vessels and at such times as the owners find advantageous. A provision in the agreement may define "minmax" limits of monthly

DEFINITION OF TECHNICAL TERMS

flows. These contracts, which are not very common, are not consummated for speculative reasons. Their purpose is to alleviate frictional unemployment and utilize ballasted capacity.

Dirty
  This term refers to crude-oil cargoes.

Fixture
  A contract for a vessel, the same as a charter.

Newbuilding
  A new vessel under construction, on order, or to be ordered.

Relet
  A relet is a sublet vessel.

Scale
  This is the English equivalent to the A.T.R.S. Since its inception there have been three revisions so the latest is Scale No. 3.

Scrapping
  Breaking up old vessels for scrap metal.

Single-Voyage (Spot) Charter
  An agreement for a single voyage between two ports. The payment is made on the basis of tons of oil delivered. The owner of the vessel is responsible for all expenses.

Tie-up or Lay-up
  These terms refer to idleness for economic reasons. When a vessel is in tie-up it is under the care of only a skeleton crew that stands watch and performs minor repairs.

Time Charter
  A contract of longer duration than a single voyage. The rent (hire) is paid usually on the basis of deadweight tons per month, and it does not include fuel for propulsion, port charges, or canal tolls.

T-2 Equivalent
  In the absence of size homogeneity, the industry is using the T-2 as a measure of capacity. To convert into T-2 equivalents, one has to multiply the deadweight by the speed of a vessel and divide by $16,500 \times 14.5$. It must be noted that the T-2 equivalent is only a rough measure of capacity.

T-2
  For the purposes of this study, we only need to know that a T-2 is a tanker of approximately 16,500 deadweight tons, achieving speeds of 14.5 to 14.6 knots.

U.S.M.C.
> As used in this study U.S.M.C. stands for the index of rates formulated in 1947 by the United States Maritime Commission for the major runs. Specific rates are expressed in terms of plus or minus percentages of the "flat" (100%) U.S.M.C. rate.

Working Petroleum Fleet
> The working petroleum fleet is equal to the total fleet less government-owned (commercial) vessels, special-purpose ships, and vessels idle either because of tie-ups or repairs of over thirty days.

Appendix B

Method for Conversion of Time-Charter Rates into Spot-Rate Equivalent

Suppose that we observe the following transaction:

A vessel of 65,000 DWT., fitted with a steam turbine and capable of traveling at 16 knots on 111 tons of Bunker "C" fuel oil per day, receives a 5-year time charter at $1.73 per DWT. per month.

We now wish to find the spot-rate equivalent of this transaction, in other words, the cost per ton of oil delivered. Under a time-charter agreement, the charterer pays for bunkers, canal tolls, and port charges, which are all paid by the owners in the case of a spot charter. Furthermore, the charterer pays a flat rate per unit of *potential gross carrying capacity* (DWT.) per month in the case of a time charter, while on a spot basis he pays for *actual* tons of oil delivered. As a result, we must choose a run, translate the tonnage of a vessel into potential tons of oil delivered, and then derive the cost per ton of oil.

If we assume that the vessel is to be used in the Curaçao–London–Curaçao run, the mechanics of such translation, with the example given as a basis are as follows:

1. Distance in miles (round-trip)	8,440	
2. Distance traveled per day (24 × 16) in miles	384	
3. Days steaming per round trip (1)/(2)	22.00	
4. Days in port for loading and unloading, including delays	3.50	
5. Total days for completing a trip	25.50	
6. Trips per year (maintenance is "off hire")		14.314
7. Carrying capacity per trip		
(a) DWT. of capacity	65,000	
(b) Less: Water and Stores	(300)	
(c) Less: Bunkers, assuming all are purchased at loading point		
(i) For steaming 111 × 22 =	(2,442)	
(ii) Safety 111 × 5 =	(555)	
(iii) Port 18 × 3.5 =	(63)	
		62,740

8. Carrying capacity per year in tons   898,000
9. Total Cost:
   (a) Fuel: $35,856 \times \$13$ per ton =   \$ 466,128
   (b) Port charges, loading ports
        $14.314 \times \$1,204 =$ 17,234
   (c) Port charges, port of discharge
        $14.314 \times \$7,294 =$ 104,406
   (d) Charter hire: $1.73 \times 65,000 \times 12 =$ 1,349,400

                                                                           \$1,937,168

10. Cost per ton of oil delivered (approximately)   \$2.16
11. Flat (100%) Scale per ton delivered   \$4.55
12. Spot-rate equivalent of time charter
     Scale $-$ [100 $-$ (10)/(11)]   Scale *minus* 52.5%

Appendix C
Coding Instructions for Data Used

1. *Charters*

Name of Field	No. of Columns	Columns From–To	Remarks
I. Code of Ship	4	1–4	Pick code from list
II. Relet or Not	1	5	Use 0 for nonrelet; Use 1 for relet
III. Date of Fixture	6	6–11	Use only 2 last digits of year
IV. Months to Delivery	2	12–13	See Detailed Instructions
V. Type of Fixture	1	14	See Detailed Instructions
VI. Duration of Fixture	3	15–17	See Detailed Instructions
VII. Tons of Cargo	6	18–23	
VIII. Type of Cargo	1	24	0 for dirty; 1 for clean; 2 for option both dirty and clean; 3 for other; 4 50% dirty 50% clean
IX. Run: From	1	25	See Detailed Instructions
X. Run: To	2	26–27	See Detailed Instructions
XI. Rate (Type)	1	28	See Detailed Instructions
XII. Amount in Terms of Index	6	29–34	See Detailed Instructions
XIII. Amount in Terms of $ or £	5	35–39	See Detailed Instructions
XIV. Followed by Type of Fixture	1	40	See Detailed Instructions
XV. Preceded by Type of Fixture	1	41	See Detailed Instructions
XVI. Charterer	2	42–43	
XVII. Whether Part Cargo	1	44	If part cargo, use 1; If full cargo, use 0
XVIII. Delivery Option	1	45	If yes, use 1
XIX. Conrad Boe Data Time Charters	1	80	Punch 1
Gulf Oil Company Data Time Charters			Punch 9

DETAILED INSTRUCTIONS

IV. *Months to Delivery:* Convert into months
   If prompt, use 0
   If within one month, use 1
   If within two months, use 2,
      and so on
   If more than 99 months, use 99

V. *Type of Fixture*
   Firm commitment:
      0 Single voyage
      1 Consecutive voyages in number
      2 Consecutive voyages in months
      3 Trading (time charter) in months (if in years convert to months)
      4 Bareboat charter in months (if in years convert to months)
   Option:
      5 Option for consecutive in number
      6 Option for consecutive in months
      7 Option for trading (time charter) in months
      8 Contract of affreightment (in M tons per year)
         See more on this under XI–XV
      9 Option single voyage

VI. *Duration of Fixture*
   Duration of V in number or months where applicable. For single voyage nothing is needed.

VII. Tons of cargo as given. Except in contracts of affreightment, the cargo is in thousand tons per year.

IX. *Run   From*
      0 U.S. Gulf
      1 Caribbean Sea, Venezuela
      2 Persian Gulf, Ras Tanura, Bahrein
      3 U.S.N.H.
      4 Sidon, Tripoli, Banias, Lebanon, Eastern Mediterranean
      5 California, San Francisco, San Pedro
      6 Sumatra, Singapore, East Indies
      7 World wide
      8 Black Sea
      9 Other

X. *Run   To*
      0 U.S.N.H. (New York)
      1 Philadelphia and Southeast Coast
      2 California
      3 Canada and N.S.
      4 Cartagena, Tenerife
      5 South America
      6 U.K. and nonspecified (other) continent
      7 Scandinavia
      8 Netherlands, Belgium, and Germany
      9 France
      10 Italy
      11 Other Mediterranean (North and South)
      12 Other Africa (excluding North Africa)
      13 Australasia

CODING INSTRUCTIONS FOR DATA 253

    14 India, Pakistan, and Ceylon
    15 Far East (excluding Japan)
    16 Japan
    17 World wide
    18 U.S. Gulf
    19 Other
    20 Caribbean
    21 Eastern Mediterranean
    22 Antarctic round voyage
    23 Western Hemisphere
    24 Central America

XI. *Rate (Type)*

No punch	Cost Plus
0	U.S.M.C.
1	Scale
2	M.O.T.
3	Dollars in lump sum (in hundreds)
4	Sterling in lump sum (in hundreds)
5	Dollars "per ton" (use always 2 decimal figures)
6	X shillings "per ton" (use always 2 decimal figures)
	27/6 as 27.50, 27/11 as 27.92
7	London Brokers' Assessment — this is expressed in terms of *Scale*
8	*Min. Max.* in Scale
9	*Min. Max.* in terms of U.S.M.C. Notice this is very, very rare. Unless it specifies U.S.M.C., *it is AFRA in Scale*

XII. *Amount in Terms of Index*

    A. Convert everything to a straight percentage of base. Use 2 decimal places.
        For example:
            Scale plus (+) 60% convert to 16000
            U.S.M.C. minus (−) 60% convert to 4000
            Same for M.O.T.

    B. Use 2 decimal figures for classifications 0, 1, 2, 5, and 6 under XI, *Rate (Type)*.

    C. For "*lump sum*" *leave out the two last digits. Namely, record sums in hundreds. No decimals here.*

    D. For classifications 8 and 9 of XI, use always 3 figures for min. (minimum) and 3 figures for max. (maximum). *No decimals here.*
        E.g., min. max. 50/85: record 150185.
              min. max. −15/−10: record 085090.
        If a decimal exists, round it.

XIII. *Amounts in Terms of Dollars or Shillings*

Wherever a rate *is given in both* index form and rate in dollars or sterling, record here the latter. *Use always 2 decimal points.*

If the rate is given in both dollars and pounds and also U.S.M.C. and Scale (U.S.M.C. is dollars and Scale is pounds), use U.S.M.C. and dollars.

If dollars or shillings are given, use 2 decimal points.
    E.g., 27/− = 2700
            27/6 = 2750 or $10.02 = 1002
            27/11 = 2792 or   8.73 = 0873

XIV.
XV. } *Followed by Type of Fixture and Preceded by Type of Fixture*

Whenever a fixture is being followed by another fixture or an option for a fixture, make a notation in Column 40 of the *first* card as to what type of fixture follows (see V), and make a *new* card for the following fixture. For each new card in Column 41, put the type of preceding fixture.

Each new card will have all the details as the original.

If a time charter or consecutive voyage is fixed for 5–7 years or 20–22 voyages, make a card for the first amount, i.e., 5 years or 20 voyages and consider the other (2 years or 2 voyages) as option.

XVI. *Charterer*

0	Not Known	16	Mitsubishi
1	Anglo-American	17	M.S.T.S.
2	Anglo-Iranian	18	Other (All Other)
3	Atlantic Refining	19	Paragon
4	British Petroleum (B.P.)	20	Petrofina
5	British Tanker Company	21	Shell
6	California Oil	22	Sinclair
7	Caltex	23	Socony Vacuum (Sovac)
8	C.F.R.	24	Soponata
9	Cities Service	25	Stanic
10	Eagle Oil (and Shipping)	26	Standard-Vacuum (Stanvac)
11	Escomberas	27	Sun Oil
12	Esso	28	Texas
13	Gulf	29	Tidewater
14	Hess	30	Union Oil
15	A. Johnson	31	Shared by Two or More

2. Tie-ups (Monthly)*

Name of Field	No. of Columns	Columns From–To	Remarks
I. Date	6	1–6	Two columns for the month, day, and year (e.g., January 1, 1948: 010148)
II. Real Tie-ups (beginning of month)	4	7–10	One decimal place (e.g., 34.2, 138.2)
III. Real Tie-ups plus Idle (beginning of month)	4	11–14	One decimal
IV. Working Petroleum Fleet	5	15–19	One decimal
V. Real Tie-ups as Percentage of Working Petroleum Fleet	3	20–22	One decimal
VI. Real Tie-ups plus Idle as Percentage of Working Petroleum Fleet	3	23–25	One decimal
VII. Item V in Period t as a Percentage of the same Item in Period $t-1$	3	26–28	No decimal. ($V_t/V_{t-1} \times 100$)
VIII. Item VI in Period t as a Percentage of the same Item in Period $t-1$	3	29–31	No decimal. ($VI_t/VI_{t-1} \times 100$)
IX. Identification	1	80	Punch 3 in Column 80

*Notes: (a) If data are missing, the number of columns called for by the FORMAT is left blank (i.e., the space key is used instead of the skip key — no hole is punched in the card).

(b) Decimals are omitted (e.g., 1266.9 would appear on card as 12669).

(c) If the data occupy less than the number of columns called for by the FORMAT, then the vacant columns are filled with zeros (e.g., if five columns are "called for" and the datum is 4173, then it would be punched as 04173).

(d) The number in Columns 25–27 for December 1951 in the Tie-ups cards should be infinity. It was made 100, as the computer cannot handle infinity.

256 APPENDIX C

3. *New Orders* (Monthly)*

Name of Field	No. of Columns	Columns From–To	Remarks
I. Date	6	1–6	Two columns for the month, day, and year
II. Orders Outstanding (beginning of month)	5	7–11	One decimal place
III. Working Petroleum Fleet	5	12–16	One decimal
IV. Orders Outstanding as Percentage of Working Petroleum Fleet	3	17–19	No decimal
V. Item IV in Period t as a Percentage of the same Item in Period $t-1$	3	20–22	No decimal. ($IV_t/IV_{t-1} \times 100$)
VI. Index of New Orders Placed (during the month)	5	23–27	One decimal. Index of new orders placed = 1000.0 + new orders placed (during the month)
VII. Item VI in Period t as a Percentage of Item II in Period $t-1$	3	28–30	No decimal. ($VI_t/II_{t-1} \times 100$)
VIII. Item VII in Period t as a Percentage of the same Item in Period $t-1$	3	31–33	No decimal. ($VII_t/VII_{t-1} \times 100$)
IX. Index of New Orders Placed as a Percentage of Working Petroleum Fleet	3	34–36	No decimal. ($VI_t/III_t \times 100$)
X. Item IX in Period t as a Percentage of same Item in Period $t-1$	3	37–39	No decimal. ($IX_t/IX_{t-1} \times 100$)
XI. Identification	1	80	Punch 4 in Column 80

* See *Notes* to Section 2.

4. *Spot Rates* (Monthly)*

Name of Field	No. of Columns	Columns From–To	Remarks
I. Date	6	1–6	Two columns for the month, day, and year
II. Average Rate Index per 1,000 Miles (a_t)	3	7–9	Two decimal places
III. Expectation Index (EI)	3	10–12	No decimal. EI = $.53 a_t/a_{t-1} + .27 a_{t-1}/a_{t-2} + .14 a_{t-2}/a_{t-3} + .06 a_{t-3}/a_{t-4}$ where a_t = average rate index per 1,000 miles
IV. Average Rate (including tolls) for Persian Gulf–U.K.	4	13–16	Two decimals
V. Average Rate (excluding tolls)† for Persian Gulf–U.K. per 1,000 Miles	3	17–19	Two decimals
VI. Average Rate (including tolls) for Persian Gulf–U.S.	4	20–23	Two decimals
VII. Average Rate (excluding tolls)‡ for Persian Gulf–U.S. per 1,000 Miles	3	24–26	Two decimals
VIII. Average Rate for Caribbean–U.K.	4	27–30	Two decimals
IX. Average Rate for Caribbean–U.K. per 1,000 Miles	3	31–33	One decimal
X. Average Rate for Caribbean–U.S.	4	34–37	Two decimals
XI. Average Rate for Caribbean–U.S. per 1,000 Miles	3	38–40	Two decimals
XII. Average Rate for U.S. Gulf–N.H.	4	41–44	Two decimals
XIII. Average Rate for U.S. Gulf–N.H. per 1,000 Miles	3	45–47	Two decimals
XIV. Average Rate Index Converted to U.S.M.C. Equivalent Based on Aruba–N.Y. Run	4	48–51	One decimal. Take average rate index per 1,000 miles (See II) and multiply by distance from Aruba to New York (1,750) and divide by 1,000. Then convert to U.S.M.C. rate
XV. Average Rate Index Converted to Scale No. 2 Equivalent Based on Aruba–N.Y. Run	4	52–55	One decimal. Same as above except convert to Scale No. 2
XVI. Identification	1	80	Punch 5 in Column 80

* See *Notes* to Section 2. † 13¢ subtracted. ‡ 10¢ subtracted.

5. Gulf Oil Company Charter Data (Format for Multiple-Correlation Card)*

Name	No. of Columns	Columns From–To	Remarks
Code	4	1–4	Serial numbers chronological
Date of Fixture	6	5–10	
Long-Term Rate (dependent variable)	3	11–13	
Lead Time	2	14–15	Independent X_1
Duration of Charter	3	16–18	Independent X_2
Size (tons of cargo)	5	19–23	Independent X_3
Short-Term Rate Index (spot)	3	24–26	Independent X_4
Index of Expectation	3	27–29	Independent X_5
New Orders (Item IV)	3	30–32	Independent X_6
New Orders (Item VIII)	3	33–35	Independent X_7
Tie-ups (Item VIII)	3	36–38	Independent X_8
Tie-ups (Item VI)	3	39–41	Independent X_9
$(X_{4t}/X_{4t-1}) \times 100$	3	42–44	Independent X_{10} (X_{10} for code 0001 = 100)
$(X_{5t}/X_{5t-1}) \times 100$	3	45–47	Independent X_{11} (X_{11} for code 0001 = 100)
Identification	1	80	Punch 9 in Column 80

* The Gulf Oil Company collected charter data for vessels of 24,000 DWT. and below only. We used these data to check on the comparable relationships derived by using Conrad Boe data. No significant differences were observed although each had transactions not recorded by the other.

Variable	Coefficient	No. of Columns†	Columns From–To	Decimals	Remarks
Dependent Y		3	11–13	2	From Deck 1, Columns 35–39. If Column 28 is 5, proceed; if 6, convert to dollars.
Independent X_1	b_1	2	14–15	0	From Deck 1, Columns 12–13
Independent X_2	b_2	3	16–18	0	From Deck 1, Columns 15–17
Independent X_3	b_3	5	19–23	0	From Deck 1, Columns 18–23
Independent X_4	b_4	3	24–26	2	From Deck 5, Columns 7–9
Independent X_5	b_5	3	27–29	0	From Deck 5, Columns 10–12

CODING INSTRUCTIONS FOR DATA

Variable	Coefficient	No. of Columns†	Columns From–To	Decimals	Remarks
Independent X_6	b_6	3	30–32	0	From Deck 4, Columns 17–19
Independent X_7	b_7	3	33–35	0	From Deck 4, Columns 31–33
Independent X_8	b_8	3	36–38	0	From Deck 3, Columns 29–31
Independent X_9	b_9	3	39–41	1	From Deck 3, Columns 23–25
Independent X_{10}	b_{10}	3	42–44	1	From Deck 9, Columns 42–44
Independent X_{11}	b_{11}	3	45–47	1	From Deck 9, Columns 45–47

† If not all spaces are needed, zeros are used.

Appendix D
Coded Data

1. *Charters*

    Headings refer to card columns. See Appendix C.1 for explanations.

2. *Tie-ups* (Monthly)

    Headings refer to card columns. See Appendix C.2 for explanation.

3. *New Orders* (Monthly)

    Headings refer to card columns. See Appendix C.3 for explanation.

4. *Spot Rates* (Monthly)

    Headings refer to card columns. See Appendix C.4 for explanation.

5. *Gulf Oil Company Charter Data*
   (*Format for Multiple-Correlation Card*)

    Headings refer to card columns. See Appendix C.5 for explanation.

1. *Charters*

6 8 10 TØ TØ TØ 7 9 11	1 TØ 4	5	12 14 TØ 13	15 TØ 17	18 24 25 TØ 23	26 28 TØ 27	29 TØ 34	35 40 41 TØ 39	42 44 45 80 TØ 43
1/31/50	1565	0	2 3	6	3500 0 0	0 6	0	3500 7 0	0 0 0 1
1/31/50	7077	0	32 3	60	13500 0 0	0 6	0	1900 0 0	0 0 0 1
2/ 1/50	7078	0	30 3	60	15000 0 0	0 6	0	1900 0 0	0 0 0 1
2/ 6/50	942	0	12 3	60	16000 0 0	0 6	0	1900 0 0	0 0 0 1
2/27/50	7029	0	40 3	84	18000 0 0	0 6	0	1900 0 0	0 0 0 1
2/27/50	7029	0	34 3	84	18000 0 0	0 6	0	1900 0 0	0 0 0 1
7/12/50	7036	0	16 3	120	16000 0 0	0 5	0	235 0 0	0 0 0 1
8/ 4/50	7081	0	1 3	3	3227 0 3	6 6	0	1900 7 0	0 0 0 1
8/10/50	2994	0	3 3	36	16460 0 0	10 5	0	300 0 0	0 0 0 1
8/14/50	7003	0	2 3	24	13000 0 0	0 6	0	2100 0 0	0 0 0 1
8/31/50	7082	0	2 1	2	10000 0 1	6 2	12000	0 3 0	0 0 0 1
8/31/50	7082	0	0 3	24	10000 0 0	0 2	10500	0 0 1	0 0 0 1
9/ 5/50	7036	0	12 3	60	12500 0 0	0 6	0	1900 0 0	0 0 0 1
9/ 5/50	162	0	36 3	60	13360 0 0	0 6	0	2206 0 3	0 0 0 1
9/ 5/50	162	0	0 3	36	13360 0 0	0 5	0	370 3 0	0 0 0 1
9/10/50	7083	0	3 3	24	14500 0 0	0 6	0	2000 0 0	0 0 0 1
9/18/50	7084	0	32 3	84	19250 0 0	0 6	0	2000 0 0	0 0 0 1
9/18/50	7084	0	27 3	84	16000 0 0	0 6	0	2000 0 0	0 0 0 1
9/18/50	7084	0	15 3	84	16250 0 0	0 6	0	2000 0 0	0 0 0 1
9/18/50	7085	0	2 3	48	16300 0 0	0 5	0	317 0 0	0 0 0 1
9/19/50	2588	0	3 3	24	10050 0 0	0 6	0	2200 0 0	0 0 0 1
10/ 5/50	7086	0	14 3	120	16000 0 0	0 5	0	265 7 0	0 0 0 1
10/18/50	232	0	1 3	12	10558 0 0	0 5	0	420 7 0	0 0 0 1
10/23/50	7087	0	24 3	60	13500 0 0	0 6	0	2000 0 0	0 0 0 1
10/31/50	7088	0	3 3	24	16460 0 0	0 5	0	450 0 0	0 0 0 1
11/ 5/50	7091	0	9 3	36	8300 0 0	0 6	0	1903 0 0	0 0 0 1
11/ 6/50	366	0	18 3	12	9800 0 0	0 5	0	355 0 3	0 0 0 1
11/ 6/50	366	0	6 3	12	9800 0 0	0 5	0	385 3 0	0 0 0 1
11/ 6/50	1671	0	1 3	6	6950 3 9	6 0	0	0 0 0	0 0 0 1
11/ 8/50	7089	0	1 3	24	9620 0 0	0 5	0	323 0 0	0 0 0 1
11/ 8/50	1353	0	6 3	36	14660 0 0	0 0	0	0 0 0	0 0 0 1
11/13/50	7090	0	12 3	24	16500 0 0	0 5	0	315 0 0	0 0 0 1
11/19/50	835	0	6 3	60	16300 0 0	0 6	0	2400 0 0	0 0 0 1
11/28/50	7092	0	24 3	60	16500 0 0	0 6	0	2006 0 0	0 0 0 1
11/28/50	7042	0	24 3	48	16300 0 0	0 6	0	2006 0 3	0 0 0 1
11/28/50	7042	0	12 3	12	16300 0 0	0 6	0	2106 3 0	0 0 0 1
12/13/50	2629	0	5 3	12	12500 1 0	0 6	0	3000 0 5	0 0 0 1
12/13/50	2629	0	17 3	48	12500 1 0	0 6	0	2500 0 3	0 0 0 1
12/13/50	2362	0	17 3	48	12500 1 0	0 6	0	2500 0 3	0 0 0 1
12/13/50	2362	0	5 3	12	12500 1 0	0 6	0	3000 3 0	0 0 0 1
12/20/50	7093	0	5 3	24	8820 0 0	0 5	0	390 0 0	0 0 0 1
12/20/50	184	0	5 3	24	14930 0 0	0 5	0	390 0 0	0 0 0 1
12/20/50	7094	0	4 1	3	5600 0 0	12 6	0	4206 0 0	0 0 0 1
12/20/50	988	0	3 1	4	7840 0 0	12 6	0	4706 0 0	0 0 0 1

Headings refer to card columns. See Appendix C.1 for explanations.

CHARTERS 263

6 TØ 7	8 TØ 9	10 TØ 11	1 TØ 4	5	12 TØ 13	14	15 TØ 17	18 TØ 23	24	25	26 TØ 27	28	29 TØ 34	35 TØ 39	40	41	42 TØ 43	44	45	80
1/ 3/51	1662	0	6	3	60		14853	0	0	0	6	0	2500	0	0	0	0	0	1
1/ 3/51	1501	0	3	3	60		14850	0	0	0	6	0	2500	0	0	0	0	0	1
1/ 4/51	7095	0	2	3	18		8495	0	0	0	5	0	370	0	0	0	0	0	1
1/ 7/51	395	0	7	3	84		12250	0	0	0	0	0	0	0	0	0	0	0	1
1/11/51	2485	0	17	3	12		18000	0	0	0	6	0	3500	0	3	0	0	0	1
1/11/51	2485	0	5	3	12		18000	0	0	0	6	0	4000	3	0	0	0	0	1
1/17/51	7025	0	22	3	60		16300	0	0	0	6	0	2300	0	0	0	0	0	1
1/20/51	467	0	1	3	0		12600	0	0	0	0	0	0	0	0	0	0	0	1
1/31/51	7096	0	31	3	60		18500	0	0	0	6	0	2206	0	0	0	0	0	1
1/31/51	444	0	45	3	46		14820	0	0	0	6	0	2300	0	3	0	0	0	1
1/31/51	444	0	7	3	38		14820	0	0	0	6	0	2500	3	0	0	0	0	1
1/31/51	1557	0	22	3	60		15900	0	0	0	0	0	0	0	0	0	0	0	1
2/ 4/51	7097	0	34	3	60		13500	0	0	0	0	0	0	0	0	0	0	0	1
2/ 5/51	7100	0	5	3	12		5800	0	0	0	6	0	3500	0	0	0	0	0	1
2/ 5/51	7100	0	17	3	6		5800	0	0	0	6	0	3206	0	0	0	0	0	1
2/15/51	7098	0	13	3	60		16000	0	0	0	6	0	2306	0	0	0	0	0	1
2/15/51	7099	0	11	3	60		16000	0	0	0	6	0	2606	0	0	0	0	0	1
2/15/51	7098	0	25	3	60		24000	0	0	0	6	0	2100	0	0	0	0	0	1
2/17/51	7038	0	24	3	60		18500	0	0	0	6	0	2206	0	0	0	0	0	1
2/17/51	3240	0	18	3	60		24750	0	0	0	6	0	2200	0	0	0	0	0	1
2/20/51	389	0	12	3	60		17500	0	0	0	6	0	2300	0	0	0	0	0	1
2/28/51	3198	0	7	3	84		16320	0	0	0	6	0	2600	0	0	0	0	0	1
2/28/51	1261	1	2	3	12		16440	0	0	0	5	0	685	0	0	0	0	0	1
3/ 5/51	7101	0	21	3	60		18500	0	0	0	5	0	325	0	0	0	0	0	1
3/ 5/51	7102	0	24	3	84		18000	0	0	0	5	0	270	7	0	0	0	0	1
3/ 8/51	3118	0	8	3	48		13025	1	0	0	6	0	2800	0	0	0	0	0	1
3/ 8/51	7036	0	12	3	48		18500	1	0	0	5	0	385	0	0	0	0	0	1
3/12/51	1968	0	13	3	36		16560	0	0	0	5	0	380	0	0	0	0	0	1
3/14/51	2668	0	7	3	60		16020	0	0	22	6	0	2306	0	0	0	0	0	1
3/14/51	7104	0	24	3	84		15500	0	0	0	6	0	2206	0	0	0	0	0	1
3/14/51	7103	0	42	3	60		15750	0	0	0	6	0	2306	0	3	0	0	0	1
3/14/51	7103	0	18	3	24		15750	1	0	0	6	0	2306	3	0	0	0	0	1
3/30/51	7066	0	29	3	60		18000	0	0	0	6	0	2206	0	0	0	0	0	1
3/30/51	7036	0	22	3	60		18500	0	0	0	6	0	2306	0	0	0	0	0	1
3/30/51	1627	0	20	3	84		13470	0	0	0	6	0	2206	0	0	0	0	0	1
4/ 3/51	7105	0	24	3	60		17500	0	0	0	5	0	317	0	0	0	0	0	1
4/ 3/51	7106	0	20	3	84		16300	0	0	0	6	0	2206	0	0	0	0	0	1
4/ 5/51	1530	0	12	3	84		14750	0	0	0	6	0	2306	0	0	0	0	0	1
4/ 5/51	1662	0	20	3	84		14833	0	0	0	6	0	2306	0	0	0	0	0	1
4/ 5/51	1646	0	20	3	84		15320	0	0	0	6	0	2306	0	0	0	0	0	1
4/ 5/51	7107	0	20	3	84		17500	0	0	0	6	0	2306	0	0	0	0	0	1
4/ 5/51	7107	0	30	3	84		18500	0	0	0	6	0	2206	0	0	0	0	0	1
4/ 5/51	7107	0	30	3	84		18500	0	0	0	6	0	2206	0	0	0	0	0	1
4/ 5/51	7107	0	30	3	84		18500	0	0	0	6	0	2206	0	0	0	0	0	1

264   APPENDIX D

```
  6   8  10    1   5   12 14   15    18 24 25  26 28    29    35 40 41 42 44 45 80
 TØ  TØ  TØ   TØ       TØ       TØ    TØ        TØ      TØ    TØ         TØ
  7   9  11    4       13       17    23        27      34    39         43

4/ 5/51  7098  0  55  3   84   29000  0  0   0  6        0   2000  0  0  0  0  0  1
4/ 6/51  2823  0  12  3   12   16738  0  7  17  5        0    300  0  0  0  0  0  1
4/10/51  3068  0  12  3   60   12835  0  0   0  5        0    303  0  0  0  0  0  1
4/10/51  7109  0  19  3   84   16000  0  0   0  6        0   2306  0  0  0  0  0  1
4/10/51  7110  0  27  3   84   18000  0  0   0  6        0   2206  0  0  0  0  0  1
4/10/51  7108  0  20  3   84   19000  0  0   0  6        0   2300  0  0  0  0  0  1
4/16/51  7025  0  38  3   84   18000  0  0   0  6        0   2106  0  0  0  0  0  1
4/16/51  7027  0  33  3  120   17500  0  0   0  0        0      0  0  0  0  0  0  1
4/17/51  7111  0  20  3   84   13250  2  0   0  6        0   2400  0  0  0  0  0  1
4/17/51  2500  0  44  3   60   14290  0  0   0  6        0   1806  0  3  0  0  0  1
4/17/51  2500  0  20  3   24   14290  0  0   0  6        0   2109  3  0  0  0  0  1
4/22/51  1761  0  18  3   60   24700  0  0   0  6        0   2300  0  2  0  0  0  1
4/22/51  1761  0   6  2   12   24700  0  0   0  2    25000      0  3  0  0  0  0  1
4/22/51  1698  0   2  3   84   13490  0  0   0  0        0      0  0  0  0  0  0  1
4/25/51  7026  0  44  3   96   30000  0  0   0  6        0   2100  0  0  0  0  0  1
4/25/51  7026  0  48  3  120   30000  0  0   0  6        0   2000  0  0  0  0  0  1
4/25/51   373  0  20  3   24   14900  0  0   0  6        0   2100  0  0  0  0  0  1
4/26/51  2906  0   3  3   24    8375  1  0   0  6        0   3500  0  0  0  0  0  1
4/26/51  7112  0  24  3   36   18100  0  0   0  6        0   2406  0  0  0  0  0  1
4/30/51  2773  0   3  3   24    9170  0  0   0  6        0   3400  0  0  0  0  0  1
4/30/51  7113  0  17  3   12    7420  0  0   0  5        0    470  0  3  0  0  0  1
4/30/51  7113  0  29  3   12    7420  0  0   0  5        0    460  0  3  0  0  0  1
4/30/51  7113  0   5  3   12    7420  0  0   0  5        0    480  3  0  0  0  0  1

5/ 7/51  7114  0  10  3   60   16500  1  0   0  5        0    390  0  0  0  0  0  1
5/14/51  1777  0  10  3   84   16200  0  0   0  6        0   2700  0  0  0  0  0  1
5/14/51  1778  0  24  3   84   16200  0  0   0  6        0   2400  0  0  0  0  0  1
5/15/51  7074  0  36  3   84   18000  0  0   0  6        0   2106  0  0  0  0  0  1
5/15/51  7115  0  99  3   24   29500  0  0   0  6        0   1900  0  3  0  0  0  1
5/15/51  7115  0  48  3  120   29500  0  0   0  6        0   2000  3  0  0  0  0  1

6/13/51  1429  0   2  3   60   16320  1  0   0  5        0    450  0  0  0  0  0  1
6/13/51  7116  0  11  3   84   16700  0  0   0  6        0   2300  0  0  0  0  0  1
6/13/51  7117  0  18  3   12   14710  0  0   0  5        0    340  0  0  0  0  0  1
6/13/51  7118  0  30  3   48   18500  0  0   0  5        0    340  0  0  0  0  0  1
6/15/51  7119  0   2  3    9   10924  0  0   0  5        0   1125  7  0  0  0  0  1
6/19/51  7081  0   1  3   12    3227  2  0   0  6        0   6400  0  0  0  0  0  1
6/30/51   341  0   1  3   60   13510  0  0   0  6        0   2506  0  0  0  0  0  1
6/30/51   336  0   1  3   60   15020  0  0   0  6        0   2500  0  0  0  0  0  1
6/30/51   338  0   2  3   60   16250  0  0   0  6        0   2600  0  0  0  0  0  1
6/30/51  7018  0  60  3   96   28000  0  0   0  0        0      0  0  0  0  0  0  1

7/ 3/51  7120  0  69  3   12   18500  0  0   0  6        0   2306  0  3  0  0  0  1
7/ 3/51  7120  0  21  3   48   18500  1  0   0  6        0   2306  3  0  0  0  0  1
7/10/51  7121  0  48  3   84   18000  0  0   0  6        0   2100  0  0  0  0  0  1
7/10/51  7122  0  21  3    0   16500  0  0   0  0        0      0  0  0  0  0  0  1
7/15/51  7123  0  32  3  144   32000  0  0   0  5        0    270  0  0  0  0  0  1
```

```
 6  8 10     1  5 12 14    15    18 24 25   26 28     29    35 40 41 42 44 45 80
TØ TØ TØ    TØ      TØ     TØ    TØ         TØ        TØ    TØ          TØ
 7  9 11     4     13      17    23         27        34    39          43

 7/22/51   7036  0  43  3   24   32000  0  0   0  5    0     400  0  0  0  0  0  1
 7/22/51   7001  0   7  3   36   16500  0  0   0  5    0     400  0  0  0  0  0  1

 8/ 3/51   2142  0   1  3   12    3080  0  0   0  4    0      75  3  0  0  0  0  1
 8/14/51   7124  0  52  3   84   32000  0  0   0  6    0    2000  0  0  0  0  0  1
 8/14/51   7107  0  48  3   84   34000  0  0   0  6    0    2006  0  0  0  0  0  1
 8/20/51   7123  1  36  3  120   32000  0  0   0  5    0     290  0  0  0  0  0  1
 8/30/51   1725  0  24  3  120   16500  0  0   0  5    0     290  0  0  0  0  0  1

 9/ 4/51   7020  0  14  3   84   16200  0  0   0  6    0    2400  0  0  0  0  0  1
 9/ 5/51   7126  0  38  3   84   18500  0  0   0  6    0    2106  0  0  0  0  0  1
 9/ 7/51   7034  0  80  3   12   17500  0  0   0  6    0    2400  0  3  0  0  0  1
 9/ 7/51   7034  0  32  3   48   17500  1  0   0  6    0    2400  3  0  0  0  0  1
 9/13/51   7127  0   1  3   10    7235  0  0   0  5    0    1200  0  0  0  0  0  1
 9/13/51   7020  0  41  3   60   16000  0  0   0  6    0    2100  0  0  0  0  0  1
 9/13/51   7036  0  12  3   84   30000  0  0   0  5    0     290  0  0  0  0  0  1
 9/13/51   7128  0  36  3  120   30000  0  0   0  5    0     295  0  0  0  0  0  1

10/ 3/51   1873  0   1  3   18    2700  0  0   0  3    0     300  0  0  0  0  0  1
10/ 9/51   7129  0   8  3   60    9900  3  1   5  5    0     525  0  0  0  0  0  1
10/14/51   7130  0  24  3   84   19000  0  7  17  5    0     390  0  0  0  0  0  1
10/14/51   7130  0  24  3   84   19000  0  7  17  5    0     390  0  0  0  0  0  1
10/14/51    807  0   8  3   42   16460  0  7  17  5    0     550  0  0  0  0  0  1
10/15/51   7036  0  20  3   60   18500  2  0   0  6    0    2600  0  0  0  0  0  1

11/21/51   7131  0  24  3   60   16500  0  0   0  5    0     350  0  0  0  0  0  1
11/21/51   7036  0  22  3   72   16400  0  0   0  5    0     425  0  0  0  0  0  1
11/21/51   1945  0  10  3   12   16110  0  0   0  5    0     425  0  0  0  0  0  1
11/21/51   7132  0   2  3   12    8800  0  0  11  0    0       0  0  0  0  0  0  1

12/ 5/51    914  0  34  3   60   15910  0  0   0  6    0    2800  0  0  0  0  0  1
12/11/51   7098  0  58  3   60   20000  0  7  17  6    0    2500  0  0  0  0  0  1
12/11/51   3059  0  51  3   60   24000  0  7  17  6    0    2400  0  0  0  0  0  1
12/11/51   3058  0  43  3   60   24380  0  7  17  6    0    2400  0  0  0  0  0  1
12/15/51   1729  0  28  3   60   13700  0  0   0  6    0    2606  7  0  0  0  0  1
12/15/51   7036  0  40  3   60   18500  0  0   0  6    0    2706  0  0  0  0  0  1
12/18/51   7101  0  54  3   60   18000  0  0   0  5    0     340  0  0  0  0  0  1
12/18/51   7133  0  28  3   60   19000  0  0   0  5    0     380  0  0  0  0  0  1
12/18/51   2426  0  36  3   60   19000  0  0   0  5    0     400  0  0  0  0  0  1
12/30/51   7028  0  24  3   60   18000  0  0   0  6    0    2800  0  0  0  0  0  1
12/30/51   7028  0  42  3   60   18000  0  0   0  6    0    2706  0  0  0  0  0  1
12/30/51   7028  0  34  3   60   18000  0  0   0  6    0    2800  0  0  0  0  0  1

 1/12/52   7107  0  24  3   60   18500  1  0   0  5    0     420  0  0  0  0  0  1
 1/12/52   7098  0  33  3   12   29000  0  0   0  5    0     315  0  0  0  0  0  1
 1/12/52   3057  0  46  3   48   24500  0  0   0  5    0     315  0  0  0  0  0  1
 1/15/52   7135  0  19  3   60   16500  0  7  17  5    0     450  0  0  0  0  0  1
 1/15/52   7027  0  22  3   84   13000  0  0   0  5    0     437  0  0  0  0  0  1
 1/17/52   7134  0  34  3   60   18500  0  0   0  6    0    2800  0  0  0  0  0  1
 1/20/52   2906  0  29  3   60   15000  0  0   0  6    0    2700  0  0  0  0  0  1
```

APPENDIX D

6 TØ 7	8 TØ 9	10 TØ 11	1 TØ 4	5	12 TØ 13	14	15 TØ 17	18 TØ 23	24	25	26 TØ 27	28	29 TØ 34	35 TØ 39	40	41	42 TØ 43	44	45	80
1/20/52	7137	0	35	3	60	16500	0	0	0	6	0	2800	0	0	0	0	0	1
1/20/52	7138	0	35	3	60	17500	0	0	0	6	0	2800	0	0	0	0	0	1
1/20/52	7137	0	24	3	60	16500	0	0	0	6	0	2800	0	2	0	0	0	1
1/20/52	7137	0	12	2	12	16500	0	0	0	2	25000	0	3	0	0	0	0	1
1/20/52	66	0	1	2	12	17000	0	0	0	2	25000	0	3	0	0	0	0	1
1/20/52	7136	0	3	2	12	17000	0	0	0	2	25000	0	3	0	0	0	0	1
1/20/52	66	0	13	3	60	17000	0	0	0	0	0	0	0	2	0	0	0	1
1/20/52	7136	0	15	3	60	17000	0	0	0	0	0	0	0	2	0	0	0	1
1/22/52	444	0	22	3	60	14820	0	0	0	5	0	403	7	0	0	0	0	1
1/22/52	7139	0	0	3	60	18000	0	0	0	5	0	450	0	0	0	0	0	1
1/25/52	7140	0	21	3	12	14580	0	0	0	5	0	425	0	0	0	0	0	1
1/25/52	2907	0	33	3	48	16320	0	0	0	5	0	450	0	0	0	0	0	1
1/28/52	7029	0	40	3	60	18000	0	0	0	6	0	2800	0	0	0	0	0	1
1/28/52	7075	0	27	3	60	18500	0	0	0	6	0	2803	0	0	0	0	0	1
1/28/52	1272	0	21	3	84	15960	0	0	0	5	0	450	0	0	0	0	0	1
1/28/52	408	0	24	3	84	24000	0	0	0	5	0	370	0	0	0	0	0	1
1/28/52	7036	0	15	3	120	38000	0	7	17	5	0	355	0	0	0	0	0	1
1/28/52	7036	0	15	2	60	38000	0	7	17	0	8500	0	0	0	0	0	0	1
2/ 5/52	182	0	30	3	60	16000	4	0	0	6	0	2800	0	2	0	0	0	1
2/ 5/52	182	0	18	2	12	16000	0	0	0	2	25000	0	3	0	0	0	0	1
2/ 8/52	7003	0	34	3	60	18000	0	0	0	6	0	2800	0	0	0	0	0	1
2/ 8/52	7141	0	28	3	60	13500	0	0	0	6	0	2800	0	2	0	0	0	1
2/ 8/52	7142	0	26	3	60	18300	0	0	0	5	0	394	0	2	0	0	0	1
2/ 8/52	7141	0	22	2	6	13500	0	0	0	2	22500	0	0	2	0	0	0	1
2/ 8/52	7141	0	18	2	4	13500	0	0	0	2	25000	0	2	0	0	0	0	1
2/ 8/52	7142	0	12	2	14	18300	0	0	0	0	0	0	3	0	0	0	0	1
2/12/52	7077	0	27	3	60	17500	0	0	0	6	0	2806	0	0	0	0	0	1
2/12/52	7143	0	28	3	60	16250	0	0	0	6	0	2800	0	2	0	0	0	1
2/12/52	7143	0	8	2	5	16250	0	0	0	2	26000	0	2	0	0	0	0	1
2/12/52	7143	0	13	2	9	16250	0	0	0	2	25000	0	0	2	0	0	0	1
2/12/52	7143	0	22	2	6	16250	0	0	0	2	22500	0	0	2	0	0	0	1
2/13/52	2484	0	29	3	48	18400	0	0	0	6	0	2806	0	0	0	0	0	1
2/13/52	7085	0	30	3	60	16000	2	0	0	6	0	2806	0	2	0	0	0	1
2/13/52	7085	0	18	2	12	16000	2	0	0	2	25000	0	3	0	0	0	0	1
2/14/52	7144	0	27	3	60	17500	0	0	0	6	0	2803	0	0	0	0	0	1
2/15/52	7145	0	34	3	60	16400	0	0	0	6	0	2709	0	0	0	0	0	1
2/25/52	7081	0	5	3	12	3250	0	0	0	6	0	6100	7	0	0	0	0	1
2/25/52	375	0	44	3	60	16320	0	0	0	6	0	2700	0	0	0	0	0	1
2/25/52	7026	0	58	3	60	32000	0	0	0	6	0	2406	0	0	0	0	0	1
2/26/52	1856	0	3	3	60	16600	0	0	0	5	0	340	0	0	0	0	0	1
2/28/52	2497	0	25	3	60	12820	0	0	0	6	0	2503	0	0	0	0	0	1
3/ 3/52	7094	0	1	3	9	5627	0	0	6	6	0	5206	7	0	0	0	0	1
3/ 5/52	1403	0	31	3	60	16225	0	0	0	5	0	384	0	0	0	0	0	1
3/ 9/52	2246	0	33	3	60	13725	0	0	0	6	0	2706	0	0	0	0	0	1

CHARTERS

6 TØ 7	8 TØ 9	10 TØ 11	1 TØ 4	5	12 TØ 13	14	15 TØ 17	18 TØ 23	24	25	26 TØ 27	28	29 TØ 34	35 TØ 39	40	41	42 TØ 43	44	45	80
3/11/52	3341	0	18	3	60		16560	0	0	0	6		0	2800	0	0	0	0	0	1
3/11/52	7146	0	16	3	60		18800	0	0	10	5		0	455	0	0	0	0	0	1
3/11/52	2522	0	2	3	6		11402	0	0	0	5		0	988	0	0	0	0	0	1
3/13/52	7147	0	26	3	60		16000	0	0	0	5		0	400	0	0	0	0	0	1
3/14/52	7034	0	36	3	60		14600	0	0	0	6		0	2706	0	0	0	0	0	1
3/14/52	7036	0	24	3	60		19000	0	0	0	5		0	349	0	0	0	0	0	1
3/14/52	3240	0	64	3	60		24850	0	0	0	6		0	2500	0	0	0	0	0	1
3/14/52	1400	0	7	2	17		12500	0	0	0	0		17800	0	0	0	0	0	0	1
3/19/52	1661	0	36	3	60		24850	0	0	0	6		0	2500	0	0	0	0	0	1
3/21/52	2655	0	14	3	44		12361	0	0	0	6		0	2500	0	0	0	0	0	1
3/19/52	1668	0	27	3	60		15400	0	0	0	6		0	2709	0	0	0	0	0	1
3/23/52	963	0	3	3	12		2700	0	0	0	6		0	7206	0	0	0	0	0	1
3/23/52	7134	0	57	3	60		32000	0	0	0	6		0	2406	0	0	0	0	0	1
3/23/52	7074	0	31	3	60		20000	0	0	0	6		0	2706	0	0	0	0	0	1
3/25/52	2048	0	21	3	60		19000	0	0	0	6		0	2906	0	0	0	0	0	1
3/25/52	7149	0	33	3	36		32850	0	0	0	5		0	400	0	0	0	0	0	1
3/25/52	7148	0	33	3	60		18700	0	0	0	3		0	714	0	0	0	0	0	1
4/15/52	2414	0	17	3	60		28000	0	0	0	5		0	370	0	0	0	0	0	1
4/24/52	7011	0	44	3	60		32000	0	0	0	6		0	2406	0	0	0	0	0	1
4/27/52	7150	0	35	3	60		18500	0	0	0	6		0	2800	0	0	0	0	0	1
4/27/52	7133	0	24	3	72		21000	0	7	17	5		0	375	0	0	0	0	0	1
5/ 5/52	2468	0	4	3	24		2800	1	1	20	5		0	1100	0	0	0	0	0	1
5/ 5/52	2867	0	24	3	60		16090	0	0	0	6		0	2800	0	0	0	0	0	1
5/19/52	7035	0	42	3	60		18250	0	0	0	6		0	2706	0	0	0	0	0	1
5/20/52	7151	0	3	3	12		10480	0	0	6	6		0	4206	0	0	0	0	0	1
6/12/52	7134	0	54	3	60		32000	0	0	0	6		0	2406	0	0	0	0	0	1
6/12/52	7032	0	30	3	60		27000	0	0	0	6		0	2708	0	2	0	0	0	1
6/12/52	7032	0	9	2	21		27000	0	0	0	2		23500	0	3	0	0	0	0	1
6/23/52	7036	0	45	3	60		24400	0	0	0	6		0	2500	0	0	0	0	0	1
6/23/52	7152	0	9	3	60		24000	0	0	0	5		0	450	0	0	0	0	0	1
7/ 9/52	864	0	11	3	60		10825	0	0	0	5		0	475	0	0	0	0	0	1
7/14/52	7062	0	20	3	60		18250	1	2	13	6		0	3109	0	0	0	0	0	1
7/21/52	7153	0	17	3	60		29000	0	0	0	5		0	350	0	0	0	0	0	1
7/24/52	7015	0	17	3	84		29000	0	0	0	5		0	350	0	0	0	0	0	1
7/25/52	1316	0	1	3	12		1422	1	1	20	5		0	1350	0	0	0	0	0	1
8/ 3/52	7154	0	24	3	60		18500	0	0	0	5		0	400	7	0	0	0	0	1
8/18/52	1037	0	1	3	60		14400	0	7	17	5		0	420	0	0	0	0	0	1
8/18/52	7036	0	20	3	60		18800	0	0	0	5		0	425	0	0	0	0	0	1
8/29/52	7003	0	14	3	60		20000	0	0	0	5		0	410	0	0	0	0	0	1
9/ 2/52	7036	0	27	3	60		20000	0	0	0	5		0	415	0	0	0	0	0	1
9/ 3/52	616	1	13	3	60		14250	0	7	17	5		0	400	0	0	0	0	0	1
9/ 3/52	2036	0	9	3	60		16900	0	0	0	5		0	410	0	0	0	0	0	1
9/ 3/52	7139	0	17	3	60		19250	0	7	17	5		0	410	0	0	0	0	0	1
10/ 1/52	1731	0	6	3	60		16400	0	0	0	6		0	3200	0	0	0	0	0	1

268 APPENDIX D

6 8 10 TØ 7 9 11	1 TØ 4	5	12 14 TØ 13	15 TØ 17	18 24 25 TØ 23	26 28 TØ 27	29 TØ 34	35 40 41 TØ 39	42 44 45 80 TØ 43
10/19/52 2457	0	4	3	60	38000 0 0	0 0	6500	0 0 0	0 0 0 1
10/20/52 228	0	4	3	60	19600 0 0	5 5	0	400 0 0	0 0 0 1
11/ 0/52 7011	0	60	3	84	32000 0 0	0 6	0	2303 0 0	0 0 0 1
12/ 3/52 3851	0	1	3	12	8760 1 0	6 6	0	3706 0 0	0 0 0 1
12/ 3/52 7156	0	0	3	12	8800 1 8	6 6	0	3706 0 0	0 0 0 1
12/ 3/52 7003	0	6	3	12	29000 0 0	0 5	0	375 0 0	0 0 0 1
12/ 3/52 7003	0	6	3	12	29000 0 0	0 5	0	375 0 0	0 0 0 1
12/ 3/52 7003	0	18	3	12	29000 0 0	0 5	0	375 0 0	0 0 0 1
12/ 3/52 7003	0	18	3	12	29000 0 0	0 5	0	375 0 0	0 0 0 1
12/16/52 7157	0	18	3	60	15750 4 0	13 6	0	2600 0 0	0 0 0 1
12/16/52 191	0	10	3	60	20000 0 0	0 5	0	385 0 0	0 0 0 1
1/ 2/53 7157	0	29	3	60	26500 0 0	0 2	9500	0 0 0	0 0 0 1
2/ 0/53 7001	0	12	3	84	29000 0 0	0 6	0	2500 0 0	0 0 0 1
2/ 0/53 7001	0	12	3	84	29000 0 0	0 6	0	2500 0 0	0 0 0 1
3/20/53 3202	0	1	3	12	11853 1 0	0 6	0	2006 0 0	0 0 0 1
4/ 0/53 7159	0	36	3	96	26800 0 0	0 6	0	2300 0 0	0 0 0 1
4/15/53 1038	0	19	3	36	18020 4 0	0 6	0	2300 0 3	0 0 0 1
4/15/53 1038	0	7	3	12	18020 1 0	0 6	0	2600 3 0	0 0 0 1
5/16/53 7003	0	12	3	84	12000 0 0	0 6	0	2400 0 0	0 0 0 1
5/18/53 1549	0	1	3	60	15255 1 7	17 6	0	2300 0 0	0 0 0 1
5/18/53 395	1	1	3	12	12324 1 0	0 6	0	2106 7 0	0 0 0 1
5/18/53 7160	0	5	3	12	13500 1 0	0 6	0	2106 7 0	0 0 0 1
6/ 2/53 1932	1	1	3	12	16500 0 0	0 5	0	300 0 0	0 0 0 1
6/ 2/53 7161	0	1	3	12	16590 0 0	0 0	0	0 0 0	0 0 0 1
6/ 6/53 1482	0	1	3	6	16738 0 0	0 5	0	240 0 0	0 0 0 1
6/13/53 1483	0	7	3	60	13500 2 0	0 6	0	2206 0 0	0 0 0 1
6/13/53 2222	0	8	3	60	13450 2 0	0 6	0	2106 7 0	0 0 0 1
6/21/53 2667	0	7	3	36	13500 2 0	0 6	0	2100 0 0	0 0 0 1
7/28/53 7162	0	17	3	60	19000 0 0	0 5	0	350 0 0	0 0 0 1
8/ 4/53 93	0	1	3	12	16410 0 0	0 5	0	250 0 0	0 0 0 1
8/17/53 1572	0	1	3	14	16729 0 0	0 6	0	1800 0 0	0 0 0 1
8/17/53 2823	0	5	3	24	16484 0 0	0 5	0	295 0 0	0 0 0 1
9/ 5/53 3955	0	2	3	24	18800 0 0	0 5	0	305 0 0	0 0 0 1
9/12/53 807	0	2	3	30	16431 0 0	0 5	0	265 0 0	0 0 0 1
9/22/53 455	0	1	3	36	12585 0 0	0 5	0	290 0 0	0 0 0 1
10/ 1/53 7036	0	20	3	120	38000 0 7	17 6	0	1800 7 0	0 0 0 1
10/ 4/53 3202	0	6	3	12	11853 0 6	15 6	0	1906 7 0	0 0 0 1
10/18/53 1692	0	1	3	6	4275 0 0	0 5	0	630 0 0	0 0 0 1
11/10/53 3130	0	8	3	60	16520 0 0	0 5	0	300 0 0	0 0 0 1
11/10/53 3124	1	4	3	60	16610 0 0	0 5	0	300 0 0	0 0 0 1
11/12/53 3129	0	5	3	36	18200 1 0	0 6	0	2100 0 0	0 0 0 1
11/15/53 1961	0	12	3	60	15900 0 0	0 5	0	305 0 0	C 0 0 1
12/ 1/53 467	0	0	3	12	12630 1 0	0 6	0	2106 7 0	0 0 0 1
12/ 1/53 1278	0	1	3	36	15720 2 0	0 6	0	1906 0 0	0 0 0 1

CHARTERS   269

```
  6  8 10     1    5    12 14    15      18 24 25   26 28      29       35 40 41 42 44 45 80
 TØ TØ TØ    TØ         TØ       TØ      TØ         TØ         TØ       TØ         TØ
  7  9 11     4         13       17      23         27         34       39         43

12/15/53   1238   0    1  3    12     9575  0  0    0  6       0     1803  0  0  0  0  0  1

 1/14/54   1372   0    1  3    12     8550  0  0    6  6       0     1609  0  0  0  0  0  1
 1/15/54   1577   0   10  3    36    18000  0  7   17  5       0      280  0  0  0  0  0  1
 1/15/54   7088   0    3  2     6    15000  0  0   10  0   14000        0  0  0  0  0  0  1

 2/ 3/54   7164   0    1  3     0     4275  3  9   12  6       0     4500  0  0  0  0  0  1
 2/ 3/54   2250   0    1  3     0     4250  3  9   12  6       0     4500  0  0  0  0  0  1

 3/23/54   2272   0    1  3    12     4071  0  0   15  6       0     4206  0  0  0  0  0  1
 3/29/54   7164   0    1  3     6     4275  0  0    0  6       0     4206  7  0  0  0  0  1
 3/29/54   3903   0    1  3     8     9800  0  8    6  6       0     1800  0  0  0  0  0  1

 4/ 6/54   7098   0   44  3   120    38000  0  0    0  6       0     1800  0  0  0  0  0  1
 4/12/54    399   0    2  3     5    13500  0  0    6  6       0     1700  0  0  0  0  0  1
 4/23/54    640   0    5  3    24    24900  0  0    0  5       0      215  0  0  0  0  0  1

 5/ 5/54   7165   0    7  3    24    19000  0  0    0  5       0      240  0  0  0  0  0  1

 6/ 8/54   1486   0   15  3    36    15472  2  0    0  6       0     1800  0  3  0  0  0  1
 6/ 8/54   1486   0    3  3    12    15472  2  0    0  6       0     1603  3  0  0  0  0  1
 6/10/54   1512   0    7  3    36    17500  0  0    0  6       0     1906  0  0  0  0  0  1

 9/ 0/54   7003   0    3  3    24    12500  0  0    0  5       0      247  0  0  0  0  0  1
 9/15/54   2753   0    1  3     7    16607  0  1   20  5       0      250  0  0  0  0  0  1
 9/20/54   7166   0    1  3     6    15000  0  0    0  5       0      250  0  0  0  0  0  1
 9/30/54   1683   0   16  3    60    16000  0  0    0  5       0      240  0  0  0  0  0  1
 9/30/54    757   0    1  3     2    13000  0  0    0  5       0      250  7  0  0  0  0  1
 9/30/54   1976   0   16  3    24    18475  0  0    0  5       0      231  0  0  0  0  0  1

10/13/54    467   0    4  3    12    12630  0  8    6  6       0     2000  0  0  0  0  0  1
10/21/54   1682   0    1  3     6    16460  0  0    0  5       0      275  0  0  0  0  0  1
10/27/54     29   0    1  3     6    16149  0  0    0  5       0      275  0  0  0  0  0  1
10/28/54   1967   0    2  3    24    13235  1  0    0  6       0     1800  0  0  0  0  0  1

11/ 1/54   1572   0    2  3    12    16729  0  0    0  6       0     1706  7  0  0  0  0  1
11/ 1/54   2995   0    2  3    12    16485  0  0    0  6       0     1706  7  0  0  0  0  1
11/ 1/54     48   0    2  3    12    15910  1  0    0  6       0     1800  7  0  0  0  0  1
11/ 3/54   1610   0    1  3     6    16460  0  0    0  5       0      285  0  0  0  0  0  1
11/ 4/54   1014   0    2  3    12    11425  1  0    0  6       0     1900  7  0  0  0  0  1
11/ 4/54   1482   0    2  3    12    16110  0  0    0  6       0     1706  7  0  0  0  0  1
11/ 5/54   1561   0    2  3    12    13500  1  0    0  6       0     1900  0  0  0  0  0  1
11/ 5/54   3149   0    2  3    12    16500  0  0    0  6       0     1900  0  0  0  0  0  1
11/ 9/54    835   1    2  3    12    16300  0  0    0  6       0     1706  7  0  0  0  0  1
11/12/54   3017   0    1  3    12    11500  1  0    5  6       0     2106  7  0  0  0  0  1
11/15/54   2947   0    1  3     6    16584  0  1   20  5       0      300  0  0  0  0  0  1
11/15/54   3013   1    2  3     8    16340  0  1   20  5       0      300  0  0  0  0  0  1
11/15/54   3266   0    1  3    12    12310  1  0    0  6       0     1705  0  0  0  0  0  1
11/17/54    150   0    0  3     6    16616  0  1   20  5       0      300  0  0  0  0  0  1
11/17/54   7044   0    1  3     6    16503  0  1   20  5       0      300  0  0  0  0  0  1
11/17/54   7167   0    1  3    12    13080  0  0   23  5       0      275  0  0  0  0  0  1
11/19/54   1796   0    1  3     5    16615  0  0   23  5       0      300  0  0  0  0  0  1
11/19/54   3089   0    1  3     1    16100  0  0   23  5       0      300  0  0  0  0  0  1
```

270 APPENDIX D

6 TØ 7	8 TØ 9	10 TØ 11	1 TØ 4	5	12 TØ 13	14	15 TØ 17	18 TØ 23	24	25	26 TØ 27	28	29 TØ 34	35 TØ 39	40	41	42 TØ 43	44	45	80
11/22/54	72	0	2	3	12	13580	1	0	0	6	0	1800	0	0	0	0	0	1
11/22/54	1773	0	2	3	12	15530	0	0	0	6	0	1706	7	0	0	0	0	1
11/22/54	2684	0	1	3	12	16220	1	0	0	6	0	1800	0	0	0	0	0	1
11/23/54	3243	0	2	3	12	15750	0	0	0	6	0	1706	7	0	0	0	0	1
11/23/54	776	0	2	3	12	16350	0	0	0	6	0	1806	7	0	0	0	0	1
11/24/54	14	0	1	3	12	16441	0	0	0	6	0	1706	7	0	0	0	0	1
11/25/54	223	0	2	3	12	13330	0	0	0	6	0	1706	7	0	0	0	0	1
11/25/54	1556	0	2	3	12	13580	1	0	0	6	0	1800	0	0	0	0	0	1
11/25/54	1475	0	2	3	12	16080	1	0	0	6	0	1800	0	0	0	0	0	1
11/25/54	1978	0	1	3	12	17610	0	0	0	6	0	1806	7	0	0	0	0	1
12/ 2/54	2485	0	2	3	12	18630	0	0	0	6	0	1706	7	0	0	0	0	1
12/ 8/54	2775	0	1	3	9	18414	0	0	0	5	0	290	0	0	0	0	0	1
12/13/54	1821	0	1	3	12	14600	0	0	0	6	0	1700	7	0	0	0	0	1
12/15/54	3230	0	7	3	24	16422	0	0	0	5	0	280	0	0	0	0	0	1
12/16/54	1807	0	1	3	12	16400	0	0	0	5	0	375	0	0	0	0	0	1
12/20/54	8	1	1	3	6	9605	0	0	0	6	0	1909	7	0	0	0	0	1
12/29/54	1372	0	1	3	2	8550	0	0	0	6	0	1906	0	0	0	0	0	1
1/ 0/55	1567	0	3	2	0	10350	0	0	22	6	0	2300	0	0	0	0	0	1
2/ 0/55	1653	0	2	3	8	10020	0	0	6	6	0	2200	0	0	0	0	0	1
2/ 0/55	933	0	0	3	12	19660	0	0	0	6	0	1906	0	0	0	0	0	1
2/ 0/55	962	0	3	3	12	24600	0	0	0	6	0	1903	0	0	0	0	0	1
2/ 0/55	389	0	2	3	60	17260	0	0	0	6	0	1906	0	0	0	0	0	1
3/ 0/55	1758	0	1	3	12	24606	0	0	0	6	0	1900	0	0	0	0	0	1
3/ 0/55	1793	0	1	3	12	12234	0	0	0	6	0	1900	0	0	0	0	0	1
3/ 0/55	3329	0	2	3	12	13550	0	0	0	6	0	1900	0	0	0	0	0	1
4/ 0/55	7003	0	3	3	60	13000	0	0	0	6	0	1900	0	0	0	0	0	1
4/ 0/55	2426	0	2	3	60	18500	0	0	0	6	0	2006	0	0	0	0	0	1
4/ 0/55	7169	0	3	3	60	24500	0	0	0	6	0	1906	0	0	0	0	0	1
4/ 0/55	7036	0	36	3	120	34000	0	0	0	6	0	1800	0	0	0	0	0	1
4/ 0/55	3355	0	1	3	8	9765	0	1	2	5	0	290	0	0	0	0	0	1
4/ 0/55	3230	0	2	3	12	16422	0	0	0	5	0	252	0	0	0	0	0	1
4/ 0/55	2727	0	2	3	12	11190	0	0	0	6	0	1509	0	0	0	0	0	1
4/ 0/55	1968	0	2	3	12	16460	0	0	0	6	0	1710	0	0	0	0	0	1
4/ 0/55	878	0	2	3	12	18500	0	0	0	5	0	280	7	0	0	0	0	1
5/ 0/55	925	0	5	3	60	17750	0	0	0	6	0	2200	0	0	0	0	0	1
5/ 0/55	1796	0	1	3	5	16615	0	1	0	5	0	285	0	0	0	0	0	1
5/ 0/55	3005	0	1	3	4	16560	0	1	0	5	0	290	0	0	0	0	0	1
5/ 0/55	1362	1	3	3	7	17400	0	0	0	6	0	1903	0	0	0	0	0	1
5/ 0/55	2441	0	2	3	12	16566	0	0	23	5	0	260	0	0	0	0	0	1
5/ 0/55	759	0	1	3	12	15170	0	0	0	6	0	1803	7	0	0	0	0	1
5/ 0/55	1424	0	1	3	12	15550	0	0	0	6	0	1806	0	0	0	0	0	1
5/ 0/55	3265	0	1	3	12	15910	0	0	0	6	0	1806	0	0	0	0	0	1
5/ 0/55	2351	0	1	3	12	16140	0	0	0	6	0	1806	7	0	0	0	0	1
5/ 0/55	3261	0	1	3	12	16580	0	0	0	6	0	1803	0	0	0	0	0	1

6 TO 7	8 TO 9	10 TO 11	1 TO 4	5	12 TO 13	14	15 TO 17	18 TO 23	24	25	26 TO 27	28	29 TO 34	35 TO 39	40	41	42 TO 43	44	45	80
5/	0/	55	2168	0	4	3	12	20000	0	0	0	6	0	1806	7	0	0	0	0	1
5/	0/	55	1778	0	1	3	24	24000	0	0	0	6	0	2006	0	0	0	0	0	1
5/	0/	55	1650	0	1	3	36	18800	0	0	0	6	0	2006	0	0	0	0	0	1
5/	0/	55	7030	0	10	3	53	24000	0	0	0	6	0	1903	0	0	0	0	0	1
6/	0/	55	3625	0	6	3	60	16202	0	0	0	6	0	2110	0	0	0	0	0	1
6/	0/	55	223	0	19	3	60	13330	0	0	0	6	0	2109	0	0	0	0	0	1
6/	0/	55	3265	0	19	3	60	15910	0	0	0	6	0	2110	0	0	0	0	0	1
6/	0/	55	3243	0	7	3	60	15750	0	0	0	6	0	2106	0	0	0	0	0	1
6/	0/	55	1424	0	19	3	60	15560	0	0	0	6	0	2200	0	0	0	0	0	1
6/	0/	55	767	0	23	3	60	15530	0	0	0	6	0	2100	0	0	0	0	0	1
6/	0/	55	759	0	19	3	60	15170	0	0	0	6	0	2100	0	0	0	0	0	1
6/	0/	55	2983	0	19	3	60	15400	0	0	0	6	0	2106	0	0	0	0	0	1
6/	0/	55	3005	0	4	3	60	16600	0	0	23	5	0	325	0	0	0	0	0	1
6/	0/	55	1683	0	7	3	60	16000	0	0	0	6	0	2103	0	0	0	0	0	1
6/	0/	55	2351	0	7	3	60	16140	0	0	0	6	0	2109	0	0	0	0	0	1
6/	0/	55	344	0	7	3	60	17600	0	0	0	6	0	2110	0	0	0	0	0	1
6/	0/	55	2268	0	10	3	60	18450	0	0	0	6	0	2100	0	0	0	0	0	1
6/	0/	55	2905	0	1	3	60	24870	0	0	0	6	0	2103	0	0	0	0	0	1
6/	0/	55	7171	0	12	3	60	19500	0	0	0	5	0	310	0	0	0	0	0	1
6/	0/	55	7036	0	12	3	60	19500	0	0	0	6	0	2203	0	0	0	0	0	1
6/	0/	55	790	0	1	3	12	16492	0	1	0	5	0	320	0	0	0	0	0	1
6/	0/	55	235	0	1	3	14	12910	0	1	0	5	0	320	0	0	0	0	0	1
6/	0/	55	2753	0	8	3	12	16560	0	0	23	5	0	280	0	0	0	0	0	1
6/	0/	55	337	0	0	3	12	17500	0	0	0	6	0	1903	7	0	0	0	0	1
6/	0/	55	1070	0	1	3	24	13750	0	0	0	6	0	2006	0	0	0	0	0	1
6/	0/	55	3227	0	2	3	36	13425	0	0	0	6	0	1906	0	0	0	0	0	1
6/	0/	55	1968	0	12	3	36	16460	0	7	17	5	0	270	0	0	0	0	0	1
6/	0/	55	24	0	1	3	36	16600	0	0	23	5	0	275	0	0	0	0	0	1
6/	0/	55	215	0	1	3	48	15626	0	0	0	6	0	2100	0	0	0	0	0	1
7/	0/	55	1572	0	18	3	60	16729	0	0	0	6	0	2200	0	0	0	0	0	1
7/	0/	55	342	0	1	3	60	16635	0	0	0	5	0	325	0	0	0	0	0	1
7/	0/	55	2775	0	3	3	60	18414	0	0	23	5	0	325	0	0	0	0	0	1
7/	0/	55	3009	0	18	3	60	13870	0	0	0	6	0	2200	0	0	0	0	0	1
7/	0/	55	20	0	22	3	60	14640	0	0	0	6	0	1936	0	0	0	0	0	1
7/	0/	55	3113	0	1	3	60	15930	0	0	0	6	0	2300	0	0	0	0	0	1
7/	0/	55	835	0	14	3	60	16150	0	0	0	6	0	2400	0	0	0	0	0	1
7/	0/	55	3230	0	15	3	60	16460	0	0	0	6	0	2203	0	0	0	0	0	1
7/	0/	55	366	0	0	3	60	16540	0	0	0	6	0	2206	0	0	0	0	0	1
7/	0/	55	7139	0	3	3	60	16600	0	0	0	6	0	2203	0	0	0	0	0	1
7/	0/	55	1540	0	15	3	60	16700	0	0	0	6	0	2209	7	0	0	0	0	1
7/	0/	55	2932	0	12	3	60	17200	0	0	0	6	0	2300	7	0	0	0	0	1
7/	0/	55	1246	0	1	3	60	18300	0	0	0	6	0	2200	0	0	0	0	0	1
7/	0/	55	244	0	2	3	60	18000	0	1	0	5	0	350	0	0	0	0	0	1
7/	0/	55	127	0	51	3	84	18625	0	0	0	6	0	2400	0	0	0	0	0	1

272 APPENDIX D

6 TØ 7	8 TØ 9	10 TØ 11	1 TØ 4	5	12 TØ 13	14	15 TØ 17	18 TØ 23	24	25	26 TØ 27	28	29 TØ 34	35 TØ 39	40	41	42 TØ 43	44	45	80
7/	0/55	7003	0	30	3	84	18500	0	0	0	6	0	2500	0	0	0	0	0	1
7/	0/55	7172	0	17	3	84	27000	0	0	0	6	0	1906	0	0	0	0	0	1
7/	0/55	7062	0	42	3	84	19000	0	0	0	6	0	2500	0	0	0	0	0	1
7/	0/55	7062	0	54	3	84	19000	0	0	0	6	0	2500	0	0	0	0	0	1
7/	0/55	7168	0	20	3	84	38000	0	0	0	6	0	1900	0	0	0	0	0	1
7/	0/55	7172	0	19	3	84	38000	0	0	0	6	0	1809	0	0	0	0	0	1
7/	0/55	7169	0	20	3	84	38000	0	0	0	5	0	235	0	0	0	0	0	1
7/	0/55	2704	0	1	3	6	16707	0	1	0	5	0	450	0	0	0	0	0	1
7/	0/55	866	0	2	3	6	16460	0	0	23	5	0	450	0	0	0	0	0	1
7/	0/55	1680	0	3	3	12	14521	0	0	0	6	0	2000	0	0	0	0	0	1
7/	0/55	1262	0	1	3	12	12620	0	0	0	6	0	1906	0	0	0	0	0	1
7/	0/55	1627	0	4	3	12	13470	1	0	0	6	0	2700	7	0	0	0	0	1
7/	0/55	7003	0	12	3	12	18000	0	0	0	6	0	2406	0	0	0	0	0	1
7/	0/55	1968	0	12	3	36	16600	0	0	0	6	0	2209	0	0	0	0	0	1
7/	0/55	93	0	18	3	48	16410	0	0	0	6	0	2209	0	0	0	0	0	1
8/	0/55	402	0	18	3	60	15630	0	0	0	6	0	2400	0	0	0	0	0	1
8/	0/55	1030	0	24	3	84	16659	0	0	0	6	0	2306	0	0	0	0	0	1
8/	0/55	339	0	1	3	6	8600	0	0	0	6	0	2409	0	0	0	0	0	1
8/	0/55	2539	0	11	3	60	16738	0	0	0	6	0	2209	0	0	0	0	0	1
8/	0/55	2441	0	14	3	60	16536	0	1	0	5	0	350	0	0	0	0	0	1
8/	0/55	1509	0	8	3	60	16475	0	0	0	6	0	2110	0	0	0	0	0	1
8/	0/55	1651	0	10	3	60	18435	0	0	0	5	0	360	7	0	0	0	0	1
8/	0/55	2506	0	3	3	60	13183	1	0	0	5	0	400	0	0	0	0	0	1
8/	0/55	264	0	1	3	60	17652	0	7	17	5	0	360	0	0	0	0	0	1
8/	0/55	1507	0	1	3	60	16620	1	0	0	6	0	2702	0	0	0	0	0	1
8/	0/55	1896	0	19	3	60	16660	0	0	0	6	0	2209	0	0	0	0	0	1
8/	0/55	2855	0	4	3	60	16250	0	0	0	6	0	2400	0	0	0	0	0	1
8/	0/55	2123	0	19	3	60	16420	0	0	0	6	0	2209	0	0	0	0	0	1
8/	0/55	7071	0	11	3	60	16400	0	0	23	5	0	325	0	0	0	0	0	1
8/	0/55	3680	1	4	3	60	17500	0	0	23	5	0	360	0	0	0	0	0	1
8/	0/55	7036	0	31	3	60	17500	0	0	0	5	0	350	0	0	0	0	0	1
8/	0/55	7003	0	2	3	60	17600	0	0	23	5	0	350	0	0	0	0	0	1
8/	0/55	132	0	8	3	60	18100	0	1	0	5	0	370	0	0	0	0	0	1
8/	0/55	3816	0	2	3	72	16500	0	0	23	5	0	360	0	0	0	0	0	1
8/	0/55	7064	0	24	3	72	19000	0	0	0	5	0	350	0	0	0	0	0	1
8/	0/55	7036	0	31	3	84	19573	0	0	0	6	0	2500	0	0	0	0	0	1
8/	0/55	1938	0	2	3	84	16200	0	0	0	6	0	2306	0	0	0	0	0	1
8/	0/55	7036	0	12	3	84	18000	0	0	0	6	0	2500	0	0	0	0	0	1
8/	0/55	7036	0	12	3	84	18000	0	0	0	6	0	2500	0	0	0	0	0	1
8/	0/55	7036	0	24	3	84	18000	0	0	0	6	0	2500	0	0	0	0	0	1
8/	0/55	1988	0	28	3	84	18050	0	0	0	6	0	2406	0	0	0	0	0	1
8/	0/55	7178	0	5	3	84	19000	0	0	0	5	0	355	0	0	0	0	0	1
8/	0/55	7176	0	24	3	84	19000	0	0	0	6	0	2500	0	0	0	0	0	1
8/	0/55	7175	0	16	3	84	19500	0	0	0	6	0	2500	0	0	0	0	0	1

6	8	10	1	5	12	14	15	18	24	25	26	28	29	35	40	41	42	44	45	80
TØ	TØ	TØ	TØ		TØ		TØ	TØ			TØ		TØ	TØ			TØ			
7	9	11	4		13		17	23			27		34	39			43			
8/	0/	55	7177	0	31	3	84	19500	0	0	0	6	0	2500	0	0	0	0	0	1
8/	0/	55	7037	0	29	3	84	32000	0	0	0	5	0	245	0	0	0	0	0	1
8/	0/	55	1628	0	10	3	96	16175	0	0	0	6	0	2303	7	0	0	0	0	1
8/	0/	55	3035	0	19	3	96	16100	0	0	0	6	0	2303	0	0	0	0	0	1
8/	0/	55	7040	0	28	3	96	19500	0	0	0	6	0	2500	0	0	0	0	0	1
8/	0/	55	7040	0	52	3	96	19500	0	0	0	6	0	2500	0	0	0	0	0	1
8/	0/	55	3342	0	4	3	28	16000	1	0	0	6	0	2506	0	0	0	0	0	1
8/	0/	55	1261	0	2	3	29	16440	0	0	0	5	0	340	0	0	0	0	0	1
8/	0/	55	2283	0	14	3	36	15570	1	1	6	6	0	2603	7	0	0	0	0	1
8/	0/	55	2588	0	2	3	36	15200	0	0	6	6	0	2006	0	0	0	0	0	1
8/	0/	55	2656	0	2	3	36	16050	0	0	0	6	0	2109	0	0	0	0	0	1
8/	0/	55	7174	0	7	3	36	25000	0	0	0	5	0	312	0	0	0	0	0	1
8/	0/	55	2023	0	1	3	48	20000	0	0	0	5	0	325	0	0	0	0	0	1
8/	0/	55	2888	0	33	3	30	14300	0	0	0	5	0	325	0	3	0	0	0	1
8/	0/	55	3358	0	26	3	36	16500	0	0	0	5	0	360	0	3	0	0	0	1
8/	0/	55	2888	0	3	3	30	14300	0	0	0	5	0	300	3	0	0	0	0	1
8/	0/	55	3358	0	2	3	24	16500	1	0	0	5	0	385	3	0	0	0	0	1
9/	0/	55	3330	0	2	3	60	14800	0	0	0	5	0	275	0	0	0	0	0	1
9/	0/	55	1495	0	19	3	60	15350	0	0	0	6	0	2109	0	0	0	0	0	1
9/	0/	55	7180	0	0	3	30	17610	0	0	0	5	0	380	0	0	0	0	0	1
9/	0/	55	1372	0	2	3	24	8550	0	0	0	6	0	2200	0	0	0	0	0	1
9/	0/	55	7088	0	18	3	60	16628	0	0	0	6	0	2209	0	0	0	0	0	1
9/	0/	55	3258	0	18	3	60	16578	0	0	0	6	0	2209	0	0	0	0	0	1
9/	0/	55	2487	0	1	3	60	18377	0	0	0	5	0	390	0	0	0	0	0	1
9/	0/	55	3609	0	22	3	60	15855	0	0	0	6	0	2400	0	0	0	0	0	1
9/	0/	55	916	0	16	3	60	16795	0	0	0	6	0	2400	0	0	0	0	0	1
9/	0/	55	1295	0	19	3	60	16631	0	0	0	6	0	2209	0	0	0	0	0	1
9/	0/	55	2499	0	23	3	60	16581	0	0	0	6	0	2209	0	0	0	0	0	1
9/	0/	55	80	0	9	3	50	16441	0	0	0	6	0	2209	0	0	0	0	0	1
9/	0/	55	7182	0	16	3	60	19250	0	0	0	6	0	2500	0	0	0	0	0	1
9/	0/	55	7036	0	25	3	60	19000	0	0	0	6	0	2500	7	0	0	0	0	1
9/	0/	55	1773	0	5	3	60	15550	0	0	0	6	0	2303	0	0	0	0	0	1
9/	0/	55	2587	0	8	3	60	16340	0	0	0	6	0	2406	0	0	0	0	0	1
9/	0/	55	7183	0	43	3	60	18250	0	0	0	6	0	2500	0	0	0	0	0	1
9/	0/	55	7184	0	36	3	60	18500	0	0	0	6	0	2510	0	0	0	0	0	1
9/	0/	55	1076	0	5	3	60	18000	0	0	0	5	0	350	0	0	0	0	0	1
9/	0/	55	7036	0	45	3	60	19000	0	0	0	6	0	2500	7	0	0	0	0	1
9/	0/	55	7036	0	49	3	60	19000	0	0	0	6	0	2500	0	0	0	0	0	1
9/	0/	55	7026	0	38	3	60	19000	0	0	0	6	0	2500	7	0	0	0	0	1
9/	0/	55	7026	0	42	3	60	19000	0	0	0	6	0	2500	7	0	0	0	0	1
9/	0/	55	7179	0	38	3	60	19000	0	0	0	6	0	2500	7	0	0	0	0	1
9/	0/	55	7181	0	6	3	60	32000	0	0	0	5	0	270	0	0	0	0	0	1
9/	0/	55	2066	0	5	3	60	32000	0	0	0	5	0	310	0	0	0	0	0	1
9/	0/	55	2348	0	1	3	72	16463	0	0	0	5	0	325	0	0	0	0	0	1

APPENDIX D

6 TØ 7	8 TØ 9	10 TØ 11	1 TØ 4	5	12 TØ 13	14	15 TØ 17	18 TØ 23	24	25	26 TØ 27	28	29 TØ 34	35 TØ 39	40	41	42 TØ 43	44	45	80
9/	0/	55	1866	0	1	3	84	15500	0	0	0	6	0	2306	0	0	0	0	0	1
9/	0/	55	355	0	4	3	84	17270	0	0	0	5	0	360	0	0	0	0	0	1
9/	0/	55	1980	0	10	3	84	18500	0	0	0	6	0	2409	0	0	0	0	0	1
9/	0/	55	7003	0	18	3	84	40000	0	0	0	5	0	235	0	0	0	0	0	1
9/	0/	55	7003	0	18	3	84	38000	0	0	0	5	0	235	0	0	0	0	0	1
9/	0/	55	7036	0	55	3	96	19000	0	0	0	6	0	2500	0	0	0	0	0	1
9/	0/	55	7042	0	60	3	96	19000	0	0	0	6	0	2500	0	0	0	0	0	1
9/	0/	55	7118	0	51	3	96	18500	0	0	0	6	0	2500	0	0	0	0	0	1
9/	0/	55	45	0	1	3	4	16409	0	1	0	5	0	450	0	0	0	0	0	1
9/	0/	55	1257	0	1	3	4	16409	0	1	0	5	0	450	0	0	0	0	0	1
9/	0/	55	3023	0	3	3	24	16225	1	0	0	6	0	2500	0	0	0	0	0	1
9/	0/	55	2613	0	13	3	36	14900	0	0	0	6	0	2003	0	0	0	0	0	1
9/	0/	55	2500	0	10	3	36	14290	0	0	0	6	0	2103	0	0	0	0	0	1
9/	0/	55	442	0	1	3	36	15030	0	0	0	6	0	2103	0	0	0	0	0	1
9/	0/	55	2668	0	21	3	18	16020	0	0	0	6	0	2306	0	3	0	0	0	1
9/	0/	55	2807	0	19	3	48	16738	0	0	0	5	0	325	0	3	0	0	0	1
9/	0/	55	7036	0	39	3	37	19500	0	0	0	6	0	2500	0	3	0	0	0	1
9/	0/	55	2667	0	16	3	5	13626	0	0	0	6	0	2203	3	0	0	0	0	1
9/	0/	55	2807	0	7	3	12	16728	0	0	0	5	0	375	3	0	0	0	0	1
9/	0/	55	1967	0	16	3	60	13235	0	0	0	0	0	0	0	0	0	0	0	1
9/	0/	55	2271	0	6	3	60	18620	0	0	0	0	0	0	0	0	0	0	0	1
9/	0/	55	2796	0	16	3	60	16500	0	0	0	0	0	0	0	0	0	0	0	1
10/	0/	55	118	0	6	3	60	16484	0	0	0	6	0	2309	0	0	0	0	0	1
10/	0/	55	1278	0	16	3	60	15750	0	0	0	6	0	2400	0	0	0	0	0	1
10/	0/	55	1946	0	8	3	60	16510	0	0	0	6	0	2309	0	0	0	0	0	1
10/	0/	55	1404	0	8	3	60	16210	0	0	0	6	0	2306	0	0	0	0	0	1
10/	0/	55	1700	0	10	3	60	17300	0	0	0	6	0	2309	0	0	0	0	0	1
10/	0/	55	925	1	2	3	60	17750	0	0	0	6	0	2800	0	0	0	0	0	1
10/	0/	55	7185	0	10	3	60	30000	0	0	0	5	0	310	0	0	0	0	0	1
10/	0/	55	7030	0	8	3	60	32000	0	0	0	5	0	315	0	0	0	0	0	1
10/	0/	55	1653	0	3	3	12	10020	0	8	6	6	0	2306	0	0	0	0	0	1
10/	0/	55	1704	0	1	3	24	12700	0	0	0	6	0	2200	0	0	0	0	0	1
10/	0/	55	121	0	9	3	36	18578	0	0	0	5	0	350	7	0	0	0	0	1
10/	0/	55	961	0	7	3	36	18626	0	0	0	5	0	350	0	0	0	0	0	1
11/	0/	55	952	0	3	3	12	12000	0	0	0	6	0	2206	7	0	0	0	0	1
11/	0/	55	181	0	3	3	12	12250	0	0	0	6	0	2206	7	0	0	0	0	1
11/	0/	55	2823	0	5	3	36	16484	0	0	0	5	0	365	0	0	0	0	0	1
11/	0/	55	7133	0	31	3	36	21000	0	0	0	6	0	2606	0	0	0	0	0	1
11/	0/	55	2245	0	22	3	48	16765	0	0	0	6	0	2309	0	0	0	0	0	1
11/	0/	55	1318	0	12	3	48	24715	0	0	0	6	0	2509	0	0	0	0	0	1
11/	0/	55	1313	0	4	3	60	12278	1	0	0	6	0	2803	0	0	0	0	0	1
11/	0/	55	3336	0	44	3	60	16300	0	0	0	6	0	2406	0	0	0	0	0	1
11/	0/	55	287	0	30	3	60	16500	0	0	0	6	0	2409	0	0	0	0	0	1
11/	0/	55	1745	0	6	3	60	16500	0	0	0	5	0	325	0	0	0	0	0	1

CHARTERS 275

6 TØ 7	8 TØ 9	10 TØ 11	1 TØ 4	5	12 TØ 13	14	15 TØ 17	18 TØ 23	24	25	26 TØ 27	28	29 TØ 34	35 TØ 39	40	41	42 TØ 43	44	45	80
11/	0/55		1396	0	38	3	60	17800	0	0	0	6	0	2409	7	0	0	0	0	1
11/	0/55		7036	0	24	3	60	19000	0	0	0	6	0	2609	7	0	0	0	0	1
11/	0/55		7036	0	36	3	60	19000	0	0	0	6	0	2609	7	0	0	0	0	1
11/	0/55		1387	0	0	3	60	28000	0	0	0	5	0	350	0	0	0	0	0	1
11/	0/55		7036	0	35	3	60	30000	0	0	0	6	0	2200	0	0	0	0	0	1
11/	0/55		7036	0	35	3	60	32000	0	0	0	6	0	2200	0	0	0	0	0	1
11/	0/55		7036	0	35	3	60	32000	0	0	0	6	0	2200	0	0	0	0	0	1
11/	0/55		7003	0	10	3	60	32000	0	0	0	6	0	2600	0	0	0	0	0	1
11/	0/55		7186	0	19	3	60	32800	0	0	0	5	0	307	0	0	0	0	0	1
11/	0/55		866	0	6	3	72	16460	0	0	0	5	0	325	0	0	0	0	0	1
11/	0/55		1786	0	5	3	72	26760	0	0	0	6	0	2206	0	0	0	0	0	1
11/	0/55		2704	0	5	3	34	16707	0	0	0	5	0	335	7	0	0	0	0	1
11/	0/55		7036	0	28	3	96	45000	0	0	0	5	0	245	7	0	0	0	0	1
11/	0/55		883	0	20	3	66	17000	0	0	0	5	0	350	0	3	0	0	0	1
11/	0/55		7036	0	4	2	24	28000	0	0	0	0	6500	0	0	0	0	0	0	1
11/	0/55		2281	0	2	3	12	8660	1	0	0	6	0	2706	0	0	0	0	0	1
11/	0/55		7133	0	34	3	36	21000	0	0	0	6	0	2606	0	0	0	0	0	1
11/	0/55		3807	0	13	3	60	15450	0	0	0	6	0	2400	0	0	0	0	0	1
11/	0/55		883	0	2	3	18	17000	1	0	0	5	0	360	3	0	0	0	0	1
12/	0/55		2785	0	6	3	60	16300	0	1	7	6	0	2600	0	0	0	0	0	1
12/	0/55		353	0	23	3	60	19260	0	0	0	6	0	2704	0	0	0	0	0	1
12/	0/55		7188	0	15	3	60	20000	0	0	0	6	0	2800	0	0	0	0	0	1
12/	0/55		7030	0	6	3	60	32000	0	0	0	5	0	325	0	0	0	0	0	1
12/	0/55		7107	0	24	3	84	32000	0	0	0	6	0	2300	0	0	0	0	0	1
12/	0/55		7036	0	30	3	96	40000	0	0	0	5	0	280	0	0	0	0	0	1
12/	0/55		1072	0	19	3	48	15880	0	0	0	6	0	2609	0	2	0	0	0	1
12/	0/55		7003	0	99	3	36	40000	0	0	0	5	0	197	0	3	0	0	0	1
12/	0/55		7003	0	99	3	36	40000	0	0	0	5	0	197	0	3	0	0	0	1
12/	0/55		7003	0	28	3	144	40000	0	0	0	5	0	230	3	0	0	0	0	1
12/	0/55		7003	0	28	3	144	40000	0	0	0	5	0	230	3	0	0	0	0	1
12/	0/55		7003	0	28	3	144	40000	0	0	0	5	0	230	3	0	0	0	0	1
12/	0/55		1072	0	7	2	12	15880	0	0	0	8	120175	0	3	0	0	0	0	1
1/	0/56		1067	0	2	3	24	16561	0	0	0	5	0	420	0	0	18	0	0	1
1/	0/56		2980	0	5	3	36	13575	0	0	0	6	0	2409	7	0	21	0	0	1
1/	0/56		3288	0	22	3	60	13550	0	0	0	6	0	2506	0	0	21	0	0	1
1/	0/56		7188	0	27	3	60	15300	0	0	0	6	0	2706	7	0	0	0	0	1
1/	0/56		1977	0	26	3	60	15314	0	0	0	6	0	2500	0	0	4	0	0	1
1/	0/56		2782	0	21	3	60	16000	0	0	0	6	0	2600	0	0	21	0	0	1
1/	0/56		1506	0	5	3	60	16290	1	0	0	6	0	2800	0	0	12	0	0	1
1/	0/56		1973	0	40	3	60	17400	0	0	0	6	0	2506	0	0	4	0	0	1
1/	0/56		7190	0	17	3	60	19000	0	0	0	6	0	2709	7	0	21	0	0	1
1/	0/56		7038	0	21	3	60	19000	0	0	0	6	0	2709	7	0	21	0	0	1
1/	0/56		7191	0	17	3	60	19000	0	0	0	6	0	2709	7	0	21	0	0	1
1/	0/56		7157	0	21	3	60	19000	0	0	0	6	0	2709	7	0	21	0	0	1

6 TO 7	8 TO 9	10 TO 11	1 TO 4	5	12 TO 13	14	15 TO 17	18 TO 23	24	25	26 TO 27	28	29 TO 34	35	40	41	42 TO 43	44	45	80
1/	0/56	7012	0	27	3	60	19000	0	0	0	6	0	2706	7	0	21	0	0	1
1/	0/56	3290	0	7	3	60	25748	0	0	0	6	0	2606	0	0	18	0	0	1
1/	0/56	2057	0	5	3	60	31688	0	0	0	5	0	375	0	0	18	0	0	1
1/	0/56	7048	0	15	3	72	19500	0	0	0	5	0	365	0	0	12	0	0	1
1/	0/56	3147	0	10	3	156	45230	0	0	0	5	0	248	0	0	13	0	0	1
1/	0/56	2880	0	18	3	54	11500	0	0	0	6	0	2400	0	2	4	0	0	1
1/	0/56	1072	0	18	3	48	15000	0	0	0	6	0	2600	0	2	4	0	0	1
1/	0/56	1647	0	18	3	48	16500	0	0	0	6	0	2906	0	2	4	0	0	1
1/	0/56	1419	0	18	3	48	17500	0	0	0	6	0	2709	0	2	4	0	0	1
1/	0/56	2216	0	7	2	7	12000	0	0	0	1	13500	0	0	2	10	0	0	1
1/	0/56	2443	0	7	2	6	19000	0	0	0	0	9000	0	0	2	18	0	0	1
1/	0/56	2216	0	1	2	6	12000	0	0	0	1	15500	0	2	0	10	0	0	1
1/	0/56	2443	0	1	2	6	19000	0	0	0	0	10500	0	2	0	18	0	0	1
1/	0/56	2880	0	12	2	6	11500	0	0	0	8	120175	0	3	0	4	0	0	1
1/	0/56	1072	0	6	2	12	15000	0	0	0	8	120175	0	3	0	4	0	0	1
1/	0/56	1647	0	6	2	12	16500	0	0	0	8	120175	0	3	0	4	0	0	1
1/	0/56	1419	0	6	2	12	17500	0	0	0	8	120175	0	3	0	4	0	0	1
1/	0/56	3649	0	4	2	24	32000	0	0	0	1	13500	0	0	0	7	0	0	1
1/	0/56	3266	0	8	2	12	11000	0	0	0	8	120175	0	0	0	4	0	0	1
1/	0/56	417	0	6	2	12	14000	0	0	0	8	120175	0	0	0	4	0	0	1
1/	0/56	337	0	7	2	12	16500	0	0	0	8	120175	0	0	0	4	0	0	1
1/	0/56	1935	0	6	2	12	17000	0	0	0	8	120175	0	0	0	4	0	0	1
1/	0/56	2133	0	10	2	18	17500	0	0	0	8	120175	0	0	0	4	0	0	1
1/	0/56	134	0	7	2	12	18500	0	0	0	8	120175	0	0	0	4	0	0	1
1/	0/56	3077	0	8	2	24	23000	0	0	0	2	11705	0	0	0	12	0	0	1
2/	0/56	1793	0	2	3	12	12282	0	0	0	6	0	2400	0	0	21	0	0	1
2/	0/56	443	0	1	3	24	13450	0	0	0	6	0	2800	0	0	12	0	0	1
2/	0/56	325	0	11	3	24	18400	0	0	0	6	0	2800	7	0	10	0	0	1
2/	0/56	3347	0	10	3	36	18160	0	0	0	6	0	2606	0	0	12	0	0	1
2/	0/56	1577	0	22	3	60	17891	0	0	0	6	0	2700	0	0	4	0	0	1
2/	0/56	7194	0	33	3	60	19000	0	0	0	6	0	2709	0	0	21	0	0	1
2/	0/56	7137	0	20	3	60	19500	0	0	0	6	0	2709	0	0	4	0	0	1
2/	0/56	7010	0	22	3	60	19000	0	0	0	6	0	2709	7	0	21	0	0	1
2/	0/56	7186	0	9	3	60	32000	0	0	0	5	0	320	0	0	12	0	0	1
2/	0/56	7016	0	11	3	60	32000	0	0	0	5	0	320	0	0	12	0	0	1
2/	0/56	7192	0	29	3	60	33000	0	0	0	6	0	2300	0	0	7	0	0	1
2/	0/56	7193	0	10	3	84	19000	0	0	0	6	0	2709	0	0	10	0	0	1
2/	0/56	7016	0	1	3	120	16300	0	0	0	6	0	2300	0	0	13	0	0	1
2/	0/56	141	0	5	3	120	16545	0	0	0	6	0	2300	0	0	13	0	0	1
2/	0/56	2987	0	1	3	120	16738	0	0	0	6	0	2300	0	0	13	0	0	1
2/	0/56	2992	0	22	3	48	17500	0	0	0	6	0	2706	0	2	4	0	0	1
2/	0/56	3712	0	21	3	48	18000	1	0	0	6	0	2600	0	2	18	0	0	1
2/	0/56	2992	0	10	2	12	17500	0	0	0	8	120175	0	3	0	4	0	0	1
2/	0/56	1772	0	6	2	12	17500	0	0	0	8	120175	0	3	0	4	0	0	1

CHARTERS 277

6 TO 7	8 TO 9	10 TO 11	1 TO 4	5	12 TO 13	14	15 TO 17	18 TO 23	24	25	26 TO 27	28	29 TO 34	35 TO 39	40	41	42 TO 43	44	45	80
2/	0/56		3712	0	6	2	15	18000	1	0	0	8	125175	0	3	0	18	0	0	1
2/	0/56		3631	0	2	2	18	32000	0	2	16	0	8000	0	0	0	0	0	0	1
2/	0/56		3355	0	0	2	36	9000	0	1	6	1	13750	0	0	0	18	0	0	1
2/	0/56		1249	0	6	2	12	11500	0	0	0	8	120175	0	0	0	4	0	0	1
2/	0/56		1516	0	6	2	12	12500	0	0	0	8	120175	0	0	0	4	0	0	1
2/	0/56		189	0	5	2	12	13500	0	0	0	8	120175	0	0	0	4	0	0	1
2/	0/56		2946	0	6	2	12	13500	0	0	0	8	120175	0	0	0	4	0	0	1
2/	0/56		2937	0	6	2	12	14000	0	0	0	8	120175	0	0	0	4	0	0	1
2/	0/56		461	0	7	2	12	14500	0	0	0	8	120175	0	0	0	4	0	0	1
2/	0/56		2501	0	5	2	12	14500	0	0	0	8	120175	0	0	0	4	0	0	1
2/	0/56		1770	0	5	2	12	15000	0	0	0	8	120175	0	0	0	4	0	0	1
2/	0/56		2653	0	6	2	12	15000	0	0	0	8	120175	0	0	0	4	0	0	1
2/	0/56		2198	0	8	2	12	15000	0	0	0	8	115200	0	0	0	7	0	0	1
2/	0/56		3267	0	6	2	12	15500	0	0	0	8	120175	0	0	0	4	0	0	1
2/	0/56		1271	0	6	2	12	17000	0	0	0	8	120175	0	0	0	4	0	0	1
2/	0/56		3677	0	7	2	12	31000	0	0	0	8	115170	0	0	0	4	0	0	1
2/	0/56		2307	0	1	2	12	15000	0	0	0	2	120175	0	0	0	12	0	0	1
2/	0/56		1433	0	8	2	12	16000	0	0	0	2	120175	0	0	0	12	0	0	1
2/	0/56		3239	0	9	2	12	17000	0	0	0	2	120175	0	0	0	12	0	0	1
2/	0/56		7037	0	10	2	36	17000	0	0	0	2	11750	0	0	0	12	0	0	1
2/	0/56		2129	0	9	2	12	18000	0	0	0	2	120175	0	6	0	12	0	0	1
2/	0/56		2126	0	21	2	12	18000	0	0	0	2	120175	0	0	2	12	0	0	1
2/	0/56		348	0	10	2	48	18500	0	0	0	2	11750	0	0	0	12	0	0	1
2/	0/56		7209	0	18	2	48	20000	0	0	0	2	11750	0	0	0	12	0	0	1
2/	0/56		1772	0	18	2	48	17500	0	0	0	6	0	2503	0	2	4	0	0	1
2/	0/56		3648	0	7	2	12	30000	0	0	0	7	9500	0	0	0	4	0	0	1
2/	1/56		7078	0	30	3	60	14500	0	0	0	6	0	1900	0	0	0	0	0	1
3/	0/56		1255	0	2	3	12	10500	0	0	0	6	0	2700	0	0	21	0	0	1
3/	0/56		2811	0	2	3	12	13360	0	0	0	6	0	2700	0	0	21	0	0	1
3/	0/56		2123	0	1	3	12	16420	0	0	0	6	0	2806	0	0	21	0	0	1
3/	0/56		1401	0	2	3	12	16460	0	0	0	6	0	2806	0	0	21	0	0	1
3/	0/56		1896	0	1	3	12	16656	0	0	0	6	0	2806	0	0	21	0	0	1
3/	0/56		3661	0	3	3	24	13500	3	0	0	5	0	475	0	0	0	0	0	1
3/	0/56		2048	0	2	3	24	20000	0	0	0	5	0	390	0	0	18	0	0	1
3/	0/56		21	0	2	3	60	20607	0	0	0	5	0	375	0	0	12	0	0	1
3/	0/56		1409	0	4	3	60	26967	0	0	0	5	0	350	0	0	18	0	0	1
3/	0/56		3654	0	2	3	60	32000	0	0	0	5	0	340	0	0	0	0	0	1
3/	0/56		1231	0	1	3	84	29402	0	0	0	5	0	350	0	0	18	0	0	1
3/	0/56		7001	0	18	3	180	40000	0	0	0	5	0	245	0	0	13	0	0	1
3/	0/56		7036	0	17	3	198	38000	0	0	0	5	0	250	0	0	13	0	0	1
3/	0/56		7195	0	48	3	120	19000	0	0	0	6	0	2600	0	0	0	0	0	1
3/	0/56		7196	0	48	3	120	19000	0	0	0	6	0	2600	0	0	0	0	0	1
3/	0/56		7110	0	48	3	120	19000	0	0	0	6	0	2600	0	0	0	0	0	1
3/	0/56		1767	0	9	2	12	17500	0	2	16	0	9000	0	0	0	0	0	0	1

APPENDIX D

6 TØ 7	8 TØ 9	10 TØ 11	1 TØ 4	5	12 TØ 13	14	15 TØ 17	18 TØ 23	24	25	26 TØ 27	28	29 TØ 34	35 TØ 39	40	41	42 TØ 43	44	45	80
3/	0/56		2214	0	9	2	12	17500	0	2	16	0	9000	0	0	0	0	0	0	1
3/	0/56		1971	0	10	2	48	17000	0	0	0	2	11750	0	0	0	12	0	0	1
3/	0/56		7011	0	15	2	48	17400	0	0	0	2	11750	0	0	0	12	0	0	1
3/	0/56		920	0	3	2	12	14000	0	2	16	0	8250	0	0	0	16	0	0	1
4/	0/56		384	0	10	3	18	13270	1	0	0	5	0	415	7	0	12	0	0	1
4/	0/56		2744	0	1	3	12	16570	0	0	0	5	0	400	0	0	21	0	0	1
4/	0/56		1510	0	1	3	24	12585	0	0	0	6	0	2709	0	0	18	0	0	1
4/	0/56		865	0	5	3	24	19000	0	0	0	6	0	3100	0	0	0	0	0	1
4/	0/56		1550	0	4	3	48	15135	0	0	0	6	0	2503	0	0	12	0	0	1
4/	0/56		1431	0	8	3	60	15609	0	0	0	6	0	2600	0	0	12	0	0	1
4/	0/56		7198	0	15	3	60	16000	4	0	0	6	0	3000	0	0	7	0	0	1
4/	0/56		280	0	17	3	60	16175	1	0	0	6	0	2700	0	0	13	0	0	1
4/	0/56		886	0	10	3	60	16691	0	0	0	6	0	2709	0	0	7	0	0	1
4/	0/56		1280	0	14	3	60	16610	0	0	0	5	0	360	0	0	12	0	0	1
4/	0/56		2055	0	2	3	60	17620	1	0	0	5	0	450	0	0	12	0	0	1
4/	0/56		7197	0	26	3	60	19300	0	0	0	6	0	410	0	0	12	0	0	1
4/	0/56		7135	0	24	3	60	19500	0	0	0	6	0	2900	0	0	7	0	0	1
4/	0/56		878	0	14	3	60	19447	0	0	0	5	0	412	0	0	18	0	0	1
4/	0/56		900	0	1	3	60	25150	0	0	0	6	0	2700	0	0	13	0	0	1
4/	0/56		908	0	1	3	60	25500	0	0	0	5	0	350	0	0	12	0	0	1
4/	0/56		7042	0	30	3	60	33600	0	0	0	6	0	2506	0	0	7	0	0	1
4/	0/56		1878	0	3	3	72	16523	0	0	0	5	0	360	0	0	12	0	0	1
4/	0/56		2502	0	3	3	78	16532	1	1	0	5	0	380	0	0	12	0	0	1
4/	0/56		1756	0	2	3	72	19284	0	0	0	5	0	395	0	0	12	0	0	1
4/	0/56		7004	0	20	3	120	25500	0	0	0	5	0	485	0	0	17	0	0	1
4/	0/56		7004	0	20	3	120	25500	0	0	0	5	0	485	0	0	17	0	0	1
4/	0/56		7004	0	20	3	120	25500	0	0	0	5	0	485	0	0	17	0	0	1
4/	0/56		7004	0	20	3	120	25500	0	0	0	5	0	485	0	0	17	0	0	1
4/	0/56		7004	0	20	3	120	25500	0	0	0	5	0	485	0	0	17	0	0	1
4/	0/56		7004	0	20	3	120	25500	0	0	0	5	0	485	0	0	17	0	0	1
4/	0/56		7004	0	20	3	120	25500	0	0	0	5	0	485	0	0	17	0	0	1
4/	0/56		7004	0	20	3	120	25500	0	0	0	5	0	485	0	0	17	0	0	1
4/	0/56		7004	0	20	3	120	25500	0	0	0	5	0	485	0	0	17	0	0	1
4/	0/56		7004	0	20	3	120	25500	0	0	0	5	0	485	0	0	17	0	0	1
4/	0/56		7030	0	26	3	120	41000	0	0	0	5	0	295	0	0	28	0	0	1
4/	0/56		7030	0	20	3	120	41000	0	0	0	5	0	298	0	0	28	0	0	1
4/	0/56		1912	0	16	3	60	14000	0	0	0	6	0	2706	0	2	7	0	0	1
4/	0/56		2135	0	21	3	60	17000	0	0	0	6	0	3000	0	2	12	0	0	1
4/	0/56		2252	0	19	2	12	11000	0	0	0	8	140225	0	0	2	21	0	0	1
4/	0/56		106	0	16	2	12	12000	0	0	0	8	125225	0	0	2	21	0	0	1
4/	0/56		776	0	21	2	12	15000	0	0	0	8	125225	0	0	2	21	0	0	1
4/	0/56		2280	0	15	2	12	15500	0	0	0	1	7000	0	0	2	7	0	0	1

CHARTERS 279

6 TO 7	8 TO 9	10 TO 11	1 TO 4	5	12 TO 13	14	15 TO 17	18 TO 23	24	25	26 TO 27	28	29 TO 34	35	40	41	42 TO 43	44	45	80
4/	0/	56	3034	0	15	2	12	16500	1	0	0	1	18000	0	0	2	26	0	0	1
4/	0/	56	997	0	20	2	12	18500	0	0	0	8	130225	0	0	2	21	0	0	1
4/	0/	56	3057	1	17	2	12	23000	0	0	0	8	125225	0	0	2	21	0	0	1
4/	0/	56	2252	0	7	2	12	11000	0	0	0	8	150250	0	2	0	21	0	0	1
4/	0/	56	106	0	4	2	12	12000	0	0	0	8	150250	0	2	0	21	0	0	1
4/	0/	56	776	0	9	2	12	15000	0	0	0	8	150250	0	2	0	21	0	0	1
4/	0/	56	2280	0	3	2	12	15500	0	0	0	1	8000	0	2	0	7	0	0	1
4/	0/	56	3034	0	3	2	12	16500	1	0	0	1	20000	0	2	0	26	0	0	1
4/	0/	56	997	0	8	2	12	18500	0	0	0	8	150250	0	2	0	21	0	0	1
4/	0/	56	3057	1	5	2	12	23000	0	0	0	8	150250	0	2	0	21	0	0	1
4/	0/	56	1912	0	4	2	12	14000	0	0	0	1	17500	0	3	0	7	0	0	1
4/	0/	56	1964	0	1	2	12	10000	0	0	0	0	13000	0	0	0	14	0	0	1
4/	0/	56	2896	0	3	2	24	12000	0	0	0	0	10500	0	0	0	18	0	0	1
4/	0/	56	7061	0	2	2	12	15500	0	0	0	0	13500	0	0	0	0	0	0	1
4/	0/	56	3705	0	4	2	12	28000	0	0	23	0	9500	0	0	0	12	0	0	1
4/	0/	56	2655	0	9	2	12	11500	0	0	0	1	20000	0	0	0	4	0	0	1
4/	0/	56	3036	0	4	2	18	12500	0	0	0	1	20000	0	0	0	21	0	0	1
4/	0/	56	457	0	3	2	12	13500	0	0	0	1	16500	0	0	0	4	0	0	1
4/	0/	56	1775	0	4	2	12	14000	0	0	0	1	17500	0	0	0	21	0	0	1
4/	0/	56	3022	0	3	2	12	15000	0	0	0	1	17500	0	0	0	7	0	0	1
4/	0/	56	2682	0	4	2	18	15000	0	0	0	1	20000	0	0	0	21	0	0	1
4/	0/	56	2627	0	3	2	18	15000	0	0	0	1	20000	0	0	0	21	0	0	1
4/	0/	56	1890	0	3	2	12	15500	0	0	0	1	17500	0	0	0	7	0	0	1
4/	0/	56	1257	0	1	2	12	15500	0	0	0	1	17500	0	0	0	7	0	0	1
4/	0/	56	3032	0	3	2	18	15500	0	0	0	1	20000	0	0	0	21	0	0	1
4/	0/	56	3281	0	2	2	12	16000	1	0	0	1	19500	0	0	0	7	0	0	1
4/	0/	56	1895	0	2	2	12	16500	0	0	0	1	17500	0	0	0	7	0	0	1
4/	0/	56	409	0	3	2	12	17000	0	0	0	1	17500	0	0	0	7	0	0	1
4/	0/	56	3697	0	3	2	18	18500	0	0	0	1	20000	0	0	0	21	0	0	1
4/	0/	56	7023	0	10	2	12	18500	0	0	0	1	20000	0	0	0	21	0	0	1
4/	0/	56	7023	0	10	2	12	18500	0	0	0	1	20000	0	0	0	21	0	0	1
4/	0/	56	151	0	4	2	12	10500	0	0	0	8	150250	0	0	0	21	0	0	1
4/	0/	56	2287	0	3	2	12	11000	0	0	0	8	150250	0	0	0	21	0	0	1
4/	0/	56	720	0	3	2	12	11500	0	0	0	8	150250	0	0	0	21	0	0	1
4/	0/	56	3675	0	3	2	12	12500	0	0	0	8	150220	0	0	0	4	0	0	1
4/	0/	56	1857	0	7	2	12	12500	0	0	0	8	150220	0	0	0	4	0	0	1
4/	0/	56	2128	0	3	2	12	14000	0	0	0	8	150220	0	0	0	4	0	0	1
4/	0/	56	1725	0	7	2	12	17000	1	0	23	8	145215	0	0	0	7	0	0	1
4/	0/	56	1876	0	3	2	12	21000	0	0	0	8	150250	0	0	0	21	0	0	1
4/	0/	56	1636	0	4	2	12	25000	0	0	0	8	150220	0	0	0	4	0	0	1
4/	0/	56	1571	0	3	2	12	30500	0	0	0	8	150250	0	0	0	21	0	0	1
4/	0/	56	2135	0	9	2	12	17000	0	0	0	2	7500	0	3	0	12	0	0	1
5/	0/	56	46	0	3	3	12	8770	0	0	0	6	0	3400	0	0	18	0	0	1
5/	0/	56	2566	0	4	3	12	16515	1	0	0	5	0	685	0	0	26	0	0	1

6 TØ 7	8 TØ 9	10 TØ 11	1 TØ 4	5	12 TØ 13	14	15 TØ 17	18 TØ 23	24	25	26 TØ 27	28	29 TØ 34	35 TØ 39	40	41	42 TØ 43	44	45	80
5/	0/	56	1283	0	1	3	12	16657	0	0	0	5	0	654	0	0	17	0	0	1
5/	0/	56	229	0	4	3	10	20090	0	0	0	5	0	425	0	0	12	0	0	1
5/	0/	56	3796	0	1	3	24	12360	0	0	0	6	0	3506	0	0	18	0	0	1
5/	0/	56	942	0	7	3	29	16385	0	0	0	6	0	2900	0	0	26	0	0	1
5/	0/	56	1786	0	17	3	24	26760	0	0	0	6	0	2509	0	0	21	0	0	1
5/	0/	56	1342	0	13	3	36	18593	0	0	0	5	0	400	0	0	26	0	0	1
5/	0/	56	3651	0	2	3	36	19205	0	0	10	5	0	450	0	0	12	0	0	1
5/	0/	56	405	0	2	3	42	15482	0	0	0	6	0	2800	0	0	21	0	0	1
5/	0/	56	450	0	18	3	60	13300	0	0	0	6	0	2806	0	0	4	0	0	1
5/	0/	56	2667	0	13	3	60	13500	0	0	0	6	0	2709	0	0	4	0	0	1
5/	0/	56	1556	0	3	3	60	13580	0	0	0	6	0	3006	0	0	20	0	0	1
5/	0/	56	7208	0	17	3	60	14800	0	0	0	6	0	2403	0	0	21	0	0	1
5/	0/	56	1912	0	16	3	60	14811	0	0	0	6	0	2706	0	0	7	0	0	1
5/	0/	56	2496	0	8	3	60	16060	0	0	0	6	0	2906	0	0	21	0	0	1
5/	0/	56	7201	0	26	3	60	17500	0	0	0	6	0	3000	0	0	7	0	0	1
5/	0/	56	7036	0	15	3	60	17500	2	0	0	6	0	3000	0	0	7	0	0	1
5/	0/	56	7036	0	15	3	60	17500	2	0	0	6	0	3000	0	0	7	0	0	1
5/	0/	56	7042	0	15	3	60	17500	0	0	0	6	0	3000	0	0	12	0	0	1
5/	0/	56	7205	0	15	3	60	17500	0	0	0	6	0	3000	0	0	12	0	0	1
5/	0/	56	1347	0	21	3	60	17660	4	0	0	6	0	2903	0	0	7	0	0	1
5/	0/	56	7200	0	13	3	60	18000	0	0	0	5	0	375	0	0	18	0	0	1
5/	0/	56	7202	0	42	3	60	19000	0	0	0	6	0	3000	0	0	21	0	0	1
5/	0/	56	7178	0	30	3	60	19000	0	0	0	6	0	2909	0	0	18	0	0	1
5/	0/	56	7030	0	36	3	60	19000	0	0	0	6	0	2900	0	0	21	0	0	1
5/	0/	56	7067	0	24	3	60	19300	4	0	0	6	0	3000	0	0	7	0	0	1
5/	0/	56	7198	0	26	3	60	19500	0	0	0	6	0	3000	0	0	7	0	0	1
5/	0/	56	7206	0	22	3	60	19700	0	0	0	6	0	3000	0	0	21	0	0	1
5/	0/	56	7203	0	25	3	60	20000	0	0	0	6	0	3000	0	0	4	0	0	1
5/	0/	56	7201	0	12	3	60	20000	0	0	0	5	0	410	0	0	12	0	0	1
5/	0/	56	431	0	2	3	60	20400	0	0	0	5	0	415	0	0	12	0	0	1
5/	0/	56	7030	0	33	3	60	24000	0	0	0	6	0	2700	0	0	23	0	0	1
5/	0/	56	7210	0	30	3	60	26770	0	0	0	6	0	2906	0	0	12	0	0	1
5/	0/	56	7204	0	36	3	60	28500	0	0	0	6	0	2600	0	0	12	0	0	1
5/	0/	56	7066	0	31	3	60	32000	0	0	0	6	0	2506	0	0	7	0	0	1
5/	0/	56	7027	0	22	3	60	32000	0	0	0	6	0	2506	0	0	7	0	0	1
5/	0/	56	7002	0	10	3	60	32000	0	0	0	5	0	430	0	0	12	0	0	1
5/	0/	56	7079	0	36	3	60	34000	0	0	0	6	0	2600	0	0	26	0	0	1
5/	0/	56	7207	0	26	3	60	34000	0	0	0	6	0	2600	0	0	26	0	0	1
5/	0/	56	84	0	3	3	72	16286	0	0	0	5	0	370	0	0	12	0	0	1
5/	0/	56	1914	0	13	3	72	16560	0	0	0	5	0	360	0	0	12	0	0	1
5/	0/	56	24	0	12	3	72	16578	0	0	0	5	0	375	0	0	12	0	0	1
5/	0/	56	2293	0	17	3	72	18500	0	0	0	5	0	390	0	0	12	0	0	1
5/	0/	56	7010	0	16	3	72	19500	0	0	0	5	0	400	0	0	12	0	0	1
5/	0/	56	933	0	1	3	72	19660	0	0	0	5	0	420	0	0	12	0	0	1

CHARTERS 281

6 TØ 7	8 TØ 9	10 TØ 11	1 TØ 4	5	12 TØ 13	14	15 TØ 17	18 TØ 23	24	25	26 TØ 27	28	29 TØ 34	35 TØ 39	40	41	42 TØ 43	44	45	80
5/	0/	56	7107	0	28	3	84	32000	0	0	0	6	0	2603	0	0	21	0	0	1
5/	0/	56	7209	0	28	3	84	32500	0	0	0	6	0	2603	0	0	21	0	0	1
5/	0/	56	7011	0	25	3	84	33700	0	0	0	6	0	2600	0	0	12	0	0	1
5/	0/	56	7026	0	60	3	84	36000	0	0	0	6	0	2506	0	0	12	0	0	1
5/	0/	56	7036	0	14	3	500	30000	0	0	0	5	0	425	0	0	12	0	0	1
5/	0/	56	7190	0	29	3	60	20000	0	0	0	6	0	3000	0	2	26	0	0	1
5/	0/	56	201	0	18	2	12	11000	1	0	0	1	18000	0	0	2	26	0	0	1
5/	0/	56	2398	0	11	2	9	14500	0	2	6	1	20000	0	0	2	21	0	0	1
5/	0/	56	1016	0	18	2	12	15000	0	0	0	8	150200	0	0	2	7	0	0	1
5/	0/	56	2129	0	25	2	6	18000	0	0	0	1	16000	0	0	2	4	0	0	1
5/	0/	56	201	0	6	2	12	11000	1	0	0	1	20000	0	2	0	26	0	0	1
5/	0/	56	2398	0	2	2	9	14500	0	2	6	1	21000	0	2	0	21	0	0	1
5/	0/	56	1016	0	6	2	12	15000	0	0	0	1	20000	0	2	0	7	0	0	1
5/	0/	56	3662	0	3	2	12	17000	0	0	0	1	20000	0	2	0	26	0	0	1
5/	0/	56	2129	0	7	2	18	18000	0	0	0	1	20000	0	2	0	4	0	0	1
5/	0/	56	2362	0	12	2	17	11500	0	0	0	1	16000	0	3	0	26	0	0	1
5/	0/	56	885	0	6	2	24	11500	0	0	0	0	14000	0	0	0	18	0	0	1
5/	0/	56	86	0	3	2	12	14500	0	0	23	0	12000	0	0	0	12	0	0	1
5/	0/	56	401	0	3	2	12	14500	0	0	23	0	12000	0	0	0	12	0	0	1
5/	0/	56	783	0	3	2	12	14500	0	0	23	0	12000	0	0	0	12	0	0	1
5/	0/	56	1079	0	3	2	12	14500	0	0	23	0	12000	0	0	0	12	0	0	1
5/	0/	56	7061	0	2	2	18	15000	0	0	0	0	13500	0	0	0	23	0	0	1
5/	0/	56	2009	0	3	2	12	15000	0	0	23	0	12000	0	0	0	12	0	0	1
5/	0/	56	2534	0	3	2	12	15000	0	0	23	0	12000	0	0	0	12	0	0	1
5/	0/	56	1436	0	3	2	12	15000	0	0	23	0	12000	0	0	0	12	0	0	1
5/	0/	56	1350	0	3	2	12	15500	0	0	0	0	13500	0	0	0	28	0	0	1
5/	0/	56	1385	0	3	2	12	15500	0	0	0	0	13500	0	0	0	28	0	0	1
5/	0/	56	7216	0	2	2	12	15500	1	0	0	0	15000	0	0	0	21	0	0	1
5/	0/	56	2751	0	3	2	12	18000	0	0	0	0	13500	0	0	0	28	0	0	1
5/	0/	56	2650	0	2	2	18	7500	0	0	0	1	19500	0	0	0	21	0	0	1
5/	0/	56	149	0	4	2	24	8500	0	0	0	1	20000	0	0	0	4	0	0	1
5/	0/	56	1802	0	2	2	18	9000	0	0	0	1	19500	0	0	0	21	0	0	1
5/	0/	56	1913	0	8	2	12	9000	0	0	0	1	20000	0	0	0	4	0	0	1
5/	0/	56	2629	0	4	2	24	11500	0	0	0	1	20000	0	0	0	4	0	0	1
5/	0/	56	1704	0	7	2	18	12000	0	0	0	1	20000	0	0	0	21	0	0	1
5/	0/	56	2717	0	1	2	24	12000	0	0	0	1	20000	0	0	0	4	0	0	1
5/	0/	56	979	0	6	2	18	13000	0	0	0	1	20000	0	0	0	21	0	0	1
5/	0/	56	1621	0	2	2	18	13500	0	0	0	1	20000	0	0	0	4	0	0	1
5/	0/	56	2125	0	4	2	12	14500	0	0	0	1	20000	0	0	0	4	0	0	1
5/	0/	56	2815	0	2	2	29	14800	0	0	0	1	14000	0	0	0	7	0	0	1
5/	0/	56	217	0	8	2	12	15000	0	0	0	1	20000	0	0	0	21	0	0	1
5/	0/	56	3126	0	5	2	24	15000	0	0	0	1	20000	0	0	0	4	0	0	1
5/	0/	56	1317	0	2	2	18	15500	0	0	0	1	20000	0	0	0	21	0	0	1
5/	0/	56	45	0	4	2	18	15500	0	0	0	1	20000	0	0	0	21	0	0	1

282 APPENDIX D

6	8	10	1 TØ 4	5	12 TØ 13	14	15 TØ 17	18 TØ 23	24	25	26 TØ 27	28	29 TØ 34	35	40	41	42 TØ 43	44	45	80
5/	0/	56	14	0	7	2	18	15500	0	0	0	1	20000	0	0	0	21	0	0	1
5/	0/	56	1817	0	2	2	18	16000	0	0	0	1	20000	0	0	0	21	0	0	1
5/	0/	56	1978	0	8	2	18	16000	0	0	0	1	20000	0	0	0	21	0	0	1
5/	0/	56	3168	0	3	2	12	17000	0	0	0	1	20000	0	0	0	4	0	0	1
5/	0/	56	3806	0	8	2	24	18000	2	0	0	1	20000	0	0	0	7	0	0	1
5/	0/	56	3153	0	4	2	24	18000	0	0	0	1	19000	0	0	0	26	0	0	1
5/	0/	56	7228	0	10	2	18	19500	0	0	0	1	20000	0	0	0	4	0	0	1
5/	0/	56	7036	0	8	2	16	30000	0	0	0	1	20000	0	0	0	21	0	0	1
5/	0/	56	1957	0	4	2	24	30000	0	0	0	1	20000	0	0	0	4	0	0	1
5/	0/	56	2555	0	2	2	16	12000	0	0	0	8	150250	0	0	0	21	0	0	1
5/	0/	56	280	1	4	2	12	15000	0	0	0	8	150250	0	0	0	21	0	0	1
5/	0/	56	1682	0	5	2	18	15500	0	0	0	8	150250	0	0	0	21	0	0	1
5/	0/	56	3002	0	2	2	12	19500	0	0	0	8	150250	0	0	0	4	0	0	1
5/	0/	56	7104	0	4	2	18	19500	0	0	0	8	150250	0	0	0	21	0	0	1
5/	0/	56	7224	0	7	2	24	30000	0	0	0	8	130200	0	7	0	21	0	0	1
5/	0/	56	1879	0	6	2	12	17000	0	0	0	2	19500	0	2	0	12	0	0	1
5/	0/	56	1879	0	18	2	12	17000	0	0	0	2	18500	0	0	2	12	0	0	1
6/	0/	56	241	0	3	3	12	16557	1	0	0	5	0	645	0	0	13	0	0	1
6/	0/	56	3026	0	1	3	12	16755	1	0	0	5	0	685	0	0	13	0	0	1
6/	0/	56	7030	0	12	3	12	33000	0	0	0	5	0	375	0	0	18	0	0	1
6/	0/	56	3261	0	1	3	36	16580	0	0	0	6	0	3500	0	0	0	0	0	1
6/	0/	56	1401	0	1	3	30	16628	0	10	0	5	0	525	0	0	0	0	0	1
6/	0/	56	2540	0	6	3	60	13250	0	0	0	6	0	3000	0	0	0	0	0	1
6/	0/	56	794	0	7	3	60	16371	0	0	0	6	0	2900	0	0	18	0	0	1
6/	0/	56	7213	0	18	3	60	18000	0	0	0	6	0	2909	0	0	21	0	0	1
6/	0/	56	7075	0	36	3	60	19000	0	0	0	6	0	3006	0	0	4	0	0	1
6/	0/	56	7025	0	36	3	60	19500	0	0	0	6	0	2900	0	0	23	0	0	1
6/	0/	56	7177	0	20	3	60	19500	0	0	0	6	0	3000	0	0	10	0	0	1
6/	0/	56	7214	0	60	3	60	19600	0	0	0	6	0	3000	0	0	0	0	0	1
6/	0/	56	7085	0	30	3	60	24300	0	0	0	6	0	2806	0	0	12	0	0	1
6/	0/	56	7008	0	7	3	60	27000	0	0	0	5	0	450	0	0	13	0	0	1
6/	0/	56	7162	0	48	3	60	29000	0	0	0	6	0	2600	0	0	21	0	0	1
6/	0/	56	1571	0	12	3	60	31000	0	0	0	5	0	425	0	0	18	0	0	1
6/	0/	56	7070	0	48	3	60	32000	0	0	0	6	0	2600	0	0	21	0	0	1
6/	0/	56	7002	0	9	3	60	32000	0	0	0	5	0	425	0	0	18	0	0	1
6/	0/	56	7211	0	13	3	60	32000	0	0	0	5	0	425	0	0	18	0	0	1
6/	0/	56	7212	0	26	3	60	39600	0	0	0	6	0	2706	0	0	12	0	0	1
6/	0/	56	458	0	19	3	72	13500	0	0	0	6	0	2900	0	0	18	0	0	1
6/	0/	56	3056	0	12	3	72	16510	0	0	0	6	0	3000	0	0	10	0	0	1
6/	0/	56	7036	0	24	3	72	40000	0	0	0	5	0	375	0	0	18	0	0	1
6/	0/	56	7174	0	38	3	84	32000	0	0	0	6	0	2600	0	0	21	0	0	1
6/	0/	56	7138	0	60	3	84	34000	0	0	0	6	0	2509	0	0	21	0	0	1
6/	0/	56	7030	0	30	3	120	45000	0	0	0	5	0	300	0	0	28	0	0	1
6/	0/	56	7230	0	32	3	42	18000	0	0	0	6	0	3000	0	2	12	0	0	1

CHARTERS 283

6 TO 7	8 TO 9	10 TO 11	1 TO 4	5	12 TO 13	14	15 TO 17	18 TO 23	24	25	26 TO 27	28	29 TO 34	35 TO 39	40	41	42 TO 43	44	45	80
6/ 0/56	7071	0	24	3	18		18500	0	0	0	5		0	500	0	2	25	0	0	1
6/ 0/56	2805	0	30	3	24		18500	0	0	0	6		0	3009	0	2	12	0	0	1
6/ 0/56	2131	0	20	3	42		19500	0	0	0	6		0	2900	0	2	4	0	0	1
6/ 0/56	2279	0	17	2	12		13500	0	0	0	8		150200	0	0	2	4	0	0	1
6/ 0/56	3089	0	14	2	12		15000	0	0	0	8		250240	0	0	2	12	0	0	1
6/ 0/56	773	0	17	2	12		15000	0	0	0	8		150200	0	0	2	4	0	0	1
6/ 0/56	1253	0	18	2	12		18500	0	0	0	1		18000	0	0	2	12	0	0	1
6/ 0/56	3756	0	28	2	12		20000	0	2	16	0		15000	0	0	2	16	0	0	1
6/ 0/56	2279	0	5	2	12		13500	0	0	0	1		20000	0	2	0	4	0	0	1
6/ 0/56	773	0	5	2	12		15000	0	0	0	1		20000	0	2	0	4	0	0	1
6/ 0/56	7270	0	12	2	12		15500	0	0	0	8		175225	0	2	0	12	0	0	1
6/ 0/56	1253	0	6	2	12		18500	0	0	0	1		20000	0	2	0	12	0	0	1
6/ 0/56	3756	0	16	2	12		20000	0	2	16	0		20000	0	2	2	16	0	0	1
6/ 0/56	3756	0	4	2	12		20000	0	2	16	0		25000	0	2	0	16	0	0	1
6/ 0/56	7270	0	24	2	12		15500	0	0	0	8		150250	0	3	2	12	0	0	1
6/ 0/56	7230	0	14	2	18		18000	0	0	0	8		150250	0	3	0	12	0	0	1
6/ 0/56	7071	0	6	2	18		18500	0	0	0	0		13000	0	3	0	25	0	0	1
6/ 0/56	2131	0	2	2	18		19500	0	0	0	1		20000	0	3	0	4	0	0	1
6/ 0/56	7229	0	5	2	24		10000	0	0	0	0		14000	0	0	0	25	0	0	1
6/ 0/56	652	0	14	2	36		13500	0	2	16	0		12500	0	0	0	0	0	0	1
6/ 0/56	3179	0	12	2	36		14000	0	2	16	0		10000	0	0	0	18	0	0	1
6/ 0/56	2448	0	1	2	17		15000	0	0	0	0		13500	0	0	0	12	0	0	1
6/ 0/56	7003	0	4	2	14		15500	0	0	0	0		13500	0	0	0	12	0	0	1
6/ 0/56	889	0	4	2	24		15500	0	0	0	0		13500	0	0	0	18	0	0	1
6/ 0/56	3781	0	6	2	24		18500	0	0	0	0		13000	0	0	0	0	0	0	1
6/ 0/56	2329	0	6	2	18		19000	0	0	0	0		13500	0	0	0	12	0	0	1
6/ 0/56	3617	1	2	2	18		20000	0	0	0	0		13500	0	0	0	12	0	0	1
6/ 0/56	38	0	7	2	36		46000	0	2	16	0		11350	0	0	0	18	0	0	1
6/ 0/56	7076	0	24	2	180		84000	0	0	0	0		5000	0	0	0	13	0	0	1
6/ 0/56	7076	0	24	2	180		84000	0	0	0	0		5000	0	0	0	13	0	0	1
6/ 0/56	7076	0	24	2	180		84000	0	0	0	0		5000	0	0	0	13	0	0	1
6/ 0/56	34	0	2	2	24		8500	0	0	0	1		20000	0	0	0	4	0	0	1
6/ 0/56	1987	0	3	2	24		11000	0	0	0	1		20000	0	0	0	4	0	0	1
6/ 0/56	3796	1	4	2	24		11500	0	0	0	1		20000	0	0	0	4	0	0	1
6/ 0/56	1369	0	3	2	18		12000	0	0	0	1		20000	0	0	0	0	0	0	1
6/ 0/56	336	0	4	2	24		13500	0	0	0	1		20000	0	0	0	4	0	0	1
6/ 0/56	3123	0	3	2	24		14000	0	0	0	1		20000	0	0	0	7	0	0	1
6/ 0/56	3128	0	3	2	24		15000	0	0	0	1		20000	0	0	0	4	0	0	1
6/ 0/56	2523	0	3	2	24		15000	0	0	0	1		20000	0	0	0	4	0	0	1
6/ 0/56	2882	0	7	2	18		15000	0	0	0	1		20000	0	0	0	0	0	0	1
6/ 0/56	177	0	2	2	24		15500	0	0	0	1		20000	0	0	0	12	0	0	1
6/ 0/56	1388	0	5	2	24		16000	0	0	0	1		20000	0	0	0	7	0	0	1
6/ 0/56	1265	0	2	2	24		16000	0	0	0	1		20000	0	0	0	4	0	0	1
6/ 0/56	2391	0	4	2	24		16500	1	0	0	1		21500	0	0	0	7	0	0	1

284   APPENDIX D

6 TO 7	8 TO 9	10 TO 11	1 TO 4	5	12 TO 13	14	15 TO 17	18 TO 23	24	25	26 TO 27	28	29 TO 34	35 TO 39	40	41	42 TO 43	44	45	80
6/	0/56	2266	0	3	2	24	18000	0	0	0	1	20000	0	0	0	4	0	0	1
6/	0/56	57	0	3	2	24	18000	0	0	0	1	20000	0	0	0	4	0	0	1
6/	0/56	1071	0	2	2	18	18500	0	0	0	1	20000	0	0	0	7	0	0	1
6/	0/56	59	0	3	2	24	23000	0	0	0	1	20000	0	0	0	4	0	0	1
6/	0/56	1857	0	15	2	12	12500	0	0	0	8	150200	0	0	0	4	0	0	1
6/	0/56	3089	0	2	2	12	15000	0	0	0	2	20000	0	2	0	12	0	0	1
6/	0/56	2805	0	6	2	24	18500	0	0	0	2	20000	0	3	0	12	0	0	1
6/	0/56	7270	0	36	2	24	15500	0	0	0	6	0	3000	0	2	12	0	0	1
7/	0/56	2304	0	17	3	36	16517	0	0	0	6	0	2900	0	0	21	0	0	1
7/	0/56	1013	0	17	3	36	16517	0	0	0	6	0	2900	0	0	21	0	0	1
7/	0/56	3650	0	33	3	36	24870	0	0	0	6	0	2000	0	0	0	0	0	1
7/	0/56	1266	0	41	3	60	15810	0	0	0	6	0	3000	0	0	4	0	0	1
7/	0/56	2668	0	41	3	60	16020	0	0	0	6	0	2900	0	0	4	0	0	1
7/	0/56	195	0	41	3	60	16189	0	0	0	6	0	2800	0	0	21	0	0	1
7/	0/56	3625	0	54	3	60	16220	0	0	0	6	0	3006	0	0	4	0	0	1
7/	0/56	2149	0	23	3	60	16490	0	0	0	6	0	2700	0	0	4	0	0	1
7/	0/56	1052	0	17	3	60	16500	0	0	0	6	0	2806	0	0	18	0	0	1
7/	0/56	1658	0	49	3	60	17000	0	0	0	6	0	3000	0	0	21	0	0	1
7/	0/56	3119	0	43	3	60	17600	0	0	0	6	0	3100	0	0	4	0	0	1
7/	0/56	2136	0	38	3	60	18560	0	0	0	6	0	2903	0	0	21	0	0	1
7/	0/56	1665	0	30	3	60	18791	0	0	0	6	0	3000	0	0	21	0	0	1
7/	0/56	7074	0	50	3	60	19000	0	0	0	6	0	3009	0	0	4	0	0	1
7/	0/56	1666	0	52	3	60	19094	0	0	0	6	0	3000	0	0	21	0	0	1
7/	0/56	1659	0	36	3	60	19108	0	0	0	6	0	3003	0	0	4	0	0	1
7/	0/56	1660	0	43	3	60	19108	0	0	0	6	0	3000	0	0	21	0	0	1
7/	0/56	362	0	48	3	60	20100	0	0	0	6	0	3000	0	0	4	0	0	1
7/	0/56	2168	0	39	3	60	20600	0	0	0	6	0	2809	0	0	4	0	0	1
7/	0/56	1667	0	45	3	60	21497	0	0	0	6	0	3000	0	0	21	0	0	1
7/	0/56	7073	0	31	3	60	24100	0	0	0	6	0	2065	0	0	12	0	0	1
7/	0/56	1661	0	44	3	60	24850	0	0	0	6	0	2706	0	0	21	0	0	1
7/	0/56	1786	0	39	3	60	26760	0	0	0	6	0	2706	0	0	21	0	0	1
7/	0/56	7071	0	15	3	60	31500	0	0	0	5	0	420	0	0	0	0	0	1
7/	0/56	7070	0	60	3	60	32000	0	0	0	6	0	2600	0	0	21	0	0	1
7/	0/56	3972	0	18	3	60	32000	0	0	0	6	0	3100	0	0	12	0	0	1
7/	0/56	3118	0	5	3	72	13025	0	0	0	6	0	3100	0	0	20	0	0	1
7/	0/56	1818	0	7	2	24	11500	0	1	6	1	20000	0	0	2	21	0	0	1
7/	0/56	2505	0	1	2	6	12000	0	1	6	1	16000	0	2	0	21	0	0	1
7/	0/56	3174	0	11	2	36	13500	0	0	0	0	10750	0	0	0	18	0	0	1
7/	0/56	3928	0	11	2	48	15500	0	2	16	0	10000	0	0	0	16	0	0	1
7/	0/56	7273	0	3	2	60	40500	0	2	16	0	10000	0	0	0	18	0	0	1
7/	0/56	1262	0	4	2	24	11500	1	0	0	1	21500	0	0	0	7	0	0	1
7/	0/56	2913	0	5	2	24	13500	0	0	0	1	20000	0	0	0	21	0	0	1
7/	0/56	2485	0	5	2	24	17000	0	0	0	1	20000	0	0	0	21	0	0	1
7/	0/56	2054	0	1	2	24	24000	0	0	0	1	20000	0	0	0	7	0	0	1

6 TO 7	8 TO 9	10 TO 11	1 TO 4	5	12 TO 13	14	15 TO 17	18 TO 23	24	25	26 TO 27	28	29 TO 34	35 TO 39	40	41	42 TO 43	44	45	80
8/ 0/56			232	0	4	3	24	13264	1	0	0	5	0	760	0	0	23	0	0	1
8/ 0/56			2314	0	0	3	42	21000	0	0	0	6	0	3400	0	0	18	0	0	1
8/ 0/56			1679	0	42	3	60	15820	0	0	0	6	0	2903	0	0	4	0	0	1
8/ 0/56			1412	0	39	3	60	16300	0	0	0	6	0	2900	0	0	4	0	0	1
8/ 0/56			2932	0	60	3	60	17300	0	0	0	6	0	3000	0	0	21	0	0	1
8/ 0/56			2353	0	53	3	60	19340	0	0	0	6	0	3000	0	0	4	0	0	1
8/ 0/56			7066	0	56	3	60	19750	0	0	0	6	0	3200	0	0	21	0	0	1
8/ 0/56			7066	0	51	3	60	25100	0	0	0	6	0	3000	0	0	21	0	0	1
8/ 0/56			1636	0	14	3	60	26746	0	0	0	5	0	490	0	0	18	0	0	1
8/ 0/56			7066	0	54	3	60	36000	0	0	0	6	0	2903	0	0	21	0	0	1
8/ 0/56			7218	0	48	3	60	36000	0	0	0	6	0	3000	0	0	12	0	0	1
8/ 0/56			7218	0	48	3	60	36000	0	0	0	6	0	3000	0	0	12	0	0	1
8/ 0/56			7067	0	38	3	60	36200	0	0	0	6	0	2900	0	0	7	0	0	1
8/ 0/56			7063	0	42	3	60	39700	0	0	0	6	0	3000	0	0	7	0	0	1
8/ 0/56			7008	0	42	3	144	40000	0	0	0	6	0	2406	0	0	18	0	0	1
8/ 0/56			2926	0	34	3	60	15000	0	0	0	6	0	3000	0	2	18	0	0	1
8/ 0/56			7221	0	60	3	48	40000	0	0	0	6	0	2800	0	3	7	0	0	1
8/ 0/56			7030	0	41	3	24	33000	0	0	0	6	0	2900	3	0	7	0	0	1
8/ 0/56			83	0	13	2	12	13500	0	0	0	8	175225	0	0	2	10	0	0	1
8/ 0/56			83	0	1	2	12	13500	0	0	0	1	20000	0	2	0	10	0	0	1
8/ 0/56			2926	0	10	2	24	15000	0	0	0	1	20000	0	3	0	18	0	0	1
8/ 0/56			2734	0	0	2	60	10500	0	0	0	0	10000	0	0	0	16	0	0	1
8/ 0/56			3229	0	5	2	26	12000	0	0	0	1	20000	0	0	0	18	0	0	1
8/ 0/56			2757	0	0	2	36	18000	0	2	16	9	90130	0	0	0	16	0	0	1
9/ 0/56			95	0	6	3	24	7320	1	0	0	6	0	5309	0	0	21	0	0	1
9/ 0/56			2056	0	6	3	42	33000	0	0	0	5	0	710	0	0	13	0	0	1
9/ 0/56			3329	0	7	3	60	13600	0	0	0	6	0	3106	0	0	21	0	0	1
9/ 0/56			1549	0	24	3	60	15135	0	0	0	6	0	3000	0	0	21	0	0	1
9/ 0/56			366	0	47	3	60	16540	0	0	0	6	0	2703	0	0	21	0	0	1
9/ 0/56			1547	0	59	3	60	22808	0	0	0	6	0	2806	0	0	21	0	0	1
9/ 0/56			1546	0	39	3	60	22808	0	0	0	6	0	2806	0	0	21	0	0	1
9/ 0/56			354	0	30	3	60	24300	0	0	0	6	0	2900	0	0	7	0	0	1
9/ 0/56			7268	0	60	3	60	33000	0	0	0	6	0	3000	0	0	21	0	0	1
9/ 0/56			7269	0	69	3	60	33000	0	0	0	6	0	3000	0	0	21	0	0	1
9/ 0/56			7065	0	44	3	60	36000	0	0	0	6	0	3000	0	0	21	0	0	1
9/ 0/56			7267	0	66	3	60	40000	0	0	0	6	0	2900	0	0	21	0	0	1
9/ 0/56			7267	0	52	3	60	40000	0	0	0	6	0	2900	0	0	21	0	0	1
9/ 0/56			7040	0	56	3	72	34000	0	0	0	6	0	1500	0	0	21	0	0	1
9/ 0/56			7254	0	40	3	72	40000	0	0	0	6	0	3000	0	0	7	0	0	1
9/ 0/56			1487	0	15	3	84	16600	0	0	0	6	0	3100	0	0	21	0	0	1
9/ 0/56			370	0	44	3	84	32900	0	0	0	5	0	400	0	0	20	0	0	1
9/ 0/56			7221	0	39	3	84	33000	0	0	0	6	0	3000	0	0	7	0	0	1
9/ 0/56			7221	0	45	3	84	36000	0	0	0	6	0	3000	0	0	7	0	0	1
9/ 0/56			7221	0	45	3	84	40000	0	0	0	6	0	2906	0	0	7	0	0	1

286 APPENDIX D

6 TØ 7	8 TØ 9	10 TØ 11	1 TØ 4	5	12 TØ 13	14	15 TØ 17	18 TØ 23	24	25	26 TØ 27	28	29 TØ 34	35 TØ 39	40	41	42 TØ 43	44	45	80
9/	0/	56	7223	0	20	3	180	40000	0	0	0	5	0	375	0	0	0	0	0	1
9/	0/	56	7263	0	20	3	180	45000	0	0	0	5	0	375	0	0	0	0	0	1
9/	0/	56	7221	0	45	3	84	45000	0	0	0	6	0	2900	0	0	7	0	0	1
9/	0/	56	72	0	24	3	36	13580	1	0	0	5	0	475	0	3	23	0	0	1
9/	0/	56	884	0	33	3	60	25000	0	0	0	6	0	3003	0	2	4	0	0	1
9/	0/	56	72	0	0	3	24	13580	1	0	0	5	0	700	3	0	23	0	0	1
9/	0/	56	2356	0	7	2	17	12000	0	0	0	8	175250	0	0	2	18	0	0	1
9/	0/	56	3013	1	7	2	19	15500	0	0	0	8	200250	0	0	2	18	0	0	1
9/	0/	56	2356	0	0	2	7	12000	0	0	0	8	225350	0	2	0	18	0	0	1
9/	0/	56	3013	1	2	2	5	15500	0	0	0	8	225350	0	2	0	18	0	0	1
9/	0/	56	884	0	15	2	12	25000	0	0	0	1	20000	0	2	0	4	0	0	1
9/	0/	56	167	0	1	2	15	8500	0	0	0	0	15000	0	0	0	0	0	0	1
9/	0/	56	2987	0	1	2	41	15000	0	0	0	0	14250	0	0	0	12	0	0	1
9/	0/	56	393	0	1	2	41	15000	0	0	0	0	14250	0	0	0	12	0	0	1
9/	0/	56	7061	0	2	2	40	15500	0	0	0	0	14250	0	0	0	12	0	0	1
9/	0/	56	1921	0	1	2	41	15500	0	0	0	0	14250	0	0	0	12	0	0	1
9/	0/	56	1309	0	2	2	24	15500	1	0	0	1	22500	0	0	0	0	0	0	1
9/	0/	56	1249	0	12	2	24	11500	0	0	0	8	150250	0	0	0	4	0	0	1
10/	0/	56	7152	0	5	3	12	33000	0	0	0	5	0	1250	0	0	26	0	0	1
10/	0/	56	3627	0	2	3	24	18500	0	0	0	6	0	5000	0	0	18	0	0	1
10/	0/	56	1579	0	8	3	24	19304	0	0	0	6	0	5206	0	0	18	0	0	1
10/	0/	56	7221	0	8	3	37	24500	0	0	0	5	0	575	0	0	16	0	0	1
10/	0/	56	2798	0	1	3	42	17230	0	0	0	5	0	645	0	0	18	0	0	1
10/	0/	56	933	0	2	3	42	19660	0	0	0	5	0	740	0	0	12	0	0	1
10/	0/	56	836	0	2	3	42	19689	0	0	0	5	0	740	0	0	12	0	0	1
10/	0/	56	3678	0	5	3	42	27500	0	0	0	6	0	5009	0	0	18	0	0	1
10/	0/	56	1771	0	20	3	60	11970	0	0	0	6	0	3100	0	0	21	0	0	1
10/	0/	56	2497	0	29	3	60	12800	0	0	0	6	0	2903	0	0	4	0	0	1
10/	0/	56	1729	0	32	3	60	13720	0	0	0	6	0	3003	0	0	21	0	0	1
10/	0/	56	33	0	31	3	60	13850	0	0	0	6	0	2800	0	0	21	0	0	1
10/	0/	56	915	0	13	3	60	15560	0	0	0	6	0	3500	0	0	21	0	0	1
10/	0/	56	1508	0	27	3	60	15075	0	0	0	6	0	2706	7	0	21	0	0	1
10/	0/	56	2377	0	39	3	60	16010	0	0	0	6	0	3200	0	0	7	0	0	1
10/	0/	56	2656	0	12	3	60	16050	0	0	0	6	0	2606	0	0	21	0	0	1
10/	0/	56	3239	0	14	3	60	18000	0	0	0	6	0	3703	0	0	21	0	0	1
10/	0/	56	3268	0	76	3	60	18178	0	0	0	6	0	3400	0	0	21	0	0	1
10/	0/	56	863	0	33	3	60	18510	0	0	0	6	0	3200	0	0	21	0	0	1
10/	0/	56	394	0	30	3	60	18530	0	0	0	6	0	3206	0	0	10	0	0	1
10/	0/	56	7125	0	39	3	60	18200	0	0	0	6	0	3400	7	0	21	0	0	1
10/	0/	56	3651	0	39	3	60	19000	0	0	0	6	0	3300	0	0	4	0	0	1
10/	0/	56	7025	0	75	3	60	19300	0	0	0	6	0	3400	0	0	21	0	0	1
10/	0/	56	7226	0	56	3	60	19500	0	0	0	6	0	3400	0	0	21	0	0	1
10/	0/	56	7226	0	68	3	60	19500	0	0	0	6	0	3400	0	0	21	0	0	1
10/	0/	56	7003	0	44	3	60	20000	0	0	0	6	0	3500	0	0	21	0	0	1

6 / 7	8 / 9	10 / 11	1 / 4	5	12 / 13	14	15 / 17	18	24	25	26 / 27	28	29 / 34	35	40	41	42 / 43	44	45	80
10	0	56	3655	0	55	3	60	24900	0	0	0	6	0	3200	0	0	4	0	0	1
10	0	56	7058	0	24	3	60	31000	0	0	0	6	0	3400	0	0	12	0	0	1
10	0	56	7032	0	26	3	60	31000	0	0	0	6	0	3400	0	0	21	0	0	1
10	0	56	7267	0	80	3	60	33000	0	0	0	6	0	2900	0	0	21	0	0	1
10	0	56	7270	0	68	3	60	34500	0	0	0	6	0	2900	0	0	21	0	0	1
10	0	56	7271	0	57	3	60	39700	0	0	0	6	0	2906	0	0	21	0	0	1
10	0	56	7032	0	50	3	60	51700	0	0	0	6	0	3000	0	0	21	0	0	1
10	0	56	1276	0	23	3	78	19260	0	0	0	6	0	3403	0	0	21	0	0	1
10	0	56	7035	0	68	3	72	34000	0	0	0	6	0	1500	0	0	21	0	0	1
10	0	56	7270	0	84	3	72	40000	0	0	0	6	0	3000	0	0	21	0	0	1
10	0	56	7270	0	44	3	84	19500	0	0	0	6	0	3400	0	0	21	0	0	1
10	0	56	7171	0	48	3	84	31500	0	0	0	6	0	3200	0	0	4	0	0	1
10	0	56	7225	0	39	3	84	34000	0	0	0	6	0	3006	0	0	7	0	0	1
10	0	56	7037	0	44	3	84	35000	0	0	0	6	0	2900	0	0	21	0	0	1
10	0	56	7037	0	52	3	84	35000	0	0	0	6	0	2900	0	0	21	0	0	1
10	0	56	7037	0	60	3	84	35000	0	0	0	6	0	2900	0	0	21	0	0	1
10	0	56	7038	0	62	3	84	35600	0	0	0	6	0	3000	0	0	21	0	0	1
10	0	56	7026	0	69	3	84	35350	0	0	0	5	0	390	0	0	20	0	0	1
10	0	56	7270	0	44	3	84	40000	0	0	0	6	0	3000	0	0	21	0	0	1
10	0	56	7221	0	44	3	120	45000	0	0	0	5	0	400	0	0	16	0	0	1
10	0	56	461	0	53	3	6	15300	0	0	0	6	0	2600	0	3	21	0	0	1
10	0	56	3023	0	26	3	60	15500	0	0	0	6	0	3003	0	2	7	0	0	1
10	0	56	2924	0	27	3	60	15500	0	0	0	6	0	2806	0	2	7	0	0	1
10	0	56	807	0	14	3	42	15500	0	0	0	6	0	2906	0	2	12	0	0	1
10	0	56	1932	0	38	3	60	15500	0	0	0	6	0	3106	0	2	7	0	0	1
10	0	56	1903	0	36	3	60	15500	0	0	0	6	0	3000	0	2	4	0	0	1
10	0	56	3267	0	36	3	60	15500	0	0	0	6	0	2906	0	2	4	0	0	1
10	0	56	2743	0	44	3	60	15500	0	0	0	6	0	3106	0	2	4	0	0	1
10	0	56	3206	0	47	3	60	16000	0	0	0	6	0	3106	0	2	7	0	0	1
10	0	56	161	0	44	3	36	16500	0	0	0	6	0	3100	0	2	26	0	0	1
10	0	56	883	0	36	3	36	16500	0	0	0	6	0	3100	0	2	26	0	0	1
10	0	56	376	0	48	3	60	18000	0	0	0	6	0	3100	0	2	4	0	0	1
10	0	56	7026	0	54	3	24	19500	0	0	0	6	0	3200	0	3	21	0	0	1
10	0	56	461	0	11	3	18	15300	0	0	0	6	0	4000	3	0	21	0	0	1
10	0	56	461	0	29	3	24	15300	0	0	0	6	0	2800	3	3	21	0	0	1
10	0	56	7026	0	18	3	12	19500	0	0	0	6	0	5100	3	0	21	0	0	1
10	0	56	7026	0	30	3	24	19500	0	0	0	6	0	3600	3	3	21	0	0	1
10	0	56	1934	0	26	2	12	9000	0	0	0	8	150250	0	0	2	4	0	0	1
10	0	56	455	0	24	2	12	11500	0	0	0	8	150250	0	0	2	4	0	0	1
10	0	56	1363	0	22	2	12	11500	0	0	0	8	150250	0	0	2	4	0	0	1
10	0	56	457	0	22	2	12	13000	0	0	0	8	150250	0	0	2	4	0	0	1
10	0	56	417	0	23	2	12	14000	0	0	0	8	150250	0	0	2	4	0	0	1
10	0	56	2102	1	7	2	20	14500	0	0	0	8	200225	0	0	2	18	0	0	1
10	0	56	42	0	23	2	12	15000	0	0	0	8	150250	0	0	2	4	0	0	1

288   APPENDIX D

6 TØ 7	8 TØ 9	10 TØ 11	1 TØ 4	5	12 TØ 13	14	15 TØ 17	18 TØ 23	24	25	26 TØ 27	28	29 TØ 34	35 TØ 39	40	41	42 TØ 43	44	45	80
10/	0/56	2584	0	26	2	6	15500	0	0	0	8	150250	0	0	2	10	0	0	1	
10/	0/56	2216	0	9	2	24	17000	0	0	0	8	200300	0	0	2	23	0	0	1	
10/	0/56	1934	0	14	2	12	9000	0	0	0	1	20000	0	2	0	4	0	0	1	
10/	0/56	455	0	12	2	12	11500	0	0	0	1	20000	0	2	0	4	0	0	1	
10/	0/56	1363	0	10	2	12	11500	0	0	0	1	20000	0	2	0	4	0	0	1	
10/	0/56	457	0	10	2	12	13000	0	0	0	1	20000	0	2	0	4	0	0	1	
10/	0/56	417	0	11	2	12	14000	0	0	0	1	20000	0	2	0	4	0	0	1	
10/	0/56	2102	1	1	2	6	14500	0	0	0	8	225350	0	2	0	18	0	0	1	
10/	0/56	42	0	11	2	12	15000	0	0	0	1	20000	0	2	0	4	0	0	1	
10/	0/56	2924	0	9	2	12	15500	0	0	0	1	20000	0	2	0	7	0	0	1	
10/	0/56	1903	0	12	2	12	15500	0	0	0	1	20000	0	2	0	4	0	0	1	
10/	0/56	3267	0	12	2	12	15500	0	0	0	1	20000	0	2	0	4	0	0	1	
10/	0/56	2743	0	26	2	12	15500	0	0	0	1	20000	0	2	0	4	0	0	1	
10/	0/56	2584	0	2	2	12	15500	0	0	0	1	23500	0	2	0	10	0	0	1	
10/	0/56	2584	0	14	2	12	15500	0	0	0	8	175275	0	2	2	10	0	0	1	
10/	0/56	2216	0	5	2	4	17000	0	0	0	8	250350	0	2	0	23	0	0	1	
10/	0/56	376	0	30	2	12	18000	0	0	0	1	20000	0	2	0	4	0	0	1	
10/	0/56	3023	0	14	2	12	15500	0	0	0	1	20000	0	3	0	7	0	0	1	
10/	0/56	1932	0	20	2	18	15500	0	0	0	1	20000	0	3	0	7	0	0	1	
10/	0/56	2924	0	21	2	6	15500	0	0	0	8	175200	0	3	2	7	0	0	1	
10/	0/56	1903	0	24	2	12	15500	0	0	0	8	150250	0	3	2	4	0	0	1	
10/	0/56	3267	0	24	2	12	15500	0	0	0	8	150250	0	3	2	4	0	0	1	
10/	0/56	2743	0	38	2	6	15500	0	0	0	8	150250	0	3	2	4	0	0	1	
10/	0/56	3206	0	29	2	18	16000	0	0	0	1	20000	0	3	0	7	0	0	1	
10/	0/56	883	0	12	2	24	16500	0	0	0	1	20000	0	3	0	26	0	0	1	
10/	0/56	161	0	20	2	24	16500	0	0	0	1	20000	0	3	0	26	0	0	1	
10/	0/56	376	0	42	2	6	18000	0	0	0	8	150250	0	3	2	4	0	0	1	
10/	0/56	1803	0	2	2	40	9500	0	0	23	0	14250	0	0	0	12	0	0	1	
10/	0/56	1911	0	4	2	24	13000	0	0	0	0	13000	0	0	0	18	0	0	1	
10/	0/56	119	0	3	2	12	31000	0	0	0	0	150250	0	0	0	13	0	0	1	
10/	0/56	7231	0	14	2	24	48000	0	0	0	0	12000	0	0	0	12	0	0	1	
10/	0/56	984	0	4	2	24	8000	0	0	0	1	20000	0	0	0	21	0	0	1	
10/	0/56	1802	0	20	2	12	9000	0	0	0	1	20000	0	0	0	21	0	0	1	
10/	0/56	2519	0	6	2	24	11000	0	0	0	1	20000	0	0	0	21	0	0	1	
10/	0/56	395	0	1	2	36	11000	1	0	0	1	23500	0	0	0	7	0	0	1	
10/	0/56	1599	0	10	2	24	11500	0	0	0	1	20000	0	0	0	21	0	0	1	
10/	0/56	7268	0	20	2	24	25000	0	0	0	1	20000	0	0	0	26	0	0	1	
10/	0/56	1687	0	2	2	12	30000	0	0	0	1	23500	0	0	0	18	0	0	1	
10/	0/56	2287	0	8	2	24	11000	0	0	0	8	150250	0	0	0	10	0	0	1	
10/	0/56	209	0	20	2	24	15000	0	0	0	8	175275	0	0	0	0	0	0	1	
10/	0/56	834	0	41	2	24	23000	0	0	0	8	75275	0	0	0	21	0	0	1	
10/	0/56	807	0	6	2	12	15500	0	0	0	2	175250	0	2	0	12	0	0	1	
10/	0/56	807	0	18	2	6	15500	0	0	0	2	160235	0	3	2	12	0	0	1	
10/	0/56	2922	0	51	2	60	12965	0	0	0	6	0	3106	0	0	21	0	0	1	

6 TO 7	8 TO 9	10 TO 11	1 TO 4	5	12 TO 13	14	15 TO 17	18 TO 23	24	25	26 TO 27	28	29 TO 34	35 TO 39	40	41	42 TO 43	44	45	80
11	0	56	3292	0	0	3	12	5737	0	0	0	6	0	5500	0	0	21	0	0	1
11	0	56	2281	0	3	3	24	8265	0	0	0	6	0	4400	0	0	0	0	0	1
11	0	56	273	0	3	3	24	10853	0	0	0	6	0	2600	0	0	0	0	0	1
11	0	56	1014	0	4	3	36	11425	1	0	0	5	0	745	0	0	23	0	0	1
11	0	56	904	0	1	3	36	16578	0	0	0	5	0	750	0	0	0	0	0	1
11	0	56	7054	0	6	3	36	17300	0	0	0	5	0	750	0	0	26	0	0	1
11	0	56	3900	0	31	3	36	18600	0	0	0	6	0	30000	0	0	0	0	0	1
11	0	56	2222	0	28	3	48	13450	0	0	0	6	0	3400	7	0	21	0	0	1
11	0	56	7008	0	0	3	40	16500	0	0	0	5	0	750	0	0	12	0	0	1
11	0	56	7008	0	0	3	40	16500	0	0	0	5	0	750	0	0	12	0	0	1
11	0	56	7008	0	0	3	40	16500	0	0	0	5	0	750	0	0	12	0	0	1
11	0	56	7008	0	0	3	40	16500	0	0	0	5	0	750	0	0	12	0	0	1
11	0	56	7008	0	0	3	40	16500	0	0	0	5	0	750	0	0	12	0	0	1
11	0	56	7008	0	0	3	40	16500	0	0	0	5	0	750	0	0	12	0	0	1
11	0	56	7008	0	0	3	40	16500	0	0	0	5	0	750	0	0	12	0	0	1
11	0	56	7008	0	0	3	40	16500	0	0	0	5	0	750	0	0	12	0	0	1
11	0	56	7008	0	0	3	40	16500	0	0	0	5	0	750	0	0	12	0	0	1
11	0	56	7057	0	4	3	42	18000	1	0	0	5	0	775	0	0	7	0	0	1
11	0	56	7008	0	0	3	40	18000	0	0	0	5	0	750	0	0	12	0	0	1
11	0	56	3624	0	53	3	60	13700	0	0	0	6	0	3309	7	0	21	0	0	1
11	0	56	1070	0	72	3	60	13750	0	0	0	6	0	3309	7	0	21	0	0	1
11	0	56	2210	0	0	3	60	13075	0	0	0	5	0	650	0	0	18	1	0	1
11	0	56	223	0	62	3	60	13300	0	0	0	6	0	3000	0	0	21	0	0	1
11	0	56	2588	0	24	3	60	15200	0	0	0	6	0	3009	0	0	21	0	0	1
11	0	56	280	0	72	3	60	16175	0	0	0	6	0	3206	0	0	21	0	0	1
11	0	56	183	0	74	3	60	16330	0	0	0	6	0	3400	0	0	21	0	0	1
11	0	56	1419	0	60	3	60	18350	0	0	0	6	0	3400	7	0	21	0	0	1
11	0	56	7017	0	79	3	60	19300	0	0	0	6	0	3400	7	0	21	0	0	1
11	0	56	7022	0	76	3	60	19300	0	0	0	6	0	3400	7	0	0	0	0	1
11	0	56	7017	0	72	3	60	19300	0	0	0	6	0	3400	7	0	21	0	0	1
11	0	56	7017	0	92	3	60	19500	0	0	0	6	0	3400	7	0	21	0	0	1
11	0	56	7272	0	49	3	60	19700	0	0	0	6	0	3400	7	0	0	0	0	1
11	0	56	7071	0	36	3	60	31000	0	0	0	6	0	3003	0	0	21	0	0	1
11	0	56	7071	0	36	3	60	31000	0	0	0	6	0	3003	0	0	21	0	0	1
11	0	56	7014	0	31	3	60	31500	0	0	0	6	0	3403	0	0	4	0	0	1
11	0	56	7017	0	92	3	60	36000	0	0	0	6	0	3003	0	0	21	0	0	1
11	0	56	7071	0	48	3	60	51700	0	0	0	6	0	3000	0	0	21	0	0	1
11	0	56	7018	0	99	3	84	19000	0	0	0	6	0	3300	0	0	21	0	0	1
11	0	56	339	0	18	3	84	25000	0	0	0	6	0	3500	0	0	21	0	0	1
11	0	56	336	0	66	3	84	28000	0	0	0	6	0	3003	0	0	21	0	0	1
11	0	56	7056	0	79	3	84	40500	0	0	0	6	0	3003	0	0	21	0	0	1
11	0	56	338	0	28	3	36	16400	0	0	0	6	0	3206	0	3	21	0	0	1

APPENDIX D

6	8	10	1	5	12	14	15	18	24	25	26	28	29	35	40	41	42	44	45	80
TØ	TØ	TØ	TØ		TØ		TØ	TØ			TØ		TØ	TØ			TØ			
7	9	11	4		13		17	23			27		34	39			43			
11/	0/56	7071	0	36	3	60	16500	0	0	0	6	0	3100	0	2	21	0	0	1
11/	0/56	7071	0	38	3	60	18000	0	0	0	6	0	3300	0	2	21	0	0	1
11/	0/56	7071	0	38	3	60	18000	0	0	0	6	0	3300	0	2	21	0	0	1
11/	0/56	3900	0	31	3	36	18600	0	0	0	6	0	3206	0	3	21	0	0	1
11/	0/56	3848	0	30	3	60	19000	0	0	0	6	0	3506	0	3	21	0	0	1
11/	0/56	7071	0	48	3	60	31500	0	0	0	6	0	3003	0	2	21	0	0	1
11/	0/56	7003	0	99	3	60	32500	0	0	0	5	0	230	0	3	26	0	0	1
11/	0/56	7016	0	99	3	60	38000	0	0	0	5	0	230	0	3	26	0	0	1
11/	0/56	338	0	4	3	24	16400	0	0	0	6	0	5306	3	0	21	0	0	1
11/	0/56	3900	0	7	3	24	18600	0	0	0	6	0	5306	3	0	21	0	0	1
11/	0/56	3848	0	6	3	24	19000	0	0	0	6	0	5509	3	0	21	0	0	1
11/	0/56	7003	0	32	3	60	32500	0	0	0	5	0	475	3	2	26	0	0	1
11/	0/56	7003	0	92	3	60	32500	0	0	0	5	0	270	3	3	26	0	0	1
11/	0/56	7016	0	32	3	60	38000	0	0	0	5	0	475	3	2	26	0	0	1
11/	0/56	7016	0	92	3	60	38000	0	0	0	5	0	270	3	3	26	0	0	1
11/	0/56	2683	0	42	2	12	10000	0	0	0	8	150250	0	0	2	21	0	0	1
11/	0/56	3850	0	13	2	28	11000	0	0	0	1	20000	0	0	2	21	0	0	1
11/	0/56	2505	0	28	2	12	12000	0	0	0	8	150250	0	0	2	21	0	0	1
11/	0/56	3036	0	42	2	312	12500	0	0	0	8	150250	0	0	2	21	0	0	1
11/	0/56	2627	0	42	2	12	15000	0	0	0	8	150250	0	0	2	21	0	0	1
11/	0/56	3032	0	42	2	12	15500	0	0	0	8	150250	0	0	2	21	0	0	1
11/	0/56	3697	0	42	2	12	18500	0	0	0	8	150250	0	0	2	21	0	0	1
11/	0/56	3796	0	42	2	12	18500	0	0	0	8	150250	0	0	2	21	0	0	1
11/	0/56	7023	0	42	2	12	18500	0	0	0	8	150250	0	0	2	21	0	0	1
11/	0/56	7023	0	42	2	12	18500	0	0	0	8	150250	0	0	2	21	0	0	1
11/	0/56	2683	0	16	2	26	10000	0	0	0	1	20000	0	2	0	21	0	0	1
11/	0/56	3850	0	5	2	8	11000	0	0	0	8	200350	0	2	0	21	0	0	1
11/	0/56	2505	0	1	2	15	12000	0	0	0	8	200350	0	2	0	21	0	0	1
11/	0/56	2505	0	16	2	12	12000	0	0	0	8	175275	0	2	2	21	0	0	1
11/	0/56	3036	0	16	2	26	12500	0	0	0	1	20000	0	2	0	21	0	0	1
11/	0/56	2627	0	16	2	26	15000	0	0	0	1	20000	0	2	0	21	0	0	1
11/	0/56	3032	0	16	2	26	15500	0	0	0	1	20000	0	2	0	21	0	0	1
11/	0/56	7071	0	8	2	8	16500	0	0	0	8	200350	0	2	0	21	0	0	1
11/	0/56	7071	0	16	2	12	16500	0	0	0	8	175275	0	2	2	21	0	0	1
11/	0/56	7071	0	2	2	12	18000	0	0	0	8	200350	0	2	0	21	0	0	1
11/	0/56	7071	0	14	2	12	18000	0	0	0	8	175275	0	2	2	21	0	0	1
11/	0/56	7071	0	2	2	12	18000	0	0	0	8	200350	0	2	0	21	0	0	1
11/	0/56	7071	0	14	2	12	18000	0	0	0	8	175275	0	2	2	21	0	0	1
11/	0/56	3697	0	16	2	26	18500	0	0	0	1	20000	0	2	0	21	0	0	1
11/	0/56	3796	0	16	2	26	18500	0	0	0	1	20000	0	2	0	21	0	0	1
11/	0/56	7023	0	16	2	26	18500	0	0	0	1	20000	0	2	0	21	0	0	1
11/	0/56	7023	0	22	2	20	18500	0	0	0	1	20000	0	2	0	21	0	0	1
11/	0/56	7071	0	28	2	16	16500	0	0	0	8	150250	0	3	2	21	0	0	1
11/	0/56	7071	0	26	2	12	18000	0	0	0	8	150250	0	3	2	21	0	0	1

6	8	10	1	5	12	14	15	18	24	25	26	28	29	35	40	41	42	44	45	80
TØ	TØ	TØ	TØ		TØ		TØ	TØ			TØ		TØ	TØ			TØ			
7	9	11	4		13		17	23			27		34	39			43			
11/ 0/56			7071	0	26	2	12	18000	0	0	0	8	150250	0	3	2	21	0	0	1
11/ 0/56			7071	0	36	2	12	31500	0	0	0	8	150250	0	3	0	21	0	0	1
11/ 0/56			7003	0	8	2	24	32500	0	0	0	0	12500	0	3	0	26	0	0	1
11/ 0/56			7016	0	20	2	12	38000	0	0	0	0	12500	0	3	0	26	0	0	1
11/ 0/56			920	0	12	2	72	14000	0	0	0	0	10500	0	0	0	18	0	0	1
11/ 0/56			7232	0	1	2	36	15500	0	0	0	0	15000	0	0	0	28	0	0	1
11/ 0/56			2244	0	2	2	12	11000	0	0	0	1	40000	0	0	0	18	0	0	1
11/ 0/56			2259	0	2	2	12	14000	0	0	0	1	41000	0	0	0	18	0	0	1
11/ 0/56			2650	0	18	2	24	8000	0	0	0	8	150250	0	0	0	21	0	0	1
12/ 0/56			862	0	9	3	36	10170	0	0	0	6	0	4000	7	0	0	0	0	1
12/ 0/56			1283	0	2	3	38	16657	0	0	0	5	0	805	0	0	18	0	0	1
12/ 0/56			7227	0	1	3	30	16700	0	4	21	5	0	725	0	0	0	0	0	1
12/ 0/56			396	0	2	3	42	16704	0	0	0	5	0	850	0	0	18	0	0	1
12/ 0/56			7006	0	48	3	60	19000	0	0	0	6	0	3500	0	0	4	0	0	1
12/ 0/56			7006	0	48	3	60	19000	0	0	0	6	0	3500	0	0	4	0	0	1
12/ 0/56			1275	0	30	3	60	19000	0	0	0	5	0	460	0	0	18	0	0	1
12/ 0/56			7249	0	48	3	60	36000	0	0	0	6	0	3400	7	0	12	0	0	1
12/ 0/56			7249	0	54	3	120	50000	0	0	0	6	0	3000	0	0	12	0	0	1
12/ 0/56			1821	0	7	2	6	13500	0	0	0	8	300400	0	0	2	18	0	0	1
12/ 0/56			442	0	22	2	12	14000	0	0	0	8	150250	0	0	2	4	0	0	1
12/ 0/56			2501	0	31	2	12	14500	0	0	0	8	150250	0	0	2	4	0	0	1
12/ 0/56			3677	0	27	2	19	30000	0	0	0	8	150250	0	0	2	4	0	0	1
12/ 0/56			7036	0	18	2	60	32000	0	2	16	0	9000	0	0	2	16	0	0	1
12/ 0/56			3783	0	10	2	3	39000	0	0	0	8	200450	0	0	2	21	0	0	1
12/ 0/56			1821	0	1	2	6	13500	0	0	0	1	45000	0	2	0	18	0	0	1
12/ 0/56			442	0	10	2	12	14000	0	0	0	8	175275	0	2	0	4	0	0	1
12/ 0/56			2501	0	7	2	12	14500	0	0	0	8	200350	0	2	0	4	0	0	1
12/ 0/56			2501	0	19	2	12	14500	0	0	0	8	175275	0	2	2	4	0	0	1
12/ 0/56			1272	0	0	2	3	15000	0	2	16	0	20000	0	2	0	16	0	0	1
12/ 0/56			1272	0	3	2	15	15000	0	2	16	0	15000	0	2	2	16	0	0	1
12/ 0/56			3677	0	10	2	5	30000	0	0	0	8	200350	0	2	0	4	0	0	1
12/ 0/56			3677	0	15	2	12	30000	0	0	0	8	175275	0	2	2	4	0	0	1
12/ 0/56			3783	0	1	2	4	39000	0	0	0	8	300450	0	2	0	21	0	0	1
12/ 0/56			3783	0	5	2	5	39000	0	0	0	8	200375	0	2	2	21	0	0	1
12/ 0/56			2557	0	1	2	24	8500	0	0	0	1	30000	0	0	0	18	0	0	1
12/ 0/56			1040	0	3	2	12	15500	0	0	0	8	300480	0	0	0	18	0	0	1
1/ 0/57			3026	0	9	3	18	16755	0	0	21	5	0	800	0	0	18	0	0	1
1/ 0/57			7004	0	2	3	12	16600	0	0	0	5	0	850	0	0	23	0	0	1
1/ 0/57			7012	0	50	3	60	25000	0	0	0	6	0	3406	0	0	4	0	0	1
1/ 0/57			7233	0	36	3	60	20000	0	0	0	6	0	3406	0	0	4	0	0	1
1/ 0/57			7014	0	46	3	60	20000	0	0	0	6	0	3500	0	0	4	0	0	1
1/ 0/57			3779	0	38	3	60	19500	0	0	0	6	0	3500	0	0	4	0	0	1
1/ 0/57			2785	0	52	3	60	16300	0	0	0	6	0	3100	0	0	4	0	0	1
1/ 0/57			2500	0	31	3	60	14290	0	0	0	6	0	2903	0	0	4	0	0	1

| 6 | 8 | 10 | 1 | 5 | 12 | 14 | 15 | 18 | 24 | 25 | 26 | 28 | 29 | 35 | 40 | 41 | 42 | 44 | 45 | 80 |
| TØ | TØ | TØ | TØ | | TØ | | TØ | TØ | | | TØ | | TØ | TØ | | | TØ | | | |
7	9	11	4		13		17	23			27		34	39			43			
1/	0/57	7026	0	48	3	84	45000	0	0	0	6		0	3006	0	0	12	0	0	1
1/	0/57	7235	0	48	3	84	47000	0	0	0	6		0	3006	0	0	12	0	0	1
1/	0/57	2785	0	52	3	60	15500	0	0	0	6		0	3100	0	2	4	0	0	1
1/	0/57	7244	0	56	3	60	18000	0	0	0	6		0	3309	0	2	4	0	0	1
1/	0/57	1238	0	8	2	6	9000	0	0	0	1		200450	0	0	2	21	0	0	1
1/	0/57	1236	0	9	2	5	9000	0	0	0	8		200450	0	0	2	21	0	0	1
1/	0/57	7246	0	25	2	1	11000	0	0	0	8		175275	0	0	2	21	0	0	1
1/	0/57	2425	0	26	2	15	11500	0	0	0	8		150250	0	0	2	4	0	0	1
1/	0/57	206	0	26	2	9	13500	0	0	0	8		150250	0	0	2	4	0	0	1
1/	0/57	2708	0	26	2	12	14000	0	0	0	8		175275	0	0	2	21	0	0	1
1/	0/57	935	0	14	2	12	14000	0	0	0	8		175275	0	0	2	21	0	0	1
1/	0/57	217	0	14	2	12	14500	0	0	0	8		175275	0	0	2	21	0	0	1
1/	0/57	381	0	27	2	12	15500	0	0	0	8		150250	0	0	2	12	0	0	1
1/	0/57	7243	0	27	2	15	17500	0	0	0	8		150250	0	0	2	4	0	0	1
1/	0/57	7064	0	42	2	36	19500	0	0	0	0		11200	0	0	2	16	0	0	1
1/	0/57	3850	0	6	2	6	30000	0	0	0	1		200450	0	0	2	21	0	0	1
1/	0/57	1238	0	2	2	6	9000	0	0	0	1		200350	0	2	0	21	0	0	1
1/	0/57	1236	0	2	2	1	9000	0	0	0	1		36000	0	2	0	21	0	0	1
1/	0/57	1236	0	3	2	6	9000	0	0	0	8		200350	0	2	2	21	0	0	1
1/	0/57	7246	0	3	2	1	11000	0	0	0	8		200450	0	2	0	21	0	0	1
1/	0/57	7246	0	15	2	4	11000	0	0	0	8		200350	0	2	2	21	0	0	1
1/	0/57	7246	0	19	2	6	11000	0	0	0	8		200450	0	2	2	21	0	0	1
1/	0/57	2425	0	5	2	9	11500	0	0	0	8		200350	0	2	0	4	0	0	1
1/	0/57	2425	0	14	2	12	11500	0	0	0	8		175275	0	2	2	4	0	0	1
1/	0/57	1369	0	15	2	12	12500	0	0	0	8		175275	0	2	0	4	0	0	1
1/	0/57	206	0	7	2	7	13500	0	0	0	8		200350	0	2	0	4	0	0	1
1/	0/57	206	0	14	2	12	13500	0	0	0	8		175275	0	2	2	4	0	0	1
1/	0/57	2708	0	8	2	18	14000	0	0	0	8		200350	0	2	0	21	0	0	1
1/	0/57	935	0	5	2	9	14000	0	0	0	8		200350	0	2	0	21	0	0	1
1/	0/57	217	0	2	2	12	14500	0	0	0	8		200375	0	2	0	21	0	0	1
1/	0/57	381	0	3	2	12	15500	0	0	0	8		200350	0	2	0	12	0	0	1
1/	0/57	381	0	15	2	12	15500	0	0	0	8		175275	0	2	2	12	0	0	1
1/	0/57	7243	0	6	2	9	17500	0	0	0	8		200350	0	2	0	4	0	0	1
1/	0/57	7243	0	15	2	12	17500	0	0	0	8		175275	0	2	2	4	0	0	1
1/	0/57	7244	0	21	2	5	18000	0	0	0	8		175275	0	2	0	4	0	0	1
1/	0/57	7064	0	6	2	36	19500	0	0	0	0		11500	0	2	0	16	0	0	1
1/	0/57	3850	0	2	2	4	30000	0	0	0	1		300450	0	2	0	21	0	0	1
1/	0/57	1369	0	27	2	14	12500	0	0	0	8		150250	0	3	2	4	0	0	1
1/	0/57	7244	0	41	2	15	18000	0	0	0	8		150250	0	3	2	4	0	0	1
1/	0/57	808	0	2	2	12	15000	0	0	0	0		17000	0	0	0	23	0	0	1
1/	0/57	7016	0	11	2	84	17000	0	2	16	0		11250	0	0	0	18	0	0	1
1/	0/57	2369	0	0	2	60	18000	0	2	16	0		11250	0	0	0	18	0	0	1
1/	0/57	2443	0	6	2	30	19000	0	2	16	0		15000	0	0	0	18	0	0	1
1/	0/57	7200	0	24	2	60	25000	1	0	0	0		12400	0	0	0	0	0	0	1

6 TØ 7	8 TØ 9	10 TØ 11	1 TØ 4	5	12 TØ 13	14	15 TØ 17	18 TØ 23	24	25	26 TØ 27	28	29 TØ 34	35 TØ 39	40	41	42 TØ 43	44	45	80
1/	0/57	7200	0	24	2	60	25000	1	0	0	0	12400	0	0	0	0	0	0	1
1/	0/57	7200	0	24	2	60	25000	1	0	0	0	12400	0	0	0	0	0	0	1
1/	0/57	7200	0	24	2	60	25000	1	0	0	0	12400	0	0	0	0	0	0	1
1/	0/57	7200	0	24	2	60	25000	0	0	0	0	11975	0	0	0	0	0	0	1
1/	0/57	7200	0	24	2	60	25000	0	0	0	0	11975	0	0	0	0	0	0	1
1/	0/57	7200	0	24	2	60	25000	0	0	0	0	11975	0	0	0	0	0	0	1
1/	0/57	7200	0	24	2	60	25000	0	0	0	0	11975	0	0	0	0	0	0	1
1/	0/57	7004	0	24	2	60	26500	0	0	0	0	13200	0	0	0	0	0	0	1
1/	0/57	7004	0	24	2	60	26500	0	0	0	0	13200	0	0	0	0	0	0	1
1/	0/57	7245	0	24	2	60	32650	0	0	0	0	12500	0	0	0	0	0	0	1
1/	0/57	7004	0	24	2	60	35000	0	0	0	0	13000	0	0	0	0	0	0	1
1/	0/57	7004	0	24	2	60	35000	0	0	0	0	13000	0	0	0	0	0	0	1
1/	0/57	7200	0	24	2	60	65000	0	0	0	0	8500	0	0	0	0	0	0	1
2/	0/57	2556	0	2	3	42	18500	0	0	0	6	0	5500	0	0	18	0	0	1
2/	0/57	1835	0	8	3	36	18000	0	0	0	6	0	5000	0	0	18	0	0	1
2/	0/57	396	0	4	3	60	16216	0	0	0	5	0	550	0	0	18	1	0	1
2/	0/57	142	0	7	3	60	9736	0	0	0	5	0	520	0	0	18	1	0	1
2/	0/57	7032	0	24	3	60	31000	0	0	0	6	0	3405	0	0	12	0	0	1
2/	0/57	7236	0	26	3	60	37000	0	0	0	6	0	3306	0	0	4	0	0	1
2/	0/57	373	0	72	3	84	32722	0	0	0	6	0	3000	0	0	20	0	0	1
2/	0/57	7002	0	36	3	120	65000	0	0	0	5	0	315	0	0	28	0	0	1
2/	0/57	7221	0	36	3	120	65000	0	0	0	5	0	300	0	0	28	0	0	1
2/	0/57	7221	0	36	3	120	65000	0	0	0	5	0	300	0	0	28	0	0	1
2/	0/57	7221	0	36	3	120	65000	0	0	0	5	0	320	0	0	28	0	0	1
2/	0/57	7009	0	36	3	120	84000	0	0	0	5	0	315	0	0	28	0	0	1
2/	0/57	2528	0	29	3	12	11000	1	0	0	5	0	550	0	3	26	0	0	1
2/	0/57	7003	0	18	3	24	20000	1	0	0	5	0	700	0	3	26	0	0	1
2/	0/57	7254	0	48	3	60	40000	0	0	0	5	0	440	0	2	12	0	0	1
2/	0/57	2528	0	5	3	12	11000	1	0	0	5	0	650	3	0	26	0	0	1
2/	0/57	2528	0	17	3	12	11000	1	0	0	5	0	600	3	3	26	0	0	1
2/	0/57	762	0	7	3	12	16779	1	0	0	5	0	750	3	0	26	0	0	1
2/	0/57	1854	0	15	2	3	11000	0	0	0	8	175275	0	0	2	21	0	0	1
2/	0/57	7003	0	14	2	6	14000	0	0	0	8	175275	0	0	2	4	0	0	1
2/	0/57	1018	0	28	2	12	17000	0	0	0	0	12500	0	0	2	18	0	0	1
2/	0/57	1854	0	7	2	8	11000	0	0	0	8	200400	0	2	0	21	0	0	1
2/	0/57	443	0	12	2	12	12500	0	0	0	1	24000	0	2	0	12	0	0	1
2/	0/57	443	0	24	2	12	12500	0	0	0	1	22000	0	2	2	12	0	0	1
2/	0/57	218	0	2	2	12	13500	0	2	16	0	15000	0	2	0	18	0	0	1
2/	0/57	218	0	14	2	12	13500	0	2	16	0	12000	0	2	2	18	0	0	1
2/	0/57	218	0	26	2	24	13500	0	2	16	0	10000	0	2	2	18	0	0	1
2/	0/57	218	0	50	2	12	13500	0	2	16	0	9500	0	2	2	18	0	0	1
2/	0/57	7003	0	8	2	6	14000	0	0	0	8	200400	0	2	0	4	0	0	1
2/	0/57	1777	0	4	2	18	15000	0	1	23	0	13750	0	2	0	18	0	0	1
2/	0/57	1018	0	4	2	12	17000	0	0	0	0	15000	0	2	0	18	0	0	1

294   APPENDIX D

6 TØ 7	8 TØ 9	10 TØ 11	1 TØ 4	5	12 TØ 13	14	15 TØ 17	18 TØ 23	24	25	26 TØ 27	28	29 TØ 34	35 TØ 39	40	41	42 TØ 43	44	45	80
2/	0/57	1018	0	16	2	12	17000	0	0	0	0	13750	0	2	2	18	0	0	1
2/	0/57	443	0	36	2	312	12500	0	0	0	1	20000	0	3	2	12	0	0	1
2/	0/57	1496	0	5	2	12	13500	0	2	16	0	18000	0	0	0	18	0	0	1
2/	0/57	7003	0	5	2	60	15000	0	2	16	0	11500	0	0	0	18	0	0	1
2/	0/57	3147	0	3	1	6	43000	0	5	16	0	12000	0	0	0	18	0	0	1
2/	0/57	2990	0	2	2	12	13500	0	0	0	8	200400	0	0	0	4	0	0	1
3/	0/57	1232	0	2	3	36	24223	0	0	0	5	0	750	0	0	13	0	0	1
3/	0/57	2429	0	19	3	60	19995	0	0	0	6	0	3400	0	0	23	0	0	1
3/	0/57	1483	0	22	3	60	13400	0	0	0	6	0	3300	0	0	23	0	0	1
3/	0/57	1861	0	3	3	60	12478	0	0	0	5	0	420	0	0	18	0	0	1
3/	0/57	7237	0	21	3	60	31000	0	0	0	5	0	480	0	0	25	0	0	1
3/	0/57	7004	0	36	3	180	40000	0	0	0	5	0	260	0	0	18	0	0	1
3/	0/57	7221	0	21	3	120	46500	0	0	0	5	0	375	0	0	23	0	0	1
3/	0/57	7008	0	42	3	120	65000	0	0	0	5	0	325	0	0	28	0	0	1
3/	0/57	7036	0	75	3	60	41000	0	0	0	6	0	3100	0	3	23	0	0	1
3/	0/57	7063	0	15	3	24	19400	0	0	0	6	0	4500	3	0	23	0	0	1
3/	0/57	1505	0	39	3	18	32100	0	0	0	6	0	3306	3	3	23	0	0	1
3/	0/57	7036	0	57	3	18	47000	0	0	0	6	0	3106	3	3	23	0	0	1
3/	0/57	2683	0	16	2	12	9000	0	0	0	8	75400	0	0	2	18	0	0	1
3/	0/57	2395	0	28	2	12	11500	0	0	0	1	20000	0	0	2	12	0	0	1
3/	0/57	3000	0	41	2	36	12500	0	0	0	0	10000	0	0	2	18	0	0	1
3/	0/57	2683	0	4	2	12	9000	0	0	0	8	200410	0	2	0	18	0	0	1
3/	0/57	2395	0	4	2	12	11500	0	0	0	1	23500	0	2	0	12	0	0	1
3/	0/57	2395	0	16	2	12	11500	0	0	0	1	21500	0	2	2	12	0	0	1
3/	0/57	3000	0	5	2	36	12500	0	0	0	0	12000	0	2	0	18	0	0	1
3/	0/57	7064	0	1	2	14	18500	0	0	0	0	15000	0	2	0	23	0	0	1
3/	0/57	2536	0	2	2	60	17500	0	0	0	0	11250	0	0	0	18	0	0	1
3/	0/57	3798	0	7	2	12	30000	0	0	0	0	14000	0	0	0	16	0	0	1
3/	0/57	7064	0	15	2	102	18000	0	0	0	5	0	395	0	2	23	0	0	1
4/	0/57	7238	0	55	3	144	45000	0	0	0	6	0	2803	0	0	0	0	0	1
4/	0/57	2994	0	1	2	12	15500	0	0	0	0	13500	0	0	0	14	0	0	1
4/	0/57	7247	0	3	2	12	32000	0	0	0	0	8000	0	0	0	71	0	0	1
4/	0/57	7009	0	0	2	120	80000	0	2	16	0	5500	0	0	0	18	0	0	1
4/	0/57	7009	0	12	2	120	100000	0	2	16	0	5500	0	0	0	18	0	0	1
5/	0/57	3129	0	12	3	60	17865	0	0	0	6	0	3400	0	0	10	0	0	1
5/	0/57	7036	0	13	3	60	40000	0	0	0	5	0	325	0	0	23	0	0	1
5/	0/57	7241	0	20	3	60	39000	0	0	0	5	0	420	0	0	7	0	0	1
5/	0/57	7240	0	44	3	180	65000	0	0	0	5	0	295	0	0	26	0	0	1
5/	0/57	3855	0	19	3	84	41000	0	0	0	6	0	3000	0	0	7	0	0	1
5/	0/57	3833	0	19	3	84	41000	0	0	0	6	0	3000	0	0	7	0	0	1
5/	0/57	3814	0	19	3	84	41000	0	0	0	6	0	3000	0	0	7	0	0	1
5/	0/57	3843	0	32	3	144	46000	0	0	0	6	0	2706	0	0	12	0	0	1
5/	0/57	7239	0	16	3	26	32800	0	0	0	5	0	690	0	3	18	0	0	1
5/	0/57	7032	0	56	3	120	50600	0	0	0	6	0	2706	0	3	12	0	0	1

CHARTERS 295

6 TØ 7	8 TØ 9	10 TØ 11	1 TØ 4	5	12 TØ 13	14	15 TØ 17	18 TØ 23	24	25	26 TØ 27	28	29 TØ 34	35 TØ 39	40	41	42 TØ 43	44	45	80
5/	0/57	2214	0	6	3	10	18774	0	0	0	5	0	690	3	0	18	0	0	1	
5/	0/57	3092	0	32	3	24	26684	0	0	0	6	0	2906	3	0	12	0	0	1	
5/	0/57	2032	0	4	2	24	15000	0	0	0	0	12000	0	0	0	17	0	0	1	
5/	0/57	7216	0	3	2	24	15500	0	0	0	0	13000	0	0	0	17	0	0	1	
5/	0/57	7216	0	3	2	24	15500	0	0	0	0	13000	0	0	0	17	0	0	1	
5/	0/57	7216	0	3	2	24	15500	0	0	0	0	13000	0	0	0	17	0	0	1	
5/	0/57	332	0	1	2	12	16000	0	0	0	0	12000	0	0	0	17	0	0	1	
5/	0/57	3321	0	2	2	12	11000	0	0	0	1	14500	0	0	0	10	0	0	1	
5/	0/57	1054	0	2	2	12	15500	0	2	10	1	14500	0	0	0	0	0	0	1	
6/	0/57	3365	0	16	3	60	16556	0	0	0	6	0	3103	0	0	18	0	0	1	
6/	0/57	7098	0	18	3	60	25000	0	0	0	6	0	3000	0	0	7	0	0	1	
6/	0/57	2947	0	1	3	13	16485	0	0	0	6	0	3906	7	0	18	0	0	1	
6/	0/57	2995	0	1	3	14	16485	0	0	0	6	0	3809	7	0	18	0	0	1	
6/	0/57	793	0	1	2	12	15000	0	1	23	0	10750	0	0	0	14	0	0	1	
7/	0/57	3346	0	13	3	60	16721	0	0	0	5	0	431	0	0	0	0	0	1	
7/	0/57	7003	0	30	3	180	68000	0	0	0	5	0	295	0	0	26	0	0	1	
7/	0/57	7263	0	12	3	180	46000	0	0	0	5	0	318	0	0	28	0	0	1	
7/	0/57	7258	0	9	3	120	40000	0	0	0	5	0	325	0	0	28	0	0	1	
7/	0/57	1255	0	1	3	36	10670	0	6	13	5	0	475	0	0	0	0	0	1	
7/	0/57	1255	0	1	3	36	10670	1	6	13	5	0	515	0	0	0	0	0	1	
7/	0/57	3139	0	0	1	6	14000	0	2	16	0	9000	0	0	1	18	0	0	1	
7/	0/57	3139	0	2	1	1	14000	0	2	16	0	5500	0	1	0	18	0	0	1	
7/	0/57	193	0	5	2	24	12000	0	9	6	0	9000	0	0	0	18	0	0	1	
7/	0/57	3788	0	2	2	12	36000	0	0	0	0	7950	0	0	0	8	0	0	1	
7/	0/57	978	0	2	2	12	9500	0	4	10	1	11500	0	0	0	13	0	0	1	
7/	0/57	2522	0	2	2	12	11000	1	0	0	2	138242	0	0	0	12	0	0	1	
7/	0/57	7002	0	3	2	12	16460	0	0	0	5	0	550	0	0	18	0	0	1	
8/	0/57	191	0	12	3	60	20641	0	0	0	5	0	385	0	0	18	0	0	1	
8/	0/57	7242	0	13	3	60	22000	0	0	0	5	0	395	0	0	18	0	0	1	
8/	0/57	3922	0	6	3	84	21500	0	0	0	6	0	2806	0	0	18	0	0	1	
8/	0/57	7258	0	24	3	84	47000	0	0	0	6	0	2406	0	0	18	0	0	1	
8/	0/57	7258	0	14	3	84	39250	0	0	0	6	0	2500	0	0	18	0	0	1	
8/	0/57	251	0	4	2	12	15000	0	0	0	0	11000	0	0	2	17	0	0	1	
8/	0/57	251	0	1	2	3	15000	0	0	0	0	10750	0	2	0	17	0	0	1	
8/	0/57	7005	0	1	2	12	10000	0	9	8	0	8900	0	0	0	0	0	0	1	
8/	0/57	262	0	1	2	24	15000	0	0	0	0	11250	0	0	0	17	0	0	1	
8/	0/57	261	0	6	2	20	15000	0	0	0	0	11000	0	0	0	17	0	0	1	
8/	0/57	2031	0	2	2	12	15000	0	0	0	0	10500	0	0	0	0	0	0	1	
8/	0/57	1301	0	1	2	12	15500	0	0	0	0	10500	0	0	0	28	0	0	1	
8/	0/57	2171	0	2	2	12	22000	0	0	0	0	10750	0	0	0	17	0	0	1	
8/	0/57	7222	0	2	2	12	30000	1	0	0	0	10750	0	0	0	17	0	0	1	
9/	0/57	7200	0	27	3	84	47800	0	0	0	6	0	2300	7	0	20	0	0	1	
9/	0/57	7003	0	4	2	30	18000	0	1	10	0	6000	0	0	0	25	0	0	1	
9/	0/57	7002	0	0	2	12	30000	0	0	0	0	5000	0	0	0	18	0	0	1	

APPENDIX D

6 TØ 7	8 TØ 9	10 TØ 11	1 TØ 4	5	12 TØ 13	14	15 TØ 17	18 TØ 23	24	25	26 TØ 27	28	29 TØ 34	35 TØ 39	40	41	42 TØ 43	44	45	80
9/	0/57	3950	0	1	2	12	10000	1	0	0	1	11500	0	0	0	26	0	0	1
9/	0/57	148	0	3	2	12	14500	0	0	10	1	8500	0	0	0	13	0	0	1
9/	0/57	3923	0	2	2	6	40000	0	0	0	1	8000	0	0	0	23	0	0	1
9/	0/57	3331	0	1	2	12	11000	1	0	9	8	130190	0	0	0	18	0	0	1
10/	0/57	3167	0	3	3	24	5325	3	0	0	5	0	675	0	0	12	0	0	1
10/	0/57	7255	0	8	3	60	26000	0	0	0	6	0	2409	0	0	18	0	0	1
10/	0/57	7001	0	3	2	12	18000	0	1	20	0	6000	0	0	0	18	0	0	1
11/	0/57	1657	0	26	3	60	19000	1	0	0	6	0	2602	0	0	26	0	0	1
11/	0/57	1273	0	24	3	60	18590	1	0	0	6	0	2602	0	0	26	0	0	1
11/	0/57	8	0	1	3	24	9605	0	0	0	6	0	2000	7	0	12	0	0	1
11/	0/57	2900	0	38	3	36	16600	0	0	0	6	0	2411	0	3	7	0	0	1
11/	0/57	1362	0	36	3	36	17360	0	0	0	6	0	2509	0	3	7	0	0	1
11/	0/57	2900	0	14	3	24	16600	0	0	0	5	0	359	3	0	7	0	0	1
11/	0/57	362	0	12	3	24	17360	0	0	0	5	0	355	3	0	7	0	0	1
11/	0/57	3055	0	11	2	10	11500	1	0	0	8	125190	0	0	0	18	0	0	1
12/	0/57	327	0	9	3	60	16875	1	0	0	6	0	2505	0	0	7	0	0	1
12/	0/57	-346	0	12	3	60	16220	1	0	0	6	0	2411	0	0	7	0	0	1
12/	0/57	3382	0	1	3	12	16460	0	1	20	5	0	280	0	0	18	0	0	1
12/	0/57	3341	0	10	3	24	16556	0	0	0	5	0	345	3	0	18	0	0	1
12/	0/57	2559	0	1	2	12	15000	0	0	9	0	7000	0	0	0	18	0	0	1
12/	0/57	1482	0	3	2	12	15500	0	2	16	0	5150	0	0	0	18	0	0	1
12/	0/57	1443	0	2	2	12	16000	0	2	16	0	5500	0	0	0	18	0	0	1
12/	0/57	1247	0	0	2	12	28000	0	0	0	0	5000	0	0	0	18	0	0	1
12/	0/57	448	0	3	1	8	11500	0	0	0	1	9500	0	6	0	18	0	0	1

2. *Tie-ups* (Monthly)

1 TØ 2	3 TØ 4	5 TØ 6	7 TØ 11	12 TØ 16	17 TØ 19	20 TØ 22	23 TØ 27	28 TØ 30	31 TØ 33	34 TØ 36	37 TØ 39	80
1/	1/49		4170	9692	43	100	10026	240	100	103	100	4
2/	1/49		4130	9673	43	100	10003	240	100	103	100	4
3/	1/49		4073	9607	42	98	9981	242	101	103	100	4
4/	1/49		4014	9640	42	100	10033	243	100	104	101	4
5/	1/49		3988	9390	42	100	10051	250	103	104	100	4
6/	1/49		3950	9113	43	102	10048	252	101	107	103	4
7/	1/49		3809	9056	42	98	9967	252	100	109	102	4
8/	1/49		3730	8994	41	98	10010	263	104	111	102	4
9/	1/49		3658	9353	39	95	9981	268	102	111	100	4
10/	1/49		3539	9679	37	95	9998	273	102	107	96	4
11/	1/49		3432	10004	28	76	10083	285	104	104	97	4
12/	1/49		3461	10386	33	118	10108	295	104	101	97	4
1/	1/50		3325	10439	32	97	9938	287	97	96	95	4
2/	1/50		3191	10603	30	94	9941	299	104	95	99	4
3/	1/50		3200	10722	30	100	10149	318	106	96	101	4
4/	1/50		3234	10906	30	100	10103	316	99	94	98	4
5/	1/50		3011	11067	28	93	9981	309	98	92	98	4
6/	1/50		3198	11106	29	104	10204	339	110	92	100	4
7/	1/50		3167	11352	28	97	10101	316	93	91	99	4
8/	1/50		3221	11427	28	100	10143	320	101	89	98	4
9/	1/50		3232	11465	28	100	10082	313	98	88	99	4
10/	1/50		3179	11656	27	96	10048	311	99	88	100	4
11/	1/50		3081	11911	26	96	10023	315	101	86	98	4
12/	1/50		3221	11879	27	104	10296	334	106	86	100	4
1/	1/51		3091	11977	26	96	9892	307	92	83	97	4
2/	1/51		3558	12130	29	112	10500	340	111	88	106	4
3/	1/51		4057	12290	33	114	10658	300	88	88	100	4
4/	1/51		4098	12345	33	100	10137	250	83	82	93	4
5/	1/51		4825	12512	39	118	10871	265	106	88	107	4
6/	1/51		5537	12459	44	113	10842	225	85	87	99	4
7/	1/51		5828	12433	47	107	10369	187	83	83	95	4
8/	1/51		6002	12570	48	102	10227	175	94	82	99	4
9/	1/51		6533	12669	52	108	10652	177	101	85	104	4
10/	1/51		6464	12731	51	98	10082	154	87	80	94	4
11/	1/51		6444	12934	50	98	10100	156	101	79	99	4
12/	1/51		7038	12875	55	110	10696	167	107	83	95	4
1/	1/52		7288	12794	57	104	10260	146	87	80	92	4
2/	1/52		8010	12991	62	109	10870	149	102	85	96	4
3/	1/52		8527	13183	65	105	10634	133	89	82	106	4
4/	1/52		8723	13241	66	102	10363	122	92	79	96	4
5/	1/52		8855	13299	67	102	10243	117	96	77	97	4
6/	1/52		9083	13414	68	101	10374	117	100	78	101	4
7/	1/52		9173	13541	68	100	10265	113	97	77	99	4
8/	1/52		9516	13392	71	104	10392	113	100	77	100	4

Headings refer to card columns. See Appendix C.2 for explanation.

298 APPENDIX D

1 TØ 2	3 TØ 4	5 TØ 6	7 TØ 11	12 TØ 16	17 TØ 19	20 TØ 22	23 TØ 27	28 TØ 30	31 TØ 33	34 TØ 36	37 TØ 39	80
9/ 1/52			9845	13419	73	103	10470	110	97	78	101	4
10/ 1/52			9792	13800	71	97	10083	102	93	75	96	4
11/ 1/52			9850	13815	71	100	10077	103	101	73	97	4
12/ 1/52			10009	13904	72	101	10368	105	102	75	103	4
1/ 1/53			9846	14045	70	97	9909	99	94	71	95	4
2/ 1/53			9636	14133	68	97	9949	101	102	71	100	4
3/ 1/53			9860	14079	70	103	10436	108	107	74	104	4
4/ 1/53			9856	14372	69	99	10236	104	96	73	99	4
5/ 1/53			9511	14534	65	94	9774	99	95	68	93	4
6/ 1/53			9476	14404	66	102	10161	107	108	70	103	4
7/ 1/53			9163	14461	63	95	9905	105	105	69	99	4
8/ 1/53			8979	14752	61	97	10014	109	104	69	100	4
9/ 1/53			8966	14837	60	98	10148	113	104	69	100	4
10/ 1/53			8709	14924	58	97	9946	111	95	67	97	4
11/ 1/53			8539	15008	57	98	10039	115	104	67	100	4
12/ 1/53			8437	15247	55	96	10212	120	104	68	199	4
1/ 1/54			8131	16405	50	91	9984	118	98	65	96	4
2/ 1/54			8002	16605	48	96	10015	123	105	60	102	4
3/ 1/54			7676	16820	46	96	9937	124	101	59	98	4
4/ 1/54			7401	16789	44	96	9960	130	105	59	100	4
5/ 1/54			7362	16542	45	102	10105	137	105	61	103	4
6/ 1/54			7235	16526	44	98	10083	137	100	61	100	4
7/ 1/54			6874	16555	42	95	9978	138	101	60	98	4
8/ 1/54			6779	16519	41	98	10015	146	106	61	102	4
9/ 1/54			6491	16953	38	93	10074	149	102	59	97	4
10/ 1/54			6185	17620	35	95	10020	154	103	57	97	4
11/ 1/54			6045	17990	34	97	10005	162	105	56	98	4
12/ 1/54			5984	18243	33	97	10242	166	102	56	100	4
1/ 1/55			5844	18650	31	94	10070	168	101	54	96	4
2/ 1/55			5956	18857	32	103	10285	176	105	55	102	4
3/ 1/55			5736	19034	30	94	10054	169	96	53	96	4
4/ 1/55			5746	19004	30	100	10157	177	105	53	100	4
5/ 1/55			5675	19075	30	100	10119	176	99	53	100	4
6/ 1/55			5926	19011	31	103	10381	183	104	55	104	4
7/ 1/55			5680	19065	30	97	9984	168	92	52	95	4
8/ 1/55			6118	19106	32	107	10416	183	109	55	106	4
9/ 1/55			6441	19342	33	103	10513	172	94	54	98	4
10/ 1/55			7040	19528	36	109	10776	167	97	55	102	4
11/ 1/55			8025	19733	41	114	11221	159	95	57	104	4
12/ 1/55			9004	20035	45	110	11132	139	87	56	98	4
1/ 1/56			9374	20340	46	102	10667	118	85	52	93	4
2/ 1/56			9800	20537	48	104	10618	113	96	52	100	4
3/ 1/56			9967	20611	48	100	10362	106	94	50	96	4
4/ 1/56			10411	20739	50	104	10600	106	100	51	102	4

TIE-UPS (MONTHLY)

1 TO 2	3 TO 4	5 TO 6	7 TO 10	11 TO 14	15 TO 19	20 TO 22	23 TO 25	26 TO 28	29 TO 31	80
5/	1/56		99	1305	20631	5	63	125	124	3
6/	1/56		87	1220	21153	4	58	80	92	3
7/	1/56		69	1219	21377	3	57	75	98	3
8/	1/56		69	1256	21567	3	58	100	102	3
9/	1/56		64	1366	21630	3	63	100	109	3
10/	1/56		53	1202	21965	2	55	67	87	3
11/	1/56		50	1033	22062	2	47	100	85	3
12/	1/56		46	790	22360	2	35	100	74	3
1/	1/57		23	653	22684	1	29	50	83	3
2/	1/57		8	667	22950	0	29	0	100	3
3/	1/57		1	648	23152	0	28	0	97	3
4/	1/57		14	1019	23166	1	44	100	157	3
5/	1/57		41	1366	23154	2	59	200	134	3
6/	1/57		87	1551	23395	4	66	200	112	3
7/	1/57		216	1610	23501	9	69	225	105	3
8/	1/57		357	1744	23667	15	74	167	107	3
9/	1/57		646	2208	23438	28	94	187	127	3
10/	1/57		888	2372	23451	38	101	136	107	3
11/	1/57		1091	2337	23616	46	99	121	98	3
12/	1/57		1248	2223	24015	52	93	113	94	3

3. *New Orders* (Monthly)

	1 TØ 2	3 TØ 4	5 TØ 6	7 TØ 10	11 TØ 14	15 TØ 19	20 TØ 22	23 TØ 25	26 TØ 28	29 TØ 31	80
1/ 1/49			68.0	1031.0	9692.0		7.0	106.0	100	105	3
2/ 1/49			68.0	1085.0	9673.0		7.0	112.0	100	106	3
3/ 1/49			87.0	1133.0	9607.0		9.0	118.0	129	105	3
4/ 1/49			128.0	1206.0	9640.0		13.0	125.0	144	106	3
5/ 1/49			196.0	1567.0	9393.0		21.0	167.0	162	134	3
6/ 1/49			480.0	2076.0	9113.0		53.0	228.0	252	137	3
7/ 1/49			577.0	2241.0	9056.0		64.0	247.0	121	108	3
8/ 1/49			523.0	2211.0	8994.0		58.0	246.0	91	100	3
9/ 1/49			513.0	1865.0	9353.0		55.0	199.0	95	81	3
10/ 1/49			505.0	1538.0	9679.0		52.0	159.0	95	80	3
11/ 1/49			496.0	1298.0	10004.0		50.0	130.0	96	82	3
12/ 1/49			496.0	910.0	10386.0		48.0	88.0	96	68	3
1/ 1/50			157.0	910.0	10439.0		15.0	87.0	31	100	3
2/ 1/50			175.0	940.0	10303.0		17.0	89.0	113	102	3
3/ 1/50			87.0	1133.0	9607.0		9.0	118.0	129	105	3
4/ 1/50			149.0	868.0	10906.0		14.0	80.0	93	96	3
5/ 1/50			115.0	1024.0	11067.0		10.0	92.0	71	115	3
6/ 1/50			120.0	1068.0	11106.0		11.0	96.0	110	104	3
7/ 1/50			60.0	962.0	11352.0		5.0	85.0	45	89	3
8/ 1/50			60.0	864.0	11427.0		5.0	76.0	100	189	3
9/ 1/50			60.0	903.0	11465.0		5.0	79.0	100	104	3
10/ 1/50			12.0	751.0	11656.0		1.0	64.0	20	81	3
11/ 1/50			12.0	550.0	11911.0		1.0	46.0	100	72	3
12/ 1/50			0.0	543.0	11879.0		0.0	46.0	0	100	3
1/ 1/51			0.0	546.0	11977.0		0.0	46.0	0	100	3
2/ 1/51			0.0	562.0	12130.0		0.0	46.0	0	100	3
3/ 1/51			0.0	540.0	12290.0		0.0	44.0	0	96	3
4/ 1/51			0.0	594.0	12345.0		0.0	848.0	0	109	3
5/ 1/51			0.0	611.0	12512.0		0.0	55.0	0	115	3
6/ 1/51			0.0	839.0	12459.0		0.0	67.0	0	122	3
7/ 1/51			0.0	891.0	12433.0		0.0	72.0	0	107	3
8/ 1/51			0.0	881.0	12570.0		0.0	70.0	0	97	3
9/ 1/51			0.0	866.0	12669.0		0.0	68.0	0	97	3
10/ 1/51			0.0	684.0	12731.0		0.0	54.0	0	79	3
11/ 1/51			0.0	619.0	12934.0		0.0	48.0	0	89	3
12/ 1/51			15.0	640.0	12875.0		1.0	50.0	100	104	3
1/ 1/52			21.0	642.0	12794.0		2.0	50.0	200	100	3
2/ 1/52			21.0	525.0	12991.0		2.0	40.0	100	80	3
3/ 1/52			25.0	586.0	13183.0		2.0	44.0	100	110	3
4/ 1/52			25.0	660.0	13241.0		2.0	50.0	100	114	3
5/ 1/52			25.0	824.0	13299.0		2.0	62.0	100	124	3
6/ 1/52			25.0	943.0	13414.0		2.0	70.0	100	113	3
7/ 1/52			30.0	1098.0	13541.0		2.0	81.0	100	116	3
8/ 1/52			35.0	1282.0	13392.0		3.0	96.0	150	119	3

Headings refer to card columns. See Appendix C.3 for explanation.

NEW ORDERS (MONTHLY)

1 TO 2	3 TO 4	5 TO 6	7 TO 10	11 TO 14	15 TO 19	20 TO 22	23 TO 25	26 TO 28	29 TO 31	80
9/	1/52		38	1290	13419	3	96	100	100	3
10/	1/52		42	1104	13800	3	80	100	83	3
11/	1/52		49	971	13815	4	70	133	88	3
12/	1/52		63	852	13904	5	61	125	87	3
1/	1/53		121	847	14045	9	60	180	98	3
2/	1/53		182	915	14133	13	65	144	108	3
3/	1/53		274	935	14079	19	66	146	102	3
4/	1/53		345	1020	14372	24	71	126	108	3
5/	1/53		499	1150	14534	34	79	142	111	3
6/	1/53		619	1405	14404	43	98	126	124	3
7/	1/53		731	1433	14461	51	99	119	101	3
8/	1/53		822	1572	14752	56	107	110	108	3
9/	1/53		865	1540	14837	58	104	104	97	3
10/	1/53		964	1532	14924	65	103	112	99	3
11/	1/53		908	1361	15008	61	91	94	88	3
12/	1/53		757	1294	15247	50	85	82	93	3
1/	1/54		880	1403	16405	54	86	108	101	3
2/	1/54		860	1340	16605	52	81	96	94	3
3/	1/54		880	1359	16820	52	81	100	100	3
4/	1/54		1020	1562	16789	61	93	117	115	3
5/	1/54		1290	2022	16542	78	122	128	131	3
6/	1/54		1570	2278	16526	95	138	122	113	3
7/	1/54		1800	2580	16555	109	156	113	113	3
8/	1/54		1980	2701	16519	120	164	105	105	3
9/	1/54		1890	2479	16953	111	146	89	89	3
10/	1/54		1560	2050	17620	89	116	79	79	3
11/	1/54		1310	1678	17990	73	93	82	80	3
12/	1/54		1030	1562	18243	56	86	77	92	3
1/	1/55		722	1277	18650	39	68	78	79	3
2/	1/55		593	1195	18857	31	63	79	93	3
3/	1/55		540	1163	19034	28	61	90	97	3
4/	1/55		558	1334	19044	29	70	104	115	3
5/	1/55		554	1644	19075	29	86	100	123	3
6/	1/55		599	1765	19011	32	93	110	108	3
7/	1/55		570	1826	19065	30	96	94	103	3
8/	1/55		495	1799	19106	26	94	87	98	3
9/	1/55		438	1724	19342	23	89	88	95	3
10/	1/55		360	1490	19528	18	76	78	85	3
11/	1/55		311	1303	19733	16	66	89	87	3
12/	1/55		215	1107	20035	11	55	69	83	3
1/	1/56		170	948	20340	8	47	73	85	3
2/	1/56		144	903	20537	7	44	88	94	3
3/	1/56		114	967	20611	6	47	86	107	3
4/	1/56		89	1058	20739	4	51	67	109	3

APPENDIX D

1 TØ 2	3 TØ 4	5 TØ 6	7 TØ 11	12 TØ 16	17 TØ 19	20 TØ 22	23 TØ 27	28 TØ 30	31 TØ 33	34 TØ 36	37 TØ 39	80
5/	1/56		11292	20631	55	110	10946	105	99	53	104	4
6/	1/56		11870	21153	56	102	10948	97	92	52	98	4
7/	1/56		12846	21377	60	107	11133	93	96	52	100	4
8/	1/56		13521	21567	63	105	10859	85	91	50	96	4
9/	1/56		14772	21630	68	108	11379	84	99	53	94	4
10/	1/56		14915	21965	68	100	10357	70	83	47	89	4
11/	1/56		15559	22062	71	104	10743	72	103	49	104	4
12/	1/56		17042	22360	76	107	11623	75	104	52	106	4
1/	1/57		19103	22684	84	111	12341	73	97	54	104	4
2/	1/57		21893	22950	95	113	13064	68	93	57	106	4
3/	1/57		22697	23152	98	103	10999	50	74	48	84	4
4/	1/57		23319	23166	101	103	10903	48	96	47	98	4
5/	1/57		23511	23154	102	101	10470	45	94	45	96	4
6/	1/57		23566	23395	101	99	10512	45	100	45	100	4
7/	1/57		23550	23501	100	99	10167	43	96	45	100	4
8/	1/57		24677	23667	104	104	11451	49	114	48	107	4
9/	1/57		26356	23438	112	108	11979	49	100	51	106	4
10/	1/57		25968	23451	111	99	9872	37	76	42	82	4
11/	1/57		25877	23616	110	99	10096	39	105	43	102	4
12/	1/57		25044	24015	104	95	9483	37	95	39	91	4

4. *Spot Rates* (Monthly)

1 TO 2	3 TO 4	5 TO 6	7 TO 9	10 TO 12	13 TO 16	17 TO 19	20 TO 23	24 TO 26	27 TO 30	31 TO 33	34 TO 37	38 TO 40	41 TO 44	45 TO 47	48 TO 51	52 TO 55	80
1/	1/49	149	102	1108	157	1175	130	650	154	0	0	245	130	967	1102	5
2/	1/49	139	97	1136	162	1080	118	612	145	0	0	233	124	900	1026	5
3/	1/49	123	92	935	131	1080	118	585	139	0	0	200	106	796	908	5
4/	1/49	102	87	0	0	953	103	0	0	0	0	188	100	660	756	5
5/	1/49	86	85	0	0	0	0	0	0	0	0	163	86	556	633	5
6/	1/49	75	72	0	0	0	0	0	0	0	0	142	75	485	553	5
7/	1/49	85	100	0	0	0	0	524	124	111	63	128	68	552	629	5
8/	1/49	68	90	0	0	572	58	0	0	128	73	137	73	441	501	5
9/	1/49	101	122	821	113	762	81	537	127	150	86	160	85	656	747	5
10/	1/49	110	116	797	109	0	0	569	135	179	102	187	99	717	817	5
11/	1/49	111	109	833	115	0	0	408	97	202	115	206	109	720	821	5
12/	1/49	124	111	858	119	0	0	536	127	222	127	236	125	804	916	5
1/	1/50	103	95	843	116	762	81	493	117	183	105	162	86	667	760	5
2/	1/50	97	95	782	107	762	81	450	107	149	85	154	82	630	718	5
3/	1/50	104	100	768	105	0	0	442	105	180	103	184	97	674	750	5
4/	1/50	101	99	811	112	0	0	473	112	158	90	168	89	656	656	5
5/	1/50	104	101	812	112	0	0	466	110	168	96	181	96	674	750	5
6/	1/50	99	98	786	108	787	84	455	108	163	93	172	91	641	730	5
7/	1/50	103	101	787	108	766	81	460	109	186	106	193	102	667	760	5
8/	1/50	124	111	831	115	1087	119	518	123	231	132	252	133	804	804	5
9/	1/50	196	136	1438	207	1497	168	788	187	347	198	371	197	1269	1446	5
10/	1/50	239	130	1769	259	0	0	988	234	404	231	419	222	1548	1775	5
11/	1/50	281	125	2208	337	2096	239	1026	243	456	261	489	259	1820	2075	5
12/	1/50	306	116	2281	326	2234	268	1064	252	553	316	626	332	2022	2263	5
1/	1/51	397	156	2621	390	3048	352	1696	402	727	415	781	414	2574	2934	5
2/	1/51	428	132	2786	415	0	0	1541	365	810	463	855	453	2772	3160	5
3/	1/51	414	114	2798	417	0	0	1828	433	724	414	746	395	2685	3061	5
4/	1/51	346	97	2554	379	0	0	1456	345	563	322	609	323	2244	2559	5
5/	1/51	193	69	1456	211	1460	164	933	221	295	169	333	177	1250	1425	5
6/	1/51	208	90	1596	232	1778	201	741	176	354	202	369	196	1348	1537	5
7/	1/51	178	87	1384	200	0	0	743	176	293	167	302	160	1156	1317	5
8/	1/51	208	104	1635	237	0	0	819	194	336	192	362	192	1348	1537	5
9/	1/51	229	108	1765	258	0	0	993	235	336	206	395	209	1485	1696	5
10/	1/51	305	122	2179	322	0	0	1371	325	504	288	534	283	1987	2255	5
11/	1/51	411	130	3170	474	0	0	1820	431	656	375	659	349	2663	3036	5
12/	1/51	430	117	3187	477	2540	292	1844	437	808	405	834	442	2787	3177	5
1/	1/52	454	111	3157	472	0	0	1792	425	809	462	834	442	2956	3357	5
2/	1/52	444	103	2975	443	0	0	1718	407	803	459	855	453	2878	3281	5
3/	1/52	400	95	2690	400	2540	292	1665	395	761	435	827	438	2593	2955	5
4/	1/52	265	80	2275	336	1270	141	1202	285	418	239	435	231	1719	1959	5
5/	1/52	183	73	1463	212	0	0	865	205	286	163	285	151	1185	1351	5
6/	1/52	188	88	1464	212	0	0	0	0	310	177	331	175	1219	1389	5
7/	1/52	163	87	1216	174	0	0	694	164	277	158	286	152	1056	1203	5
8/	1/52	153	93	0	0	1222	135	0	0	274	157	315	167	1096	1132	5

Headings refer to card columns. See Appendix C.4 for explanation.

APPENDIX D

	1 TØ 2	3 TØ 4	5 TØ 6	7 TØ 9	10 TØ 12	13 TØ 16	17 TØ 19	20 TØ 23	24 TØ 26	27 TØ 30	31 TØ 33	34 TØ 37	38 TØ 40	41 TØ 44	45 TØ 47	48 TØ 51	52 TØ 55	80
9/ 1/52				169	102	0	0	0	0	660	156	296	169	343	182	1040	1250	5
10/ 1/52				149	95	0	0	1058	116	637	151	246	141	312	165	967	1112	5
11/ 1/52				154	99	0	0	1016	111	637	151	265	151	345	183	1000	1140	5
12/ 1/52				146	97	1017	143	1032	113	603	143	257	147	312	165	948	1081	5
1/ 1/53				128	92	890	124	0	0	455	108	205	117	263	239	830	946	5
2/ 1/53				108	88	831	115	857	92	432	102	166	95	209	111	700	798	5
3/ 1/53				99	89	721	98	762	81	0	0	160	91	173	92	641	730	5
4/ 1/53				103	97	728	99	656	68	0	0	201	115	231	122	667	760	5
5/ 1/53				98	96	682	92	698	73	412	98	176	101	214	113	637	727	5
6/ 1/53				88	93	627	83	0	0	377	98	148	85	171	91	570	650	5
7/ 1/53				75	89	385	46	656	68	364	86	158	90	190	101	485	553	5
8/ 1/53				86	102	578	76	635	65	0	0	165	94	205	109	559	638	5
9/ 1/53				80	98	601	79	0	0	0	0	135	77	160	85	519	591	5
10/ 1/53				91	107	673	90	0	0	359	85	161	92	182	97	589	671	5
11/ 1/53				95	106	697	94	0	0	0	0	165	94	181	96	615	701	5
12/ 1/53				98	104	691	93	0	0	421	100	173	99	195	103	638	727	5
1/ 1/54				99	103	708	96	698	73	400	95	176	101	203	108	641	730	5
2/ 1/54				108	106	754	103	0	0	456	108	193	110	206	109	700	798	5
3/ 1/54				102	100	780	107	0	0	466	110	155	89	192	102	660	754	5
4/ 1/54				79	88	596	79	476	47	345	82	140	80	168	89	511	583	5
5/ 1/54				74	90	506	65	0	0	296	70	129	74	166	88	481	549	5
6/ 1/54				63	87	406	58	476	47	296	70	104	59	137	72	407	464	5
7/ 1/54				57	89	388	47	444	43	227	54	88	50	153	81	370	422	5
8/ 1/54				73	110	572	75	508	50	240	57	188	67	177	94	474	549	5
9/ 1/54				97	123	638	85	0	0	371	88	177	101	211	112	630	718	5
10/ 1/54				95	111	641	85	674	70	372	88	186	106	224	119	615	701	5
11/ 1/54				99	108	654	87	791	84	376	89	184	105	235	125	641	730	5
12/ 1/54				131	120	876	122	1027	112	455	108	257	147	300	159	848	967	5
1/ 1/55				134	110	923	129	867	93	544	129	241	138	301	160	870	993	5
2/ 1/55				149	111	1080	153	1111	122	566	134	275	157	299	159	967	1104	5
3/ 1/55				111	92	781	107	826	88	457	108	163	93	257	136	720	821	5
4/ 1/55				86	83	588	77	627	65	339	80	183	82	212	112	559	638	5
5/ 1/55				88	92	607	80	611	63	323	77	177	101	211	112	570	650	5
6/ 1/55				83	93	570	75	578	59	323	77	141	81	207	110	537	612	5
7/ 1/55				108	113	770	105	0	0	411	97	206	118	204	108	700	798	5
8/ 1/55				107	107	761	104	847	91	463	110	177	101	221	117	694	790	5
9/ 1/55				107	104	741	101	831	89	439	104	186	106	235	125	694	790	5
10/ 1/55				109	103	827	114	900	97	457	108	189	108	202	107	709	809	5
11/ 1/55				218	153	561	227	1715	194	912	216	415	237	393	208	1415	1613	5
12/ 1/55				291	145	1968	289	0	0	1131	268	512	293	576	305	1885	2149	5
1/ 1/56				184	119	1267	182	1513	170	709	168	339	194	374	198	1193	1359	5
2/ 1/56				146	97	1029	145	1099	121	559	132	238	136	323	171	948	1081	5
3/ 1/56				144	94	1058	150	1080	118	566	134	265	151	284	151	933	1064	5
4/ 1/56				186	112	1180	168	1372	153	659	156	432	247	403	214	1207	1376	5

5. Gulf Oil Company Charter Data
(Format for Multiple-Correlation Card)

1 TO 4	5 TO 6	7 TO 8	9 TO 10	11 TO 13	14 TO 15	16 TO 18	19 TO 23	24 TO 26	27 TO 29	30 TO 32	33 TO 35	36 TO 38	39 TO 41	42 TO 44	45 TO 47	80
1	1/	1/49	400	6	60	16440	149	102	43	100	105	106	100	100	9
2	1/	1/49	280	30	36	16500	149	102	43	100	105	106	100	100	9
4	1/	1/49	290	33	36	16200	149	102	43	100	105	106	100	100	9
5	2/	1/49	266	24	36	13500	139	97	43	100	106	112	93	95	9
6	2/	1/49	266	24	36	12500	139	97	43	100	106	112	100	100	9
7	2/	1/49	290	30	36	16000	139	97	43	100	106	112	100	100	9
8	2/	1/49	280	24	36	15800	139	97	43	100	106	112	100	100	9
9	2/	1/49	260	1	60	11900	139	97	43	100	106	112	100	100	9
10	2/	1/49	260	1	36	16000	139	97	43	100	106	112	100	100	9
11	2/	1/49	270	24	36	16500	139	97	43	100	106	112	100	100	9
12	2/	1/49	325	18	96	15000	139	97	43	100	106	112	100	100	9
13	3/	1/49	265	12	36	15000	123	92	42	101	105	118	88	95	9
14	11/	1/49	300	4	24	16400	111	109	28	104	82	130	90	118	9
15	11/	1/49	285	4	60	15300	111	109	28	104	82	130	100	100	9
16	11/	1/49	265	3	60	12600	111	109	28	104	82	130	100	100	9
17	1/	1/50	265	24	60	16000	103	95	32	97	82	87	93	87	9
18	1/	1/50	265	24	60	16000	103	95	32	97	100	87	100	100	9
19	1/	1/50	265	24	60	16000	103	95	32	97	100	87	100	100	9
20	1/	1/50	280	36	96	16000	103	95	32	97	100	87	100	100	9
21	2/	8/50	266	24	60	13500	97	95	30	104	100	89	94	100	9
22	2/	8/50	266	24	60	15900	97	95	30	104	102	89	100	100	9
23	2/	1/50	265	8	60	16000	97	95	30	104	102	89	100	100	9
24	5/	4/50	266	24	84	16000	104	101	28	98	102	92	107	106	9
25	7/	1/50	255	6	60	16000	103	101	28	93	115	85	99	100	9
26	8/	1/50	300	4	36	16400	124	111	28	101	89	76	120	110	9
27	9/	1/50	280	3	24	14500	196	136	28	98	89	79	158	123	9
28	9/	1/50	280	12	84	16250	196	136	28	98	104	79	100	100	9
29	9/	1/50	280	24	84	16300	196	136	28	98	104	79	100	100	9
30	9/	1/50	280	36	84	19000	196	136	28	98	104	79	100	100	9
31	9/	1/50	310	3	24	10100	196	136	28	98	104	79	100	100	9
32	11/	1/50	450	3	24	16400	281	125	26	101	72	46	143	92	9

Headings refer to card columns. See Appendix C.5 for explanation.

APPENDIX D

1 TØ 4	5 TØ 6	7 TØ 8	9 TØ 10	11 TØ 13	14 TØ 15	16 TØ 18	19 TØ 23	24 TØ 26	27 TØ 29	30 TØ 32	33 TØ 35	36 TØ 38	39 TØ 41	42 TØ 44	45 TØ 47	80
33	11/ 1/50	370	3	24	9700	281	125	26	101	72	46	100	100	9
34	11/ 8/50	280	18	60	13500	281	125	26	101	72	46	100	100	9
35	11/21/50	304	12	24	17000	281	125	26	101	72	46	100	100	9
36	11/21/50	308	18	24	17500	281	125	26	101	72	46	100	100	9
37	12/ 1/50	335	6	60	16300	306	116	27	106	100	46	109	93	9
40	12/ 1/50	390	6	24	14900	306	116	27	106	100	46	100	100	9
41	12/ 1/50	385	5	60	12500	306	116	27	106	100	46	100	100	9
42	1/ 1/51	390	5	36	18000	397	156	26	92	100	46	130	134	9
43	1/ 1/51	320	18	60	16300	397	156	26	92	100	46	100	100	9
44	1/ 9/50	350	3	60	14000	397	156	26	92	100	46	100	100	9
45	2/15/51	280	36	84	18000	428	132	29	111	100	46	109	85	9
46	2/ 1/51	322	18	60	16000	428	132	29	111	100	46	100	100	9
47	2/ 1/51	335	18	84	14800	428	132	29	111	100	46	100	100	9
48	3/ 1/51	330	12	84	15700	414	114	33	88	96	44	97	86	9
49	3/ 1/51	330	12	24	15700	414	114	33	88	96	44	100	100	9
50	3/ 1/51	210	24	84	15500	414	114	33	88	96	44	100	100	9
51	3/ 1/51	385	12	60	18000	414	114	33	88	96	44	100	100	9
52	3/ 1/51	320	12	60	16000	414	114	33	88	96	44	100	100	9
53	3/ 1/51	370	9	60	16000	414	114	33	88	96	44	100	100	9
54	3/ 1/51	365	6	84	16000	414	114	33	88	96	44	100	100	9
55	3/ 1/51	380	2	36	15500	414	114	33	88	96	44	100	100	9
56	3/ 1/51	270	24	112	18000	414	114	33	88	96	44	100	100	9
57	3/ 1/51	310	24	60	18000	414	114	33	88	96	44	100	100	9
58	3/ 1/51	320	12	84	13500	414	114	33	88	96	44	100	100	9
59	3/ 1/51	330	12	60	16000	414	114	33	88	96	44	100	100	9
60	3/ 1/51	320	24	60	18000	414	114	33	88	96	44	100	100	9
61	3/ 1/51	392	9	48	13200	414	114	33	88	96	44	100	100	9
62	3/14/51	315	30	84	16250	414	114	33	88	96	44	100	100	9
63	4/ 6/51	304	24	60	17000	346	97	33	83	109	48	84	85	9
64	4/ 6/51	315	18	84	14000	346	97	33	83	109	48	100	100	9
65	4/ 6/51	325	18	60	18000	346	97	33	83	109	48	100	100	9
66	4/ 6/51	329	12	84	14750	346	97	33	83	109	48	100	100	9
67	4/13/51	299	12	60	12835	346	97	33	83	109	48	100	100	9
68	4/20/51	322	18	84	19000	346	97	33	83	109	48	100	100	9
69	4/20/51	305	18	84	16250	346	97	33	83	109	48	100	100	9
70	4/23/51	315	18	84	18000	346	97	33	83	109	48	100	100	9
71	4/23/51	336	18	84	13250	346	97	33	83	109	48	100	100	9

GULF OIL COMPANY CHARTER DATA

1 TO 4	5 TO 6	7 TO 8	9 TO 10	11 TO 13	14 TO 15	16 TO 18	19 TO 23	24 TO 26	27 TO 29	30 TO 32	33 TO 35	36 TO 38	39 TO 41	42 TO 44	45 TO 47	80
72	4/23/51			315	24	84	18000	346	97	33	83	109	48	100	100	9
73	4/23/51			329	18	84	16300	346	97	33	83	109	48	100	100	9
74	4/23/51			301	24	84	18000	346	97	33	83	109	48	100	100	9
75	4/26/51			343	30	36	18000	346	97	33	83	109	48	100	100	9
76	5/23/51			315	30	48	18000	193	69	39	106	115	55	56	71	9
77	5/23/51			390	12	60	16500	193	69	39	106	115	55	100	100	9
78	5/ 1/51			390	12	36	16000	193	69	39	106	115	55	100	100	9
79	5/ 1/51			335	24	84	15000	193	69	39	106	115	55	100	100	9
80	5/ 1/51			336	24	84	18500	193	69	39	106	115	55	100	100	9
81	6/ 1/51			325	18	84	16500	208	90	44	85	122	67	108	130	9
82	6/ 1/51			340	18	60	14700	208	90	44	85	122	67	100	100	9
83	6/ 1/51			350	1	60	15000	208	90	44	85	122	67	100	100	9
84	6/ 1/51			355	2	60	13500	208	90	44	85	122	67	100	100	9
85	6/ 1/51			365	2	60	16200	208	90	44	85	122	67	100	100	9
86	6/ 1/51			301	36	84	18000	208	90	44	85	122	67	100	100	9
87	7/ 1/51			330	24	60	18500	178	87	47	83	107	72	86	97	9
88	7/ 1/51			330	24	60	18500	178	87	47	83	107	72	100	100	9
89	7/ 1/51			450	6	60	16000	178	87	47	83	107	72	100	100	9
90	7/ 1/51			295	48	84	18500	178	87	47	83	107	72	100	100	9
91	9/ 1/51			290	18	120	16500	229	108	52	101	97	68	129	124	9
92	9/ 1/51			335	12	84	16200	229	108	52	101	97	68	100	100	9
93	9/ 1/51			335	36	60	17400	229	108	52	101	97	68	100	100	9
94	9/ 1/51			300	36	84	18500	229	108	52	101	97	68	100	100	9
95	10/ 1/51			365	18	60	18000	305	122	51	87	79	54	133	113	9
96	10/ 1/51			365	24	60	18500	305	122	51	87	79	54	100	100	9
97	10/ 1/51			390	18	84	18000	305	122	51	87	79	54	100	100	9
98	11/ 1/51			550	7	48	16400	411	130	50	101	89	48	135	107	9
99	11/ 1/51			390	48	84	18000	411	130	50	101	89	48	100	100	9
100	11/ 1/51			390	6	84	18000	411	130	50	101	89	48	100	100	9
101	11/ 1/51			350	30	60	16500	411	130	50	101	89	48	100	100	9
102	12/ 1/51			425	30	84	16000	430	117	55	107	104	50	105	90	9
103	12/ 1/51			350	24	60	20000	430	117	55	107	104	50	100	100	9
104	12/ 1/51			500	24	60	9000	430	117	55	107	104	50	100	100	9
105	12/ 1/51			385	24	60	18500	430	117	55	107	104	50	100	100	9
106	12/ 1/51			370	24	60	13000	430	117	55	107	104	50	100	100	9

APPENDIX D

1 TO 4	5 TO 6	7 TO 8	9 TO 10	11 TO 13	14 TO 15	16 TO 18	19 TO 23	24 TO 26	27 TO 29	30 TO 32	33 TO 35	36 TO 38	39 TO 41	42 TO 44	45 TO 47	80
107	12/	1/51		390	24	60	19000	430	117	55	107	104	50	100	100	9
108	12/	1/51		395	24	60	18000	430	117	55	107	104	50	100	100	9
109	12/	1/51		395	24	60	18000	430	117	55	107	104	50	100	100	9
110	12/	1/51		395	24	60	18000	430	117	55	107	104	50	100	100	9
111	12/	1/51		392	36	60	15910	430	117	55	107	104	50	100	100	9
112	12/	1/51		400	36	60	18500	430	117	55	107	104	50	100	100	9
113	1/	9/52		340	48	60	18000	454	111	57	87	100	50	106	95	9
114	1/	9/52		400	36	60	19000	454	111	57	87	100	50	100	100	9
115	1/30/52			420	24	60	17000	454	111	57	87	100	50	100	100	9
116	1/30/52			390	1	60	18300	454	111	57	87	100	50	100	100	9
117	1/30/52			392	1	60	16000	454	111	57	87	100	50	100	100	9
118	1/30/52			392	24	60	16000	454	111	57	87	100	50	100	100	9
119	1/30/52			392	36	60	18500	454	111	57	87	100	50	100	100	9
120	1/30/52			432	24	84	13500	454	111	57	87	100	50	100	100	9
121	1/30/52			450	18	60	16500	454	111	57	87	100	50	100	100	9
122	1/30/52			378	24	60	15000	454	111	57	87	100	50	100	100	9
123	1/30/52			385	36	60	17500	454	111	57	87	100	50	100	100	9
124	1/30/52			399	24	60	14820	454	111	57	87	100	50	100	100	0
125	1/30/52			425	18	60	14000	454	111	57	87	100	50	100	100	9
126	1/30/52			450	36	60	16000	454	111	57	87	100	50	100	100	9
127	2/	6/52		399	36	60	18500	444	103	62	102	80	40	98	93	9
128	2/	6/52		450	18	84	15960	444	103	62	102	80	40	100	100	9
129	2/	6/52		425	12	84	14580	444	103	62	102	80	40	100	100	9
130	2/	6/52		392	1	60	16200	444	103	62	102	80	40	100	100	9
131	2/	6/52		392	1	60	13500	444	103	62	102	80	40	100	100	9
132	2/20/52			392	1	60	16200	444	103	62	102	80	40	100	100	9
133	2/20/52			400	24	60	17600	444	103	62	102	80	40	100	100	9
134	2/20/52			396	24	60	17500	444	103	62	102	80	40	100	100	9
135	2/20/52			399	24	48	19000	444	103	62	102	80	40	100	100	9
136	2/20/52			399	1	60	16300	444	103	62	102	80	40	100	100	9
137	2/20/52			399	1	60	16300	444	103	62	102	80	40	100	100	9
138	2/21/52			389	24	60	16400	444	103	62	102	80	40	100	100	9
139	2/21/52			392	36	60	18500	444	103	62	102	80	40	100	100	9
140	2/29/52			400	36	60	18500	444	103	62	102	80	40	100	100	9
141	2/	1/52		400	30	60	17500	444	103	62	102	80	40	100	100	9
142	3/19/52			370	24	84	16225	400	95	65	89	110	44	90	92	9
143	3/19/52			392	36	60	13300	400	95	65	89	110	44	100	100	9
144	3/19/52			380	30	60	16225	400	95	65	89	110	44	100	100	9
145	3/19/52			392	18	60	16556	400	95	65	89	110	44	100	100	9

GULF OIL COMPANY CHARTER DATA

1 TO 4	5 TO 6	7 TO 8	9 TO 10	11 TO 13	14 TO 15	16 TO 18	19 TO 23	24 TO 26	27 TO 29	30 TO 32	33 TO 35	36 TO 38	39 TO 41	42 TO 44	45 TO 47	80
146	3/21/52	389	30	60	15000	400	95	65	89	110	44	100	100	9
147	3/27/52	350	2	36	12460	400	95	65	89	110	44	100	100	9
148	3/27/52	385	30	60	20000	400	95	65	89	110	44	100	100	9
149	3/ 1/52	455	18	60	18800	400	95	65	89	110	44	100	100	9
150	3/ 1/52	380	36	60	16300	400	95	65	89	110	44	100	100	9
151	4/ 4/52	413	18	60	19500	265	80	66	92	114	50	66	84	9
152	5/12/52	375	24	60	21000	183	73	67	96	124	62	69	91	9
153	5/12/52	392	24	60	16090	183	73	67	96	124	62	100	100	9
154	5/ 1/52	385	36	60	14700	183	73	67	96	124	62	100	100	9
155	5/ 1/52	385	36	60	18200	183	73	67	96	124	62	100	100	9
156	6/ 1/52	385	36	60	18200	188	88	68	100	113	70	103	121	9
157	6/ 1/52	435	24	60	19800	188	88	68	100	113	70	100	100	9
158	7/14/52	440	24	60	18250	163	87	68	97	116	81	87	99	9
159	7/ 1/52	475	12	60	10800	163	87	68	97	116	81	100	100	9
160	7/ 1/52	510	9	60	9600	163	87	68	97	116	81	100	100	9
161	7/ 1/52	450	9	60	16500	163	87	68	97	116	81	100	100	9
162	9/10/52	410	12	60	16900	169	102	73	97	100	96	104	117	9
163	9/14/52	336	12	84	16200	169	102	73	97	100	96	100	100	9
164	9/17/52	400	12	60	14250	169	102	73	97	100	96	100	100	9
165	9/17/52	410	24	60	19250	169	102	73	97	100	96	100	100	9
166	10/ 3/52	400	6	60	20000	149	95	71	93	83	80	88	93	9
167	10/ 1/52	450	12	60	16400	149	95	71	93	83	80	100	100	9
168	10/ 1/52	385	18	30	15900	149	95	71	93	83	80	100	100	9
169	10/ 1/52	400	30	36	20000	149	95	71	93	83	80	100	100	9
170	11/21/52	400	1	60	20300	154	99	71	101	88	70	103	104	9
171	12/ 3/52	364	18	60	15750	146	97	72	102	87	61	95	98	9
172	1/ 2/53	385	1	48	20300	128	92	70	94	98	60	88	95	9
173	2/26/53	340	3	60	15500	108	88	68	102	108	65	84	96	9
174	3/ 1/53	330	12	120	18000	99	89	70	107	102	66	92	101	9
175	3/ 1/53	325	12	120	18000	99	89	70	107	102	66	100	100	9
176	5/18/53	336	24	84	12000	98	96	65	95	111	79	99	108	9

APPENDIX D

1 TO 4	5 TO 6	7 TO 8	9 TO 10	11 TO 13	14 TO 15	16 TO 18	19 TO 23	24 TO 26	27 TO 29	30 TO 32	33 TO 35	36 TO 38	39 TO 41	42 TO 44	45 TO 47	80
177	6/ 2/53	323	1	60			15135	88	93	66	108	124	98	90	97	9
178	6/17/53	315	7	60			13500	88	93	66	108	124	98	100	100	9
179	7/ 1/53	301	6	60			13500	75	89	63	105	101	99	85	96	9
180	7/ 1/53	294	6	36			13500	75	89	63	105	101	99	100	100	9
181	7/ 1/53	292	6	60			15500	75	89	63	105	101	99	100	100	9
182	7/ 1/53	295	5	24			15500	75	89	63	105	101	99	100	100	9
183	9/11/53	305	4	24			18000	80	98	60	104	97	104	107	110	9
184	9/17/53	265	2	30			15500	80	98	60	104	97	104	100	100	9
185	9/25/53	290	1	36			12585	80	98	60	104	97	104	100	100	9
187	11/18/53	300	12	60			16610	95	106	57	104	88	91	119	108	9
188	11/18/53	300	12	60			16520	95	106	57	104	88	91	100	100	9
189	11/13/53	294	6	36			18000	95	106	57	104	88	91	100	100	9
190	12/ 1/53	273	1	36			15750	98	104	55	104	93	85	103	98	9
191	12/ 4/53	320	4	60			19000	98	104	55	104	93	85	100	100	9
192	12/ 1/53	280	6	24			16422	98	104	55	104	93	85	100	100	9
193	1/17/54	280	9	36			18000	99	103	50	98	101	86	101	99	9
194	5/ 4/54	240	8	24			19000	74	90	45	105	131	122	75	87	9
195	5/ 6/54	273	6	36			17500	74	90	45	105	131	122	100	100	9
196	6/12/54	236	3	48			15472	63	87	44	100	113	138	85	97	9
197	6/ 8/54	273	9	36			17000	63	87	44	100	113	138	100	100	9
198	9/28/54	232	15	24			18475	97	123	38	102	89	146	154	141	9
199	10/28/54	252	3	24			13235	95	111	35	103	79	116	98	90	9
200	11/ 1/54	245	2	18			15500	99	108	34	105	80	93	104	97	9
201	11/ 1/54	245	1	18			15500	99	108	34	105	80	93	100	100	9
202	11/ 2/54	252	2	18			15000	99	108	34	105	80	93	100	100	9
203	11/ 2/54	266	3	18			11425	99	108	34	105	80	93	100	100	9
204	11/ 4/54	245	2	18			16563	99	108	34	105	80	93	100	100	9
205	11/22/54	245	2	18			15500	99	108	34	105	80	93	100	100	9
206	11/23/54	245	2	18			15700	99	108	34	105	80	93	100	100	9
207	11/24/54	259	1	18			16350	99	108	34	105	80	93	100	100	9
208	11/25/54	259	1	18			18000	99	108	34	105	80	93	100	100	9

GULF OIL COMPANY CHARTER DATA

1 TO 4	5 TO 6	7 TO 8	9 TO 10	11 TO 13	14 TO 15	16 TO 18	19 TO 23	24 TO 26	27 TO 29	30 TO 32	33 TO 35	36 TO 38	39 TO 41	42 TO 44	45 TO 47	80
209	11/25/54	245	1	18	16441	99	108	34	105	80	93	100	100	9
210	11/25/54	245	1	18	13330	99	108	34	105	80	93	100	100	9
211	12/ 3/54	245	1	18	18000	131	120	33	102	92	86	132	111	9
212	12/14/54	238	1	18	14500	131	120	33	102	92	86	100	100	9
213	3/24/55	273	1	60	17260	111	92	30	96	97	61	85	77	9
214	4/14/55	287	2	60	19000	86	83	30	105	115	70	77	90	9
215	4/16/55	285	2	24	18000	86	83	30	105	115	70	100	100	9
216	4/30/55	287	12	36	18800	86	83	30	105	115	70	100	100	9
217	4/30/55	269	2	60	17400	86	83	30	105	115	70	100	100	9
218	5/ 4/55	259	2	18	16140	88	92	30	99	123	86	102	111	9
219	5/19/55	315	12	60	17500	88	92	30	99	123	86	100	100	9
220	5/20/55	287	4	24	16200	88	92	30	99	123	86	100	100	9
221	5/20/55	259	1	18	20000	88	92	30	99	123	86	100	100	9
222	6/ 1/55	297	1	60	16000	83	93	31	104	108	93	94	101	9
223	6/ 9/55	297	1	36	16460	83	93	31	104	108	93	100	100	9
224	6/13/55	306	4	60	16000	83	93	31	104	108	93	100	100	9
225	6/14/55	294	7	48	15626	83	93	31	104	108	93	100	100	9
226	6/22/55	304	1	60	16140	83	93	31	104	108	93	100	100	9
227	6/22/55	273	6	36	13425	83	93	31	104	108	93	100	100	9
228	6/22/55	294	1	60	18450	83	93	31	104	108	93	100	100	9
229	6/23/55	301	18	60	15700	83	93	31	104	108	93	100	100	9
230	6/27/55	306	1	60	17600	83	93	31	104	108	93	100	100	9
231	6/27/55	294	6	60	15170	83	93	31	104	108	93	100	100	9
232	6/29/55	306	18	60	16000	83	93	31	104	108	93	100	100	9
233	6/29/55	308	18	60	13870	83	93	31	104	108	93	100	100	9
234	6/29/55	304	18	60	13330	83	93	31	104	108	93	100	100	9
235	6/30/55	304	18	60	15530	83	93	31	104	108	93	100	100	9
236	6/30/55	308	18	60	15560	83	93	31	104	108	93	100	100	9
237	6/30/55	294	18	60	15530	83	93	31	104	108	93	100	100	9
238	6/30/55	301	24	60	15400	83	93	31	104	108	93	100	100	9
239	7/ 1/55	345	3	60	16800	108	113	30	92	103	96	130	122	9
240	7/ 6/55	325	1	60	16635	108	113	30	92	103	96	100	100	9
241	7/ 6/55	259	24	60	9867	108	113	30	92	103	96	100	100	9
242	7/ 8/55	308	18	60	16729	108	113	30	92	103	96	100	100	9
243	7/ 8/55	308	1	60	18300	108	113	30	92	103	96	100	100	9
244	7/11/55	325	1	60	17850	108	113	30	92	103	96	100	100	9

APPENDIX D

1 TO 4	5 TO 6	7 TO 8	9 TO 10	11 TO 13	14 TO 15	16 TO 18	19 TO 23	24 TO 26	27 TO 29	30 TO 32	33 TO 35	36 TO 38	39 TO 41	42 TO 44	45 TO 47	80
245	7/14/55			311	1	60	15930	108	113	30	92	103	96	100	100	9
246	7/19/55			318	18	60	16410	108	113	30	92	103	96	100	100	9
247	7/22/55			318	12	36	16600	108	113	30	92	103	96	100	100	9
248	7/25/55			315	1	60	16540	108	113	30	92	103	96	100	100	9
249	7/25/55			336	54	84	18000	108	113	30	92	103	96	100	100	9
250	7/25/55			350	54	84	19000	108	113	30	92	103	96	100	100	9
251	7/25/55			350	42	84	19000	108	113	30	92	103	96	100	100	9
252	7/28/55			318	24	84	16403	108	113	30	92	103	96	100	100	9
253	8/ 2/55			336	12	60	15260	107	107	32	109	98	94	99	95	9
254	8/ 2/55			318	18	60	16656	107	107	32	109	98	94	100	100	9
255	8/22/55			318	18	60	16420	107	107	32	109	98	94	100	100	9
256	8/ 5/55			273	12	24	12620	107	107	32	109	98	94	100	100	9
257	8/ 5/55			318	12	60	16738	107	107	32	109	98	94	100	100	9
258	8/ 5/55			306	8	60	16475	107	107	32	109	98	94	100	100	9
259	8/ 5/55			329	2	84	16200	107	107	32	109	98	94	100	100	9
260	8/ 5/55			360	3	60	17500	107	107	32	109	98	94	100	100	9
261	8/11/55			350	18	72	19000	107	107	32	109	98	94	100	100	9
262	8/11/55			329	18	84	16659	107	107	32	109	98	94	100	100	9
263	8/15/55			326	12	96	16175	107	107	32	109	98	94	100	100	9
264	8/15/55			326	18	96	16100	107	107	32	109	98	94	100	100	9
265	8/15/55			350	24	96	18000	107	107	32	109	98	94	100	100	9
266	8/15/55			350	48	96	18000	107	107	32	109	98	94	100	100	9
267	8/17/55			336	16	60	16250	107	107	32	109	98	94	100	100	9
268	8/17/55			287	1	60	15200	107	107	32	109	98	94	100	100	9
269	8/17/55			400	2	60	13200	107	107	32	109	98	94	100	100	9
270	8/18/55			304	1	36	16050	107	107	32	109	98	94	100	100	9
271	8/22/55			350	12	60	16536	107	107	32	109	98	94	100	100	9
272	8/23/55			380	1	60	16620	107	107	32	109	98	94	100	100	9
273	8/23/55			350	36	84	18000	107	107	32	109	98	94	100	100	9
274	8/23/55			350	36	84	19500	107	107	32	109	98	94	100	100	9
275	8/24/55			370	2	72	16500	107	107	32	109	98	94	100	100	9
276	8/24/55			370	12	60	18435	107	107	32	109	98	94	100	100	9
277	8/25/55			358	7	60	18158	107	107	32	109	98	94	100	100	9
278	8/25/55			352	3	36	16440	107	107	32	109	98	94	100	100	9
279	8/27/55			370	2	60	16500	107	107	32	109	98	94	100	100	9
280	8/30/55			368	14	36	16000	107	107	32	109	98	94	100	100	9
281	8/31/55			370	1	60	17600	107	107	32	109	98	94	100	100	9
282	8/31/55			350	30	84	19570	107	107	32	109	98	94	100	100	9
283	8/31/55			343	24	84	18000	107	107	32	109	98	94	100	100	9
284	9/ 1/55			370	42	84	17270	107	104	33	94	95	89	100	97	9

1 TO 4	5 TO 6	7 TO 8	9 TO 10	11 TO 13	14 TO 15	16 TO 18	19 TO 23	24 TO 26	27 TO 29	30 TO 32	33 TO 35	36 TO 38	39 TO 41	42 TO 44	45 TO 47	80
285	9/ 2/55	298	10	36	14290	107	104	33	94	95	89	100	100	9
286	9/ 2/55	318	24	60	16560	107	104	33	94	95	89	100	100	9
287	9/ 2/55	326	18	60	15500	107	104	33	94	95	89	100	100	9
288	9/ 2/55	326	18	60	15500	107	104	33	94	95	89	100	100	9
289	9/ 2/55	350	24	84	19000	107	104	33	94	95	89	100	100	9
290	9/ 6/55	318	9	60	16441	107	104	33	94	95	89	100	100	9
291	9/ 6/55	318	9	60	16441	107	104	33	94	95	89	100	100	9
292	9/ 6/55	350	4	84	18500	107	104	33	94	95	89	100	100	9
293	9/ 7/55	358	4	60	19200	107	104	33	94	95	89	100	100	9
294	9/ 7/55	350	36	72	19500	107	104	33	94	95	89	100	100	9
295	9/ 7/55	350	36	66	19000	107	104	33	94	95	89	100	100	9
296	9/ 7/55	350	42	90	19000	107	104	33	94	95	89	100	100	9
297	9/ 7/55	350	48	96	19000	107	104	33	94	95	89	100	100	9
298	9/16/55	390	1	60	18300	107	104	33	94	95	89	100	100	9
299	9/16/55	336	18	60	17000	107	104	33	94	95	89	100	100	9
300	9/16/55	297	12	36	14000	107	104	33	94	95	89	100	100	9
301	9/16/55	350	48	96	19000	107	104	33	94	95	89	100	100	9
302	9/19/55	363	5	60	17000	107	104	33	94	95	89	100	100	9
303	9/19/55	338	7	60	15500	107	104	33	94	95	89	100	100	9
304	9/19/55	308	2	60	14800	107	104	33	94	95	89	100	100	9
305	9/21/55	318	18	60	16738	107	104	33	94	95	89	100	100	9
306	9/21/55	318	18	60	16628	107	104	33	94	95	89	100	100	9
307	9/21/55	338	2	72	16463	107	104	33	94	95	89	100	100	9
308	9/21/55	336	24	60	16000	107	104	33	94	95	89	100	100	9
309	9/21/55	350	48	96	19000	107	104	33	94	95	89	100	100	9
310	9/21/55	350	36	78	19000	107	104	33	94	95	89	100	100	9
311	9/28/55	343	6	60	16340	107	104	33	94	95	89	100	100	9
312	9/28/55	329	1	84	15680	107	104	33	94	95	89	100	100	9
313	10/ 5/55	350	12	60	15000	109	103	36	97	85	76	102	99	9
314	10/66/55	350	2	24	16225	109	103	36	97	85	76	100	100	9
315	10/14/55	392	2	60	18500	109	103	36	97	85	76	100	100	9
316	10/14/55	350	6	36	18624	109	103	36	97	85	76	100	100	9
317	10/17/55	350	6	36	18500	109	103	36	97	85	76	100	100	9
318	10/17/55	350	6	60	17300	109	103	36	97	85	76	100	100	9
319	10/18/55	332	9	60	16510	109	103	36	97	85	76	100	100	9
320	10/26/55	350	6	60	16300	109	103	36	97	85	76	100	100	9
321	10/27/55	332	6	60	16484	109	103	36	97	85	76	100	100	9
322	10/28/55	329	9	60	16210	109	103	36	97	85	76	100	100	9
323	11/ 1/55	345	30	60	16500	218	153	41	95	87	66	200	149	9
324	11/ 1/55	343	42	60	16300	218	153	41	95	87	66	100	100	9

APPENDIX D

1 TØ 4	5 TØ 6	7 TØ 8	9 TØ 10	11 TØ 13	14 TØ 15	16 TØ 18	19 TØ 23	24 TØ 26	27 TØ 29	30 TØ 32	33 TØ 35	36 TØ 38	39 TØ 41	42 TØ 44	45 TØ 47	80
325	11/ 3/55	345	36	60	17500	218	153	41	95	87	66	100	100	9
326	11/ 9/55	350	36	84	19500	218	153	41	95	87	66	100	100	9
327	11/15/55	395	6	60	12000	218	153	41	95	87	66	100	100	9
328	11/16/55	332	24	48	16460	218	153	41	95	87	66	100	100	9
329	11/16/55	336	12	72	15450	218	153	41	95	87	66	100	100	9
330	11/22/55	371	36	36	21000	218	153	41	95	87	66	100	100	9
331	11/22/55	371	36	36	21000	218	153	41	95	87	66	100	100	9
332	11/23/55	374	24	78	19130	218	153	41	95	87	66	100	100	9
333	11/23/55	374	42	78	19130	218	153	41	95	87	66	100	100	9
334	11/28/55	352	3	84	17300	218	153	41	95	87	66	100	100	9
335	11/29/55	365	4	36	16484	218	153	41	95	87	66	100	100	9
336	12/ 8/55	364	1	60	16300	291	145	45	87	83	55	133	95	9
337	12/21/55	382	24	60	18500	291	145	45	87	83	55	100	100	9
338	12/21/55	389	24	60	18500	291	145	45	87	83	55	100	100	9
339	12/28/55	392	12	60	20000	291	145	45	87	83	55	100	100	9
340	1/11/56	392	1	60	16290	184	119	46	85	85	47	63	82	9
342	1/18/56	385	24	72	19000	184	119	46	85	85	47	100	100	9
343	1/18/56	388	18	48	18350	184	119	46	85	85	47	100	100	9
344	1/18/56	374	6	48	15880	184	119	46	85	85	47	100	100	9
345	1/18/56	350	24	60	15314	184	119	46	85	85	47	100	100	9
346	1/18/56	357	36	60	17400	184	119	46	85	85	47	100	100	9
348	1/23/56	420	2	24	16561	184	119	46	85	85	47	100	100	9
349	1/25/56	365	12	72	19500	184	119	46	85	85	47	100	100	9
350	1/26/56	388	18	72	19000	184	119	46	85	85	47	100	100	9
351	1/26/56	388	18	72	18000	184	119	46	85	85	47	100	100	9
352	1/26/56	388	24	72	19200	184	119	46	85	85	47	100	100	9
353	1/26/56	364	24	60	16014	184	119	46	85	85	47	100	100	9
354	1/26/56	365	12	72	19500	184	119	46	85	85	47	100	100	9
355	1/26/56	357	7	60	13550	184	119	46	85	85	47	100	100	9
356	1/27/56	346	4	60	13575	184	119	46	85	85	47	100	100	9
357	2/ 1/56	388	18	72	19000	146	97	48	96	94	44	79	82	9
358	2/ 1/56	392	1	24	12300	146	97	48	96	94	44	100	100	9
359	2/ 1/56	388	22	72	19000	146	97	48	96	94	44	100	100	9
360	2/ 1/56	388	24	72	15300	146	97	48	96	94	44	100	100	9
364	2/ 8/56	388	18	60	19500	146	97	48	96	94	44	100	100	9
365	2/ 8/56	325	1	120	19000	146	97	48	96	94	44	100	100	9
366	2/ 8/56	378	24	60	17890	146	97	48	96	94	44	100	100	9
368	2/15/56	359	30	60	18500	146	97	48	96	94	44	100	100	9
369	2/15/56	392	12	24	18400	146	97	48	96	94	44	100	100	9

GULF OIL COMPANY CHARTER DATA   315

1 TO 4	5 TO 6	7 TO 8	9 TO 10	11 TO 13	14 TO 15	16 TO 18	19 TO 23	24 TO 26	27 TO 29	30 TO 32	33 TO 35	36 TO 38	39 TO 41	42 TO 44	45 TO 47	80
370	2/16/56	388	12	84	19000	146	97	48	96	94	44	100	100	9
371	2/21/56	371	8	36	18160	146	97	48	96	94	44	100	100	9
372	3/14/56	378	1	24	12585	144	94	48	94	107	47	98	97	9
373	3/21/56	475	3	24	13500	144	94	48	94	107	47	100	100	9
374	3/12/56	390	1	24	20200	144	94	48	94	107	47	100	100	9
375	3/27/56	375	1	60	20600	144	94	48	94	107	47	100	100	9
377	4/ 4/56	354	5	48	15135	186	112	50	100	109	51	100	100	9
378	4/ 4/56	365	8	60	15650	186	112	50	100	109	51	100	100	9
379	4/11/56	378	3	60	23000	186	112	50	100	109	51	100	100	9
380	4/23/56	525	1	30	16657	186	112	50	100	109	51	100	100	9
381	4/20/56	434	6	24	19000	186	112	50	100	109	51	100	100	9
382	4/23/56	360	4	60	16523	186	112	50	100	109	51	100	100	9
383	4/23/56	360	9	60	16610	186	112	50	100	109	51	100	100	9
384	4/24/56	415	9	24	13270	186	112	50	100	109	51	100	100	9
385	4/24/56	410	10	60	19500	186	112	50	100	109	51	100	100	9
386	4/25/56	399	1	72	19284	186	112	50	100	109	51	100	100	9
387	4/26/56	450	2	60	17620	186	112	50	100	109	51	100	100	9
388	4/27/56	360	2	78	15500	186	112	50	100	109	51	100	100	9
389	4/27/56	420	15	60	15200	186	112	50	100	109	51	100	100	9
390	4/27/56	389	6	60	15500	186	112	50	100	109	51	100	100	9
391	4/30/56	406	27	60	19500	186	112	50	100	109	51	100	100	9
392	4/30/56	389	8	60	16636	186	112	50	100	109	51	100	100	9
393	5/ 2/56	390	18	72	18519	229	119	55	99	124	63	123	106	9
394	5/ 2/56	360	8	60	16505	229	119	55	99	124	63	100	100	9
395	5/ 3/56	360	20	60	15500	229	119	55	99	124	63	100	100	9
396	5/ 3/56	400	18	72	19500	229	119	55	99	124	63	100	100	9
397	5/ 4/56	420	4	72	19660	229	119	55	99	124	63	100	100	9
398	5/ 4/56	370	4	72	16629	229	119	55	99	124	63	100	100	9
399	5/ 8/56	420	24	60	17500	229	119	55	99	124	63	100	100	9
400	5/ 8/56	410	12	60	17500	229	119	55	99	124	63	100	100	9
401	5/ 8/56	415	1	60	20320	229	119	55	99	124	63	100	100	9
402	5/ 8/56	410	12	60	20320	229	119	55	99	124	63	100	100	9
403	5/10/56	420	24	84	19000	229	119	55	99	124	63	100	100	9
404	5/14/56	389	14	60	13500	229	119	55	99	124	63	100	100	9
405	5/14/56	420	24	60	18300	229	119	55	99	124	63	100	100	9
406	5/16/56	497	1	24	12360	229	119	55	99	124	63	100	100	9
407	5/16/56	420	18	60	19700	229	119	55	99	124	63	100	100	9
408	5/16/56	420	24	60	20000	229	119	55	99	124	63	100	100	9
409	5/16/56	420	15	60	17500	229	119	55	99	124	63	100	100	9

APPENDIX D

1 TØ 4	5 TØ 6	7 TØ 8	9 TØ 10	11 TØ 13	14 TØ 15	16 TØ 18	19 TØ 23	24 TØ 26	27 TØ 29	30 TØ 32	33 TØ 35	36 TØ 38	39 TØ 41	42 TØ 44	45 TØ 47	80
410	5/16/56	420	15	60	17500	229	119	55	99	124	63	100	100	9
411	5/16/56	427	2	60	13580	229	119	55	99	124	63	100	100	9
412	5/17/56	417	30	60	19000	229	119	55	99	124	63	100	100	9
413	5/17/56	420	4	48	13500	229	119	55	99	124	63	100	100	9
414	5/18/56	425	4	60	20090	229	119	55	99	124	63	100	100	9
415	5/22/56	413	8	60	16400	229	119	55	99	124	63	100	100	9
416	5/22/56	399	18	60	13250	229	119	55	99	124	63	100	100	9
417	5/22/56	420	24	60	19786	229	119	55	99	124	63	100	100	9
418	5/23/56	420	24	60	19300	229	119	55	99	124	63	100	100	9
419	5/24/56	400	12	36	18500	229	119	55	99	124	63	100	100	9
420	5/28/56	329	2	66	15400	229	119	55	99	124	63	100	100	9
421	5/29/56	406	36	60	19000	229	119	55	99	124	63	100	100	9
422	5/30/56	340	16	60	14735	229	119	55	99	124	63	100	100	9
423	5/30/56	420	24	60	19300	229	119	55	99	124	63	100	100	9
424	5/31/56	389	24	84	22000	229	119	55	99	124	63	100	100	9
425	5/31/56	389	24	84	22000	229	119	55	99	124	63	100	100	9
426	6/ 6/56	420	12	72	16510	221	109	56	92	92	58	97	92	9
427	6/11/56	490	1	36	16000	221	109	56	92	92	58	100	100	9
428	6/13/56	525	1	24	16628	221	109	56	92	92	58	100	100	9
429	6/13/56	406	36	60	19600	221	109	56	92	92	58	100	100	9
431	6/14/56	406	18	72	13550	221	109	56	92	92	58	100	100	9
434	6/20/56	420	24	60	19500	221	109	56	92	92	58	100	100	9
435	7/ 2/56	434	5	72	13025	201	99	60	96	98	57	91	91	9
436	7/ 3/56	427	36	60	19500	201	99	60	96	98	57	100	100	9
437	7/ 4/56	420	36	60	18125	201	99	60	96	98	57	100	100	9
438	7/ 8/56	420	36	60	15810	201	99	60	96	98	57	100	100	9
439	7/11/56	420	5	60	13025	201	99	60	96	98	57	100	100	9
440	7/11/56	420	60	60	19500	201	99	60	96	98	57	100	100	9
441	7/12/56	420	48	60	20100	201	99	60	96	98	57	100	100	9
442	7/12/56	430	48	60	21000	201	99	60	96	98	57	100	100	9
443	7/13/56	424	36	60	19078	201	99	60	96	98	57	100	100	9
444	7/13/56	378	24	60	16490	201	99	60	96	98	57	100	100	9
445	7/19/56	409	36	60	19000	201	99	60	96	98	57	100	100	9
446	7/23/56	399	10	60	16500	201	99	60	96	98	57	100	100	9
447	7/23/56	406	36	60	16020	201	99	60	96	98	57	100	100	9
448	7/24/56	427	60	60	16000	201	99	60	96	98	57	100	100	9
449	7/25/56	434	48	60	17600	201	99	60	96	98	57	100	100	9
450	7/25/56	406	12	36	16588	201	99	60	96	98	57	100	100	9
451	7/27/56	406	15	36	16588	201	99	60	96	98	57	100	100	9
452	7/31/56	392	36	60	16000	201	99	60	96	98	57	100	100	9

1 TO 4	5 TO 6	7 TO 8	9 TO 10	11 TO 13	14 TO 15	16 TO 18	19 TO 23	24 TO 26	27 TO 29	30 TO 32	33 TO 35	36 TO 38	39 TO 41	42 TO 44	45 TO 47	80
453	7/30/56	420	42	60	19100	201	99	60	96	98	57	100	100	9
454	7/30/56	420	48	60	19100	201	99	60	96	98	57	100	100	9
455	7/30/56	420	30	60	18970	201	99	60	96	98	57	100	100	9
456	7/30/56	420	48	60	17590	201	99	60	96	98	57	100	100	9
457	8/ 5/56	420	48	60	19250	201	98	63	91	102	58	100	100	9
458	8/ 9/56	406	36	60	16300	201	98	63	91	102	58	100	100	9
459	8/ 9/56	409	42	60	15820	201	98	63	91	102	58	100	100	9
460	8/14/56	420	60	60	17300	201	98	63	91	102	58	100	100	9
461	8/17/56	760	3	24	13264	201	98	63	91	102	58	100	100	9
462	8/21/56	448	48	60	19750	201	98	63	91	102	58	100	100	9
464	9/ 6/56	441	7	60	13600	249	111	68	99	109	63	124	113	9
465	9/ 6/56	381	48	60	16540	249	111	68	99	109	63	100	100	9
466	9/ 7/56	420	24	60	15135	249	111	68	99	109	63	100	100	9
467	9/ 7/56	399	60	60	22808	249	111	68	99	109	63	100	100	9
468	9/ 7/56	399	36	60	22760	249	111	68	99	109	63	100	100	9
469	9/14/56	565	1	60	13000	249	111	68	99	109	63	100	100	9
470	9/26/56	434	12	60	16687	249	111	68	99	109	63	100	100	9
471	10/ 1/56	423	12	60	16225	281	113	68	83	87	55	113	102	9
472	10/ 5/56	490	12	60	15000	281	113	68	83	87	55	100	100	9
473	10/ 5/56	399	6	60	16000	281	113	68	83	87	55	100	100	9
475	10/ 5/56	476	36	84	19500	281	113	68	83	87	55	100	100	9
476	10/ 5/56	476	48	60	19500	281	113	68	83	87	55	100	100	9
477	10/ 8/56	735	12	24	19300	281	113	68	83	87	55	100	100	9
478	10/ 8/56	451	12	48	15300	281	113	68	83	87	55	100	100	9
479	10/ 9/56	441	18	60	15000	281	113	68	83	87	55	100	100	9
480	10/10/56	406	12	60	16450	281	113	68	83	87	55	100	100	9
482	10/10/56	522	12	60	18200	281	113	68	83	87	55	100	100	9
483	10/10/56	641	12	42	17230	281	113	68	83	87	55	100	100	9
484	10/10/56	441	24	60	16850	281	113	68	83	87	55	100	100	9
485	10/11/56	423	30	60	13720	281	113	68	83	87	55	100	100	9
486	10/11/56	448	36	60	16010	281	113	68	83	87	55	100	100	9
487	10/11/56	455	36	60	15810	281	113	68	83	87	55	100	100	9
488	10/15/56	441	24	60	16500	281	113	68	83	87	55	100	100	9
489	10/15/56	476	36	60	18200	281	113	68	83	87	55	100	100	9
490	10/17/56	371	24	60	16050	281	113	68	83	87	55	100	100	9
491	10/17/56	496	18	36	16698	281	113	68	83	87	55	100	100	9
492	10/19/56	480	24	68	18956	281	113	68	83	87	55	100	100	9
494	10/19/56	434	24	36	17620	281	113	68	83	87	55	100	100	9
495	10/19/56	434	18	60	19021	281	113	68	83	87	55	100	100	9

1	5 TØ 6	7 TØ 8	9 TØ 10	11 TØ 13	14 TØ 15	16 TØ 18	19 TØ 23	24 TØ 26	27 TØ 29	30 TØ 32	33 TØ 35	36 TØ 38	39 TØ 41	42 TØ 44	45 TØ 47	80
496	10/22/56			389	66	60	18178	281	113	68	83	87	55	100	100	9
497	10/22/56			476	72	60	19300	281	113	68	83	87	55	100	100	9
498	10/22/56			462	36	60	19000	281	113	68	83	87	55	100	100	9
499	10/24/56			392	30	60	13850	281	113	68	83	87	55	100	100	9
500	10/24/56			441	48	60	12965	281	113	68	83	87	55	100	100	9
501	10/24/56			410	30	60	12820	281	113	68	83	87	55	100	100	9
502	10/24/56			468	24	60	19000	281	113	68	83	87	55	100	100	9
503	10/24/56			455	30	60	18530	281	113	68	83	87	55	100	100	9
504	10/24/56			700	3	24	18500	281	113	68	83	87	55	100	100	9
505	10/26/56			476	48	60	19000	281	113	68	83	87	55	100	100	9
506	10/26/56			476	48	60	19000	281	113	68	83	87	55	100	100	9
507	10/29/56			476	48	60	19000	281	113	68	83	87	55	100	100	9
508	10/29/56			385	24	72	15075	281	113	68	83	87	55	100	100	9
509	10/29/56			448	36	60	18510	281	113	68	83	87	55	100	100	9
510	10/29/56			434	24	60	11970	281	113	68	83	87	55	100	100	9
511	10/30/56			650	1	60	13075	281	113	68	83	87	55	100	100	9
512	11/ 2/56			455	72	60	16400	441	137	71	103	85	47	157	121	9
513	11/ 9/56			750	1	39	15500	441	137	71	103	85	47	100	100	9
514	11/ 9/56			750	1	39	15500	441	137	71	103	85	47	100	100	9
515	11/ 9/56			750	1	39	15500	441	137	71	103	85	47	100	100	9
516	11/ 9/56			750	1	39	15500	441	137	71	103	85	47	100	100	9
517	11/ 9/56			750	1	39	15500	441	137	71	103	85	47	100	100	9
518	11/ 9/56			750	1	39	15500	441	137	71	103	85	47	100	100	9
519	11/ 9/56			750	1	39	15500	441	137	71	103	85	47	100	100	9
520	11/ 7/56			476	60	60	18350	441	137	71	103	85	47	100	100	9
521	11/ 7/56			476	78	60	19300	441	137	71	103	85	47	100	100	9
522	11/13/56			476	24	54	13450	441	137	71	103	85	47	100	100	9
523	11/13/56			473	72	72	13750	441	137	71	103	85	47	100	100	9
524	11/13/56			473	60	72	13500	441	137	71	103	85	47	100	100	9
525	11/13/56			487	72	72	19300	441	137	71	103	85	47	100	100	9
526	11/13/56			487	84	72	19300	441	137	71	103	85	47	100	100	9
527	11/13/56			487	96	72	19500	441	137	71	103	85	47	100	100	9
528	11/13/56			749	3	24	16250	441	137	71	103	85	47	100	100	9
530	11/13/56			249	6	24	18600	441	137	71	103	85	47	100	100	9
532	11/13/56			781	4	24	19000	441	137	71	103	85	47	100	100	9
534	11/13/56			462	96	84	19000	441	137	71	103	85	47	100	100	9
535	11/19/56			750	1	36	16578	441	137	71	103	85	47	100	100	9
536	11/14/56			431	24	60	15200	441	137	71	103	85	47	100	100	9
537	11/14/56			476	72	60	16330	441	137	71	103	85	47	100	100	9
538	11/14/56			426	60	60	13330	441	137	71	103	85	47	100	100	9
539	11/14/56			476	36	72	19500	441	137	71	103	85	47	100	100	9

GULF OIL COMPANY CHARTER DATA 319

1 TO 4	5 TO 6	7 TO 8	9 TO 10	11 TO 13	14 TO 15	16 TO 18	19 TO 23	24 TO 26	27 TO 29	30 TO 32	33 TO 35	36 TO 38	39 TO 41	42 TO 44	45 TO 47	80
540	11/19/56	745	2	36	11425	441	137	71	103	85	47	100	100	9
541	12/ 6/56	460	30	60	18500	470	122	76	104	74	35	107	89	9
544	12/31/56	490	48	60	19000	470	122	76	104	74	35	100	100	9
545	1/ 4/57	410	24	60	14290	388	101	84	97	83	29	83	83	9
546	1/ 1/57	483	36	60	20000	388	101	84	97	83	29	100	100	9
547	1/ 7/57	560	7	42	10170	388	101	84	97	83	29	100	100	9
549	1/16/57	490	36	60	18000	388	101	84	97	83	29	100	100	9
551	2/ 8/57	770	2	36	18500	405	101	95	93	100	29	104	100	9
552	2/13/57	527	7	60	9736	405	101	95	93	100	29	100	100	9
553	2/20/57	442	60	72	20000	405	101	95	93	100	29	100	100	9
554	3/29/57	420	1	60	12428	311	87	98	74	97	28	77	86	9
555	5/24/57	476	12	60	17865	98	60	102	94	134	59	32	69	9
556	5/24/57	490	5	60	18000	98	60	102	94	134	59	100	100	9
557	6/ 5/57	438	16	60	16556	97	79	101	100	112	66	99	132	9
558	7/23/57	515	1	24	10670	102	93	100	96	105	69	105	118	9
559	7/30/57	429	12	60	16721	102	93	100	96	105	69	100	100	9
560	8/ 9/57	399	6	84	21400	80	87	104	114	107	74	78	94	9
561	8/31/57	395	7	60	20300	80	87	104	114	107	74	100	100	9
562	8/31/57	395	12	60	22000	80	87	104	114	107	74	100	100	9
563	11/18/57	366	12	60	18590	87	102	110	105	98	99	109	117	9
564	11/14/57	366	12	60	19200	87	102	110	105	98	99	100	100	9
565	11/14/57	348	3	60	16900	87	102	110	105	98	99	100	100	9
566	11/18/57	280	1	30	9605	87	102	110	105	98	99	100	100	9
567	11/25/57	360	12	60	17360	87	102	110	105	98	99	100	100	9
568	12/20/57	355	9	60	16875	83	99	104	95	94	93	95	97	9

Appendix E

Sources of Data Used in Figures

Figures 2.1–2.5: Theoretical.

Figures 4.1–4.3: *Number of Fixtures:* Maritime Research Inc., New York, up to December 1957; Davies & Newman, Ltd., London, for 1958. *Rates:* Index of Rates developed as explained in Chapter 10. *Data:* U.S. Maritime Administration 1948–1956; Addison Outwater and Associates, New York, and Dietz, Inc., New York, for 1957; Addison Outwater and Associates, New York, for 1958.

Figures 5.1–5.5: *Rates:* same as in Figure 4.1. *New Orders Placed:* Transportation Coordination Department, Standard Oil Company (New Jersey).

Figure 5.6: *Cost of Vessels:* Fairplay Index (see *Fairplay* semiannual issues).

Figures 5.7–5.18, 6.1–6.3: *Rates:* Same as in Figure 4.1.

Figures 8.1–8.2, 9.1: *Deliveries, Orders Outstanding, Size of Fleet, Number, Age, and Size of Vessels Scrapped, Repairs, Idle Fleet, and Tie-ups:* Transportation Coordination Department, Standard Oil Company (New Jersey).

Figures 9.2–9.3: *Charters:* Conrad Boe, Ltd., Shipbrokers, Oslo; R. S. Platou, A/S, Shipbrokers, Oslo. For method of conversion of time-charter rates to spot-rate equivalent see Appendix B.

Figure 11.1: *Cost of Operation:* Marine Brokerage, New York.

Selected Bibliography

Books

Allen, R. G. D., *Mathematical Economics,* Macmillan & Co., Ltd., London, England, 1957.

Arkin, Herbert, and Raymond Colton, *Statistical Methods,* Barnes & Noble, Inc., New York, 1957.

Baumol, J. W., *Economic Dynamics,* The Macmillan Company, New York, 1957.

Birkhoff, Garrett, and Saunders MacLane, *A Survey of Modern Algebra,* The Macmillan Company, New York, 1949.

Bes, J., *Chartering Shipping Terms,* C. De Boer, Jr., Hilversum, Netherlands, Fourth Edition, 1956.

———, *Tanker Chartering and Management,* C. De Boer, Jr., Hilversum, Netherlands, 1956.

Chow, Gregory C., *Demand for Automobiles in the United States,* North-Holland Publishing Company, Amsterdam, Netherlands, 1957.

Fisher, Irving, *The Theory of Interest,* The Macmillan Company, New York, 1930.

Frankel, P. H., *Essentials of Petroleum,* Chapman & Hall Ltd., London, England, 1946.

Gayer, Arthur D., W. W. Rostow, and Anna J. Schwartz, *The Growth and Fluctuation of the British Economy 1790–1850,* Two Volumes, Oxford University Press, Oxford, 1953.

Hicks, J. R., *Value and Capital,* Second Edition, Oxford University Press, London, England, 1953.

Hoel, Paul G., *Introduction to Mathematical Statistics,* Second Edition, John Wiley & Sons, Inc., New York, 1954.

Kalecki, M., *Studies in Economic Dynamics,* Allen and Unwin, Ltd., London, England, 1943.

Keynes, J. M., *The General Theory of Employment, Interest and Money,* Macmillan & Co., Ltd., London, England, 1936.

Koopmans, Tjalling C., *Tanker Freight Rates and Tankship Building.* Haarlem, Netherlands, 1939.

Koyck, L. M., *Distributed Lags and Investment Analysis,* North-Holland Publishing Company, Amsterdam, Netherlands, 1954.

Manning, George C., *The Theory and Technique of Ship Design,* The Technology Press of the Massachusetts Institute of Technology, Cambridge, Massachusetts, 1956.

Marshall, Alfred, *Principles of Economics,* Eighth Edition, Macmillan & Co., Ltd., London, England, 1956.

Metcalfe, James V., *Principles of Ocean Transportation,* Simmons-Boardman, New York, 1959.

Mosac, Jacob L., *General Equilibrium Theory in International Trade,* The Principia Press, Inc., Bloomington, Indiana, 1944.

Robinson, Joan, *The Economics of Imperfect Competition,* Macmillan & Co., Ltd., London, England, 1933.

Rostow, W. W., *British Economy in the Nineteenth Century,* Oxford University Press, Oxford, England, 1948.

Samuelson, Paul, *Economics,* Fourth Edition, McGraw-Hill Book Company, New York, 1958.

―――, *Foundations of Economic Analysis,* Harvard University Press, Cambridge, Massachusetts, 1947.

Shackle, G. L. S., *Time in Economics,* North-Holland Publishing Company, Amsterdam, Netherlands, 1958.

Tinbergen, Jan, *Selected Papers,* L. H. Klaasen *et al.* Editors, North-Holland Publishing Company, Amsterdam, Netherlands, 1959.

Viner, Jacob, *The Long View and the Short,* The Free Press, Glencoe, Illinois, 1958.

Public Documents

Nerlove, Marc, *Distributed Lags and Demand Analysis for Agricultural and Other Commodities,* U.S. Government Printing Office, Washington 25, D. C., June 1958.

Organization for European Economic Cooperation, *Oil, The Outlook for Europe,* Paris, 1955, Chapter XI.

―――, *Europe's Need for Oil,* Paris, 1958, Chapter VI.

Secretariat of the Economic Commission for Europe, *Produits Pétroliers en Europe Occidentale,* United Nations, Geneva, March 1955.

U.S. Government Printing Office, Committee on the Judiciary, U.S. Senate, *Petroleum, The Antitrust Laws and Government Policies,* S. Res. 57, Washington 25, D. C., August 27, 1957.

―――, *New Ship Construction Program,* Pursuant to S. Res. 13, April 21–22, 1955.

―――, Subcommittee of the Committee on Interstate and Foreign Commerce hearings before the United States Senate, *Merchant Marine Study and Investigation,* Pursuant to S. Res. 50, June 21–22, 1949.

―――, *Tanker and Cargo Tankship Charter and Construction,* On S. 3877, June 13, 1956.

Articles

Akerman, Gustav, "The Cobweb Theorem: A Reconsideration," *The Quarterly Journal of Economics,* Vol. LXXI, No. 1, February 1957.

Arrow, Kenneth J., and Maurice McManus, "A Note of Dynamic Stability," *Econometrica,* Vol. 26, No. 3, July 1958.

Benford, Harry, *Engineering Economy in Tanker Design,* Society of Naval Architects and Marine Engineers, paper presented at the December 1956 meeting.

Buchanan, Norman S., "A Reconsideration of the Cobweb Theorem," *Journal of Political Economy,* February 1939.

Enthoven, Alain C., and Kenneth J. Arrow, "A Theorem on Expectations and Stability of Equilibrium," *Econometrica,* Vol. 24, No. 3, July 1956.

Ezekiel, Mordecai, "The Cobweb Theorem," *The Quarterly Journal of Economics,* Vol. LII, 1938.

Jung, Ingvar, and Gunnar Ohlsson, "Technical and Economic Data for Turbine-Powered Tankers," *International Shipbuilding Progress,* Vol. 4, No. 38, October 1957.

Kaldor, Nicholas, "Economics of Imperfect Competition," *Economica,* Vol. 1, Nos. 1–4, 1934.

McIntosh, A. F., "Petroleum Demand Past and Future," *Petroleum Press Service,* London, January 1958.

Metzler, Lloyd A., "Stability of Multiple Markets: The Hicks Condition," *Econometrica,* Vol. 13, No. 4, October 1945.

Mills, Edwin S., "The Use of Adaptive Expectations in Stability Analysis: Comment," *The Quarterly Journal of Economics,* Vol. LXXV, No. 2, May 1961.

Nerlove, Marc, "Adaptive Expectations and Cobweb Phenomena," *The Quarterly Journal of Economics,* Vol. LXXIII, No. 2, May 1958.

Ozanne, H., "Super-Tankers Threaten U.S. with $2 Middle East Oil," *World Oil,* April 1949.

Robbins, Lionel, "On a Certain Ambiguity in the Conception of Stationary Equilibrium," *Economic Journal,* June 1930.

Samuelson, Paul, "Dynamics, Statics and the Stationary State," *Review of Economic Statistics,* February 1943.

Reports

Ebasco Services, *Survey of the Future of the Suez Canal Company,* Ebasco Services, New York, 1957.

Kahle and Kelley, *The Role of Sea Transportation in the Petroleum Industry,* paper presented at the Fifth World Petroleum Congress, May 30, 1959.

Møller-Guldberg, *Comparison Between Steam-Turbine and Diesel-Driven Tankers of 24,000 D.W.T.,* Burmeister & Wain, Copenhagen, Denmark, 1956.

Shields and Company, *Financing the United States Merchant Marine,* Shields and Company, New York, May 1958.

Unpublished Material

Bishop, Robert L., *Unpublished Manuscript,* Book II, Chapter 1.

Periodicals and Reports

Fairplay, London, England.
Financial Times, "Outlook for Shipping," by Stavros Niarchos, April 17, 1958.
International Shipbuilding Progress, The, London, England.
Lloyd's Register of Shipping, London, England.
Marine News, New York.
Motorship, The, London, England.
Oil Forum, The, Vol. IV, No. 3, March 1950.
Oil and Gas Journal, The, Tulsa, Oklahoma.
Petroleum Press Service, London, England.
Petroleum Times, The, London, England.
Register of Tank Vessels of the World, Standard Oil Company of New Jersey.
Shipping World and World Shipbuilding, The, London, England.
U.S.M.C. Rate Schedule, Robert T. Jones, Inc., New York.
Westinform Shipping Reports and *Monthly Tanker Bulletins,* W. G. Weston, Ltd., London, England.
World Tanker Fleet Review, John I. Jacobs & Co., London, England.

Tankship Brokers' Reports

Addison Outwater and Associates, New York.
Clarkson, Ltd., London, England.
Conrad Boe, Ltd., A/S, Oslo, Norway.
Davies & Newman, Ltd., London, England.
Dietz, Inc., New York.
E. A. Gibson & Co., Ltd., London, England.
Howard Houlder & Partners, Ltd., London, England.
Lambert Brothers, Ltd., London, England.
R. S. Platou, A/S, Oslo, Norway.

Index

AALL and Co., Ltd., 98
Addison Outwater and Associates, 92, 120, 125n
Adjustment, index of, 216–218
Adjustment paths, *see under* Cobweb theorem
AFRA, 246, 253
  definition of, 246
Age distribution of vessels, *see under* Tankships
Akerman, Gustav, 189, 191n
Allen, R. G. D., 10, 30, 52
Allen-Hicks formulation, 10, *see also* Slutsky-Hicks formulation
Allied/Ashland, 62, 66, 70
Andreadis, S. G., 63, 67, 71
Antwerp, 129, 133, 148, 150, 151, 168
Archimedean property, 15
Arkin, Herbert, 222n
Arrow, Kenneth J., 8, 11
Association of Ship Brokers and Agents, Inc., 150
Atlantic Refining, 62, 66, 70, 254
A.T.R.S., definition of, 246
Australia, 82, 252

Backlog of orders, *see under* Orders placed
Backward-bending supply, 84
Ballasted traffic, 162–164, 168, 169
  institutional factors and, 162
  short-run supply schedule and, 162
Barber Oil, 63, 67, 71
Bareboat, 3, 246
  see also Charters
Baumol, J. W., 1, 6, 22, 80, 109n, 196n
Belgium, 82, 252
Benford, Harry, 127n
Bes, J., 138n, 155n, 207n, 208, 213n
Bimodalities, significance in time-charter rates, 227, 229–230
Birkhoff, Garrett, 15
Bishop, R. L., 161n
Britain, *see* United Kingdom
British Petroleum, 62, 66, 70, 107, 129, 254
Brokerage fees, 151
Buchanan, Norman S., 189n, 190n

"Budget" effects, 9, 19, 25, 54n, 55, 81–82, 86
  and expectations of buyers, 25, 81–82
  empirical evidence, 86
  impact on suppliers, 19
  see also Income effect
Building, *see* Shipbuilding
Buyers and sellers, behavior of, 6–34, 97, 116, 187, 205, 239
  asymmetry in, 20–21
  expectations and, 6–34, 187, 205
  supply and demand interactions under elastic expectations, 21–29
  interperiod maximization of profit or utility, mathematical formulation, 30–34

Caltex, 62, 66, 70, 215n, 254
Canada, 82, 252
Cancellations of orders in 1958, *see under* Orders placed
Capacity, tankship, 4, 50–76, 94–169, 170–173, 222, 225, 240, 249
  ballasted traffic and, 162–163, 168, 169
  carrying, *see* Carrying capacity
  contraction in, reasons for, 116–126
  contributions from outside, 165–166
  definition of, 167–169
  demand schedule and, 240
  dry cargo ships and, 50
  excess of, 25, 57n, 96, 100, 129n
  factors affecting it, 160–169
  future increments in, 80, 113
  idle for repairs, 138, 140–143, 222, 225, *see also* Tie-ups and idle capacity
  in short run, 50
  in spot market, 94
  maximum usable, 168
  owned vs. chartered, ratio of, 75
  ownership of, *see* Ownership shares
  point of full capacity 108, 167–173
  potential gross carrying, 249
  shipbuilding and, 50
  spot, 187
  see also Supply schedule
Cape route, 133

325

Caribbean, 194n, 216, 253
Carras, J. C., 63, 67, 71
Carrying capacity, 46, 47, 72, 163, 168, 249
  adjustment in, 47
  and ballasted traffic, 163
  feasible level, 168
  ownership of, 72
Carrying charges and excess inventory, 31
Charter agreement, duration of, 208–213
  and charter rate long-term, 208–213
Charter rate, long-term, in long run, 231–238, 245
  cost of operation and, 233, 236, 238
  economies of scale and, 232
  existence of many rates, 233, 238
  size of vessel and, 233–238
    "time-charter cost of operation" for vessels of different sizes, 233, 235, 236–238
  trend in, 238, 245
  voyage rate equivalent of, 236n
Charter rate, long-term in short run, 5, 52, 202–230, 244, 249–250
  analysis of highs and lows, 229
  and short-term rates, 203–205, 210, 227, 230, 244, 249–250
  conversion into spot-rate equivalent of, 211, 235, 249–250
  currency, type of and, 214
  definition of, 202n
  determination of, 219–226, 245
  duration of charter agreement and, 208–213
    bimodality of, 227–230
    empirical evidence, 212
  economics of tanker propulsion and, 206–208
  economies of scale and, 205
  equation for, 231
  expectations of buyers and, 202, 205
  factors affecting it, 202, 231
  formation of, see determination of
  heterogeneity of tankship markets and, 211
  idle capacity and, 222
  lead time and, 213
  "normal rate," 210
  orders and, 205
  sample size, 219
  short-term rate and, 203–205, 210, 227
  size of vessel and, 204, 227–230
    bimodality of, 227–230
  statistical model for, 215–230
    beta coefficients, 222
    index of spot rates, 215–217
    logarithmic formulation, 219–226
    regression equation, 220, 224
    significance of variables, 223
  tie-ups and, 205
Charter rate, short-term, 41–49, 51, 55, 75n, 76–93, 96, 103, 104, 110–159, 165, 176, 186–201, 203–205, 210, 211, 215–218, 227, 230, 235, 249–250
  adjustments in, short-run, 188–201, 210, 216, 243–244
  and age of vessel retired, 117, 120
  and construction costs, 55, 242n
  and expectations, see Expectations
  and long-term rates, 203–205, 210, 227, 230, 244, 249–250
  and scrappings, 242
  and size of vessels retired, 126
  and slowdowns, 126–134
  and tie-ups, 144–159
  and transactions, 42–49, 165
  average, 103, 104
  boundaries of oscillations in, 193, 196–201
  changes in, 46, 53, 75
  convergence of, in short run, 196, 197
  conversion of time-charter rates into, 211, 235, 249–250
  conversions of vessels and, 134
  cyclical, 24n, 44
  deliveries and, 110–116, 118
  determination of, 50, 186–201, 243
  empirical observations, 199
  explosive movements of, see Cobweb theorem
  Fairplay index versus, 83
  fixtures transacted versus, 42, 43, 47
  formation of, see determination of
  high levels of, reasons for, 194
  idle tonnage and, 157
  index of, 215–216
  index of adjustment and, 216–218
  instability of in long run, 196–198
  investment opportunity schedule and, 55
  lead time between contract and vessel delivery and, 213
  long-run cost and, 103, 104
  market behavior and, 176
  operating fleet capacity and, 169
  orders for new vessels and, 50, 51, 59, 61, 76–93, 111, 115–116, 205
    backlog of, 76
    net changes in, 115
    scatter diagrams for, 83–87, 115–116
  oscillations in, 2, 10, 86, 95, 98, 108, 193, 196–201
  peaks of, 110–114
  random walk, nonexistence of in, 200
  reflecting barriers, 201
  repairs and, 135–144
  scatter diagrams for, see Scatter diagrams
  seaborne trade and, 113
  statistics for, 80
  technical innovation and, 122
  upper limit of, 193
Chartering activity, 42–49, 99, 165
  expectations and, 165
  high rates and, 165
  independents vs. oil companies and, 99
  see also Tankship markets
Charters, 3, 44, 53, 94, 95, 99, 107, 219–226, 240, 246, 247, 249
  bareboat, 3

Charters (*continued*)
  consecutive voyage, 3, 99, 240
    definition of, 240
  definition of, 246
  demand for, *see* Demand schedule, chartering
  long-term, 3, 5, 165, 219–226, 244
    definition of, 3
  period, *see* Charters, time
  rate for, *see* Charter rate, long-term, and Charter rate, short-term
  single-voyage, 3, 44, 159, 247
    definition of, 3, 247
  spot, *see* Charters, single-voyage
  time, 3, 94n, 101, 103, 107, 247
    definition of, 3
    duration of, 103, 107
    revenue of, 101
Chow, Gregory C., 216n
Cities Service, 62, 66, 70, 254
Clean cargo, definition of, 246
"Clean" trade, 214
  vs. "dirty," 214
Clemence, Richard V., 189n
Cobweb theorem, 9, 189–201, 210, 216, 243–244
  adjustment paths, 192–197, 210
  applicability in short-term tankship rate formation, 189–192
Coefficients of expectations, 8, 17, 21, 22, 54n, 55
  braid effect, 21
  smoothing functions, 22
Colton, Raymond, 222
Competition in tankship markets, 176–184, 190, 243
  cobweb assumptions and, 190
  ease of entry and, 180–182
    reasons for, 182
  mobility and, 179–180
  and artificial controls, 183
  ownership and, 176
  size of optimal unit, 181–183
  vessel is the firm, 182
Complementarities in tankship markets, *see under* Tankship markets
Conrad Boe, Ltd., 120, 234, 254
Consecutive voyage charters, *see under* Charters
Conservatism, principle of, 109
  asymmetry of anguish vs. joy, 109
  implications of, 109n
Construction statistics, timing of, 76n
Continental Oil Co., 62, 66, 70
Contract of affreightment, 163, 246
Contracts, *see* Charters
Contractual bargaining, long-term, 68
Controls, absence of in tankship markets, 183
Conversions of vessels, 126, 134, 165
  cost of, 134, 165
  extent of, 134
Cooper, M. D., 129n
Cosmopolitan Transit Lines, 107, 144
Cost of capital, 8, 16, 31, 57n, 102

Costs, 38, 54n, 57–60, 75n, 76, 79, 83, 87, 95, 98–99, 100, 101, 102, 103, 104, 105–107, 117, 133n, 151, 167, 210, 233, 236
  and analysis of time-charter rates, 233, 236
  average spot rate and long-run cost, 103, 104
  long-run, 210
    and long-term rates, 102
  marginal operating, 167
  of delivered vessel, 98–99, 105–107
  of fuel, *see under* Slowdowns
  of idleness, 59, 105, 153
  of lay-up, 58, 133n
  of recommissioning, 59
  of tie-up, *see under* Tie-ups
  out-of-pocket, 60, 87, 117, 133n, 151
  per unit of capacity, 60
  shipbuilding, *see under* Shipbuilding
  time-fixity of, 167
  variable, average, 57–59
Cross price effects, 12, 13
Crosshauling, 178
Currency, type of and charter rate, 214
Curaçao, 211, 249
Cyclical demand, *see under* Demand schedule
Cyclical rates, *see under* Charter rates, short-term

Davies and Newman, Ltd., 42n, 152n, 174
Deliveries, *see under* Shipbuilding
Demand
  dynamic shifts in, *see under* Demand schedule, chartering, and Demand schedule, shipbuilding
  excess in, 49, 101
  for future deliveries, *see* Interperiod substitutions, and *under* Shipbuilding, now vs. later decisions
  for petroleum, reasons for inelasticity of, 35
  stationary, 31, 35
Demand schedule, chartering, 2, 6–17, 17–29, 30–34, 35–41, 41–42, 43, 44, 51n, 61, 74, 77, 78, 81, 83, 93, 94–97, 108, 113, 134, 143, 192–194, 239–241
  adjusting oscillation, 24
  alternation of sign of slope, 240
  and interperiod substitution, 16–19, 24, 192, 194, 239
  and seaborne trade, 113
  "budget" effects and technology, 51n
  clockwise rotation of, 24
  comparison with shipbuilding, 94–97
  consecutive shifts in, 241
  cyclical, 75, 241
  difficulties in establishing it, 38
  double-valued, 40
  dynamic impacts, 3, 23, 40
  effective, 78
  elasticity of, 2, 61, 74
  empirical, 41–42, 239–240
  external primary effects on, 40

328   INDEX

Demand schedule, chartering (*continued*)
 for future deliveries, 101
 hypothetical, 18
 reversibility of, 25, 43, 83, 93, 194
  reasons for, 83
 segments of, 17
 sequential shifts in, 108
 shifts in, 24, 40, 44, 78, 81, 95, 143, 239
  and idle capacity, 143
  and observed patterns, 44
  consequences of, 24
 short term, 192, 194
  interperiod substitutions, 192, 194
  reversibility of, 194
 slope, sign of, 20, 44, 78
 slowdowns, 134
 static, 31, 35
 theoretical discussion, 6–41, 192–194
 turning points in, 43, 96, 194n
Demand schedule, shipbuilding, 6–34, 52, 54, 56, 61, 75, 76, 94–97, 104, 134, 143, 187, 229, 240, 241
 and interperiod substitutions, 239
 and tonnage, 240
 comparison with chartering, 94–97
 consecutive shifts in, 241
 construction lead time, 239
 cyclical, 75, 241
 elasticity of, 13, 16, 52, 54, 56, 61, 76
  future building elasticity, 54
  income elasticity, 13, 16, 56
  price elasticity, 13, 54
  spot-rate elasticity, 52
 empirical shape of, 239, 240
 hypothetical, 18
 impact of expectations, 239
 market vs. derived, 104
 orders placed, *see* Orders placed
 shifts in, 95, 143
 slowdowns, 134
 spot rates, 52, 187
 theoretical discussion, 6–34
 turning points in, 84–86, 96–97, 194n
Denmark, 82, 107
Depletion allowance, U.S., 69n
Depressed periods, 95, 148, 150
 yield during, 148
 withdrawals during, 150
Diesel vs. steam turbine, 206–208
Dirty cargo, definition of, 247
"Dirty" trade, 214
 vs. "clean," 214
Distress rates, 147
Dry cargo, 50, 126

Ebasco Services, 163
Economic life and retirements, 51, 59
Economics of tanker propulsion, 206–208
 and charter rate, 206–208
Economies of scale, 61, 74, 86, 87, 122, 124–125, 162, 180, 195, 198, 205, 232, 233, 236
 administrative and financial, 180
 and charter rates, 205, 232
 and vessel size, 233
 in crew costs, 236
 in tankship building, 74, 86, 236
 in tankship operation, 74, 86, 236
 of supertankers, 124, 236
 technological, 61, 125, 198
Economies of specialization, 154n
Elastic expectations, *see under* Expectations, elasticity of
Elasticity of expectations, *see* Expectations, elasticity of
Einarsen's data, 119
Enthoven, A. C., 8, 11
Escalation clauses, 79, 105n
Excess capacity, 25, 57n, 96, 100, 129n
Expectations, 1, 3, 7–29, 31, 40, 42–49, 53, 54n, 55, 59, 60, 77–80, 81, 83, 84, 87, 93, 95, 97, 99, 100, 102–105, 107, 116, 117, 187, 190, 193, 205, 225n, 239
 adaptive, 9
 and behavior of buyers and sellers, 7–29
 and changes in demand schedule, 24, 44, 78
 and chartering activity, 193
 and fixtures, 52
 and market fluctuations, 26
 and spot rates, 42–49, 117
 and stability of rates, 239
 asymmetrical pattern of, 20, 104
 building cost, 100, 241
 coefficient of, 8, 17, 21, 22, 26, 54n, 55
 cycle in, 21
 dynamic, 8, 9, 13, 21, 23, 31, 40n, 53, 55, 87, 116
  and length of production cycle, 23
 elasticity of, *see* Expectations, elasticity of
 impact of, 7–29, 40, 42–49, 53, 95
  on buyers and sellers, 7–29
  on contracts, 95
  on quantity demanded, 40, 53
  on spot rates, 42–49
 in nonmonetary markets, 7
 in tankship building markets, 79n, 107
 index of, 88
 "intermediate," 225n
 lag in, 99n
 manifested vs. real symmetry in schedules of, 28
 of buyers, 19, 25, 53, 77–82, 84, 93, 97, 187, 205
  and charter rates, 205
  and demand schedules, 25
  rate elasticity for, 53, 187
 of buyers and sellers, 7–29, 77–80, 84, 97, 239
  symmetry between, 7, 8, 19, 84, 97, 239
 of charterers, 103
  rate elasticity for, 103
 of derived factor costs, 104
 of future price levels, 1, 7, 8, 11, 12, 14, 17, 31
 of independents, 100, 105
  for rates, 100, 105
  for shipbuilding costs, 100

INDEX 329

Expectations (*continued*)
of operatives, *see* of buyers and sellers
of sellers, 7–29, 84, 97, 239
rate, 16, 44, 49, 59, 60, 64, 77, 79, 86, 100, 105, 193, 239, 241
and chartering activity, 59, 60, 193
and excess demand, 49
and price movements, 239
elasticity of, *see* Expectations, elasticity of
real vs. manifested schedules for, 28
reversals in, 24
schedules of oil companies vs. independents, 99
shipbuilding costs and, 102
static, 9, 12, 13
"temporary changes in," 84
Expectations, elasticity of, 1, 4, 6–9, 13–16, 19–21, 24, 25, 27, 28, 40, 43, 44, 53–56, 61, 68, 77n, 80, 84, 89, 90, 93, 94n, 95, 100, 103–105, 147, 154n, 165, 171, 185, 187, 193, 194
and depressions, 95
and interperiod substitutions, 54, 194
and surpluses, 187n
and tie-ups, 147
change in, 19
charter-rate elasticity, 100
definition of, 6
destabilizing, 28
elastic, 6–9, 14–16, 19, 20, 23, 24, 27, 40, 43, 61, 64, 68, 80, 84, 94n, 95, 104, 171, 184
followership of leader and, 184
price elastic, 14, 16, 23, 24, 27, 84, 94n, 95
uniformly elastic, 61
"final market rate" inelasticity, 105
income elasticity, 13, 16, 53, 54, 56
inelastic, 19, 21
measurement of, 40
price elasticity, 1, 4, 7, 10, 13, 14, 16, 23, 53, 54, 84, 93, 94
defined, 13, 95, 165
rate elasticity, 44, 64, 90, 95, 103, 187
of buyers, 53, 187
of charterers, 103
of orders, 90
unit elastic, 7, 14, 40
Expected cost of idleness, 59
Expected level of future prices, 17
Expected replacement, total cost for, 60
Expected revenue, 58
Expected total cost, per unit of capacity, 60
Ezekiel, Mordecai, 189n

"Fair rate," 87
Fairplay index, 83, 105–107
50% Rule, 218, 227
Fisher, Irving, 60n
Fixtures, 42, 43, 46, 48, 247
and spot rates, 42, 46
average number contracted, 48
carrying capacity, 46
definition of, 247

impact of rates on, 46
in month equivalent, 46
number of, 42, 43
"Flat" U.S.M.C., 248
see also U.S.M.C.
Fleet, petroleum, 53, 64, 67, 71, 114, 115, 139, 150, 162, 164n, 165–169, 218, 248
and repairs, 139
capacity of, *see* Capacity, tankship
composition of and short-term supply, 162
in the spot market, 164n, 165n
and Suez crisis, 165n
operating, 167–169
and spot rates, 169
as percentage of total fleet, 168
ownership pattern of, 51, 64–76, 242
specialized, 165
total, 114, 115
withdrawal of, 83, 84, 150, 171
working, 114, 115, 139, 168, 169, 218, 248
definition of, 248
Foreign repair yards, *see under* Repair yards
Formosa, 82
France, 82, 107, 183, 252
Frankel, P. H., 37n
Fuel consumption, *see* Slowdowns
Full capacity, 57, 108, 167–173
definition of, 108n
point of, 57, 108, 167–173
see also Capacity
Fundamental equation of value, 10, 11, 30, 33, 51, 52, 240
see also Slutsky-Hicks formulation
Fundamental theory of value, *see* Fundamental equation of value
Future price elasticity of demand, *see* Expectations, elasticity of

Gayer, Arthur D., 80n
Geographical constraints operating in oil markets, 37
Giffen's paradox, 2, 54n
Goulandris, M. P., 63, 67, 71
Government commercial fleet, 63, 67, 71
Greece, 82
Greek shipowners, 100
Gulf Oil Company, 62, 66, 70, 97n, 125n, 254
charter data, 254

Hendy, Joshua, 63, 67, 71
Hess, 62, 66, 70, 254
Hicks, J. R., 1, 6, 10, 21, 22, 30, 80n, 203n
Hicks' formulation, 18
"Hidden surplus," 134
Higgins, E. A., 37n
Hoel, P. G., 220, 223n

Idle capacity, 59, 60, 141–143, 150, 153, 157–159
and rates, 157–158
equation for, 157–158

Idle capacity (*continued*)
  and repairs, 157n
  days for repairs, 150
  lag behind rates, reasons for, 159
  opportunity cost of, 153
  pattern of, 143
  periodicity in, 142
  recommissioning cost, 59, 60
  see also Tie-ups
Idle port time, 166
Idle tonnage, *see* Idle capacity
Income determination, accrual principle for, 61n
Income effect, 10–29, 49n, 52–56, 58, 61, 65, 85, 96, 196, 221, 240–241
  for suppliers of consumer goods, 18
  impact on demand schedules, 10–29, 240
  impact on supply schedules, 22, 52–56, 85, 96, 241
  negative, 14, 55
  of own price change, 14, 22, 56, 96
  positive, 61, 65
  static effects, 53, 55, 58
  vs. substitution effect, 85
Income realized, 61n
Independents, 53, 56n, 63, 65n, 67, 69, 71, 72, 74, 75, 97–110, 125, 153, 174, 175, 190, 242
  and arbitrage, 104
  and transportation service, 99
  as pure competitors, 190
  behavior of and tanker rates, 107
  expectations of, 7–29, 100, 104–106
    elastic, 104
    for charter rates, 100, 105, 106
    for shipbuilding costs, 100, 102
  manifest behavior of, 242
  ownership, share of, 53, 69, 72, 74, 174, 175
  reactions of to rate changes, 75
  vs. oil companies, 97–110, 125, 133, 153, 242
Index of expectations, 88
  see also Expectations and Adjustment, index of
Indifference curves, static, 54n
Inferior good, 14, 32, 54
Institutional factors, 37, 51, 68, 75, 243
  and ballasted traffic, 162
  influence of on new capacity, 51
  operating in oil markets, 37–38
  operating in tankship markets, 174–185
Interperiod maximization of utility or profit, 11, 30–34
Interperiod substitutions, 7–10, 12–14, 16, 17, 19, 24, 30, 32, 33, 38, 44, 54, 55, 192, 194, 196, 240
  and elasticity of expectations, 54
  and empirical demand schedule, 240
  and equilibrium, 32
  and fundamental equation of value, 30, 33, 51, 52, 240
  caused by expectations, 17
  dynamic, 12
  effect on short-term rate oscillations, 196

impact of, 33n, 192, 194, 196
Inventory carrying cost, 7, 16
Investment possibility schedules, 27, 53, 55
Iraq, 100n
Iraq Petroleum Company, 100n
Italian yards, 77
Italy, 82, 107, 183, 252

Jacobs, John I., *see* John I. Jacobs and Company, Ltd.
Japan, 80, 82, 96, 97n, 98, 125n, 183, 253
Japanese Ministry of Commerce, export statistics, 98
Japanese shipbuilders, 84
Japanese yards, 80
John I. Jacobs and Company, Ltd., 68n, 79n, 96n, 100n, 106n, 111

Kahle, L. F., and Kelley, A. J., Jr., 186
Kaldor, N., 4
Kalecki, M., 203n
Karchere, Alvin, 215n
Keynes, J. M., 203n
Koopmans, Tjalling C., 9, 38n, 45n, 65n, 111, 113n, 115n, 118, 119, 153n, 155n, 162
Korean War, 24, 38, 77, 83n, 140, 142, 199
Koyck, L. M., 216n
Kulukundis, M. E., 63, 67, 71
Kure Shipbuilding Company, 97n
Kurz, C., 63, 67, 71

Lagrange multiplier, 31
Lags, 38, 40, 48, 66n, 89, 98n, 99n, 110, 111, 114, 146, 159, 242n
  between rates and tie-ups, 146
  in expectations, 99n
  in initiation and announcement of orders, 114
  of building costs behind rates, 96, 242n
  of deliveries behind orders, 110, 111
  of deliveries behind rates, 110, 111
  of idle capacity behind rates, 159
  of shipbuilding behind chartering activities, 94–97
Lay-up, *see* Tie-ups
Lead time, 27, 48, 52, 59, 77, 103, 110n, 111, 165, 213, 239
  and loan value of charter, 213n
  and spot rates, 213
  between charter contract and vessel delivery, 52, 107, 165, 213
  and impact on long-term rate, 213
  data for 1950–1957, 107
  between input and output in production, 27
  between ship order and delivery, 52, 59, 72, 110n, 111, 213, 239
  equality to charter duration, 53
Lemos, G. Ch., 63, 67, 71
Liberia, 107
Livanos, M. G., 63, 67, 71

INDEX

Logarithmic formulation of time-charter rate, 219–226
Long-term rate, *see* Charter rate, long-term
Ludwig, 124

McIntosh, A. F., 36
MacLane, Saunders, 15
McManus, M., 8
Management policy suggestions, 245
Managerial information system suggestions, 245
Manning, George C., 126
Manufacturing time cycles, 30
Maracaibo, 148, 150, 151, 159, 163, 168
Marginal cost of oil and final price, 36
Marginal operating costs and average tie-up costs, 167
"Marginal" sales and "net back," 37
Marginal utility of money, 32
Marginal vessel, 87, 145, 171, 187, 243
   average lay-up rate of, 171
   in rate determination, 145
   out-of-pocket cost for, 87
   tie-up cost of, 243
Marine Brokerage Company, 129n, 130, 132, 144, 147, 150, 235
Marine Transportation Department, Socony Mobil Oil Company, 164, 165
Market
   depressed conditions of, and governmental restrictions, 75
   long-run instability of, 101
   tankship, *see* Tankship markets
Market fluctuations and elastic expectations, 25, 106
Marshall, A., 2, 161n
Marshall's laws of derived demand, 37n
Metcalf, James V., 151
Metzler, L. A., 8
Metzler's theorem, 8
Middle East, 48, 100, 125n
Mills, E. S., 9
Mobility in tankship markets, 179, 180
   see also Tankship markets
Monetary markets, 14
Monetary resources, 15
Mosac, Jacob L., 10n, 30
Moving averages of orders placed, 89n
Multiple regression, 89n, 215
   and correlation 704 program, 88
   for long-term rates, 215

National Bulk Carriers, Inc., 63, 67, 71, 124
Negative correlation, 61
   short-term rates and orders, 61
Nerlove, Marc, 8, 11, 189, 216n
"Net back," 37
   and "marginal" sales, 37
   and transportation rates, 37n
   to producers, 37
Netherlands, 82, 252
New orders, *see* Orders placed
Newbuilding, definition of, 247

Niarchos, S., 63, 67, 71, 124
Nicolaou, N. G., 63, 67, 71
Nomikos, P. M., 63, 67, 71
Normal speed and shaft horsepower, 108n
Norway, 82, 107, 120, 234

Obsolescence of vessels, 50, 57, 59, 126
"Off-hire" repairs, *see* Repairs
Oil companies, 62, 66, 70, 74, 77, 87n, 97–110, 125, 127, 129, 133, 152n, 153, 154, 177, 178, 184, 185, 242, 243
   and low rates, 74
   and refusal rates, 152n, *see also* Refusal rate
   and slowdowns, 127, 129
   and tonnage surpluses, 74
   and total world fleet, 99n
   and transportation services, 99
   behavior of, 106, *see also* Buyers and sellers, behavior of
   charters of during Suez crisis, 101
   charters to independents, 100n
   covariance of transportation needs of, 185
   delayed response of, 99n
   dual role of, 153
   employment policy of, 152n
   FOB vs. CIF, 177
   following leader, 184
   individual action of, 69n
   need of for crosshauling, 178
   opportunity costs for, 100
   orders of, for "supertankers," 77
   orders of, for vessels, *see* Orders placed
   ownership share, 69, 72, 74, 125, 174, 175
   of big vessels, 125
   profit maximization by, 108
   penalty minimization by, 108
   policy planners of, 108, 110
   reaction to fluctuations in transportation costs, 177
   self-sufficiency of, 176, 243
   tanker rates and behavior of, 75, 107–110
   tie-ups by at low rates, 154
   vs. independents, 97–110, 125, 133, 153, 242
Oil fleet, *see* Fleet, petroleum
Oil markets, 38
Oil movements and transportation needs, 113
Oil prices, 37, 69
Oligopoly in tankship markets, 174
Onassis, A., 63, 67, 71, 124
One-way stable equilibria, 19
Operating petroleum fleet, *see under* Fleet, petroleum
Opportunity costs, 37, 109n
Orders placed, 50–51, 53, 54, 59, 61, 64, 68, 74–76, 80, 87, 90, 93, 94, 98, 99, 103, 110, 111, 114, 118, 123, 205, 242
   and charter rates, 50, 51, 59, 61, 76–93, 111, 115–116, 205

332 INDEX

Orders placed (*continued*)
  and deliveries, 110, 111
  and pattern of ownership, 242
  and replacements, 118
  and retirements, 123
  and scrappings, 242
  and surplus production, 74
  backlog of, 76, 80, 94
  cancellations, 68, 86
  changes in, defined, 89n
  converted to dry cargo orders, 68n
  correlation with spot rates, 51, 61, 87
  cost of, 98–99, 105–107
  during downturn in demand, 103
  factors affecting, 50–51
  impact of rates on, 114
  income elasticity of, 53, 54, 56
  negative net, 93
  number of, 64, 68, 75
    and market conditions, 75
  oscillating, 64
  point of zero orders, 90n
  rate elasticity of, 90
  scatter diagrams for, 83–87, 93, 115–116, 118, 119
  substitute for charters, 53
  time series for, 114
  see also Shipbuilding
Out-of-pocket losses, 59, 60, 117, 133n
Own price changes, see Prices
Ownership pattern, 51, 64–76, 242
Ownership shares of transportation facilities, 51, 64–76, 174, 176
  and competition, 176
  of independents, 69, 72
  of oil companies, 69, 72
Ozanne, Henry, 100n

Paragon Oil Company, 62, 66, 70, 254
Pattern of expectations, see Expectations
Pattern of ownership, 51, 64–76, 242
Period charter, see Charters
Period rates, see Charter rate
Persian Gulf, 125n, 147, 148, 150, 151, 152, 156, 163, 168, 194n, 216, 233
Petrofina, 62, 66, 70, 254
Petroleum fleet, working, see under Fleet, petroleum
Planning horizon for building now vs. later decisions, five parts of, 101–102
Port Arthur, 129, 148, 150, 151
Portugal, 82
Prices, 8–10, 12–14, 16–19, 22, 26, 28, 34, 38n, 40, 52, 80, 84, 99n
  changes in, 10, 14, 22, 26, 34, 38n, 40, 52
    and income effects, 10, 14, 22, 52
    and quantity demanded, 34, 40
    and substitution effect, 10, 52
    own price change, 38n
  cross effects of, 12, 13
  cycles in, 9, 26, 99n
  expectations of, see Expectations
  explosive patterns of, 8, 13, 16, 28, 80, see also Cobweb theorem
  of bunker C, 129–133
  of oil, 37, 69
  range of instability, 18
  re-entry, 19
  refusal, 19
  regions of, 16, 40, 84
  see also Charter rate and Shipbuilding, costs
Production plans, 30, 38
  and input costs, 38
  current, 30
Production possibility schedules, 55
Profit function, present value of, 31
"Profit-squeeze," 60
Profit maximization in oil companies, 108
Protectionist premium, 156n
Pure Oil, 62, 66, 70

Random walk in spot rates, 200–201
Ras Tanura, 129, 130, 133
Rate, see Charter rate
Rate cycles, 42, 46, 95, 194n
  amplitude of, 46
  defined, 42
  in short-term rates, 42
  turning points of, 194n
Rate, determination of, see under Charter rate, long-term, and Charter rate, short-term
Rate elasticity of expectations, see under Expectations, elasticity of
Rate elasticity of orders, 90
Rate expectations, see under Expectations, and Expectations, elasticity of
Rate, long-term, see Charter rate, long-term
Rate of return, subjective, 60n, 102
Rate of scrapping, 57
Rate, period, see Charter rate, long-term
Rate, refusal, see Refusal rate
Rate, spot, see Charter rate, short-term
Rate, time-charter, see Charter rate, long-term
Rates and chartering activity, 42–49, 165
  see also under Charter rate, short-term
Reaction cycle of suppliers, 23
Reactivation, cost of, 59, 137n
  consideration in replacement decisions, 59
Recommissioning cost, see Reactivation, cost of
Recontracting, 38, 49, 56n, 145
Reflecting barriers in rates, 201
Refusal rate, 19, 87, 151–159, 167, 170. 171
  and average rates, 151, 152
  and oil companies, 152n
  empirical evidence, 155–159
  for extended time period, 151
  for T-2, 151, 171
  lower limit of, 151
  of marginal vessel, 171
Region of strict static relevance, 12, 13, 17, 35, 64, 85
Regression analysis
  coefficients of, 90

Regression analysis (*continued*)
  logarithmic, 90, 219–226
  multiple, 89n
  of long-term rates, 219–226
    equation for, 220, 224
  of rates and orders, 90
    equation for, 90
  simple, 89n
Regulating agencies, 36, 65
"Relet," 97n, 247
Remaining capacity, costs per unit of, 58
Repair yards, 135
  foreign, 135
  technology of, 135
  U.S., 135
Repairs, 126, 135–144, 150, 157n, 161, 166, 167, 242
  analysis of data for, 141
  and idle capacity (tie-ups), 139
  and seasonality in trade, 13, 140, 143
  and spot rates, 137, 143
  and technology, 136, 137
  capacity lost to, 139
  determinants of levels of, 135
  duration of, 135, 139, 150
    distribution of durations, 135n
  efficiency of, in post-Korean period, 140
  expectations and, 141
  idleness for, 135, 139, 150, 161
  incidence of, 143
    and spot rates, 143
  information available on, 138
  level of, and spot rates, 135, 138, 142
  level of, and technology, 135, 138, 142, 143
Replacements, 36, 57–64, 74, 121–125
  and retirements, 121–125
  cost of, 36
    distribution over time, 36n
  impact of, 59
  orders for, 58, 122
    and economic value, 122
  programs for, 57
  timing of, 58
Retirements, 57–64, 74, 117, 118, 120–126, 161, 162
  and orders placed, 118, 123
  and rates, 59, 118, 120–126
  and replacements, 118, 121
  average age of vessel at, 118, 120, 125
    and rates, 120
  programs for, 57
  supply schedule, impact of on, 162
Reversal in expectations, *see under* Expectations
Richfield, 62, 66, 70
Risk function of sellers, 45
Risk minimization, preference for, 109, 110
Robert T. Jones, Inc., 147
Robinson, J., 4
Rostow, W. W., 80n

Samuelson, P. A., 37n, 40n
Scale, definition of, 247, 253
  No. 3, definition of, 247

Scatter diagrams, 42–48, 83–87, 93, 115–116, 118–119, 155–159, 169–173
  changes in orders vs. spot rates, 115–116, 118, 119
  fixtures vs. spot rates, 42–48
  idle capacity vs. spot rates, 157–159
  operating fleet vs. spot rates, 169–173
  orders placed vs. spot rates, 83–87
  tie-ups vs. spot rates, 155–156
Schwartz, Anna J., 80n
Scrappings, 57–64, 116–126, 242, 247
  and orders, 242
  and spot rates, 116–126, 242
  definition of, 247
  of old ship, 58
  rate of, 57
  value of, 57n, 60n
Sellers, *see* Buyers and sellers
Sellers' refusal price, 19
  see also Refusal rate
Shackle, G. L. S., 108n
Share of ownership, *see* Ownership shares
Shell Oil Company, 62, 66, 70, 107, 129, 254
Shillinglaw, Gordon, 35n
Shipbuilding, 44, 50–57, 64, 69–116, 135, 161, 187n
  backlog of orders, 76
  budgets for, 55
  contracts, nature of, 95
  costs, 44, 50–57, 64, 75, 76–82, 83, 95–100, 102, 105–107
    and elasticity of expectations, 51, 64
    and expectations of independents, 100, 102
    and expectations of shipbuilders, 97
    availability of information, 95
    changes in, 55, 56
    current, 81
    Fairplay indices of, 105–107
    fluctuations in, 98
    impact of on new capacity, 51
    substitute measures for tanker rates, 83
    time series for, 76, 83
  cycle in, 44, 50
  decisions for, 95
  deliveries, 107, 110–116, 161, 187n
  demand for, *see* Demand schedule, shipbuilding
  economies of scale in, *see* Economies of scale
  flag registry of deliveries, 107
  lead time, 58, 59, 110n, 111
  markets of, *see* Tankship markets, building
  now vs. later decisions, 101–102
  orders, *see* Orders placed
  prices, 96
  service, 53
    complementarity to transportation service, 53
  shifts in schedule of, 78
  "short-selling," 45, 187n
  statistics, timing of, 76n

Shipbuilding (*continued*)
  time delay in, 95
  time-series index of cost of, 76, 83
  vs. chartering, 94–97
Shipyards, 44, 57n, 77, 80, 135
"Short-chartering," 94
Shortest short run, 59n
Short-term, definition of, 3
Short-term supply, *see* Supply schedule, short-term
"Shut-in" capacities, 36
Sinclair Refining, 62, 66, 70, 254
Single-voyage, synonymity with "spot" transaction, 3n
Single voyage rate, synonymity with "spot" rate, 3n
Size indivisibilities, 74
Slowdowns, 126–134, 164–165
  bunker prices and, 130
  capacity and, 127, 128, 133
    formula for, 128
  costs, out-of-pocket and, 133n
  critical spot rate, 133
  demand schedule and, 134
  dynamic considerations, 134
  economics of, 126, 164–165, 242
  fuel savings in, 127–130
    formula for, 128n
  lay-up and, 133n
  speed vs. fuel savings, 128n, 164–165
    formula for, 128n
  spot rates and, 126–134
    critical rate, 133
  Suez crisis and, 129
Slutsky-Hicks formulation, 10, 11, 33, 51, 52, 240
Smoothing functions, 22
  see also Coefficients of expectations
Socony Mobil Oil Company, 62, 66, 70, 164, 165
Spain, 82
Speed and shaft horsepower, 108n
Speed, economics of, 164–165
  see also Slowdowns
Speed-ups, *see* Slowdowns
Spot rates, *see* Charter rate, short-term
Spot transactions, definition of, 3
Standard Oil Co. (California), 62, 66, 70
Standard Oil Co. (Indiana), 62, 66, 70
Standard Oil Co. (New Jersey), 62, 66, 70, 73, 81, 82, 92, 111n, 120, 122, 129, 133, 137, 146
Standard-Vacuum, 62, 66, 70, 125, 254
Stationary-state requirements, 64
Steam turbine vs. diesel, 207
"Stockboat," 105
  and Fairplay index, 105
  and premium during high rates, 105
  price of, 105
Straight-line depreciation, formula for, 61n
Strict static relevance, region of, 12, 13, 17, 35, 64, 85
Subjective rate of return, 60n
Substitutes, 13
Substitution effect, 6–34, 52, 53, 59
  dynamic, 59
  in demand schedules, 240–241
  in supply schedules, 241
  positive, 53
  static, 54
  vs. income effect, 85
  see also Slutsky-Hicks formulation, and Interperiod substitutions
Substitution, interperiod, *see* Interperiod substitutions
Substitution of sources of energy, 35
Substitution, own, 40n
Suez Canal, 10, 24, 48n, 56n, 69, 75n, 77, 86, 95, 98, 100, 101, 114, 115, 124, 129, 142, 163, 165n, 194n, 199n
  closure of, 48
  crisis of, 10, 24, 48n, 56n, 75n, 77, 86, 98, 100, 101, 114, 115, 124, 129, 142, 163, 165, 194n, 199n
  post-crisis period, 65, 74, 112, 124
  tolls, 129, 130
Suez Canal Company, 163
Sun Oil, 62, 66, 70, 254
"Supertankers," 77, 98, 130n
Supply schedule, 18, 24, 50–171, 187–188, 241
  backward bending, 84
  beyond full capacity level, 126, 160
  conversions and, 134
  counterclockwise rotation of, 24
  deliveries and, 110–116
  downward shift of, 161n
  elasticity of and working petroleum fleet, 168–173
  empirical determination, 160
  of tankship building, 39, 51–64, 76–94
  of tankship service, 77, 94–97, 116, 241
  pattern of ownership and, 64–76
  relationship of long-run to short-run, 187–188
  repairs and, 136–144
  retirements and, 57–65
  slowdowns and, 126–134
  tie-ups and, 144–159
Supply schedule, long-term, *see* Supply schedule
Supply schedule, short-term, 126, 160–173, 187–196, 243
  adjustment paths of, 188
  and ballasted traffic, 162
  and composition of fleet, 162
  and idleness, 166
  and operating fleet, 171
    equation for, 171
  and point of full capacity, 171
  and retirements, 161–162
  and theoretical full capacity, 161, 166, 167, 171
  backward bending, 170
  cobweb assumptions for, 189–196
  definition of, 161
  elastic part, width of, 170
  elasticity of, 167–173, 191
    statistical measures for, 171
  equilibria at low rates, 188

Supply schedule (*continued*)
  factors affecting it, 126, 243
  reversibility of, 191, 192
    empirical evidence, 194
  shape of, 187
  shift of, reasons for, 195
  stability of, 187
  see also Supply schedule
Suppliers, 23, 26
  reaction of, 23, 26
    instantaneous, 26
    delayed, 26
Surpluses, 74, 187, 195
  and deliveries, 187n
  and elasticity of expectations, 187n
  and short-term rates, 195
  short-selling, 187n
Sweden, 82, 107

Tanker, *see* Tankships
Tankship building, *see* Shipbuilding
Tankship capacity, *see* Capacity, tankship, and Fleet, petroleum
Tankship deliveries, *see* Shipbuilding, deliveries
Tankship fleet, composition, *see* Fleet, petroleum, and Capacity, tankship
Tankship markets, 2, 9, 10, 13, 18, 48n, 69, 82, 104, 126, 156n, 174–185, 189–201
  analysis of, 18
  building, *see* Tankship markets, building
  characteristics of, 104, 174–185
  cobweb theorem and, 189–201, 243–244
  competition in, *see* Competition in tankship markets
  complementarities in, 2, 9, 10, 13, 183
  cyclical prices in, 241
    and cyclical demand, 241
  depressions in, 48n, 126
  ease of entry to, 180, 181
  economies of scale in, 180
  existence of, 65n, 174–185, 243
    reasons for, 65n, 184–185, 243
  fluctuations in, 69, 82
  leadership in, 184
  mobility in, 179, 180
  service, *see* Tankship markets, service
  size of operational unit in, 181–183
  technology, commonness of, 183
  see also Demand schedule, and Supply schedule
Tankship markets, building, 52–57, 64–124, 126, 161–171, 188–199, 202–214, 241–244
  ancillary technologies and, 74
  competitiveness of, 64
  deliveries and, 110–116
  depressed condition of and government efforts, 75
  empirical data, 77–93
    qualitative, 77–82
    quantitative, 82–93
  expectations of buyers in, 93, 106–108, 113
  independents vs. oil companies and, 97–110
  "now vs. later" decisions in, 101–110
  orders placed, *see* Orders placed
  pattern of ownership and, 64–76
  rates and, 188–189, 202–214
  secrecy of data in, 82
  supply schedule in, *see* Supply schedule
  vessels scrapped and, 116–124
  violent fluctuations, existence of in, 82
  vs. chartering, 52, 94–97
Tankship markets, service, 3, 9, 29, 35, 45, 52, 55n, 69, 79n, 81, 83, 86, 94, 95, 96, 121, 174–185, 188–201, 202–213, 242, 243, 244, 245
  characteristics of, 174–185
  cobweb assumptions for, 189–190
  competition in, *see* Competition in tankship markets
  competitiveness of, 176
  demand in, *see* Demand schedule, chartering
  economies of scale, 86
  investment in, reasons for, 198
  management policy in, 245
  oscillations in, 9, 196
    boundaries of, 196
  rates and, 188–213, 215–238
  spatial utility, 35
  supply in, *see* Supply schedule
Tankship propulsion, economics of, 206–208
  and charter rate, 206–208
Tankship rates
  see Charter rates
Tankships, 2, 3, 9, 50, 51, 61, 76–93, 97, 107, 110–116, 120–122, 126
  age distribution of, 9, 50, 86
  and inferior goods, 2
  building of, *see* Shipbuilding
  cleaning cost of, 3
  deliveries of, 107, 110–116, 122
  dry cargo, 126
  economic life of, 2, 9, 51, 120–122
  entry into other trades, reasons for, 97
  in tie-ups, *see* Tie-ups
  marginal, *see* Marginal vessel
  markets of, *see* Tankship markets
  orders for, 50, 51, 61, 76–93, 111, 115–116, *see also* Orders placed
  rates for, *see* Charter rates
  replacements of, *see* Replacements
  retirements of, *see* Retirements
Taxes, impact of, 61n
Technological change, 57
Technological economies of scale, 61, 124, 125, 198
Technological innovations, 60, 122
Technological obsolescence, 50, 57, 59, 126
Technology, 61, 74, 108, 142, 183
  ancillary, 74, 108
  and level of repairs, 142

Technology (*continued*)
  commonness of, 183
  economies of, 61, 125, 198
Texas Co., 63, 67, 71, 125n, 254
Theoretical full capacity, 161, 166, 167, 171
Tidewater, 63, 67, 71, 254
Tie-ups, 57, 58, 59, 126, 129n, 135, 136, 138, 140, 144–159, 167, 171, 174, 205, 242, 243, 247
  and age of vessels tied up, December 1958, 152n
  and marginal vessel, 145
  and size of vessel, 145
  cost of, 57–59, 137n, 144, 146, 151, 167, 243
    data on, 144
    for marginal vessel, 243
    size fixity of, 167
  critical rates for, 148
  definition of, 247
  during depressed conditions, 144, 153, 154
  empirical schedule for, 153, 243
  inelasticity of expectations and, 144, 147
  lags of behind rate movements, 146
  lay-up rate, *see* Refusal rate
  rate of, *see* Refusal rate
  reluctance for, 148
  vs. rates, 155, 156, 205
    diagram for, 155
    equation for, 155, 156
Time charter, *see* Charters, time
Time-charter rates, *see* Charter rate, long-term
Time equivalents of transactions, 38, 39
Time series, 40, 48, 76, 89, 98n, 114
  analysis, 40
  index of for shipbuilding cost, 76
  of all transactions, 48
  of consecutive-voyage charters, 48
  of costs, 98n
  of orders, 114
  of spot rates, 48, 98n, 114
  of time charters, 48
  shifts in, 89
Tinbergen, J., 9, 111, 115n
Tonnage, *see* Capacity, and Fleet, petroleum
Transactions, 37, 38–39, 41, 42–49, 94n, 95, 249
  and actual demand, 49
  and short-term rates, 41
  futures and non-futures, 3
  period, definition of, 3
  present vs. future, 7, 94n, 95
  spot, definition of, 3
  spot-rate equivalent, calculation of, 249–250

tabulation of, 42
time equivalents of, 38–39
Transportation capacity, *see* Capacity and Fleet, petroleum
Transportation needs and oil movements, 113
Transportation rates, *see* Charter rate
Transportation self-sufficiency of oil companies, *see under* Oil companies
T-2, definition of, 247
T-2 equivalent, definition of, 247

Union Oil, 63, 67, 71, 254
United Kingdom, 82, 107, 147, 156, 216, 233, 252
United States, 69n, 76, 82, 99, 124n, 125n, 135, 148n, 152, 156n, 163, 183, 216, 252
  coastal trade, 148n, 152, 156
  depletion allowance, 69n
  flag vessels, 76, 148n
  government, 124n
  market operations, 156n
  Maritime Administration, 92n, 120, 137n, 139
  shipyards, 99, 135
Universe Tankship Company, Inc., 97n, 124
U.S. Gulf, 147, 216, 253
U.S.M.C., 87, 129, 130, 146, 147, 150–152, 159, 253
  definition of, 248
  "flat" U.S.M.C., definition of, 248
Utility function, 30, 31
Utility surface, 110n

Variable cost, average, 57–59
Variance analysis, 48, 219, 227–230
  and elastic expectations, 48
  of charter duration, 48
  of lead times, 48
  of time-charter rate, 219, 228
Vergottis, Ltd., 63, 67, 71
Vessel, *see* Tankships
Viner, Jacob, 161n
Voyage rate equivalent, 236n

Wang, K., 63, 67, 71
Weston, W. G., 112n
W. G. Weston, Ltd., 2, 112n
Withdrawals, 83, 84, 150, 171
  and elastic expectations, 171
  and out-of-pocket costs, 150
  "temporary for reappraisals," 84
  see also Tie-ups
Working petroleum fleet, *see under* Fleet, petroleum
World commercial fleet, *see* Fleet, petroleum

Yugoslavia, 82